I0839590

Jane Addams

The Greatest Works of Jane Addams

Madison & Adams Press 2019

Charles Ball
Fifty Years in Chains-Life of an American Slave

Jane Addams
Democracy and Social Ethics

Millicent Garrett Fawcett
The Women's Victory and After

John Stuart Mill
The Political Theory of John Stuart Mill: 7 Book Collection

Elizabeth Cady Stanton
Eighty Years and More: Memoirs of Elizabeth Cady Stanton (1815-1897)

Jane Addams
The Greatest Works of Jane Addams

Democracy and Social Ethics, The Spirit of Youth and the City Streets, A New Conscience and An Ancient Evil, Why Women Should Vote, Belated Industry, Twenty Years at Hull-House

Madison & Adams Press, 2019.
Contact: info@madisonadamspress.com

ISBN 978-80-273-3418-6

This is a publication of Madison & Adams Press. Our production consists of thoroughly prepared educational & informative editions: Advice & How-To Books, Encyclopedias, Law Anthologies, Declassified Documents, Legal & Criminal Files, Historical Books, Scientific & Medical Publications, Technical Handbooks and Manuals. All our publications are meticulously edited and formatted to the highest digital standard. The main goal of Madison & Adams Press is to make all informative books and records accessible to everyone in a high quality digital and print form.

Contents

Democracy and Social Ethics

Prefatory Note

The following pages present the substance of a course of twelve lectures on "Democracy and Social Ethics" which have been delivered at various colleges and university extension centres.

In putting them into the form of a book, no attempt has been made to change the somewhat informal style used in speaking. The "we" and "us" which originally referred to the speaker and her audience are merely extended to possible readers.

Acknowledgment for permission to reprint is extended to *The Atlantic Monthly*, *The International Journal of Ethics*, *The American Journal of Sociology*, and to *The Commons*.

Chapter I
Introduction

It is well to remind ourselves, from time to time, that "Ethics" is but another word for "righteousness," that for which many men and women of every generation have hungered and thirsted, and without which life becomes meaningless.

Certain forms of personal righteousness have become to a majority of the community almost automatic. It is as easy for most of us to keep from stealing our dinners as it is to digest them, and there is quite as much voluntary morality involved in one process as in the other. To steal would be for us to fall sadly below the standard of habit and expectation which makes virtue easy. In the same way we have been carefully reared to a sense of family obligation, to be kindly and considerate to the members of our own households, and to feel responsible for their well-being. As the rules of conduct have become established in regard to our self-development and our families, so they have been in regard to limited circles of friends. If the fulfilment of these claims were all that a righteous life required, the hunger and thirst would be stilled for many good men and women, and the clew of right living would lie easily in their hands.

But we all know that each generation has its own test, the contemporaneous and current standard by which alone it can adequately judge of its own moral achievements, and that it may not legitimately use a previous and less vigorous test. The advanced test must indeed include that which has already been attained; but if it includes no more, we shall fail to go forward, thinking complacently that we have "arrived" when in reality we have not yet started.

To attain individual morality in an age demanding social morality, to pride one's self on the results of personal effort when the time demands social adjustment, is utterly to fail to apprehend the situation.

It is perhaps significant that a German critic has of late reminded us that the one test which the most authoritative and dramatic portrayal of the Day of Judgment offers, is the social test. The stern questions are not in regard to personal and family relations, but did ye visit the poor, the criminal, the sick, and did ye feed the hungry?

All about us are men and women who have become unhappy in regard to their attitude toward the social order itself; toward the dreary round of uninteresting work, the pleasures narrowed down to those of appetite, the declining consciousness of brain power, and the lack of mental food which characterizes the lot of the large proportion of their fellow-citizens. These men and women have caught a moral challenge raised by the exigencies of contemporaneous life; some are bewildered, others who are denied the relief which sturdy action brings are even seeking an escape, but all are increasingly anxious concerning their actual relations to the basic organization of society.

The test which they would apply to their conduct is a social test. They fail to be content with the fulfilment of their family and personal obligations, and find themselves striving to respond to a new demand involving a social obligation; they have become conscious of another requirement, and the contribution they would make is toward a code of social ethics. The conception of life which they hold has not yet expressed itself in social changes or legal enactment, but rather in a mental attitude of maladjustment, and in a sense of divergence between their consciences and their conduct. They desire both a clearer definition of the code of morality adapted to present day demands and a part in its fulfilment, both a creed and a practice of social morality. In the perplexity of this intricate situation at least one thing is becoming clear: if the latter day moral ideal is in reality that of a social morality, it is inevitable that those who desire it must be brought in contact with the moral experiences of the many in order to procure an adequate social motive.

These men and women have realized this and have disclosed the fact in their eagerness for a wider acquaintance with and participation in the life about them. They believe that experience gives the easy and trustworthy impulse toward right action in the broad as well as in the narrow relations. We may indeed imagine many of them saying: "Cast our experiences in a larger mould if our lives are to be animated by the larger social aims. We have met the obligations of our family life, not because we had made resolutions to that end, but spontaneously, because of a common fund of memories and affections, from which the obligation naturally develops, and we see no other way in which to prepare ourselves for the larger social duties." Such a demand is reasonable, for by our daily experience we have discovered that we cannot mechanically hold up a moral standard, then jump at it in rare moments of exhilaration when we have the strength for it, but that even as the ideal itself must be a rational development of life, so the strength to attain it must be secured from interest in life itself. We slowly learn that life consists of processes as well as results, and that failure may come quite as easily from ignoring the adequacy of one's method as from selfish or ignoble aims. We are thus brought to a conception of Democracy not merely as a sentiment which desires the well-being of all men, nor yet as a creed which believes in the essential dignity and equality of all men, but as that which affords a rule of living as well as a test of faith.

We are learning that a standard of social ethics is not attained by travelling a sequestered byway, but by mixing on the thronged and common road where all must turn out for one another, and at least see the size of one another's burdens. To follow the path of social morality results perforce in the temper if not the practice of the democratic spirit, for it implies that diversified human experience and resultant sympathy which are the foundation and guarantee of Democracy.

There are many indications that this conception of Democracy is growing among us. We have come to have an enormous interest in human life as such, accompanied by confidence in its essential soundness. We do not believe that genuine experience can lead us astray any more than scientific data can.

We realize, too, that social perspective and sanity of judgment come only from contact with social experience; that such contact is the surest corrective of opinions concerning the social order, and concerning efforts, however humble, for its improvement. Indeed, it is a consciousness of the illuminating and dynamic value of this wider and more thorough human experience which explains in no small degree that new curiosity regarding human life which has more of a moral basis than an intellectual one.

The newspapers, in a frank reflection of popular demand, exhibit an omniverous curiosity equally insistent upon the trivial and the important. They are perhaps the most obvious manifestations of that desire to know, that "What is this?" and "Why do you do that?" of the child. The first dawn of the social consciousness takes this form, as the dawning intelligence of the child takes the form of constant question and insatiate curiosity.

Literature, too, portrays an equally absorbing though better adjusted desire to know all kinds of life. The popular books are the novels, dealing with life under all possible conditions, and they are widely read not only because they are entertaining, but also because they in a measure satisfy an unformulated belief that to see farther, to know all sorts of men, in an indefinite way, is a preparation for better social adjustment-for the remedying of social ills.

Doubtless one under the conviction of sin in regard to social ills finds a vague consolation in reading about the lives of the poor, and derives a sense of complicity in doing good. He likes to feel that he knows about social wrongs even if he does not remedy them, and in a very genuine sense there is a foundation for this belief.

Partly through this wide reading of human life, we find in ourselves a new affinity for all men, which probably never existed in the world before. Evil itself does not shock us as it once did, and we count only that man merciful in whom we recognize an understanding of the criminal. We have learned as common knowledge that much of the insensibility and hardness of the world is due to the lack of imagination which prevents a realization of the experiences of other people. Already there is a conviction that we are under a moral obligation in choosing our experiences, since the result of those experiences must ultimately determine our understanding of life. We know instinctively that if we grow contemptuous of our fellows, and consciously limit our intercourse to certain kinds of people whom we have previously decided to respect, we not only tremendously circumscribe our range of life, but limit the scope of our ethics.

We can recall among the selfish people of our acquaintance at least one common characteristic, —the conviction that they are different from other men and women, that they need
peculiar consideration because they are more sensitive or more refined. Such people "refuse
to be bound by any relation save the personally luxurious ones of love and admiration, or the
identity of political opinion, or religious creed." We have learned to recognize them as selfish,
although we blame them not for the will which chooses to be selfish, but for a narrowness of
interest which deliberately selects its experience within a limited sphere, and we say that they
illustrate the danger of concentrating the mind on narrow and unprogressive issues.

We know, at last, that we can only discover truth by a rational and democratic interest in life,
and to give truth complete social expression is the endeavor upon which we are entering. Thus
the identification with the common lot which is the essential idea of Democracy becomes the
source and expression of social ethics. It is as though we thirsted to drink at the great wells of
human experience, because we knew that a daintier or less potent draught would not carry us
to the end of the journey, going forward as we must in the heat and jostle of the crowd.

The six following chapters are studies of various types and groups who are being impelled
by the newer conception of Democracy to an acceptance of social obligations involving in each
instance a new line of conduct. No attempt is made to reach a conclusion, nor to offer advice
beyond the assumption that the cure for the ills of Democracy is more Democracy, but the
quite unlooked-for result of the studies would seem to indicate that while the strain and perplexity of the situation is felt most keenly by the educated and self-conscious members of the
community, the tentative and actual attempts at adjustment are largely coming through those
who are simpler and less analytical.

Chapter II
Charitable Effort

All those hints and glimpses of a larger and more satisfying democracy, which literature and our own hopes supply, have a tendency to slip away from us and to leave us sadly unguided and perplexed when we attempt to act upon them.

Our conceptions of morality, as all our other ideas, pass through a course of development; the difficulty comes in adjusting our conduct, which has become hardened into customs and habits, to these changing moral conceptions. When this adjustment is not made, we suffer from the strain and indecision of believing one hypothesis and acting upon another.

Probably there is no relation in life which our democracy is changing more rapidly than the charitable relation-that relation which obtains between benefactor and beneficiary; at the same time there is no point of contact in our modern experience which reveals so clearly the lack of that equality which democracy implies. We have reached the moment when democracy has made such inroads upon this relationship, that the complacency of the old-fashioned charitable man is gone forever; while, at the same time, the very need and existence of charity, denies us the consolation and freedom which democracy will at last give.

It is quite obvious that the ethics of none of us are clearly defined, and we are continually obliged to act in circles of habit, based upon convictions which we no longer hold. Thus our estimate of the effect of environment and social conditions has doubtless shifted faster than our methods of administrating charity have changed. Formerly when it was believed that poverty was synonymous with vice and laziness, and that the prosperous man was the righteous man, charity was administered harshly with a good conscience; for the charitable agent really blamed the individual for his poverty, and the very fact of his own superior prosperity gave him a certain consciousness of superior morality. We have learned since that time to measure by other standards, and have ceased to accord to the money-earning capacity exclusive respect; while it is still rewarded out of all proportion to any other, its possession is by no means assumed to imply the possession of the highest moral qualities. We have learned to judge men by their social virtues as well as by their business capacity, by their devotion to intellectual and disinterested aims, and by their public spirit, and we naturally resent being obliged to judge poor people so solely upon the industrial side. Our democratic instinct instantly takes alarm. It is largely in this modern tendency to judge all men by one democratic standard, while the old charitable attitude commonly allowed the use of two standards, that much of the difficulty adheres. We know that unceasing bodily toil becomes wearing and brutalizing, and our position is totally untenable if we judge large numbers of our fellows solely upon their success in maintaining it.

The daintily clad charitable visitor who steps into the little house made untidy by the vigorous efforts of her hostess, the washerwoman, is no longer sure of her superiority to the latter; she recognizes that her hostess after all represents social value and industrial use, as over against her own parasitic cleanliness and a social standing attained only through status.

The only families who apply for aid to the charitable agencies are those who have come to grief on the industrial side; it may be through sickness, through loss of work, or for other guiltless and inevitable reasons; but the fact remains that they are industrially ailing, and must be bolstered and helped into industrial health. The charity visitor, let us assume, is a young college woman, well-bred and open-minded; when she visits the family assigned to her, she is often embarrassed to find herself obliged to lay all the stress of her teaching and advice upon the industrial virtues, and to treat the members of the family almost exclusively as factors in the industrial system. She insists that they must work and be self-supporting, that the most dangerous of all situations is idleness, that seeking one's own pleasure, while ignoring claims and responsibilities, is the most ignoble of actions. The members of her assigned family may have other charms and virtues-they may possibly be kind and considerate of each other, generous to their friends, but it is her business to stick to the industrial side. As she daily holds up these standards, it often occurs to the mind of the sensitive visitor, whose conscience has been made tender by much talk of brotherhood and equality, that she has no right to say these things; that her untrained hands are no more fitted to cope with actual conditions than those of her broken-down family.

The grandmother of the charity visitor could have done the industrial preaching very well, because she did have the industrial virtues and housewifely training. In a generation our experiences have changed, and our views with them; but we still keep on in the old methods, which could be applied when our consciences were in line with them, but which are daily becoming more difficult as we divide up into people who work with their hands and those who do not. The charity visitor belonging to the latter class is perplexed by recognitions and suggestions which the situation forces upon her. Our democracy has taught us to apply our moral teaching all around, and the moralist is rapidly becoming so sensitive that when his life does not exemplify his ethical convictions, he finds it difficult to preach.

Added to this is a consciousness, in the mind of the visitor, of a genuine misunderstanding of her motives by the recipients of her charity, and by their neighbors. Let us take a neighborhood of poor people, and test their ethical standards by those of the charity visitor, who comes with the best desire in the world to help them out of their distress. A most striking incongruity, at once apparent, is the difference between the emotional kindness with which relief is given by one poor neighbor to another poor neighbor, and the guarded care with which relief is given by a charity visitor to a charity recipient. The neighborhood mind is at once confronted not only by the difference of method, but by an absolute clashing of two ethical standards.

A very little familiarity with the poor districts of any city is sufficient to show how primitive and genuine are the neighborly relations. There is the greatest willingness to lend or borrow anything, and all the residents of the given tenement know the most intimate family affairs of all the others. The fact that the economic condition of all alike is on a most precarious level makes the ready outflow of sympathy and material assistance the most natural thing in the world. There are numberless instances of self-sacrifice quite unknown in the circles where greater economic advantages make that kind of intimate knowledge of one's neighbors impossible. An Irish family in which the man has lost his place, and the woman is struggling to eke out the scanty savings by day's work, will take in the widow and her five children who have been turned into the street, without a moment's reflection upon the physical discomforts involved. The most maligned landlady who lives in the house with her tenants is usually ready to lend a scuttle full of coal to one of them who may be out of work, or to share her supper. A woman for whom the writer had long tried in vain to find work failed to appear at the appointed time when employment was secured at last. Upon investigation it transpired that a neighbor further down the street was taken ill, that the children ran for the family friend, who went of course, saying simply when reasons for her non-appearance were demanded, "It broke me heart to leave the place, but what could I do?" A woman whose husband was sent up to the city prison for the maximum term, just three months, before the birth of her child found herself penniless at the end of that time, having gradually sold her supply of household furniture. She took refuge with a friend whom she supposed to be living in three rooms in another part of town. When she arrived, however, she discovered that her friend's husband had been out of work so long that they had been reduced to living in one room. The friend, however, took her in, and the friend's husband was obliged to sleep upon a bench in the park every night for a week, which he did uncomplainingly if not cheerfully. Fortunately it was summer, "and it only rained one night." The writer could not discover from the young mother that she had any special claim upon the "friend" beyond the fact that they had formerly worked together in the same factory. The husband she had never seen until the night of her arrival, when he at once went forth in search of a midwife who would consent to come upon his promise of future payment.

The evolutionists tell us that the instinct to pity, the impulse to aid his fellows, served man at a very early period, as a rude rule of right and wrong. There is no doubt that this rude rule still holds among many people with whom charitable agencies are brought into contact, and that their ideas of right and wrong are quite honestly outraged by the methods of these agencies.

When they see the delay and caution with which relief is given, it does not appear to them a conscientious scruple, but as the cold and calculating action of a selfish man. It is not the aid that they are accustomed to receive from their neighbors, and they do not understand why the impulse which drives people to "be good to the poor" should be so severely supervised. They feel, remotely, that the charity visitor is moved by motives that are alien and unreal. They may be superior motives, but they are different, and they are "agin nature." They cannot comprehend why a person whose intellectual perceptions are stronger than his natural impulses, should go into charity work at all. The only man they are accustomed to see whose intellectual perceptions are stronger than his tenderness of heart, is the selfish and avaricious man who is frankly "on the make." If the charity visitor is such a person, why does she pretend to like the poor? Why does she not go into business at once?

We may say, of course, that it is a primitive view of life, which thus confuses intellectuality and business ability; but it is a view quite honestly held by many poor people who are obliged to receive charity from time to time. In moments of indignation the poor have been known to say: "What do you want, anyway? If you have nothing to give us, why not let us alone and stop your questionings and investigations?" "They investigated me for three weeks, and in the end gave me nothing but a black character," a little woman has been heard to assert. This indignation, which is for the most part taciturn, and a certain kindly contempt for her abilities, often puzzles the charity visitor. The latter may be explained by the standard of worldly success which the visited families hold. Success does not ordinarily go, in the minds of the poor, with charity and kind-heartedness, but rather with the opposite qualities. The rich landlord is he who collects with sternness, who accepts no excuse, and will have his own. There are moments of irritation and of real bitterness against him, but there is still admiration, because he is rich and successful. The good-natured landlord, he who pities and spares his poverty-pressed tenants, is seldom rich. He often lives in the back of his house, which he has owned for a long time, perhaps has inherited; but he has been able to accumulate little. He commands the genuine love and devotion of many a poor soul, but he is treated with a certain lack of respect. In one sense he is a failure. The charity visitor, just because she is a person who concerns herself with the poor, receives a certain amount of this good-natured and kindly contempt, sometimes real affection, but little genuine respect. The poor are accustomed to help each other and to respond according to their kindliness; but when it comes to worldly judgment, they use industrial success as the sole standard. In the case of the charity visitor who has neither natural kindness nor dazzling riches, they are deprived of both standards, and they find it of course utterly impossible to judge of the motive of organized charity.

Even those of us who feel most sorely the need of more order in altruistic effort and see the end to be desired, find something distasteful in the juxtaposition of the words "organized" and "charity." We say in defence that we are striving to turn this emotion into a motive, that pity is capricious, and not to be depended on; that we mean to give it the dignity of conscious duty. But at bottom we distrust a little a scheme which substitutes a theory of social conduct for the natural promptings of the heart, even although we appreciate the complexity of the situation. The poor man who has fallen into distress, when he first asks aid, instinctively expects tenderness, consideration, and forgiveness. If it is the first time, it has taken him long to make up his mind to take the step. He comes somewhat bruised and battered, and instead of being met with warmth of heart and sympathy, he is at once chilled by an investigation and an intimation that he ought to work. He does not recognize the disciplinary aspect of the situation.

The only really popular charity is that of the visiting nurses, who by virtue of their professional training render services which may easily be interpreted into sympathy and kindness, ministering as they do to obvious needs which do not require investigation.

The state of mind which an investigation arouses on both sides is most unfortunate; but the perplexity and clashing of different standards, with the consequent misunderstandings, are not so bad as the moral deterioration which is almost sure to follow.

When the agent or visitor appears among the poor, and they discover that under certain conditions food and rent and medical aid are dispensed from some unknown source, every man, woman, and child is quick to learn what the conditions may be, and to follow them. Though in their eyes a glass of beer is quite right and proper when taken as any self-respecting man should take it; though they know that cleanliness is an expensive virtue which can be required of few; though they realize that saving is well-nigh impossible when but a few cents can be laid by at a time; though their feeling for the church may be something quite elusive of definition and quite apart from daily living: to the visitor they gravely laud temperance and cleanliness and thrift and religious observance. The deception in the first instances arises from a wondering inability to understand the ethical ideals which can require such impossible virtues, and from an innocent desire to please. It is easy to trace the development of the mental suggestions thus received. When A discovers that B, who is very little worse off than he, receives good things from an inexhaustible supply intended for the poor at large, he feels that he too has a claim for his share, and step by step there is developed the competitive spirit which so horrifies charity visitors when it shows itself in a tendency to "work" the relief-giving agencies.

The most serious effect upon the poor comes when dependence upon the charitable society is substituted for the natural outgoing of human love and sympathy, which, happily, we all possess in some degree. The spontaneous impulse to sit up all night with the neighbor's sick child is turned into righteous indignation against the district nurse, because she goes home at six o'clock, and doesn't do it herself. Or the kindness which would have prompted the quick purchase of much needed medicine is transformed into a voluble scoring of the dispensary, because it gives prescriptions and not drugs; and "who can get well on a piece of paper?"

If a poor woman knows that her neighbor next door has no shoes, she is quite willing to lend her own, that her neighbor may go decently to mass, or to work; for she knows the smallest item about the scanty wardrobe, and cheerfully helps out. When the charity visitor comes in, all the neighbors are baffled as to what her circumstances may be. They know she does not need a new pair of shoes, and rather suspect that she has a dozen pairs at home; which, indeed, she sometimes has. They imagine untold stores which they may call upon, and her most generous gift is considered niggardly, compared with what she might do. She ought to get new shoes for the family all round, "she sees well enough that they need them." It is no more than the neighbor herself would do, has practically done, when she lent her own shoes. The charity visitor has broken through the natural rule of giving, which, in a primitive society, is bounded only by the need of the recipient and the resources of the giver; and she gets herself into untold trouble when she is judged by the ethics of that primitive society.

The neighborhood understands the selfish rich people who stay in their own part of town, where all their associates have shoes and other things. Such people don't bother themselves about the poor; they are like the rich landlords of the neighborhood experience. But this lady visitor, who pretends to be good to the poor, and certainly does talk as though she were kind-hearted, what does she come for, if she does not intend to give them things which are so plainly needed?

The visitor says, sometimes, that in holding her poor family so hard to a standard of thrift she is really breaking down a rule of higher living which they formerly possessed; that saving, which seems quite commendable in a comfortable part of town, appears almost criminal in a poorer quarter where the next-door neighbor needs food, even if the children of the family do not.

She feels the sordidness of constantly being obliged to urge the industrial view of life. The benevolent individual of fifty years ago honestly believed that industry and self-denial in youth would result in comfortable possessions for old age. It was, indeed, the method he had practised in his own youth, and by which he had probably obtained whatever fortune he possessed. He therefore reproved the poor family for indulging their children, urged them to work long hours, and was utterly untouched by many scruples which afflict the contemporary charity visitor. She says sometimes, "Why must I talk always of getting work and saving money, the things I know nothing about? If it were anything else I had to urge, I could do it; anything like Latin prose, which I had worried through myself, it would not be so hard." But she finds it difficult to connect the experiences of her youth with the experiences of the visited family.

Because of this diversity in experience, the visitor is continually surprised to find that the safest platitude may be challenged. She refers quite naturally to the "horrors of the saloon," and discovers that the head of her visited family does not connect them with "horrors" at all. He remembers all the kindnesses he has received there, the free lunch and treating which goes on, even when a man is out of work and not able to pay up; the loan of five dollars he got there when the charity visitor was miles away and he was threatened with eviction. He may listen politely to her reference to "horrors," but considers it only "temperance talk."

The charity visitor may blame the women for lack of gentleness toward their children, for being hasty and rude to them, until she learns that the standard of breeding is not that of gentleness toward the children so much as the observance of certain conventions, such as the punctilious wearing of mourning garments after the death of a child. The standard of gentleness each mother has to work out largely by herself, assisted only by the occasional shame-faced remark of a neighbor, "That they do better when you are not too hard on them"; but the wearing of mourning garments is sustained by the definitely expressed sentiment of every woman in the street. The mother would have to bear social blame, a certain social ostracism, if she failed to comply with that requirement. It is not comfortable to outrage the conventions of those among whom we live, and, if our social life be a narrow one, it is still more difficult. The visitor may choke a little when she sees the lessened supply of food and the scanty clothing provided for the remaining children in order that one may be conventionally mourned, but she doesn't talk so strongly against it as she would have done during her first month of experience with the family since bereaved.

The subject of clothes indeed perplexes the visitor constantly, and the result of her reflections may be summed up somewhat in this wise: The girl who has a definite social standing, who has been to a fashionable school or to a college, whose family live in a house seen and known by all her friends and associates, may afford to be very simple, or even shabby as to her clothes, if she likes. But the working girl, whose family lives in a tenement, or moves from one small apartment to another, who has little social standing and has to make her own place, knows full well how much habit and style of dress has to do with her position. Her income goes into her clothing, out of all proportion to the amount which she spends upon other things. But, if social advancement is her aim, it is the most sensible thing she can do. She is judged largely by her clothes. Her house furnishing, with its pitiful little decorations, her scanty supply of books, are never seen by the people whose social opinions she most values. Her clothes are her background, and from them she is largely judged. It is due to this fact that girls' clubs succeed best in the business part of town, where "working girls" and "young ladies" meet upon an equal footing, and where the clothes superficially look very much alike. Bright and ambitious girls will come to these down-town clubs to eat lunch and rest at noon, to study all sorts of subjects and listen to lectures, when they might hesitate a long time before joining a club identified with their own neighborhood, where they would be judged not solely on their own merits and the unconscious social standing afforded by good clothes, but by other surroundings which are not nearly up to these. For the same reason, girls' clubs are infinitely more difficult to organize in little towns and villages, where every one knows every one else, just how the front parlor is furnished, and the amount of mortgage there is upon the house. These facts get in the way of a clear and unbiassed judgment; they impede the democratic relationship and add to the self-consciousness of all concerned. Every one who has had to do with down-town girls' clubs has had the experience of going into the home of some bright, well-dressed girl, to discover it uncomfortable and perhaps wretched, and to find the girl afterward carefully avoiding her, although the working girl may not have been at home when the call was made, and the visitor may have carried herself with the utmost courtesy throughout. In some very successful down-town clubs the home address is not given at all, and only the "business address" is required. Have we worked out our democracy further in regard to clothes than anything else?

The charity visitor has been rightly brought up to consider it vulgar to spend much money upon clothes, to care so much for "appearances." She realizes dimly that the care for personal decoration over that for one's home or habitat is in some way primitive and undeveloped; but she is silenced by its obvious need. She also catches a glimpse of the fact that the disproportionate expenditure of the poor in the matter of clothes is largely due to the exclusiveness of the rich who hide from them the interior of their houses, and their more subtle pleasures, while of necessity exhibiting their street clothes and their street manners. Every one who goes shopping at the same time may see the clothes of the richest women in town, but only those invited to her receptions see the Corot on her walls or the bindings in her library. The poor naturally try to bridge the difference by reproducing the street clothes which they have seen. They are striving to conform to a common standard which their democratic training presupposes belongs to all of us. The charity visitor may regret that the Italian peasant woman has laid aside her picturesque kerchief and substituted a cheap street hat. But it is easy to recognize the first attempt toward democratic expression.

The charity visitor finds herself still more perplexed when she comes to consider such problems as those of early marriage and child labor; for she cannot deal with them according to economic theories, or according to the conventions which have regulated her own life. She finds both of these fairly upset by her intimate knowledge of the situation, and her sympathy for those into whose lives she has gained a curious insight. She discovers how incorrigibly bourgeois her standards have been, and it takes but a little time to reach the conclusion that she cannot insist so strenuously upon the conventions of her own class, which fail to fit the bigger, more emotional, and freer lives of working people. The charity visitor holds well-grounded views upon the imprudence of early marriages, quite naturally because she comes from a family and circle of professional and business people. A professional man is scarcely equipped and started in his profession before he is thirty. A business man, if he is on the road to success, is much nearer prosperity at thirty-five than twenty-five, and it is therefore wise for these men not to marry in the twenties; but this does not apply to the workingman. In many trades he is laid upon the shelf at thirty-five, and in nearly all trades he receives the largest wages in his life between twenty and thirty. If the young workingman has all his wages to himself, he will probably establish habits of personal comfort, which he cannot keep up when he has to divide with a family-habits which he can, perhaps, never overcome.

The sense of prudence, the necessity for saving, can never come to a primitive, emotional man with the force of a conviction; but the necessity of providing for his children is a powerful incentive. He naturally regards his children as his savings-bank; he expects them to care for him when he gets old, and in some trades old age comes very early. A Jewish tailor was quite lately sent to the Cook County poorhouse, paralyzed beyond recovery at the age of thirty-five. Had his little boy of nine been but a few years older, he might have been spared this sorrow of public charity. He was, in fact, better able to well support a family when he was twenty than when he was thirty-five, for his wages had steadily grown less as the years went on. Another tailor whom I know, who is also a Socialist, always speaks of saving as a bourgeois virtue, one quite impossible to the genuine workingman. He supports a family consisting of himself, a wife and three children, and his two parents on eight dollars a week. He insists it would be criminal not to expend every penny of this amount upon food and shelter, and he expects his children later to care for him.

This economic pressure also accounts for the tendency to put children to work overyoung and thus cripple their chances for individual development and usefulness, and with the avaricious parent also leads to exploitation. "I have fed her for fourteen years, now she can help me pay my mortgage" is not an unusual reply when a hardworking father is expostulated with because he would take his bright daughter out of school and put her into a factory.

It has long been a common error for the charity visitor, who is strongly urging her "family" toward self-support, to suggest, or at least connive, that the children be put to work early, although she has not the excuse that the parents have. It is so easy, after one has been taking the industrial view for a long time, to forget the larger and more social claim; to urge that the boy go to work and support his parents, who are receiving charitable aid. She does not realize what a cruel advantage the person who distributes charity has, when she gives advice.

The manager in a huge mercantile establishment employing many children was able to show during a child-labor investigation, that the only children under fourteen years of age in his employ were protégés who had been urged upon him by philanthropic ladies, not only acquaintances of his, but valued patrons of the establishment. It is not that the charity visitor is less wise than other people, but she has fixed her mind so long upon the industrial lameness of her family that she is eager to seize any crutch, however weak, which may enable them to get on.

She has failed to see that the boy who attempts to prematurely support his widowed mother may lower wages, add an illiterate member to the community, and arrest the development of a capable workingman. As she has failed to see that the rules which obtain in regard to the age of marriage in her own family may not apply to the workingman, so also she fails to understand that the present conditions of employment surrounding a factory child are totally unlike those which obtained during the energetic youth of her father.

The child who is prematurely put to work is constantly oppressed by this never ending question of the means of subsistence, and even little children are sometimes almost crushed with the cares of life through their affectionate sympathy. The writer knows a little Italian lad of six to whom the problems of food, clothing, and shelter have become so immediate and pressing that, although an imaginative child, he is unable to see life from any other standpoint. The goblin or bugaboo, feared by the more fortunate child, in his mind, has come to be the need of coal which caused his father hysterical and demonstrative grief when it carried off his mother's inherited linen, the mosaic of St. Joseph, and, worst of all, his own rubber boots. He once came to a party at Hull-House, and was interested in nothing save a gas stove which he saw in the kitchen. He became excited over the discovery that fire could be produced without fuel. "I will tell my father of this stove. You buy no coal, you need only a match. Anybody will give you a match." He was taken to visit at a country-house and at once inquired how much rent was paid for it. On being told carelessly by his hostess that they paid no rent for that house, he came back quite wild with interest that the problem was solved. "Me and my father will go to the country. You get a big house, all warm, without rent." Nothing else in the country interested him but the subject of rent, and he talked of that with an exclusiveness worthy of a single taxer.

The struggle for existence, which is so much harsher among people near the edge of pauperism, sometimes leaves ugly marks on character, and the charity visitor finds these indirect results most mystifying. Parents who work hard and anticipate an old age when they can no longer earn, take care that their children shall expect to divide their wages with them from the very first. Such a parent, when successful, impresses the immature nervous system of the child thus tyrannically establishing habits of obedience, so that the nerves and will may not depart from this control when the child is older. The charity visitor, whose family relation is lifted quite out of this, does not in the least understand the industrial foundation for this family tyranny.

The head of a kindergarten training-class once addressed a club of working women, and spoke of the despotism which is often established over little children. She said that the so-called determination to break a child's will many times arose from a lust of dominion, and she urged the ideal relationship founded upon love and confidence. But many of the women were puzzled. One of them remarked to the writer as she came out of the club room, "If you did not keep control over them from the time they were little, you would never get their wages when they are grown up." Another one said, "Ah, of course she (meaning the speaker) doesn't have to depend upon her children's wages. She can afford to be lax with them, because even if they don't give money to her, she can get along without it."

There are an impressive number of children who uncomplainingly and constantly hand over their weekly wages to their parents, sometimes receiving back ten cents or a quarter for spending-money, but quite as often nothing at all; and the writer knows one girl of twenty-five who for six years has received two cents a week from the constantly falling wages which she earns in a large factory. Is it habit or virtue which holds her steady in this course? If love and tenderness had been substituted for parental despotism, would the mother have had enough affection, enough power of expression to hold her daughter's sense of money obligation through all these years? This girl who spends her paltry two cents on chewing-gum and goes plainly clad in clothes of her mother's choosing, while many of her friends spend their entire wages on those clothes which factory girls love so well, must be held by some powerful force.

The charity visitor finds these subtle and elusive problems most harrowing. The head of a family she is visiting is a man who has become black-listed in a strike. He is not a very good workman, and this, added to his agitator's reputation, keeps him out of work for a long time. The fatal result of being long out of work follows: he becomes less and less eager for it, and gets a "job" less and less frequently. In order to keep up his self-respect, and still more to keep his wife's respect for him, he yields to the little self-deception that this prolonged idleness follows because he was once blacklisted, and he gradually becomes a martyr. Deep down in his heart perhaps-but who knows what may be deep down in his heart? Whatever may be in his wife's, she does not show for an instant that she thinks he has grown lazy, and accustomed to see her earn, by sewing and cleaning, most of the scanty income for the family. The charity visitor, however, does see this, and she also sees that the other men who were in the strike have gone back to work. She further knows by inquiry and a little experience that the man is not skilful. She cannot, however, call him lazy and good-for-nothing, and denounce him as worthless as her grandmother might have done, because of certain intellectual conceptions at which she has arrived. She sees other workmen come to him for shrewd advice; she knows that he spends many more hours in the public library reading good books than the average workman has time to do. He has formed no bad habits and has yielded only to those subtle temptations toward a life of leisure which come to the intellectual man. He lacks the qualifications which would induce his union to engage him as a secretary or organizer, but he is a constant speaker at workingmen's meetings, and takes a high moral attitude on the questions discussed there. He contributes a certain intellectuality to his friends, and he has undoubted social value. The neighboring women confide to the charity visitor their sympathy with his wife, because she has to work so hard, and because her husband does not "provide." Their remarks are sharpened by a certain resentment toward the superiority of the husband's education and gentle manners. The charity visitor is ashamed to take this point of view, for she knows that it is not altogether fair. She is reminded of a college friend of hers, who told her that she was not going to allow her literary husband to write unworthy potboilers for the sake of earning a living. "I insist that we shall live within my own income; that he shall not publish until he is ready, and can give his genuine message." The charity visitor recalls what she has heard of another acquaintance, who urged her husband to decline a lucrative position as a railroad attorney, because she wished him to be free to take municipal positions, and handle public questions without the inevitable suspicion which unaccountably attaches itself in a corrupt city to a corporation attorney. The action of these two women seemed noble to her, but in their cases they merely lived on a lesser income. In the case of the workingman's wife, she faced living on no income at all, or on the precarious one which she might be able to get together.

She sees that this third woman has made the greatest sacrifice, and she is utterly unwilling to condemn her while praising the friends of her own social position. She realizes, of course, that the situation is changed by the fact that the third family needs charity, while the other two do not; but, after all, they have not asked for it, and their plight was only discovered through an accident to one of the children. The charity visitor has been taught that her mission is to preserve the finest traits to be found in her visited family, and she shrinks from the thought of convincing the wife that her husband is worthless and she suspects that she might turn all this beautiful devotion into complaining drudgery. To be sure, she could give up visiting the family altogether, but she has become much interested in the progress of the crippled child who eagerly anticipates her visits, and she also suspects that she will never know many finer women than the mother. She is unwilling, therefore, to give up the friendship, and goes on bearing her perplexities as best she may.

The first impulse of our charity visitor is to be somewhat severe with her shiftless family for spending money on pleasures and indulging their children out of all proportion to their means. The poor family which receives beans and coal from the county, and pays for a bicycle on the instalment plan, is not unknown to any of us. But as the growth of juvenile crime becomes gradually understood, and as the danger of giving no legitimate and organized pleasure to the child becomes clearer, we remember that primitive man had games long before he cared for a house or regular meals.

There are certain boys in many city neighborhoods who form themselves into little gangs with a leader who is somewhat more intrepid than the rest. Their favorite performance is to break into an untenanted house, to knock off the faucets, and cut the lead pipe, which they sell to the nearest junk dealer. With the money thus procured they buy beer and drink it in little free-booter's groups sitting in the alley. From beginning to end they have the excitement of knowing that they may be seen and caught by the "coppers," and are at times quite breathless with suspense. It is not the least unlike, in motive and execution, the practice of country boys who go forth in squads to set traps for rabbits or to round up a coon.

It is characterized by a pure spirit for adventure, and the vicious training really begins when they are arrested, or when an older boy undertakes to guide them into further excitements. From the very beginning the most enticing and exciting experiences which they have seen have been connected with crime. The policeman embodies all the majesty of successful law and established government in his brass buttons and dazzlingly equipped patrol wagon.

The boy who has been arrested comes back more or less a hero with a tale to tell of the interior recesses of the mysterious police station. The earliest public excitement the child remembers is divided between the rattling fire engines, "the time there was a fire in the next block," and all the tense interest of the patrol wagon "the time the drunkest lady in our street was arrested."

In the first year of their settlement the Hull-House residents took fifty kindergarten children to Lincoln Park, only to be grieved by their apathetic interest in trees and flowers. As they came back with an omnibus full of tired and sleepy children, they were surprised to find them galvanized into sudden life because a patrol wagon rattled by. Their eager little heads popped out of the windows full of questioning: "Was it a man or a woman?" "How many policemen inside?" and eager little tongues began to tell experiences of arrests which baby eyes had witnessed.

The excitement of a chase, the chances of competition, and the love of a fight are all centred in the outward display of crime. The parent who receives charitable aid and yet provides pleasure for his child, and is willing to indulge him in his play, is blindly doing one of the wisest things possible; and no one is more eager for playgrounds and vacation schools than the conscientious charity visitor.

This very imaginative impulse and attempt to live in a pictured world of their own, which seems the simplest prerogative of childhood, often leads the boys into difficulty. Three boys aged seven, nine, and ten were once brought into a neighboring police station under the charge of pilfering and destroying property. They had dug a cave under a railroad viaduct in which they had spent many days and nights of the summer vacation. They had "swiped" potatoes and other vegetables from hucksters' carts, which they had cooked and eaten in true brigand fashion; they had decorated the interior of the excavation with stolen junk, representing swords and firearms, to their romantic imaginations. The father of the ringleader was a janitor living in a building five miles away in a prosperous portion of the city. The landlord did not want an active boy in the building, and his mother was dead; the janitor paid for the boy's board and lodging to a needy woman living near the viaduct. She conscientiously gave him his breakfast and supper, and left something in the house for his dinner every morning when she went to work in a neighboring factory; but was too tired by night to challenge his statement that he "would rather sleep outdoors in the summer," or to investigate what he did during the day. In the meantime the three boys lived in a world of their own, made up from the reading of adventurous stories and their vivid imaginations, steadily pilfering more and more as the days went by, and actually imperilling the safety of the traffic passing over the street on the top of the viaduct. In spite of vigorous exertions on their behalf, one of the boys was sent to the Reform School, comforting himself with the conclusive remark, "Well, we had fun anyway, and maybe they will let us dig a cave at the School; it is in the country, where we can't hurt anything."

In addition to books of adventure, or even reading of any sort, the scenes and ideals of the theatre largely form the manners and morals of the young people. "Going to the theatre" is indeed the most common and satisfactory form of recreation. Many boys who conscientiously give all their wages to their mothers have returned each week ten cents to pay for a seat in the gallery of a theatre on Sunday afternoon. It is their one satisfactory glimpse of life-the moment when they "issue forth from themselves" and are stirred and thoroughly interested. They quite simply adopt as their own, and imitate as best they can, all that they see there. In moments of genuine grief and excitement the words and the gestures they employ are those copied from the stage, and the tawdry expression often conflicts hideously with the fine and genuine emotion of which it is the inadequate and vulgar vehicle.

As in the matter of dress, more refined and simpler manners and mode of expressions are unseen by them, and they must perforce copy what they know.

If we agree with a recent definition of Art, as that which causes the spectator to lose his sense of isolation, there is no doubt that the popular theatre, with all its faults, more nearly fulfils the function of art for the multitude of working people than all the "free galleries" and picture exhibits combined.

The greatest difficulty is experienced when the two standards come sharply together, and when both sides make an attempt at understanding and explanation. The difficulty of making clear one's own ethical standpoint is at times insurmountable. A woman who had bought and sold school books stolen from the school fund, —books which are all plainly marked with a red stamp, —came to Hull House one morning in great distress because she had been arrested, and begged a resident "to speak to the judge." She gave as a reason the fact that the House had known her for six years, and had once been very good to her when her little girl was buried. The resident more than suspected that her visitor knew the school books were stolen when buying them, and any attempt to talk upon that subject was evidently considered very rude. The visitor wished to get out of her trial, and evidently saw no reason why the House should not help her. The alderman was out of town, so she could not go to him. After a long conversation the visitor entirely failed to get another point of view and went away grieved and disappointed at a refusal, thinking the resident simply disobliging; wondering, no doubt, why such a mean woman had once been good to her; leaving the resident, on the other hand, utterly baffled and in the state of mind she would have been in, had she brutally insisted that a little child should lift weights too heavy for its undeveloped muscles.

Such a situation brings out the impossibility of substituting a higher ethical standard for a lower one without similarity of experience, but it is not as painful as that illustrated by the following example, in which the highest ethical standard yet attained by the charity recipient is broken down, and the substituted one not in the least understood: —

A certain charity visitor is peculiarly appealed to by the weakness and pathos of forlorn old age. She is responsible for the well-being of perhaps a dozen old women to whom she sustains a sincerely affectionate and almost filial relation. Some of them learn to take her benefactions quite as if they came from their own relatives, grumbling at all she does, and scolding her with a family freedom. One of these poor old women was injured in a fire years ago. She has but the fragment of a hand left, and is grievously crippled in her feet. Through years of pain she had become addicted to opium, and when she first came under the visitor's care, was only held from the poorhouse by the awful thought that she would there perish without her drug. Five years of tender care have done wonders for her. She lives in two neat little rooms, where with her thumb and two fingers she makes innumerable quilts, which she sells and gives away with the greatest delight. Her opium is regulated to a set amount taken each day, and she has been drawn away from much drinking. She is a voracious reader, and has her head full of strange tales made up from books and her own imagination. At one time it seemed impossible to do anything for her in Chicago, and she was kept for two years in a suburb, where the family of the charity visitor lived, and where she was nursed through several hazardous illnesses. She now lives a better life than she did, but she is still far from being a model old woman. The neighbors are constantly shocked by the fact that she is supported and comforted by a "charity lady," while at the same time she occasionally "rushes the growler," scolding at the boys lest they jar her in her tottering walk. The care of her has broken through even that second standard, which the neighborhood had learned to recognize as the standard of charitable societies, that only the "worthy poor" are to be helped; that temperance and thrift are the virtues which receive the plums of benevolence. The old lady herself is conscious of this criticism. Indeed, irate neighbors tell her to her face that she doesn't in the least deserve what she gets. In order to disarm them, and at the same time to explain what would otherwise seem loving-kindness so colossal as to be abnormal, she tells them that during her sojourn in the suburb she discovered an awful family secret,—a horrible scandal connected with the long-suffering charity visitor; that it is in order to prevent the divulgence of this that she constantly receives her ministrations. Some of her perplexed neighbors accept this explanation as simple and offering a solution of this vexed problem. Doubtless many of them have a glimpse of the real state of affairs, of the love and patience which ministers to need irrespective of worth. But the standard is too high for most of them, and it sometimes seems unfortunate to break down the second standard, which holds that people who "rush the growler" are not worthy of charity, and that there is a certain justice attained when they go to the poorhouse. It is certainly dangerous to break down the lower, unless the higher is made clear.

Just when our affection becomes large enough to care for the unworthy among the poor as we would care for the unworthy among our own kin, is certainly a perplexing question. To say that it should never be so, is a comment upon our democratic relations to them which few of us would be willing to make.

Of what use is all this striving and perplexity? Has the experience any value? It is certainly genuine, for it induces an occasional charity visitor to live in a tenement house as simply as the other tenants do. It drives others to give up visiting the poor altogether, because, they claim, it is quite impossible unless the individual becomes a member of a sisterhood, which requires, as some of the Roman Catholic sisterhoods do, that the member first take the vows of obedience and poverty, so that she can have nothing to give save as it is first given to her, and thus she is not harassed by a constant attempt at adjustment.

Both the tenement-house resident and the sister assume to have put themselves upon the industrial level of their neighbors, although they have left out the most awful element of poverty, that of imminent fear of starvation and a neglected old age.

The young charity visitor who goes from a family living upon a most precarious industrial level to her own home in a prosperous part of the city, if she is sensitive at all, is never free from perplexities which our growing democracy forces upon her.

We sometimes say that our charity is too scientific, but we would doubtless be much more correct in our estimate if we said that it is not scientific enough. We dislike the entire arrangement of cards alphabetically classified according to streets and names of families, with the unrelated and meaningless details attached to them. Our feeling of revolt is probably not unlike that which afflicted the students of botany and geology in the middle of the last century, when flowers were tabulated in alphabetical order, when geology was taught by colored charts and thin books. No doubt the students, wearied to death, many times said that it was all too scientific, and were much perplexed and worried when they found traces of structure and physiology which their so-called scientific principles were totally unable to account for. But all this happened before science had become evolutionary and scientific at all, before it had a principle of life from within. The very indications and discoveries which formerly perplexed, later illumined and made the study absorbing and vital.

We are singularly slow to apply this evolutionary principle to human affairs in general, although it is fast being applied to the education of children. We are at last learning to follow the development of the child; to expect certain traits under certain conditions; to adapt methods and matter to his growing mind. No "advanced educator" can allow himself to be so absorbed in the question of what a child ought to be as to exclude the discovery of what he is. But in our charitable efforts we think much more of what a man ought to be than of what he is or of what he may become; and we ruthlessly force our conventions and standards upon him, with a sternness which we would consider stupid indeed did an educator use it in forcing his mature intellectual convictions upon an undeveloped mind.

Let us take the example of a timid child, who cries when he is put to bed because he is afraid of the dark. The "soft-hearted" parent stays with him, simply because he is sorry for him and wants to comfort him. The scientifically trained parent stays with him, because he realizes that the child is in a stage of development in which his imagination has the best of him, and in which it is impossible to reason him out of a belief in ghosts. These two parents, wide apart in point of view, after all act much alike, and both very differently from the pseudo-scientific parent, who acts from dogmatic conviction and is sure he is right. He talks of developing his child's self-respect and good sense, and leaves him to cry himself to sleep, demanding powers of self-control and development which the child does not possess. There is no doubt that our development of charity methods has reached this pseudo-scientific and stilted stage. We have learned to condemn unthinking, ill-regulated kind-heartedness, and we take great pride in mere repression much as the stern parent tells the visitor below how admirably he is rearing the child, who is hysterically crying upstairs and laying the foundation for future nervous disorders. The pseudo-scientific spirit, or rather, the undeveloped stage of our philanthropy, is perhaps most clearly revealed in our tendency to lay constant stress on negative action. "Don't give;" "don't break down self-respect," we are constantly told. We distrust the human impulse as well as the teachings of our own experience, and in their stead substitute dogmatic rules for conduct. We forget that the accumulation of knowledge and the holding of convictions must finally result in the application of that knowledge and those convictions to life itself; that the necessity for activity and a pull upon the sympathies is so severe, that all the knowledge in the possession of the visitor is constantly applied, and she has a reasonable chance for an ultimate intellectual comprehension. Indeed, part of the perplexity in the administration of charity comes from the fact that the type of person drawn to it is the one who insists that her convictions shall not be unrelated to action. Her moral concepts constantly tend to float away from her, unless they have a basis in the concrete relation of life. She is confronted with the task of reducing her scruples to action, and of converging many wills, so as to unite the strength of all of them into one accomplishment, the value of which no one can foresee.

On the other hand, the young woman who has succeeded in expressing her social compunction through charitable effort finds that the wider social activity, and the contact with the larger experience, not only increases her sense of social obligation but at the same time recasts her social ideals. She is chagrined to discover that in the actual task of reducing her social scruples to action, her humble beneficiaries are far in advance of her, not in charity or singleness of purpose, but in self-sacrificing action. She reaches the old-time virtue of humility by a social process, not in the old way, as the man who sits by the side of the road and puts dust upon his head, calling himself a contrite sinner, but she gets the dust upon her head because she has stumbled and fallen in the road through her efforts to push forward the mass, to march with her fellows. She has socialized her virtues not only through a social aim but by a social process.

The Hebrew prophet made three requirements from those who would join the great forward-moving procession led by Jehovah. "To love mercy" and at the same time "to do justly" is the difficult task; to fulfil the first requirement alone is to fall into the error of indiscriminate giving with all its disastrous results; to fulfil the second solely is to obtain the stern policy of withholding, and it results in such a dreary lack of sympathy and understanding that the establishment of justice is impossible. It may be that the combination of the two can never be attained save as we fulfil still the third requirement —"to walk humbly with God," which may mean to walk for many dreary miles beside the lowliest of His creatures, not even in that peace of mind which the company of the humble is popularly supposed to afford, but rather with the pangs and throes to which the poor human understanding is subjected whenever it attempts to comprehend the meaning of life.

Chapter III
Filial Relations

There are many people in every community who have not felt the "social compunction," who do not share the effort toward a higher social morality, who are even unable to sympathetically interpret it. Some of these have been shielded from the inevitable and salutary failures which the trial of new powers involve, because they are content to attain standards of virtue demanded by an easy public opinion, and others of them have exhausted their moral energy in attaining to the current standard of individual and family righteousness.

Such people, who form the bulk of contented society, demand that the radical, the reformer, shall be without stain or question in his personal and family relations, and judge most harshly any deviation from the established standards. There is a certain justice in this: it expresses the inherent conservatism of the mass of men, that none of the established virtues which have been so slowly and hardly acquired shall be sacrificed for the sake of making problematic advance; that the individual, in his attempt to develop and use the new and exalted virtue, shall not fall into the easy temptation of letting the ordinary ones slip through his fingers.

This instinct to conserve the old standards, combined with a distrust of the new standard, is a constant difficulty in the way of those experiments and advances depending upon the initiative of women, both because women are the more sensitive to the individual and family claims, and because their training has tended to make them content with the response to these claims alone.

There is no doubt that, in the effort to sustain the moral energy necessary to work out a more satisfactory social relation, the individual often sacrifices the energy which should legitimately go into the fulfilment of personal and family claims, to what he considers the higher claim.

In considering the changes which our increasing democracy is constantly making upon various relationships, it is impossible to ignore the filial relation. This chapter deals with the relation between parents and their grown-up daughters, as affording an explicit illustration of the perplexity and mal-adjustment brought about by the various attempts of young women to secure a more active share in the community life. We constantly see parents very much disconcerted and perplexed in regard to their daughters when these daughters undertake work lying quite outside of traditional and family interests. These parents insist that the girl is carried away by a foolish enthusiasm, that she is in search of a career, that she is restless and does not know what she wants. They will give any reason, almost, rather than the recognition of a genuine and dignified claim. Possibly all this is due to the fact that for so many hundreds of years women have had no larger interests, no participation in the affairs lying quite outside personal and family claims. Any attempt that the individual woman formerly made to subordinate or renounce the family claim was inevitably construed to mean that she was setting up her own will against that of her family's for selfish ends. It was concluded that she could have no motive larger than a desire to serve her family, and her attempt to break away must therefore be wilful and self-indulgent.

The family logically consented to give her up at her marriage, when she was enlarging the family tie by founding another family. It was easy to understand that they permitted and even promoted her going to college, travelling in Europe, or any other means of self-improvement, because these merely meant the development and cultivation of one of its own members. When, however, she responded to her impulse to fulfil the social or democratic claim, she violated every tradition.

The mind of each one of us reaches back to our first struggles as we emerged from self-willed childhood into a recognition of family obligations. We have all gradually learned to respond to them, and yet most of us have had at least fleeting glimpses of what it might be to disregard them and the elemental claim they make upon us. We have yielded at times to the temptation of ignoring them for selfish aims, of considering the individual and not the family convenience, and we remember with shame the self-pity which inevitably followed. But just as we have learned to adjust the personal and family claims, and to find an orderly development impossible without recognition of both, so perhaps we are called upon now to make a second adjustment between the family and the social claim, in which neither shall lose and both be ennobled.

The attempt to bring about a healing compromise in which the two shall be adjusted in proper relation is not an easy one. It is difficult to distinguish between the outward act of him who in following one legitimate claim has been led into the temporary violation of another, and the outward act of him who deliberately renounces a just claim and throws aside all obligation for the sake of his own selfish and individual development. The man, for instance, who deserts his family that he may cultivate an artistic sensibility, or acquire what he considers more fulness of life for himself, must always arouse our contempt. Breaking the marriage tie as Ibsen's "Nora" did, to obtain a larger self-development, or holding to it as George Eliot's "Romola" did, because of the larger claim of the state and society, must always remain two distinct paths. The collision of interests, each of which has a real moral basis and a right to its own place in life, is bound to be more or less tragic. It is the struggle between two claims, the destruction of either of which would bring ruin to the ethical life. Curiously enough, it is almost exactly this contradiction which is the tragedy set forth by the Greek dramatist, who asserted that the gods who watch over the sanctity of the family bond must yield to the higher claims of the gods of the state. The failure to recognize the social claim as legitimate causes the trouble; the suspicion constantly remains that woman's public efforts are merely selfish and captious, and are not directed to the general good. This suspicion will never be dissipated until parents, as well as daughters, feel the democratic impulse and recognize the social claim.

Our democracy is making inroads upon the family, the oldest of human institutions, and a claim is being advanced which in a certain sense is larger than the family claim. The claim of the state in time of war has long been recognized, so that in its name the family has given up sons and husbands and even the fathers of little children. If we can once see the claims of society in any such light, if its misery and need can be made clear and urged as an explicit claim, as the state urges its claims in the time of danger, then for the first time the daughter who desires to minister to that need will be recognized as acting conscientiously. This recognition may easily come first through the emotions, and may be admitted as a response to pity and mercy long before it is formulated and perceived by the intellect.

The family as well as the state we are all called upon to maintain as

the highest institutions which the race has evolved for its safeguard and protection. But merely to preserve these institutions is not enough. There come periods of reconstruction, during which the task is laid upon a passing generation, to enlarge the function and carry forward the ideal of a long-established institution. There is no doubt that many women, consciously and unconsciously, are struggling with this task. The family, like every other element of human life, is susceptible of progress, and from epoch to epoch its tendencies and aspirations are enlarged, although its duties can never be abrogated and its obligations can never be cancelled. It is impossible to bring about the higher development by any self-assertion or breaking away of the individual will. The new growth in the plant swelling against the sheath, which at the same time imprisons and protects it, must still be the truest type of progress. The family in its entirety must be carried out into the larger life. Its various members together must recognize and acknowledge the validity of the social obligation. When this does not occur we have a most flagrant example of the ill-adjustment and misery arising when an ethical code is applied too rigorously and too conscientiously to conditions which are no longer the same as when the code was instituted, and for which it was never designed. We have all seen parental control and the family claim assert their authority in fields of effort which belong to the adult judgment of the child and pertain to activity quite outside the family life. Probably the distinctively family tragedy of which we all catch glimpses now and then, is the assertion of this authority through all the entanglements of wounded affection and misunderstanding. We see parents and children acting from conscientious motives and with the tenderest affection, yet bringing about a misery which can scarcely be hidden.

Such glimpses remind us of that tragedy enacted centuries ago in Assisi, when the eager young noble cast his very clothing at his father's feet, dramatically renouncing his filial allegiance, and formally subjecting the narrow family claim to the wider and more universal duty. All the conflict of tragedy ensued which might have been averted, had the father recognized the higher claim, and had he been willing to subordinate and adjust his own claim to it. The father considered his son disrespectful and hard-hearted, yet we know St. Francis to have been the most tender and loving of men, responsive to all possible ties, even to those of inanimate nature. We know that by his affections he freed the frozen life of his time. The elements of tragedy lay in the narrowness of the father's mind; in his lack of comprehension and his lack of sympathy with the power which was moving his son, and which was but part of the religious revival which swept Europe from end to end in the early part of the thirteenth century; the same power which built the cathedrals of the North, and produced the saints and sages of the South. But the father's situation was nevertheless genuine; he felt his heart sore and angry, and his dignity covered with disrespect. He could not, indeed, have felt otherwise, unless he had been touched by the fire of the same revival, and lifted out of and away from the contemplation of himself and his narrower claim. It is another proof that the notion of a larger obligation can only come through the response to an enlarged interest in life and in the social movements around us.

The grown-up son has so long been considered a citizen with well-defined duties and a need of "making his way in the world," that the family claim is urged much less strenuously in his case, and as a matter of authority, it ceases gradually to be made at all. In the case of the grown-up daughter, however, who is under no necessity of earning a living, and who has no strong artistic bent, taking her to Paris to study painting or to Germany to study music, the years immediately following her graduation from college are too often filled with a restlessness and unhappiness which might be avoided by a little clear thinking, and by an adaptation of our code of family ethics to modern conditions.

It is always difficult for the family to regard the daughter otherwise than as a family possession. From her babyhood she has been the charm and grace of the household, and it is hard to think of her as an integral part of the social order, hard to believe that she has duties outside of the family, to the state and to society in the larger sense. This assumption that the daughter is solely an inspiration and refinement to the family itself and its own immediate circle, that her delicacy and polish are but outward symbols of her father's protection and prosperity, worked very smoothly for the most part so long as her education was in line with it. When there was absolutely no recognition of the entity of woman's life beyond the family, when the outside claims upon her were still wholly unrecognized, the situation was simple, and the finishing school harmoniously and elegantly answered all requirements. She was fitted to grace the fireside and to add lustre to that social circle which her parents selected for her. But this family assumption has been notably broken into, and educational ideas no longer fit it. Modern education recognizes woman quite apart from family or society claims, and gives her the training which for many years has been deemed successful for highly developing a man's individuality and freeing his powers for independent action. Perplexities often occur when the daughter returns from college and finds that this recognition has been but partially accomplished. When she attempts to act upon the assumption of its accomplishment, she finds herself jarring upon ideals which are so entwined with filial piety, so rooted in the tenderest affections of which the human heart is capable, that both daughter and parents are shocked and startled when they discover what is happening, and they scarcely venture to analyze the situation. The ideal for the education of woman has changed under the pressure of a new claim. The family has responded to the extent of granting the education, but they are jealous of the new claim and assert the family claim as over against it.

The modern woman finds herself educated to recognize a stress of social obligation which her family did not in the least anticipate when they sent her to college. She finds herself, in addition, under an impulse to act her part as a citizen of the world. She accepts her family inheritance with loyalty and affection, but she has entered into a wider inheritance as well, which, for lack of a better phrase, we call the social claim. This claim has been recognized for four years in her training, but after her return from college the family claim is again exclusively and strenuously asserted. The situation has all the discomfort of transition and compromise. The daughter finds a constant and totally unnecessary conflict between the social and the family claims. In most cases the former is repressed and gives way to the family claim, because the latter is concrete and definitely asserted, while the social demand is vague and unformulated. In such instances the girl quietly submits, but she feels wronged whenever she allows her mind to dwell upon the situation. She either hides her hurt, and splendid reserves of enthusiasm and capacity go to waste, or her zeal and emotions are turned inward, and the result is an unhappy woman, whose heart is consumed by vain regrets and desires.

If the college woman is not thus quietly reabsorbed, she is even reproached for her discontent. She is told to be devoted to her family, inspiring and responsive to her social circle, and to give the rest of her time to further self-improvement and enjoyment. She expects to do this, and responds to these claims to the best of her ability, even heroically sometimes. But where is the larger life of which she has dreamed so long? That life which surrounds and completes the individual and family life? She has been taught that it is her duty to share this life, and her highest privilege to extend it. This divergence between her self-centred existence and her best convictions becomes constantly more apparent. But the situation is not even so simple as a conflict between her affections and her intellectual convictions, although even that is tumultuous enough, also the emotional nature is divided against itself. The social claim is a demand upon the emotions as well as upon the intellect, and in ignoring it she represses not only her convictions but lowers her springs of vitality. Her life is full of contradictions. She looks out into the world, longing that some demand be made upon her powers, for they are too untrained to furnish an initiative. When her health gives way under this strain, as it often does, her physician invariably advises a rest. But to be put to bed and fed on milk is not what she requires. What she needs is simple, health-giving activity, which, involving the use of all her faculties, shall be a response to all the claims which she so keenly feels.

It is quite true that the family often resents her first attempts to be part of a life quite outside their own, because the college woman frequently makes these first attempts most awkwardly; her faculties have not been trained in the line of action. She lacks the ability to apply her knowledge and theories to life itself and to its complicated situations. This is largely the fault of her training and of the one-sidedness of educational methods. The colleges have long been full of the best ethical teaching, insisting that the good of the whole must ultimately be the measure of effort, and that the individual can only secure his own rights as he labors to secure those of others. But while the teaching has included an ever-broadening range of obligation and has insisted upon the recognition of the claims of human brotherhood, the training has been singularly individualistic; it has fostered ambitions for personal distinction, and has trained the faculties almost exclusively in the direction of intellectual accumulation. Doubtless, woman's education is at fault, in that it has failed to recognize certain needs, and has failed to cultivate and guide the larger desires of which all generous young hearts are full.

During the most formative years of life, it gives the young girl no contact with the feebleness of childhood, the pathos of suffering, or the needs of old age. It gathers together crude youth in contact only with each other and with mature men and women who are there for the purpose of their mental direction. The tenderest promptings are bidden to bide their time. This could only be justifiable if a definite outlet were provided when they leave college. Doubtless the need does not differ widely in men and women, but women not absorbed in professional or business life, in the years immediately following college, are baldly brought face to face with the deficiencies of their training. Apparently every obstacle is removed, and the college woman is at last free to begin the active life, for which, during so many years, she has been preparing. But during this so-called preparation, her faculties have been trained solely for accumulation, and she has learned to utterly distrust the finer impulses of her nature, which would naturally have connected her with human interests outside of her family and her own immediate social circle. All through school and college the young soul dreamed of self-sacrifice, of succor to the helpless and of tenderness to the unfortunate. We persistently distrust these desires, and, unless they follow well-defined lines, we repress them with every device of convention and caution.

One summer the writer went from a two weeks' residence in East London, where she had become sick and bewildered by the sights and sounds encountered there, directly to Switzerland. She found the beaten routes of travel filled with young English men and women who could walk many miles a day, and who could climb peaks so inaccessible that the feats received honorable mention in Alpine journals,—a result which filled their families with joy and pride. These young people knew to a nicety the proper diet and clothing which would best contribute toward endurance. Everything was very fine about them save their motive power. The writer does not refer to the hard-worked men and women who were taking a vacation, but to the leisured young people, to whom this period was the most serious of the year, and filled with the most strenuous exertion. They did not, of course, thoroughly enjoy it, for we are too complicated to be content with mere exercise. Civilization has bound us too closely with our brethren for any one of us to be long happy in the cultivation of mere individual force or in the accumulation of mere muscular energy.

With Whitechapel constantly in mind, it was difficult not to advise these young people to use some of this muscular energy of which they were so proud, in cleaning neglected alleys and paving soggy streets. Their stores of enthusiasm might stir to energy the listless men and women of East London and utilize latent social forces. The exercise would be quite as good, the need of endurance as great, the care for proper dress and food as important; but the motives for action would be turned from selfish ones into social ones. Such an appeal would doubtless be met with a certain response from the young people, but would never be countenanced by their families for an instant.

Fortunately a beginning has been made in another direction, and a few parents have already begun to consider even their little children in relation to society as well as to the family. The young mothers who attend "Child Study" classes have a larger notion of parenthood and expect given characteristics from their children, at certain ages and under certain conditions. They quite calmly watch the various attempts of a child to assert his individuality, which so often takes the form of opposition to the wishes of the family and to the rule of the household. They recognize as acting under the same law of development the little child of three who persistently runs away and pretends not to hear his mother's voice, the boy of ten who violently, although temporarily, resents control of any sort, and the grown-up son who, by an individualized and trained personality, is drawn into pursuits and interests quite alien to those of his family.

This attempt to take the parental relation somewhat away from mere personal experience, as well as the increasing tendency of parents to share their children's pursuits and interests, will doubtless finally result in a better understanding of the social obligation. The understanding, which results from identity of interests, would seem to confirm the conviction that in the complicated life of to-day there is no education so admirable as that education which comes from participation in the constant trend of events. There is no doubt that most of the misunderstandings of life are due to partial intelligence, because our experiences have been so unlike that we cannot comprehend each other. The old difficulties incident to the clash of two codes of morals must drop away, as the experiences of various members of the family become larger and more identical.

At the present moment, however, many of those difficulties still exist and may be seen all about us. In order to illustrate the situation baldly, and at the same time to put it dramatically, it may be well to take an instance concerning which we have no personal feeling. The tragedy of King Lear has been selected, although we have been accustomed so long to give him our sympathy as the victim of the ingratitude of his two older daughters, and of the apparent coldness of Cordelia, that we have not sufficiently considered the weakness of his fatherhood, revealed by the fact that he should get himself into so entangled and unhappy a relation to all of his children. In our pity for Lear, we fail to analyze his character. The King on his throne exhibits utter lack of self-control. The King in the storm gives way to the same emotion, in repining over the wickedness of his children, which he formerly exhibited in his indulgent treatment of them.

It might be illuminating to discover wherein he had failed, and why his old age found him roofless in spite of the fact that he strenuously urged the family claim with his whole conscience. At the opening of the drama he sat upon his throne, ready for the enjoyment which an indulgent parent expects when he has given gifts to his children. From the two elder, the responses for the division of his lands were graceful and fitting, but he longed to hear what Cordelia, his youngest and best beloved child, would say. He looked toward her expectantly, but instead of delight and gratitude there was the first dawn of character. Cordelia made the awkward attempt of an untrained soul to be honest and scrupulously to express her inmost feeling. The king was baffled and distressed by this attempt at self-expression. It was new to him that his daughter should be moved by a principle obtained outside himself, which even his imagination could not follow; that she had caught the notion of an existence in which her relation as a daughter played but a part. She was transformed by a dignity which recast her speech and made it self-contained. She found herself in the sweep of a feeling so large that the immediate loss of a kingdom seemed of little consequence to her. Even an act which might be construed as disrespect to her father was justified in her eyes, because she was vainly striving to fill out this larger conception of duty. The test which comes sooner or later to many parents had come to Lear, to maintain the tenderness of the relation between father and child, after that relation had become one between adults, to be content with the responses made by the adult child to the family claim, while at the same time she responded to the claims of the rest of life. The mind of Lear was not big enough for this test; he failed to see anything but the personal slight involved, and the ingratitude alone reached him. It was impossible for him to calmly watch his child developing beyond the stretch of his own mind and sympathy.

That a man should be so absorbed in his own indignation as to fail to apprehend his child's thought, that he should lose his affection in his anger, simply reveals the fact that his own emotions are dearer to him than his sense of paternal obligation. Lear apparently also ignored the common ancestry of Cordelia and himself, and forgot her royal inheritance of magnanimity. He had thought of himself so long as a noble and indulgent father that he had lost the faculty by which he might perceive himself in the wrong. Even in the midst of the storm he declared himself more sinned against than sinning. He could believe any amount of kindness and goodness of himself, but could imagine no fidelity on the part of Cordelia unless she gave him the sign he demanded.

At length he suffered many hardships; his spirit was buffeted and broken; he lost his reason as well as his kingdom; but for the first time his experience was identical with the experience of the men around him, and he came to a larger conception of life. He put himself in the place of "the poor naked wretches," and unexpectedly found healing and comfort. He took poor Tim in his arms from a sheer desire for human contact and animal warmth, a primitive and genuine need, through which he suddenly had a view of the world which he had never had from his throne, and from this moment his heart began to turn toward Cordelia.

In reading the tragedy of King Lear, Cordelia receives a full share of our censure. Her first words are cold, and we are shocked by her lack of tenderness. Why should she ignore her father's need for indulgence, and be unwilling to give him what he so obviously craved? We see in the old king "the over-mastering desire of being beloved, selfish, and yet characteristic of the selfishness of a loving and kindly nature alone." His eagerness produces in us a strange pity for him, and we are impatient that his youngest and best-beloved child cannot feel this, even in the midst of her search for truth and her newly acquired sense of a higher duty. It seems to us a narrow conception that would break thus abruptly with the past and would assume that her father had no part in the new life. We want to remind her "that pity, memory, and faithfulness are natural ties," and surely as much to be prized as is the development of her own soul. We do not admire the Cordelia who through her self-absorption deserts her father, as we later admire the same woman who comes back from France that she may include her father in her happiness and freer life. The first had selfishly taken her salvation for herself alone, and it was not until her conscience had developed in her new life that she was driven back to her father, where she perished, drawn into the cruelty and wrath which had now become objective and tragic.

Historically considered, the relation of Lear to his children was archaic and barbaric, indicating merely the beginning of a family life since developed. His paternal expression was one of domination and indulgence, without the perception of the needs of his children, without any anticipation of their entrance into a wider life, or any belief that they could have a worthy life apart from him. If that rudimentary conception of family life ended in such violent disaster, the fact that we have learned to be more decorous in our conduct does not demonstrate that by following the same line of theory we may not reach a like misery.

Wounded affection there is sure to be, but this could be reduced to a modicum if we could preserve a sense of the relation of the individual to the family, and of the latter to society, and if we had been given a code of ethics dealing with these larger relationships, instead of a code designed to apply so exclusively to relationships obtaining only between individuals.

Doubtless the clashes and jars which we all feel most keenly are those which occur when two standards of morals, both honestly held and believed in, are brought sharply together. The awkwardness and constraint we experience when two standards of conventions and manners clash but feebly prefigure this deeper difference.

Chapter IV
Household Adjustment

If we could only be judged or judge other people by purity of motive, life would be much simplified, but that would be to abandon the contention made in the first chapter, that the processes of life are as important as its aims. We can all recall acquaintances of whose integrity of purpose we can have no doubt, but who cause much confusion as they proceed to the accomplishment of that purpose, who indeed are often insensible to their own mistakes and harsh in their judgments of other people because they are so confident of their own inner integrity.

This tendency to be so sure of integrity of purpose as to be unsympathetic and hardened to the means by which it is accomplished, is perhaps nowhere so obvious as in the household itself. It nowhere operates as so constant a force as in the minds of the women who in all the perplexity of industrial transition are striving to administer domestic affairs. The ethics held by them are for the most part the individual and family codes, untouched by the larger social conceptions.

These women, rightly confident of their household and family integrity and holding to their own code of morals, fail to see the household in its social aspect. Possibly no relation has been so slow to respond to the social ethics which we are now considering, as that between the household employer and the household employee, or, as it is still sometimes called, that between mistress and servant.

This persistence of the individual code in relation to the household may be partly accounted for by the fact that orderly life and, in a sense, civilization itself, grew from the concentration of interest in one place, and that moral feeling first became centred in a limited number of persons. From the familiar proposition that the home began because the mother was obliged to stay in one spot in order to cherish the child, we can see a foundation for the belief that if women are much away from home, the home itself will be destroyed and all ethical progress endangered.

We have further been told that the earliest dances and social gatherings were most questionable in their purposes, and that it was, therefore, the good and virtuous women who first stayed at home, until gradually the two-the woman who stayed at home and the woman who guarded her virtue-became synonymous. A code of ethics was thus developed in regard to woman's conduct, and her duties were logically and carefully limited to her own family circle. When it became impossible to adequately minister to the needs of this circle without the help of many people who did not strictly belong to the family, although they were part of the household, they were added as aids merely for supplying these needs. When women were the brewers and bakers, the fullers, dyers, spinners, and weavers, the soap and candle makers, they administered large industries, but solely from the family point of view. Only a few hundred years ago, woman had complete control of the manufacturing of many commodities which now figure so largely in commerce, and it is evident that she let the manufacturing of these commodities go into the hands of men, as soon as organization and a larger conception of their production were required. She felt no responsibility for their management when they were taken from the home to the factory, for deeper than her instinct to manufacture food and clothing for her family was her instinct to stay with them, and by isolation and care to guard them from evil.

She had become convinced that a woman's duty extended only to her own family, and that the world outside had no claim upon her. The British matron ordered her maidens aright, when they were spinning under her own roof, but she felt no compunction of conscience when the morals and health of young girls were endangered in the overcrowded and insanitary factories. The code of family ethics was established in her mind so firmly that it excluded any notion of social effort.

It is quite possible to accept this explanation of the origin of morals, and to believe that the preservation of the home is at the foundation of all that is best in civilization, without at the same time insisting that the separate preparation and serving of food is an inherent part of the structure and sanctity of the home, or that those who minister to one household shall minister to that exclusively. But to make this distinction seems difficult, and almost invariably the sense of obligation to the family becomes confused with a certain sort of domestic management. The moral issue involved in one has become inextricably combined with the industrial difficulty involved in the other, and it is at this point that so many perplexed housekeepers, through the confusion of the two problems, take a difficult and untenable position.

There are economic as well as ethical reasons for this survival of a simpler code. The wife of a workingman still has a distinct economic value to her husband. She cooks, cleans, washes, and mends-services for which, before his marriage, he paid ready money. The wife of the successful business or professional man does not do this. He continues to pay for his cooking, house service, and washing. The mending, however, is still largely performed by his wife; indeed, the stockings are pathetically retained and their darning given an exaggerated importance, as if women instinctively felt that these mended stockings were the last remnant of the entire household industry, of which they were formerly mistresses. But one industry, the cooking and serving of foods to her own family, woman has never relinquished. It has, therefore, never been organized, either by men or women, and is in an undeveloped state. Each employer of household labor views it solely from the family standpoint. The ethics prevailing in regard to it are distinctly personal and unsocial, and result in the unique isolation of the household employee.

As industrial conditions have changed, the household has simplified, from the mediæval affair of journeymen, apprentices, and maidens who spun and brewed to the family proper; to those who love each other and live together in ties of affection and consanguinity. Were this process complete, we should have no problem of household employment. But, even in households comparatively humble, there is still one alien, one who is neither loved nor loving.

The modern family has dropped the man who made its shoes, the woman who spun its clothes, and, to a large extent, the woman who washes them, but it stoutly refuses to drop the woman who cooks its food and ministers directly to its individual comfort; it strangely insists that to do that would be to destroy the family life itself. The cook is uncomfortable, the family is uncomfortable; but it will not drop her as all her fellow-workers have been dropped, although the cook herself insists upon it. So far has this insistence gone that every possible concession is made to retain her. The writer knows an employer in one of the suburbs who built a bay at the back of her house so that her cook might have a pleasant room in which to sleep, and another in which to receive her friends. This employer naturally felt aggrieved when the cook refused to stay in her bay. Viewed in an historic light, this employer might quite as well have added a bay to her house for her shoemaker, and then deemed him ungrateful because he declined to live in it.

A listener, attentive to a conversation between two employers of household labor, —and we certainly all have opportunity to hear such conversations, —would often discover a tone implying that the employer was abused and put upon; that she was struggling with the problem solely because she was thus serving her family and performing her social duties; that otherwise it would be a great relief to her to abandon the entire situation, and "never have a servant in her house again." Did she follow this impulse, she would simply yield to the trend of her times and accept the present system of production. She would be in line with the industrial organization of her age. Were she in line ethically, she would have to believe that the sacredness and beauty of family life do not consist in the processes of the separate preparation of food, but in sharing the corporate life of the community, and in making the family the unit of that life.

The selfishness of a modern mistress, who, in her narrow social ethics, insists that those who minister to the comforts of her family shall minister to it alone, that they shall not only be celibate, but shall be cut off, more or less, from their natural social ties, excludes the best working-people from her service.

A man of dignity and ability is quite willing to come into a house to tune a piano. Another man of mechanical skill will come to put up window shades. Another of less skill, but of perfect independence, will come to clean and relay a carpet. These men would all resent the situation and consider it quite impossible if it implied the giving up of their family and social ties, and living under the roof of the household requiring their services.

The isolation of the household employee is perhaps inevitable so long as the employer holds her belated ethics; but the situation is made even more difficult by the character and capacity of the girls who enter this industry. In any great industrial change the workmen who are permanently displaced are those who are too dull to seize upon changed conditions. The workmen who have knowledge and insight, who are in touch with their time, quickly reorganize.

The general statement may be made that the enterprising girls of the community go into factories, and the less enterprising go into households, although there are many exceptions. It is not a question of skill, of energy, of conscientious work, which will make a girl rise industrially while she is in the household; she is not in the rising movement. She is belated in a class composed of the unprogressive elements of the community, which is recruited constantly by those from the ranks of the incompetent, by girls who are learning the language, girls who are timid and slow, or girls who look at life solely from the savings-bank point of view. The distracted housekeeper struggles with these unprogressive girls, holding to them not even the well-defined and independent relation of employer and employed, but the hazy and constantly changing one of mistress to servant.

The latter relation is changing under pressure from various directions. In our increasing democracy the notion of personal service is constantly becoming more distasteful, conflicting, as it does, with the more modern notion of personal dignity. Personal ministration to the needs of childhood, illness, and old age seem to us reasonable, and the democratic adjustment in regard to them is being made. The first two are constantly raised nearer to the level of a profession, and there is little doubt that the third will soon follow. But personal ministrations to a normal, healthy adult, consuming the time and energy of another adult, we find more difficult to reconcile to our theories of democracy.

A factory employer parts with his men at the factory gates at the end of a day's work; they go to their homes as he goes to his, in the assumption that they both do what they want and spend their money as they please; but this solace of equality outside of working hours is denied the bewildered employer of household labor.

She is obliged to live constantly in the same house with her employee, and because of certain equalities in food and shelter she is brought more sharply face to face with the mental and social inequalities.

The difficulty becomes more apparent as the character of the work performed by the so-called servant is less absolutely useful and may be merely time consuming. A kind-hearted woman who will complacently take an afternoon drive, leaving her cook to prepare the five courses of a "little dinner for only ten guests," will not be nearly so comfortable the next evening when she speeds her daughter to a dance, conscious that her waitress must spend the evening in dull solitude on the chance that a caller or two may ring the door-bell.

A conscientious employer once remarked to the writer: "In England it must be much easier; the maid does not look and dress so like your daughter, and you can at least pretend that she doesn't like the same things. But really, my new waitress is quite as pretty and stylish as my daughter is, and her wistful look sometimes when Mary goes off to a frolic quite breaks my heart."

Too many employers of domestic service have always been exempt from manual labor, and therefore constantly impose exacting duties upon employees, the nature of which they do not understand by experience; there is thus no curb of rationality imposed upon the employer's requirements and demands. She is totally unlike the foreman in a shop, who has only risen to his position by way of having actually performed with his own hands all the work of the men he directs. There is also another class of employers of domestic labor, who grow capricious and over-exacting through sheer lack of larger interests to occupy their minds; it is equally bad for them and the employee that the duties of the latter are not clearly defined. Tolstoy contends that an exaggerated notion of cleanliness has developed among such employers, which could never have been evolved among usefully employed people. He points to the fact that a serving man, in order that his hands may be immaculately clean, is kept from performing the heavier work of the household, and then is supplied with a tray, upon which to place a card, in order that even his clean hands may not touch it; later, even his clean hands are covered with a pair of clean white gloves, which hold the tray upon which the card is placed.

If it were not for the undemocratic ethics used by the employers of domestics, much work now performed in the household would be done outside, as is true of many products formerly manufactured in the feudal household. The worker in all other trades has complete control of his own time after the performance of definitely limited services, his wages are paid altogether in money which he may spend in the maintenance of a separate home life, and he has full opportunity to organize with the other workers in his trade.

The domestic employee is retained in the household largely because her "mistress" fatuously believes that she is thus maintaining the sanctity of family life.

The household employee has no regular opportunity for meeting other workers of her trade, and of attaining with them the dignity of a corporate body. The industrial isolation of the household employee results, as isolation in a trade must always result, in a lack of progress in the methods and products of that trade, and a lack of aspiration and education in the workman. Whether we recognize this isolation as a cause or not, we are all ready to acknowledge that household labor has been in some way belated; that the improvements there have not kept up with the improvement in other occupations. It is said that the last revolution in the processes of cooking was brought about by Count Rumford, who died a hundred years ago. This is largely due to the lack of *esprit de corps* among the employees, which keeps them collectively from fresh achievements, as the absence of education in the individual keeps her from improving her implements.

Under this isolation, not only must one set of utensils serve divers purposes, and, as a consequence, tend to a lessened volume and lower quality of work, but, inasmuch as the appliances are not made to perform the fullest work, there is an amount of capital invested disproportionate to the product when measured by the achievement in other branches of industry. More important than this is the result of the isolation upon the worker herself. There is nothing more devastating to the inventive faculty, nor fatal to a flow of mind and spirit, than the constant feeling of loneliness and the absence of that fellowship which makes our public opinion. If an angry foreman reprimands a girl for breaking a machine, twenty other girls hear him, and the culprit knows perfectly well their opinion as to the justice or injustice of her situation. In either case she bears it better for knowing that, and not thinking it over in solitude. If a household employee breaks a utensil or a piece of porcelain and is reprimanded by her employer, too often the invisible jury is the family of the latter, who naturally uphold her censorious position and intensify the feeling of loneliness in the employee.

The household employee, in addition to her industrial isolation, is also isolated socially. It is well to remember that the household employees for the better quarters of the city and suburbs are largely drawn from the poorer quarters, which are nothing if not gregarious. The girl is born and reared in a tenement house full of children. She goes to school with them, and there she learns to march, to read, and write in companionship with forty others. When she is old enough to go to parties, those she attends are usually held in a public hall and are crowded with dancers. If she works in a factory, she walks home with many other girls, in much the same spirit as she formerly walked to school with them. She mingles with the young men she knows, in frank, economic, and social equality. Until she marries she remains at home with no special break or change in her family and social life. If she is employed in a household, this is not true. Suddenly all the conditions of her life are altered. This change may be wholesome for her, but it is not easy, and thought of the savings-bank does not cheer one much, when one is twenty. She is isolated from the people with whom she has been reared, with whom she has gone to school, and among whom she expects to live when she marries. She is naturally lonely and constrained away from them, and the "new maid" often seems "queer" to her employer's family. She does not care to mingle socially with the people in whose house she is employed, as the girl from the country often does, but she surfers horribly from loneliness.

This wholesome, instinctive dread of social isolation is so strong that, as every city intelligence-office can testify, the filling of situations is easier, or more difficult, in proportion as the place offers more or less companionship. Thus, the easy situation to fill is always the city house, with five or six employees, shading off into the more difficult suburban home, with two, and the utterly impossible lonely country house.

There are suburban employers of household labor who make heroic efforts to supply domestic and social life to their employees; who take the domestic employee to drive, arrange to have her invited out occasionally; who supply her with books and papers and companionship. Nothing could be more praiseworthy in motive, but it is seldom successful in actual operation, resulting as it does in a simulacrum of companionship. The employee may have a genuine friendship for her employer, and a pleasure in her companionship, or she may not have, and the unnaturalness of the situation comes from the insistence that she has, merely because of the propinquity.

The unnaturalness of the situation is intensified by the fact that the employee is practically debarred by distance and lack of leisure from her natural associates, and that her employer sympathetically insists upon filling the vacancy in interests and affections by her own tastes and friendship. She may or may not succeed, but the employee should not be thus dependent upon the good will of her employer. That in itself is undemocratic.

The difficulty is increasing by a sense of social discrimination which the household employee keenly feels is against her and in favor of the factory girls, in the minds of the young men of her acquaintance. Women seeking employment, understand perfectly well this feeling among mechanics, doubtless quite unjustifiable, but it acts as a strong inducement toward factory labor. The writer has long ceased to apologize for the views and opinions of working people, being quite sure that on the whole they are quite as wise and quite as foolish as the views and opinions of other people, but that this particularly foolish opinion of young mechanics is widely shared by the employing class can be easily demonstrated. The contrast is further accentuated by the better social position of the factory girl, and the advantages provided for her in the way of lunch clubs, social clubs, and vacation homes, from which girls performing household labor are practically excluded by their hours of work, their geographical situation, and a curious feeling that they are not as interesting as factory girls.

This separation from her natural social ties affects, of course, her opportunity for family life. It is well to remember that women, as a rule, are devoted to their families; that they want to live with their parents, their brothers and sisters, and kinsfolk, and will sacrifice much to accomplish this. This devotion is so universal that it is impossible to ignore it when we consider women as employees. Young unmarried women are not detached from family claims and requirements as young men are, and are more ready and steady in their response to the needs of aged parents and the helpless members of the family. But women performing labor in households have peculiar difficulties in responding to their family claims, and are practically dependent upon their employers for opportunities of even seeing their relatives and friends.

Curiously enough the same devotion to family life and quick response to its claims, on the part of the employer, operates against the girl employed in household labor, and still further contributes to her isolation.

The employer of household labor, in her zeal to preserve her own family life intact and free from intrusion, acts inconsistently and grants to her cook, for instance, but once or twice a week, such opportunity for untrammelled association with her relatives as the employer's family claims constantly. This in itself is undemocratic, in that it makes a distinction between the value of family life for one set of people as over against another; or, rather, claims that one set of people are of so much less importance than another, that a valuable side of life pertaining to them should be sacrificed for the other.

This cannot be defended theoretically, and no doubt much of the talk among the employers of household labor, that their employees are carefully shielded and cared for, and that it is so much better for a girl's health and morals to work in a household than to work in a factory, comes from a certain uneasiness of conscience, and from a desire to make up by individual scruple what would be done much more freely and naturally by public opinion if it had an untrammelled chance to assert itself. One person, or a number of isolated persons, however conscientious, cannot perform this office of public opinion. Certain hospitals in London have contributed statistics showing that seventy-eight per cent of illegitimate children born there are the children of girls working in households. These girls are certainly not less virtuous than factory girls, for they come from the same families and have had the same training, but the girls who remain at home and work in factories meet their lovers naturally and easily, their fathers and brothers know the men, and unconsciously exercise a certain supervision and a certain direction in their choice of companionship. The household employees living in another part of the city, away from their natural family and social ties, depend upon chance for the lovers whom they meet. The lover may be the young man who delivers for the butcher or grocer, or the solitary friend, who follows the girl from her own part of town and pursues unfairly the advantage which her social loneliness and isolation afford him. There is no available public opinion nor any standard of convention which the girl can apply to her own situation.

It would be easy to point out many inconveniences arising from the fact that the old economic forms are retained when moral conditions which befitted them have entirely disappeared, but until employers of domestic labor become conscious of their narrow code of ethics, and make a distinct effort to break through the status of mistress and servant, because it shocks their moral sense, there is no chance of even beginning a reform.

A fuller social and domestic life among household employees would be steps toward securing their entrance into the larger industrial organizations by which the needs of a community are most successfully administered. Many a girl who complains of loneliness, and who relinquishes her situation with that as her sole excuse, feebly tries to formulate her sense of restraint and social mal-adjustment. She sometimes says that she "feels so unnatural all the time." The writer has known the voice of a girl to change so much during three weeks of "service" that she could not recognize it when the girl returned to her home. It alternated between the high falsetto in which a shy child "speaks a piece" and the husky gulp with which the *globus hystericus* is swallowed. The alertness and *bonhomie* of the voice of the tenement-house child had totally disappeared. When such a girl leaves her employer, her reasons are often incoherent and totally incomprehensible to that good lady, who naturally concludes that she wishes to get away from the work and back to her dances and giddy life, content, if she has these, to stand many hours in an insanitary factory. The charge of the employer is only half a truth. These dances may be the only organized form of social life which the disheartened employee is able to mention, but the girl herself, in her discontent and her moving from place to place, is blindly striving to respond to a larger social life. Her employer thinks that she should be able to consider only the interests and conveniences of her employer's family, because the employer herself is holding to a family outlook, and refuses to allow her mind to take in the larger aspects of the situation.

Although this household industry survives in the midst of the factory system, it must, of course, constantly compete with it. Women with little children, or those with invalids depending upon them, cannot enter either occupation, and they are practically confined to the sewing trades; but to all other untrained women seeking employment a choice is open between these two forms of labor.

There are few women so dull that they cannot paste labels on a box, or do some form of factory work; few so dull that some perplexed housekeeper will not receive them, at least for a trial, in her household. Household labor, then, has to compete with factory labor, and women seeking employment, more or less consciously compare these two forms of labor in point of hours, in point of permanency of employment, in point of wages, and in point of the advantage they afford for family and social life. Three points are easily disposed of. First, in regard to hours, there is no doubt that the factory has the advantage. The average factory hours are from seven in the morning to six in the evening, with the chance of working overtime in busy seasons. This leaves most of the evenings and Sundays entirely free. The average hours of household labor are from six in the morning until eight at night, with little difference in seasons. There is one afternoon a week, with an occasional evening, but Sunday is seldom wholly free. Even these evenings and afternoons take the form of a concession from the employer. They are called "evenings out," as if the time really belonged to her, but that she was graciously permitting her employee to use it. This attitude, of course, is in marked contrast to that maintained by the factory operative, who, when she works evenings is paid for "over-time."

Second, in regard to permanency of position, the advantage is found clearly on the side of the household employee, if she proves in any measure satisfactory to her employer, for she encounters much less competition.

Third, in point of wages, the household is again fairly ahead, if we consider not the money received, but the opportunity offered for saving money. This is greater among household employees, because they do not pay board, the clothing required is simpler, and the temptation to spend money in recreation is less frequent. The minimum wages paid an adult in household labor may be fairly put at two dollars and a half a week; the maximum at six dollars, this excluding the comparatively rare opportunities for women to cook at forty dollars a month, and the housekeeper's position at fifty dollars a month.

The factory wages, viewed from the savings-bank point of view, may be smaller in the average, but this is doubtless counterbalanced in the minds of the employees by the greater chance which the factory offers for increased wages. A girl over sixteen seldom works in a factory for less than four dollars a week, and always cherishes the hope of at last being a forewoman with a permanent salary of from fifteen to twenty-five dollars a week. Whether she attains this or not, she runs a fair chance of earning ten dollars a week as a skilled worker. A girl finds it easier to be content with three dollars a week, when she pays for board, in a scale of wages rising toward ten dollars, than to be content with four dollars a week and pay no board, in a scale of wages rising toward six dollars; and the girl well knows that there are scores of forewomen at sixty dollars a month for one forty-dollar cook or fifty-dollar housekeeper. In many cases this position is well taken economically, for, although the opportunity for saving may be better for the employees in the household than in the factory, her family saves more when she works in a factory and lives with them. The rent is no more when she is at home. The two dollars and a half a week which she pays into the family fund more than covers the cost of her actual food, and at night she can often contribute toward the family labor by helping her mother wash and sew.

The fourth point has already been considered, and if the premise in regard to the isolation of the household employee is well taken, and if the position can be sustained that this isolation proves the determining factor in the situation, then certainly an effort should be made to remedy this, at least in its domestic and social aspects. To allow household employees to live with their own families and among their own friends, as factory employees now do, would be to relegate more production to industrial centres administered on the factory system, and to secure shorter hours for that which remains to be done in the household.

In those cases in which the household employees have no family ties, doubtless a remedy against social isolation would be the formation of residence clubs, at least in the suburbs, where the isolation is most keenly felt. Indeed, the beginnings of these clubs are already seen in the servants' quarters at the summer hotels. In these residence clubs, the household employee could have the independent life which only one's own abiding place can afford. This, of course, presupposes a higher grade of ability than household employees at present possess; on the other hand, it is only by offering such possibilities that the higher grades of intelligence can be secured for household employment. As the plan of separate clubs for household employees will probably come first in the suburbs, where the difficulty of securing and holding "servants" under the present system is most keenly felt, so the plan of buying cooked food from an outside kitchen, and of having more and more of the household product relegated to the factory, will probably come from the comparatively poor people in the city, who feel most keenly the pressure of the present system. They already consume a much larger proportion of canned goods and bakers' wares and "prepared meats" than the more prosperous people do, because they cannot command the skill nor the time for the more tedious preparation of the raw material. The writer has seen a tenement-house mother pass by a basket of green peas at the door of a local grocery store, to purchase a tin of canned peas, because they could be easily prepared for supper and "the children liked the tinny taste."

It is comparatively easy for an employer to manage her household industry with a cook, a laundress, a waitress. The difficulties really begin when the family income is so small that but one person can be employed in the household for all these varied functions, and the difficulties increase and grow almost insurmountable as they fall altogether upon the mother of the family, who is living in a flat, or, worse still, in a tenement house, where one stove and one set of utensils must be put to all sorts of uses, fit or unfit, making the living room of the family a horror in summer, and perfectly insupportable on rainy washing-days in winter. Such a woman, rather than the prosperous housekeeper, uses factory products, and thus no high standard of quality is established.

The problem of domestic service, which has long been discussed in the United States and England, is now coming to prominence in France. As a well-known economist has recently pointed out, the large defection in the ranks of domestics is there regarded as a sign of revolt against an "unconscious slavery," while English and American writers appeal to the statistics which point to the absorption of an enormous number of the class from which servants were formerly recruited into factory employments, and urge, as the natural solution, that more of the products used in households be manufactured in factories, and that personal service, at least for healthy adults, be eliminated altogether. Both of these lines of discussion certainly indicate that domestic service is yielding to the influence of a democratic movement, and is emerging from the narrower code of family ethics into the larger code governing social relations. It still remains to express the ethical advance through changed economic conditions by which the actual needs of the family may be supplied not only more effectively but more in line with associated effort. To fail to apprehend the tendency of one's age, and to fail to adapt the conditions of an industry to it, is to leave that industry ill-adjusted and belated on the economic side, and out of line ethically.

Chapter V
Industrial Amelioration

There is no doubt that the great difficulty we experience in reducing to action our imperfect code of social ethics arises from the fact that we have not yet learned to act together, and find it far from easy even to fuse our principles and aims into a satisfactory statement. We have all been at times entertained by the futile efforts of half a dozen highly individualized people gathered together as a committee. Their aimless attempts to find a common method of action have recalled the wavering motion of a baby's arm before he has learned to coördinate his muscles.

If, as is many times stated, we are passing from an age of individualism to one of association, there is no doubt that for decisive and effective action the individual still has the best of it. He will secure efficient results while committees are still deliberating upon the best method of making a beginning. And yet, if the need of the times demand associated effort, it may easily be true that the action which appears ineffective, and yet is carried out upon the more highly developed line of associated effort, may represent a finer social quality and have a greater social value than the more effective individual action. It is possible that an individual may be successful, largely because he conserves all his powers for individual achievement and does not put any of his energy into the training which will give him the ability to act with others. The individual acts promptly, and we are dazzled by his success while only dimly conscious of the inadequacy of his code. Nowhere is this illustrated more clearly than in industrial relations, as existing between the owner of a large factory and his employees.

A growing conflict may be detected between the democratic ideal, which urges the workmen to demand representation in the administration of industry, and the accepted position, that the man who owns the capital and takes the risks has the exclusive right of management. It is in reality a clash between individual or aristocratic management, and corporate or democratic management. A large and highly developed factory presents a sharp contrast between its socialized form and individualistic ends.

It is possible to illustrate this difference by a series of events which occurred in Chicago during the summer of 1894. These events epitomized and exaggerated, but at the same time challenged, the code of ethics which regulates much of our daily conduct, and clearly showed that so-called social relations are often resting upon the will of an individual, and are in reality regulated by a code of individual ethics.

As this situation illustrates a point of great difficulty to which we have arrived in our development of social ethics, it may be justifiable to discuss it at some length. Let us recall the facts, not as they have been investigated and printed, but as they remain in our memories.

A large manufacturing company had provided commodious workshops, and, at the instigation of its president, had built a model town for the use of its employees. After a series of years it was deemed necessary, during a financial depression, to reduce the wages of these employees by giving each workman less than full-time work "in order to keep the shops open." This reduction was not accepted by the men, who had become discontented with the factory management and the town regulations, and a strike ensued, followed by a complete shut-down of the works. Although these shops were non-union shops, the strikers were hastily organized and appealed for help to the American Railway Union, which at that moment was holding its biennial meeting in Chicago. After some days' discussion and some futile attempts at arbitration, a sympathetic strike was declared, which gradually involved railway men in all parts of the country, and orderly transportation was brought to a complete standstill. In the excitement which followed, cars were burned and tracks torn up. The police of Chicago did not cope with the disorder, and the railway companies, apparently distrusting the Governor of the State, and in order to protect the United States mails, called upon the President of the United States for the federal troops, the federal courts further enjoined all persons against any form of interference with the property or operation of the railroads, and the situation gradually assumed the proportions of internecine warfare. During all of these events the president of the manufacturing company first involved, steadfastly refused to have the situation submitted to arbitration, and this attitude naturally provoked much discussion. The discussion was broadly divided between those who held that the long kindness of the president of the company had been most ungratefully received, and those who maintained that the situation was the inevitable outcome of the social consciousness developing among working people. The first defended the president of the company in his persistent refusal to arbitrate, maintaining that arbitration was impossible after the matter had been taken up by other than his own employees, and they declared that a man must be allowed to run his own business. They considered the firm stand of the president a service to the manufacturing interests of the entire country. The others claimed that a large manufacturing concern has ceased to be a private matter; that not only a number of workmen and stockholders are concerned in its management, but that the interests of the public are so involved that the officers of the company are in a real sense administering a public trust.

This prolonged strike clearly puts in a concrete form the ethics of an individual, in this case a benevolent employer, and the ethics of a mass of men, his employees, claiming what they believed to be their moral rights.

These events illustrate the difficulty of managing an industry which has become organized into a vast social operation, not with the coöperation of the workman thus socialized, but solely by the dictation of the individual owning the capital. There is a sharp divergence between the social form and the individual aim, which becomes greater as the employees are more highly socialized and dependent. The president of the company under discussion went further than the usual employer does. He socialized not only the factory, but the form in which his workmen were living. He built, and in a great measure regulated, an entire town, without calling upon the workmen either for self-expression or self-government. He honestly believed that he knew better than they what was for their good, as he certainly knew better than they how to conduct his business. As his factory developed and increased, making money each year under his direction, he naturally expected the town to prosper in the same way.

He did not realize that the men submitted to the undemocratic conditions of the factory organization because the economic pressure in our industrial affairs is so great that they could not do otherwise. Under this pressure they could be successfully discouraged from organization, and systematically treated on the individual basis.

Social life, however, in spite of class distinctions, is much freer than industrial life, and the men resented the extension of industrial control to domestic and social arrangements. They felt the lack of democracy in the assumption that they should be taken care of in these matters, in which even the humblest workman has won his independence. The basic difficulty lay in the fact that an individual was directing the social affairs of many men without any consistent effort to find out their desires, and without any organization through which to give them social expression. The president of the company was, moreover, so confident of the righteousness of his aim that he had come to test the righteousness of the process by his own feelings and not by those of the men. He doubtless built the town from a sincere desire to give his employees the best surroundings. As it developed, he gradually took toward it the artist attitude toward his own creation, which has no thought for the creation itself but is absorbed in the idea it stands for, and he ceased to measure the usefulness of the town by the standard of the men's needs. This process slowly darkened his glints of memory, which might have connected his experience with that of his men. It is possible to cultivate the impulses of the benefactor until the power of attaining a simple human relationship with the beneficiaries, that of frank equality with them, is gone, and there is left no mutual interest in a common cause. To perform too many good deeds may be to lose the power of recognizing good in others; to be too absorbed in carrying out a personal plan of improvement may be to fail to catch the great moral lesson which our times offer.

The president of this company fostered his employees for many years; he gave them sanitary houses and beautiful parks; but in their extreme need, when they were struggling with the most difficult situation which the times could present to them, he lost his touch and had nothing wherewith to help them. The employer's conception of goodness for his men had been cleanliness, decency of living, and, above all, thrift and temperance. Means had been provided for all this, and opportunities had also been given for recreation and improvement. But this employer suddenly found his town in the sweep of a world-wide moral impulse. A movement had been going on about him and among his working men, of which he had been unconscious, or concerning which he had heard only by rumor.

Outside the ken of philanthropists the proletariat had learned to say in many languages, that "the injury of one is the concern of all." Their watchwords were brotherhood, sacrifice, the subordination of individual and trade interests, to the good of the working classes, and they were moved by a determination to free that class from the untoward conditions under which they were laboring.

Compared to these watchwords, the old ones which this philanthropic employer had given his town were negative and inadequate. He had believed strongly in temperance and steadiness of individual effort, but had failed to apprehend the greater movement of combined abstinence and concerted action. With all his fostering, the president had not attained to a conception of social morality for his men and had imagined that virtue for them largely meant absence of vice.

When the labor movement finally stirred his town, or, to speak more fairly, when, in their distress and perplexity, his own employees appealed to an organized manifestation of this movement, they were quite sure that simply because they were workmen in distress they would not be deserted by it. This loyalty on the part of a widely ramified and well-organized union toward the workmen in a "non-union shop," who had contributed nothing to its cause, was certainly a manifestation of moral power.

In none of his utterances or correspondence did the president for an instant recognize this touch of nobility, although one would imagine that he would gladly point out this bit of virtue, in what he must have considered the moral ruin about him. He stood throughout for the individual virtues, those which had distinguished the model workmen of his youth; those which had enabled him and so many of his contemporaries to rise in life, when "rising in life" was urged upon every promising boy as the goal of his efforts.

Of the code of social ethics he had caught absolutely nothing. The morals he had advocated in selecting and training his men did not fail them in the hour of confusion. They were self-controlled, and they themselves destroyed no property. They were sober and exhibited no drunkenness, even although obliged to hold their meetings in the saloon hall of a neighboring town. They repaid their employer in kind, but he had given them no rule for the life of association into which they were plunged.

The president of the company desired that his employees should possess the individual and family virtues, but did nothing to cherish in them the social virtues which express themselves in associated effort.

Day after day, during that horrible time of suspense, when the wires constantly reported the same message, "the President of the Company holds that there is nothing to arbitrate," one was forced to feel that the ideal of one-man rule was being sustained in its baldest form. A demand from many parts of the country and from many people was being made for social adjustment, against which the commercial training and the individualistic point of view held its own successfully.

The majority of the stockholders, not only of this company but of similar companies, and many other citizens, who had had the same commercial experience, shared and sustained this position. It was quite impossible for them to catch the other point of view. They not only felt themselves right from the commercial standpoint, but had gradually accustomed themselves also to the philanthropic standpoint, until they had come to consider their motives beyond reproach. Habit held them persistent in this view of the case through all changing conditions.

A wise man has said that "the consent of men and your own conscience are two wings given you whereby you may rise to God." It is so easy for the good and powerful to think that they can rise by following the dictates of conscience, by pursuing their own ideals, that they are prone to leave those ideals unconnected with the consent of their fellow-men. The president of the company thought out within his own mind a beautiful town. He had power with which to build this town, but he did not appeal to nor obtain the consent of the men who were living in it. The most unambitious reform, recognizing the necessity for this consent, makes for slow but sane and strenuous progress, while the most ambitious of social plans and experiments, ignoring this, is prone to failure.

The man who insists upon consent, who moves with the people, is bound to consult the "feasible right" as well as the absolute right. He is often obliged to attain only Mr. Lincoln's "best possible," and then has the sickening sense of compromise with his best convictions. He has to move along with those whom he leads toward a goal that neither he nor they see very clearly till they come to it. He has to discover what people really want, and then "provide the channels in which the growing moral force of their lives shall flow." What he does attain, however, is not the result of his individual striving, as a solitary mountain-climber beyond that of the valley multitude but it is sustained and upheld by the sentiments and aspirations of many others. Progress has been slower perpendicularly, but incomparably greater because lateral. He has not taught his contemporaries to climb mountains, but he has persuaded the villagers to move up a few feet higher; added to this, he has made secure his progress. A few months after the death of the promoter of this model town, a court decision made it obligatory upon the company to divest itself of the management of the town as involving a function beyond its corporate powers. The parks, flowers, and fountains of this far-famed industrial centre were dismantled, with scarcely a protest from the inhabitants themselves.

The man who disassociates his ambition, however disinterested, from the coöperation of his fellows, always takes this risk of ultimate failure. He does not take advantage of the great conserver and guarantee of his own permanent success which associated efforts afford. Genuine experiments toward higher social conditions must have a more democratic faith and practice than those which underlie private venture. Public parks and improvements, intended for the common use, are after all only safe in the hands of the public itself; and associated effort toward social progress, although much more awkward and stumbling than that same effort managed by a capable individual, does yet enlist deeper forces and evoke higher social capacities.

The successful business man who is also the philanthropist is in more than the usual danger of getting widely separated from his employees. The men already have the American veneration for wealth and successful business capacity, and, added to this, they are dazzled by his good works. The workmen have the same kindly impulses as he, but while they organize their charity into mutual benefit associations and distribute their money in small amounts in relief for the widows and insurance for the injured, the employer may build model towns, erect college buildings, which are tangible and enduring, and thereby display his goodness in concentrated form.

By the very exigencies of business demands, the employer is too often cut off from the social ethics developing in regard to our larger social relationships, and from the great moral life springing from our common experiences. This is sure to happen when he is good "to" people rather than "with" them, when he allows himself to decide what is best for them instead of consulting them. He thus misses the rectifying influence of that fellowship which is so big that it leaves no room for sensitiveness or gratitude. Without this fellowship we may never know how great the divergence between ourselves and others may become, nor how cruel the misunderstandings.

During a recent strike of the employees of a large factory in Ohio, the president of the company expressed himself as bitterly disappointed by the results of his many kindnesses, and evidently considered the employees utterly unappreciative. His state of mind was the result of the fallacy of ministering to social needs from an individual impulse and expecting a socialized return of gratitude and loyalty. If the lunch-room was necessary, it was a necessity in order that the employees might have better food, and, when they had received the better food, the legitimate aim of the lunch-room was met. If baths were desirable, and the fifteen minutes of calisthenic exercise given the women in the middle of each half day brought a needed rest and change to their muscles, then the increased cleanliness and the increased bodily comfort of so many people should of themselves have justified the experiment.

To demand, as a further result, that there should be no strikes in the factory, no revolt against the will of the employer because the employees were filled with loyalty as the result of the kindness, was of course to take the experiment from an individual basis to a social one.

Large mining companies and manufacturing concerns are constantly appealing to their stockholders for funds, or for permission to take a percentage of the profits, in order that the money may be used for educational and social schemes designed for the benefit of the employees. The promoters of these schemes use as an argument and as an appeal, that better relations will be thus established, that strikes will be prevented, and that in the end the money returned to the stockholders will be increased. However praiseworthy this appeal may be in motive, it involves a distinct confusion of issues, and in theory deserves the failure it so often meets with in practice. In the clash which follows a strike, the employees are accused of an ingratitude, when there was no legitimate reason to expect gratitude; and useless bitterness, which has really a factitious basis, may be developed on both sides.

Indeed, unless the relation becomes a democratic one, the chances of misunderstanding are increased, when to the relation of employer and employees is added the relation of benefactor to beneficiaries, in so far as there is still another opportunity for acting upon the individual code of ethics.

There is no doubt that these efforts are to be commended, not only from the standpoint of their social value but because they have a marked industrial significance. Failing, as they do, however, to touch the question of wages and hours, which are almost invariably the points of trades-union effort, the employers confuse the mind of the public when they urge the amelioration of conditions and the kindly relation existing between them and their men as a reason for the discontinuance of strikes and other trades-union tactics. The men have individually accepted the kindness of the employers as it was individually offered, but quite as the latter urges his inability to increase wages unless he has the coöperation of his competitors, so the men state that they are bound to the trades-union struggle for an increase in wages because it can only be undertaken by combinations of labor.

Even the much more democratic effort to divide a proportion of the profits at the end of the year among the employees, upon the basis of their wages and efficiency, is also exposed to a weakness, from the fact that the employing side has the power of determining to whom the benefit shall accrue.

Both individual acts of self-defence on the part of the wage earner and individual acts of benevolence on the part of the employer are most useful as they establish standards to which the average worker and employer may in time be legally compelled to conform. Progress must always come through the individual who varies from the type and has sufficient energy to express this variation. He first holds a higher conception than that held by the mass of his fellows of what is righteous under given conditions, and expresses this conviction in conduct, in many instances formulating a certain scruple which the others share, but have not yet defined even to themselves. Progress, however, is not secure until the mass has conformed to this new righteousness. This is equally true in regard to any advance made in the standard of living on the part of the trades-unionists or in the improved conditions of industry on the part of reforming employers. The mistake lies, not in overpraising the advance thus inaugurated by individual initiative, but in regarding the achievement as complete in a social sense when it is still in the realm of individual action. No sane manufacturer regards his factory as the centre of the industrial system. He knows very well that the cost of material, wages, and selling prices are determined by industrial conditions completely beyond his control. Yet the same man may quite calmly regard himself and his own private principles as merely self-regarding, and expect results from casual philanthropy which can only be accomplished through those common rules of life and labor established by the community for the common good.

Outside of and surrounding these smaller and most significant efforts are the larger and irresistible movements operating toward combination. This movement must tend to decide upon social matters from the social standpoint. Until then it is difficult to keep our minds free from a confusion of issues. Such a confusion occurs when the gift of a large sum to the community for a public and philanthropic purpose, throws a certain glamour over all the earlier acts of a man, and makes it difficult for the community to see possible wrongs committed against it, in the accumulation of wealth so beneficently used. It is possible also that the resolve to be thus generous unconsciously influences the man himself in his methods of accumulation. He keeps to a certain individual rectitude, meaning to make an individual restitution by the old paths of generosity and kindness, whereas if he had in view social restitution on the newer lines of justice and opportunity, he would throughout his course doubtless be watchful of his industrial relationships and his social virtues.

The danger of professionally attaining to the power of the righteous man, of yielding to the ambition "for doing good" on a large scale, compared to which the ambition for politics, learning, or wealth, are vulgar and commonplace, ramifies through our modern life; and those most easily beset by this temptation are precisely the men best situated to experiment on the larger social lines, because they so easily dramatize their acts and lead public opinion. Very often, too, they have in their hands the preservation and advancement of large vested interests, and often see clearly and truly that they are better able to administer the affairs of the community than the community itself: sometimes they see that if they do not administer them sharply and quickly, as only an individual can, certain interests of theirs dependent upon the community will go to ruin.

The model employer first considered, provided a large sum in his will with which to build and equip a polytechnic school, which will doubtless be of great public value. This again shows the advantage of individual management, in the spending as well as in the accumulating of wealth, but this school will attain its highest good, in so far as it incites the ambition to provide other schools from public funds. The town of Zurich possesses a magnificent polytechnic institute, secured by the vote of the entire people and supported from public taxes. Every man who voted for it is interested that his child should enjoy its benefits, and, of course, the voluntary attendance must be larger than in a school accepted as a gift to the community.

In the educational efforts of model employers, as in other attempts toward social amelioration, one man with the best of intentions is trying to do what the entire body of employees should have undertaken to do for themselves. The result of his efforts will only attain its highest value as it serves as an incentive to procure other results by the community as well as for the community.

There are doubtless many things which the public would never demand unless they were first supplied by individual initiative, both because the public lacks the imagination, and also the power of formulating their wants. Thus philanthropic effort supplies kindergartens, until they become so established in the popular affections that they are incorporated in the public school system. Churches and missions establish reading rooms, until at last the public library system dots the city with branch reading rooms and libraries. For this willingness to take risks for the sake of an ideal, for those experiments which must be undertaken with vigor and boldness in order to secure didactic value in failure as well as in success, society must depend upon the individual possessed with money, and also distinguished by earnest and unselfish purpose. Such experiments enable the nation to use the Referendum method in its public affairs. Each social experiment is thus tested by a few people, given wide publicity, that it may be observed and discussed by the bulk of the citizens before the public prudently makes up its mind whether or not it is wise to incorporate it into the functions of government. If the decision is in its favor and it is so incorporated, it can then be carried on with confidence and enthusiasm.

But experience has shown that we can only depend upon successful men for a certain type of experiment in the line of industrial amelioration and social advancement. The list of those who found churches, educational institutions, libraries, and art galleries, is very long, as is again the list of those contributing to model dwellings, recreation halls, and athletic fields. At the present moment factory employers are doing much to promote "industrial betterment" in the way of sanitary surroundings, opportunities for bathing, lunch rooms provided with cheap and wholesome food, club rooms, and guild halls. But there is a line of social experiment involving social righteousness in its most advanced form, in which the number of employers and the "favored class" are so few that it is plain society cannot count upon them for continuous and valuable help. This lack is in the line of factory legislation and that sort of social advance implied in shorter hours and the regulation of wages; in short, all that organization and activity that is involved in such a maintenance and increase of wages as would prevent the lowering of the standard of life.

A large body of people feel keenly that the present industrial system is in a state of profound disorder, and that there is no guarantee that the pursuit of individual ethics will ever right it. They claim that relief can only come through deliberate corporate effort inspired by social ideas and guided by the study of economic laws, and that the present industrial system thwarts our ethical demands, not only for social righteousness but for social order. Because they believe that each advance in ethics must be made fast by a corresponding advance in politics and legal enactment, they insist upon the right of state regulation and control. While many people representing all classes in a community would assent to this as to a general proposition, and would even admit it as a certain moral obligation, legislative enactments designed to control industrial conditions have largely been secured through the efforts of a few citizens, mostly those who constantly see the harsh conditions of labor and who are incited to activity by their sympathies as well as their convictions.

This may be illustrated by the series of legal enactments regulating the occupations in which children may be allowed to work, also the laws in regard to the hours of labor permitted in those occupations, and the minimum age below which children may not be employed. The first child labor laws were enacted in England through the efforts of those members of parliament whose hearts were wrung by the condition of the little parish apprentices bound out to the early textile manufacturers of the north; and through the long years required to build up the code of child labor legislation which England now possesses, knowledge of the conditions has always preceded effective legislation. The efforts of that small number in every community who believe in legislative control have always been reënforced by the efforts of trades-unionists rather than by the efforts of employers. Partly because the employment of workingmen in the factories brings them in contact with the children who tend to lower wages and demoralize their trades, and partly because workingmen have no money nor time to spend in alleviating philanthropy, and must perforce seize upon agitation and legal enactment as the only channel of redress which is open to them.

We may illustrate by imagining a row of people seated in a moving street-car, into which darts a boy of eight, calling out the details of the last murder, in the hope of selling an evening newspaper. A comfortable looking man buys a paper from him with no sense of moral shock; he may even be a trifle complacent that he has helped along the little fellow, who is making his way in the world. The philanthropic lady sitting next to him may perhaps reflect that it is a pity that such a bright boy is not in school. She may make up her mind in a moment of compunction to redouble her efforts for various newsboys' schools and homes, that this poor child may have better teaching, and perhaps a chance at manual training. She probably is convinced that he alone, by his unaided efforts, is supporting a widowed mother, and her heart is moved to do all she can for him. Next to her sits a workingman trained in trades-union methods. He knows that the boy's natural development is arrested, and that the abnormal activity of his body and mind uses up the force which should go into growth; moreover, that this premature use of his powers has but a momentary and specious value. He is forced to these conclusions because he has seen many a man, entering the factory at eighteen and twenty, so worn out by premature work that he was "laid on the shelf" within ten or fifteen years. He knows very well that he can do nothing in the way of ameliorating the lot of this particular boy; that his only possible chance is to agitate for proper child-labor laws; to regulate, and if possible prohibit, street-vending by children, in order that the child of the poorest may have his school time secured to him, and may have at least his short chance for growth.

These three people, sitting in the street car, are all honest and upright, and recognize a certain duty toward the forlorn children of the community. The self-made man is encouraging one boy's own efforts; the philanthropic lady is helping on a few boys; the workingman alone is obliged to include all the boys of his class. Workingmen, because of their feebleness in all but numbers, have been forced to appeal to the state, in order to secure protection for themselves and for their children. They cannot all rise out of their class, as the occasionally successful man has done; some of them must be left to do the work in the factories and mines, and they have no money to spend in philanthropy.

Both public agitation and a social appeal to the conscience of the community is necessary in order to secure help from the state, and, curiously enough, child-labor laws once enacted and enforced are a matter of great pride, and even come to be regarded as a register of the community's humanity and enlightenment. If the method of public agitation could find quiet and orderly expression in legislative enactment, and if labor measures could be submitted to the examination and judgment of the whole without a sense of division or of warfare, we should have the ideal development of the democratic state.

But we judge labor organizations as we do other living institutions, not by their declaration of principles, which we seldom read, but by their blundering efforts to apply their principles to actual conditions, and by the oft-time failure of their representatives, when the individual finds himself too weak to become the organ of corporate action.

The very blunders and lack of organization too often characterizing a union, in marked contrast to the orderly management of a factory, often confuse us as to the real issues involved, and we find it hard to trust uncouth and unruly manifestations of social effort. The situation is made even more complicated by the fact that those who are formulating a code of associated action so often break through the established code of law and order. As society has a right to demand of the reforming individual that he be sternly held to his personal and domestic claims, so it has a right to insist that labor organizations shall keep to the hardly won standards of public law and order; and the community performs but its plain duty when it registers its protest every time law and order are subverted, even in the interest of the so-called social effort. Yet in moments of industrial stress and strain the community is confronted by a moral perplexity which may arise from the mere fact that the good of yesterday is opposed to the good of today, and that which may appear as a choice between virtue and vice is really but a choice between virtue and virtue. In the disorder and confusion sometimes incident to growth and progress, the community may be unable to see anything but the unlovely struggle itself.

The writer recalls a conversation between two workingmen who were leaving a lecture on "Organic Evolution." The first was much puzzled, and anxiously inquired of the second "if evolution could mean that one animal turned into another." The challenged workman stopped in the rear of the hall, put his foot upon a chair, and expounded what he thought evolution did mean; and this, so nearly as the conversation can be recalled, is what he said: "You see a lot of fishes are living in a stream, which overflows in the spring and strands some of them upon the bank. The weak ones die up there, but others make a big effort to get back into the water. They dig their fins into the sand, breathe as much air as they can with their gills, and have a terrible time. But after a while their fins turn into legs and their gills into lungs, and they have become frogs. Of course they are further along than the sleek, comfortable fishes who sail up and down the stream waving their tails and despising the poor damaged things thrashing around on the bank. He-the lecturer-did not say anything about men, but it is easy enough to think of us poor devils on the dry bank, struggling without enough to live on, while the comfortable fellows sail along in the water with all they want and despise us because we thrash about." His listener did not reply, and was evidently dissatisfied both with the explanation and the application. Doubtless the illustration was bungling in more than its setting forth, but the story is suggestive.

At times of social disturbance the law-abiding citizen is naturally so anxious for peace and order, his sympathies are so justly and inevitably on the side making for the restoration of law, that it is difficult for him to see the situation fairly. He becomes insensible to the unselfish impulse which may prompt a sympathetic strike in behalf of the workers in a non-union shop, because he allows his mind to dwell exclusively on the disorder which has become associated with the strike. He is completely side-tracked by the ugly phases of a great moral movement. It is always a temptation to assume that the side which has respectability, authority, and superior intelligence, has therefore righteousness as well, especially when the same side presents concrete results of individual effort as over against the less tangible results of associated effort.

It is as yet most difficult for us to free ourselves from the individualistic point of view sufficiently to group events in their social relations and to judge fairly those who are endeavoring to produce a social result through all the difficulties of associated action. The philanthropist still finds his path much easier than do those who are attempting a social morality. In the first place, the public, anxious to praise what it recognizes as an undoubted moral effort often attended with real personal sacrifice, joyfully seizes upon this manifestation and overpraises it, recognizing the philanthropist as an old friend in the paths of righteousness, whereas the others are strangers and possibly to be distrusted as aliens. It is easy to confuse the response to an abnormal number of individual claims with the response to the social claim. An exaggerated personal morality is often mistaken for a social morality, and until it attempts to minister to a social situation its total inadequacy is not discovered. To attempt to attain a social morality without a basis of democratic experience results in the loss of the only possible corrective and guide, and ends in an exaggerated individual morality but not in social morality at all. We see this from time to time in the care-worn and overworked philanthropist, who has taxed his individual will beyond the normal limits and has lost his clew to the situation among a bewildering number of cases. A man who takes the betterment of humanity for his aim and end must also take the daily experiences of humanity for the constant correction of his process. He must not only test and guide his achievement by human experience, but he must succeed or fail in proportion as he has incorporated that experience with his own. Otherwise his own achievements become his stumbling-block, and he comes to believe in his own goodness as something outside of himself. He makes an exception of himself, and thinks that he is different from the rank and file of his fellows. He forgets that it is necessary to know of the lives of our contemporaries, not only in order to believe in their integrity, which is after all but the first beginnings of social morality, but in order to attain to any mental or moral integrity for ourselves or any such hope for society.

Chapter VI
Educational Methods

As democracy modifies our conception of life, it constantly raises the value and function of each member of the community, however humble he may be. We have come to believe that the most "brutish man" has a value in our common life, a function to perform which can be fulfilled by no one else. We are gradually requiring of the educator that he shall free the powers of each man and connect him with the rest of life. We ask this not merely because it is the man's right to be thus connected, but because we have become convinced that the social order cannot afford to get along without his special contribution. Just as we have come to resent all hindrances which keep us from untrammelled comradeship with our fellows, and as we throw down unnatural divisions, not in the spirit of the eighteenth-century reformers, but in the spirit of those to whom social equality has become a necessity for further social development, so we are impatient to use the dynamic power residing in the mass of men, and demand that the educator free that power. We believe that man's moral idealism is the constructive force of progress, as it has always been; but because every human being is a creative agent and a possible generator of fine enthusiasm, we are sceptical of the moral idealism of the few and demand the education of the many, that there may be greater freedom, strength, and subtilty of intercourse and hence an increase of dynamic power. We are not content to include all men in our hopes, but have become conscious that all men are hoping and are part of the same movement of which we are a part.

Many people impelled by these ideas have become impatient with the slow recognition on the part of the educators of their manifest obligation to prepare and nourish the child and the citizen for social relations. The educators should certainly conserve the learning and training necessary for the successful individual and family life, but should add to that a preparation for the enlarged social efforts which our increasing democracy requires. The democratic ideal demands of the school that it shall give the child's own experience a social value; that it shall teach him to direct his own activities and adjust them to those of other people. We are not willing that thousands of industrial workers shall put all of their activity and toil into services from which the community as a whole reaps the benefit, while their mental conceptions and code of morals are narrow and untouched by any uplift which the consciousness of social value might give them.

We are impatient with the schools which lay all stress on reading and writing, suspecting them to rest upon the assumption that the ordinary experience of life is worth little, and that all knowledge and interest must be brought to the children through the medium of books. Such an assumption fails to give the child any clew to the life about him, or any power to usefully or intelligently connect himself with it. This may be illustrated by observations made in a large Italian colony situated in Chicago, the children from which are, for the most part, sent to the public schools.

The members of the Italian colony are largely from South Italy, —Calabrian and Sicilian peasants, or Neapolitans from the workingmen's quarters of that city. They have come to America with the distinct aim of earning money, and finding more room for the energies of themselves and their children. In almost all cases they mean to go back again, simply because their imaginations cannot picture a continuous life away from the old surroundings. Their experiences in Italy have been those of simple outdoor activity, and their ideas have come directly to them from their struggle with Nature, —such a hand-to-hand struggle as takes place when each man gets his living largely through his own cultivation of the soil, or with tools simply fashioned by his own hands. The women, as in all primitive life, have had more diversified activities than the men. They have cooked, spun, and knitted, in addition to their almost equal work in the fields. Very few of the peasant men or women can either read or write. They are devoted to their children, strong in their family feeling, even to remote relationships, and clannish in their community life.

The entire family has been upheaved, and is striving to adjust itself to its new surroundings. The men, for the most part, work on railroad extensions through the summer, under the direction of a *padrone*, who finds the work for them, regulates the amount of their wages, and supplies them with food. The first effect of immigration upon the women is that of idleness. They no longer work in the fields, nor milk the goats, nor pick up faggots. The mother of the family buys all the clothing, not only already spun and woven but made up into garments, of a cut and fashion beyond her powers. It is, indeed, the most economical thing for her to do. Her house-cleaning and cooking are of the simplest; the bread is usually baked outside of the house, and the macaroni bought prepared for boiling. All of those outdoor and domestic activities, which she would naturally have handed on to her daughters, have slipped away from her. The domestic arts are gone, with their absorbing interests for the children, their educational value, and incentive to activity. A household in a tenement receives almost no raw material. For the hundreds of children who have never seen wheat grow, there are dozens who have never seen bread baked. The occasional washings and scrubbings are associated only with discomfort. The child of such a family receives constant stimulus of most exciting sort from his city street life, but he has little or no opportunity to use his energies in domestic manufacture, or, indeed, constructively in any direction. No activity is supplied to take the place of that which, in Italy, he would naturally have found in his own surroundings, and no new union with wholesome life is made for him.

Italian parents count upon the fact that their children learn the English language and American customs before they do themselves, and the children act not only as interpreters of the language, but as buffers between them and Chicago, resulting in a certain almost pathetic dependence of the family upon the child. When a child of the family, therefore, first goes to school, the event is fraught with much significance to all the others. The family has no social life in any structural form and can supply none to the child. He ought to get it in the school and give it to his family, the school thus becoming the connector with the organized society about them. It is the children aged six, eight, and ten, who go to school, entering, of course, the primary grades. If a boy is twelve or thirteen on his arrival in America, his parents see in him a wage-earning factor, and the girl of the same age is already looking toward her marriage.

Let us take one of these boys, who has learned in his six or eight years to speak his native language, and to feel himself strongly identified with the fortunes of his family. Whatever interest has come to the minds of his ancestors has come through the use of their hands in the open air; and open air and activity of body have been the inevitable accompaniments of all their experiences. Yet the first thing that the boy must do when he reaches school is to sit still, at least part of the time, and he must learn to listen to what is said to him, with all the perplexity of listening to a foreign tongue. He does not find this very stimulating, and is slow to respond to the more subtle incentives of the schoolroom. The peasant child is perfectly indifferent to showing off and making a good recitation. He leaves all that to his schoolfellows, who are more sophisticated and equipped with better English. His parents are not deeply interested in keeping him in school, and will not hold him there against his inclination. Their experience does not point to the good American tradition that it is the educated man who finally succeeds. The richest man in the Italian colony can neither read nor write-even Italian. His cunning and acquisitiveness, combined with the credulity and ignorance of his countrymen, have slowly brought about his large fortune. The child himself may feel the stirring of a vague ambition to go on until he is as the other children are; but he is not popular with his schoolfellows, and he sadly feels the lack of dramatic interest. Even the pictures and objects presented to him, as well as the language, are strange.

If we admit that in education it is necessary to begin with the experiences which the child already has and to use his spontaneous and social activity, then the city streets begin this education for him in a more natural way than does the school. The South Italian peasant comes from a life of picking olives and oranges, and he easily sends his children out to pick up coal from railroad tracks, or wood from buildings which have been burned down. Unfortunately, this process leads by easy transition to petty thieving. It is easy to go from the coal on the railroad track to the coal and wood which stand before a dealer's shop; from the potatoes which have rolled from a rumbling wagon to the vegetables displayed by the grocer. This is apt to be the record of the boy who responds constantly to the stimulus and temptations of the street, although in the beginning his search for bits of food and fuel was prompted by the best of motives.

The school has to compete with a great deal from the outside in addition to the distractions of the neighborhood. Nothing is more fascinating than that mysterious "down town," whither the boy longs to go to sell papers and black boots, to attend theatres, and, if possible, to stay all night on the pretence of waiting for the early edition of the great dailies. If a boy is once thoroughly caught in these excitements, nothing can save him from over-stimulation and consequent debility and worthlessness; he arrives at maturity with no habits of regular work and with a distaste for its dulness.

On the other hand, there are hundreds of boys of various nationalities who conscientiously remain in school and fulfil all the requirements of the early grades, and at the age of fourteen are found in factories, painstakingly performing their work year after year. These later are the men who form the mass of the population in every industrial neighborhood of every large city; but they carry on the industrial processes year after year without in the least knowing what it is all about. The one fixed habit which the boy carries away with him from the school to the factory is the feeling that his work is merely provisional. In school the next grade was continually held before him as an object of attainment, and it resulted in the conviction that the sole object of present effort is to get ready for something else. This tentative attitude takes the last bit of social stimulus out of his factory work; he pursues it merely as a necessity, and his very mental attitude destroys his chance for a realization of its social value. As the boy in school contracted the habit of doing his work in certain hours and taking his pleasure in certain other hours, so in the factory he earns his money by ten hours of dull work and spends it in three hours of lurid and unprofitable pleasure in the evening. Both in the school and in the factory, in proportion as his work grows dull and monotonous, his recreation must become more exciting and stimulating. The hopelessness of adding evening classes and social entertainments as a mere frill to a day filled with monotonous and deadening drudgery constantly becomes more apparent to those who are endeavoring to bring a fuller life to the industrial members of the community, and who are looking forward to a time when work shall cease to be senseless drudgery with no self-expression on the part of the worker. It sometimes seems that the public schools should contribute much more than they do to the consummation of this time. If the army of school children who enter the factories every year possessed thoroughly vitalized faculties, they might do much to lighten this incubus of dull factory work which presses so heavily upon so large a number of our fellow-citizens. Has our commercialism been so strong that our schools have become insensibly commercialized, whereas we supposed that our industrial life was receiving the broadening and illuminating effects of the schools? The training of these children, so far as it has been vocational at all, has been in the direction of clerical work. It is possible that the business men, whom we in America so tremendously admire, have really been dictating the curriculum of our public schools, in spite of the conventions of educators and the suggestions of university professors. The business man, of course, has not said, "I will have the public schools train office boys and clerks so that I may have them easily and cheaply," but he has sometimes said, "Teach the children to write legibly and to figure accurately and quickly; to acquire habits of punctuality and order; to be prompt to obey; and you will fit them to make their way in the world as I have made mine." Has the workingman been silent as to what he desires for his children, and allowed the business man to decide for him there, as he has allowed the politician to manage his municipal affairs, or has the workingman so far shared our universal optimism that he has really believed that his children would never need to go into industrial life at all, but that all of his sons would become bankers and merchants?

Certain it is that no sufficient study has been made of the child who enters into industrial life early and stays there permanently, to give him some offset to its monotony and dulness, some historic significance of the part he is taking in the life of the community.

It is at last on behalf of the average workingmen that our increasing democracy impels us to make a new demand upon the educator. As the political expression of democracy has claimed for the workingman the free right of citizenship, so a code of social ethics is now insisting that he shall be a conscious member of society, having some notion of his social and industrial value.

The early ideal of a city that it was a market-place in which to exchange produce, and a mere trading-post for merchants, apparently still survives in our minds and is constantly reflected in our schools. We have either failed to realize that cities have become great centres of production and manufacture in which a huge population is engaged, or we have lacked sufficient presence of mind to adjust ourselves to the change. We admire much more the men who accumulate riches, and who gather to themselves the results of industry, than the men who actually carry forward industrial processes; and, as has been pointed out, our schools still prepare children almost exclusively for commercial and professional life.

Quite as the country boy dreams of leaving the farm for life in town and begins early to imitate the travelling salesman in dress and manner, so the school boy within the town hopes to be an office boy, and later a clerk or salesman, and looks upon work in the factory as the occupation of ignorant and unsuccessful men. The schools do so little really to interest the child in the life of production, or to excite his ambition in the line of industrial occupation, that the ideal of life, almost from the very beginning, becomes not an absorbing interest in one's work and a consciousness of its value and social relation, but a desire for money with which unmeaning purchases may be made and an unmeaning social standing obtained.

The son of a workingman who is successful in commercial life, impresses his family and neighbors quite as does the prominent city man when he comes back to dazzle his native town. The children of the working people learn many useful things in the public schools, but the commercial arithmetic, and many other studies, are founded on the tacit assumption that a boy rises in life by getting away from manual labor, —that every promising boy goes into business or a profession. The children destined for factory life are furnished with what would be most useful under other conditions, quite as the prosperous farmer's wife buys a folding-bed for her huge four-cornered "spare room," because her sister, who has married a city man, is obliged to have a folding-bed in the cramped limits of her flat Partly because so little is done for him educationally, and partly because he must live narrowly and dress meanly, the life of the average laborer tends to become flat and monotonous, with nothing in his work to feed his mind or hold his interest. Theoretically, we would all admit that the man at the bottom, who performs the meanest and humblest work, so long as the work is necessary, performs a useful function; but we do not live up to our theories, and in addition to his hard and uninteresting work he is covered with a sort of contempt, and unless he falls into illness or trouble, he receives little sympathy or attention. Certainly no serious effort is made to give him a participation in the social and industrial life with which he comes in contact, nor any insight and inspiration regarding it.

Apparently we have not yet recovered manual labor from the deep distrust which centuries of slavery and the feudal system have cast upon it. To get away from menial work, to do obviously little with one's hands, is still the desirable status. This may readily be seen all along the line. A workingman's family will make every effort and sacrifice that the brightest daughter be sent to the high school and through the normal school, quite as much because a teacher in the family raises the general social standing and sense of family consequence, as that the returns are superior to factory or even office work. "Teacher" in the vocabulary of many children is a synonym for women-folk gentry, and the name is indiscriminately applied to women of certain dress and manner. The same desire for social advancement is expressed by the purchasing of a piano, or the fact that the son is an office boy, and not a factory hand. The overcrowding of the professions by poorly equipped men arises from much the same source, and from the conviction that "an education" is wasted if a boy goes into a factory or shop.

A Chicago manufacturer tells a story of twin boys, whom he befriended and meant to give a start in life. He sent them both to the Athenæum for several winters as a preparatory business training, and then took them into his office, where they speedily became known as the bright one and the stupid one. The stupid one was finally dismissed after repeated trials, when to the surprise of the entire establishment, he quickly betook himself into the shops, where he became a wide-awake and valuable workman. His chagrined benefactor, in telling the story, admits that he himself had fallen a victim to his own business training and his early notion of rising in life. In reality he had merely followed the lead of most benevolent people who help poor boys. They test the success of their efforts by the number whom they have taken out of factory work into some other and "higher occupation."

Quite in line with this commercial ideal are the night schools and institutions of learning most accessible to working people. First among them is the business college which teaches largely the mechanism of type-writing and book-keeping, and lays all stress upon commerce and methods of distribution. Commodities are treated as exports and imports, or solely in regard to their commercial value, and not, of course, in relation to their historic development or the manufacturing processes to which they have been subjected. These schools do not in the least minister to the needs of the actual factory employee, who is in the shop and not in the office. We assume that all men are searching for "puddings and power," to use Carlyle's phrase, and furnish only the schools which help them to those ends.

The business college man, or even the man who goes through an academic course in order to prepare for a profession, comes to look on learning too much as an investment from which he will later reap the benefits in earning money. He does not connect learning with industrial pursuits, nor does he in the least lighten or illuminate those pursuits for those of his friends who have not risen in life. "It is as though nets were laid at the entrance to education, in which those who by some means or other escape from the masses bowed down by labor, are inevitably caught and held from substantial service to their fellows." The academic teaching which is accessible to workingmen through University Extension lectures and classes at settlements, is usually bookish and remote, and concerning subjects completely divorced from their actual experiences. The men come to think of learning as something to be added to the end of a hard day's work, and to be gained at the cost of toilsome mental exertion. There are, of course, exceptions, but many men who persist in attending classes and lectures year after year find themselves possessed of a mass of inert knowledge which nothing in their experience fuses into availability or realization.

Among the many disappointments which the settlement experiment has brought to its promoters, perhaps none is keener than the fact that they have as yet failed to work out methods of education, specialized and adapted to the needs of adult working people in contra-distinction to those employed in schools and colleges, or those used in teaching children. There are many excellent reasons and explanations for this failure. In the first place, the residents themselves are for the most part imbued with academic methods and ideals, which it is most difficult to modify. To quote from a late settlement report, "The most vaunted educational work in settlements amounts often to the stimulation mentally of a select few who are, in a sense, of the academic type of mind, and who easily and quickly respond to the academic methods employed." These classes may be valuable, but they leave quite untouched the great mass of the factory population, the ordinary workingman of the ordinary workingman's street, whose attitude is best described as that of "acquiescence," who lives through the aimless passage of the years without incentive "to imagine, to design, or to aspire." These men are totally untouched by all the educational and philanthropic machinery which is designed for the young and the helpless who live on the same streets with them. They do not often drink to excess, they regularly give all their wages to their wives, they have a vague pride in their superior children; but they grow prematurely old and stiff in all their muscles, and become more and more taciturn, their entire energies consumed in "holding a job."

Various attempts have been made to break through the inadequate educational facilities sup-plied by commercialism and scholarship, both of which have followed their own ideals and have failed to look at the situation as it actually presents itself. The most noteworthy attempt has been the movement toward industrial education, the agitation for which has been ably sec-onded by manufacturers of a practical type, who have from time to time founded and endowed technical schools, designed for workingmen's sons. The early schools of this type inevitably reflected the ideal of the self-made man. They succeeded in transferring a few skilled workers into the upper class of trained engineers, and a few less skilled workers into the class of trained mechanics, but did not aim to educate the many who are doomed to the unskilled work which the permanent specialization of the division of labor demands.

The Peter Coopers and other good men honestly believed that if intelligence could be added to industry, each workingman who faithfully attended these schools could walk into increased skill and wages, and in time even become an employer himself. Such schools are useful be-yond doubt; but so far as educating workingmen is concerned or in any measure satisfying the democratic ideal, they plainly beg the question.

Almost every large city has two or three polytechnic institutions founded by rich men, anx-ious to help "poor boys." These have been captured by conventional educators for the pur-pose of fitting young men for the colleges and universities. They have compromised by merely adding to the usual academic course manual work, applied mathematics, mechanical drawing and engineering. Two schools in Chicago, plainly founded for the sons of workingmen, afford an illustration of this tendency and result. On the other hand, so far as schools of this type have been captured by commercialism, they turn out trained engineers, professional chemists, and electricians. They are polytechnics of a high order, but do not even pretend to admit the workingman with his meagre intellectual equipment. They graduate machine builders, but not educated machine tenders. Even the textile schools are largely seized by young men who ex-pect to be superintendents of factories, designers, or manufacturers themselves, and the textile worker who actually "holds the thread" is seldom seen in them; indeed, in one of the largest schools women are not allowed, in spite of the fact that spinning and weaving have traditionally been woman's work, and that thousands of women are at present employed in the textile mills.

It is much easier to go over the old paths of education with "manual training" thrown in, as it were; it is much simpler to appeal to the old ambitions of "getting on in life," or of "preparing for a profession," or "for a commercial career," than to work out new methods on democratic lines. These schools gradually drop back into the conventional courses, modified in some slight degree, while the adaptation to workingmen's needs is never made, nor, indeed, vigorously attempted. In the meantime, the manufacturers continually protest that engineers, especially trained for devising machines, are not satisfactory. Three generations of workers have invented, but we are told that invention no longer goes on in the workshop, even when it is artificially stimulated by the offer of prizes, and that the inventions of the last quarter of the nineteenth century have by no means fulfilled the promise of the earlier three-quarters.

Every foreman in a large factory has had experience with two classes of men: first with those who become rigid and tolerate no change in their work, partly because they make more money "working by the piece," when they stick to that work which they have learned to do rapidly, and partly because the entire muscular and nervous system has become by daily use adapted to particular motions and resents change. Secondly, there are the men who float in and out of the factory, in a constantly changing stream. They "quit work" for the slightest reason or none at all, and never become skilled at anything. Some of them are men of low intelligence, but many of them are merely too nervous and restless, too impatient, too easily "driven to drink," to be of any use in a modern factory. They are the men for whom the demanded adaptation is impossible.

The individual from whom the industrial order demands ever larger drafts of time and energy, should be nourished and enriched from social sources, in proportion as he is drained. He, more than other men, needs the conception of historic continuity in order to reveal to him the purpose and utility of his work, and he can only be stimulated and dignified as he obtains a conception of his proper relation to society. Scholarship is evidently unable to do this for him; for, unfortunately, the same tendency to division of labor has also produced over-specialization in scholarship, with the sad result that when the scholar attempts to minister to a worker, he gives him the result of more specialization rather than an offset from it. He cannot bring healing and solace because he himself is suffering from the same disease. There is indeed a deplorable lack of perception and adaptation on the part of educators all along the line.

It will certainly be embarrassing to have our age written down triumphant in the matter of inventions, in that our factories were filled with intricate machines, the result of advancing mathematical and mechanical knowledge in relation to manufacturing processes, but defeated in that it lost its head over the achievement and forgot the men. The accusation would stand, that the age failed to perform a like service in the extension of history and art to the factory employees who ran the machines; that the machine tenders, heavy and almost dehumanized by monotonous toil, walked about in the same streets with us, and sat in the same cars; but that we were absolutely indifferent and made no genuine effort to supply to them the artist's perception or student's insight, which alone could fuse them into social consciousness. It would further stand that the scholars among us continued with yet more research, that the educators were concerned only with the young and the promising, and the philanthropists with the criminals and helpless.

There is a pitiful failure to recognize the situation in which the majority of working people are placed, a tendency to ignore their real experiences and needs, and, most stupid of all, we leave quite untouched affections and memories which would afford a tremendous dynamic if they were utilized.

We constantly hear it said in educational circles, that a child learns only by "doing," and that education must proceed "through the eyes and hands to the brain"; and yet for the vast number of people all around us who do not need to have activities artificially provided, and who use their hands and eyes all the time, we do not seem able to reverse the process. We quote the dictum, "What is learned in the schoolroom must be applied in the workshop," and yet the skill and handicraft constantly used in the workshop have no relevance or meaning given to them by the school; and when we do try to help the workingman in an educational way, we completely ignore his everyday occupation. Yet the task is merely one of adaptation. It is to take actual conditions and to make them the basis for a large and generous method of education, to perform a difficult idealization doubtless, but not an impossible one.

We apparently believe that the workingman has no chance to realize life through his vocation. We easily recognize the historic association in regard to ancient buildings. We say that "generation after generation have stamped their mark upon them, have recorded their thoughts in them, until they have become the property of all." And yet this is even more true of the instruments of labor, which have constantly been held in human hands. A machine really represents the "seasoned life of man" preserved and treasured up within itself, quite as much as an ancient building does. At present, workmen are brought in contact with the machinery with which they work as abruptly as if the present set of industrial implements had been newly created. They handle the machinery day by day, without any notion of its gradual evolution and growth. Few of the men who perform the mechanical work in the great factories have any comprehension of the fact that the inventions upon which the factory depends, the instruments which they use, have been slowly worked out, each generation using the gifts of the last and transmitting the inheritance until it has become a social possession. This can only be understood by a man who has obtained some idea of social progress. We are still childishly pleased when we see the further subdivision of labor going on, because the quantity of the output is increased thereby, and we apparently are unable to take our attention away from the product long enough to really focus it upon the producer. Theoretically, "the division of labor" makes men more interdependent and human by drawing them together into a unity of purpose. "If a number of people decide to build a road, and one digs, and one brings stones, and another breaks them, they are quite inevitably united by their interest in the road. But this naturally presupposes that they know where the road is going to, that they have some curiosity and interest about it, and perhaps a chance to travel upon it." If the division of labor robs them of interest in any part of it, the mere mechanical fact of interdependence amounts to nothing.

The man in the factory, as well as the man with the hoe, has a grievance beyond being overworked and disinherited, in that he does not know what it is all about. We may well regret the passing of the time when the variety of work performed in the unspecialized workshop naturally stimulated the intelligence of the workingmen and brought them into contact both with the raw material and the finished product. But the problem of education, as any advanced educator will tell us, is to supply the essentials of experience by a short cut, as it were. If the shop constantly tends to make the workman a specialist, then the problem of the educator in regard to him is quite clear: it is to give him what may be an offset from the over-specialization of his daily work, to supply him with general information and to insist that he shall be a cultivated member of society with a consciousness of his industrial and social value.

As sad a sight as an old hand-loom worker in a factory attempting to make his clumsy machine compete with the flying shuttles about him, is a workingman equipped with knowledge so meagre that he can get no meaning into his life nor sequence between his acts and the far-off results.

Manufacturers, as a whole, however, when they attempt educational institutions in connection with their factories, are prone to follow conventional lines, and to exhibit the weakness of imitation. We find, indeed, that the middle-class educator constantly makes the mistakes of the middle-class moralist when he attempts to aid working people. The latter has constantly and traditionally urged upon the workingman the specialized virtues of thrift, industry, and sobriety-all virtues pertaining to the individual. When each man had his own shop, it was perhaps wise to lay almost exclusive stress upon the industrial virtues of diligence and thrift; but as industry has become more highly organized, life becomes incredibly complex and interdependent. If a workingman is to have a conception of his value at all, he must see industry in its unity and entirety; he must have a conception that will include not only himself and his immediate family and community, but the industrial organization as a whole. It is doubtless true that dexterity of hand becomes less and less imperative as the invention of machinery and subdivision of labor proceeds; but it becomes all the more necessary, if the workman is to save his life at all, that he should get a sense of his individual relation to the system. Feeding a machine with a material of which he has no knowledge, producing a product, totally unrelated to the rest of his life, without in the least knowing what becomes of it, or its connection with the community, is, of course, unquestionably deadening to his intellectual and moral life. To make the moral connection it would be necessary to give him a social consciousness of the value of his work, and at least a sense of participation and a certain joy in its ultimate use; to make the intellectual connection it would be essential to create in him some historic conception of the development of industry and the relation of his individual work to it.

Workingmen themselves have made attempts in both directions, which it would be well for moralists and educators to study. It is a striking fact that when workingmen formulate their own moral code, and try to inspire and encourage each other, it is always a large and general doctrine which they preach. They were the first class of men to organize an international association, and the constant talk at a modern labor meeting is of solidarity and of the identity of the interests of workingmen the world over. It is difficult to secure a successful organization of men into the simplest trades organization without an appeal to the most abstract principles of justice and brotherhood. As they have formulated their own morals by laying the greatest stress upon the largest morality, so if they could found their own schools, it is doubtful whether they would be of the mechanic institute type. Courses of study arranged by a group of workingmen are most naïve in their breadth and generality. They will select the history of the world in preference to that of any period or nation. The "wonders of science" or "the story of evolution" will attract workingmen to a lecture when zoölogy or chemistry will drive them away. The "outlines of literature" or "the best in literature" will draw an audience when a lecturer in English poetry will be solitary. This results partly from a wholesome desire to have general knowledge before special knowledge, and is partly a rebound from the specialization of labor to which the workingman is subjected. When he is free from work and can direct his own mind, he tends to roam, to dwell upon large themes. Much the same tendency is found in programmes of study arranged by Woman's Clubs in country places. The untrained mind, wearied with meaningless detail, when it gets an opportunity to make its demand heard, asks for general philosophy and background.

In a certain sense commercialism itself, at least in its larger aspect, tends to educate the workingman better than organized education does. Its interests are certainly world-wide and democratic, while it is absolutely undiscriminating as to country and creed, coming into contact with all climes and races. If this aspect of commercialism were utilized, it would in a measure counterbalance the tendency which results from the subdivision of labor.

The most noteworthy attempt to utilize this democracy of commerce in relation to manufacturing is found at Dayton, Ohio, in the yearly gatherings held in a large factory there. Once a year the entire force is gathered together to hear the returns of the business, not so much in respect to the profits, as in regard to its extension. At these meetings, the travelling salesmen from various parts of the world-from Constantinople, from Berlin, from Rome, from Hong Kong-report upon the sales they have made, and the methods of advertisement and promotion adapted to the various countries.

Stereopticon lectures are given upon each new country as soon as it has been successfully invaded by the product of the factory. The foremen in the various departments of the factory give accounts of the increased efficiency and the larger output over former years. Any man who has made an invention in connection with the machinery of the factory, at this time publicly receives a prize, and suggestions are approved that tend to increase the comfort and social facilities of the employees. At least for the moment there is a complete esprit de corps, and the youngest and least skilled employee sees himself in connection with the interests of the firm, and the spread of an invention. It is a crude example of what might be done in the way of giving a large framework of meaning to factory labor, and of putting it into a sentient background, at least on the commercial side.

It is easy to indict the educator, to say that he has gotten entangled in his own material, and has fallen a victim to his own methods; but granting this, what has the artist done about it-he who is supposed to have a more intimate insight into the needs of his contemporaries, and to minister to them as none other can?

It is quite true that a few writers are insisting that the growing desire for labor, on the part of many people of leisure, has its counterpart in the increasing desire for general knowledge on the part of many laborers. They point to the fact that the same duality of conscience which seems to stifle the noblest effort in the individual because his intellectual conception and his achievement are so difficult to bring together, is found on a large scale in society itself, when we have the separation of the people who think from those who work. And yet, since Ruskin ceased, no one has really formulated this in a convincing form. And even Ruskin's famous dictum, that labor without art brutalizes, has always been interpreted as if art could only be a sense of beauty or joy in one's own work, and not a sense of companionship with all other workers. The situation demands the consciousness of participation and well-being which comes to the individual when he is able to see himself "in connection and cooperation with the whole"; it needs the solace of collective art inherent in collective labor.

As the poet bathes the outer world for us in the hues of human feeling, so the workman needs some one to bathe his surroundings with a human significance-some one who shall teach him to find that which will give a potency to his life. His education, however simple, should tend to make him widely at home in the world, and to give him a sense of simplicity and peace in the midst of the triviality and noise to which he is constantly subjected. He, like other men, can learn to be content to see but a part, although it must be a part of something.

It is because of a lack of democracy that we do not really incorporate him in the hopes and advantages of society, and give him the place which is his by simple right. We have learned to say that the good must be extended to all of society before it can be held secure by any one person or any one class; but we have not yet learned to add to that statement, that unless all men and all classes contribute to a good, we cannot even be sure that it is worth having. In spite of many attempts we do not really act upon either statement.

Chapter VII
Political Reform

Throughout this volume we have assumed that much of our ethical maladjustment in social affairs arises from the fact that we are acting upon a code of ethics adapted to individual relationships, but not to the larger social relationships to which it is bunglingly applied. In addition, however, to the consequent strain and difficulty, there is often an honest lack of perception as to what the situation demands.

Nowhere is this more obvious than in our political life as it manifests itself in certain quarters of every great city. It is most difficult to hold to our political democracy and to make it in any sense a social expression and not a mere governmental contrivance, unless we take pains to keep on common ground in our human experiences. Otherwise there is in various parts of the community an inevitable difference of ethical standards which becomes responsible for much misunderstanding.

It is difficult both to interpret sympathetically the motives and ideals of those who have acquired rules of conduct in experience widely different from our own, and also to take enough care in guarding the gains already made, and in valuing highly enough the imperfect good so painfully acquired and, at the best, so mixed with evil. This wide difference in daily experience exhibits itself in two distinct attitudes toward politics. The well-to-do men of the community think of politics as something off by itself; they may conscientiously recognize political duty as part of good citizenship, but political effort is not the expression of their moral or social life. As a result of this detachment, "reform movements," started by business men and the better element, are almost wholly occupied in the correction of political machinery and with a concern for the better method of administration, rather than with the ultimate purpose of securing the welfare of the people. They fix their attention so exclusively on methods that they fail to consider the final aims of city government. This accounts for the growing tendency to put more and more responsibility upon executive officers and appointed commissions at the expense of curtailing the power of the direct representatives of the voters. Reform movements tend to become negative and to lose their educational value for the mass of the people. The reformers take the rôle of the opposition. They give themselves largely to criticisms of the present state of affairs, to writing and talking of what the future must be and of certain results which should be obtained. In trying to better matters, however, they have in mind only political achievements which they detach in a curious way from the rest of life, and they speak and write of the purification of politics as of a thing set apart from daily life.

On the other hand, the real leaders of the people are part of the entire life of the community which they control, and so far as they are representative at all, are giving a social expression to democracy. They are often politically corrupt, but in spite of this they are proceeding upon a sounder theory. Although they would be totally unable to give it abstract expression, they are really acting upon a formulation made by a shrewd English observer; namely, that, "after the enfranchisement of the masses, social ideals enter into political programmes, and they enter not as something which at best can be indirectly promoted by government, but as something which it is the chief business of government to advance directly."

Men living near to the masses of voters, and knowing them intimately, recognize this and act upon it; they minister directly to life and to social needs. They realize that the people as a whole are clamoring for social results, and they hold their power because they respond to that demand. They are corrupt and often do their work badly; but they at least avoid the mistake of a certain type of business men who are frightened by democracy, and have lost their faith in the people. The two standards are similar to those seen at a popular exhibition of pictures where the cultivated people care most for the technique of a given painting, the moving mass for a subject that shall be domestic and human.

This difference may be illustrated by the writer's experience in a certain ward of Chicago, during three campaigns, when efforts were made to dislodge an alderman who had represented the ward for many years. In this ward there are gathered together fifty thousand people, representing a score of nationalities; the newly emigrated Latin, Teuton, Celt, Greek, and Slav who live there have little in common save the basic experiences which come to men in all countries and under all conditions. In order to make fifty thousand people, so heterogeneous in nationality, religion, and customs, agree upon any demand, it must be founded upon universal experiences which are perforce individual and not social.

An instinctive recognition of this on the part of the alderman makes it possible to understand the individualistic basis of his political success, but it remains extremely difficult to ascertain the reasons for the extreme leniency of judgment concerning the political corruption of which he is constantly guilty.

This leniency is only to be explained on the ground that his constituents greatly admire individual virtues, and that they are at the same time unable to perceive social outrages which the alderman may be committing. They thus free the alderman from blame because his corruption is social, and they honestly admire him as a great man and hero, because his individual acts are on the whole kindly and generous.

In certain stages of moral evolution, a man is incapable of action unless the results will benefit himself or some one of his acquaintances, and it is a long step in moral progress to set the good of the many before the interest of the few, and to be concerned for the welfare of a community without hope of an individual return. How far the selfish politician befools his constituents into believing that their interests are identical with his own; how far he presumes upon their inability to distinguish between the individual and social virtues, an inability which he himself shares with them; and how far he dazzles them by the sense of his greatness, and a conviction that they participate therein, it is difficult to determine.

Morality certainly develops far earlier in the form of moral fact than in the form of moral ideas, and it is obvious that ideas only operate upon the popular mind through will and character, and must be dramatized before they reach the mass of men, even as the biography of the saints have been after all "the main guide to the stumbling feet of thousands of Christians to whom the Credo has been but mysterious words."

Ethics as well as political opinions may be discussed and disseminated among the sophisticated by lectures and printed pages, but to the common people they can only come through example-through a personality which seizes the popular imagination. The advantage of an unsophisticated neighborhood is, that the inhabitants do not keep their ideas as treasures-they are untouched by the notion of accumulating them, as they might knowledge or money, and they frankly act upon those they have. The personal example promptly rouses to emulation. In a neighborhood where political standards are plastic and undeveloped, and where there has been little previous experience in self-government, the office-holder himself sets the standard, and the ideas that cluster around him exercise a specific and permanent influence upon the political morality of his constituents.

Nothing is more certain than that the quality which a heterogeneous population, living in one of the less sophisticated wards, most admires is the quality of simple goodness; that the man who attracts them is the one whom they believe to be a good man. We all know that children long "to be good" with an intensity which they give to no other ambition. We can all remember that the earliest strivings of our childhood were in this direction, and that we venerated grown people because they had attained perfection.

Primitive people, such as the South Italian peasants, are still in this stage. They want to be good, and deep down in their hearts they admire nothing so much as the good man. Abstract virtues are too difficult for their untrained minds to apprehend, and many of them are still simple enough to believe that power and wealth come only to good people.

The successful candidate, then, must be a good man according to the morality of his constituents. He must not attempt to hold up too high a standard, nor must he attempt to reform or change their standards. His safety lies in doing on a large scale the good deeds which his constituents are able to do only on a small scale. If he believes what they believe and does what they are all cherishing a secret ambition to do, he will dazzle them by his success and win their confidence. There is a certain wisdom in this course. There is a common sense in the mass of men which cannot be neglected with impunity, just as there is sure to be an eccentricity in the differing and reforming individual which it is perhaps well to challenge.

The constant kindness of the poor to each other was pointed out in a previous chapter, and that they unfailingly respond to the need and distresses of their poorer neighbors even when in danger of bankruptcy themselves. The kindness which a poor man shows his distressed neighbor is doubtless heightened by the consciousness that he himself may be in distress next week; he therefore stands by his friend when he gets too drunk to take care of himself, when he loses his wife or child, when he is evicted for non-payment of rent, when he is arrested for a petty crime. It seems to such a man entirely fitting that his alderman should do the same thing on a larger scale-that he should help a constituent out of trouble, merely because he is in trouble, irrespective of the justice involved.

The alderman therefore bails out his constituents when they are arrested, or says a good word to the police justice when they appear before him for trial, uses his pull with the magistrate when they are likely to be fined for a civil misdemeanor, or sees what he can do to "fix up matters" with the state's attorney when the charge is really a serious one, and in doing this he follows the ethics held and practised by his constituents. All this conveys the impression to the simple-minded that law is not enforced, if the lawbreaker have a powerful friend. One may instance the alderman's action in standing by an Italian padrone of the ward when he was indicted for violating the civil service regulations. The commissioners had sent out notices to certain Italian day-laborers who were upon the eligible list that they were to report for work at a given day and hour. One of the padrones intercepted these notifications and sold them to the men for five dollars apiece, making also the usual bargain for a share of their wages. The padrone's entire arrangement followed the custom which had prevailed for years before the establishment of civil service laws. Ten of the laborers swore out warrants against the padrone, who was convicted and fined seventy-five dollars. This sum was promptly paid by the alderman, and the padrone, assured that he would be protected from any further trouble, returned uninjured to the colony. The simple Italians were much bewildered by this show of a power stronger than that of the civil service, which they had trusted as they did the one in Italy. The first violation of its authority was made, and various sinister acts have followed, until no Italian who is digging a sewer or sweeping a street for the city feels quite secure in holding his job unless he is backed by the friendship of the alderman. According to the civil service law, a laborer has no right to a trial; many are discharged by the foreman, and find that they can be reinstated only upon the aldermanic recommendation. He thus practically holds his old power over the laborers working for the city. The popular mind is convinced that an honest administration of civil service is impossible, and that it is but one more instrument in the hands of the powerful.

It will be difficult to establish genuine civil service among these men, who learn only by experience, since their experiences have been of such a nature that their unanimous vote would certainly be that "civil service" is "no good."

As many of his constituents in this case are impressed with the fact that the aldermanic power is superior to that of government, so instances of actual lawbreaking might easily be cited. A young man may enter a saloon long after midnight, the legal closing hour, and seat himself at a gambling table, perfectly secure from interruption or arrest, because the place be-longs to an alderman; but in order to secure this immunity the policeman on the beat must pretend not to see into the windows each time that he passes, and he knows, and the young man knows that he knows, that nothing would embarrass "Headquarters" more than to have an arrest made on those premises. A certain contempt for the whole machinery of law and order is thus easily fostered.

Because of simple friendliness the alderman is expected to pay rent for the hard-pressed tenant when no rent is forthcoming, to find "jobs" when work is hard to get, to procure and divide among his constituents all the places which he can seize from the city hall. The alderman of the ward we are considering at one time could make the proud boast that he had twenty-six hundred people in his ward upon the public pay-roll. This, of course, included day laborers, but each one felt under distinct obligations to him for getting a position. When we reflect that this is one-third of the entire vote of the ward, we realize that it is very important to vote for the right man, since there is, at the least, one chance out of three for securing work.

If we recollect further that the franchise-seeking companies pay respectful heed to the applicants backed by the alderman, the question of voting for the successful man becomes as much an industrial one as a political one. An Italian laborer wants a "job" more than anything else, and quite simply votes for the man who promises him one. It is not so different from his relation to the padrone, and, indeed, the two strengthen each other.

The alderman may himself be quite sincere in his acts of kindness, for an office seeker may begin with the simple desire to alleviate suffering, and this may gradually change into the desire to put his constituents under obligations to him; but the action of such an individual becomes a demoralizing element in the community when kindly impulse is made a cloak for the satisfaction of personal ambition, and when the plastic morals of his constituents gradually conform to his own undeveloped standards.

The alderman gives presents at weddings and christenings. He seizes these days of family festivities for making friends. It is easiest to reach them in the holiday mood of expansive good-will, but on their side it seems natural and kindly that he should do it. The alderman procures passes from the railroads when his constituents wish to visit friends or attend the funerals of distant relatives; he buys tickets galore for benefit entertainments given for a widow or a consumptive in peculiar distress; he contributes to prizes which are awarded to the handsomest lady or the most popular man. At a church bazaar, for instance, the alderman finds the stage all set for his dramatic performance. When others are spending pennies, he is spending dollars. When anxious relatives are canvassing to secure votes for the two most beautiful children who are being voted upon, he recklessly buys votes from both sides, and laughingly declines to say which one he likes best, buying off the young lady who is persistently determined to find out, with five dollars for the flower bazaar, the posies, of course, to be sent to the sick of the parish. The moral atmosphere of a bazaar suits him exactly. He murmurs many times, "Never mind, the money all goes to the poor; it is all straight enough if the church gets it, the poor won't ask too many questions." The oftener he can put such sentiments into the minds of his constituents, the better he is pleased. Nothing so rapidly prepares them to take his view of money getting and money spending. We see again the process disregarded, because the end itself is considered so praiseworthy.

There is something archaic in a community of simple people in their attitude toward death and burial. There is nothing so easy to collect money for as a funeral, and one involuntarily remembers that the early religious tithes were paid to ward off death and ghosts. At times one encounters almost the Greek feeling in regard to burial. If the alderman seizes upon times of festivities for expressions of his good-will, much more does he seize upon periods of sorrow. At a funeral he has the double advantage of ministering to a genuine craving for comfort and solace, and at the same time of assisting a bereaved constituent to express that curious feeling of remorse, which is ever an accompaniment of quick sorrow, that desire to "make up" for past delinquencies, to show the world how much he loved the person who has just died, which is as natural as it is universal.

In addition to this, there is, among the poor, who have few social occasions, a great desire for a well-arranged funeral, the grade of which almost determines their social standing in the neighborhood. The alderman saves the very poorest of his constituents from that awful horror of burial by the county; he provides carriages for the poor, who otherwise could not have them. It may be too much to say that all the relatives and friends who ride in the carriages provided by the alderman's bounty vote for him, but they are certainly influenced by his kindness, and talk of his virtues during the long hours of the ride back and forth from the suburban cemetery. A man who would ask at such a time where all the money thus spent comes from would be considered sinister. The tendency to speak lightly of the faults of the dead and to judge them gently is transferred to the living, and many a man at such a time has formulated a lenient judgment of political corruption, and has heard kindly speeches which he has remembered on election day. "Ah, well, he has a big Irish heart. He is good to the widow and the fatherless." "He knows the poor better than the big guns who are always talking about civil service and reform."

Indeed, what headway can the notion of civic purity, of honesty of administration make against this big manifestation of human friendliness, this stalking survival of village kindness? The notions of the civic reformer are negative and impotent before it. Such an alderman will keep a standing account with an undertaker, and telephone every week, and sometimes more than once, the kind of funeral he wishes provided for a bereaved constituent, until the sum may roll up into "hundreds a year." He understands what the people want, and ministers just as truly to a great human need as the musician or the artist. An attempt to substitute what we might call a later standard was made at one time when a delicate little child was deserted in the Hull-House nursery. An investigation showed that it had been born ten days previously in the Cook County hospital, but no trace could be found of the unfortunate mother. The little child lived for several weeks, and then, in spite of every care, died. It was decided to have it buried by the county authorities, and the wagon was to arrive at eleven o'clock; about nine o'clock in the morning the rumor of this awful deed reached the neighbors. A half dozen of them came, in a very excited state of mind, to protest. They took up a collection out of their poverty with which to defray a funeral. The residents of Hull-House were then comparatively new in the neighborhood and did not realize that they were really shocking a genuine moral sentiment of the community. In their crudeness they instanced the care and tenderness which had been expended upon the little creature while it was alive; that it had had every attention from a skilled physician and a trained nurse, and even intimated that the excited members of the group had not taken part in this, and that it now lay with the nursery to decide that it should be buried as it had been born, at the county's expense. It is doubtful if Hull-House has ever done anything which injured it so deeply in the minds of some of its neighbors. It was only forgiven by the most indulgent on the ground that the residents were spinsters, and could not know a mother's heart. No one born and reared in the community could possibly have made a mistake like that. No one who had studied the ethical standards with any care could have bungled so completely.

We are constantly underestimating the amount of sentiment among simple people. The songs which are most popular among them are those of a reminiscent old age, in which the ripened soul calmly recounts and regrets the sins of his youth, songs in which the wayward daughter is forgiven by her loving parents, in which the lovers are magnanimous and faithful through all vicissitudes. The tendency is to condone and forgive, and not hold too rigidly to a standard. In the theatres it is the magnanimous man, the kindly reckless villain who is always applauded. So shrewd an observer as Samuel Johnson once remarked that it was surprising to find how much more kindness than justice society contained.

On the same basis the alderman manages several saloons, one down town within easy access of the city hall, where he can catch the more important of his friends. Here again he has seized upon an old tradition and primitive custom, the good fellowship which has long been best expressed when men drink together. The saloons offer a common meeting ground, with stimulus enough to free the wits and tongues of the men who meet there.

He distributes each Christmas many tons of turkeys not only to voters, but to families who are represented by no vote. By a judicious management some families get three or four turkeys apiece; but what of that, the alderman has none of the nagging rules of the charitable societies, nor does he declare that because a man wants two turkeys for Christmas, he is a scoundrel who shall never be allowed to eat turkey again. As he does not distribute his Christmas favors from any hardly acquired philanthropic motive, there is no disposition to apply the carefully evolved rules of the charitable societies to his beneficiaries. Of course, there are those who suspect that the benevolence rests upon self-seeking motives, and feel themselves quite freed from any sense of gratitude; others go further and glory in the fact that they can thus "soak the alderman." An example of this is the young man who fills his pockets with a handful of cigars, giving a sly wink at the others. But this freedom from any sense of obligation is often the first step downward to the position where he is willing to sell his vote to both parties, and then scratch his ticket as he pleases. The writer recalls a conversation with a man in which he complained quite openly, and with no sense of shame, that his vote had "sold for only two dollars this year," and that he was "awfully disappointed." The writer happened to know that his income during the nine months previous had been but twenty-eight dollars, and that he was in debt thirty-two dollars, and she could well imagine the eagerness with which he had counted upon this source of revenue. After some years the selling of votes becomes a commonplace, and but little attempt is made upon the part of the buyer or seller to conceal the fact, if the transaction runs smoothly.

A certain lodging-house keeper at one time sold the votes of his entire house to a political party and was "well paid for it too"; but being of a grasping turn, he also sold the house for the same election to the rival party. Such an outrage could not be borne. The man was treated to a modern version of tar and feathers, and as a result of being held under a street hydrant in November, contracted pneumonia which resulted in his death. No official investigation took place, since the doctor's certificate of pneumonia was sufficient for legal burial, and public sentiment sustained the action. In various conversations which the writer had concerning the entire transaction, she discovered great indignation concerning his duplicity and treachery, but none whatever for his original offence of selling out the votes of his house.

A club will be started for the express purpose of gaining a reputation for political power which may later be sold out. The president and executive committee of such a club, who will naturally receive the funds, promise to divide with "the boys" who swell the size of the membership. A reform movement is at first filled with recruits who are active and loud in their assertions of the number of votes they can "deliver." The reformers are delighted with this display of zeal, and only gradually find out that many of the recruits are there for the express purpose of being bought by the other side; that they are most active in order to seem valuable, and thus raise the price of their allegiance when they are ready to sell. Reformers seeing them drop away one by one, talk of desertion from the ranks of reform, and of the power of money over well-meaning men, who are too weak to withstand temptation; but in reality the men are not deserters because they have never actually been enrolled in the ranks. The money they take is neither a bribe nor the price of their loyalty, it is simply the consummation of a long-cherished plan and a well-earned reward. They came into the new movement for the purpose of being bought out of it, and have successfully accomplished that purpose.

Hull-House assisted in carrying on two unsuccessful campaigns against the same alderman. In the two years following the end of the first one, nearly every man who had been prominent in it had received an office from the reëlected alderman. A printer had been appointed to a clerkship in the city hall; a driver received a large salary for services in the police barns; the candidate himself, a bricklayer, held a position in the city construction department. At the beginning of the next campaign, the greatest difficulty was experienced in finding a candidate, and each one proposed, demanded time to consider the proposition. During this period he invariably became the recipient of the alderman's bounty. The first one, who was foreman of a large factory, was reported to have been bought off by the promise that the city institutions would use the product of his firm. The second one, a keeper of a grocery and family saloon, with large popularity, was promised the aldermanic nomination on the regular ticket at the expiration of the term of office held by the alderman's colleague, and it may be well to state in passing that he was thus nominated and successfully elected. The third proposed candidate received a place for his son in the office of the city attorney.

Not only are offices in his gift, but all smaller favors as well. Any requests to the council, or special licenses, must be presented by the alderman of the ward in which the person desiring the favor resides. There is thus constant opportunity for the alderman to put his constituents under obligations to him, to make it difficult for a constituent to withstand him, or for one with large interests to enter into political action at all. From the Italian pedler who wants a license to peddle fruit in the street, to the large manufacturing company who desires to tunnel an alley for the sake of conveying pipes from one building to another, everybody is under obligations to his alderman, and is constantly made to feel it. In short, these very regulations for presenting requests to the council have been made, by the aldermen themselves, for the express purpose of increasing the dependence of their constituents, and thereby augmenting aldermanic power and prestige.

The alderman has also a very singular hold upon the property owners of his ward. The paving, both of the streets and sidewalks throughout his district, is disgraceful; and in the election speeches the reform side holds him responsible for this condition, and promises better paving under another régime. But the paving could not be made better without a special assessment upon the property owners of the vicinity, and paying more taxes is exactly what his constituents do not want to do. In reality, "getting them off," or at the worst postponing the time of the improvement, is one of the genuine favors which he performs. A movement to have the paving done from a general fund would doubtless be opposed by the property owners in other parts of the city who have already paid for the asphalt bordering their own possessions, but they have no conception of the struggle and possible bankruptcy which repaving may mean to the small property owner, nor how his chief concern may be to elect an alderman who cares more for the feelings and pocket-books of his constituents than he does for the repute and cleanliness of his city.

The alderman exhibited great wisdom in procuring from certain of his down-town friends the sum of three thousand dollars with which to uniform and equip a boys' temperance brigade which had been formed in one of the ward churches a few months before his campaign. Is it strange that the good leader, whose heart was filled with innocent pride as he looked upon these promising young scions of virtue, should decline to enter into a reform campaign? Of what use to suggest that uniforms and bayonets for the purpose of promoting temperance, bought with money contributed by a man who was proprietor of a saloon and a gambling house, might perhaps confuse the ethics of the young soldiers? Why take the pains to urge that it was vain to lecture and march abstract virtues into them, so long as the "champion boodler" of the town was the man whom the boys recognized as a loyal and kindhearted friend, the public-spirited citizen, whom their fathers enthusiastically voted for, and their mothers called "the friend of the poor." As long as the actual and tangible success is thus embodied, marching whether in kindergartens or brigades, talking whether in clubs or classes, does little to change the code of ethics.

The question of where does the money come from which is spent so successfully, does of course occur to many minds. The more primitive people accept the truthful statement of its sources without any shock to their moral sense. To their simple minds he gets it "from the rich" and, so long as he again gives it out to the poor as a true Robin Hood, with open hand, they have no objections to offer. Their ethics are quite honestly those of the merry-making foresters. The next less primitive people of the vicinage are quite willing to admit that he leads the "gang" in the city council, and sells out the city franchises; that he makes deals with the franchise-seeking companies; that he guarantees to steer dubious measures through the council, for which he demands liberal pay; that he is, in short, a successful "boodler." When, however, there is intellect enough to get this point of view, there is also enough to make the contention that this is universally done, that all the aldermen do it more or less successfully, but that the alderman of this particular ward is unique in being so generous; that such a state of affairs is to be deplored, of course; but that that is the way business is run, and we are fortunate when a kind-hearted man who is close to the people gets a large share of the spoils; that he serves franchised companies who employ men in the building and construction of their enterprises, and that they are bound in return to give work to his constituents. It is again the justification of stealing from the rich to give to the poor. Even when they are intelligent enough to complete the circle, and to see that the money comes, not from the pockets of the companies' agents, but from the street-car fares of people like themselves, it almost seems as if they would rather pay two cents more each time they ride than to give up the consciousness that they have a big, warm-hearted friend at court who will stand by them in an emergency. The sense of just dealing comes apparently much later than the desire for protection and indulgence. On the whole, the gifts and favors are taken quite simply as an evidence of genuine loving-kindness. The alderman is really elected because he is a good friend and neighbor. He is corrupt, of course, but he is not elected because he is corrupt, but rather in spite of it. His standard suits his constituents. He exemplifies and exaggerates the popular type of a good man. He has attained what his constituents secretly long for.

At one end of the ward there is a street of good houses, familiarly called "Con Row." The term is perhaps quite unjustly used, but it is nevertheless universally applied, because many of these houses are occupied by professional office holders. This row is supposed to form a happy hunting-ground of the successful politician, where he can live in prosperity, and still maintain his vote and influence in the ward. It would be difficult to justly estimate the influence which this group of successful, prominent men, including the alderman who lives there, have had upon the ideals of the youth in the vicinity. The path which leads to riches and success, to civic prominence and honor, is the path of political corruption. We might compare this to the path laid out by Benjamin Franklin, who also secured all of these things, but told young men that they could be obtained only by strenuous effort and frugal living, by the cultivation of the mind, and the holding fast to righteousness; or, again, we might compare it to the ideals which were held up to the American youth fifty years ago, lower, to be sure, than the revolutionary ideal, but still fine and aspiring toward honorable dealing and careful living. They were told that the career of the self-made man was open to every American boy, if he worked hard and saved his money, improved his mind, and followed a steady ambition. The writer remembers that when she was ten years old, the village schoolmaster told his little flock, without any mitigating clauses, that Jay Gould had laid the foundation of his colossal fortune by always saving bits of string, and that, as a result, every child in the village assiduously collected party-colored balls of twine. A bright Chicago boy might well draw the inference that the path of the corrupt politician not only leads to civic honors, but to the glories of benevolence and philanthropy. This lowering of standards, this setting of an ideal, is perhaps the worst of the situation, for, as we said in the first chapter, we determine ideals by our daily actions and decisions not only for ourselves, but largely for each other.

We are all involved in this political corruption, and as members of the community stand indicted. This is the penalty of a democracy, —that we are bound to move forward or retrograde together. None of us can stand aside; our feet are mired in the same soil, and our lungs breathe the same air.

That the alderman has much to do with setting the standard of life and desirable prosperity may be illustrated by the following incident: During one of the campaigns a clever cartoonist drew a poster representing the successful alderman in portraiture drinking champagne at a table loaded with pretentious dishes and surrounded by other revellers. In contradistinction was his opponent, a bricklayer, who sat upon a half-finished wall, eating a meagre dinner from a workingman's dinner-pail, and the passer-by was asked which type of representative he preferred, the presumption being that at least in a workingman's district the bricklayer would come out ahead. To the chagrin of the reformers, however, it was gradually discovered that, in the popular mind, a man who laid bricks and wore overalls was not nearly so desirable for an alderman as the man who drank champagne and wore a diamond in his shirt front. The district wished its representative "to stand up with the best of them," and certainly some of the constituents would have been ashamed to have been represented by a bricklayer. It is part of that general desire to appear well, the optimistic and thoroughly American belief, that even if a man is working with his hands to-day, he and his children will quite likely be in a better position in the swift coming to-morrow, and there is no need of being too closely associated with common working people. There is an honest absence of class consciousness, and a naïve belief that the kind of occupation quite largely determines social position. This is doubtless exaggerated in a neighborhood of foreign people by the fact that as each nationality becomes more adapted to American conditions, the scale of its occupation rises. Fifty years ago in America "a Dutchman" was used as a term of reproach, meaning a man whose language was not understood, and who performed menial tasks, digging sewers and building railroad embankments. Later the Irish did the same work in the community, but as quickly as possible handed it on to the Italians, to whom the name "dago" is said to cling as a result of the digging which the Irishman resigned to him. The Italian himself is at last waking up to this fact. In a political speech recently made by an Italian padrone, he bitterly reproached the alderman for giving the-four-dollars-a-day "jobs" of sitting in an office to Irishmen and the-dollar-and-a-half-a-day "jobs" of sweeping the streets to the Italians. This general struggle to rise in life, to be at least politically represented by one of the best, as to occupation and social status, has also its negative side. We must remember that the imitative impulse plays an important part in life, and that the loss of social estimation, keenly felt by all of us, is perhaps most dreaded by the humblest, among whom freedom of individual conduct, the power to give only just weight to the opinion of neighbors, is but feebly developed. A form of constraint, gentle, but powerful, is afforded by the simple desire to do what others do, in order to share with them the approval of the community. Of course, the larger the number of people among whom an habitual mode of conduct obtains, the greater the constraint it puts upon the individual will. Thus it is that the political corruption of the city presses most heavily where it can be least resisted, and is most likely to be imitated.

According to the same law, the positive evils of corrupt government are bound to fall heaviest upon the poorest and least capable. When the water of Chicago is foul, the prosperous buy water bottled at distant springs; the poor have no alternative but the typhoid fever which comes from using the city's supply. When the garbage contracts are not enforced, the well-to-do pay for private service; the poor suffer the discomfort and illness which are inevitable from a foul atmosphere. The prosperous business man has a certain choice as to whether he will treat with the "boss" politician or preserve his independence on a smaller income; but to an Italian day laborer it is a choice between obeying the commands of a political "boss" or practical starvation. Again, a more intelligent man may philosophize a little upon the present state of corruption, and reflect that it is but a phase of our commercialism, from which we are bound to emerge; at any rate, he may give himself the solace of literature and ideals in other directions, but the more ignorant man who lives only in the narrow present has no such resource; slowly the conviction enters his mind that politics is a matter of favors and positions, that self-government means pleasing the "boss" and standing in with the "gang." This slowly acquired knowledge he hands on to his family. During the month of February his boy may come home from school with rather incoherent tales about Washington and Lincoln, and the father may for the moment be fired to tell of Garibaldi, but such talk is only periodic, and the long year round the fortunes of the entire family, down to the opportunity to earn food and shelter, depend upon the "boss."

In a certain measure also, the opportunities for pleasure and recreation depend upon him. To use a former illustration, if a man happens to have a taste for gambling, if the slot machine affords him diversion, he goes to those houses which are protected by political influence. If he and his friends like to drop into a saloon after midnight, or even want to hear a little music while they drink together early in the evening, he is breaking the law when he indulges in either of them, and can only be exempt from arrest or fine because the great political machine is friendly to him and expects his allegiance in return.

During the campaign, when it was found hard to secure enough local speakers of the moral tone which was desired, orators were imported from other parts of the town, from the so-called "better element." Suddenly it was rumored on all sides that, while the money and speakers for the reform candidate were coming from the swells, the money which was backing the corrupt alderman also came from a swell source; that the president of a street-car combination, for whom he performed constant offices in the city council, was ready to back him to the extent of fifty thousand dollars; that this president, too, was a good man, and sat in high places; that he had recently given a large sum of money to an educational institution and was therefore as philanthropic, not to say good and upright, as any man in town; that the corrupt alderman had the sanction of the highest authorities, and that the lecturers who were talking against corruption, and the selling and buying of franchises, were only the cranks, and not the solid business men who had developed and built up Chicago.

All parts of the community are bound together in ethical development. If the so-called more enlightened members accept corporate gifts from the man who buys up the council, and the so-called less enlightened members accept individual gifts from the man who sells out the council, we surely must take our punishment together. There is the difference, of course, that in the first case we act collectively, and in the second case individually; but is the punishment which follows the first any lighter or less far-reaching in its consequences than the more obvious one which follows the second?

Have our morals been so captured by commercialism, to use Mr. Chapman's generalization, that we do not see a moral dereliction when business or educational interests are served thereby, although we are still shocked when the saloon interest is thus served?

The street-car company which declares that it is impossible to do business without managing the city council, is on exactly the same moral level with the man who cannot retain political power unless he has a saloon, a large acquaintance with the semi-criminal class, and questionable money with which to debauch his constituents. Both sets of men assume that the only appeal possible is along the line of self-interest. They frankly acknowledge money getting as their own motive power, and they believe in the cupidity of all the men whom they encounter. No attempt in either case is made to put forward the claims of the public, or to find a moral basis for action. As the corrupt politician assumes that public morality is impossible, so many business men become convinced that to pay tribute to the corrupt aldermen is on the whole cheaper than to have taxes too high; that it is better to pay exorbitant rates for franchises, than to be made unwilling partners in transportation experiments. Such men come to regard political reformers as a sort of monomaniac, who are not reasonable enough to see the necessity of the present arrangement which has slowly been evolved and developed, and upon which business is safely conducted. A reformer who really knew the people and their great human needs, who believed that it was the business of government to serve them, and who further recognized the educative power of a sense of responsibility, would possess a clew by which he might analyze the situation. He would find out what needs, which the alderman supplies, are legitimate ones which the city itself could undertake, in counter-distinction to those which pander to the lower instincts of the constituency. A mother who eats her Christmas turkey in a reverent spirit of thankfulness to the alderman who gave it to her, might be gradually brought to a genuine sense of appreciation and gratitude to the city which supplies her little children with a Kindergarten, or, to the Board of Health which properly placarded a case of scarlet-fever next door and spared her sleepless nights and wearing anxiety, as well as the money paid with such difficulty to the doctor and the druggist. The man who in his emotional gratitude almost kneels before his political friend who gets his boy out of jail, might be made to see the kindness and good sense of the city authorities who provided the boy with a playground and reading room, where he might spend his hours of idleness and restlessness, and through which his temptations to petty crime might be averted. A man who is grateful to the alderman who sees that his gambling and racing are not interfered with, might learn to feel loyal and responsible to the city which supplied him with a gymnasium and swimming tank where manly and well-conducted sports are possible. The voter who is eager to serve the alderman at all times, because the tenure of his job is dependent upon aldermanic favor, might find great relief and pleasure in working for the city in which his place was secured by a well-administered civil service law.

After all, what the corrupt alderman demands from his followers and largely depends upon is a sense of loyalty, a standing-by the man who is good to you, who understands you, and who gets you out of trouble. All the social life of the voter from the time he was a little boy and played "craps" with his "own push," and not with some other "push," has been founded on this sense of loyalty and of standing in with his friends. Now that he is a man, he likes the sense of being inside a political organization, of being trusted with political gossip, of belonging to a set of fellows who understand things, and whose interests are being cared for by a strong friend in the city council itself. All this is perfectly legitimate, and all in the line of the development of a strong civic loyalty, if it were merely socialized and enlarged. Such a voter has already proceeded in the forward direction in so far as he has lost the sense of isolation, and has abandoned the conviction that city government does not touch his individual affairs. Even Mill claims that the social feelings of man, his desire to be at unity with his fellow-creatures, are the natural basis for morality, and he defines a man of high moral culture as one who thinks of himself, not as an isolated individual, but as a part in a social organism.

Upon this foundation it ought not to be difficult to build a structure of civic virtue. It is only necessary to make it clear to the voter that his individual needs are common needs, that is, public needs, and that they can only be legitimately supplied for him when they are supplied for all. If we believe that the individual struggle for life may widen into a struggle for the lives of all, surely the demand of an individual for decency and comfort, for a chance to work and obtain the fulness of life may be widened until it gradually embraces all the members of the community, and rises into a sense of the common weal.

In order, however, to give him a sense of conviction that his individual needs must be merged into the needs of the many, and are only important as they are thus merged, the appeal cannot be made along the line of self-interest. The demand should be universalized; in this process it would also become clarified, and the basis of our political organization become perforce social and ethical.

Would it be dangerous to conclude that the corrupt politician himself, because he is democratic in method, is on a more ethical line of social development than the reformer, who believes that the people must be made over by "good citizens" and governed by "experts"? The former at least are engaged in that great moral effort of getting the mass to express itself, and of adding this mass energy and wisdom to the community as a whole.

The wide divergence of experience makes it difficult for the good citizen to understand this point of view, and many things conspire to make it hard for him to act upon it. He is more or less a victim to that curious feeling so often possessed by the good man, that the righteous do not need to be agreeable, that their goodness alone is sufficient, and that they can leave the arts and wiles of securing popular favor to the self-seeking. This results in a certain repellent manner, commonly regarded as the apparel of righteousness, and is further responsible for the fatal mistake of making the surroundings of "good influences" singularly unattractive; a mistake which really deserves a reprimand quite as severe as the equally reprehensible deed of making the surroundings of "evil influences" so beguiling. Both are akin to that state of mind which narrows the entrance into a wider morality to the eye of a needle, and accounts for the fact that new moral movements have ever and again been inaugurated by those who have found themselves in revolt against the conventionalized good.

The success of the reforming politician who insists upon mere purity of administration and upon the control and suppression of the unruly elements in the community, may be the easy result of a narrowing and selfish process. For the painful condition of endeavoring to minister to genuine social needs, through the political machinery, and at the same time to remodel that machinery so that it shall be adequate to its new task, is to encounter the inevitable discomfort of a transition into a new type of democratic relation. The perplexing experiences of the actual administration, however, have a genuine value of their own. The economist who treats the individual cases as mere data, and the social reformer who labors to make such cases impossible, solely because of the appeal to his reason, may have to share these perplexities before they feel themselves within the grasp of a principle of growth, working outward from within; before they can gain the exhilaration and uplift which comes when the individual sympathy and intelligence is caught into the forward intuitive movement of the mass. This general movement is not without its intellectual aspects, but it has to be transferred from the region of perception to that of emotion before it is really apprehended. The mass of men seldom move together without an emotional incentive. The man who chooses to stand aside, avoids much of the perplexity, but at the same time he loses contact with a great source of vitality.

Perhaps the last and greatest difficulty in the paths of those who are attempting to define and attain a social morality, is that which arises from the fact that they cannot adequately test the value of their efforts, cannot indeed be sure of their motives until their efforts are reduced to action and are presented in some workable form of social conduct or control. For action is indeed the sole medium of expression for ethics. We continually forget that the sphere of morals is the sphere of action, that speculation in regard to morality is but observation and must remain in the sphere of intellectual comment, that a situation does not really become moral until we are confronted with the question of what shall be done in a concrete case, and are obliged to act upon our theory. A stirring appeal has lately been made by a recognized ethical lecturer who has declared that "It is insanity to expect to receive the data of wisdom by looking on. We arrive at moral knowledge only by tentative and observant practice. We learn how to apply the new insight by having attempted to apply the old and having found it to fail."

This necessity of reducing the experiment to action throws out of the undertaking all timid and irresolute persons, more than that, all those who shrink before the need of striving forward shoulder to shoulder with the cruder men, whose sole virtue may be social effort, and even that not untainted by self-seeking, who are indeed pushing forward social morality, but who are doing it irrationally and emotionally, and often at the expense of the well-settled standards of morality.

The power to distinguish between the genuine effort and the adventitious mistakes is perhaps the most difficult test which comes to our fallible intelligence. In the range of individual morals, we have learned to distrust him who would reach spirituality by simply renouncing the world, or by merely speculating upon its evils. The result, as well as the process of virtues attained by repression, has become distasteful to us. When the entire moral energy of an individual goes into the cultivation of personal integrity, we all know how unlovely the result may become; the character is upright, of course, but too coated over with the result of its own endeavor to be attractive. In this effort toward a higher morality in our social relations, we must demand that the individual shall be willing to lose the sense of personal achievement, and shall be content to realize his activity only in connection with the activity of the many.

The cry of "Back to the people" is always heard at the same time, when we have the prophet's demand for repentance or the religious cry of "Back to Christ," as though we would seek refuge with our fellows and believe in our common experiences as a preparation for a new moral struggle.

As the acceptance of democracy brings a certain life-giving power, so it has its own sanctions and comforts. Perhaps the most obvious one is the curious sense which comes to us from time to time, that we belong to the whole, that a certain basic well being can never be taken away from us whatever the turn of fortune. Tolstoy has portrayed the experience in "Master and Man." The former saves his servant from freezing, by protecting him with the heat of his body, and his dying hours are filled with an ineffable sense of healing and well-being. Such experiences, of which we have all had glimpses, anticipate in our relation to the living that peace of mind which envelopes us when we meditate upon the great multitude of the dead. It is akin to the assurance that the dead understand, because they have entered into the Great Experience, and therefore must comprehend all lesser ones; that all the misunderstandings we have in life are due to partial experience, and all life's fretting comes of our limited intelligence; when the last and Great Experience comes, it is, perforce, attended by mercy and forgiveness. Consciously to accept Democracy and its manifold experiences is to anticipate that peace and freedom.

The Spirit of Youth and the City Streets

TO MY DEAR FRIEND

Louise de Koben Bowen

WITH SINCERE ADMIRATION FOR HER UNDERSTANDING
OF THE NEEDS OF CITY CHILDREN AND WITH WARM
APPRECIATION OF HER SERVICE AS PRESIDENT
OF THE JUVENILE PROTECTIVE ASSOCIATION
OF CHICAGO

Foreword

Much of the material in the following pages has appeared in current publications. It is here presented in book form in the hope that it may prove of value to those groups of people who in many cities are making a gallant effort to minimize the dangers which surround young people and to provide them with opportunities for recreation.

Chapter I
Youth in the City

Nothing is more certain than that each generation longs for a reassurance as to the value and charm of life, and is secretly afraid lest it lose its sense of the youth of the earth. This is doubtless one reason why it so passionately cherishes its poets and artists who have been able to explore for themselves and to reveal to others the perpetual springs of life's self-renewal.

And yet the average man cannot obtain this desired reassurance through literature, nor yet through glimpses of earth and sky. It can come to him only through the chance embodiment of joy and youth which life itself may throw in his way. It is doubtless true that for the mass of men the message is never so unchallenged and so invincible as when embodied in youth itself. One generation after another has depended upon its young to equip it with gaiety and enthusiasm, to persuade it that living is a pleasure, until men everywhere have anxiously provided channels through which this wine of life might flow, and be preserved for their delight. The classical city promoted play with careful solicitude, building the theater and stadium as it built the market place and the temple. The Greeks held their games so integral a part of religion and patriotism that they came to expect from their poets the highest utterances at the very moments when the sense of pleasure released the national life. In the medieval city the knights held their tourneys, the guilds their pageants, the people their dances, and the church made festival for its most cherished saints with gay street processions, and presented a drama in which no less a theme than the history of creation became a matter of thrilling interest. Only in the modern city have men concluded that it is no longer necessary for the municipality to provide for the insatiable desire for play. In so far as they have acted upon this conclusion, they have entered upon a most difficult and dangerous experiment; and this at the very moment when the city has become distinctly industrial, and daily labor is continually more monotonous and subdivided. We forget how new the modern city is, and how short the span of time in which we have assumed that we can eliminate public provision for recreation.

A further difficulty lies in the fact that this industrialism has gathered together multitudes of eager young creatures from all quarters of the earth as a labor supply for the countless factories and workshops, upon which the present industrial city is based. Never before in civilization have such numbers of young girls been suddenly released from the protection of the home and permitted to walk unattended upon city streets and to work under alien roofs; for the first time they are being prized more for their labor power than for their innocence, their tender beauty, their ephemeral gaiety. Society cares more for the products they manufacture than for their immemorial ability to reaffirm the charm of existence. Never before have such numbers of young boys earned money independently of the family life, and felt themselves free to spend it as they choose in the midst of vice deliberately disguised as pleasure.

This stupid experiment of organizing work and failing to organize play has, of course, brought about a fine revenge. The love of pleasure will not be denied, and when it has turned into all sorts of malignant and vicious appetites, then we, the middle aged, grow quite distracted and resort to all sorts of restrictive measures. We even try to dam up the sweet fountain itself because we are affrighted by these neglected streams; but almost worse than the restrictive measures is our apparent belief that the city itself has no obligation in the matter, an assumption upon which the modern city turns over to commercialism practically all the provisions for public recreation.

Quite as one set of men has organized the young people into industrial enterprises in order to profit from their toil, so another set of men and also of women, I am sorry to say, have entered the neglected field of recreation and have organized enterprises which make profit out of this invincible love of pleasure.

In every city arise so-called "places" —"gin-palaces," they are called in fiction; in Chicago we euphemistically say merely "places," —in which alcohol is dispensed, not to allay thirst, but, ostensibly to stimulate gaiety, it is sold really in order to empty pockets. Huge dance halls are opened to which hundreds of young people are attracted, many of whom stand wistfully outside a roped circle, for it requires five cents to procure within it for five minutes the sense of allurement and intoxication which is sold in lieu of innocent pleasure. These coarse and illicit merrymakings remind one of the unrestrained jollities of Restoration London, and they are indeed their direct descendants, properly commercialized, still confusing joy with lust, and gaiety with debauchery. Since the soldiers of Cromwell shut up the people's playhouses and destroyed their pleasure fields, the Anglo-Saxon city has turned over the provision for public recreation to the most evil-minded and the most unscrupulous members of the community. We see thousands of girls walking up and down the streets on a pleasant evening with no chance to catch a sight of pleasure even through a lighted window, save as these lurid places provide it. Apparently the modern city sees in these girls only two possibilities, both of them commercial: first, a chance to utilize by day their new and tender labor power in its factories and shops, and then another chance in the evening to extract from them their petty wages by pandering to their love of pleasure.

As these overworked girls stream along the street, the rest of us see only the self-conscious walk, the giggling speech, the preposterous clothing. And yet through the huge hat, with its wilderness of bedraggled feathers, the girl announces to the world that she is here. She demands attention to the fact of her existence, she states that she is ready to live, to take her place in the world. The most precious moment in human development is the young creature's assertion that he is unlike any other human being, and has an individual contribution to make to the world. The variation from the established type is at the root of all change, the only possible basis for progress, all that keeps life from growing unprofitably stale and repetitious.

Is it only the artists who really see these young creatures as they are-the artists who are themselves endowed with immortal youth? Is it our disregard of the artist's message which makes us so blind and so stupid, or are we so under the influence of our *Zeitgeist* that we can detect only commercial values in the young as well as in the old? It is as if our eyes were holden to the mystic beauty, the redemptive joy, the civic pride which these multitudes of young people might supply to our dingy towns.

The young creatures themselves piteously look all about them in order to find an adequate means of expression for their most precious message: One day a serious young man came to Hull-House with his pretty young sister who, he explained, wanted to go somewhere every single evening, "although she could only give the flimsy excuse that the flat was too little and too stuffy to stay in." In the difficult rôle of elder brother, he had done his best, stating that he had taken her "to all the missions in the neighborhood, that she had had a chance to listen to some awful good sermons and to some elegant hymns, but that some way she did not seem to care for the society of the best Christian people." The little sister reddened painfully under this cruel indictment and could offer no word of excuse, but a curious thing happened to me. Perhaps it was the phrase "the best Christian people," perhaps it was the delicate color of her flushing cheeks and her swimming eyes, but certain it is, that instantly and vividly there appeared to my mind the delicately tinted piece of wall in a Roman catacomb where the early Christians, through a dozen devices of spring flowers, skipping lambs and a shepherd tenderly guiding the young, had indelibly written down that the Christian message is one of inexpressible joy. Who is responsible for forgetting this message delivered by the "best Christian people" two thousand years ago? Who is to blame that the lambs, the little ewe lambs, have been so caught upon the brambles?

But quite as the modern city wastes this most valuable moment in the life of the girl, and drives into all sorts of absurd and obscure expressions her love and yearning towards the world in which she forecasts her destiny, so it often drives the boy into gambling and drinking in order to find his adventure.

Of Lincoln's enlistment of two and a half million soldiers, a very large number were under twenty-one, some of them under eighteen, and still others were mere children under fifteen.

Even in those stirring times when patriotism and high resolve were at the flood, no one responded as did "the boys," and the great soul who yearned over them, who refused to shoot the sentinels who slept the sleep of childhood, knew, as no one else knew, the precious glowing stuff of which his army was made. But what of the millions of boys who are now searching for adventurous action, longing to fulfil the same high purpose?

One of the most pathetic sights in the public dance halls of Chicago is the number of young men, obviously honest young fellows from the country, who stand about vainly hoping to make the acquaintance of some "nice girl." They look eagerly up and down the rows of girls, many of whom are drawn to the hall by the same keen desire for pleasure and social intercourse which the lonely young men themselves feel.

One Sunday night at twelve o'clock I had occasion to go into a large public dance hall. As I was standing by the rail looking for the girl I had come to find, a young man approached me and quite simply asked me to introduce him to some "nice girl," saying that he did not know any one there. On my replying that a public dance hall was not the best place in which to look for a nice girl, he said: "But I don't know any other place where there is a chance to meet any kind of a girl. I'm awfully lonesome since I came to Chicago." And then he added rather defiantly: "Some nice girls do come here! It's one of the best halls in town." He was voicing the "bitter loneliness" that many city men remember to have experienced during the first years after they had "come up to town." Occasionally the right sort of man and girl meet each other in these dance halls and the romance with such a tawdry beginning ends happily and respectably. But, unfortunately, mingled with the respectable young men seeking to form the acquaintance of young women through the only channel which is available to them, are many young fellows of evil purpose, and among the girls who have left their lonely boarding houses or rigid homes for a "little fling" are likewise women who openly desire to make money from the young men whom they meet, and back of it all is the desire to profit by the sale of intoxicating and "doctored" drinks.

Perhaps never before have the pleasures of the young and mature become so definitely separated as in the modern city. The public dance halls filled with frivolous and irresponsible young people in a feverish search for pleasure, are but a sorry substitute for the old dances on the village green in which all of the older people of the village participated. Chaperonage was not then a social duty but natural and inevitable, and the whole courtship period was guarded by the conventions and restraint which were taken as a matter of course and had developed through years of publicity and simple propriety.

The only marvel is that the stupid attempt to put the fine old wine of traditional country life into the new bottles of the modern town does not lead to disaster oftener than it does, and that the wine so long remains pure and sparkling.

We cannot afford to be ungenerous to the city in which we live without suffering the penalty which lack of fair interpretation always entails. Let us know the modern city in its weakness and wickedness, and then seek to rectify and purify it until it shall be free at least from the grosser temptations which now beset the young people who are living in its tenement houses and working in its factories. The mass of these young people are possessed of good intentions and they are equipped with a certain understanding of city life. This itself could be made a most valuable social instrument toward securing innocent recreation and better social organization. They are already serving the city in so far as it is honeycombed with mutual benefit societies, with "pleasure clubs," with organizations connected with churches and factories which are filling a genuine social need. And yet the whole apparatus for supplying pleasure is wretchedly inadequate and full of danger to whomsoever may approach it. Who is responsible for its inadequacy and dangers? We certainly cannot expect the fathers and mothers who have come to the city from farms or who have emigrated from other lands to appreciate or rectify these dangers. We cannot expect the young people themselves to cling to conventions which are totally unsuited to modern city conditions, nor yet to be equal to the task of forming new conventions through which this more agglomerate social life may express itself. Above all we cannot hope that they will understand the emotional force which seizes them and which, when it does not find the traditional line of domesticity, serves as a cancer in the very tissues of society and as a disrupter of the securest social bonds. No attempt is made to treat the manifestations of this fundamental instinct with dignity or to give it possible social utility. The spontaneous joy, the clamor for pleasure, the desire of the young people to appear finer and better and altogether more lovely than they really are, the idealization not only of each other but of the whole earth which they regard but as a theater for their noble exploits, the unworldly ambitions, the romantic hopes, the make-believe world in which they live, if properly utilized, what might they not do to make our sordid cities more beautiful, more companionable? And yet at the present moment every city is full of young people who are utterly bewildered and uninstructed in regard to the basic experience which must inevitably come to them, and which has varied, remote, and indirect expressions.

Even those who may not agree with the authorities who claim that it is this fundamental sex susceptibility which suffuses the world with its deepest meaning and beauty, and furnishes the momentum towards all art, will perhaps permit me to quote the classical expression of this view as set forth in that ancient and wonderful conversation between Socrates and the wise woman Diotima. Socrates asks: "What are they doing who show all this eagerness and heat which is called love? And what is the object they have in view? Answer me." Diotima replies: "I will teach you. The object which they have in view is birth in beauty, whether of body or soul.... For love, Socrates, is not as you imagine the love of the beautiful only ... but the love of birth in beauty, because to the mortal creature generation is a sort of eternity and immortality."

To emphasize the eternal aspects of love is not of course an easy undertaking, even if we follow the clue afforded by the heart of every generous lover. His experience at least in certain moments tends to pull him on and out from the passion for one to an enthusiasm for that highest beauty and excellence of which the most perfect form is but an inadequate expression. Even the most loutish tenement-house youth vaguely feels this, and at least at rare intervals reveals it in his talk to his "girl." His memory unexpectedly brings hidden treasures to the surface of consciousness and he recalls the more delicate and tender experiences of his childhood and earlier youth. "I remember the time when my little sister died, that I rode out to the cemetery feeling that everybody in Chicago had moved away from the town to make room for that kid's funeral, everything was so darned lonesome and yet it was kind of peaceful too." Or, "I never had a chance to go into the country when I was a kid, but I remember one day when I had to deliver a package way out on the West Side, that I saw a flock of sheep in Douglas Park. I had never thought that a sheep could be anywhere but in a picture, and when I saw those big white spots on the green grass beginning to move and to turn into sheep, I felt exactly as if Saint Cecilia had come out of her frame over the organ and was walking in the park." Such moments come into the life of the most prosaic youth living in the most crowded quarters of the cities. What do we do to encourage and to solidify those moments, to make them come true in our dingy towns, to give them expression in forms of art?

We not only fail in this undertaking but even debase existing forms of art. We are informed by high authority that there is nothing in the environment to which youth so keenly responds as to music, and yet the streets, the vaudeville shows, the five-cent theaters are full of the most blatant and vulgar songs. The trivial and obscene words, the meaningless and flippant airs run through the heads of hundreds of young people for hours at a time while they are engaged in monotonous factory work. We totally ignore that ancient connection between music and morals which was so long insisted upon by philosophers as well as poets. The street music has quite broken away from all control, both of the educator and the patriot, and we have grown singularly careless in regard to its influence upon young people. Although we legislate against it in saloons because of its dangerous influence there, we constantly permit music on the street to incite that which should be controlled, to degrade that which should be exalted, to make sensuous that which might be lifted into the realm of the higher imagination.

Our attitude towards music is typical of our carelessness towards all those things which make for common joy and for the restraints of higher civilization on the streets. It is as if our cities had not yet developed a sense of responsibility in regard to the life of the streets, and continually forget that recreation is stronger than vice, and that recreation alone can stifle the lust for vice.

Perhaps we need to take a page from the philosophy of the Greeks to whom the world of fact was also the world of the ideal, and to whom the realization of what ought to be, involved not the destruction of what was, but merely its perfecting upon its own lines. To the Greeks virtue was not a hard conformity to a law felt as alien to the natural character, but a free expression of the inner life. To treat thus the fundamental susceptibility of sex which now so bewilders the street life and drives young people themselves into all sorts of difficulties, would mean to loosen it from the things of sense and to link it to the affairs of the imagination. It would mean to fit to this gross and heavy stuff the wings of the mind, to scatter from it "the clinging mud of banality and vulgarity," and to speed it on through our city streets amid spontaneous laughter, snatches of lyric song, the recovered forms of old dances, and the traditional rondels of merry games. It would thus bring charm and beauty to the prosaic city and connect it subtly with the arts of the past as well as with the vigor and renewed life of the future.

Chapter II
The Wrecked Foundations of Domesticity

>"Sense with keenest edge unused
> Yet unsteel'd by scathing fire:
> Lovely feet as yet unbruised
> On the ways of dark desire!"

These words written by a poet to his young son express the longing which has at times seized all of us, to guard youth from the mass of difficulties which may be traced to the obscure manifestation of that fundamental susceptibility of which we are all slow to speak and concerning which we evade public responsibility, although it brings its scores of victims into the police courts every morning.

At the very outset we must bear in mind that the senses of youth are singularly acute, and ready to respond to every vivid appeal. We know that nature herself has sharpened the senses for her own purposes, and is deliberately establishing a connection between them and the newly awakened susceptibility of sex; for it is only through the outward senses that the selection of an individual mate is made and the instinct utilized for nature's purposes. It would seem, however, that nature was determined that the force and constancy of the instinct must make up for its lack of precision, and that she was totally unconcerned that this instinct ruthlessly seized the youth at the moment when he was least prepared to cope with it; not only because his powers of self-control and discrimination are unequal to the task, but because his senses are helplessly wide open to the world. These early manifestations of the sex susceptibility are for the most part vague and formless, and are absolutely without definition to the youth himself. Sometimes months and years elapse before the individual mate is selected and determined upon, and during the time when the differentiation is not complete-and it often is not-there is of necessity a great deal of groping and waste.

This period of groping is complicated by the fact that the youth's power for appreciating is far ahead of his ability for expression. "The inner traffic fairly obstructs the outer current," and it is nothing short of cruelty to over-stimulate his senses as does the modern city. This period is difficult everywhere, but it seems at times as if a great city almost deliberately increased its perils. The newly awakened senses are appealed to by all that is gaudy and sensual, by the flippant street music, the highly colored theater posters, the trashy love stories, the feathered hats, the cheap heroics of the revolvers displayed in the pawn-shop windows. This fundamental susceptibility is thus evoked without a corresponding stir of the higher imagination, and the result is as dangerous as possible. We are told upon good authority that "If the imagination is retarded, while the senses remain awake, we have a state of esthetic insensibility," —in other words, the senses become sodden and cannot be lifted from the ground. It is this state of "esthetic insensibility" into which we allow the youth to fall which is so distressing and so unjustifiable. Sex impulse then becomes merely a dumb and powerful instinct without in the least awakening the imagination or the heart, nor does it overflow into neighboring fields of consciousness. Every city contains hundreds of degenerates who have been over-mastered and borne down by it; they fill the casual lodging houses and the infirmaries. In many instances it has pushed men of ability and promise to the bottom of the social scale. Warner, in his *American Charities*, designates it as one of the steady forces making for failure and poverty, and contends that "the inherent uncleanness of their minds prevents many men from rising above the rank of day laborers and finally incapacitates them even for that position." He also suggests that the modern man has a stronger imagination than the man of a few hundred years ago and that sensuality destroys him the more rapidly.

It is difficult to state how much evil and distress might be averted if the imagination were utilized in its higher capacities through the historic paths. An English moralist has lately asserted that "much of the evil of the time may be traced to outraged imagination. It is the strongest quality of the brain and it is starved. Children, from their earliest years, are hedged in with facts; they are not trained to use their minds on the unseen."

In failing to diffuse and utilize this fundamental instinct of sex through the imagination, we not only inadvertently foster vice and enervation, but we throw away one of the most precious implements for ministering to life's highest needs. There is no doubt that this ill adjusted function consumes quite unnecessarily vast stores of vital energy, even when we contemplate it in its immature manifestations which are infinitely more wholesome than the dumb swamping process. Every high school boy and girl knows the difference between the concentration and the diffusion of this impulse, although they would be hopelessly bewildered by the use of the terms. They will declare one of their companions to be "in love" if his fancy is occupied by the image of a single person about whom all the newly found values gather, and without whom his solitude is an eternal melancholy. But if the stimulus does not appear as a definite image, and the values evoked are dispensed over the world, the young person suddenly seems to have discovered a beauty and significance in many things-he responds to poetry, he becomes a lover of nature, he is filled with religious devotion or with philanthropic zeal. Experience, with young people, easily illustrates the possibility and value of diffusion.

It is neither a short nor an easy undertaking to substitute the love of beauty for mere desire, to place the mind above the senses; but is not this the sum of the immemorial obligation which rests upon the adults of each generation if they would nurture and restrain the youth, and has not the whole history of civilization been but one long effort to substitute psychic impulsion for the driving force of blind appetite?

Society has recognized the "imitative play" impulse of children and provides them with tiny bricks with which to "build a house," and dolls upon which they may lavish their tenderness. We exalt the love of the mother and the stability of the home, but in regard to those difficult years between childhood and maturity we beg the question and unless we repress, we do nothing. We are so timid and inconsistent that although we declare the home to be the foundation of society, we do nothing to direct the force upon which the continuity of the home depends. And yet to one who has lived for years in a crowded quarter where men, women and children constantly jostle each other and press upon every inch of space in shop, tenement and street, nothing is more impressive than the strength, the continuity, the varied and powerful manifestations, of family affection. It goes without saying that every tenement house contains women who for years spend their hurried days in preparing food and clothing and pass their sleepless nights in tending and nursing their exigent children, with never one thought for their own comfort or pleasure or development save as these may be connected with the future of their families. We all know as a matter of course that every shop is crowded with workingmen who year after year spend all of their wages upon the nurture and education of their children, reserving for themselves but the shabbiest clothing and a crowded place at the family table.

"Bad weather for you to be out in," you remark on a February evening, as you meet rheumatic Mr. S. hobbling home through the freezing sleet without an overcoat. "Yes, it is bad," he assents: "but I've walked to work all this last year. We've sent the oldest boy back to high school, you know," and he moves on with no thought that he is doing other than fulfilling the ordinary lot of the ordinary man.

These are the familiar and the constant manifestations of family affection which are so intimate a part of life that we scarcely observe them.

In addition to these we find peculiar manifestations of family devotion exemplifying that touching affection which rises to unusual sacrifice because it is close to pity and feebleness. "My cousin and his family had to go back to Italy. He got to Ellis Island with his wife and five children, but they wouldn't let in the feeble-minded boy, so of course they all went back with him. My cousin was fearful disappointed."

Or, "These are the five children of my brother. He and his wife, my father and mother, were all done for in the bad time at Kishinef. It's up to me all right to take care of the kids, and I'd no more go back on them than I would on my own." Or, again: "Yes, I have seven children of my own. My husband died when Tim was born. The other three children belong to my sister, who died the year after my husband. I get on pretty well. I scrub in a factory every night from six to twelve, and I go out washing four days a week. So far the children have all gone through the eighth grade before they quit school," she concludes, beaming with pride and joy.

That wonderful devotion to the child seems at times, in the midst of our stupid social and industrial arrangements, all that keeps society human, the touch of nature which unites it, as it was that same devotion which first lifted it out of the swamp of bestiality. The devotion to the child is "the inevitable conclusion of the two premises of the practical syllogism, the devotion of man to woman." It is, of course, this tremendous force which makes possible the family, that bond which holds society together and blends the experience of generations into a continuous story. The family has been called "the fountain of morality," "the source of law," "the necessary prelude to the state" itself; but while it is continuous historically, this dual bond must be made anew a myriad times in each generation, and the forces upon which its formation depend must be powerful and unerring. It would be too great a risk to leave it to a force whose manifestations are intermittent and uncertain. The desired result is too grave and fundamental.

One Sunday evening an excited young man came to see me, saying that he must have advice; some one must tell him at once what to do, as his wife was in the state's prison serving a sentence for a crime which he himself had committed. He had seen her the day before, and though she had been there only a month he was convinced that she was developing consumption. She was "only seventeen, and couldn't stand the hard work and the 'low down' women" whom she had for companions. My remark that a girl of seventeen was too young to be in the state penitentiary brought out the whole wretched story.

He had been unsteady for many years and the despair of his thoroughly respectable family who had sent him West the year before. In Arkansas he had fallen in love with a girl of sixteen and married her. His mother was far from pleased, but had finally sent him money to bring his bride to Chicago, in the hope that he might settle there. *En route* they stopped at a small town for the naïve reason that he wanted to have an aching tooth pulled. But the tooth gave him an excellent opportunity to have a drink, and before he reached the office of the country practitioner he was intoxicated. As they passed through the vestibule he stole an overcoat hanging there, although the little wife piteously begged him to let it alone. Out of sheer bravado he carried it across his arm as they walked down the street, and was, of course, immediately arrested "with the goods upon him." In sheer terror of being separated from her husband, the wife insisted that she had been an accomplice, and together they were put into the county jail awaiting the action of the Grand Jury. At the end of the sixth week, on one of the rare occasions when they were permitted to talk to each other through the grating which separated the men's visiting quarters from the women's, the young wife told her husband that she made up her mind to swear that she had stolen the overcoat. What could she do if he were sent to prison and she were left free? She was afraid to go to his people and could not possibly go back to hers. In spite of his protest, that very night she sent for the state's attorney and made a full confession, giving her age as eighteen in the hope of making her testimony more valuable. From that time on they stuck to the lie through the indictment, the trial and her conviction. Apparently it had seemed to him only a well-arranged plot until he had visited the penitentiary the day before, and had really seen her piteous plight. Remorse had seized him at last, and he was ready to make every restitution. She, however, had no notion of giving up-on the contrary, as she realized more clearly what prison life meant, she was daily more determined to spare him the experience. Her letters, written in the unformed hand of a child-for her husband had himself taught her to read and write-were filled with a riot of self-abnegation, the martyr's joy as he feels the iron enter the flesh. Thus had an illiterate, neglected girl through sheer devotion to a worthless sort of young fellow inclined to drink, entered into that noble company of martyrs.

When girls "go wrong" what happens? How has this tremendous force, valuable and necessary for the foundation of the family, become misdirected? When its manifestations follow the legitimate channels of wedded life we call them praiseworthy; but there are other manifestations quite outside the legal and moral channels which yet compel our admiration.

A young woman of my acquaintance was married to a professional criminal named Joe. Three months after the wedding he was arrested and "sent up" for two years. Molly had always been accustomed to many lovers, but she remained faithful to her absent husband for a year. At the end of that time she obtained a divorce which the state law makes easy for the wife of a convict, and married a man who was "rich and respectable" —in fact, he owned the small manufacturing establishment in which her mother did the scrubbing. He moved his bride to another part of town six miles away, provided her with a "steam-heated flat," furniture upholstered in "cut velvet," and many other luxuries of which Molly heretofore had only dreamed. One day as she was wheeling a handsome baby carriage up and down the prosperous street, her brother, who was "Joe's pal," came to tell her that Joe was "out," had come to the old tenement and was "mighty sore" because "she had gone back on him." Without a moment's hesitation Molly turned the baby carriage in the direction of her old home and never stopped wheeling it until she had compassed the entire six miles. She and Joe rented the old room and went to housekeeping. The rich and respectable husband made every effort to persuade her to come back, and then another series of efforts to recover his child, before he set her free through a court proceeding. Joe, however, steadfastly refused to marry her, still "sore" because she had not "stood by." As he worked only intermittently, and was too closely supervised by the police to do much at his old occupation, Molly was obliged to support the humble ménage by scrubbing in a neighboring lodging house and by washing "the odd shirts" of the lodgers. For five years, during which time two children were born, when she was constantly subjected to the taunts of her neighbors, and when all the charitable agencies refused to give help to such an irregular household, Molly happily went on her course with no shade of regret or sorrow. "I'm all right as long as Joe keeps out of the jug," was her slogan of happiness, low in tone, perhaps, but genuine and "game." Her surroundings were as sordid as possible, consisting of a constantly changing series of cheap "furnished rooms" in which the battered baby carriage was the sole witness of better days. But Molly's heart was full of courage and happiness, and she was never desolate until her criminal lover was "sent up" again, this time on a really serious charge.

These irregular manifestations form a link between that world in which each one struggles to "live respectable," and that nether world in which are also found cases of devotion and of enduring affection arising out of the midst of the folly and the shame. The girl there who through all tribulation supports her recreant "lover," or the girl who overcomes, her drink and opium habits, who renounces luxuries and goes back to uninteresting daily toil for the sake of the good opinion of a man who wishes her to "appear decent," although he never means to marry her, these are also impressive.

One of our earliest experiences at Hull-House had to do with a lover of this type and the charming young girl who had become fatally attached to him. I can see her now running for protection up the broad steps of the columned piazza then surrounding Hull-House. Her slender figure was trembling with fright, her tear-covered face swollen and bloodstained from the blows he had dealt her. "He is apt to abuse me when he is drunk," was the only explanation, and that given by way of apology, which could be extracted from her. When we discovered that there had been no marriage ceremony, that there were no living children, that she had twice narrowly escaped losing her life, it seemed a simple matter to insist that the relation should be broken off. She apathetically remained at Hull-House for a few weeks, but when her strength had somewhat returned, when her lover began to recover from his prolonged debauch of whiskey and opium, she insisted upon going home every day to prepare his meals and to see that the little tenement was clean and comfortable because "Pierre is always so sick and weak after one of those long ones." This of course meant that she was drifting back to him, and when she was at last restrained by that moral compulsion, by that overwhelming of another's will which is always so ruthlessly exerted by those who are conscious that virtue is struggling with vice, her mind gave way and she became utterly distraught.

A poor little Ophelia, I met her one night wandering in the hall half dressed in the tawdry pink gown "that Pierre liked best of all" and groping on the blank wall to find the door which might permit her to escape to her lover. In a few days it was obvious that hospital restraint was necessary, but when she finally recovered we were obliged to admit that there is no civic authority which can control the acts of a girl of eighteen. From the hospital she followed her heart directly back to Pierre, who had in the meantime moved out of the Hull-House neighborhood. We knew later that he had degraded the poor child still further by obliging her to earn money for his drugs by that last method resorted to by a degenerate man to whom a woman's devotion still clings.

It is inevitable that a force which is enduring enough to withstand the discouragements, the suffering and privation of daily living, strenuous enough to overcome and rectify the impulses which make for greed and self-indulgence, should be able, even under untoward conditions, to lift up and transfigure those who are really within its grasp and set them in marked contrast to those who are merely playing a game with it or using it for gain. But what has happened to these wretched girls? Why has this beneficent current cast them upon the shores of death and destruction when it should have carried them into the safe port of domesticity? Through whose fault has this basic emotion served merely to trick and deride them?

Older nations have taken a well defined line of action in regard to it.

Among the Hull-House neighbors are many of the Latin races who employ a careful chaperonage over their marriageable daughters and provide husbands for them at an early age. "My father will get a husband for me this winter," announces Angelina, whose father has brought her to a party at Hull-House, and she adds with a toss of her head, "I saw two already, but my father says they haven't saved enough money to marry me." She feels quite as content in her father's wisdom and ability to provide her with a husband as she does in his capacity to escort her home safely from the party. He does not permit her to cross the threshold after nightfall unaccompanied by himself, and unless the dowry and the husband are provided before she is eighteen he will consider himself derelict in his duty towards her. "Francesca can't even come to the Sodality meeting this winter. She lives only across from the church but her mother won't let her come because her father is out West working on a railroad," is a comment one often hears. The system works well only when it is carried logically through to the end of an early marriage with a properly-provided husband.

Even with the Latin races, when the system is tried in America it often breaks down, and when the Anglo-Saxons anywhere imitate this régime it is usually utterly futile. They follow the first part of the program as far as repression is concerned, but they find it impossible to follow the second because all sorts of inherited notions deter them. The repressed girl, if she is not one of the languishing type, takes matters into her own hands, and finds her pleasures in illicit ways, without her parents' knowledge. "I had no idea my daughter was going to public dances. She always told me she was spending the night with her cousin on the South Side. I hadn't a suspicion of the truth," many a broken-hearted mother explains. An officer who has had a long experience in the Juvenile Court of Chicago, and has listened to hundreds of cases involving wayward girls, gives it as his deliberate impression that a large majority of cases are from families where the discipline had been rigid, where they had taken but half of the convention of the Old World and left the other half.

Unless we mean to go back to these Old World customs which are already hopelessly broken, there would seem to be but one path open to us in America. That path implies freedom for the young people made safe only through their own self-control. This, in turn, must be based upon knowledge and habits of clean companionship. In point of fact no course between the two is safe in a modern city, and in the most crowded quarters the young people themselves are working out a protective code which reminds one of the instinctive protection that the free-ranging child in the country learns in regard to poisonous plants and "marshy places," or of the cautions and abilities that the mountain child develops in regard to ice and precipices. This statement, of course, does not hold good concerning a large number of children in every crowded city quarter who may be classed as degenerates, the children of careless or dissolute mothers who fall into all sorts of degenerate habits and associations before childhood is passed, who cannot be said to have "gone wrong" at any one moment because they have never been in the right path even of innocent childhood; but the statement is sound concerning thousands of girls who go to and from work every day with crowds of young men who meet them again and again in the occasional evening pleasures of the more decent dance halls or on a Sunday afternoon in the parks.

The mothers who are of most use to these normal city working girls are the mothers who develop a sense of companionship with the changing experiences of their daughters, who are willing to modify ill-fitting social conventions into rules of conduct which are of actual service to their children in their daily lives of factory work and of city amusements. Those mothers, through their sympathy and adaptability, substitute keen present interests and activity for solemn warnings and restraint, self-expression for repression. Their vigorous family life allies itself by a dozen bonds to the educational, the industrial and the recreational organizations of the modern city, and makes for intelligent understanding, industrial efficiency and sane social pleasures.

By all means let us preserve the safety of the home, but let us also make safe the street in which the majority of our young people find their recreation and form their permanent relationships. Let us not forget that the great processes of social life develop themselves through influences of which each participant is unconscious as he struggles alone and unaided in the strength of a current which seizes him and bears him along with myriads of others, a current which may so easily wreck the very foundations of domesticity.

Chapter III
The Quest for Adventure

A certain number of the outrages upon the spirit of youth may be traced to degenerate or careless parents who totally neglect their responsibilities; a certain other large number of wrongs are due to sordid men and women who deliberately use the legitimate pleasure-seeking of young people as lures into vice. There remains, however, a third very large class of offenses for which the community as a whole must be held responsible if it would escape the condemnation, "Woe unto him by whom offenses come." This class of offenses is traceable to a dense ignorance on the part of the average citizen as to the requirements of youth, and to a persistent blindness on the part of educators as to youth's most obvious needs.

The young people are overborne by their own undirected and misguided energies. A mere temperamental outbreak in a brief period of obstreperousness exposes a promising boy to arrest and imprisonment, an accidental combination of circumstances too complicated and overwhelming to be coped with by an immature mind, condemns a growing lad to a criminal career. These impulsive misdeeds may be thought of as dividing into two great trends somewhat obscurely analogous to the two historic divisions of man's motive power, for we are told that all the activities of primitive man and even those of his more civilized successors may be broadly traced to the impulsion of two elemental appetites. The first drove him to the search for food, the hunt developing into war with neighboring tribes and finally broadening into barter and modern commerce; the second urged him to secure and protect a mate, developing into domestic life, widening into the building of homes and cities, into the cultivation of the arts and a care for beauty.

In the life of each boy there comes a time when these primitive instincts urge him to action, when he is himself frightened by their undefined power. He is faced by the necessity of taming them, of reducing them to manageable impulses just at the moment when "a boy's will is the wind's will," or, in the words of a veteran educator, at the time when "it is almost impossible for an adult to realize the boy's irresponsibility and even moral neurasthenia." That the boy often fails may be traced in those pitiful figures which show that between two and three times as much incorrigibility occurs between the ages of thirteen and sixteen as at any other period of life.

The second division of motive power has been treated in the preceding chapter. The present chapter is an effort to point out the necessity for an understanding of the first trend of motives if we would minimize the temptations of the struggle and free the boy from the constant sense of the stupidity and savagery of life. To set his feet in the worn path of civilization is not an easy task, but it may give us a clue for the undertaking to trace his misdeeds to the unrecognized and primitive spirit of adventure corresponding to the old activity of the hunt, of warfare, and of discovery.

To do this intelligently, we shall have to remember that many boys in the years immediately following school find no restraint either in tradition or character. They drop learning as a childish thing and look upon school as a tiresome task that is finished. They demand pleasure as the right of one who earns his own living. They have developed no capacity for recreation demanding mental effort or even muscular skill, and are obliged to seek only that depending upon sight, sound and taste. Many of them begin to pay board to their mothers, and make the best bargain they can, that more money may be left to spend in the evening. They even bait the excitement of "losing a job," and often provoke a foreman if only to see "how much he will stand." They are constitutionally unable to enjoy anything continuously and follow their vagrant wills unhindered. Unfortunately the city lends itself to this distraction. At the best, it is difficult to know what to select and what to eliminate as objects of attention among its thronged streets, its glittering shops, its gaudy advertisements of shows and amusements. It is perhaps to the credit of many city boys that the very first puerile spirit of adventure looking abroad in the world for material upon which to exercise itself, seems to center about the railroad. The impulse is not unlike that which excites the coast-dwelling lad to dream of

> "The beauty and mystery of the ships
> And the magic of the sea."

I cite here a dozen charges upon which boys were brought into the Juvenile Court of Chicago, all of which might be designated as deeds of adventure. A surprising number, as the reader will observe, are connected with railroads. They are taken from the court records and repeat the actual words used by police officers, irate neighbors, or discouraged parents, when the boys were brought before the judge. (1) Building fires along the railroad tracks; (2) flagging trains; (3) throwing stones at moving train windows; (4) shooting at the actors in the Olympic Theatre with sling shots; (5) breaking signal lights on the railroad; (6) stealing linseed oil barrels from the railroad to make a fire; (7) taking waste from an axle box and burning it upon the railroad tracks; (8) turning a switch and running a street car off the track; (9) staying away from home to sleep in barns; (10) setting fire to a barn in order to see the fire engines come up the street; (11) knocking down signs; (12) cutting Western Union cable.

Another dozen charges also taken from actual court records might be added as illustrating the spirit of adventure, for although stealing is involved in all of them, the deeds were doubtless inspired much more by the adventurous impulse than by a desire for the loot itself:

(1) Stealing thirteen pigeons from a barn; (2) stealing a bathing suit; (3) stealing a tent; (4) stealing ten dollars from mother with which to buy a revolver; (5) stealing a horse blanket to use at night when it was cold sleeping on the wharf; (6) breaking a seal on a freight car to steal "grain for chickens"; (7) stealing apples from a freight car; (8) stealing a candy peddler's wagon "to be full up just for once"; (9) stealing a hand car; (10) stealing a bicycle to take a ride; (11) stealing a horse and buggy and driving twenty-five miles into the country; (12) stealing a stray horse on the prairie and trying to sell it for twenty dollars.

Of another dozen it might be claimed that they were also due to this same adventurous spirit, although the first six were classed as disorderly conduct: (1) Calling a neighbor a "scab"; (2) breaking down a fence; (3) flipping cars; (4) picking up coal from railroad tracks; (5) carrying a concealed "dagger," and stabbing a playmate with it; (6) throwing stones at a railroad employee. The next three were called vagrancy: (1) Loafing on the docks; (2) "sleeping out" nights; (3) getting "wandering spells." One, designated petty larceny, was cutting telephone wires under the sidewalk and selling them; another, called burglary, was taking locks off from basement doors; and the last one bore the dignified title of "resisting an officer" because the boy, who was riding on the fender of a street car, refused to move when an officer ordered him off.

Of course one easily recalls other cases in which the manifestations were negative. I remember an exasperated and frightened mother who took a boy of fourteen into court upon the charge of incorrigibility. She accused him of "shooting craps," "smoking cigarettes," "keeping bad company," "being idle." The mother regrets it now, however, for she thinks that taking a boy into court only gives him a bad name, and that "the police are down on a boy who has once been in court, and that that makes it harder for him." She hardly recognizes her once troublesome charge in the steady young man of nineteen who brings home all his wages and is the pride and stay of her old age.

I recall another boy who worked his way to New York and back again to Chicago before he was quite fourteen years old, skilfully escaping the truant officers as well as the police and special railroad detectives. He told his story with great pride, but always modestly admitted that he could never have done it if his father had not been a locomotive engineer so that he had played around railroad tracks and "was onto them ever since he was a small kid."

There are many of these adventurous boys who exhibit a curious incapacity for any effort which requires sustained energy. They show an absolute lack of interest in the accomplishment of what they undertake, so marked that if challenged in the midst of their activity, they will be quite unable to tell you the end they have in view. Then there are those tramp boys who are the despair of every one who tries to deal with them.

I remember the case of a boy who traveled almost around the world in the years lying between the ages of eleven and fifteen. He had lived for six months in Honolulu where he had made up his mind to settle when the irresistible "Wanderlust" again seized him. He was scrupulously neat in his habits and something of a dandy in appearance. He boasted that he had never stolen, although he had been arrested several times on the charge of vagrancy, a fate which befell him in Chicago and landed him in the Detention Home connected with the Juvenile Court. The judge gained a personal hold upon him, and the lad tried with all the powers of his untrained moral nature to "make good and please the judge." Monotonous factory work was not to be thought of in connection with him, but his good friend the judge found a place for him as a bell-boy in a men's club, where it was hoped that the uniform and the variety of experience might enable him to take the first steps toward regular pay and a settled life. Through another bell-boy, however, he heard of the find of a diamond carelessly left in one of the wash rooms of the club. The chance to throw out mysterious hints of its whereabouts, to bargain for its restoration, to tell of great diamond deals he had heard of in his travels, inevitably laid him open to suspicion which resulted in his dismissal, although he had had nothing to do with the matter beyond gloating over its adventurous aspects. In spite of skilful efforts made to detain him, he once more started on his travels, throwing out such diverse hints as that of "a trip into Old Mexico," or "following up Roosevelt into Africa."

There is an entire series of difficulties directly traceable to the foolish and adventurous persistence of carrying loaded firearms. The morning paper of the day in which I am writing records the following:

> "A party of boys, led by Daniel O'Brien, thirteen years old, had gathered in front of the house and O'Brien was throwing stones at Nieczgodzki in revenge for a whipping that he received at his hands about a month ago. The Polish boy ordered them away and threatened to go into the house and get a revolver if they did not stop. Pfister, one of the boys in O'Brien's party, called him a coward, and when he pulled a revolver from his pocket, dared him to put it away and meet him in a fist fight in the street. Instead of accepting the challenge, Nieczgodzki aimed his revolver at Pfister and fired. The bullet crashed through the top of his head and entered the brain. He was rushed to the Alexian Brothers' Hospital, but died a short time after being received there. Nieczgodzki was arrested and held without bail."

This tale could be duplicated almost every morning; what might be merely a boyish scrap is turned into a tragedy because some boy has a revolver.

Many citizens in Chicago have been made heartsick during the past month by the knowledge that a boy of nineteen was lodged in the county jail awaiting the death penalty. He had shot and killed a policeman during the scrimmage of an arrest, although the offense for which he was being "taken in" was a trifling one. His parents came to Chicago twenty years ago from a little farm in Ohio, the best type of Americans, whom we boast to be the backbone of our cities. The mother, who has aged and sickened since the trial, can only say that "Davie was never a bad boy until about five years ago when he began to go with this gang who are always looking out for fun."

Then there are those piteous cases due to a perfervid imagination which fails to find material suited to its demands. I can recall misadventures of children living within a few blocks of Hull-House which may well fill with chagrin those of us who are trying to administer to their deeper needs. I remember a Greek boy of fifteen who was arrested for attempting to hang a young Turk, stirred by some vague notion of carrying on a traditional warfare, and of adding another page to the heroic annals of Greek history. When sifted, the incident amounted to little more than a graphic threat and the lad was dismissed by the court, covered with confusion and remorse that he had brought disgrace upon the name of Greece when he had hoped to add to its glory.

I remember with a lump in my throat the Bohemian boy of thirteen who committed suicide because he could not "make good" in school, and wished to show that he too had "the stuff" in him, as stated in the piteous little letter left behind. This same love of excitement, the desire to jump out of the humdrum experience of life, also induces boys to experiment with drinks and drugs to a surprising extent. For several years the residents of Hull-House struggled with the difficulty of prohibiting the sale of cocaine to minors under a totally inadequate code of legislation, which has at last happily been changed to one more effective and enforcible. The long effort brought us into contact with dozens of boys who had become victims of the cocaine habit. The first group of these boys was discovered in the house of "Army George." This one-armed man sold cocaine on the streets and also in the levee district by a system of signals so that the word cocaine need never be mentioned, and the style and size of the package was changed so often that even a vigilant police found it hard to locate it. What could be more exciting to a lad than a traffic in a contraband article, carried on in this mysterious fashion? I recall our experience with a gang of boys living on a neighboring street. There were eight of them altogether, the eldest seventeen years of age, the youngest thirteen, and they practically lived the life of vagrants. What answered to their club house was a corner lot on Harrison and Desplaines Streets, strewn with old boilers, in which they slept by night and many times by day. The gang was brought to the attention of Hull-House during the summer of 1904 by a distracted mother, who suspected that they were all addicted to some drug. She was terribly frightened over the state of her youngest boy of thirteen, who was hideously emaciated and his mind reduced almost to vacancy. I remember the poor woman as she sat in the reception room at Hull-House, holding the unconscious boy in her arms, rocking herself back and forth in her fright and despair, saying: "I have seen them go with the drink, and eat the hideous opium, but I never knew anything like this."

An investigation showed that cocaine had first been offered to these boys on the street by a colored man, an agent of a drug store, who had given them samples and urged them to try it. In three or four months they had become hopelessly addicted to its use, and at the end of six months, when they were brought to Hull-House, they were all in a critical condition. At that time not one of them was either going to school or working. They stole from their parents, "swiped junk," pawned their clothes and shoes, —did any desperate thing to "get the dope," as they called it.

Of course they continually required more, and had spent as much as eight dollars a night for cocaine, which they used to "share and share alike." It sounds like a large amount, but it really meant only four doses each during the night, as at that time they were taking twenty-five cents' worth at once if they could possibly secure it. The boys would tell nothing for three or four days after they were discovered, in spite of the united efforts of their families, the police, and the residents of Hull-House. But finally the superior boy of the gang, the manliest and the least debauched, told his tale, and the others followed in quick succession. They were willing to go somewhere to be helped, and were even eager if they could go together, and finally seven of them were sent to the Presbyterian Hospital for four weeks' treatment and afterwards all went to the country together for six weeks more. The emaciated child gained twenty pounds during his sojourn in the hospital, the head of which testified that at least three of the boys could have stood but little more of the irregular living and doping. At the present moment they are all, save one, doing well, although they were rescued so late that they seemed to have but little chance. One is still struggling with the appetite on an Iowa farm and dares not trust himself in the city because he knows too well how cocaine may be procured in spite of better legislation. It is doubtful whether these boys could ever have been pulled through unless they had been allowed to keep together through the hospital and convalescing period, —unless we had been able to utilize the gang spirit and to turn its collective force towards overcoming the desire for the drug.

The desire to dream and see visions also plays an important part with the boys who habitually use cocaine. I recall a small hut used by boys for this purpose. They washed dishes in a neighboring restaurant and as soon as they had earned a few cents they invested in cocaine which they kept pinned underneath their suspenders. When they had accumulated enough for a real debauch they went to this hut and for several days were dead to the outside world. One boy told me that in his dreams he saw large rooms paved with gold and silver money, the walls papered with greenbacks, and that he took away in buckets all that he could carry.

This desire for adventure also seizes girls. A group of girls ranging in age from twelve to seventeen was discovered in Chicago last June, two of whom were being trained by older women to open tills in small shops, to pick pockets, to remove handkerchiefs, furs and purses and to lift merchandise from the counters of department stores. All the articles stolen were at once taken to their teachers and the girls themselves received no remuneration, except occasional sprees to the theaters or other places of amusement. The girls gave no coherent reason for their actions beyond the statement that they liked the excitement and the fun of it. Doubtless to the thrill of danger was added the pleasure and interest of being daily in the shops and the glitter of "down town." The boys are more indifferent to this downtown life, and are apt to carry on their adventures on the docks, the railroad tracks or best of all upon the unoccupied prairie.

This inveterate demand of youth that life shall afford a large element of excitement is in a measure well founded. We know of course that it is necessary to accept excitement as an inevitable part of recreation, that the first step in recreation is "that excitement which stirs the worn or sleeping centers of a man's body and mind." It is only when it is followed by nothing else that it defeats its own end, that it uses up strength and does not create it. In the actual experience of these boys the excitement has demoralized them and led them into law-breaking. When, however, they seek legitimate pleasure, and say with great pride that they are "ready to pay for it," what they find is legal but scarcely more wholesome, —it is still merely excitement. "Looping the loop" amid shrieks of simulated terror or dancing in disorderly saloon halls, are perhaps the natural reactions to a day spent in noisy factories and in trolley cars whirling through the distracting streets, but the city which permits them to be the acme of pleasure and recreation to its young people, commits a grievous mistake.

May we not assume that this love for excitement, this desire for adventure, is basic, and will be evinced by each generation of city boys as a challenge to their elders? And yet those of us who live in Chicago are obliged to confess that last year there were arrested and brought into court fifteen thousand young people under the age of twenty, who had failed to keep even the common law of the land. Most of these young people had broken the law in their blundering efforts to find adventure and in response to the old impulse for self-expression. It is said indeed that practically the whole machinery of the grand jury and of the criminal courts is maintained and operated for the benefit of youths between the ages of thirteen and twenty-five. Men up to ninety years of age, it is true, commit crimes, but they are not characterized by the recklessness, the bravado and the horror which have stained our records in Chicago. An adult with the most sordid experience of life and the most rudimentary notion of prudence, could not possibly have committed them. Only a utilization of that sudden burst of energy belonging partly to the future could have achieved them, only a capture of the imagination and of the deepest emotions of youth could have prevented them!

Possibly these fifteen thousand youths were brought to grief because the adult population assumed that the young would be able to grasp only that which is presented in the form of sensation; as if they believed that youth could thus early become absorbed in a hand to mouth existence, and so entangled in materialism that there would be no reaction against it. It is as though we were deaf to the appeal of these young creatures, claiming their share of the joy of life, flinging out into the dingy city their desires and aspirations after unknown realities, their unutterable longings for companionship and pleasure. Their very demand for excitement is a protest against the dullness of life, to which we ourselves instinctively respond.

Chapter IV
The House of Dreams

To the preoccupied adult who is prone to use the city street as a mere passageway from one hurried duty to another, nothing is more touching than his encounter with a group of children and young people who are emerging from a theater with the magic of the play still thick upon them. They look up and down the familiar street scarcely recognizing it and quite unable to determine the direction of home. From a tangle of "make believe" they gravely scrutinize the real world which they are so reluctant to reënter, reminding one of the absorbed gaze of a child who is groping his way back from fairy-land whither the story has completely transported him.

"Going to the show" for thousands of young people in every industrial city is the only possible road to the realms of mystery and romance; the theater is the only place where they can satisfy that craving for a conception of life higher than that which the actual world offers them. In a very real sense the drama and the drama alone performs for them the office of art as is clearly revealed in their blundering demand stated in many forms for "a play unlike life." The theater becomes to them a "veritable house of dreams" infinitely more real than the noisy streets and the crowded factories.

This first simple demand upon the theater for romance is closely allied to one more complex which might be described as a search for solace and distraction in those moments of first awakening from the glamour of a youth's interpretation of life to the sterner realities which are thrust upon his consciousness. These perceptions which inevitably "close around" and imprison the spirit of youth are perhaps never so grim as in the case of the wage-earning child. We can all recall our own moments of revolt against life's actualities, our reluctance to admit that all life was to be as unheroic and uneventful as that which we saw about us, it was too unbearable that "this was all there was" and we tried every possible avenue of escape. As we made an effort to believe, in spite of what we saw, that life was noble and harmonious, as we stubbornly clung to poesy in contradiction to the testimony of our senses, so we see thousands of young people thronging the theaters bent in their turn upon the same quest. The drama provides a transition between the romantic conceptions which they vainly struggle to keep intact and life's cruelties and trivialities which they refuse to admit. A child whose imagination has been cultivated is able to do this for himself through reading and reverie, but for the overworked city youth of meager education, perhaps nothing but the theater is able to perform this important office.

The theater also has a strange power to forecast life for the youth. Each boy comes from our ancestral past not "in entire forgetfulness," and quite as he unconsciously uses ancient war-cries in his street play, so he longs to reproduce and to see set before him the valors and vengeances of a society embodying a much more primitive state of morality than that in which he finds himself. Mr. Patten has pointed out that the elemental action which the stage presents, the old emotions of love and jealousy, of revenge and daring take the thoughts of the spectator back into deep and well worn channels in which his mind runs with a sense of rest afforded by nothing else. The cheap drama brings cause and effect, will power and action, once more into relation and gives a man the thrilling conviction that he may yet be master of his fate. The youth of course, quite unconscious of this psychology, views the deeds of the hero simply as a forecast of his own future and it is this fascinating view of his own career which draws the boy to "shows" of all sorts. They can scarcely be too improbable for him, portraying, as they do, his belief in his own prowess. A series of slides which has lately been very popular in the five-cent theaters of Chicago, portrayed five masked men breaking into a humble dwelling, killing the father of the family and carrying away the family treasure. The golden-haired son of the house, aged seven, vows eternal vengeance on the spot, and follows one villain after another to his doom. The execution of each is shown in lurid detail, and the last slide of the series depicts the hero, aged ten, kneeling upon his father's grave counting on the fingers of one hand the number of men that he has killed, and thanking God that he has been permitted to be an instrument of vengeance.

In another series of slides, a poor woman is wearily bending over some sewing, a baby is crying in the cradle, and two little boys of nine and ten are asking for food. In despair the mother sends them out into the street to beg, but instead they steal a revolver from a pawn shop and with it kill a Chinese laundry-man, robbing him of $200. They rush home with the treasure which is found by the mother in the baby's cradle, whereupon she and her sons fall upon their knees and send up a prayer of thankfulness for this timely and heaven-sent assistance.

Is it not astounding that a city allows thousands of its youth to fill their impressionable minds with these absurdities which certainly will become the foundation for their working moral codes and the data from which they will judge the proprieties of life?

It is as if a child, starved at home, should be forced to go out and search for food, selecting, quite naturally, not that which is nourishing but that which is exciting and appealing to his outward sense, often in his ignorance and foolishness blundering into substances which are filthy and poisonous.

Out of my twenty years' experience at Hull-House I can recall all sorts of pilferings, petty larcenies, and even burglaries, due to that never ceasing effort on the part of boys to procure theater tickets. I can also recall indirect efforts towards the same end which are most pitiful. I remember the remorse of a young girl of fifteen who was brought into the Juvenile Court after a night spent weeping in the cellar of her home because she had stolen a mass of artificial flowers with which to trim a hat. She stated that she had taken the flowers because she was afraid of losing the attention of a young man whom she had heard say that "a girl has to be dressy if she expects to be seen." This young man was the only one who had ever taken her to the theater and if he failed her, she was sure that she would never go again, and she sobbed out incoherently that she "couldn't live at all without it." Apparently the blankness and grayness of life itself had been broken for her only by the portrayal of a different world.

One boy whom I had known from babyhood began to take money from his mother from the time he was seven years old, and after he was ten she regularly gave him money for the play Saturday evening. However, the Saturday performance, "starting him off like," he always went twice again on Sunday, procuring the money in all sorts of illicit ways. Practically all of his earnings after he was fourteen were spent in this way to satisfy the insatiable desire to know of the great adventures of the wide world which the more fortunate boy takes out in reading Homer and Stevenson.

In talking with his mother, I was reminded of my experience one Sunday afternoon in Russia when the employees of a large factory were seated in an open-air theater, watching with breathless interest the presentation of folk stories. I was told that troupes of actors went from one manufacturing establishment to another presenting the simple elements of history and literature to the illiterate employees. This tendency to slake the thirst for adventure by viewing the drama is, of course, but a blind and primitive effort in the direction of culture, for "he who makes himself its vessel and bearer thereby acquires a freedom from the blindness and soul poverty of daily existence."

It is partly in response to this need that more sophisticated young people often go to the theater, hoping to find a clue to life's perplexities. Many times the bewildered hero reminds one of Emerson's description of Margaret Fuller, "I don't know where I am going, follow me"; nevertheless, the stage is dealing with the moral themes in which the public is most interested.

And while many young people go to the theater if only to see represented, and to hear discussed, the themes which seem to them so tragically important, there is no doubt that what they hear there, flimsy and poor as it often is, easily becomes their actual moral guide. In moments of moral crisis they turn to the sayings of the hero who found himself in a similar plight. The sayings may not be profound, but at least they are applicable to conduct. In the last few years scores of plays have been put upon the stage whose titles might be easily translated into proper headings for sociological lectures or sermons, without including the plays of Ibsen, Shaw and Hauptmann, which deal so directly with moral issues that the moralists themselves wince under their teachings and declare them brutal. But it is this very brutality which the over-refined and complicated city dwellers often crave. Moral teaching has become so intricate, creeds so metaphysical, that in a state of absolute reaction they demand definite instruction for daily living. Their whole-hearted acceptance of the teaching corroborates the statement recently made by an English playwright that "The theater is literally making the minds of our urban populations to-day. It is a huge factory of sentiment, of character, of points of honor, of conceptions of conduct, of everything that finally determines the destiny of a nation. The theater is not only a place of amusement, it is a place of culture, a place where people learn how to think, act, and feel." Seldom, however, do we associate the theater with our plans for civic righteousness, although it has become so important a factor in city life.

One Sunday evening last winter an investigation was made of four hundred and sixty six theaters in the city of Chicago, and it was discovered that in the majority of them the leading theme was revenge; the lover following his rival; the outraged husband seeking his wife's paramour; or the wiping out by death of a blot on a hitherto unstained honor. It was estimated that one sixth of the entire population of the city had attended the theaters on that day. At that same moment the churches throughout the city were preaching the gospel of good will. Is not this a striking commentary upon the contradictory influences to which the city youth is constantly subjected?

This discrepancy between the church and the stage is at times apparently recognized by the five-cent theater itself, and a blundering attempt is made to suffuse the songs and moving pictures with piety. Nothing could more absurdly demonstrate this attempt than a song, illustrated by pictures, describing the adventures of a young man who follows a pretty girl through street after street in the hope of "snatching a kiss from her ruby lips." The young man is overjoyed when a sudden wind storm drives the girl to shelter under an archway, and he is about to succeed in his attempt when the good Lord, "ever watchful over innocence," makes the same wind "blow a cloud of dust into the eyes of the rubberneck," and "his foul purpose is foiled." This attempt at piety is also shown in a series of films depicting Bible stories and the Passion Play at Oberammergau, forecasting the time when the moving film will be viewed as a mere mechanical device for the use of the church, the school and the library, as well as for the theater.

At present, however, most improbable tales hold the attention of the youth of the city night after night, and feed his starved imagination as nothing else succeeds in doing. In addition to these fascinations, the five-cent theater is also fast becoming the general social center and club house in many crowded neighborhoods. It is easy of access from the street the entire family of parents and children can attend for a comparatively small sum of money and the performance lasts for at least an hour; and, in some of the humbler theaters, the spectators are not disturbed for a second hour.

The room which contains the mimic stage is small and cozy, and less formal than the regular theater, and there is much more gossip and social life as if the foyer and pit were mingled. The very darkness of the room, necessary for an exhibition of the films, is an added attraction to many young people, for whom the space is filled with the glamour of love making.

Hundreds of young people attend these five-cent theaters every evening in the week, including Sunday, and what is seen and heard there becomes the sole topic of conversation, forming the ground pattern of their social life. That mutual understanding which in another social circle is provided by books, travel and all the arts, is here compressed into the topics suggested by the play.

The young people attend the five-cent theaters in groups, with something of the "gang" instinct, boasting of the films and stunts in "our theater." They find a certain advantage in attending one theater regularly, for the *habitués* are often invited to come upon the stage on "amateur nights," which occur at least once a week in all the theaters. This is, of course, a most exciting experience. If the "stunt" does not meet with the approval of the audience, the performer is greeted with jeers and a long hook pulls him off the stage; if, on the other hand, he succeeds in pleasing the audience, he may be paid for his performance and later register with a booking agency, the address of which is supplied by the obliging manager, and thus he fancies that a lucrative and exciting career is opening before him. Almost every night at six o'clock a long line of children may be seen waiting at the entrance of these booking agencies, of which there are fifteen that are well known in Chicago.

Thus, the only art which is constantly placed before the eyes of "the temperamental youth" is a debased form of dramatic art, and a vulgar type of music, for the success of a song in these theaters depends not so much upon its musical rendition as upon the vulgarity of its appeal. In a song which held the stage of a cheap theater in Chicago for weeks, the young singer was helped out by a bit of mirror from which she threw a flash of light into the faces of successive boys whom she selected from the audience as she sang the refrain, "You are my Affinity." Many popular songs relate the vulgar experiences of a city man wandering from amusement park to bathing beach in search of flirtations. It may be that these "stunts" and recitals of city adventure contain the nucleus of coming poesy and romance, as the songs and recitals of the early minstrels sprang directly from the life of the people, but all the more does the effort need help and direction, both in the development of its technique and the material of its themes.

The few attempts which have been made in this direction are astonishingly rewarding to those who regard the power of self-expression as one of the most precious boons of education. The Children's Theater in New York is the most successful example, but every settlement in which dramatics have been systematically fostered can also testify to a surprisingly quick response to this form of art on the part of young people. The Hull-House Theater is constantly besieged by children clamoring to "take part" in the plays of Schiller, Shakespeare, and Molière, although they know it means weeks of rehearsal and the complete memorizing of "stiff" lines. The audiences sit enthralled by the final rendition and other children whose tastes have supposedly been debased by constant vaudeville, are pathetically eager to come again and again. Even when still more is required from the young actors, research into the special historic period, copying costumes from old plates, hours of labor that the "th" may be restored to its proper place in English speech, their enthusiasm is unquenched. But quite aside from its educational possibilities one never ceases to marvel at the power of even a mimic stage to afford to the young a magic space in which life may be lived in efflorescence, where manners may be courtly and elaborate without exciting ridicule, where the sequence of events is impressive and comprehensible. Order and beauty of life is what the adolescent youth craves above all else as the younger child indefatigably demands his story. "Is this where the most beautiful princess in the world lives?" asks a little girl peering into the door of the Hull-House Theater, or "Does Alice in Wonderland always stay here?" It is much easier for her to put her feeling into words than it is for the youth who has enchantingly rendered the gentle poetry of Ben Jonson's "Sad Shepherd," or for him who has walked the boards as Southey's Wat Tyler. His association, however, is quite as clinging and magical as is the child's although he can only say, "Gee, I wish I could always feel the way I did that night. Something would be doing then." Nothing of the artist's pleasure, nor of the revelation of that larger world which surrounds and completes our own, is lost to him because a careful technique has been exacted, —on the contrary this has only dignified and enhanced it. It would also be easy to illustrate youth's eagerness for artistic expression from the recitals given by the pupils of the New York Music School Settlement, or by those of the Hull-House Music School. These attempts also combine social life with the training of the artistic sense and in this approximate the fascinations of the five-cent theater.

This spring a group of young girls accustomed to the life of a five-cent theater, reluctantly refused an invitation to go to the country for a day's outing because the return on a late train would compel them to miss one evening's performance. They found it impossible to tear themselves away not only from the excitements of the theater itself but from the gaiety of the crowd of young men and girls invariably gathered outside discussing the sensational posters.

A steady English shopkeeper lately complained that unless he provided his four, daughters with the money for the five-cent theaters every evening they would steal it from his till, and he feared that they might be driven to procure it in even more illicit ways. Because his entire family life had been thus disrupted he gloomily asserted that "this cheap show had ruined his 'ome and was the curse of America." This father was able to formulate the anxiety of many immigrant parents who are absolutely bewildered by the keen absorption of their children in the cheap theater. This anxiety is not, indeed, without foundation. An eminent alienist of Chicago states that he has had a number of patients among neurotic children whose emotional natures have been so over-wrought by the crude appeal to which they had been so constantly subjected in the theaters, that they have become victims of hallucination and mental disorder. The statement of this physician may be the first note of alarm which will awaken the city to its duty in regard to the theater, so that it shall at least be made safe and sane for the city child whose senses are already so abnormally developed.

This testimony of a physician that the conditions are actually pathological, may at last induce us to bestir ourselves in regard to procuring a more wholesome form of public recreation. Many efforts in social amelioration have been undertaken only after such exposures; in the meantime, while the occasional child is driven distraught, a hundred children permanently injure their eyes watching the moving films, and hundreds more seriously model their conduct upon the standards set before them on this mimic stage.

Three boys, aged nine, eleven and thirteen years, who had recently seen depicted the adventures of frontier life including the holding up of a stage coach and the lassoing of the driver, spent weeks planning to lasso, murder, and rob a neighborhood milkman, who started on his route at four o'clock in the morning. They made their headquarters in a barn and saved enough money to buy a revolver, adopting as their watchword the phrase "Dead Men Tell no Tales." One spring morning the conspirators, with their faces covered with black cloth, lay "in ambush" for the milkman. Fortunately for him, as the lariat was thrown the horse shied, and, although the shot was appropriately fired, the milkman's life was saved. Such a direct influence of the theater is by no means rare, even among older boys. Thirteen young lads were brought into the Municipal Court in Chicago during the first week that "Raffles, the Amateur Cracksman" was upon the stage, each one with an outfit of burglar's tools in his possession, and each one shamefacedly admitting that the gentlemanly burglar in the play had suggested to him a career of similar adventure.

In so far as the illusions of the theater succeed in giving youth the rest and recreation which comes from following a more primitive code of morality, it has a close relation to the function performed by public games. It is, of course, less valuable because the sense of participation is largely confined to the emotions and the imagination, and does not involve the entire nature.

We might illustrate by the "Wild West Show" in which the onlooking boy imagines himself an active participant. The scouts, the Indians, the bucking ponies, are his real intimate companions and occupy his entire mind. In contrast with this we have the omnipresent game of tag which is, doubtless, also founded upon the chase. It gives the boy exercise and momentary echoes of the old excitement, but it is barren of suggestion and quickly degenerates into horse-play.

Well considered public games easily carried out in a park or athletic field, might both fill the mind with the imaginative material constantly supplied by the theater, and also afford the activity which the cramped muscles of the town dweller so sorely need. Even the unquestioned ability which the theater possesses to bring men together into a common mood and to afford them a mutual topic of conversation, is better accomplished with the one national game which we already possess, and might be infinitely extended through the organization of other public games.

The theater even now by no means competes with the baseball league games which are attended by thousands of men and boys who, during the entire summer, discuss the respective standing of each nine and the relative merits of every player. During the noon hour all the employees of a city factory gather in the nearest vacant lot to cheer their own home team in its practice for the next game with the nine of a neighboring manufacturing establishment and on a Saturday afternoon the entire male population of the city betakes itself to the baseball field; the ordinary means of transportation are supplemented by gay stage-coaches and huge automobiles, noisy with blowing horns and decked with gay pennants. The enormous crowd of cheering men and boys are talkative, good-natured, full of the holiday spirit, and absolutely released from the grind of life. They are lifted out of their individual affairs and so fused together that a man cannot tell whether it is his own shout or another's that fills his ears; whether it is his own coat or another's that he is wildly waving to celebrate a victory. He does not call the stranger who sits next to him his "brother" but he unconsciously embraces him in an overwhelming outburst of kindly feeling when the favorite player makes a home run. Does not this contain a suggestion of the undoubted power of public recreation to bring together all classes of a community in the modern city unhappily so full of devices for keeping men apart?

Already some American cities are making a beginning toward more adequate public recreation. Boston has its municipal gymnasiums, cricket fields, and golf grounds. Chicago has seventeen parks with playing fields, gymnasiums and baths, which at present enroll thousands of young people. These same parks are provided with beautiful halls which are used for many purposes, rent free, and are given over to any group of young people who wish to conduct dancing parties subject to city supervision and chaperonage. Many social clubs have deserted neighboring saloon halls for these municipal drawing rooms beautifully decorated with growing plants supplied by the park greenhouses, and flooded with electric lights supplied by the park power house. In the saloon halls the young people were obliged to "pass money freely over the bar," and in order to make the most of the occasion they usually stayed until morning. At such times the economic necessity itself would override the counsels of the more temperate, and the thrifty door keeper would not insist upon invitations but would take in any one who had the "price of a ticket." The free rent in the park hall, the good food in the park restaurant, supplied at cost, have made three parties closing at eleven o'clock no more expensive than one party breaking up at daylight, too often in disorder.

Is not this an argument that the drinking, the late hours, the lack of decorum, are directly traceable to the commercial enterprise which ministers to pleasure in order to drag it into excess because excess is more profitable? To thus commercialize pleasure is as monstrous as it is to commercialize art. It is intolerable that the city does not take over this function of making provision for pleasure, as wise communities in Sweden and South Carolina have taken the sale of alcohol out of the hands of enterprising publicans.

We are only beginning to understand what might be done through the festival, the street procession, the band of marching musicians, orchestral music in public squares or parks, with the magic power they all possess to formulate the sense of companionship and solidarity. The experiments which are being made in public schools to celebrate the national holidays, the changing seasons, the birthdays of heroes, the planting of trees, are slowly developing little ceremonials which may in time work out into pageants of genuine beauty and significance. No other nation has so unparalleled an opportunity to do this through its schools as we have, for no other nation has so wide-spreading a school system, while the enthusiasm of children and their natural ability to express their emotions through symbols, gives the securest possible foundation to this growing effort.

The city schools of New York have effected the organization of high school girls into groups for folk dancing. These old forms of dancing which have been worked out in many lands and through long experiences, safeguard unwary and dangerous expression and yet afford a vehicle through which the gaiety of youth may flow. Their forms are indeed those which lie at the basis of all good breeding, forms which at once express and restrain, urge forward and set limits.

One may also see another center of growth for public recreation and the beginning of a pageantry for the people in the many small parks and athletic fields which almost every American city is hastening to provide for its young. These small parks have innumerable athletic teams, each with its distinctive uniform, with track meets and match games arranged with the teams from other parks and from the public schools; choruses of trade unionists or of patriotic societies fill the park halls with eager listeners. Labor Day processions are yearly becoming more carefully planned and more picturesque in character, as the desire to make an overwhelming impression with mere size gives way to a growing ambition to set forth the significance of the craft and the skill of the workman. At moments they almost rival the dignified showing of the processions of the German Turn Vereins which are also often seen in our city streets.

The many foreign colonies which are found in all American cities afford an enormous reserve of material for public recreation and street festival. They not only celebrate the feasts and holidays of the fatherland, but have each their own public expression for their mutual benefit societies and for the observance of American anniversaries. From the gay celebration of the Scandinavians when war was averted and two neighboring nations were united, to the equally gay celebration of the centenary of Garibaldi's birth; from the Chinese dragon cleverly trailing its way through the streets, to the Greek banners flung out in honor of immortal heroes, there is an infinite variety of suggestions and possibilities for public recreation and for the corporate expression of stirring emotions. After all, what is the function of art but to preserve in permanent and beautiful form those emotions and solaces which cheer life and make it kindlier, more heroic and easier to comprehend; which lift the mind of the worker from the harshness and loneliness of his task, and, by connecting him with what has gone before, free him from a sense of isolation and hardship?

Were American cities really eager for municipal art, they would cherish as genuine beginnings the tarentella danced so interminably at Italian weddings; the primitive Greek pipe played throughout the long summer nights; the Bohemian theaters crowded with eager Slavophiles; the Hungarian musicians strolling from street to street; the fervid oratory of the young Russian preaching social righteousness in the open square.

Many Chicago citizens who attended the first annual meeting of the National Playground Association of America, will never forget the long summer day in the large playing field filled during the morning with hundreds of little children romping through the kindergarten games, in the afternoon with the young men and girls contending in athletic sports; and the evening light made gay by the bright colored garments of Italians, Lithuanians, Norwegians, and a dozen other nationalities, reproducing their old dances and festivals for the pleasure of the more stolid Americans. Was this a forecast of what we may yet see accomplished through a dozen agencies promoting public recreation which are springing up in every city of America, as they already are found in the large towns of Scotland and England?

Let us cherish these experiments as the most precious beginnings of an attempt to supply the recreational needs of our industrial cities. To fail to provide for the recreation of youth, is not only to deprive all of them of their natural form of expression, but is certain to subject some of them to the overwhelming temptation of illicit and soul-destroying pleasures. To insist that young people shall forecast their rose-colored future only in a house of dreams, is to deprive the real world of that warmth and reassurance which it so sorely needs and to which it is justly entitled; furthermore, we are left outside with a sense of dreariness, in company with that shadow which already lurks only around the corner for most of us —a skepticism of life's value.

Chapter V
The Spirit of Youth and Industry

As it is possible to establish a connection between the lack of public recreation and the vicious excitements and trivial amusements which become their substitutes, so it may be illuminating to trace the connection between the monotony and dullness of factory work and the petty immoralities which are often the youth's protest against them.

There are many city neighborhoods in which practically every young person who has attained the age of fourteen years enters a factory. When the work itself offers nothing of interest, and when no public provision is made for recreation, the situation becomes almost insupportable to the youth whose ancestors have been rough-working and hard-playing peasants.

In such neighborhoods the joy of youth is well nigh extinguished; and in that long procession of factory workers, each morning and evening, the young walk almost as wearily and listlessly as the old. Young people working in modern factories situated in cities still dominated by the ideals of Puritanism face a combination which tends almost irresistably to overwhelm the spirit of youth. When the Puritan repression of pleasure was in the ascendant in America the people it dealt with lived on farms and villages where, although youthful pleasures might be frowned upon and crushed out, the young people still had a chance to find self-expression in their work. Plowing the field and spinning the flax could be carried on with a certain joyousness and vigor which the organization of modern industry too often precludes. Present industry based upon the inventions of the nineteenth century has little connection with the old patterns in which men have worked for generations. The modern factory calls for an expenditure of nervous energy almost more than it demands muscular effort, or at least machinery so far performs the work of the massive muscles, that greater stress is laid upon fine and exact movements necessarily involving nervous strain. But these movements are exactly of the type to which the muscles of a growing boy least readily respond, quite as the admonition to be accurate and faithful is that which appeals the least to his big primitive emotions. The demands made upon his eyes are complicated and trivial, the use of his muscles is fussy and monotonous, the relation between cause and effect is remote and obscure. Apparently no one is concerned as to what may be done to aid him in this process and to relieve it of its dullness and difficulty, to mitigate its strain and harshness.

Perhaps never before have young people been expected to work from motives so detached from direct emotional incentive. Never has the age of marriage been so long delayed; never has the work of youth been so separated from the family life and the public opinion of the community. Education alone can repair these losses. It alone has the power of organizing a child's activities with some reference to the life he will later lead and of giving him a clue as to what to select and what to eliminate when he comes into contact with contemporary social and industrial conditions. And until educators take hold of the situation, the rest of the community is powerless.

In vast regions of the city which are completely dominated by the factory, it is as if the development of industry had outrun all the educational and social arrangements.

The revolt of youth against uniformity and the necessity of following careful directions laid down by some one else, many times results in such nervous irritability that the youth, in spite of all sorts of prudential reasons, "throws up his job," if only to get outside the factory walls into the freer street, just as the narrowness of the school inclosure induces many a boy to jump the fence.

When the boy is on the street, however, and is "standing around on the corner" with the gang to which he mysteriously attaches himself, he finds the difficulties of direct untrammeled action almost as great there as they were in the factory, but for an entirely different set of reasons. The necessity so strongly felt in the factory for an outlet to his sudden and furious bursts of energy, his overmastering desire to prove that he could do things "without being bossed all the time," finds little chance for expression, for he discovers that in whatever really active pursuit he tries to engage, he is promptly suppressed by the police. After several futile attempts at self-expression, he returns to his street corner subdued and so far discouraged that when he has the next impulse to vigorous action he concludes that it is of no use, and sullenly settles back into inactivity. He thus learns to persuade himself that it is better to do nothing, or, as the psychologist would say, "to inhibit his motor impulses."

When the same boy, as an adult workman, finds himself confronted with an unusual or an untoward condition in his work, he will fall back into this habit of inhibition, of making no effort toward independent action. When "slack times" come, he will be the workman of least value, and the first to be dismissed, calmly accepting his position in the ranks of the unemployed because it will not be so unlike the many hours of idleness and vacuity to which he was accustomed as a boy. No help having been extended to him in the moment of his first irritable revolt against industry, his whole life has been given a twist toward idleness and futility. He has not had the chance of recovery which the school system gives a like rebellious boy in a truant school.

The unjustifiable lack of educational supervision during the first years of factory work makes it quite impossible for the modern educator to offer any real assistance to young people during that trying transitional period between school and industry. The young people themselves who fail to conform can do little but rebel against the entire situation, and the expressions of revolt roughly divide themselves into three classes. The first, resulting in idleness, may be illustrated from many a sad story of a boy or a girl who has spent in the first spurt of premature and uninteresting work, all the energy which should have carried them through years of steady endeavor.

I recall a boy who had worked steadily for two years as a helper in a smelting establishment, and had conscientiously brought home all his wages, one night suddenly announcing to his family that he "was too tired and too hot to go on." As no amount of persuasion could make him alter his decision, the family finally threatened to bring him into the Juvenile Court on a charge of incorrigibility, whereupon the boy disappeared and such efforts as the family have been able to make in the two years since, have failed to find him. They are convinced that "he is trying a spell of tramping" and wish that they "had let him have a vacation the first summer when he wanted it so bad." The boy may find in the rough outdoor life the healing which a wise physician would recommend for nervous exhaustion, although the tramp experiment is a perilous one.

This revolt against factory monotony is sometimes closely allied to that "moral fatigue" which results from assuming responsibility prematurely. I recall the experience of a Scotch girl of eighteen who, with her older sister, worked in a candy factory, their combined earnings supporting a paralytic father. The older girl met with an accident involving the loss of both eyes, and the financial support of the whole family devolved upon the younger girl, who worked hard and conscientiously for three years, supplementing her insufficient factory wages by evening work at glove making. In the midst of this devotion and monotonous existence she made the acquaintance of a girl who was a chorus singer in a cheap theater and the contrast between her monotonous drudgery and the glitter of the stage broke down her allegiance to her helpless family. She left the city, absolutely abandoning the kindred to whom she had been so long devoted, and announced that if they all starved she would "never go into a factory again." Every effort failed to find her after the concert troupe left Milwaukee and although the pious Scotch father felt that "she had been ensnared by the Devil," and had brought his "gray hairs in sorrow to the grave," I could not quite dismiss the case with this simple explanation, but was haunted by all sorts of social implications.

The second line of revolt manifests itself in an attempt to make up for the monotony of the work by a constant change from one occupation to another. This is an almost universal experience among thousands of young people in their first impact with the industrial world.

The startling results of the investigation undertaken in Massachusetts by the Douglas Commission showed how casual and demoralizing the first few years of factory life become to thousands of unprepared boys and girls; in their first restlessness and maladjustment they change from one factory to another, working only for a few weeks or months in each, and they exhibit no interest in any of them save for the amount of wages paid. At the end of their second year of employment many of them are less capable than when they left school and are actually receiving less wages. The report of the commission made clear that while the two years between fourteen and sixteen were most valuable for educational purposes, they were almost useless for industrial purposes, that no trade would receive as an apprentice a boy under sixteen, that no industry requiring skill and workmanship could utilize these untrained children and that they not only demoralized themselves, but in a sense industry itself.

An investigation of one thousand tenement children in New York who had taken out their "working papers" at the age of fourteen, reported that during the first working year a third of them had averaged six places each. These reports but confirm the experience of those of us who live in an industrial neighborhood and who continually see these restless young workers, in fact there are moments when this constant changing seems to be all that saves them from the fate of those other children who hold on to a monotonous task so long that they finally incapacitate themselves for all work. It often seems to me an expression of the instinct of self-preservation, as in the case of a young Swedish boy who during a period of two years abandoned one piece of factory work after another, saying "he could not stand it," until in the chagrin following the loss of his ninth place he announced his intention of leaving the city and allowing his mother and little sisters to shift for themselves. At this critical juncture a place was found for him as lineman in a telephone company; climbing telephone poles and handling wires apparently supplied him with the elements of outdoor activity and danger which were necessary to hold his interest, and he became the steady support of his family.

But while we know the discouraging effect of idleness upon the boy who has thrown up his job and refuses to work again, and we also know the restlessness and lack of discipline resulting from the constant change from one factory to another, there is still a third manifestation of maladjustment of which one's memory and the Juvenile Court records unfortunately furnish many examples. The spirit of revolt in these cases has led to distinct disaster. Two stories will perhaps be sufficient in illustration although they might be multiplied indefinitely from my own experience.

A Russian girl who went to work at an early age in a factory, pasting labels on mucilage bottles, was obliged to surrender all her wages to her father who, in return, gave her only the barest necessities of life. In a fit of revolt against the monotony of her work, and "that nasty sticky stuff," she stole from her father $300 which he had hidden away under the floor of his kitchen, and with this money she ran away to a neighboring city for a spree, having first bought herself the most gorgeous clothing a local department store could supply. Of course, this preposterous beginning could have but one ending and the child was sent to the reform school to expiate not only her own sins but the sins of those who had failed to rescue her from a life of grinding monotony which her spirit could not brook.

"I know the judge thinks I am a bad girl," sobbed a poor little prisoner, put under bonds for threatening to kill her lover, "but I have only been bad for one week and before that I was good for six years. I worked every day in Blank's factory and took home all my wages to keep the kids in school. I met this fellow in a dance hall. I just had to go to dances sometimes after pushing down the lever of my machine with my right foot and using both my arms feeding it for ten hours a day-nobody knows how I felt some nights. I agreed to go away with this man for a week but when I was ready to go home he tried to drive me out on the street to earn money for him and, of course, I threatened to kill him-any decent girl would," she concluded, as unconscious of the irony of the reflection as she was of the connection between her lurid week and her monotonous years.

Knowing as educators do that thousands of the city youth will enter factory life at an age as early as the state law will permit; instructed as the modern teacher is as to youth's requirements for a normal mental and muscular development, it is hard to understand the apathy in regard to youth's inevitable experience in modern industry. Are the educators, like the rest of us, so caught in admiration of the astonishing achievements of modern industry that they forget the children themselves?

A Scotch educator who recently visited America considered it very strange that with a remarkable industrial development all about us, affording such amazing educational opportunities, our schools should continually cling to a past which did not fit the American temperament, was not adapted to our needs, and made no vigorous pull upon our faculties. He concluded that our educators, overwhelmed by the size and vigor of American industry, were too timid to seize upon the industrial situation, and to extract its enormous educational value. He lamented that this lack of courage and initiative failed not only to fit the child for an intelligent and conscious participation in industrial life, but that it was reflected in the industrial development itself; that industry had fallen back into old habits, and repeated traditional mistakes until American cities exhibited stupendous extensions of the medievalisms in the traditional Ghetto, and of the hideousness in the Black Country of Lancashire.

He contended that this condition is the inevitable result of separating education from contemporary life. Education becomes unreal and far fetched, while industry becomes ruthless and materialistic. In spite of the severity of the indictment, one much more severe and well deserved might have been brought against us. He might have accused us not only of wasting, but of misusing and of trampling under foot the first tender instincts and impulses which are the source of all charm and beauty and art, because we fail to realize that by premature factory work, for which the youth is unprepared, society perpetually extinguishes that variety and promise, that bloom of life, which is the unique possession of the young. He might have told us that our cities would continue to be traditionally cramped and dreary until we comprehend that youth alone has the power to bring to reality the vision of the "Coming City of Mankind, full of life, full of the spirit of creation."

A few educational experiments are carried on in Cincinnati, in Boston and in Chicago, in which the leaders of education and industry unite in a common aim and purpose. A few more are carried on by trade unionists, who in at least two of the trades are anxious to give to their apprentices and journeymen the wider culture afforded by the "capitalistic trade schools" which they suspect of preparing strike-breakers; still a few other schools have been founded by public spirited citizens to whom the situation has become unendurable, and one or two more such experiments are attached to the public school system itself. All of these schools are still blundering in method and unsatisfactory in their results, but a certain trade school for girls, in New York, which is preparing young girls of fourteen for the sewing trade, already so overcrowded and subdivided that there remains very little education for the worker, is conquering this difficult industrial situation by equipping each apprentice with "the informing mind." If a child goes into a sewing factory with a knowledge of the work she is doing in relation to the finished product; if she is informed concerning the material she is manipulating and the processes to which it is subjected; if she understands the design she is elaborating in its historic relation to art and decoration, her daily life is lifted from drudgery to one of self-conscious activity, and her pleasure and intelligence is registered in her product.

I remember a little colored girl in this New York school who was drawing for the pattern she was about to embroider, a carefully elaborated acanthus leaf. Upon my inquiry as to the design, she replied: "It is what the Egyptians used to put on everything, because they saw it so much growing in the Nile; and then the Greeks copied it, and sometimes you can find it now on the buildings downtown." She added, shyly: "Of course, I like it awfully well because it was first used by people living in Africa where the colored folks come from." Such a reasonable interest in work not only reacts upon the worker, but is, of course, registered in the product itself. Such genuine pleasure is in pitiful contrast to the usual manifestation of the play spirit as it is found in the factories, where, at the best, its expression is illicit and often is attended with great danger.

There are many touching stories by which this might be illustrated. One of them comes from a large steel mill of a boy of fifteen whose business it was to throw a lever when a small tank became filled with molton metal. During the few moments when the tank was filling it was his foolish custom to catch the reflection of the metal upon a piece of looking-glass, and to throw the bit of light into the eyes of his fellow workmen. Although an exasperated foreman had twice dispossessed him of his mirror, with a third fragment he was one day flicking the gloom of the shop when the neglected tank overflowed, almost instantly burning off both his legs. Boys working in the stock yards, during their moments of wrestling and rough play, often slash each other painfully with the short knives which they use in their work, but in spite of this the play impulse is too irrepressible to be denied.

If educators could go upon a voyage of discovery into that army of boys and girls who enter industry each year, what values might they not discover; what treasures might they not conserve and develop if they would direct the play instinct into the art impulse and utilize that power of variation which industry so sadly needs. No force will be sufficiently powerful and widespread to redeem industry from its mechanism and materialism save the freed power in every single individual.

In order to do this, however, we must go back a little over the educational road to a training of the child's imagination, as well as to his careful equipment with a technique. A little child makes a very tottering house of cardboard and calls it a castle. The important feature there lies in the fact that he has expressed a castle, and it is not for his teacher to draw undue attention to the fact that the corners are not well put together, but rather to listen to and to direct the story which centers about this effort at creative expression. A little later, however, it is clearly the business of the teacher to call attention to the quality of the dovetailing in which the boy at the manual training bench is engaged, for there is no value in dovetailing a box unless it is accurately done. At one point the child's imagination is to be emphasized, and at another point his technique is important-and he will need both in the industrial life ahead of him.

There is no doubt that there is a third period, when the boy is not interested in the making of a castle, or a box, or anything else, unless it appears to him to bear a direct relation to the future; unless it has something to do with earning a living. At this later moment he is chiefly anxious to play the part of a man and to take his place in the world. The fact that a boy at fourteen wants to go out and earn his living makes that the moment when he should be educated with reference to that interest, and the records of many high schools show that if he is not thus educated, he bluntly refuses to be educated at all. The forces pulling him to "work" are not only the overmastering desire to earn money and be a man, but, if the family purse is small and empty, include also his family loyalty and affection, and over against them, we at present place nothing but a vague belief on the part of his family and himself that education is a desirable thing and may eventually help him "on in the world." It is of course difficult to adapt education to this need; it means that education must be planned so seriously and definitely for those two years between fourteen and sixteen that it will be actual trade training so far as it goes, with attention given to the condition under which money will be actually paid for industrial skill; but at the same time, that the implications, the connections, the relations to the industrial world, will be made clear. A man who makes, year after year, but one small wheel in a modern watch factory, may, if his education has properly prepared him, have a fuller life than did the old watchmaker who made a watch from beginning to end. It takes thirty-nine people to make a coat in a modern tailoring establishment, yet those same thirty-nine people might produce a coat in a spirit of "team work" which would make the entire process as much more exhilarating than the work of the old solitary tailor, as playing in a baseball nine gives more pleasure to a boy than that afforded by a solitary game of hand ball on the side of the barn. But it is quite impossible to imagine a successful game of baseball in which each player should be drilled only in his own part, and should know nothing of the relation of that part to the whole game. In order to make the watch wheel, or the coat collar interesting, they must be connected with the entire product-must include fellowship as well as the pleasures arising from skilled workmanship and a cultivated imagination.

When all the young people working in factories shall come to use their faculties intelligently, and as a matter of course to be interested in what they do, then our manufactured products may at last meet the demands of a cultivated nation, because they will be produced by cultivated workmen. The machine will not be abandoned by any means, but will be subordinated to the intelligence of the man who manipulates it, and will be used as a tool. It may come about in time that an educated public will become inexpressibly bored by manufactured objects which reflect absolutely nothing of the minds of the men who made them, that they may come to dislike an object made by twelve unrelated men, even as we do not care for a picture which has been painted by a dozen different men, not because we have enunciated a theory in regard to it, but because such a picture loses all its significance and has no meaning or message. We need to apply the same principle but very little further until we shall refuse to be surrounded by manufactured objects which do not represent some gleam of intelligence on the part of the producer. Hundreds of people have already taken that step so far as all decoration and ornament are concerned, and it would require but one short step more. In the meantime we are surrounded by stupid articles which give us no pleasure, and the young people producing them are driven into all sorts of expedients in order to escape work which has been made impossible because all human interest has been extracted from it. That this is not mere theory may be demonstrated by the fact that many times the young people may be spared the disastrous effects of this third revolt against the monotony of industry if work can be found for them in a place where the daily round is less grinding and presents more variety. Fortunately, in every city there are places outside of factories where occupation of a more normal type of labor may be secured, and often a restless boy can be tided over this period if he is put into one of these occupations. The experience in every boys' club can furnish illustrations of this.

A factory boy who had been brought into the Juvenile Court many times because of his persistent habit of borrowing the vehicles of physicians as they stood in front of houses of patients, always meaning to "get back before the doctor came out," led a contented and orderly life after a place had been found for him as a stable boy in a large livery establishment where his love for horses could be legitimately gratified.

Still another boy made the readjustment for himself in spite of the great physical suffering involved. He had lost both legs at the age of seven, "flipping cars." When he went to work at fourteen with two good cork legs, which he vainly imagined disguised his disability, his employer kindly placed him where he might sit throughout the entire day, and his task was to keep tally on the boxes constantly hoisted from the warehouse into cars. The boy found this work so dull that he insisted upon working in the yards, where the cars were being loaded and switched. He would come home at night utterly exhausted, more from the extreme nervous tension involved in avoiding accidents than from the tremendous exertion, and although he would weep bitterly from sheer fatigue, nothing could induce him to go back to the duller and safer job. Fortunately he belonged to a less passionate race than the poor little Italian girl in the Hull-House neighborhood who recently battered her head against the wall so long and so vigorously that she had to be taken to a hospital because of her serious injuries. So nearly as dull "grown-ups" could understand, it had been an hysterical revolt against factory work by day and "no fun in the evening."

America perhaps more than any other country in the world can demonstrate what applied science has accomplished for industry; it has not only made possible the utilization of all sorts of unpromising raw material, but it has tremendously increased the invention and elaboration of machinery. The time must come, however, if indeed the moment has not already arrived, when applied science will have done all that it can do for the development of machinery. It may be that machines cannot be speeded up any further without putting unwarranted strain upon the nervous system of the worker; it may be that further elaboration will so sacrifice the workman who feeds the machine that industrial advance will lie not in the direction of improvement in machinery, but in the recovery and education of the workman. This refusal to apply "the art of life" to industry continually drives out of it many promising young people. Some of them, impelled by a creative impulse which will not be denied, avoid industry altogether and demand that their ambitious parents give them lessons in "china painting" and "art work," which clutters the overcrowded parlor of the more prosperous workingman's home with useless decorated plates, and handpainted "drapes," whereas the plates upon the table and the rugs upon the floor used daily by thousands of weary housewives are totally untouched by the beauty and variety which this ill-directed art instinct might have given them had it been incorporated into industry.

I could cite many instances of high-spirited young people who suffer a veritable martyrdom in order to satisfy their artistic impulse.

A young girl of fourteen whose family had for years displayed a certain artistic aptitude, the mother having been a singer and the grandmother, with whom the young girl lived, a clever worker in artificial flowers, had her first experience of wage earning in a box factory. She endured it only for three months, and then gave up her increasing wage in exchange for $1.50 a week which she earns by making sketches of dresses, cloaks and hats for the advertisements of a large department store.

A young Russian girl of my acquaintance starves on the irregular pay which she receives for her occasional contributions to the Sunday newspapers-meanwhile writing her novel-rather than return to the comparatively prosperous wages of a necktie factory which she regards with horror. Another girl washes dishes every evening in a cheap boarding house in order to secure the leisure in which to practise her singing lessons, rather than to give them up and return to her former twelve-dollar-a-week job in an electrical factory.

The artistic expression in all these cases is crude, but the young people are still conscious of that old sacrifice of material interest which art has ever demanded of those who serve her and which doubtless brings its own reward. That the sacrifice is in vain makes it all the more touching and is an indictment of the educator who has failed to utilize the art instinct in industry.

Something of the same sort takes place among many lads who find little opportunity in the ordinary factories to utilize the "instinct for workmanship"; or, among those more prosperous young people who establish "studios" and "art shops," in which, with a vast expenditure of energy, they manufacture luxurious articles.

The educational system in Germany is deliberately planned to sift out and to retain in the service of industry, all such promising young people. The method is as yet experimental, and open to many objections, but it is so far successful that "Made in Germany" means made by a trained artisan and in many cases by a man working with the freed impulse of the artist.

The London County Council is constantly urging plans which may secure for the gifted children in the Board Schools support in Technological institutes. Educators are thus gradually developing the courage and initiative to conserve for industry the young worker himself so that his mind, his power of variation, his art instinct, his intelligent skill, may ultimately be reflected in the industrial product. That would imply that industry must be seized upon and conquered by those educators, who now either avoid it altogether by taking refuge in the caves of classic learning or beg the question by teaching the tool industry advocated by Ruskin and Morris in their first reaction against the present industrial system. It would mean that educators must bring industry into "the kingdom of the mind"; and pervade it with the human spirit.

The discovery of the labor power of youth was to our age like the discovery of a new natural resource, although it was merely incidental to the invention of modern machinery and the consequent subdivision of labor. In utilizing it thus ruthlessly we are not only in danger of quenching the divine fire of youth, but we are imperiling industry itself when we venture to ignore these very sources of beauty, of variety and of suggestion.

Chapter VI
The Thirst for Righteousness

Even as we pass by the joy and beauty of youth on the streets without dreaming it is there, so we may hurry past the very presence of august things without recognition. We may easily fail to sense those spiritual realities, which, in every age, have haunted youth and called to him without ceasing. Historians tell us that the extraordinary advances in human progress have been made in those times when "the ideals of freedom and law, of youth and beauty, of knowledge and virtue, of humanity and religion, high things, the conflicts between which have caused most of the disruptions and despondences of human society, seem for a generation or two to lie in the same direction."

Are we perhaps at least twice in life's journey dimly conscious of the needlessness of this disruption and of the futility of the despondency? Do we feel it first when young ourselves we long to interrogate the "transfigured few" among our elders whom we believe to be carrying forward affairs of gravest import? Failing to accomplish this are we, for the second time, dogged by a sense of lost opportunity, of needless waste and perplexity, when we too, as adults, see again the dreams of youth in conflict with the efforts of our own contemporaries? We see idealistic endeavor on the one hand lost in ugly friction; the heat and burden of the day borne by mature men and women on the other hand, increased by their consciousness of youth's misunderstanding and high scorn. It may relieve the mind to break forth in moments of irritation against "the folly of the coming generation," but whoso pauses on his plodding way to call even his youngest and rashest brother a fool, ruins thereby the joy of his journey, —for youth is so vivid an element in life that unless it is cherished, all the rest is spoiled. The most praiseworthy journey grows dull and leaden unless companioned by youth's iridescent dreams. Not only that, but the mature of each generation run a grave risk of putting their efforts in a futile direction, in a blind alley as it were, unless they can keep in touch with the youth of their own day and know at least the trend in which eager dreams are driving them-those dreams that fairly buffet our faces as we walk the city streets.

At times every one possessed with a concern for social progress is discouraged by the formless and unsubdued modern city, as he looks upon that complicated life which drives men almost without their own volition, that life of ingenuous enterprises, great ambitions, political jealousies, where men tend to become mere "slaves of possessions." Doubtless these striving men are full of weakness and sensitiveness even when they rend each other, and are but caught in the coils of circumstance; nevertheless, a serious attempt to ennoble and enrich the content of city life that it may really fill the ample space their ruthless wills have provided, means that we must call upon energies other than theirs. When we count over the resources which are at work "to make order out of casualty, beauty out of confusion, justice, kindliness and mercy out of cruelty and inconsiderate pressure," we find ourselves appealing to the confident spirit of youth. We know that it is crude and filled with conflicting hopes, some of them unworthy and most of them doomed to disappointment, yet these young people have the advantage of "morning in their hearts"; they have such power of direct action, such ability to stand free from fear, to break through life's trammelings, that in spite of ourselves we become convinced that

> "They to the disappointed earth shall give
> The lives we meant to live."

That this solace comes to us only in fugitive moments, and is easily misleading, may be urged as an excuse for our blindness and insensitiveness to the august moral resources which the youth of each city offers to those who are in the midst of the city's turmoil. A further excuse is afforded in the fact that the form of the dreams for beauty and righteousness change with each generation and that while it is always difficult for the fathers to understand the sons, at those periods when the demand of the young is one of social reconstruction, the misunderstanding easily grows into bitterness.

The old desire to achieve, to improve the world, seizes the ardent youth to-day with a stern command to bring about juster social conditions. Youth's divine impatience with the world's inheritance of wrong and injustice makes him scornful of "rose water for the plague" prescriptions, and he insists upon something strenuous and vital.

One can find innumerable illustrations of this idealistic impatience with existing conditions among the many Russian subjects found in the foreign quarters of every American city. The idealism of these young people might be utilized to a modification of our general culture and point of view, somewhat as the influence of the young Germans who came to America in the early fifties, bringing with them the hopes and aspirations embodied in the revolutions of 1848, made a profound impression upon the social and political institutions of America. Long before they emigrated, thousands of Russian young people had been caught up into the excitements and hopes of the Russian revolution in Finland, in Poland, in the Russian cities, in the university towns. Life had become intensified by the consciousness of the suffering and starvation of millions of their fellow subjects. They had been living with a sense of discipline and of preparation for a coming struggle which, although grave in import, was vivid and adventurous. Their minds had been seized by the first crude forms of social theory and they had cherished a vague belief that they were the direct instruments of a final and ideal social reconstruction. When they come to America they sadly miss this sense of importance and participation in a great and glorious conflict against a recognized enemy. Life suddenly grows stale and unprofitable; the very spirit of tolerance which characterizes American cities is that which strikes most unbearably upon their ardent spirits. They look upon the indifference all about them with an amazement which rapidly changes to irritation. Some of them in a short time lose their ardor, others with incredible rapidity make the adaptation between American conditions and their store of enthusiasm, but hundreds of them remain restless and ill at ease. Their only consolation, almost their only real companionship, is when they meet in small groups for discussion or in larger groups to welcome a well known revolutionist who brings them direct news from the conflict, or when they arrange for a demonstration in memory of "The Red Sunday" or the death of Gershuni. Such demonstrations, however, are held in honor of men whose sense of justice was obliged to seek an expression quite outside the regular channels of established government. Knowing that Russia has forced thousands of her subjects into this position, one would imagine that patriotic teachers in America would be most desirous to turn into governmental channels all that insatiable desire for juster relations in industrial and political affairs. A distinct and well directed campaign is necessary if this gallant enthusiasm is ever to be made part of that old and still incomplete effort to embody in law —"the law that abides and falters not, ages long" —the highest aspirations for justice.

Unfortunately, we do little or nothing with this splendid store of youthful ardor and creative enthusiasm. Through its very isolation it tends to intensify and turn in upon itself, and no direct effort is made to moralize it, to discipline it, to make it operative upon the life of the city. And yet it is, perhaps, what American cities need above all else, for it is but too true that Democracy —"a people ruling" —the very name of which the Greeks considered so beautiful, no longer stirs the blood of the American youth, and that the real enthusiasm for self-government must be found among the groups of young immigrants who bring over with every ship a new cargo of democratic aspirations. That many of these young men look for a consummation of these aspirations to a social order of the future in which the industrial system as well as government shall embody democratic relations, simply shows that the doctrine of Democracy like any other of the living faiths of men, is so essentially mystical that it continually demands new formulation. To fail to recognize it in a new form, to call it hard names, to refuse to receive it, may mean to reject that which our fathers cherished and handed on as an inheritance not only to be preserved but also to be developed.

We allow a great deal of this precious stuff-this *Welt-Schmerz* of which each generation has need-not only to go unutilized, but to work havoc among the young people themselves. One of the saddest illustrations of this, in my personal knowledge, was that of a young Russian girl who lived with a group of her compatriots on the west side of Chicago. She recently committed suicide at the same time that several others in the group tried it and failed. One of these latter, who afterwards talked freely of the motives which led her to this act, said that there were no great issues at stake in this country; that America was wholly commercial in its interests and absorbed in money making; that Americans were not held together by any historic bonds nor great mutual hopes, and were totally ignorant of the stirring social and philosophic movements of Europe; that her life here had been a long, dreary, economic struggle, unrelieved by any of the higher interests; that she was tired of getting seventy-five cents for trimming a hat that sold for twelve dollars and was to be put upon the empty head of some one who had no concern for the welfare of the woman who made it. The statement doubtless reflected something of "The Sorrows of Werther," but the entire tone was nobler and more highly socialized.

It is difficult to illustrate what might be accomplished by reducing to action the ardor of those youths who so bitterly arraign our present industrial order. While no part of the social system can be changed rapidly, we would all admit that the present industrial arrangements in America might be vastly improved and that we are failing to meet the requirements of our industrial life with courage and success simply because we do not realize that unless we establish that humane legislation which has its roots in a consideration for human life, our industrialism itself will suffer from inbreeding, growing ever more unrestrained and ruthless. It would seem obvious that in order to secure relief in a community dominated by industrial ideals, an appeal must be made to the old spiritual sanctions for human conduct, that we must reach motives more substantial and enduring than the mere fleeting experiences of one phase of modern industry which vainly imagines that its growth would be curtailed if the welfare of its employees were guarded by the state. It would be an interesting attempt to turn that youthful enthusiasm to the aid of one of the most conservative of the present social efforts, the almost world-wide movement to secure protective legislation for women and children in industry, in which America is so behind the other nations. Fourteen of the great European powers protect women from all night work, from excessive labor by day, because paternalistic governments prize the strength of women for the bearing and rearing of healthy children to the state. And yet in a republic it is the citizens themselves who must be convinced of the need of this protection unless they would permit industry to maim the very mothers of the future.

In one year in the German Empire one hundred thousand children were cared for through money paid from the State Insurance fund to their widowed mothers or to their invalided fathers. And yet in the American states it seems impossible to pass a most rudimentary employers' liability act, which would be but the first step towards that code of beneficent legislation which protects "the widow and fatherless" in Germany and England. Certainly we shall have to bestir ourselves if we would care for the victims of the industrial order as well as do other nations. We shall be obliged speedily to realize that in order to secure protective legislation from a governmental body in which the most powerful interests represented are those of the producers and transporters of manufactured goods, it will be necessary to exhort to a care for the defenseless from the religious point of view. To take even the non-commercial point of view would be to assert that evolutionary progress assumes that a sound physique is the only secure basis of life, and to guard the mothers of the race is simple sanity.

And yet from lack of preaching we do not unite for action because we are not stirred to act at all, and protective legislation in America is shamefully inadequate. Because it is always difficult to put the championship of the oppressed above the counsels of prudence, we say in despair sometimes that we are a people who hold such varied creeds that there are not enough of one religious faith to secure anything, but the truth is that it is easy to unite for action people whose hearts have once been filled by the fervor of that willing devotion which may easily be generated in the youthful breast. It is comparatively easy to enlarge a moral concept, but extremely difficult to give it to an adult for the first time. And yet when we attempt to appeal to the old sanctions for disinterested conduct, the conclusion is often forced upon us that they have not been engrained into character, that they cannot be relied upon when they are brought into contact with the arguments of industrialism, that the colors of the flag flying over the fort of our spiritual resources wash out and disappear when the storm actually breaks. It is because the ardor of youth has not been attracted to the long effort to modify the ruthlessness of industry by humane enactments, that we sadly miss their resourceful enthusiasm and that at the same time groups of young people who hunger and thirst after social righteousness are breaking their hearts because the social reform is so long delayed and an unsympathetic and hardhearted society frustrates all their hopes. And yet these ardent young people who obscure the issue by their crying and striving and looking in the wrong place, might be of inestimable value if so-called political leaders were in any sense social philosophers. To permit these young people to separate themselves from the contemporaneous efforts of ameliorating society and to turn their vague hopes solely toward an ideal commonwealth of the future, is to withdraw from an experimental self-government founded in enthusiasm, the very stores of enthusiasm which are needed to sustain it. The championship of the oppressed came to be a spiritual passion with the Hebrew prophets. They saw the promises of religion, not for individuals but in the broad reaches of national affairs and in the establishment of social justice. It is quite possible that such a spiritual passion is again to be found among the ardent young souls of our cities. They see a vision, not of a purified nation but of a regenerated and a reorganized society. Shall we throw all this into the future, into the futile prophecy of those who talk because they cannot achieve, or shall we commingle their ardor, their overmastering desire for social justice, with that more sober effort to modify existing conditions? Are we once more forced to appeal to the educators? Is it so difficult to utilize this ardor because educators have failed to apprehend the spiritual quality of their task?

It would seem a golden opportunity for those to whom is committed the task of spiritual instruction, for to preach and seek justice in human affairs is one of the oldest obligations of religion and morality. All that would be necessary would be to attach this teaching to the contemporary world in such wise that the eager youth might feel a tug upon his faculties, and a sense of participation in the moral life about him. To leave it unattached to actual social movements means that the moralist is speaking in incomprehensible terms. Without this connection, the religious teachers may have conscientiously carried out their traditional duties and yet have failed utterly to stir the fires of spiritual enthusiasm.

Each generation of moralists and educators find themselves facing an inevitable dilemma; first, to keep the young committed to their charge "unspotted from the world," and, second, to connect the young with the ruthless and materialistic world all about them in such wise that they may make it the arena for their spiritual endeavor. It is fortunate for these teachers that sometime during "The Golden Age" the most prosaic youth is seized by a new interest in remote and universal ends, and that if but given a clue by which he may connect his lofty aims with his daily living, he himself will drag the very heavens into the most sordid tenement. The perpetual difficulty consists in finding the clue for him and placing it in his hands, for, if the teaching is too detached from life, it does not result in any psychic impulsion at all. I remember as an illustration of the saving power of this definite connection, a tale told me by a distinguished labor leader in England. His affections had been starved, even as a child, for he knew nothing of his parents, his earliest memories being associated with a wretched old woman who took the most casual care of him. When he was nine years old he ran away to sea and for the next seven years led the rough life of a dock laborer, until he became much interested in a little crippled boy, who by the death of his father had been left solitary on a freight boat. My English friend promptly adopted the child as his own and all the questionings of life centered about his young protégé. He was constantly driven to attend evening meetings where he heard discussed those social conditions which bear so hard upon the weak and sick. The crippled boy lived until he was fifteen and by that time the regeneration of his foster father was complete, the young docker was committed for life to the bettering of social conditions. It is doubtful whether any abstract moral appeal could have reached such a roving nature. Certainly no attempt to incite his ambition would have succeeded. Only a pull upon his deepest sympathies and affections, his desire to protect and cherish a weaker thing, could possibly have stimulated him and connected him with the forces making for moral and social progress.

This, of course, has ever been the task of religion, to make the sense of obligation personal, to touch morality with enthusiasm, to bathe the world in affection-and on all sides we are challenging the teachers of religion to perform this task for the youth of the city.

For thousands of years definite religious instruction has been given by authorized agents to the youth of all nations, emphasized through tribal ceremonials, the assumption of the Roman toga, the Barmitzvah of the Jews, the First Communion of thousands of children in Catholic Europe, the Sunday Schools of even the least formal of the evangelical sects. It is as if men had always felt that this expanding period of human life must be seized upon for spiritual ends, that the tender tissue and newly awakened emotions must be made the repository for the historic ideals and dogmas which are, after all, the most precious possessions of the race. How has it come about that so many of the city youth are not given their share in our common inheritance of life's best goods? Why are their tender feet so often ensnared even when they are going about youth's legitimate business? One would suppose that in such an age as ours moral teachers would be put upon their mettle, that moral authority would be forced to speak with no uncertain sound if only to be heard above the din of machinery and the roar of industrialism; that it would have exerted itself as never before to convince the youth of the reality of the spiritual life. Affrighted as the moralists must be by the sudden new emphasis placed upon wealth, despairing of the older men and women who are already caught by its rewards, one would say that they would have seized upon the multitude of young people whose minds are busied with issues which lie beyond the portals of life, as the only resource which might save the city from the fate of those who perish through lack of vision.

Yet because this inheritance has not been attached to conduct, the youth of Jewish birth may have been taught that prophets and statesmen for three thousand years declared Jehovah to be a God of Justice who hated oppression and desired righteousness, but there is no real appeal to his spirit of moral adventure unless he is told that the most stirring attempts to translate justice into the modern social order have been inaugurated and carried forward by men of his own race, and that until he joins in the contemporary manifestations of that attempt he is recreant to his highest traditions and obligations.

The Christian youth may have been taught that man's heartbreaking adventure to find justice in the order of the universe moved the God of Heaven himself to send a Mediator in order that the justice man craves and the mercy by which alone he can endure his weakness might be reconciled, but he will not make the doctrine his own until he reduces it to action and tries to translate the spirit of his Master into social terms.

The youth who calls himself an "Evolutionist" —it is rather hard to find a name for this youth, but there are thousands of him and a fine fellow he often is-has read of that struggle beginning with the earliest tribal effort to establish just relations between man and man, but he still needs to be told that after all justice can only be worked out upon this earth by those who will not tolerate a wrong to the feeblest member of the community, and that it will become a social force only in proportion as men steadfastly strive to establish it.

If these young people who are subjected to varied religious instruction are also stirred to action, or rather, if the instruction is given validity because it is attached to conduct, then it may be comparatively easy to bring about certain social reforms so sorely needed in our industrial cities. We are at times obliged to admit, however, that both the school and the church have failed to perform this office, and are indicted by the young people themselves. Thousands of young people in every great city are either frankly hedonistic, or are vainly attempting to work out for themselves a satisfactory code of morals. They cast about in all directions for the clue which shall connect their loftiest hopes with their actual living.

Several years ago a committee of lads came to see me in order to complain of a certain high school principal because "He never talks to us about life." When urged to make a clearer statement, they added, "He never asks us what we are going to be; we can't get a word out of him, excepting lessons and keeping quiet in the halls."

Of the dozens of young women who have begged me to make a connection for them between their dreams of social usefulness and their actual living, I recall one of the many whom I had sent back to her clergyman, returning with this remark: "His only suggestion was that I should be responsible every Sunday for fresh flowers upon the altar. I did that when I was fifteen and liked it then, but when you have come back from college and are twenty-two years old, it doesn't quite fit in with the vigorous efforts you have been told are necessary in order to make our social relations more Christian."

All of us forget how very early we are in the experiment of founding self-government in this trying climate of America, and that we are making the experiment in the most materialistic period of all history, having as our court of last appeal against that materialism only the wonderful and inexplicable instinct for justice which resides in the hearts of men, —which is never so irresistible as when the heart is young. We may cultivate this most precious possession, or we may disregard it. We may listen to the young voices rising-clear above the roar of industrialism and the prudent councils of commerce, or we may become hypnotized by the sudden new emphasis placed upon wealth and power, and forget the supremacy of spiritual forces in men's affairs. It is as if we ignored a wistful, over-confident creature who walked through our city streets calling out, "I am the spirit of Youth! With me, all things are possible!" We fail to understand what he wants or even to see his doings, although his acts are pregnant with meaning, and we may either translate them into a sordid chronicle of petty vice or turn them into a solemn school for civic righteousness.

We may either smother the divine fire of youth or we may feed it. We may either stand stupidly staring as it sinks into a murky fire of crime and flares into the intermittent blaze of folly or we may tend it into a lambent flame with power to make clean and bright our dingy city streets.

A New Conscience and An Ancient Evil

Preface

The following material, much of which has been published in *McClure's Magazine*, was written, not from the point of view of the expert, but because of my own need for a counter-knowledge to a bewildering mass of information which came to me through the Juvenile Protective Association of Chicago. The reports which its twenty field officers daily brought to its main office adjoining Hull House became to me a revelation of the dangers implicit in city conditions and of the allurements which are designedly placed around many young girls in order to draw them into an evil life.

As head of the Publication Committee, I read the original documents in a series of special investigations made by the Association on dance halls, theatres, amusement parks, lake excursion boats, petty gambling, the home surroundings of one hundred Juvenile Court children and the records of four thousand parents who clearly contributed to the delinquency of their own families. The Association also collected the personal histories of two hundred department-store girls, of two hundred factory girls, of two hundred immigrant girls, of two hundred office girls, and of girls employed in one hundred hotels and restaurants.

While this experience was most distressing, I was, on the other hand, much impressed and at times fairly startled by the large and diversified number of people to whom the very existence of the white slave traffic had become unendurable and who promptly responded to any appeal made on behalf of its victims. City officials, policemen, judges, attorneys, employers, trades unionists, physicians, teachers, newly arrived immigrants, clergymen, railway officials, and newspaper men, as under a profound sense of compunction, were unsparing of time and effort when given an opportunity to assist an individual girl, to promote legislation designed for her protection, or to establish institutions for her rescue.

I therefore venture to hope that in serving my own need I may also serve the need of a rapidly growing public when I set down for rational consideration the temptations surrounding multitudes of young people and when I assemble, as best I may, the many indications of a new conscience, which in various directions is slowly gathering strength and which we may soberly hope will at last successfully array itself against this incredible social wrong, ancient though it may be.

Hull House,
Chicago.

Chapter I
An Analogy

In every large city throughout the world thousands of women are so set aside as outcasts from decent society that it is considered an impropriety to speak the very word which designates them. Lecky calls this type of woman "the most mournful and the most awful figure in history": he says that "she remains, while creeds and civilizations rise and fall, the eternal sacrifice of humanity, blasted for the sins of the people." But evils so old that they are imbedded in man's earliest history have been known to sway before an enlightened public opinion and in the end to give way to a growing conscience, which regards them first as a moral affront and at length as an utter impossibility. Thus the generation just before us, our own fathers, uprooted the enormous upas of slavery, "the tree that was literally as old as the race of man," although slavery doubtless had its beginnings in the captives of man's earliest warfare, even as this existing evil thus originated.

Those of us who think we discern the beginnings of a new conscience in regard to this twin of slavery, as old and outrageous as slavery itself and even more persistent, find a possible analogy between certain civic, philanthropic and educational efforts directed against the very existence of this social evil and similar organized efforts which preceded the overthrow of slavery in America. Thus, long before slavery was finally declared illegal, there were international regulations of its traffic, state and federal legislation concerning its extension, and many extra legal attempts to control its abuses; quite as we have the international regulations concerning the white slave traffic, the state and interstate legislation for its repression, and an extra legal power in connection with it so universally given to the municipal police that the possession of this power has become one of the great sources of corruption in every American city.

Before society was ready to proceed against the institution of slavery as such, groups of men and women by means of the underground railroad cherished and educated individual slaves; it is scarcely necessary to point out the similarity to the rescue homes and preventive associations which every great city contains.

It is always easy to overwork an analogy, and yet the economist who for years insisted that slave labor continually and arbitrarily limited the wages of free labor and was therefore a detriment to national wealth was a forerunner of the economist of to-day who points out the economic basis of the social evil, the connection between low wages and despair, between over-fatigue and the demand for reckless pleasure.

Before the American nation agreed to regard slavery as unjustifiable from the standpoint of public morality, an army of reformers, lecturers, and writers set forth its enormity in a never-ceasing flow of invective, of appeal, and of portrayal concerning the human cruelty to which the system lent itself. We can discern the scouts and outposts of a similar army advancing against this existing evil: the physicians and sanitarians who are committed to the task of ridding the race from contagious diseases, the teachers and lecturers who are appealing to the higher morality of thousands of young people; the growing literature, not only biological and didactic, but of a popular type more closely approaching "Uncle Tom's Cabin."

Throughout the agitation for the abolition of slavery in America, there were statesmen who gradually became convinced of the political and moral necessity of giving to the freedman the protection of the ballot. In this current agitation there are at least a few men and women who would extend a greater social and political freedom to all women if only because domestic control has proved so ineffectual.

We may certainly take courage from the fact that our contemporaries are fired by social compassions and enthusiasms, to which even our immediate predecessors were indifferent. Such compunctions have ever manifested themselves in varying degrees of ardor through different groups in the same community. Thus among those who are newly aroused to action in regard to the social evil are many who would endeavor to regulate it and believe they can minimize its dangers, still larger numbers who would eliminate all trafficking of unwilling victims in connection with it, and yet others who believe that as a quasi-legal institution it may be absolutely abolished. Perhaps the analogy to the abolition of slavery is most striking in that these groups, in their varying points of view, are like those earlier associations which differed widely in regard to chattel slavery. Only the so-called extremists, in the first instance, stood for abolition and they were continually told that what they proposed was clearly impossible. The legal and commercial obstacles, bulked large, were placed before them and it was confidently asserted that the blame for the historic existence of slavery lay deep within human nature itself. Yet gradually all of these associations reached the point of view of the abolitionist and before the war was over even the most lukewarm unionist saw no other solution of the nation's difficulty. Some such gradual conversion to the point of view of abolition is the experience of every society or group of people who seriously face the difficulties and complications of the social evil. Certainly all the national organizations-the National Vigilance Committee, the American Purity Federation, the Alliance for the Suppression and Prevention of the White Slave Traffic and many others-stand for the final abolition of commercialized vice. Local vice commissions, such as the able one recently appointed in Chicago, although composed of members of varying beliefs in regard to the possibility of control and regulation, united in the end in recommending a law enforcement looking towards final abolition. Even the most sceptical of Chicago citizens, after reading the fearless document, shared the hope of the commission that "the city, when aroused to the truth, would instantly rebel against the social evil in all its phases." A similar recommendation of ultimate abolition was recently made unanimous by the Minneapolis vice commission after the conversion of many of its members. Doubtless all of the national societies have before them a task only less gigantic than that faced by those earlier associations in America for the suppression of slavery, although it may be legitimate to remind them that the best-known anti-slavery society in America was organized by the New England abolitionists in 1836, and only thirty-six years later, in 1872, was formally disbanded because its object had been accomplished. The long struggle ahead of these newer associations will doubtless claim its martyrs and its heroes, has indeed already claimed them during the last thirty years. Few righteous causes have escaped baptism with blood; nevertheless, to paraphrase Lincoln's speech, if blood were exacted drop by drop in measure to the tears of anguished mothers and enslaved girls, the nation would still be obliged to go into the struggle.

Throughout this volume the phrase "social evil" is used to designate the sexual commerce permitted to exist in every large city, usually in a segregated district, wherein the chastity of women is bought and sold. Modifications of legal codes regarding marriage and divorce, moral judgments concerning the entire group of questions centring about illicit affection between men and women, are quite other questions which are not considered here. Such problems must always remain distinct from those of commercialized vice, as must the treatment of an irreducible minimum of prostitution, which will doubtless long exist, quite as society still retains an irreducible minimum of murders. This volume does not deal with the probable future of prostitution, and gives only such historical background as is necessary to understand the present situation. It endeavors to present the contributory causes, as they have become registered in my consciousness through a long residence in a crowded city quarter, and to state the indications, as I have seen them, of a new conscience with its many and varied manifestations.

Nothing is gained by making the situation better or worse than it is, nor in anywise different from what it is. This ancient evil is indeed social in the sense of community responsibility and can only be understood and at length remedied when we face the fact and measure the resources which may at length be massed against it. Perhaps the most striking indication that our generation has become the bearer of a new moral consciousness in regard to the existence of commercialized vice is the fact that the mere contemplation of it throws the more sensitive men and women among our contemporaries into a state of indignant revolt. It is doubtless an instinctive shrinking from this emotion and an unconscious dread that this modern sensitiveness will be outraged, which justifies to themselves so many moral men and women in their persistent ignorance of the subject. Yet one of the most obvious resources at our command, which might well be utilized at once, if it is to be utilized at all, is the overwhelming pity and sense of protection which the recent revelations in the white slave traffic have aroused for the thousands of young girls, many of them still children, who are yearly sacrificed to the "sins of the people." All of this emotion ought to be made of value, for quite as a state of emotion is invariably the organic preparation for action, so it is certainly true that no profound spiritual transformation can take place without it.

After all, human progress is deeply indebted to a study of imperfections, and the counsels of despair, if not full of seasoned wisdom, are at least fertile in suggestion and a desperate spur to action. Sympathetic knowledge is the only way of approach to any human problem, and the line of least resistance into the jungle of human wretchedness must always be through that region which is most thoroughly explored, not only by the information of the statistician, but by sympathetic understanding. We are daily attaining the latter through such authors as Sudermann and Elsa Gerusalem, who have enabled their readers to comprehend the so-called "fallen" woman through a skilful portrayal of the reaction of experience upon personality. Their realism has rescued her from the sentimentality surrounding an impossible Camille quite as their fellow-craftsmen in realism have replaced the weeping Amelias of the Victorian period by reasonable women transcribed from actual life.

The treatment of this subject in American literature is at present in the pamphleteering stage, although an ever-increasing number of short stories and novels deal with it. On the other hand, the plays through which Bernard Shaw constantly places the truth before the public in England as Brieux is doing for the public in France, produce in the spectators a disquieting sense that society is involved in commercialized vice and must speedily find a way out. Such writing is like the roll of the drum which announces the approach of the troops ready for action.

Some of the writers who are performing this valiant service are related to those great artists who in every age enter into a long struggle with existing social conditions, until after many years they change the outlook upon life for at least a handful of their contemporaries. Their readers find themselves no longer mere bewildered spectators of a given social wrong, but have become conscious of their own hypocrisy in regard to it, and they realize that a veritable horror, simply because it was hidden, had come to seem to them inevitable and almost normal.

Many traces of this first uneasy consciousness regarding the social evil are found in contemporary literature, for while the business of literature is revelation and not reformation, it may yet perform for the men and women now living that purification of the imagination and intellect which the Greeks believed to come through pity and terror.

Secure in the knowledge of evolutionary processes, we have learned to talk glibly of the obligations of race progress and of the possibility of racial degeneration. In this respect certainly we have a wider outlook than that possessed by our fathers, who so valiantly grappled with chattel slavery and secured its overthrow. May the new conscience gather force until men and women, acting under its sway, shall be constrained to eradicate this ancient evil!

Chapter II
Recent Legal Enactments

At the present moment even the least conscientious citizens agree that, first and foremost, the organized traffic in what has come to be called white slaves must be suppressed and that those traffickers who procure their victims for purely commercial purposes must be arrested and prosecuted. As it is impossible to rescue girls fraudulently and illegally detained, save through governmental agencies, it is naturally through the line of legal action that the most striking revelations of the white slave traffic have come. For the sake of convenience, we may divide this legal action into those cases dealing with the international trade, those with the state and interstate traffic, and the regulations with which the municipality alone is concerned.

First in value to the white slave commerce is the girl imported from abroad who from the nature of the case is most completely in the power of the trader. She is literally friendless and unable to speak the language and at last discouraged she makes no effort to escape. Many cases of the international traffic were recently tried in Chicago and the offenders convicted by the federal authorities. One of these cases, which attracted much attention throughout the country, was of Marie, a French girl, the daughter of a Breton stone mason, so old and poor that he was obliged to take her from her convent school at the age of twelve years. He sent her to Paris, where she became a little household drudge and nurse-maid, working from six in the morning until eight at night, and for three years sending her wages, which were about a franc a day, directly to her parents in the Breton village. One afternoon, as she was buying a bottle of milk at a tiny shop, she was engaged in conversation by a young man who invited her into a little patisserie where, after giving her some sweets, he introduced her to his friend, Monsieur Paret, who was gathering together a theatrical troupe to go to America. Paret showed her pictures of several young girls gorgeously arrayed and announcements of their coming tour, and Marie felt much flattered when it was intimated that she might join this brilliant company. After several clandestine meetings to perfect the plan, she left the city with Paret and a pretty French girl to sail for America with the rest of the so-called actors. Paret escaped detection by the immigration authorities in New York, through his ruse of the "Kinsella troupe," and took the girls directly to Chicago. Here they were placed in a disreputable house belonging to a man named Lair, who had advanced the money for their importation. The two French girls remained in this house for several months until it was raided by the police, when they were sent to separate houses. The records which were later brought into court show that at this time Marie was earning two hundred and fifty dollars a week, all of which she gave to her employers. In spite of this large monetary return she was often cruelly beaten, was made to do the household scrubbing, and was, of course, never allowed to leave the house. Furthermore, as one of the methods of retaining a reluctant girl is to put her hopelessly in debt and always to charge against her the expenses incurred in securing her, Marie as an imported girl had begun at once with the huge debt of the ocean journey for Paret and herself. In addition to this large sum she was charged, according to universal custom, with exorbitant prices for all the clothing she received and with any money which Paret chose to draw against her account. Later, when Marie contracted typhoid fever, she was sent for treatment to a public hospital and it was during her illness there, when a general investigation was made of the white slave traffic, that a federal officer visited her. Marie, who thought she was going to die, freely gave her testimony, which proved to be most valuable.

The federal authorities following up her statements at last located Paret in the city prison at Atlanta, Georgia, where he had been convicted on a similar charge. He was brought to Chicago and on his testimony Lair was also convicted and imprisoned.

Marie has since married a man who wishes to protect her from the influence of her old life, but although not yet twenty years old and making an honest effort, what she has undergone has apparently so far warped and weakened her will that she is only partially successful in keeping her resolutions, and she sends each month to her parents in France ten or twelve dollars, which she confesses to have earned illicitly. It is as if the shameful experiences to which this little convent-bred Breton girl was forcibly subjected, had finally become registered in every fibre of her being until the forced demoralization has become genuine. She is as powerless now to save herself from her subjective temptations as she was helpless five years ago to save herself from her captors.

Such demoralization is, of course, most valuable to the white slave trader, for when a girl has become thoroughly accustomed to the life and testifies that she is in it of her own free will, she puts herself beyond the protection of the law. She belongs to a legally degraded class, without redress in courts of justice for personal outrages.

Marie, herself, at the end of her third year in America, wrote to the police appealing for help, but the lieutenant who in response to her letter visited the house, was convinced by Lair that she was there of her own volition and that therefore he could do nothing for her. It is easy to see why it thus becomes part of the business to break down a girl's moral nature by all those horrible devices which are constantly used by the owner of a white slave. Because life is so often shortened for these wretched girls, their owners degrade them morally as quickly as possible, lest death release them before their full profit has been secured. In addition to the quantity of sacrificed virtue, to the bulk of impotent suffering, which these white slaves represent, our civilization becomes permanently tainted with the vicious practices designed to accelerate the demoralization of unwilling victims in order to make them commercially valuable. Moreover, a girl thus rendered more useful to her owner, will thereafter fail to touch either the chivalry of men or the tenderness of women because good men and women have become convinced of her innate degeneracy, a word we have learned to use with the unction formerly placed upon original sin. The very revolt of society against such girls is used by their owners as a protection to the business.

The case against the captors of Marie, as well as twenty-four other cases, was ably and vigorously conducted by Edwin W. Sims, United States District Attorney in Chicago. He prosecuted under a clause of the immigration act of 1908, which was unfortunately declared unconstitutional early the next year, when for the moment federal authorities found themselves unable to proceed directly against this international traffic. They could not act under the international white slave treaty signed by the contracting powers in Paris in 1904, and proclaimed by the President of the United States in 1908, because it was found impossible to carry out its provisions without federal police. The long consideration of this treaty by Congress made clear to the nation that it is in matters of this sort that navies are powerless and that as our international problems become more social, other agencies must be provided, a point which arbitration committees have long urged. The discussion of the international treaty brought the subject before the entire country as a matter for immediate legislation and for executive action, and the White Slave Traffic Act was finally passed by Congress in 1910, under which all later prosecutions have since been conducted. When the decision on the immigration clause rendered in 1909 threw the burden of prosecution back upon the states, Mr. Clifford Roe, then assistant State's Attorney, within one year investigated 348 such cases, domestic and foreign, and successfully prosecuted 91, carrying on the vigorous policy inaugurated by United States Attorney Sims. In 1908 Illinois passed the first pandering law in this country, changing the offence from disorderly conduct to a misdemeanor, and greatly increasing the penalty. In many states pandering is still so little defined as to make the crime merely a breach of manners and to put it in the same class of offences as selling a street-car transfer.

As a result of this vigorous action, Chicago became the first city to look the situation squarely in the face, and to make a determined business-like fight against the procuring of girls. An office was established by public-spirited citizens where Mr. Roe was placed in charge and empowered to follow up the clues of the traffic wherever found and to bring the traffickers to justice; in consequence the white slave traders have become so frightened that the foreign importation of girls to Chicago has markedly declined. It is estimated by Mr. Roe that since 1909 about one thousand white slave traders, of whom thirty or forty were importers of foreign girls, have been driven away from the city.

Throughout the Congressional discussions of the white slave traffic, beginning with the Howell-Bennett Act in 1907, it was evident that the subject was closely allied to immigration, and when the immigration commission made a partial report to Congress in December, 1909, upon "the importation and harboring of women for immoral purposes," their finding only emphasized the report of the Commissioner General of Immigration made earlier in the year. His report had traced the international traffic directly to New York, Chicago, Boston, Buffalo, New Orleans, Denver, Seattle, Portland, Salt Lake City, Ogden, and Butte. As the list of cities was comparatively small, it seemed not unreasonable to hope that the international traffic might be rigorously prosecuted, with the prospect of finally doing away with it in spite of its subtle methods, its multiplied ramifications, and its financial resources. Only officials of vigorous conscience can deal with this traffic; but certainly there can be no nobler service for federal and state officers to undertake than this protection of immigrant girls.

It is obvious that a foreign girl who speaks no English, who has not the remotest idea in what part of the city her fellow-countrymen live, who does not know the police station or any agency to which she may apply, is almost as valuable to a white slave trafficker as a girl imported directly for the trade. The trafficker makes every effort to intercept such a girl before she can communicate with her relations. Although great care is taken at Ellis Island, the girl's destination carefully indicated upon her ticket and her friends communicated with, after she boards the train the governmental protection is withdrawn and many untoward experiences may befall a girl between New York and her final destination. Only this year a Polish mother of the Hull House neighborhood failed to find her daughter on a New York train upon which she had been notified to expect her, because the girl had been induced to leave the New York train at South Chicago, where she was met by two young men, one of them well known to the police, and the other a young Pole, purporting to have been sent by the girl's mother.

The immigrant girl also encounters dangers upon the very moment of her arrival. The cab-men and expressmen are often unscrupulous. One of the latter was recently indicted in Chicago upon the charge of regularly procuring immigrant girls for a disreputable hotel. The non-English speaking girl handing her written address to a cabman has no means of knowing whither he will drive her, but is obliged to place herself implicitly in his hands. The Immigrants' Protective League has brought about many changes in this respect, but has upon its records some piteous tales of girls who were thus easily deceived.

An immigrant girl is occasionally exploited by her own lover whom she has come to America to marry. I recall the case of a Russian girl thus decoyed into a disreputable life by a man deceiving her through a fake marriage ceremony. Although not found until a year later, the girl had never ceased to be distressed and rebellious. Many Slovak and Polish girls, coming to America without their relatives, board in houses already filled with their countrymen who have also preceded their own families to the land of promise, hoping to earn money enough to send for them later. The immigrant girl is thus exposed to dangers at the very moment when she is least able to defend herself. Such a girl, already bewildered by the change from an old world village to an American city, is unfortunately sometimes convinced that the new country freedom does away with the necessity for a marriage ceremony. Many others are told that judgment for a moral lapse is less severe in America than in the old country. The last month's records of the Municipal Court in Chicago, set aside to hear domestic relation cases, show sixteen unfortunate girls, of whom eight were immigrant girls representing eight different nationalities. These discouraged and deserted girls become an easy prey for the procurers who have sometimes been in league with their lovers.

Even those girls who immigrate with their families and sustain an affectionate relation with them are yet often curiously free from chaperonage. The immigrant mothers do not know where their daughters work, save that it is in a vague "over there" or "down town." They themselves were guarded by careful mothers and they would gladly give the same oversight to their daughters, but the entire situation is so unlike that of their own peasant girlhoods that, discouraged by their inability to judge it, they make no attempt to understand their daughters' lives. The girls, realizing this inability on the part of their mothers, elated by that sense of independence which the first taste of self-support always brings, sheltered from observation during certain hours, are almost as free from social control as is the traditional young man who comes up from the country to take care of himself in a great city. These immigrant parents are, of course, quite unable to foresee that while a girl feels a certain restraint of public opinion from the tenement house neighbors among whom she lives, and while she also responds to the public opinion of her associates in a factory where she works, there is no public opinion at all operating as a restraint upon her in the hours which lie between the two, occupied in the coming and going to work through the streets of a city large enough to offer every opportunity for concealment. So much of the recreation which is provided by commercial agencies, even in its advertisements, deliberately plays upon the interest of sex because it is under such excitement and that of alcohol that money is most recklessly spent. The great human dynamic, which it has been the long effort of centuries to limit to family life, is deliberately utilized for advertising purposes, and it is inevitable that many girls yield to such allurements.

On the other hand, one is filled with admiration for the many immigrant girls who in the midst of insuperable difficulties resist all temptations. Such admiration was certainly due Olga, a tall, handsome girl, a little passive and slow, yet with that touch of dignity which a continued mood of introspection so often lends to the young. Olga had been in Chicago for a year living with an aunt who, when she returned to Sweden, placed her niece in a boarding-house which she knew to be thoroughly respectable. But a friendless girl of such striking beauty could not escape the machinations of those who profit by the sale of girls. Almost immediately Olga found herself beset by two young men who continually forced themselves upon her attention, although she refused all their invitations to shows and dances. In six months the frightened girl had changed her boarding-place four times, hoping that the men would not be able to follow her. She was also obliged constantly to look for a cheaper place, because the dull season in the cloak-making trade came early that year. In the fifth boarding-house she finally found herself so hopelessly in arrears that the landlady, tired of waiting for the "new cloak making to begin," at length fulfilled a long-promised threat, and one summer evening at nine o'clock literally put Olga into the street, retaining her trunk in payment of the debt. The girl walked the street for hours, until she fancied that she saw one of her persecutors in the distance, when she hastily took refuge in a sheltered doorway, crouching in terror. Although no one approached her, she sat there late into the night, apparently too apathetic to move. With the curious inconsequence of moody youth, she was not aroused to action by the situation in which she found herself. The incident epitomized to her the everlasting riddle of the universe to which she could see no solution and she drearily decided to throw herself into the lake. As she left the doorway at daybreak for this pitiful purpose, she attracted the attention of a passing policeman. In response to his questions, kindly at first but becoming exasperated as he was convinced that she was either "touched in her wits" or "guying" him, he obtained a confused story of the persecutions of the two young men, and in sheer bewilderment he finally took her to the station on the very charge against the thought of which she had so long contended.

The girl was doubtless sullen in court the next morning; she was resentful of the policeman's talk, she was oppressed and discouraged and therefore taciturn. She herself said afterwards that she "often got still that way." She so sharply felt the disgrace of arrest, after her long struggle for respectability, that she gave a false name and became involved in a story to which she could devote but half her attention, being still absorbed in an undercurrent of speculative thought which continually broke through the flimsy tale she was fabricating.

With the evidence before him, the judge felt obliged to sustain the policeman's charge, and as Olga could not pay the fine imposed, he sentenced her to the city prison. The girl, however, had appeared so strangely that the judge was uncomfortable and gave her in charge of a representative of the Juvenile Protective Association in the hope that she could discover the whole situation, meantime suspending the sentence. It took hours of patient conversation with the girl and the kindly services of a well-known alienist to break into her dangerous state of mind and to gain her confidence. Prolonged medical treatment averted the threatened melancholia and she was at last rescued from the meaningless despondency so hostile to life itself, which has claimed many young victims.

It is strange that we are so slow to learn that no one can safely live without companionship and affection, that the individual who tries the hazardous experiment of going without at least one of them is prone to be swamped by a black mood from within. It is as if we had to build little islands of affection in the vast sea of impersonal forces lest we be overwhelmed by them. Yet we know that in every large city there are hundreds of men whose business it is to discover girls thus hard pressed by loneliness and despair, to urge upon them the old excuse that "no one cares what you do," to fill them with cheap cynicism concerning the value of virtue, all to the end that a business profit may be secured.

Had Olga yielded to the solicitations of bad men and had the immigration authorities in the federal building of Chicago discovered her in the disreputable hotel in which her captors wanted to place her, she would have been deported to Sweden, sent home in disgrace from the country which had failed to protect her. Certainly the immigration laws might do better than to send a girl back to her parents, diseased and disgraced because America has failed to safeguard her virtue from the machinations of well-known but unrestrained criminals. The possibility of deportation on the charge of prostitution is sometimes utilized by jealous husbands or rejected lovers. Only last year a Russian girl came to Chicago to meet her lover and was deceived by a fake marriage. Although the man basely deserted her within a few weeks he became very jealous a year later when he discovered that she was about to be married to a prosperous fellow-countryman, and made charges against her to the federal authorities concerning her life in Russia. It was with the greatest difficulty that the girl was saved from deportation to Russia under circumstances which would have compelled her to take out a red ticket in Odessa, and to live forevermore the life with which her lover had wantonly charged her.

May we not hope that in time the nation's policy in regard to immigrants will become less negative and that a measure of protection will be extended to them during the three years when they are so liable to prompt deportation if they become criminals or paupers?

While it may be difficult for the federal authorities to accomplish this protection and will doubtless require an extension of the powers of the Department of Immigration, certainly no one will doubt that it is the business of the city itself to extend much more protection to young girls who so thoughtlessly walk upon its streets. Yet, in spite of the grave consequences which lack of proper supervision implies, the municipal treatment of commercialized vice not only differs in each city but varies greatly in the same city under changing administrations.

The situation is enormously complicated by the pharisaic attitude of the public which wishes to have the comfort of declaring the social evil to be illegal, while at the same time it expects the police department to regulate it and to make it as little obvious as possible. In reality the police, as they themselves know, are not expected to serve the public in this matter but to consult the desires of the politicians; for, next to the fast and loose police control of gambling, nothing affords better political material than the regulation of commercialized vice. First in line is the ward politician who keeps a disorderly saloon which serves both as a meeting-place for the vicious young men engaged in the traffic and as a market for their wares. Back of this the politician higher up receives his share of the toll which this business pays that it may remain undisturbed. The very existence of a segregated district under police regulation means, of course, that the existing law must be nullified or at least rendered totally inoperative. When police regulation takes the place of law enforcement a species of municipal blackmail inevitably becomes intrenched. The police are forced to regulate an illicit trade, but because the men engaged in an unlawful business expect to pay money for its protection, the corruption of the police department is firmly established and, as the Chicago vice commission report points out, is merely called "protection to the business." The practice of grafting thereafter becomes almost official. On the other hand, any man who attempts to show mercy to the victims of that business, or to regulate it from the victim's point of view, is considered a traitor to the cause. Quite recently a former inspector of police in Chicago established a requirement that every young girl who came to live in a disreputable house within a prescribed district must be reported to him within an hour after her arrival. Each one was closely questioned as to her reasons for entering into the life. If she was very young, she was warned of its inevitable consequences and urged to abandon her project. Every assistance was offered her to return to work and to live a normal life. Occasionally a girl was desperate and it was sometimes necessary that she be forcibly detained in the police station until her friends could be communicated with. More often she was glad to avail herself of the chance of escape; practically always, unless she had already become romantically entangled with a disreputable young man, whom she firmly believed to be her genuine lover and protector.

One day a telephone message came to Hull House from the inspector asking us to take charge of a young girl who had been brought into the station by an older woman for registration. The girl's youth and the innocence of her replies to the usual questions convinced the inspector that she was ignorant of the life she was about to enter and that she probably believed she was simply registering her choice of a boarding-house. Her story which she told at Hull House was as follows: She was a Milwaukee factory girl, the daughter of a Bohemian carpenter. Ten days before she had met a Chicago young man at a Milwaukee dance hall and after a brief courtship had promised to marry him, arranging to meet him in Chicago the following week. Fearing that her Bohemian mother would not approve of this plan, which she called "the American way of getting married," the girl had risen one morning even earlier than factory work necessitated and had taken the first train to Chicago. The young man met her at the station, took her to a saloon where he introduced her to a friend, an older woman, who, he said, would take good care of her. After the young man disappeared, ostensibly for the marriage license, the woman professed to be much shocked that the little bride had brought no luggage, and persuaded her that she must work a few weeks in order to earn money for her trousseau, and that she, an older woman who knew the city, would find a boarding-house and a place in a factory for her. She further induced her to write postal cards to six of her girl friends in Milwaukee, telling them of the kind lady in Chicago, of the good chances for work, and urging them to come down to the address which she sent. The woman told the unsuspecting girl that, first of all, a newcomer must register her place of residence with the police, as that was the law in Chicago. It was, of course, when the woman took her to the police station that the situation was disclosed. It needed but little investigation to make clear that the girl had narrowly escaped a well-organized plot and that the young man to whom she was engaged was an agent for a disreputable house. Mr. Clifford Roe took up the case with vigor, and although all efforts failed to find the young man, the woman who was his accomplice was fined one hundred and fifty dollars and costs.

The one impression which the trial left upon our minds was that all the men concerned in the prosecution felt a keen sense of outrage against the method employed to secure the girl, but took for granted that the life she was about to lead was in the established order of things, if she had chosen it voluntarily. In other words, if the efforts of the agent had gone far enough to involve her moral nature, the girl, who although unsophisticated, was twenty-one years old, could have remained, quite unchallenged, in the hideous life. The woman who was prosecuted was well known to the police and was fined, not for her daily occupation, but because she had become involved in interstate white slave traffic. One touch of nature redeemed the trial, for the girl suffered much more from the sense that she had been deserted by her lover than from horror over the fate she had escaped, and she was never wholly convinced that he had not been genuine. She asserted constantly, in order to account for his absence, that some accident must have befallen him. She felt that he was her natural protector in this strange Chicago to which she had come at his behest and continually resented any imputation of his motives. The betrayal of her confidence, the playing upon her natural desire for a home of her own, was a ghastly revelation that even when this hideous trade is managed upon the most carefully calculated commercial principles, it must still resort to the use of the oldest of the social instincts as its basis of procedure.

This Chicago police inspector, whose desire to protect young girls was so genuine and so successful, was afterward indicted by the grand jury and sent to the penitentiary on the charge of accepting "graft" from saloon-keepers and proprietors of the disreputable houses in his district. His experience was a dramatic and tragic portrayal of the position into which every city forces its police. When a girl who has been secured for the life is dissuaded from it, her rescue represents a definite monetary loss to the agency which has secured her and incurs the enmity of those who expected to profit by her. When this enmity has sufficiently accumulated, the active official is either "called down" by higher political authority, or brought to trial for those illegal practices which he shares with his fellow-officials. It is, therefore, easy to make such an inspector as ours suffer for his virtues, which are individual, by bringing charges against his grafting, which is general and almost official. So long as the customary prices for protection are adhered to, no one feels aggrieved; but the sentiment which prompts an inspector "to side with the girls" and to destroy thousands of dollars' worth of business is unjustifiable. He has not stuck to the rules of the game and the pack of enraged gamesters, under full cry of "morality," can very easily run him to ground, the public meantime being gratified that police corruption has been exposed and the offender punished. Yet hundreds of girls, who could have been discovered in no other way, were rescued by this man in his capacity of police inspector. On the other hand, he did little to bring to justice those responsible for securing the girls, and while he rescued the victim, he did not interfere with the source of supply. Had he been brought to trial for this indifference, it would have been impossible to find a grand jury to sustain the indictment. He was really brought to trial because he had broken the implied contract with the politicians; he had devised illicit and damaging methods to express that instinct for protecting youth and innocence, which every man on the police force doubtless possesses. Were this instinct freed from all political and extra legal control, it would in and of itself be a tremendous force against commercialized vice which is so dependent upon the exploitation of young girls. Yet the fortunes of the police are so tied up to those who profit by this trade and to their friends, the politicians, that the most well-meaning man upon the force is constantly handicapped. Several illustrations of this occur to me. Two years ago, when very untoward conditions were discovered in connection with a certain five-cent theatre, a young policeman arrested the proprietor, who was later brought before the grand jury, indicted and released upon bail for nine thousand dollars. The crime was a heinous one, involving the ruin of fourteen little girls; but so much political influence had been exerted on behalf of the proprietor, who was a relative of the republican committeeman of his ward, that although the license of the theatre was immediately revoked, it was reissued to his wife within a very few days and the man continued to be a menace to the community. When the young policeman who had made the arrest saw him in the neighborhood of the theatre talking to little girls and reported him, the officer was taken severely to task by the highest republican authority in the city. He was reprimanded for his activity and ordered transferred to the stockyards, eleven miles away. The policeman well understood that this was but the first step in the process called "breaking;" that after he had moved his family to the stockyards, in a few weeks he would be transferred elsewhere, and that this change of beat would be continued until he should at last be obliged to resign from the force. His offence, as he was plainly told, had been his ignorance of the fact that the theatre was under political protection. In short, the young officer had naïvely undertaken to serve the public without waiting for his instructions from the political bosses.

A flagrant example of the collusion of the police with vice is instanced by United States District Attorney Sims, who recently called upon the Chicago police to make twenty-four arrests on behalf of the United States government for violations of the white slave law, when all of the men liable to arrest left town two hours after the warrants were issued. To quote Mr. Sims: "We sent the secret service men who had been working in conjunction with the police back to Washington and brought in a fresh supply. These men did not work with the police, and within two weeks after the first set of secret service men had left Chicago, the men we wanted were back in town, and without the aid of the city police we arrested all of them."

When the legal control of commercialized vice is thus tied up with city politics the functions of the police become legislative, executive and judicial in regard to street solicitation: in a sense they also have power of license, for it lies with them to determine the number of women who are allowed to ply their trade upon the street. Some of these women are young earthlings, as it were, hoping to earn money for much-desired clothing or pleasure. Others are desperate creatures making one last effort before they enter a public hospital to face a miserable end; but by far the larger number are sent out under the protection of the men who profit by their earnings, or they are utilized to secure patronage for disreputable houses. The police regard the latter "as regular," and while no authoritative order is ever given, the patrolman understands that they are protected. On the other hand, "the straggler" is liable to be arrested by any officer who chooses, and she is subjected to a fine upon his unsupported word. In either case the police regard all such women as literally "abandoned," deprived of ordinary rights, obliged to live in specified residences, and liable to have their personal liberties invaded in a way that no other class of citizens would tolerate.

The recent establishment of the Night Court in New York registers an advance in regard to the treatment of these wretched women. Not only does the public gradually become cognizant of the treatment accorded them, but some attempt at discrimination is made between the first offenders and those hardened by long practice in that most hideous of occupations. Furthermore, an adult probation system is gradually being substituted for the system of fines which at present are levied in such wise as to virtually constitute a license and a partnership with the police department.

While American cities cannot be said to have adopted a policy either of suppression or one of regulation, because the police consider the former impracticable and the latter intolerable to public opinion, we may perhaps claim for America a little more humanity in its dealing with this class of women, a little less ruthlessness than that exhibited by the continental cities where regimentation is relentlessly assumed.

The suggestive presence of such women on the streets is perhaps one of the most demoralizing influences to be found in a large city, and such vigorous efforts as were recently made by a former chief of police in Chicago when he successfully cleared the streets of their presence, demonstrates that legal suppression is possible. At least this obvious temptation to young men and boys who are idly walking the streets might be avoided, for in an old formula one such woman "has cast down many wounded; yea, many strong men have been slain by her." Were the streets kept clear, many young girls would be spared familiar knowledge that such a method of earning money is open to them. I have personally known several instances in which young girls have begun street solicitation through sheer imitation. A young Polish woman found herself in dire straits after the death of her mother. Her only friends in America had moved to New York, she was in debt for her mother's funeral, and as it was the slack season of the miserable sweat-shop sewing she had been doing, she was unable to find work. One evening when she was quite desperate with hunger, she stopped several men upon the street, as she had seen other girls do, and in her broken English asked them for something to eat. Only after a young man had given her a good meal at a restaurant did she realize the price she was expected to pay and the horrible things which the other girls were doing. Even in her shocked revolt she could not understand, of course, that she herself epitomized that hideous choice between starvation and vice which is perhaps the crowning disgrace of civilization.

The legal suppression of street solicitation would not only protect girls but would enormously minimize the risk and temptation to boys. The entire system of recruiting for commercialized vice is largely dependent upon boys who are scarcely less the victims of the system than are the girls themselves. Certainly this aspect of the situation must be seriously considered.

In 1908, when Mr. Clifford Roe conducted successful prosecutions against one hundred and fifty of these disreputable young men in Chicago, nearly all of them were local boys who had used their personal acquaintance to secure their victims. The accident of a long acquaintance with one of these boys, born in the Hull-House neighborhood, filled me with questionings as to how far society may be responsible for these wretched lads, many of them beginning a vicious career when they are but fifteen or sixteen years of age. Because the trade constantly demands very young girls, the procurers require the assistance of immature boys, for in this game above all others "youth calls to youth." Such a boy is often incited by the professional procurer to ruin a young girl, because the latter's position is much safer if the character of the girl is blackened before he sells her, and if he himself cannot be implicated in her downfall. He thus keeps himself within the letter of the law, and when he is even more cautious, he induces the boy to go through the ceremony of a legal marriage by promising him a percentage of his wife's first earnings.

Only yesterday I received a letter from a young man whom I had known from his early boyhood, written in the state penitentiary, where he is serving a life sentence. His father was a drunkard, but his mother was a fine woman, devoted to her children, and she had patiently supported her son Jim far beyond his school age. At the time of his trial, she pawned all her personal possessions and mortgaged her furniture in order to get three hundred dollars for his lawyer. Although Jim usually led the life of a loafer and had never supported his mother, he was affectionately devoted to her and always kindly and good-natured. Perhaps it was because he had been so long dependent upon a self-sacrificing woman that it became easy for him to be dependent upon his wife, a girl whom he met when he was temporarily acting as porter in a disreputable hotel. Through his long familiarity with vice, and the fact that many of his companions habitually lived upon the earnings of "their girls," he easily consented that his wife should continue her life, and he constantly accepted the money which she willingly gave him. After his marriage he still lived in his mother's house and refused to take more money from her, but she had no idea of the source of his income. One day he called at the hotel, as usual, to ask for his wife's earnings, and in a quarrel over the amount with the landlady of the house, he drew a revolver and killed her. Although the plea of self-defense was urged in the trial, his abominable manner of life so outraged both judge and jury that he received the maximum sentence. His mother still insists that he sincerely loved the girl, whom he so impulsively married and that he constantly tried to dissuade her from her evil life. Certain it is that Jim's wife and mother are both filled with genuine sorrow for his fate and that in some wise the educational and social resources in the city of his birth failed to protect him from his own lower impulses and from the evil companionship whose influence he could not withstand. He is but one of thousands of weak boys, who are constantly utilized to supply the white slave trafficker with young girls, for it has been estimated that at any given moment the majority of the girls utilized by the trade are under twenty years of age and that most of them were procured when younger. We cannot assume that the youths who are hired to entice and entrap these girls are all young fiends, degenerate from birth; the majority of them are merely out-of-work boys, idle upon the streets, who readily lend themselves to these base demands because nothing else is presented to them.

All the recent investigations have certainly made clear that the bulk of the entire traffic is conducted with the youth of the community, and that the social evil, ancient though it may be, must be renewed in our generation through its younger members. The knowledge of the youth of its victims doubtless in a measure accounts for the new sense of compunction which fills the community.

Chapter III
Amelioration of Economic Conditions

It may be possible to extract some small degree of comfort from the recent revelations of the white slave traffic when we reflect that at the present moment, in the midst of a freedom such as has never been accorded to young women in the history of the world, under an economic pressure grinding down upon the working girl at the very age when she most wistfully desires to be taken care of, it is necessary to organize a widespread commercial enterprise in order to procure a sufficient number of girls for the white slave market.

Certainly the larger freedom accorded to woman by our changing social customs and the phenomenal number of young girls who are utilized by modern industry, taken in connection with this lack of supply, would seem to show that the chastity of women is holding its own in that slow-growing civilization which ever demands more self-control and conscious direction on the part of the individuals sharing it.

Successive reports of the United States census indicate that self-supporting girls are increasing steadily in number each decade, until 59 per cent. of all the young women in the nation between the ages of sixteen and twenty, are engaged in some gainful occupation. Year after year, as these figures increase, the public views them with complacency, almost with pride, and confidently depends upon the inner restraint and training of this girlish multitude to protect it from disaster. Nevertheless, the public is totally unable to determine at what moment these safeguards, evolved under former industrial conditions, may reach a breaking point, not because of economic freedom, but because of untoward economic conditions.

For the first time in history multitudes of women are laboring without the direct stimulus of family interest or affection, and they are also unable to proportion their hours of work and intervals of rest according to their strength; in addition to this for thousands of them the effort to obtain a livelihood fairly eclipses the very meaning of life itself. At the present moment no student of modern industrial conditions can possibly assert how far the superior chastity of woman, so rigidly maintained during the centuries, has been the result of her domestic surroundings, and certainly no one knows under what degree of economic pressure the old restraints may give way.

In addition to the monotony of work and the long hours, the small wages these girls receive have no relation to the standard of living which they are endeavoring to maintain. Discouraged and over-fatigued, they are often brought into sharp juxtaposition with the women who are obtaining much larger returns from their illicit trade. Society also ventures to capitalize a virtuous girl at much less than one who has yielded to temptation, and it may well hold itself responsible for the precarious position into which, year after year, a multitude of frail girls is placed.

The very valuable report recently issued by the vice commission of Chicago leaves no room for doubt upon this point. The report estimates the yearly profit of this nefarious business as conducted in Chicago to be between fifteen and sixteen millions of dollars. Although these enormous profits largely accrue to the men who conduct the business side of prostitution, the report emphasizes the fact that the average girl earns very much more in such a life than she can hope to earn by any honest work. It points out that the capitalized value of the average working girl is six thousand dollars, as she ordinarily earns six dollars a week, which is three hundred dollars a year, or five per cent. on that sum. A girl who sells drinks in a disreputable saloon, earning in commissions for herself twenty-one dollars a week, is capitalized at a value of twenty-two thousand dollars. The report further estimates that the average girl who enters an illicit life under a protector or manager is able to earn twenty-five dollars a week, representing a capital of twenty-six thousand dollars. In other words, a girl in such a life "earns more than four times as much as she is worth as a factor in the social and industrial economy, where brains, intelligence, virtue and womanly charm should bring a premium." The argument is specious in that it does not record the economic value of the many later years in which the honest girl will live as wife and mother, in contrast to the premature death of the woman in the illicit trade, but the girl herself sees only the difference in the immediate earning possibilities in the two situations.

Nevertheless the supply of girls for the white slave traffic so far falls below the demand that large business enterprises have been developed throughout the world in order to secure a sufficient number of victims for this modern market. Over and over again in the criminal proceedings against the men engaged in this traffic, when questioned as to their motives, they have given the simple reply "that more girls are needed", and that they were "promised big money for them". Although economic pressure as a reason for entering an illicit life has thus been brought out in court by the evidence in a surprising number of cases, there is no doubt that it is often exaggerated; a girl always prefers to think that economic pressure is the reason for her downfall, even when the immediate causes have been her love of pleasure, her desire for finery, or the influence of evil companions. It is easy for her, as for all of us, to be deceived as to real motives. In addition to this the wretched girl who has entered upon an illicit life finds the experience so terrible that, day by day, she endeavors to justify herself with the excuse that the money she earns is needed for the support of some one dependent upon her, thus following habits established by generations of virtuous women who cared for feeble folk. I know one such girl living in a disreputable house in Chicago who has adopted a delicate child afflicted with curvature of the spine, whom she boards with respectable people and keeps for many weeks out of each year in an expensive sanitarium that it may receive medical treatment. The mother of the child, an inmate of the house in which the ardent foster-mother herself lives, is quite indifferent to the child's welfare and also rather amused at such solicitude. The girl has persevered in her course for five years, never however allowing the little invalid to come to the house in which she and the mother live. The same sort of devotion and self-sacrifice is often poured out upon the miserable man who in the beginning was responsible for the girl's entrance into the life and who constantly receives her earnings. She supports him in the luxurious life he may be living in another part of the town, takes an almost maternal pride in his good clothes and general prosperity, and regards him as the one person in all the world who understands her plight.

Most of the cases of economic responsibility, however, are not due to chivalric devotion, but arise from a desire to fulfill family obligations such as would be accepted by any conscientious girl. This was clearly revealed in conversations which were recently held with thirty-four girls, who were living at the same time in a rescue home, when twenty-two of them gave economic pressure as the reason for choosing the life which they had so recently abandoned. One piteous little widow of seventeen had been supporting her child and had been able to leave the life she had been leading only because her married sister offered to take care of the baby without the money formerly paid her. Another had been supporting her mother and only since her recent death was the girl sure that she could live honestly because she had only herself to care for.

The following story, fairly typical of the twenty-two involving economic reasons, is of a girl who had come to Chicago at the age of fifteen, from a small town in Indiana. Her father was too old to work and her mother was a dependent invalid. The brother who cared for the parents, with the help of the girl's own slender wages earned in the country store of the little town, became ill with rheumatism. In her desire to earn more money the country girl came to the nearest large city, Chicago, to work in a department store. The highest wage she could earn, even though she wore long dresses and called herself "experienced," was five dollars a week. This sum was of course inadequate even for her own needs and she was constantly filled with a corroding worry for "the folks at home." In a moment of panic, a fellow clerk who was "wise" showed her that it was possible to add to her wages by making appointments for money in the noon hour at down-town hotels. Having earned money in this way for a few months, the young girl made an arrangement with an older woman to be on call in the evenings whenever she was summoned by telephone, thus joining that large clandestine group of apparently respectable girls, most of whom yield to temptation only when hard pressed by debt incurred during illness or non-employment, or when they are facing some immediate necessity. This practice has become so general in the larger American cities as to be systematically conducted. It is perhaps the most sinister outcome of the economic pressure, unless one cites its corollary —the condition of thousands of young men whose low salaries so cruelly and unjustifiably postpone their marriages. For a long time the young saleswoman kept her position in the department store, retaining her honest wages for herself, but sending everything else to her family. At length however, she changed from her clandestine life to an openly professional one when she needed enough money to send her brother to Hot Springs, Arkansas, where she maintained him for a year. She explained that because he was now restored to health and able to support the family once more, she had left the life "forever and ever", expecting to return to her home in Indiana. She suspected that her brother knew of her experience, although she was sure that her parents did not, and she hoped that as she was not yet seventeen, she might be able to make a fresh start. Fortunately the poor child did not know how difficult that would be.

It is perhaps in the department store more than anywhere else that every possible weakness in a girl is detected and traded upon. For while it is true that "wherever many girls are gathered together more or less unprotected and embroiled in the struggle for a livelihood, near by will be hovering the procurers and evil-minded", no other place of employment is so easy of access as the department store. No visitor is received in a factory or office unless he has definite business there, whereas every purchaser is welcome at a department store, even a notorious woman well known to represent the demi-monde trade is treated with marked courtesy if she spends large sums of money. The primary danger lies in the fact that the comely saleswomen are thus easy of access. The disreputable young man constantly passes in and out, making small purchases from every pretty girl, opening an acquaintance with complimentary remarks; or the procuress, a fashionably-dressed woman, buys clothing in large amounts, sometimes for a young girl by her side, ostensibly her daughter. She condoles with the saleswoman upon her hard lot and lack of pleasure, and in the rôle of a kindly, prosperous matron invites her to come to her own home for a good time. The girl is sometimes subjected to temptation through the men and women in her own department, who tell her how invitations to dinners and theatres may be procured. It is not surprising that so many of these young, inexperienced girls are either deceived or yield to temptation in spite of the efforts made to protect them by the management and by the older women in the establishment.

The department store has brought together, as has never been done before in history, a bewildering mass of delicate and beautiful fabrics, jewelry and household decorations such as women covet, gathered skilfully from all parts of the world, and in the midst of this bulk of desirable possessions is placed an untrained girl with careful instructions as to her conduct for making sales, but with no guidance in regard to herself. Such a girl may be bitterly lonely, but she is expected to smile affably all day long upon a throng of changing customers. She may be without adequate clothing, although she stands in an emporium where it is piled about her, literally as high as her head. She may be faint for want of food but she may not sit down lest she assume "an attitude of inertia and indifference," which is against the rules. She may have a great desire for pretty things, but she must sell to other people at least twenty-five times the amount of her own salary, or she will not be retained. Because she is of the first generation of girls which has stood alone in the midst of trade, she is clinging and timid, and yet the only person, man or woman, in this commercial atmosphere who speaks to her of the care and protection which she craves, is seeking to betray her. Because she is young and feminine, her mind secretly dwells upon a future lover, upon a home, adorned with the most enticing of the household goods about her, upon a child dressed in the filmy fabrics she tenderly touches, and yet the only man who approaches her there acting upon the knowledge of this inner life of hers, does it with the direct intention of playing upon it in order to despoil her. Is it surprising that the average human nature of these young girls cannot, in many instances, endure this strain? Of fifteen thousand women employed in the down-town department stores of Chicago, the majority are Americans. We all know that the American girl has grown up in the belief that the world is hers from which to choose, that there is ordinarily no limit to her ambition or to her definition of success. She realizes that she is well mannered and well dressed and does not appear unlike most of her customers. She sees only one aspect of her countrywomen who come shopping, and she may well believe that the chief concern of life is fashionable clothing. Her interest and ambition almost inevitably become thoroughly worldly, and from the very fact that she is employed down town, she obtains an exaggerated idea of the luxury of the illicit life all about her, which is barely concealed.

The fifth volume of the report of "Women and Child Wage Earners" in the United States gives the result of a careful inquiry into "the relation of wages to the moral condition of department store women." In connection with this, the investigators secured "the personal histories of one hundred immoral women," of whom ten were or had been employed in a department store. They found that while only one of the ten had been directly induced to leave the store for a disreputable life, six of them said that they had found "it was easier to earn money that way." The report states that the average employee in a department store earns about seven dollars a week, and that the average income of the one hundred immoral women covered by the personal histories, ranged from fifty dollars a week to one hundred dollars a week in exceptional cases. It is of these exceptional cases that the department store girl hears, and the knowledge becomes part of the unreality and glittering life that is all about her.

Another class of young women which is especially exposed to this alluring knowledge is the waitress in down-town cafés and restaurants. A recent investigation of girls in the segregated district of a neighboring city places waiting in restaurants and hotels as highest on the list of "previous occupations." Many waitresses are paid so little that they gratefully accept any fee which men may offer them. It is also the universal habit for customers to enter into easy conversation while being served. Some of them are lonely young men who have few opportunities to speak to women. The girl often quite innocently accepts an invitation for an evening, spent either in a theatre or dance hall, with no evil results, but this very lack of social convention exposes her to danger. Even when the proprietor means to protect the girls, a certain amount of familiarity must be borne, lest their resentment should diminish the patronage of the café. In certain restaurants, moreover, the waitresses doubtless suffer because the patrons compare them with the girls who ply their trade in disreputable saloons under the guise of serving drinks.

The following story would show that mere friendly propinquity may constitute a danger. Last summer an honest, straightforward girl from a small lake town in northern Michigan was working in a Chicago café, sending every week more than half of her wages of seven dollars to her mother and little sister, ill with tuberculosis, at home. The mother owned the little house in which she lived, but except for the vegetables she raised in her own garden and an occasional payment for plain sewing, she and her younger daughter were dependent upon the hard-working girl in Chicago. The girl's heart grew heavier week by week as the mother's letters reported that the sister was daily growing weaker. One hot day in August she received a letter from her mother telling her to come at once if she "would see sister before she died." At noon that day when sickened by the hot air of the café, and when the clatter of dishes, the buzz of conversation, the orders shouted through the slide seemed but a hideous accompaniment to her tormented thoughts, she was suddenly startled by hearing the name of her native town, and realized that one of her regular patrons was saying to her that he meant to take a night boat to M. at 8 o'clock and get out of this "infernal heat." Almost involuntarily she asked him if he would take her with him. Although the very next moment she became conscious what his consent implied, she did not reveal her fright, but merely stipulated that if she went with him he must agree to buy her a return ticket. She reached home twelve hours before her sister died, but when she returned to Chicago a week later burdened with the debt of an undertaker's bill, she realized that she had discovered a means of payment.

All girls who work down town are at a disadvantage as compared to factory girls, who are much less open to direct inducement and to the temptations which come through sheer imitation. Factory girls also have the protection of working among plain people who frankly designate an irregular life, in harsh, old-fashioned terms. If a factory girl catches sight of the vicious life at all, she sees its miserable victims in all the wretchedness and sordidness of their trade in the poorer parts of the city. As she passes the opening doors of a disreputable saloon she may see for an instant three or four listless girls urging liquor upon men tired out with the long day's work and already sodden with drink. As she hurries along the street on a rainy night she may hear a sharp cry of pain from a sick-looking girl whose arm is being brutally wrenched by a rough man, and if she stops for a moment she catches his muttered threats in response to the girl's pleading "that it is too bad a night for street work." She sees a passing policeman shrug his shoulders as he crosses the street, and she vaguely knows that the sick girl has put herself beyond the protection of the law, and that the rough man has an understanding with the officer on the beat. She has been told that certain streets are "not respectable," but a furtive look down the length of one of them reveals only forlorn and ill-looking houses, from which all suggestion of homely domesticity has long since gone; a slovenly woman with hollow eyes and a careworn face holding up the lurching bulk of a drunken man is all she sees of its "denizens," although she may have known a neighbor's daughter who came home to die of a mysterious disease said to be the result of a "fast life," and whose disgraced mother "never again held up her head."

Yet in spite of all this corrective knowledge, the increasing nervous energy to which industrial processes daily accommodate themselves, and the speeding up constantly required of the operators, may at any moment so register their results upon the nervous system of a factory girl as to overcome her powers of resistance. Many a working girl at the end of a day is so hysterical and overwrought that her mental balance is plainly disturbed. Hundreds of working girls go directly to bed as soon as they have eaten their suppers. They are too tired to go from home for recreation, too tired to read and often too tired to sleep. A humane forewoman recently said to me as she glanced down the long room in which hundreds of young women, many of them with their shoes beside them, were standing: "I hate to think of all the aching feet on this floor; these girls all have trouble with their feet, some of them spend the entire evening bathing them in hot water." But aching feet are no more usual than aching backs and aching heads. The study of industrial diseases has only this year been begun by the federal authorities, and doubtless as more is known of the nervous and mental effect of over-fatigue, many moral breakdowns will be traced to this source. It is already easy to make the connection in definite cases: "I was too tired to care," "I was too tired to know what I was doing," "I was dead tired and sick of it all," "I was dog tired and just went with him," are phrases taken from the lips of reckless girls, who are endeavoring to explain the situation in which they find themselves.

Only slowly are laws being enacted to limit the hours of working women, yet the able brief presented to the United States supreme court on the constitutionality of the Oregon ten-hour law for women, based its plea upon the results of overwork as affecting women's health, the grave medical statement constantly broken into by a portrayal of the disastrous effects of over-fatigue upon character. It is as yet difficult to distinguish between the results of long hours and the results of overstrain. Certainly the constant sense of haste is one of the most nerve-racking and exhausting tests to which the human system can be subjected. Those girls in the sewing industry whose mothers thread needles for them far into the night that they may sew without a moment's interruption during the next day; those girls who insert eyelets into shoes, for which they are paid two cents a case, each case containing twenty-four pairs of shoes, are striking victims of the over-speeding which is so characteristic of our entire factory system.

Girls working in factories and laundries are also open to the possibilities of accidents. The loss of only two fingers upon the right hand, or a broken wrist, may disqualify an operator from continuing in the only work in which she is skilled and make her struggle for respectability even more difficult. Varicose veins and broken arches in the feet are found in every occupation in which women are obliged to stand for hours, but at any moment either one may develop beyond purely painful symptoms into crippling incapacity. One such girl recently returning home after a long day's work deliberately sat down upon the floor of a crowded street car, explaining defiantly to the conductor and the bewildered passengers that "her feet would not hold out another minute." A young woman who only last summer broke her hand in a mangle was found in a rescue home in January, explaining her recent experience by the phrase that she was "up against it when leaving the hospital in October."

In spite of many such heart-breaking instances the movement for safeguarding machinery and securing indemnity for industrial accidents proceeds all too slowly. At a recent exhibition in Boston the knife of a miniature guillotine fell every ten seconds to indicate the rate of industrial accidents in the United States. Grisly as was the device, its hideousness might well have been increased had it been able to demonstrate the connection between certain of these accidents and the complete moral disaster which overtook their victims.

Yet factory girls who are subjected to this overstrain and overtime often find their greatest discouragement in the fact that after all their efforts they earn too little to support themselves. One girl said that she had first yielded to temptation when she had become utterly discouraged because she had tried in vain for seven months to save enough money for a pair of shoes. She habitually spent two dollars a week for her room, three dollars for her board, and sixty cents a week for carfare, and she had found the forty cents remaining from her weekly wage of six dollars inadequate to do more than re-sole her old shoes twice. When the shoes became too worn to endure a third soling and she possessed but ninety cents towards a new pair, she gave up her struggle; to use her own contemptuous phrase, she "sold out for a pair of shoes."

Usually the phrases are less graphic, but after all they contain the same dreary meaning: "Couldn't make both ends meet," "I had always been used to having nice things," "Couldn't make enough money to live on," "I got sick and ran behind," "Needed more money," "Impossible to feed and clothe myself," "Out of work, hadn't been able to save." Of course a girl in such a strait does not go out deliberately to find illicit methods of earning money, she simply yields in a moment of utter weariness and discouragement to the temptations she has been able to withstand up to that moment. The long hours, the lack of comforts, the low pay, the absence of recreation, the sense of "good times" all about her which she cannot share, the conviction that she is rapidly losing health and charm, rouse the molten forces within her. A swelling tide of self-pity suddenly storms the banks which have hitherto held her and finally overcomes her instincts for decency and righteousness, as well as the habit of clean living, established by generations of her forebears.

The aphorism that "morals fluctuate with trade" was long considered cynical, but it has been demonstrated in Berlin, in London, in Japan, as well as in several American cities, that there is a distinct increase in the number of registered prostitutes during periods of financial depression and even during the dull season of leading local industries. Out of my own experience I am ready to assert that very often all that is necessary to effectively help the girl who is on the edge of wrong-doing is to lend her money for her board until she finds work, provide the necessary clothing for which she is in such desperate need, persuade her relatives that she should have more money for her own expenditures, or find her another place at higher wages. Upon such simple economic needs does the tried virtue of a good girl sometimes depend.

Here again the immigrant girl is at a disadvantage. The average wage of two hundred newly arrived girls of various nationalities, Poles, Italians, Slovaks, Bohemians, Russians, Galatians, Croatians, Lithuanians, Roumanians, Germans, and Swedes, who were interviewed by the Immigrants' Protective League, was four dollars and a half a week for the first position which they had been able to secure in Chicago. It often takes a girl several weeks to find her first place. During this period of looking for work the immigrant girl is subjected to great dangers. It is at such times that immigrants often exhibit symptoms of that type of disordered mind which alienists pronounce "due to conflict through poor adaptation." I have known several immigrant young men as well as girls who became deranged during the first year of life in America. A young Russian who came to Chicago in the hope of obtaining the freedom and self-development denied him at home, after three months of bitter disillusionment, with no work and insufficient food, was sent to the hospital for the insane. He only recovered after a group of his young countrymen devotedly went to see him each week with promises of work, the companionship at last establishing a sense of unbroken association. I also recall a Polish girl who became utterly distraught after weeks of sleeplessness and anxiety because she could not repay fifty dollars which she had borrowed from a countryman in Chicago for the purpose of bringing her sister to America. Her case was declared hopeless, but when the creditor made reassuring visits to the patient she began to mend and now, five years later, is not only free from debt, but has brought over the rest of the family, whose united earnings are slowly paying for a house and lot. Psychiatry is demonstrating the after-effects of fear upon the minds of children, but little has yet been done to show how far that fear of the future, arising from economic insecurity in the midst of new surroundings, has superinduced insanity among newly arrived immigrants. Such a state of nervous bewilderment and fright, added to that sense of expectation which youth always carries into new surroundings, often makes it easy to exploit the virtue of an immigrant girl. It goes without saying that she is almost always exploited industrially. A Russian girl recently took a place in a Chicago clothing factory at twenty cents a day, without in the least knowing that she was undercutting the wages of even that ill-paid industry. This girl rented a room for a dollar a week and all that she had to eat was given her by a friend in the same lodging house, who shared her own scanty fare with the newcomer.

In the clothing industry trade unionism has already established a minimum wage limit for thousands of women who are receiving the protection and discipline of trade organization and responding to the tonic of self-help. Low wages will doubtless in time be modified by Minimum Wage Boards representing the government's stake in industry, such as have been in successful operation for many years in certain British colonies and are now being instituted in England itself. As yet Massachusetts is the only state which has appointed a special commission to consider this establishment for America, although the Industrial Commission of Wisconsin is empowered to investigate wages and their effect upon the standard of living.

Anyone who has lived among working people has been surprised at the docility with which grown-up children give all of their earnings to their parents. This is, of course, especially true of the daughters. The fifth volume of the governmental report upon "Women and Child Wage Earners in the United States," quoted earlier, gives eighty-four per cent. as the proportion of working girls who turn in all of their wages to the family fund. In most cases this is done voluntarily and cheerfully, but in many instances it is as if the tradition of woman's dependence upon her family for support held long after the actual fact had changed, or as if the tyranny established through generations when daughters could be starved into submission to a father's will, continued even after the rôles had changed, and the wages of the girl child supported a broken and dissolute father.

An over-restrained girl, from whom so much is exacted, will sometimes begin to deceive her family by failing to tell them when she has had a raise in her wages. She will habitually keep the extra amount for herself, as she will any overtime pay which she may receive. All such money is invariably spent upon her own clothing, which she, of course, cannot wear at home, but which gives her great satisfaction upon the streets.

The girl of the crowded tenements has no room in which to receive her friends or to read the books through which she shares the lives of assorted heroines, or, better still, dreams of them as of herself. Even if the living-room is not full of boarders or children or washing, it is comfortable neither for receiving friends nor for reading, and she finds upon the street her entire social field; the shop windows with their desirable garments hastily clothe her heroines as they travel the old roads of romance, the street cars rumbling noisily by suggest a delectable somewhere far away, and the young men who pass offer possibilities of the most delightful acquaintance. It is not astonishing that she insists upon clothing which conforms to the ideals of this all-absorbing street and that she will unhesitatingly deceive an uncomprehending family which does not recognize its importance.

One such girl had for two years earned money for clothing by filling regular appointments in a disreputable saloon between the hours of six and half-past seven in the evening. With this money earned almost daily she bought the clothes of her heart's desire, keeping them with the saloon-keeper's wife. She demurely returned to her family for supper in her shabby working clothes and presented her mother with her unopened pay envelope every Saturday night. She began this life at the age of fourteen after her Polish mother had beaten her because she had "elbowed" the sleeves and "cut out" the neck of her ungainly calico gown in a vain attempt to make it look "American." Her mother, who had so conscientiously punished a daughter who was "too crazy for clothes," could never of course comprehend how dangerous a combination is the girl with an unsatisfied love for finery and the opportunities for illicit earning afforded on the street. Yet many sad cases may be traced to such lack of comprehension. Charles Booth states that in England a large proportion of parents belonging to the working and even lower middle classes, are unacquainted with the nature of the lives led by their own daughters, a result doubtless of the early freedom of the street accorded city children. Too often the mothers themselves are totally ignorant of covert dangers. A few days ago I held in my hand a pathetic little pile of letters written by a desperate young girl of fifteen before she attempted to commit suicide. These letters were addressed to her lover, her girl friends, and to the head of the rescue home, but none to her mother towards whom she felt a bitter resentment "because she did not warn me." The poor mother after the death of her husband had gone to live with a married daughter, but as the son-in-law would not "take in two" she had told the youngest daughter, who had already worked for a year as an apprentice in a dressmaking establishment, that she must find a place to live with one of her girl friends. The poor child had found this impossible, and three days after the breaking up of her home she had fallen a victim to a white slave trafficker, who had treated her most cruelly and subjected her to unspeakable indignities. It was only when her "protector" left the city, frightened by the unwonted activity of the police, due to a wave of reform, that she found her way to the rescue home, and in less than five months after the death of her father she had purchased carbolic acid and deliberately "courted death for the nameless child" and herself.

Another experience during which a girl faces a peculiar danger is when she has lost one "job" and is looking for another. Naturally she loses her place in the slack season and pursues her search at the very moment when positions are hardest to find, and her un-employment is therefore most prolonged. Perhaps nothing in our social order is so unorganized and inchoate as our method, or rather lack of method, of placing young people in industry. This is obvious from the point of view of their first positions when they leave school at the unstable age of fourteen, or from the innumerable places they hold later, often as high as ten a year, when they are dismissed or change voluntarily through sheer restlessness. Here again a girl's difficulty is often increased by the lack of sympathy and understanding on the part of her parents. A girl is often afraid to say that she has lost her place and pretends to go to work each morning while she is looking for a new one; she postpones telling them at home day by day, growing more frantic as the usual pay-day approaches. Some girls borrow from loan sharks in order to take the customary wages to their parents, others fall victims to unscrupulous employment agencies in their eagerness to take the first thing offered.

The majority of these girls answer the advertisements in the daily papers as affording the cheapest and safest way to secure a position. These out-of-work girls are found, sometimes as many as forty or fifty at a time, in the rest rooms of the department stores, waiting for the new edition of the newspapers after they have been the rounds of the morning advertisements and have found nothing.

Of course such a possible field as these rest rooms is not overlooked by the procurer, who finds it very easy to establish friendly relations through the offer of the latest edition of the newspaper. Even pennies are precious to a girl out of work and she is also easily grateful to anyone who expresses an interest in her plight and tells her of a position. Two representatives of the Juvenile Protective Association of Chicago, during a period of three weeks, arrested and convicted seventeen men and three women who were plying their trades in the rest rooms of nine department stores. The managers were greatly concerned over this exposure and immediately arranged both for more intelligent matrons and greater vigilance. One of the less scrupulous stores voluntarily gave up a method of advertising carried on in the rest room itself where a demonstrator from "the beauty counter" made up the faces of the patrons of the rest room with the powder and paint procurable in her department below. The out-of-work girls especially availed themselves of this privilege and hoped that their search would be easier when their pale, woe-begone faces were "made beautiful." The poor girls could not know that a face thus made up enormously increased their risks.

A number of girls also came early in the morning as soon as the rest rooms were open. They washed their faces and arranged their hair and then settled to sleep in the largest and easiest chairs the room afforded. Some of these were out-of-work girls also determined to take home their wages at the end of the week, each pretending to her mother that she had spent the night with a girl friend and was working all day as usual. How much of this deception is due to parental tyranny and how much to a sense of responsibility for younger children or invalids, it is impossible to estimate until the number of such recorded cases is much larger. Certain it is that the long habit of obedience, as well as the feeling of family obligation established from childhood, is often utilized by the white slave trafficker.

Difficult as is the position of the girl out of work when her family is exigent and uncomprehending, she has incomparably more protection than the girl who is living in the city without home ties. Such girls form sixteen per cent. of the working women of Chicago. With absolutely every penny of their meagre wages consumed in their inadequate living, they are totally unable to save money. That loneliness and detachment which the city tends to breed in its inhabitants is easily intensified in such a girl into isolation and a desolating feeling of belonging nowhere. All youth resents the sense of the enormity of the universe in relation to the insignificance of the individual life, and youth, with that intense self-consciousness which makes each young person the very centre of all emotional experience, broods over this as no older person can possibly do. At such moments a black oppression, the instinctive fear of solitude, will send a lonely girl restlessly to walk the streets even when she is "too tired to stand," and when her desire for companionship in itself constitutes a grave danger. Such a girl living in a rented room is usually without any place in which to properly receive callers. An investigation was recently made in Kansas City of 411 lodging-houses in which young girls were living; less than 30 per cent. were found with a parlor in which guests might be received. Many girls quite innocently permit young men to call upon them in their bedrooms, pitifully disguised as "sitting-rooms," but the danger is obvious, and the standards of the girl gradually become lowered.

Certainly during the trying times when a girl is out of work she should have much more intelligent help than is at present extended to her; she should be able to avail herself of the state employment agencies much more than is now possible, and the work of the newly established vocational bureaus should be enormously extended.

When once we are in earnest about the abolition of the social evil, society will find that it must study industry from the point of view of the producer in a sense which has never been done before. Such a study with reference to industrial legislation will ally itself on one hand with the trades-union movement, which insists upon a living wage and shorter hours for the workers, and also upon an opportunity for self-direction, and on the other hand with the efficiency movement, which would refrain from over-fatiguing an operator as it would from over-speeding a machine. In addition to legislative enactment and the historic trade-union effort, the feebler and newer movement on the part of the employers is being reinforced by the welfare secretary, who is not only devising recreational and educational plans, but is placing before the employer much disturbing information upon the cost of living in relation to the pitiful wages of working girls. Certainly employers are growing ashamed to use the worn-out, hypocritical pretence of employing only the girl "protected by home influences" as a device for reducing wages. Help may also come from the consumers, for an increasing number of them, with compunctions in regard to tempted young employees, are not only unwilling to purchase from the employer who underpays his girls and thus to share his guilt, but are striving in divers ways to modify existing conditions.

As working women enter fresh fields of labor which ever open up anew as the old fields are submerged behind them, society must endeavor to speedily protect them by an amelioration of the economic conditions which are now so unnecessarily harsh and dangerous to health and morals. The world-wide movement for establishing governmental control of industrial conditions is especially concerned for working women. Fourteen of the European countries prohibit all night work for women and almost every civilized country in the world is considering the number of hours and the character of work in which women may be permitted to safely engage.

Although amelioration comes about so slowly that many young girls are sacrificed each year under conditions which could so easily and reasonably be changed, nevertheless it is apparently better to overcome the dangers in this new and freer life, which modern industry has opened to women, than it is to attempt to retreat into the domestic industry of the past; for all statistics of prostitution give the largest number of recruits for this life as coming from domestic service and the second largest number from girls who live at home with no definite occupation whatever. Therefore, although in the economic aspect of the social evil more than in any other, do we find ground for despair, at the same time we discern, as nowhere else, the young girl's stubborn power of resistance. Nevertheless, the most superficial survey of her surroundings shows the necessity for ameliorating, as rapidly as possible, the harsh economic conditions which now environ her.

That steadily increasing function of the state by which it seeks to protect its workers from their own weakness and degradation, and insists that the livelihood of the manual laborer shall not be beaten down below the level of efficient citizenship, assumes new forms almost daily. From the human as well as the economic standpoint there is an obligation resting upon the state to discover how many victims of the white slave traffic are the result of social neglect, remedial incapacity, and the lack of industrial safeguards, and how far discontinuous employment and non-employment are factors in the breeding of discouragement and despair.

Is it because our modern industrialism is so new that we have been slow to connect it with the poverty and vice all about us? The socialists talk constantly of the relation of economic law to destitution and point out the connection between industrial maladjustment and individual wrongdoing, but certainly the study of social conditions, the obligation to eradicate vice, cannot belong to one political party or to one economic school. It must be recognized as a solemn obligation of existing governments, and society must realize that economic conditions can only be made more righteous and more human by the unceasing devotion of generations of men.

Chapter IV
Moral Education and Legal Protection of Children

No great wrong has ever arisen more clearly to the social consciousness of a generation than has that of commercialized vice in the consciousness of ours, and that we are so slow to act is simply another evidence that human nature has a curious power of callous indifference towards evils which have been so entrenched that they seem part of that which has always been. Educators of course share this attitude; at moments they seem to intensify it, although at last an educational movement in the direction of sex hygiene is beginning in the schools and colleges. Primary schools strive to satisfy the child's first questionings regarding the beginnings of human life and approach the subject through simple biological instruction which at least places this knowledge on a par with other natural facts. Such teaching is an enormous advance for the children whose curiosity would otherwise have been satisfied from poisonous sources and who would have learned of simple physiological matters from such secret undercurrents of corrupt knowledge as to have forever perverted their minds. Yet this first direct step towards an adequate educational approach to this subject has been surprisingly difficult owing to the self-consciousness of grown-up people; for while the children receive the teaching quite simply, their parents often take alarm. Doubtless co-operation with parents will be necessary before the subject can fall into its proper place in the schools. In Chicago, the largest women's club in the city has established normal courses in sex hygiene attended both by teachers and mothers, the National and State Federations of Women's Clubs are gradually preparing thousands of women throughout America for fuller co-operation with the schools in this difficult matter. In this, as in so many other educational movements, Germany has led the way. Two publications are issued monthly in Berlin, which promote not only more effective legislation but more adequate instruction in the schools on this basic subject. These journals are supported by men and women anxious for light for the sake of their children. Some of them were first stirred to action by Wedekind's powerful drama "The Awakening of Spring," which, with Teutonic grimness, thrusts over the footlights the lesson that death and degradation may be the fate of a group of gifted school-children, because of the cowardly reticence of their parents.

A year ago the Bishop of London gathered together a number of influential people and laid before them his convictions that the root of the social evil lay in so-called "parental modesty," and that in the quickening of the parental conscience lay the hope for the "lifting up of England's moral tone which has for so long been the despair of England's foremost men."

In America the eighth year-book of the National Society for the Scientific Study of Education treats of this important subject with great ability, massing the agencies and methods in impressive array. Many other educational journals and organized societies could be cited as expressing a new conscience in regard to this world-old evil. The expert educational opinion which they represent is practically agreed that for older children the instruction should not be confined to biology and hygiene, but may come quite naturally in history and literature, which record and portray the havoc wrought by the sexual instinct when uncontrolled, and also show that, when directed and spiritualized, it has become an inspiration to the loftiest devotions and sacrifices. The youth thus taught sees this primal instinct not only as an essential to the continuance of the race, but also, when it is transmuted to the highest ends, as a fundamental factor in social progress. The entire subject is broadened out in his mind as he learns that his own struggle is a common experience. He is able to make his own interpretations and to combat the crude inferences of his patronizing companions. After all, no young person will be able to control his impulses and to save himself from the grosser temptations, unless he has been put under the sway of nobler influences. Perhaps we have yet to learn that the inhibitions of character as well as its reinforcements come most readily through idealistic motives.

Certainly all the great religions of the world have recognized youth's need of spiritual help during the trying years of adolescence. The ceremonies of the earliest religions deal with this instinct almost to the exclusion of others, and all later religions attempt to provide the youth with shadowy weapons for the struggle which lies ahead of him, for the wise men in every age have known that only the power of the spirit can overcome the lusts of the flesh. In spite of this educational advance, courses of study in many public and private schools are still prepared exactly as if educators had never known that at fifteen or sixteen years of age, the will power being still weak, the bodily desires are keen and insistent. The head master of Eton, Mr. Lyttleton, who has given much thought to this gap in the education of youth says, "The certain result of leaving an enormous majority of boys unguided and uninstructed in a matter where their strongest passions are concerned, is that they grow up to judge of all questions connected with it, from a purely selfish point of view." He contends that this selfishness is due to the fact that any single suggestion or hint which boys receive on the subject comes from other boys or young men who are under the same potent influences of ignorance, curiosity and the claims of self. No wholesome counter-balance of knowledge is given, no attempt is made to invest the subject with dignity or to place it in relation to the welfare of others and to universal law. Mr. Lyttleton contends that this alone can explain the peculiarly brutal attitude towards "outcast" women which is a sustained cruelty to be discerned in no other relation of English life. To quote him again: "But when the victims of man's cruelty are not birds or beasts but our own countrywomen, doomed by the hundred thousand to a life of unutterable shame and hopeless misery, then and then only the general average tone of young men becomes hard and brutally callous or frivolous with a kind of coarse frivolity not exhibited in relation to any other form of human suffering." At the present moment thousands of young people in our great cities possess no other knowledge of this grave social evil which may at any moment become a dangerous personal menace, save what is imparted to them in this brutal flippant spirit. It has been said that the child growing up in the midst of civilization receives from its parents and teachers something of the accumulated experience of the world on all other subjects save upon that of sex. On this one subject alone each generation learns little from its predecessors.

An educator has lately pointed out that it is an old lure of vice to pretend that it alone deals with manliness and reality, and he complains that it is always difficult to convince youth that the higher planes of life contain anything but chilly sentiments. He contends that young people are therefore prone to receive moralizing and admonitions with polite attention, but when it comes to action, they carefully observe the life about them in order to conduct themselves in such wise as to be part of the really desirable world inhabited by men of affairs. Owing to this attitude, many young people living in our cities at the present moment have failed to apprehend the admonitions of religion and have never responded to its inner control. It is as if the impact of the world had stunned their spiritual natures, and as if this had occurred at the very time that a most dangerous experiment is being tried. The public gaieties formerly allowed in Catholic countries where young people were restrained by the confessional, are now permitted in cities where this restraint is altogether unknown to thousands of young people, and only faintly and traditionally operative upon thousands of others. The puritanical history of American cities assumes that these gaieties are forbidden, and that the streets are sober and decorous for conscientious young men and women who need no external protection. This ungrounded assumption, united to the fact that no adult has the confidence of these young people, who are constantly subjected to a multitude of imaginative impressions, is almost certain to result disastrously.

The social relationships in a modern city are so hastily made and often so superficial, that the old human restraints of public opinion, long sustained in smaller communities, have also broken down. Thousands of young men and women in every great city have received none of the lessons in self-control which even savage tribes imparted to their children when they taught them to master their appetites as well as their emotions. These young people are perhaps further from all community restraint and genuine social control than the youth of the community have ever been in the long history of civilization. Certainly only the modern city has offered at one and the same time every possible stimulation for the lower nature and every opportunity for secret vice. Educators apparently forget that this unrestrained stimulation of young people, so characteristic of our cities, although developing very rapidly, is of recent origin, and that we have not yet seen the outcome. The present education of the average young man has given him only the most unreal protection against the temptations of the city. Schoolboys are subjected to many lures from without just at the moment when they are filled with an inner tumult which utterly bewilders them and concerning which no one has instructed them save in terms of empty precept and unintelligible warning.

We are authoritatively told that the physical difficulties are enormously increased by uncontrolled or perverted imaginations, and all sound advice to young men in regard to this subject emphasizes a clean mind, exhorts an imagination kept free from sensuality and insists upon days filled with wholesome athletic interests. We allow this régime to be exactly reversed for thousands of young people living in the most crowded and most unwholesome parts of the city. Not only does the stage in its advertisements exhibit all the allurements of sex to such an extent that a play without a "love interest" is considered foredoomed to failure, but the novels which form the sole reading of thousands of young men and girls deal only with the course of true or simulated love, resulting in a rose-colored marriage, or in variegated misfortunes.

Often the only recreation possible for young men and young women together is dancing, in which it is always easy to transgress the proprieties. In many public dance halls, however, improprieties are deliberately fostered. The waltzes and two-steps are purposely slow, the couples leaning heavily on each other barely move across the floor, all the jollity and bracing exercise of the peasant dance is eliminated, as is all the careful decorum of the formal dance. The efforts to obtain pleasure or to feed the imagination are thus converged upon the senses which it is already difficult for young people to understand and to control. It is therefore not remarkable that in certain parts of the city groups of idle young men are found whose evil imaginations have actually inhibited their power for normal living. On the streets or in the pool-rooms where they congregate their conversation, their tales of adventure, their remarks upon women who pass by, all reveal that they have been caught in the toils of an instinct so powerful and primal that when left without direction it can easily overwhelm its possessor and swamp his faculties. These young men, who do no regular work, who expect to be supported by their mothers and sisters and to get money for the shows and theatres by any sort of disreputable undertaking, are in excellent training for the life of the procurer, and it is from such groups that they are recruited. There is almost a system of apprenticeship, for boys when very small act as "look-outs" and are later utilized to make acquaintances with girls in order to introduce them to professionals. From this they gradually learn the method of procuring girls and at last do an independent business. If one boy is successful in such a life, throughout his acquaintance runs the rumor that a girl is an asset that will bring a larger return than can possibly be earned in hard-working ways. Could the imaginations of these young men have been controlled and cultivated, could the desire for adventure have been directed into wholesome channels, could these idle boys have been taught that, so far from being manly they were losing all virility, could higher interests have been aroused and standards given them in relation to this one aspect of life, the entire situation of commercialized vice would be a different thing.

The girls with a desire for adventure seem confined to this one dubious outlet even more than the boys, although there are only one-eighth as many delinquent girls as boys brought into the juvenile court in Chicago, the charge against the girls in almost every instance involves a loss of chastity. One of them who was vainly endeavoring to formulate the causes of her downfall, concentrated them all in the single statement that she wanted the other girls to know that she too was a "good Indian." Such a girl, while she is not an actual member of a gang of boys, is often attached to one by so many loyalties and friendships that she will seldom testify against a member, even when she has been injured by him. She also depends upon the gang when she requires bail in the police court or the protection that comes from political influence, and she is often very proud of her quasi-membership. The little girls brought into the juvenile court are usually daughters of those poorest immigrant families living in the worst type of city tenements, who are frequently forced to take boarders in order to pay the rent. A surprising number of little girls have first become involved in wrong-doing through the men of their own households. A recent inquiry among 130 girls living in a sordid red light district disclosed the fact that a majority of them had thus been victimized and the wrong had come to them so early that they had been despoiled at an average age of eight years. Looking upon the forlorn little creatures, who are often brought into the Chicago juvenile court to testify against their own relatives, one is seized with that curious compunction Goethe expressed in the now hackneyed line from "Mignon:"

"Was hat Man dir, du armes Kind, gethan?"

One is also inclined to reproach educators for neglecting to give children instruction in play when one sees the unregulated amusement parks which are apparently so dangerous to little girls twelve or fourteen years old. Because they are childishly eager for amusement and totally unable to pay for a ride on the scenic railway or for a ticket to an entertainment, these disappointed children easily accept many favors from the young men who are standing near the entrances for the express purpose of ruining them. The hideous reward which is demanded from them later in the evening, after they have enjoyed the many "treats" which the amusement park offers, apparently seems of little moment. Their childish minds are filled with the memory of the lurid pleasures to the oblivion of the later experience, and they eagerly tell their companions of this possibility "of getting in to all the shows." These poor little girls pass unnoticed amidst a crowd of honest people seeking recreation after a long day's work, groups of older girls walking and talking gaily with young men of their acquaintance, and happy children holding their parents' hands. This cruel exploitation of the childish eagerness for pleasure is, of course, possible only among a certain type of forlorn city children who are totally without standards and into whose colorless lives a visit to the amusement park brings the acme of delirious excitement. It is possible that these children are the inevitable product of city life; in Paris, little girls at local fêtes wishing to ride on the hobby horse frequently buy the privilege at a fearful price from the man directing the machinery, and a physician connected with the New York Society for the Prevention of Cruelty to Children writes: "It is horribly pathetic to learn how far a nickel or a quarter will go towards purchasing the virtue of these children."

The home environment of such children has been similar to that of many others who come to grief through the five-cent theatres. These eager little people, to whom life has offered few pleasures, crowd around the door hoping to be taken in by some kind soul and, when they have been disappointed over and over again and the last performance is about to begin, a little girl may be induced unthinkingly to barter her chastity for an entrance fee.

Many children are also found who have been decoyed into their first wrong-doing through the temptation of the saloon, in spite of the fact that one of the earliest regulations in American cities for the protection of children was the prohibition of the sale of liquor to minors. That children may be easily demoralized by the influence of a disorderly saloon was demonstrated recently in Chicago; one of these saloons was so situated that the pupils of a public school were obliged to pass it and from the windows of the schoolhouse itself could see much of what was passing within the place. An effort was made by the Juvenile Protective Association to have it closed by the chief of police, but although he did so, it was opened again the following day. The Association then took up the matter with the mayor, who refused to interfere, insisting that the objectionable features had been eliminated. Through months of effort, during which time the practices of the place remained quite unchanged, one group after another of public-spirited citizens endeavored to suppress what had become a public scandal, only to find that the place was protected by brewery interests which were more powerful, both financially and politically, than themselves. At last, after a peculiarly flagrant case involving a little girl, the mothers of the neighborhood arranged a mass meeting in the schoolhouse itself, inviting local officials to be present. The mothers then produced a mass of testimony which demonstrated that dozens and hundreds of children had been directly or indirectly affected by the place whose removal they demanded. A meeting so full of genuine anxiety and righteous indignation could not well be disregarded, and the compulsory education department was at last able to obtain a revocation of the license. The many people who had so long tried to do away with this avowedly disreputable saloon received a fresh impression of the menace to children who became sophisticated by daily familiarity with vice. Yet many mothers, hard pressed by poverty, are obliged to rent houses next to vicious neighborhoods and their children very early become familiar with all the outer aspects of vice. Among them are the children of widows who make friends with their dubious neighbors during the long days while their mothers are at work. I recall two sisters in one family whose mother had moved her household to the borders of a Chicago segregated district, apparently without knowing the character of the neighborhood. The little sisters, twelve and eight years old, accepted many invitations from a kind neighbor to come into her house to see her pretty things. The older girl was delighted to be "made up" with powder and paint and to try on long dresses, while the little one who sang very prettily was taught some new songs, happily without understanding their import. The tired mother knew nothing of what the children did during her absence, until an honest neighbor who had seen the little girls going in and out of the district, interfered on their behalf. The frightened mother moved back to her old neighborhood which she had left in search of cheaper rent, her pious soul stirred to its depths that the children for whom she patiently worked day by day had so narrowly escaped destruction.

Who cannot recall at least one of these desperate mothers, overworked and harried through a long day, prolonged by the family washing and cooking into the evening, followed by a night of foreboding and misgiving because the very children for whom her life is sacrificed are slowly slipping away from her control and affection? Such a spectacle forces one into an agreement with Wells, that it is a "monstrous absurdity" that women who are "discharging their supreme social function, that of rearing children, should do it in their spare time, as it were, while they 'earn their living' by contributing some half-mechanical element to some trivial industrial product." Nevertheless, such a woman whose wages are fixed on the basis of individual subsistence, who is quite unable to earn a family wage, is still held by a legal obligation to support her children with the desperate penalty of forfeiture if she fail.

I can recall a very intelligent woman who long brought her children to the Hull House day nursery with this result at the end of ten years of devotion: the little girl is almost totally deaf owing to neglect following a case of measles, because her mother could not stop work in order to care for her; the youngest boy has lost a leg flipping cars; the oldest boy has twice been arrested for petty larceny; the twin boys, in spite of prolonged sojourns in the parental school, have been such habitual truants that their natural intelligence has secured little aid from education. Of the five children three are now in semi-penal institutions, supported by the state. It would not therefore have been so un-economical to have boarded them with their own mother, requiring a standard of nutrition and school attendance at least up to that national standard of nurture which the more advanced European governments are establishing.

The recent Illinois law, providing that the children of widows may be supported by public funds paid to the mother upon order of the juvenile court, will eventually restore a mother's care to these poor children; but in the meantime, even the poor mother who is receiving such aid, in her forced search for cheap rent may be continually led nearer to the notoriously evil districts. Many appeals made to landlords of disreputable houses in Chicago on behalf of the children living adjacent to such property have never secured a favorable response. It is apparently difficult for the average property owner to resist the high rents which houses in certain districts of the city can command if rented for purposes of vice. I recall two small frame houses identical in type and value standing side by side. One which belonged to a citizen without scruples was rented for $30.00 a month, the other belonging to a conscientious man was rented for $9.00 a month. The supposedly respectable landlords defend themselves behind the old sophistry: "If I did not rent my house for such a purpose, someone else would," and the more hardened ones say that "It is all in the line of business." Both of them are enormously helped by the secrecy surrounding the ownership of such houses, although it is hoped that the laws requiring the name of the owner and the agent of every multiple house to be posted in the public hallway will at length break through this protection, and the discovered landlords will then be obliged to pay the fine to which the law specifically states they have made themselves liable. In the meantime, women forced to find cheap rents are subjected to one more handicap in addition to the many others poverty places upon them. Such experiences may explain the fact that English figures show a very large proportion of widows and deserted women among the prostitutes in those large towns which maintain segregated districts.

The deprivation of a mother's care is most frequently experienced by the children of the poorest colored families who are often forced to live in disreputable neighborhoods because they literally cannot rent houses anywhere else. Both because rents are always high for colored people and because the colored mothers are obliged to support their children, seven times as many of them, in proportion to their entire number, as of the white mothers, the actual number of colored children neglected in the midst of temptation is abnormally large. So closely is child life founded upon the imitation of what it sees that the child who knows all evil is almost sure in the end to share it. Colored children seldom roam far from their own neighborhoods: in the public playgrounds, which are theoretically open to them, they are made so uncomfortable by the slights of other children that they learn to stay away, and, shut out from legitimate recreation, are all the more tempted by the careless, luxurious life of a vicious neighborhood. In addition to the colored girls who have thus from childhood grown familiar with the outer aspects of vice, are others who are sent into the district in the capacity of domestic servants by unscrupulous employment agencies who would not venture to thus treat a white girl. The community forces the very people who have confessedly the shortest history of social restraint, into a dangerous proximity with the vice districts of the city. This results, as might easily be predicted, in a very large number of colored girls entering a disreputable life. The negroes themselves believe that the basic cause for the high percentage of colored prostitutes is the recent enslavement of their race with its attendant unstable marriage and parental status, and point to thousands of slave sales that but two generations ago disrupted the negroes' attempts at family life. Knowing this as we do, it seems all the more unjustifiable that the nation which is responsible for the broken foundations of this family life should carelessly permit the negroes, making their first struggle towards a higher standard of domesticity, to be subjected to the most flagrant temptations which our civilization tolerates.

The imaginations of even very young children may easily be forced into sensual channels. A little girl, twelve years old, was one day brought to the psychopathic clinic connected with the Chicago juvenile court. She had been detained under police surveillance for more than a week, while baffled detectives had in vain tried to verify the statements she had made to her Sunday-school teacher in great detail of certain horrible experiences which had befallen her. For at least a week no one concerned had the remotest idea that the child was fabricating. The police thought that she had merely grown confused as to the places to which she had been "carried unconscious." The mother gave the first clue when she insisted that the child had never been away from her long enough to have had these experiences, but came directly home from school every afternoon for her tea, of which she habitually drank ten or twelve cups. The skilful questionings at the clinic, while clearly establishing the fact of a disordered mind, disclosed an astonishing knowledge of the habits of the underworld.

Even children who live in respectable neighborhoods and are guarded by careful parents so that their imaginations are not perverted, but only starved, constantly conduct a search for the magical and impossible which leads them into moral dangers. An astonishing number of them consult palmists, soothsayers, and fortune tellers. These dealers in futurity, who sell only love and riches, the latter often dependent upon the first, are sometimes in collusion with disreputable houses, and at the best make the path of normal living more difficult for their eager young patrons. There is something very pathetic in the sheepish, yet radiant, faces of the boy and girl, often together, who come out on the street from a dingy doorway which bears the palmist's sign of the spread-out hand. This remnant of primitive magic is all they can find with which to feed their eager imaginations, although the city offers libraries and galleries, crowned with man's later imaginative achievements. One hard-working girl of my acquaintance, told by a palmist that "diamonds were coming to her soon," afterwards accepted without a moment's hesitation a so-called diamond ring from a man whose improper attentions she had hitherto withstood.

In addition to these heedless young people, pulled into a sordid and vicious life through their very search for romance, are many little children ensnared by means of the most innocent playthings and pleasures of childhood. Perhaps one of the saddest aspects of the social evil as it exists to-day in the modern city, is the procuring of little girls who are too young to have received adequate instruction of any sort and whose natural safeguard of modesty and reserve has been broken down by the overcrowding of tenement house life. Any educator who has made a careful study of the children from the crowded districts is impressed with the numbers of them whose moral natures are apparently unawakened. While there are comparatively few of these non-moral children in any one neighborhood, in the entire city their number is far from negligible. Such children are used by disreputable people to invite their more normal playmates to house parties, which they attend again and again, lured by candy and fruit, until they gradually learn to trust the vicious hostess. The head of one such house, recently sent to the penitentiary upon charges brought against her by the Juvenile Protective Association, founded her large and successful business upon the activities of three or four little girls who, although they had gradually come to understand her purpose, were apparently so chained to her by the goodies and favors which they received, that they were quite indifferent to the fate of their little friends. Such children, when brought to the psychopathic clinic attached to the Chicago juvenile court, are sometimes found to have incipient epilepsy or other physical disabilities from which their conduct may be at least partially accounted for. Sometimes they come from respectable families, but more often from families where they have been mistreated and where dissolute parents have given them neither affection nor protection. Many of these children whose relatives have obviously contributed to their delinquency are helped by the enforcement of the adult delinquency law.

One looks upon these hardened little people with a sense of apology that educational forces have not been able to break into their first ignorance of life before it becomes toughened into insensibility, and one knows that, whatever may be done for them later, because of this early neglect, they will probably always remain impervious to the gentler aspects of life, as if vice seared their tender minds with red-hot irons. Our public-school education is so nearly universal, that if the entire body of the teachers seriously undertook to instruct all American youth in regard to this most important aspect of life, why should they not in time train their pupils to continence and self-direction, as they already discipline their minds with knowledge in regard to many other matters? Certainly the extreme youth of the victims of the white slave traffic, both boys and girls, places a great responsibility upon the educational forces of the community.

The state which supports the public school is also coming to the rescue of children through protective legislation. This is another illustration that the beginnings of social advance have often resulted from the efforts to defend the weakest and least-sheltered members of the community. The widespread movement which would protect children from premature labor, also prohibits them from engaging in occupations in which they are subjected to moral dangers. Several American cities have of late become much concerned over the temptations to which messenger boys, delivery boys, and newsboys are constantly subjected when their business takes them into vicious districts. The Chicago vice commission makes a plea for these "children of the night" that they shall be protected by law from those temptations which they are too young and too untrained to withstand. New York and Wisconsin are the only states which have raised the legal age of messenger boys employed late at night to twenty-one years. Under the inadequate sixteen-year limit, which regulates night work for children in Illinois, boys constantly come to grief through their familiarity with the social evil. One of these, a delicate boy of seventeen, had been put into the messenger service by his parents when their family doctor had recommended out-of-door work. Because he was well-bred and good-looking, he became especially popular with the inmates of disreputable houses. They gave him tips of a dollar and more when he returned from the errands which he had executed for them, such as buying candy, cocaine or morphine. He was inevitably flattered by their attentions and pleased with his own popularity. Although his mother knew that his duties as a messenger boy occasionally took him to disreputable houses, she fervently hoped his early training might keep him straight, but in the end realized the foolhardiness of subjecting an immature youth to these temptations. The vice commission report gives various detailed instances of similar experiences on the part of other lads, one of them being a high-school boy who was merely earning extra money as a messenger boy during the rush of Christmas week.

The regulations in Boston, New York, Cincinnati, Milwaukee and St. Louis for the safeguarding of these children may be but a forecast of the care which the city will at last learn to devise for youth under special temptations. Because the various efforts made in Chicago to obtain adequate legislation for the protection of street-trading children have not succeeded, incidents like the following have not only occurred once, but are constantly repeated: a pretty little girl, the only child of a widowed mother, sold newspapers after school hours from the time she was seven years old. Because her home was near a vicious neighborhood and because the people in the disreputable hotels seldom asked for change when they bought a paper and good-naturedly gave her many little presents, her mother permitted her to gain a clientele within the district on the ground that she was too young to understand what she might see. This continued familiarity, in spite of her mother's admonitions, not to talk to her customers, inevitably resulted in so vitiating the standard of the growing girl, that at the age of fourteen she became an inmate of one of the houses. A similar instance concerns three little girls who habitually sold gum in one of the segregated districts. Because they had repeatedly been turned away by kind-hearted policemen who felt that they ought not to be in such a neighborhood, each one of these children had obtained a special permit from the mayor of the city in order to protect herself from "police interference." While the mayor had no actual authority to issue such permits, naturally the piece of paper bearing his name, when displayed by a child, checked the activity of the police officer. The incident was but one more example of the old conflict between mistaken kindness to the individual child in need of money, and the enforcement of those regulations which may seem to work a temporary hardship upon one child, but save a hundred others from entering occupations which can only lead into blind alleys. Because such occupations inevitably result in increasing the number of unemployables, the educational system itself must be challenged.

A royal commission has recently recommended to the English Parliament that "the legally permissible hours for the employment of boys be shortened, that they be required to spend the hours so set free, in physical and technological training, that the manufacturing of the unemployable may cease." Certainly we are justified in demanding from our educational system, that the interest and capacity of each child leaving school to enter industry, shall have been studied with reference to the type of work he is about to undertake. When vocational bureaus are properly connected with all the public schools, a girl will have an intelligent point of departure into her working life, and a place to which she may turn in time of need, for help and advice through those long and dangerous periods of unemployment which are now so inimical to her character.

This same British commission divided all of the unemployed, the under-employed, and the unemployable as the results of three types of trades: first, the subsidized labor trades, wherein women and children are paid wages insufficient to maintain them at the required standard of health and industrial efficiency, so that their wages must be supplemented by relatives or charity; second, labor deteriorating trades, which have sapped the energy, the capacity, the character, of workers; third, bare subsistence trades, where the worker is forced to such a low level in his standard of life that he continually falls below self-support. We have many trades of these three types in America, all of them demanding the work of young and untrained girls. Yet, in spite of the obvious dangers surrounding every girl who enters one of them, little is done to guide the multitude of children who leave school prematurely each year into reasonable occupations.

Unquestionably the average American child has received a more expensive education than has yet been accorded to the child of any other nation. The girls working in department stores have been in the public schools on an average of eight years, while even the factory girls, who so often leave school from the lower grades, have yet averaged six and two-tenths years of education at the public expense, before they enter industrial life. Certainly the community that has accomplished so much could afford them help and oversight for six and a half years longer, which is the average length of time that a working girl is employed. The state might well undertake this, if only to secure its former investment and to save that investment from utter loss.

Our generation, said to have developed a new enthusiasm for the possibilities of child life, and to have put fresh meaning into the phrase "children's rights," may at last have the courage to insist upon a child's right to be well born and to start in life with its tiny body free from disease. Certainly allied to this new understanding of child life and a part of the same movement is the new science of eugenics with its recently appointed university professors. Its organized societies publish an ever-increasing mass of information as to that which constitutes the inheritance of well-born children. When this new science makes clear to the public that those diseases which are a direct outcome of the social evil are clearly responsible for race deterioration, effective indignation may at last be aroused, both against the preventable infant mortality for which these diseases are responsible, and against the ghastly fact that the survivors among these afflicted children infect their contemporaries and hand on the evil heritage to another generation. Public societies for the prevention of blindness are continually distributing information on the care of new-born children and may at length answer that old, confusing question "Did this man sin or his parents, that he was born blind?" Such knowledge is becoming more widespread every day and the rising interest in infant welfare must in time react upon the very existence of the social-evil itself.

This new public concern for the welfare of little children in certain American cities has resulted in a municipal milk supply; in many German cities, in free hospitals and nurseries. New York, Chicago, Boston and other large towns, employ hundreds of nurses each summer to instruct tenement-house mothers upon the care of little children. Doubtless all of this enthusiasm for the nurture of children will at last arouse public opinion in regard to the transmission of that one type of disease which thousands of them annually inherit, and which is directly traceable to the vicious living of their parents or grandparents. This slaughter of the innocents, this infliction of suffering upon the new-born, is so gratuitous and so unfair, that it is only a question of time until an outraged sense of justice shall be aroused on behalf of these children. But even before help comes through chivalric sentiments, governmental and municipal agencies will decline to spend the tax-payers' money for the relief of suffering infants, when by the exertion of the same authority they could easily provide against the possibility of the birth of a child so afflicted. It is obvious that the average tax-payer would be moved to demand the extermination of that form of vice which has been declared illegal, although it still flourishes by official connivance, did he once clearly apprehend that it is responsible for the existence of these diseases which cost him so dear. It is only his ignorance which makes him remain inert until each victim of the white slave traffic shall be avenged unto the third and fourth generation of them that bought her. It is quite possible that the tax-payer will himself contend that, as the state does not legalize a marriage without a license officially recorded, that the status of children may be clearly defined, so the state would need to go but one step further in the same direction, to insist upon health certificates from the applicant for a marriage license, that the health of future children might in a certain measure, be guaranteed. Whether or not this step may be predicted, the mere discussion of this matter in itself, is an indication of the changing public opinion, as is the fact that such legislation has already been enacted in two states, which are only now putting into action the recommendation made centuries ago by such social philosophers as Plato and Sir Thomas More. A sense of justice outraged by the wanton destruction of new-born children, may in time unite with that ardent tide of rising enthusiasm for the nurture of the young, until the old barriers of silence and inaction, behind which the social evil has so long intrenched itself, shall at last give way.

Certainly it will soon be found that the sentiment of pity, so recently aroused throughout the country on behalf of the victims of the white slave traffic, will be totally unable to afford them protection unless it becomes incorporated in government. It is possible that we are on the eve of a series of legislative enactments similar to those which resulted from the attempts to regulate child labor. Through the entire course of the last century, in that anticipation of coming changes which does so much to bring changes about, the friends of the children were steadily engaged in making a new state, from the first child labor law passed in the English parliament in 1803 to the final passage of the so-called children's charter in 1909. During the long century of transforming pity into political action there was created that social sympathy which has become one of the greatest forces in modern legislation, and to which we may confidently appeal in this new crusade against the social evil.

Another point of similarity to the child labor movement is obvious, for the friends of the children early found that they needed much statistical information and that the great problem of the would-be reformer is not so much overcoming actual opposition-the passing of time gradually does that for him-as obtaining and formulating accurate knowledge and fitting that knowledge into the trend of his time. From this point of view and upon the basis of what has already been accomplished for "the protection of minors," the many recent investigations which have revealed the extreme youth of the victims of the white slave traffic, should make legislation on their behalf all the more feasible. Certainly no reformer could ever more legitimately make an emotional appeal to the higher sensibility of the public.

In the rescue homes recently opened in Chicago by the White Slave Traffic Committee of the League of Cook County Clubs, the tender ages of the little girls who were brought there horrified the good clubwomen more than any other aspect of the situation. A number of the little inmates in the home wanted to play with dolls and several of them brought dolls of their own, which they had kept with them through all their vicissitudes. There is something literally heart-breaking in the thought of these little children who are ensnared and debauched when they are still young enough to have every right to protection and care. Quite recently I visited a home for semi-delinquent girls against each one of whom stood a grave charge involving the loss of her chastity. Upon each of the little white beds or on one of the stiff chairs standing by its side was a doll belonging to a delinquent owner still young enough to love and cherish this supreme toy of childhood. I had come to the home prepared to "lecture to the inmates." I remained to dress dolls with a handful of little girls who eagerly asked questions about the dolls I had once possessed in a childhood which seemed to them so remote. Looking at the little victims who supply the white slave trade, one is reminded of the burning words of Dr. Howard Kelly uttered in response to the demand that the social evil be legalized and its victims licensed. He says: "Where shall we look to recruit the ever-failing ranks of these poor creatures as they die yearly by the tens of thousands? Which of the little girls of our land shall we designate for this traffic? Mark their sweet innocence to-day as they run about in our streets and parks prattling and playing, ever busy about nothing; which of them shall we snatch as they approach maturity, to supply this foul mart?"

It is incomprehensible that a nation whose chief boast is its free public education, that a people always ready to respond to any moral or financial appeal made in the name of children, should permit this infamy against childhood to continue! Only the protection of all children from the menacing temptations which their youth is unable to withstand, will prevent some of them from falling victims to the white slave traffic; only when moral education is made effective and universal will there be hope for the actual abolition of commercialized vice. These are illustrations perhaps of that curious solidarity of which society is so rapidly becoming conscious.

Chapter V
Philanthropic Rescue and Prevention

There is no doubt that philanthropy often reflects and dramatizes the modern sensitiveness of the community in relation to a social wrong, because those engaged in the rescue of the victims are able to apprehend, through their daily experiences, many aspects of a recognized evil concerning which the public are ignorant and therefore indifferent. However ancient a wrong may be, in each generation it must become newly embodied in living people and the social custom into which it has hardened through the years, must be continued in individual lives. Unless the contemporaries of such unhappy individuals are touched to tenderness or stirred to indignation by the actual embodiments of the old wrong in their own generation, effective action cannot be secured.

The social evil has, on the whole, received less philanthropic effort than any other well-recognized menace to the community, largely because there is something peculiarly distasteful and distressing in personal acquaintance with its victims; a distaste and distress that sometimes leads to actual nervous collapse. A distinguished Englishman has recently written "that sober-minded people who, from motives of pity, have looked the hideous evil full in the face, have often asserted that nothing in their experience has seemed to threaten them so nearly with a loss of reason."

Nevertheless, this comparative lack of philanthropic effort is the more remarkable because the average age of the recruits to prostitution is between sixteen and eighteen years, the age at which girls are still minors under the law in respect to all matters of property. We allow a minor to determine for herself whether or not she will live this most abominable life, although if she resolve to be a thief she will, if possible, be apprehended and imprisoned; if she become a vagrant she will be restrained; even if she become a professional beggar, she will be interfered with; but the decision to lead this evil life, disastrous alike to herself and the community, although well known to the police, is openly permitted. If a man has seized upon a moment of weakness in a girl and obtained her consent, although she may thereafter be in dire need of help she is put outside all protection of the law. The courts assume that such a girl has deliberately decided for herself and that because she is not "of previous chaste life and character," she is lost to all decency. Yet every human being knows deep down in his heart that his own moral energy ebbs and flows, that he could not be judged fairly by his hours of defeat, and that after revealing moments of weakness, although shocked and frightened, he is the same human being, struggling as he did before. Nevertheless in some states, a little girl as young as ten years of age may make this irrevocable decision for herself.

Modern philanthropy, continually discovering new aspects of prostitution through the aid of economics, sanitary science, statistical research, and many other agencies, finds that this increase of knowledge inevitably leads it from the attempt to rescue the victims of white slavery to a consideration of the abolition of the monstrous wrong itself. At the present moment philanthropy is gradually impelled to a consideration of prostitution in relation to the welfare and the orderly existence of society itself. If the moral fire seems at times to be dying out of certain good old words, such as charity, it is filling with new warmth such words as social justice, which belong distinctively to our own time. It is also true that those for whom these words contain most of hope and warmth are those who have been long mindful of the old tasks and obligations, as if the great basic emotion of human compassion had more than held its own. Certainly the youth of many of the victims of the white slave traffic, and the helplessness of the older girls who find themselves caught in the grip of an enormous force which they cannot comprehend, make a most pitiful appeal. Philanthropy moreover discovers many young girls, who if they had not been rescued by protective agencies would have become permanent outcasts, although they would have entered a disreputable life through no fault of their own.

The illustrations in this chapter are all taken from the Juvenile Protective Association of Chicago in connection with its efforts to save girls from overwhelming temptation. Doubtless many other associations could offer equally convincing testimony, for in recent years the number of people to whom the very existence of the white slave traffic has become unendurable and who are determinedly working against it, has enormously increased.

A surprising number of country girls have been either brought to Chicago under false pretences, or have been decoyed into an evil life very soon after their arrival in the city. Mr. Clifford Roe estimates that more than half of the girls who have been recruited into a disreputable life in Chicago have come from the farms and smaller towns in Illinois and from neighboring states. This estimate is borne out by the records of Paris and other metropolitan cities in which it is universally estimated that a little less than one-third of the prostitutes found in them, at any given moment, are city born.

The experience of a pretty girl who came to the office of the Juvenile Protective Association, a year ago, is fairly typical of the argument many of these country girls offer in their own defense. This girl had been a hotel chambermaid in an Iowa town where many of the traveling patrons of the hotel had made love to her, one of them occasionally offering her protection if she would leave with him. At first she indignantly refused, but was at length convinced that the acceptance of such offers must be a very general practice and that, whatever might be the custom in the country, no one in a city made personal inquiries. She finally consented to accompany a young man to Seattle, both because she wanted to travel and because she was discouraged in her attempts to "be good." A few weeks later, when in Chicago, she had left the young man, acting from what she considered a point of honor, as his invitation had been limited to the journey which was now completed. Feeling too disgraced to go home and under the glamour of the life of idleness she had been leading, she had gone voluntarily into a disreputable house, in which the police had found her and sent her to the Association. She could not be persuaded to give up her plan, but consented to wait for a few days to "think it over." As she was leaving the office in company with a representative of the Association, they met the young man, who had been distractedly searching for her and had just discovered her whereabouts. She was married the very same day and of course the Association never saw her again.

From the point of view of the traffickers in white slaves, it is much cheaper and safer to procure country girls after they have reached the city. Such girls are in constant danger because they are much more easily secreted than girls procured from the city. A country girl entering a vicious life quickly feels the disgrace and soon becomes too broken-spirited and discouraged to make any effort to escape into the unknown city which she believes to be full of horrors similar to those she has already encountered. She desires above all things to deceive her family at home, often sending money to them regularly and writing letters describing a fictitious life of hard work. Perhaps the most flagrant case with which the Association ever dealt, was that of two young girls who had come to Chicago from a village in West Virginia, hoping to earn large wages in order to help their families. They arrived in the city penniless, having been robbed en route of their one slender purse. As they stood in the railway station, utterly bewildered, they were accosted by a young man who presented the advertising card of a boarding-house and offered to take them there. They quite innocently accepted his invitation, but an hour later, finding themselves in a locked room, they became frightened and realized they had been duped. Fortunately the two agile country girls had no difficulty in jumping from a second-story window, but upon the street they were of course much too frightened to speak to anyone again and wandered about for hours. The house from which they had escaped bore the sign "rooms to rent," and they therefore carefully avoided all houses whose placards offered shelter. Finally, when they were desperate with hunger, they went into a saloon for a "free lunch," not in the least realizing that they were expected to take a drink in order to receive it. A policeman, seeing two young girls in a saloon "without escort," arrested them and took them to the nearest station where they spent the night in a wretched cell.

At the hearing the next morning, where, much frightened, they gave a very incoherent account of their adventures, the judge fined them each fifteen dollars and costs, and as they were unable to pay the fine, they were ordered sent to the city prison. When they were escorted from the court room, another man approached them and offered to pay their fines if they would go with him. Frightened by their former experience, they stoutly declined his help, but were over-persuaded by his graphic portrayal of prison horrors and the disgrace that their imprisonment would bring upon "the folks at home." He also made clear that when they came out of prison, thirty days later, they would be no better off than they were now, save that they would have the added stigma of being jail-birds. The girls at last reluctantly consented to go with him, when a representative of the Juvenile Protective Association, who had followed them from the court room and had listened to the conversation, insisted upon the prompt arrest of the white slave trader. When the entire story, finally secured from the girls, was related to the judge, he reversed his decision, fined the man $100.00, which he was abundantly able to pay, and insisted that the girls be sent back to their mothers in Virginia. They were farmers' daughters, strong and capable of taking care of themselves in an environment that they understood, but in constant danger because of their ignorance of city life.

The methods employed to secure city girls must be much more subtle and complicated than those employed with the less sophisticated country girl. Although the city girl, once procured, is later allowed more freedom than is accorded either to a country girl or to an immigrant girl, every effort is made to demoralize her completely before she enters the life. Because she may, at any moment, escape into the city which she knows so well, it is necessary to obtain her inner consent. Those whose profession it is to procure girls for the white slave trade apparently find it possible to decoy and demoralize most easily that city girl whose need for recreation has led her to the disreputable public dance hall or other questionable places of amusement.

Gradually those philanthropic agencies that are endeavoring to be of service to the girls learn to know the dangers in these places. Many parents are utterly indifferent or ignorant of the pleasures that their children find for themselves. From the time these children were five years old, such parents were accustomed to see them take care of themselves on the street and at school, and it seems but natural that when the children are old enough to earn money, they should be able to find their own amusements.

The girls are attracted to the unregulated dance halls not only by a love of pleasure but by a sense of adventure, and it is in these places that they are most easily recruited for a vicious life. Unfortunately there are three hundred and twenty-eight public dance halls in Chicago, one hundred and ninety of them connect directly with saloons, while liquor is openly sold in most of the others. This consumption of liquor enormously increases the danger to young people. A girl after a long day's work is easily induced to believe that a drink will dispel her lassitude. There is plenty of time between the dances to persuade her, as the intermissions are long, fifteen to twenty minutes, and the dances short, occupying but four or five minutes; moreover the halls are hot and dusty and it is almost impossible to obtain a drink of water. Often the entire purpose of the dance hall, with its carefully arranged intermissions, is the selling of liquor to the people it has brought together. After the girl has begun to drink, the way of the procurer, who is often in league with the "spieler" who frequents the dance hall, is comparatively easy. He assumes one of two rôles, that of the sympathetic older man or that of the eager young lover. In the character of the former, he tells "the down-trodden working girl" that her wages are a mere pittance and that he can procure a better place for her with higher wages if she will trust him. He often makes allusions to the shabbiness or cheapness of her clothing and considers it "a shame that such a pretty girl cannot dress better." In the second rôle he apparently falls in love with her, tells of his rich parents, complaining that they want him to marry, "a society swell," but that he really prefers a working girl like herself. In either case he establishes friendly relations, exalted in the girl's mind, through the excitement of the liquor and the dance, into a new sense of intimate understanding and protection.

Later in the evening, she leaves the hall with him for a restaurant because, as he truthfully says, she is exhausted and in need of food. At the supper, however, she drinks much more, and it is not surprising that she is at last persuaded that it is too late to go home and in the end consents to spend the rest of the night in a nearby lodging house. Six young girls, each accompanied by a "spieler" from a dance hall, were recently followed to a chop suey restaurant and then to a lodging-house, which the police were instigated to raid and where the six girls, more or less intoxicated, were found. If no one rescues the girl after such an experience, she sometimes does not return home at all, or if she does, feels herself initiated into a new world where it is possible to obtain money at will, to easily secure the pleasures it brings, and she comes at length to consider herself superior to her less sophisticated companions. Of course this latter state of mind is untenable for any length of time and the girl is soon found openly leading a disreputable life.

The girls attending the cheap theatres and the vaudeville shows are most commonly approached through their vanity. They readily listen to the triumphs of a stage career, sure to be attained by such a "good looker," and a large number of them follow a young man to the woman with whom he is in partnership, under the promise of being introduced to a theatrical manager. There are also theatrical agencies in league with disreputable places, who advertise for pretty girls, promising large salaries. Such an agency operating with a well-known "near theatre" in the state capital was recently prosecuted in Chicago and its license revoked. In this connection the experience of two young English girls is not unusual. They were sisters possessed of an extraordinary skill in juggling, who were brought to this country by a relative acting as their manager. Although he exploited them for his own benefit for three years, paying them the most meager salaries and supplying them with the simplest living in the towns which they "toured," he had protected them from all immorality, and they had preserved the clean living of the family of acrobats to which they belonged. Last October, when appearing in San Francisco, the girls, then sixteen and seventeen years of age, demanded more pay than the dollar and twenty cents a week each had been receiving, representing the five shillings with which they had started from home. The manager, who had become discouraged with his American experience, refused to accede to their demands, gave them each a ticket for Chicago, and heartlessly turned them adrift. Arriving in the city, they quite naturally at once applied to a theatrical agency, through which they were sent to a disreputable house where a vaudeville program was given each night. Delighted that they had found work so quickly, they took the position in good faith. During the very first performance, however, they became frightened by the conduct of the girls who preceded them on the program and by the hilarity of the audience. They managed to escape from the dressing-room, where they were waiting their turn, and on the street appealed to the first policeman, who brought them to the Juvenile Protective Association. They were detained for several days as witnesses against the theatrical agency, entering into the legal prosecution with that characteristic British spirit which is ever ready to protest against an imposition, before they left the city with a travelling company, each on a weekly salary of twenty dollars.

The methods pursued on excursion boats are similar to those of the dance halls, in that decent girls are induced to drink quantities of liquor to which they are unaccustomed. On the high seas, liquor is sold usually in original packages, which enormously increases the amount consumed. It is not unusual to see a boy and girl drinking between them an entire bottle of whiskey. Some of these excursion boats carry five thousand people and in the easy breakdown of propriety which holiday-making often implies, and the absence of police, to which city young people are unaccustomed, the utmost freedom and license is often indulged in. Thus the lake excursions, one of the most delightful possibilities for recreation in Chicago, through lack of proper policing and through the sale of liquor, are made a menace to thousands of young people to whom they should be a great resource.

When a philanthropic association, with a knowledge of the commercial exploitation of youth's natural response to gay surroundings, attempts to substitute innocent recreation, it finds the undertaking most difficult. In Chicago the Juvenile Protective Association, after a thorough investigation of public dance halls, amusement parks, five-cent theatres, and excursion boats, is insisting upon more vigorous enforcement of the existing legislation, and is also urging further legal regulation; Kansas City has instituted a Department of Public Welfare with power to regulate places of amusement; a New York committee has established model dance halls; Milwaukee is urging the appointment of commissions on public recreation, while New York and Columbus have already created them.

Perhaps nothing in actual operation is more valuable than the small parks of Chicago in which the large halls are used every evening for dancing and where outdoor sports, swimming pools and gymnasiums daily attract thousands of young people. Unless cities make some such provision for their youth, those who sell the facilities for amusement in order to make a profit will continue to exploit the normal desire of all young people for recreation and pleasure. The city of Chicago contains at present eight hundred and fourteen thousand minors, all eager for pleasure. It is not surprising that commercial enterprise undertakes to supply this demand and that penny arcades, slot machines, candy stores, ice-cream parlors, moving-picture shows, skating rinks, cheap theatres and dance halls are trying to attract young people with every device known to modern advertising. Their promoters are, of course, careless of the moral effect upon their young customers if they can but secure their money. Until municipal provisions adequately meet this need, philanthropic and social organizations must be committed to the establishment of more adequate recreational facilities.

Although many dangers are encountered by the pleasure-loving girl who demands that each evening shall bring her some measure of recreation, a large number of girls meet with difficulties and temptations while soberly at work. Many of these tempted girls are newly-arrived immigrant girls between the ages of sixteen and twenty, who find their first work in hotels. Polish girls especially are utilized in hotel kitchens and laundries, and for the interminable scrubbing of halls and lobbies where a knowledge of the English language is not necessary, but where their peasant strength is in demand. The work is very heavy and fatiguing and until the Illinois law limited the work of women to ten hours a day, it often lasted late into the night. Even now the girls report themselves so tired that at the end of the day, they crowd into the dormitories and fall upon their beds undressed. When food and shelter is given them, their wages are from $14.00 to $18.00 a month, most of which is usually sent back to the old country, that the remaining members of the family may be brought to America. Such positions are surrounded by temptations of every sort. Even the hotel housekeepers, who are honestly trying to protect the girls, admit that it is impossible to do it adequately. One of these housekeepers recently said "that it takes a girl who knows the world to work in any hotel," and regretted that the sophisticated English-speaking girl who might protect herself, was unable to endure the hard work. She added that as soon as a girl learned English she promoted her from the laundry to the halls and from there to the position of chambermaid, but that the latter position was the most dangerous of all, as the girls were constantly exposed to insults from the guests. In the less respectable hotels these newly-arrived immigrant girls, inevitably seeing a great deal of the life of the underworld and the apparent ease with which money may be earned in illicit ways, find their first impression of the moral standards of life in America most bewildering. One young Polish girl had worked for two years in a down-town hotel, and had steadfastly resisted all improper advances even sometimes by the aid of her own powerful fist. She yielded at last to the suggestions of the life about her when she received a telegram from Ellis Island stating that her mother had arrived in New York, but was too ill to be sent on to Chicago. All of her money had gone for the steamer ticket and as the thought of her old country mother, ill and alone among strangers, was too much for her long fortitude, she made the best bargain possible with the head waiter whose importunities she had hitherto resisted, accepted the little purse the other Polish girls in the hotel collected for her and arrived in New York only to find that her mother had died the night before.

The simple obedience to parents on the part of these immigrant girls, working in hotels and restaurants, often miscarries pathetically. Their unspoiled human nature, not yet immune to the poisons of city life, when thrust into the midst of that unrelieved drudgery which lies at the foundation of all complex luxury, often results in the most fatal reactions. A young German woman, the proprietor of what is considered a successful "house" in the most notorious district in Chicago, traces her career directly to a desperate attempt to conform to the standard of "bringing home good wages" maintained by her numerous brothers and sisters. One requirement of her home was rigid: all money earned by a child must be paid into the family income until "legal age" was attained. The slightly neurotic, very pretty girl of seventeen heartily detested the dish-washing in a restaurant, which constituted her first place in America, and quite honestly declared that the heavy lifting was beyond her strength. Such insubordination was not tolerated at home, and every Saturday night when her meager wages, reduced by sick days "off," were compared with what the others brought in, she was regularly scolded, "sometimes slapped," by her parents, jeered at by her more vigorous sisters and bullied by her brothers. She tried to shorten her hours by doing "rush-work" as a waitress at noon, but she found this still beyond her strength, and worst of all, the pay of two dollars and a half insufficient to satisfy her mother. Confiding her troubles to the other waitresses, one of them good-naturedly told her how she could make money through appointments in a nearby disreputable hotel, and so take home an increased amount of money easily called "a raise in wages." So strong was the habit of obedience, that the girl continued to take money home every Saturday night until her eighteenth birthday, in spite of the fact that she gave up the restaurant in less than six weeks after her first experience. Although all of this happened ten years ago and the German mother is long since dead, the daughter bitterly ended the story with the infamous hope that "the old lady was now suffering the torments of the lost, for making me what I am." Such a girl was subjected to temptations to which society has no right to expose her.

A dangerous cynicism regarding the value of virtue, a cynicism never so unlovely as in the young, sometimes seizes a girl who, because of long hours and overwork, has been unable to preserve either her health or spirits and has lost all measure of joy in life. That this premature cynicism may be traced to an unhappy and narrow childhood is suggested by the fact that a large number of these girls come from families in which there has been little affection and the poor substitute of parental tyranny.

A young Italian girl who earned four dollars a week in a tailor shop pulling out hastings, when asked why she wore a heavy woolen gown on one of the hottest days of last summer, replied that she was obliged to earn money for her clothes by scrubbing for the neighbors after hours; that she had found no such work lately and that her father would not allow her anything from her wages for clothes or for carfare, because he was buying a house.

This parental control sometimes exercised in order to secure all of a daughter's wages, is often established with the best intentions in the world. I recall a French dressmaker who had frugally supported her two daughters until they were of working age, when she quite naturally expected them to conform to the careful habits of living necessary during her narrow years. In order to save carfare, she required her daughters to walk a long distance to the department store in which one was a bundle wrapper and the other a clerk at the ribbon counter. They dressed in black as being the most economical color and a penny spent in pleasure was never permitted. One day a young man who was buying ribbon from the older girl gave her a yard with the remark that she was much too young and pretty to be so somberly dressed. She wore the ribbon at work, never of course at home, but it opened a vista of delightful possibilities and she eagerly accepted a pair of gloves the following week from the same young man, who afterwards asked her to dine with him. This was the beginning of a winter of surreptitious pleasures on the part of the two sisters. They were shrewd enough never to be out later than ten o'clock and always brought home so-called overtime pay to their mother. In the spring the older girl, finding herself worn out by her dissipation and having resolved to cut loose from her home, came to the office of the Juvenile Protective Association to ask help for her younger sister. It was discovered that the mother was totally ignorant of the semi-professional life her daughters had been leading. She reiterated over and over again that she had always guarded them carefully and had given them no money to spend. It took months of constant visiting on the part of a representative of the Association before she was finally persuaded to treat the younger girl more generously.

While this family is fairly typical of those in which over-restraint is due to the lack of under-standing, it is true that in most cases the family tyranny is exercised by an old-country father in an honest attempt to guard his daughter against the dangers of a new world. The worst instances, however, are those in which the father has fallen into the evil ways of drink, and not only demands all of his daughter's wages, but treats her with great brutality when those wages fall below his expectations. Many such daughters have come to grief because they have been afraid to go home at night when their wage envelopes contained less than usual, either because a new system of piece work had reduced the amount or because, in a moment of weakness, they had taken out five cents with which to attend a show, or ten cents for the much-desired pleasure of riding back and forth the full length of an elevated railroad, or because they had in a thirsty moment taken out a nickel for a drink of soda water, or worst of all, had fallen a victim to the installment plan of buying a new hat or a pair of shoes. These girls, in their fear of beatings and scoldings, although they are sure of shelter and food and often have a mother who is trying to protect them from domestic storms, have almost no money for clothing, and are inevitably subject to moments of sheer revolt, their rebellion intensified by the fact that after a girl earns her own money and is accustomed to come and go upon the streets as an independent wage earner, she finds unsympathetic control much harder to bear than do schoolgirls of the same age who have never broken the habits of their childhood and are still economically dependent upon their parents.

In spite of the fact that domestic service is always suggested by the average woman as an alternative for the working girl whose life is beset with danger, the federal report on "Women and Child Wage Earners in the United States" gives the occupation of the majority of girls who go wrong as that of domestic service, and in this it confirms the experience of every matron in a rescue home and the statistics in the maternity wards of the public hospitals. The report suggests that the danger comes from the general conditions of work: "These general conditions are the loneliness of the life, the lack of opportunities for making friends and securing recreation and amusement in safe surroundings, the monotonous and uninteresting nature of the work done as these untrained girls do it, the lack of external stimulus to pride and self-respect, and the absolutely unguarded state of the girl, except when directly under the eye of her mistress."

In addition to these reasons, the girls realize that the opportunities for marriage are less in domestic service than in other occupations, and after all, the great business of youth is securing a mate, as the young instinctively understand. Unlike the working girl who lives at home and constantly meets young men of her own neighborhood and factory life, the girl in domestic service is brought into contact with very few possible lovers. Even the men of her former acquaintance, however slightly Americanized, do not like to call on a girl in someone else's kitchen, and find the entire situation embarrassing. The girl's mistress knows that for her own daughters mutual interests and recreation are the natural foundations for friendship with young men, which may or may not lead to marriage, but which is the prerogative of every young girl. The mistress does not, however, apply this worldly wisdom to the maid in her service, only eighteen or nineteen years old, utterly dependent upon her for social life save during one afternoon and evening a week.

The majority of domestics are employed in families where there is only one, and the tired and dispirited girl, often without a taste for reading, spends many lonely hours. That most fundamental and powerful of all instincts has therefore no chance for diffusion or social expression and like all confined forces, tends to degenerate. The girl is equipped with no weapon with which to contend with those poisonous images which arise from the senses, and these images, bred of fatigue and loneliness, make a girl an easy victim. This is especially true of the colored girl, who because of her traditions, is often treated with so little respect by white men, that she is constantly subjected to insult. Even the colored servants in the New York apartment houses, who live at home and thus avoid this loneliness, because their hours extend until nine in the evening, are obliged to seek their pleasures late into the night. American cities offer occupation to more colored women than colored men and this surplus of women, in some cities as large as one hundred and thirty or forty women to one hundred men, affords an opportunity to the procurer which he quickly seizes. He is often in league with certain employment bureaus, who make a business of advancing the railroad or boat fare to colored girls coming from the South to enter into domestic service. The girl, in debt and unused to the city, is often put into a questionable house and kept there until her debt is paid many times over. In some respects her position is not unlike that of the imported white slave, for although she has the inestimable advantage of speaking the language, she finds it even more difficult to have her story credited. This contemptuous attitude places her at a disadvantage, for so universally are colored girls in domestic service suspected of blackmail that the average court is slow to credit their testimony when it is given against white men. The field of employment for colored girls is extremely limited. They are seldom found in factories and workshops. They are not wanted in department stores nor even as waitresses in hotels. The majority of them therefore are engaged in domestic service and often find the position of maid in a house of prostitution or of chambermaid in a disreputable hotel, the best-paying position open to them.

When a girl who has been in domestic service loses her health, or for any other reason is unable to carry on her occupation, she is often curiously detached and isolated, because she has had so little opportunity for normal social relationships and friendships. One of the saddest cases ever brought to my personal knowledge was that of an orphan Norwegian girl who, coming to America at the age of seventeen, had been for three years in one position as general housemaid, during which time she had drawn only such part of her wages as was necessary for her simple clothing. At the end of three years, when she was sent to a public hospital with nervous prostration, her employer refused to pay her accumulated wages, on the ground that owing to her ill health she had been of little use during the last year. When she left the hospital, practically penniless, advised by the physician to find some outdoor work, she sold a patented egg-beater for six months, scarcely earning enough for her barest necessities and in constant dread lest she could not "keep respectable." When she was found wandering upon the street she not only had no capital with which to renew her stock, but had been without food for two days and had resolved to drown herself. Every effort was made to restore the half-crazed girl, but unfortunately hospital restraint was not considered necessary, and a month later, in spite of the vigilance of her new employer, her body was taken from the lake. One more of those gentle spirits who had found the problem of life insoluble, had sought refuge in death.

A surprising number of suicides occur among girls who have been in domestic service, when they discover that they have been betrayed by their lovers. Perhaps nothing is more astonishing than the attitude of the mistress when the situation of such a forlorn girl is discovered, and it would be interesting to know how far this attitude has influenced these girls either to suicide or to their reckless choice of a disreputable life, which statistics show so many of their number have elected. The mistress almost invariably promptly dismisses such a girl, assuring her that she is disgraced forever and too polluted to remain for another hour in a good home. In full command of the situation, she usually succeeds in convincing the wretched girl that she is irreparably ruined. Her very phraseology, although unknown to herself, is a remnant of that earlier historic period when every woman was obliged in her own person to protect her home and to secure the status of her children. The indignant woman is trying to exercise alone that social restraint which should have been exercised by the community and which would have naturally protected the girl, if she had not been so withdrawn from it, in order to serve exclusively the interests of her mistress's family. Such a woman seldom follows the ruined girl through the dreary weeks after her dismissal; her difficulty in finding any sort of work, the ostracism of her former friends added to her own self-accusation, the poverty and loneliness, the final ten days in the hospital, and the great temptation which comes after that, to give away her child. The baby farmer who haunts the public hospitals for such cases tells her that upon the payment of forty or fifty dollars, he will take care of the child for a year and that "maybe it won't live any longer than that," and unless the hospital is equipped with a social service department, such as the one at the Massachusetts General, the girl leaves it weak and low-spirited and too broken to care what becomes of her. It is in moments such as these that many a poor girl, convinced that all the world is against her, decides to enter a disreputable house. Here at least she will find food and shelter, she will not be despised by the other inmates and she can earn money for the support of her child. Often she has received the address of such a house from one of her companions in the maternity ward where, among the fifty per cent, of the unmarried mothers, at least two or three sophisticated girls are always to be found, eager to "put wise" the girls who are merely unfortunate. Occasionally a girl who follows such baneful advice still insists upon keeping her child. I recall a pathetic case in the juvenile court of Chicago when such a mother of a five-year-old child was pronounced by the judge to be an "improper guardian." The agonized woman was told that she might retain her child if she would completely change her way of life; but she insisted that such a requirement was impossible, that she had no other means of earning her living, and that she had become too idle and broken for regular work. The child clung piteously to the mother, and, having gathered from the evidence that she was considered "bad," assured the judge over and over again that she was "the bestest mother in the world." The poor mother, who had begun her wretched mode of life for her child's sake, found herself so demoralized by her hideous experiences that she could not leave the life, even for the sake of the same child, still her most precious possession. Only six years before, this mother had been an honest girl cheerfully working in the household of a good woman, whose sense of duty had expressed itself in dismissing "the outcast."

These discouraged girls, who so often come from domestic service to supply the vice demands of the city, are really the last representatives of those thousands of betrayed girls who for many years met the entire demand of the trade; for, while a procurer of some sort has performed his office for centuries, only in the last fifty years has the white slave market required the services of extended business enterprises in order to keep up the supply. Previously the demand had been largely met by the girls who had voluntarily entered a disreputable life because they had been betrayed. While the white slave traffic was organized primarily for profit it could of course never have flourished unless there had been a dearth of these discouraged girls. Is it not also significant that the surviving representatives of the girls who formerly supplied the demand are drawn most largely from the one occupation which is farthest from the modern ideal of social freedom and self-direction? Domestic service represents, in the modern world, more nearly than any other of the gainful occupations open to women, the ancient labor conditions under which woman's standard of chastity was developed and for so long maintained. It would seem obvious that both the girl over-restrained at home, as well as the girl in domestic service, had been too much withdrawn from the healthy influence of public opinion, and it is at least significant that domestic control has so broken down that the girls most completely under its rule are shown to be those in the greatest danger. Such a statement undoubtedly needs the modification that the girls in domestic service are frequently those who are unadapted to skilled labor and are least capable of taking care of themselves, yet the fact remains that they are belated morally as well as industrially. As they have missed the industrial discipline that comes from regular hours of systematized work, so they have missed the moral training of group solidarity, the ideals and restraints which the friendships and companionships of other working girls would have brought them.

When the judgment of her peers becomes not less firm but more kindly, the self-supporting girl will have a safeguard and restraint many times more effective than the individual control which has become so inadequate, or the family discipline that, with the best intentions in the world, cannot cope with existing social conditions.

The most perplexing case that comes before the philanthropic organizations trying to aid and rescue the victims of the white slave traffic, is of the type which involves a girl who has been secured by the trafficker when so lonely, detached and discouraged that she greedily seized whatever friendship was offered her. Such a girl has been so eager for affection that she clings to even the wretched simulacrum of it, afforded by the man who calls himself her "protector," and she can only be permanently detached from the life to which he holds her, when she is put under the influence of more genuine affections and interests. That is doubtless one reason it is always more possible to help the girl who has become the mother of a child. Although she unjustly faces a public opinion much more severe than that encountered by the childless woman who also endeavors to "reform," the mother's sheer affection and maternal absorption enables her to overcome the greater difficulties more easily than the other woman, without the new warmth of motive, overcomes the lesser ones. The Salvation Army in their rescue homes have long recognized this need for an absorbing interest, which should involve the Magdalen's deepest affections and emotions, and therefore often utilize the rescued girl to save others.

Certainly no philanthropic association, however rationalistic and suspicious of emotional appeal, can hope to help a girl once overwhelmed by desperate temptation, unless it is able to pull her back into the stream of kindly human fellowship and into a life involving normal human relations. Such an association must needs remember those wise words of Count Tolstoy: "We constantly think that there are circumstances in which a human being can be treated without affection, and there are no such circumstances."

Chapter VI
Increased Social Control

When certain groups in a community, to whom a social wrong has become intolerable, prepare for definite action against it, they almost invariably discover unexpected help from contemporaneous social movements with which they later find themselves allied. The most immediate help in this new campaign against the social evil will probably come thus indirectly from those streams of humanitarian effort which are ever widening and which will in time slowly engulf into their rising tide of enthusiasm for human betterment, even the victims of the white slave traffic.

Foremost among them is the world-wide movement to preserve and prolong the term of human life, coupled with the determination on the part of the medical profession to eliminate all forms of germ diseases. The same physicians and sanitarians who have practically rid the modern city of small-pox and cholera and are eliminating tuberculosis, well know that the social evil is directly responsible for germ diseases more prevalent than any of the others, and also communicable. Over and over again in the history of large cities, Vienna, Paris, St. Louis, the medical profession has been urged to control the diseases resulting from the commercialized vice which the municipal authorities themselves permitted. But the experiments in segregation, in licensed systems, and certification have not been considered successful. The medical profession, hitherto divided in opinion as to the feasibility of such undertakings, is virtually united in the conclusion that so long as commercialized vice exists, physicians cannot guarantee a city against the spread of the contagious poison generated by it, which is fatal alike to the individual and to his offspring. The medical profession agrees that, as the victims of the social evil inevitably become the purveyors of germ diseases of a very persistent and incurable type, safety in this regard lies only in the extinction of commercialized vice. They point out the indirect ways in which this contagion can spread exactly as any other can, but insist that its control is enormously complicated by the fact that the victims of these diseases are most unwilling to be designated and quarantined. The medical profession is at last taking the position that the community wishing to protect itself against this contagion will in the end be driven to the extermination of the very source itself. A well-known authority states the one breeding-place of these disease germs, without exception, is the social institution designated as prostitution, but, once bred and cultivated there, they then spread through the community, attacking alike both the innocent and the guilty.

We can imagine, after a dozen years of vigorous and able propaganda of this opinion on the part of public-spirited physicians and sanitarians, that a city might well appeal to the medical profession to exterminate prostitution on the very ground that it is a source of constant danger to the health and future of the community. Such a city might readily give to the board of health ordered to undertake this extermination more absolute authority than is now accorded to it in a small-pox epidemic. Of course, no city could reach such a view unless the education of the public proceeded much more rapidly than at present, although the newly-established custom of careful medical examination of school-children and of employees in factories and commercial establishments must result in the discovery of many such cases, and in the end adequate provision must be made for their isolation. A child was recently discovered in a Chicago school with an open sore upon her lip, which made her a most dangerous source of infection. She was just fourteen years of age, too old to be admitted into that most pathetic and most unlovely of all children's wards, where children must suffer for "the sins of their fathers," and too young and innocent to be put into the women's ward in which the public takes care of those wrecks of dissolute living who are no longer valuable to the commerce which once secured them, and have become merely worthless stock which pays no dividend. The disease of the little girl was in too virulent a stage to admit her to that convalescent home lately established in Chicago for those infected children who are dismissed from the county hospital, but whom it is impossible to return to their old surroundings. A philanthropic association was finally obliged to pay her board for weeks to a woman who carefully followed instructions as to her treatment. This is but one example of a child who was discovered and provided for, but it is evident that the public cannot long remain indifferent to the care of such cases when it has already established the means for detecting them. In twenty-seven months over six hundred children passed through this most piteous children's ward in Chicago's public hospital. All but twenty-nine of these children were under ten years of age, and doubtless a number of them had been victims of that wretched tradition that a man afflicted with this incurable disease might cure himself at the expense of innocence.

Crusades against other infectious diseases, such as small-pox and cholera, imply well-considered sanitary precautions, dependent upon widespread education and an aroused public opinion. To establish such education and to arouse the public in regard to this present menace apparently presents insuperable difficulties. Many newspapers, so ready to deal with all other forms of vice and misery, never allow these evils to be mentioned in their columns except in the advertisements of quack remedies; the clergy, unlike the founder of the Christian religion and the early apostles, seldom preach against the sin of which these contagions are an inevitable consequence: the physicians, bound by a rigorous medical etiquette, tell nothing of the prevalence of these maladies, use a confusing nomenclature in the hospitals, and write only contributory causes upon the very death certificates of the victims.

Yet it is easy to predict that a society committed to the abolition of infectious germs, to a higher degree of public health, and to a better standard of sanitation will not forever permit these highly communicable diseases to spread unchecked in its midst, and that a public, convinced that sanitary science, properly supported, might rid our cities of this type of disease, will at length insist upon its accomplishment. When we consider the many things undertaken in the name of health and sanitation it becomes easy to make the prediction, for public health is a magic word which ever grows more potent, as society realizes that the very existence of the modern city would be an impossibility had it not been discovered that the health of the individual is largely controlled by the hygienic condition of his surroundings. Since the first commission to inquire into the conditions of great cities was appointed in Manchester in 1844, sanitary science, both in knowledge and municipal authority, has progressed until advocates of the most advanced measures in city hygiene and preventive sanitary science boldly state that neglected childhood and neglected disease are the most potent causes of social insufficiency.

Certainly a plea could be made for the women and children who are often the innocent victims of these diseases. Quite recently in Chicago there was brought to my attention the incredibly pathetic plight of a widow with four children who was in such constant fear of spreading the infection for which her husband had been responsible, that she touchingly offered to leave her children forevermore, if there was no other way to save them from the horrible suffering she herself was enduring. In spite of thousands of such cases Utah is the pioneer and only state with a law which requires that this infection shall be reported and controlled, as are other contagious maladies, and which also authorizes boards of health to take adequate measures in order to secure protection.

Another humanitarian movement from which assistance will doubtless come to the crusade against the social evil, is the great movement against alcoholism with its recent revival in every civilized country of the world. A careful scientist has called alcohol the indispensable vehicle of the business transacted by the white slave traders, and has asserted that without its use this trade could not long continue. Whoever has tried to help a girl making an effort to leave the irregular life she has been leading, must have been discouraged by the victim's attempts to overcome the habit of using alcohol and drugs. Such a girl has commonly been drawn into the life in the first place when under the influence of liquor and has continued to drink that she might be able to live through each day. Furthermore, the drinking habit grows upon her because she is constantly required to sell liquor and to be "treated."

It is estimated that the liquor sold by such girls nets a profit to the trade of two hundred and fifty per cent. over and above the girl's own commission. Chicago made at least one honest effort to divorce the sale of liquor from prostitution, when the superintendent of police last year ruled that no liquor should be sold in any disreputable house. The difficulty of enforcing such an order is greatly increased because such houses, as well as the questionable dance halls, commonly obtain a special permit to sell liquor under a federal license, which is not only cheaper than the saloon license obtained from the city, but has the added advantage to the holder that he can sell after one o'clock in the morning, at which time the city closes all saloons.

The aggregate annual profit of the two hundred and thirty-six disorderly saloons recently investigated in Chicago by the Vice Commission was $4,307,000. This profit on the sale of liquor can be traced all along the line in connection with the white slave traffic and is no less disastrous from the point of view of young men than of the girls. Even a slight exhilaration from alcohol relaxes the moral sense and throws a sentimental or adventurous glamor over an aspect of life from which a decent young man would ordinarily recoil, and its continued use stimulates the senses at the very moment when the intellectual and moral inhibitions are lessened. May we not conclude that both chastity and self-restraint are more firmly established in the modern city than we realize, when the white slave traders find it necessary both forcibly to detain their victims and to ply young men with alcohol that they may profit thereby? General Bingham, who as Police Commissioner of New York certainly knew whereof he spoke, says: "There is not enough depravity in human nature to keep alive this very large business. The immorality of women and the brutishness of men have to be persuaded, coaxed and constantly stimulated in order to keep the social evil in its present state of business prosperity."

We may soberly hope that some of the experiments made by governmental and municipal authorities to control and regulate the sale of liquor will at last meet with such a measure of success that the existence of public prostitution, deprived of its artificial stimulus of alcohol, will in the end be imperilled. The Chicago Vice Commission has made a series of valuable suggestions for the regulation of saloons and for the separation of the sale of liquor from dance halls and from all other places known as recruiting grounds for the white slave traffic. There is still need for a much wider and more thorough education of the public in regard to the historic connection between commercialized vice and alcoholism, of the close relation between politics and the liquor interests, behind which the social evil so often entrenches itself.

In addition to the movements against germ diseases and the suppression of alcoholism, both of which are mitigating the hard fate of the victims of the white slave traffic, other public movements mysteriously affecting all parts of the social order will in time threaten the very existence of commercialized vice. First among these, perhaps, is the equal suffrage movement. On the horizon everywhere are signs that woman will soon receive the right to exercise political power, and it is believed that she will show her efficiency most conspicuously in finding means for enhancing and preserving human life, if only as the result of her age-long experiences. That primitive maternal instinct, which has always been as ready to defend as it has been to nurture, will doubtless promptly grapple with certain crimes connected with the white slave traffic; women with political power would not brook that men should live upon the wages of captured victims, should openly hire youths to ruin and debase young girls, should be permitted to transmit poison to unborn children. Life is full of hidden remedial powers which society has not yet utilized, but perhaps nowhere is the waste more flagrant than in the matured deductions and judgments of the women, who are constantly forced to share the social injustices which they have no recognized power to alter. If political rights were once given to women, if the situation were theirs to deal with as a matter of civic responsibility, one cannot imagine that the existence of the social evil would remain unchallenged in its semi-legal protection. Those women who are already possessed of political power have in many ways registered their conscience in regard to it. The Norwegian women, for instance, have guaranteed to every illegitimate child the right of inheritance to its father's name and property by a law which also provides for the care of its mother. This is in marked contrast to the usual treatment of the mother of an illegitimate child, who even when the paternity of her child is acknowledged receives from the father but a pitiful sum for its support; moreover, if the child dies before birth and the mother conceals this fact, although perfectly guiltless of its death, she can be sent to jail for a year.

The age of consent is eighteen years in all of the states in which women have had the ballot, although in only eight of the others is it so high. In the majority of the latter the age of consent is between fourteen and sixteen, and in some of them it is as low as ten. These legal regulations persist in spite of the well-known fact that the mass of girls enter a disreputable life below the age of eighteen. In equal suffrage states important issues regarding women and children, whether of the sweat-shop or the brothel, have always brought out the women voters in great numbers.

Certainly enfranchised women would offer some protection to the white slaves themselves who are tolerated and segregated, but who, because their very existence is illegal, may be arrested whenever any police captain chooses, may be brought before a magistrate, fined and imprisoned. A woman so arrested may be obliged to answer the most harassing questions put to her by a city attorney with no other woman near to protect her from insult. She may be subjected to the most trying examinations in the presence of policemen with no matron to whom to appeal. These things constantly happen everywhere save in Scandinavian countries, where juries of women sit upon such cases and offer the protection of their presence to the prisoners. Without such protection even an innocent woman, made to appear a member of this despised class, receives no consideration. A girl of fifteen recently acting in a South Chicago theatre attracted the attention of a milkman who gradually convinced her that he was respectable. Walking with him one evening to the door of her lodging-house, the girl told him of her difficulties and quite innocently accepted money for the payment of her room rent. The following morning as she was leaving the house the milkman met her at the door and asked her for the five dollars he had given her the night before. When she said she had used it to pay her debt to the landlady, he angrily replied that unless she returned the money at once he would call a policeman and arrest her on a charge of theft. The girl, helpless because she had already disposed of the money, was taken to court, where, frightened and confused, she was unable to give a convincing account of the interview the night before; except for the prompt intervention on the part of a woman, she would either have been obliged to put herself in the power of the milkman, who offered to pay her fine, or she would have been sent to the city prison, not because the proof of her guilt was conclusive, but because her connection with a cheap theatre and the hour of the so-called offence had convinced the court that she belonged to a class of women who are regarded as no longer entitled to legal protection.

Several years ago in Colorado the disreputable women of Denver appealed to a large political club of women against the action of the police who were forcing them to register under the threat of arrest in order later to secure their votes for a corrupt politician. The disreputable women, wishing to conceal their real names and addresses, did not want to be registered, in this respect at least differing from the lodging-house men whose venal votes play such an important part in every municipal election. The women's political club responded to this appeal, and not only stopped the coercion, but finally turned out of office the chief of police responsible for it.

The very fact that the conditions and results of the social evil lie so far away from the knowledge of good women is largely responsible for the secrecy and hypocrisy upon which it thrives. Most good women will probably never consent to break through their ignorance save under a sense of duty which has ever been the incentive to action to which even timid women have responded. At least a promising beginning would be made toward a more effective social control, if the mass of conscientious women were once thoroughly convinced that a knowledge of local vice conditions was a matter of civic obligation, if the entire body of conventional women, simply because they held the franchise, felt constrained to inform themselves concerning the social evil throughout the cities of America. Perhaps the most immediate result would be a change in the attitude toward prostitution on the part of elected officials, responding to that of their constituency. Although good and bad men alike prize chastity in women, and although good men require it of themselves, almost all men are convinced that it is impossible to require it of thousands of their fellow-citizens, and hence connive at the policy of the officials who permit commercialized vice to flourish.

As the first organized Women's Rights movement was inaugurated by the women who were refused seats in the world's Anti-Slavery convention held in London in 1840, although they had been the very pioneers in the organization of the American Abolitionists, so it is quite possible that an equally energetic attempt to abolish white slavery will bring many women into the Equal Suffrage movement, simply because they too will discover that without the use of the ballot they are unable to work effectively for the eradication of a social wrong.

Women are said to have been historically indifferent to social injustices, but it may be possible that, if they once really comprehend the actual position of prostitutes the world over, their sense of justice will at last be freed, and become forevermore a new force in the long struggle for social righteousness. The wind of moral aspiration now dies down and now blows with unexpected force, urging on the movements of social destiny; but never do the sails of the ship of state push forward with such assured progress as when filled by the mighty hopes of a newly enfranchised class. Those already responsible for existing conditions have come to acquiesce in them, and feel obliged to adduce reasons explaining the permanence and so-called necessity of the most evil conditions. On the other hand, the newly enfranchised view existing conditions more critically, more as human beings and less as politicians.

After all, why should the woman voter concur in the assumption that every large city must either set aside well-known districts for the accommodation of prostitution, as Chicago does, or continually permit it to flourish in tenement and apartment houses, as is done in New York? Smaller communities and towns throughout the land are free from at least this semi-legal organization of it, and why should it be accepted as a permanent aspect of city life? The valuable report of the Chicago Vice Commission estimates that twenty thousand of the men daily responsible for this evil in Chicago live outside of the city. They are the men who come from other towns to Chicago in order to see the sights. They are supposedly moral at home, where they are well known and subjected to the constant control of public opinion. The report goes on to state that during conventions or "show" occasions the business of commercialized vice is enormously increased. The village gossip with her vituperative tongue after all performs a valuable function both of castigation and retribution; but her fellow-townsman, although quite unconscious of her restraint, coming into a city hotel often experiences a great sense of relief which easily rises to a mood of exhilaration. In addition to this he holds an exaggerated notion of the wickedness of the city. A visiting countryman is often shown museums and questionable sights reserved largely for his patronage, just as tourists are conducted to lurid Parisian revels and indecencies sustained primarily for their horrified contemplation. Such a situation would indicate that, because control is much more difficult in a large city than in a small town, the city deliberately provides for its own inability in this direction.

During a recent military encampment in Chicago large numbers of young girls were attracted to it by that glamour which always surrounds the soldier. On the complaint of several mothers, investigators discovered that the girls were there without the knowledge of their parents, some of them having literally climbed out of windows after their parents had supposed them asleep. A thorough investigation disclosed not only an enormous increase of business in the restricted districts, but the downfall of many young girls who had hitherto been thoroughly respectable and able to resist the ordinary temptations of city life, but who had completely lost their heads over the glitter of a military camp. One young girl was seen by an investigator in the late evening hurrying away from the camp. She was so absorbed in her trouble and so blinded by her tears that she fairly ran against him and he heard her praying, as she frantically clutched the beads around her neck, "Oh, Mother of God, what have I done! What have I done!" The Chicago encampment was finally brought under control through the combined efforts of the park commissioners, the city police, and the military authorities, but not without a certain resentment from the last toward "civilian interference." Such an encampment may be regarded as an historic survival representing the standing armies sustained in Europe since the days of the Roman Empire. These large bodies of men, deprived of domestic life, have always afforded centres in which contempt for the chastity of women has been fostered. The older centres of militarism have established prophylactic measures designed to protect the health of the soldiers, but evince no concern for the fate of the ruined women. It is a matter of recent history that Josephine Butler and the men and women associated with her, subjected themselves to unspeakable insult for eight years before they finally induced the English Parliament to repeal the infamous Contagious Disease Acts relating to the garrison towns of Great Britain, through which the government itself not only permitted vice, but legally provided for it within certain specified limits.

The primary difficulty of military life lies in the withdrawal of large numbers of men from normal family life, and hence from the domestic restraints and social checks which are operative upon the mass of human beings. The great peace propagandas have emphasized the unjustifiable expense involved in the maintenance of the standing armies of Europe, the social waste in the withdrawal of thousands of young men from industrial, commercial and professional pursuits into the barren negative life of the barracks. They might go further and lay stress upon the loss of moral sensibility, the destruction of romantic love, the perversion of the longing for wife and child. The very stability and refinement of the social order depend upon the preservation of these basic emotions.

Social customs are instituted so slowly and even imperceptibly, so far as the conforming individual is concerned, that the mass of men submit to control in spite of themselves, and it is therefore always difficult to determine how far the average upright living is the result of external props, until they are suddenly withdrawn. This is especially true of domestic life. Even the sordid marriages in which the senses have forestalled the heart almost always end in some form of family affection. The young couple who may have been brought together in marriage upon the most primitive plane, after twenty years of hard work in meagre, unlovely surroundings, in spite of stupidity and many mistakes, in the face of failure and even wrongdoing, will have unfolded lives of unassuming affection and family devotion to a group of children. They will have faithfully fulfilled that obligation which falls to the lot of the majority of men and women, with its high rewards and painful sacrifices. These rewards as well as the restraints of family life are denied to the soldier. A somewhat similar situation is found in every large construction camp, and in the crowded city tenements occupied by thousands of immigrant men who have preceded their families to America.

In the light of the history of prostitution in relation to militarism, nothing could be more absurd than the familiar statement that virtuous women could not safely walk the streets unless opportunity for secret vice were offered to the men of the city. It is precisely the men who have not submitted to self-control who are dangerous and they only, as the court records themselves make clear.

In addition to the large social movements for the betterment of Public Health, for the establishment of Temperance, for the promotion of Equal Suffrage, and for the hastening of Peace and Arbitration is the world-wide organization and active propaganda of International Socialism. It has always included the abolition of this ancient evil in its program of social reconstruction, and since the publication of Bebel's great book, nearly thirty years ago, the leaders of the Socialist party have never ceased to discuss the economics of prostitution with its psychological and moral resultants. The Socialists contend that commercialized vice is fundamentally a question of poverty, a by-product of despair, which will disappear only with the abolition of poverty itself; that it persists not primarily from inherent weakness in human nature, but is a vice arising from a defective organization of social life; that with a reorganization of society, at least all of prostitution which is founded upon the hunger of the victims and upon the profits of the traffickers, will disappear.

Whether we are Socialists or not, we will all admit that every level of culture breeds its own particular brand of vice and uncovers new weaknesses as well as new nobilities in human nature; that a given social development-such, for instance as the conditions of life for thousands of young people in crowded city quarters-may produce such temptations and present such snares to virtue, that average human nature cannot withstand them.

The very fact that the existence of the social evil is semi-legal in large cities is an admission that our individual morality is so uncertain that it breaks down when social control is withdrawn and the opportunity for secrecy is offered. The situation indicates either that the best conscience of the community fails to translate itself into civic action or that our cities are too large to be civilized in a social sense. These difficulties have been enormously augmented during the past century so marked by the rapid growth of cities, because the great principle of liberty has been translated not only into the unlovely doctrine of commercial competition, but also has fostered in many men the belief that personal development necessitates a rebellion against existing social laws. To the opportunity for secrecy which the modern city offers, such men are able to add a high-sounding justification for their immoralities. Fortunately, however, for our moral progress, the specious and illegitimate theories of freedom are constantly being challenged, and a new form of social control is slowly establishing itself on the principle, so widespread in contemporary government, that the state has a responsibility for conditions which determine the health and welfare of its own members; that it is in the interest of social progress itself that hard-won liberties must be restrained by the demonstrable needs of society.

This new and more vigorous development of social control, while reflecting something of that wholesome fear of public opinion which the intimacies of a small community maintain, is much more closely allied to the old communal restraints and mutual protections to which the human will first yielded. Although this new control is based upon the voluntary co-operation of self-directed individuals, in contrast to the forced submission that characterized the older forms of social restraint, nevertheless in predicting the establishment of adequate social control over the instinct which the modern novelists so often describe as "uncontrollable," there is a certain sanction in this old and well-nigh forgotten history.

The most superficial student of social customs quickly discovers the practically unlimited extent to which public opinion has always regulated marriage. If the traditions of one tribe were endogamous, all the men dutifully married within it; but if the customs of another decreed that wives must be secured by capture or purchase, all the men of that tribe fared forth in order to secure their mates. From the primitive Australian who obtains his wives in exchange for his sisters or daughters, and never dreams of obtaining them in any other way, to the sophisticated young Frenchman, who without objection marries the bride his careful parents select for him; from the ancient Hebrew, who contentedly married the widow of his deceased brother because it was according to the law, to the modern Englishman who refused to marry his deceased wife's sister because the law forbade it, the entire pathway of the so-called uncontrollable instinct has been gradually confined between carefully clipped hedges and has steadily led up to a house of conventional domesticity. Men have fallen in love with their cousins or declined to fall in love with them, very much as custom declared marriages between cousins to be desirable or undesirable, as they formerly married their sisters and later absolutely ceased to desire to marry them. In fact, regulation of this great primitive instinct goes back of the human race itself. All the higher tribes of monkeys are strictly monogamous, and many species of birds are faithful to one mate, season after season. According to the great authority, Forel, prostitution never became established among primitive peoples. Even savage tribes designated the age at which their young men were permitted to assume paternity because feeble children were a drag upon their communal resources. As primitive control lessened with the disappearance of tribal organization and later of the patriarchal family, a social control, not less binding, was slowly established, until throughout the centuries, in spite of many rebellious individuals, the mass of men have lived according to the dictates of the church, the legal requirements of the state, and the surveillance of the community, if only because they feared social ostracism. It is easy, however, to forget these men and their prosaic virtues because history has so long busied herself in recording court amours and the gentle dalliances of the overlord.

The great primitive instinct, so responsive to social control as to be almost an example of social docility, has apparently broken with all the restraints and decencies under two conditions: first and second, when the individual felt that he was above social control and when the individual has had an opportunity to hide his daily living. Prostitution upon a commercial basis in a measure embraces the two conditions, for it becomes possible only in a society so highly complicated that social control may be successfully evaded and the individual thus feels superior to it. When a city is so large that it is extremely difficult to fix individual responsibility, that which for centuries was considered the luxury of the king comes within the reach of every office-boy, and that lack of community control which belonged only to the overlord who felt himself superior to the standards of the people, may be seized upon by any city dweller who can evade his acquaintances. Against such moral aggression, the old types of social control are powerless.

Fortunately, the same crowded city conditions which make moral isolation possible, constantly tend to develop a new restraint founded upon the mutual dependences of city life and its daily necessities. The city itself socializes the very instruments that constitute the apparatus of social control-Law, Publicity, Literature, Education and Religion. Through their socialization, the desirability of chastity, which has hitherto been a matter of individual opinion and decision, comes to be regarded, not only as a personal virtue indispensable in women and desirable in men, but as a great basic requirement which society has learned to demand because it has been proven necessary for human welfare. To the individual restraints is added the conviction of social responsibility and the whole determination of chastity is reinforced by social sanctions. Such a shifting to social grounds is already obviously taking place in regard to the chastity of women. Formerly all that the best woman possessed was a negative chastity which had been carefully guarded by her parents and duennas. The chastity of the modern woman of self-directed activity and of a varied circle of interests, which gives her an acquaintance with many men as well as women, has therefore a new value and importance in the establishment of social standards. There was a certain basis for the belief that if a woman lost her personal virtue, she lost all; when she had no activity outside of domestic life, the situation itself afforded a foundation for the belief that a man might claim praise for his public career even when his domestic life was corrupt. As woman, however, fulfills her civic obligations while still guarding her chastity, she will be in position as never before to uphold the "single standard," demanding that men shall add the personal virtues to their performance of public duties. Women may at last force men to do away with the traditional use of a public record as a cloak for a wretched private character, because society will never permit a woman to make such excuses for herself.

Every movement therefore which tends to increase woman's share of civic responsibility undoubtedly forecasts the time when a social control will be extended over men, similar to the historic one so long established over women. As that modern relationship between men and women, which the Romans called "virtue between equals" increases, while it will continue to make women freer and nobler, less timid of reputation and more human, will also inevitably modify the standards of men.

On the other hand, there is no doubt that this new freedom from domestic and community control, with the opportunity for escaping observation which the city affords, is often utilized unworthily by women. The report of the Chicago vice commission tells of numerous girls living in small cities and country towns, who come to Chicago from time to time under arrangements made with the landlady of a seemingly respectable apartment. They remain long enough to earn money for a spring or fall wardrobe and return to their home towns, where their acquaintances are quite without suspicion of the methods they have employed to secure the much-admired costumes brought from the city. Often an unattached country girl, who has come to live in a city, has gradually fallen into a vicious life from sheer lack of social restraint. Such a girl, when living in a smaller community, realized that good behavior was a protective measure and that any suspicion of immorality would quickly ruin her social standing; but when removed from such surveillance, she hopes to be able to pass from her regular life to an irregular one and back again before the fact has been noted, quite as many young men are trying to do.

Perhaps no young woman is more exposed to temptation of this sort than the one who works in an office where she may be the sole woman employed and where the relation to her employer and to her fellow-clerks is almost on a social basis. Many office girls have taken "business courses" in their native towns and have come to the city in search of the large salaries which have no parallels at home. Such a position is not only new to the individual, but it is so recent an outcome of modern business methods, that it has not yet been conventionalized. The girl is without the wholesome social restraint afforded by the companionship of other working-women and her isolation in itself constitutes a danger. An investigation disclosed that a startling number of Chicago girls had found their positions through advertisements and had no means of ascertaining the respectability of their employers. In addition to this, the girls who seek such positions are sometimes vain and pretentious, and will take any sort of office work because it seems to them "more ladylike." A girl of this sort came to Chicago from the country three years ago at the age of seventeen and secured a position as a stenographer with a large firm of lawyers. She was pretty and attractive, and in her desire to see more of the wonderful city to which she had come, she accepted many invitations to dinners and theatres from a younger member of the firm. The other girls in the office, representing the more capable type of business women, among whom a careful code of conduct is developing, although at present it is often manifested only by the social ostracism of the one of their number who has broken the conventions, protested against her conduct, first to the girl and then to the head of the office. The usual story developed rapidly, the girl lost her position, her brother-in-law, learning the cause, refused her a home and she became absolutely dependent upon the man. As their relations became notorious, he at length was requested to withdraw from the firm. When brought to my knowledge she had already been deserted for a year. The only people she had known during that time were those in the disreputable hotel in which she had been living when her lover disappeared, and it was through their mistaken kindness in making an opportunity for her in the only life with which they were familiar, that she had been drawn into the worst vice of the city.

She was but one of thousands of young women whose undisciplined minds are fatally assailed by the subtleties and sophistries of city life, and who have lost their bearings in the midst of a multitude of new imaginative impressions. It is hard for a girl, thrilled by the mere propinquity of city excitements and eager to share them, to keep to the gray and monotonous path of regular work. Almost every such girl of the hundreds who have come to grief, "begins" by accepting invitations to dinners and places of amusement. She is always impressed with the ease for concealment which the city affords, although at the same time vaguely resentful that it is so indifferent to her individual existence. It is impossible to estimate the amount of clandestine prostitution which the modern city contains, but there is no doubt that the growth of the social evil at the present moment, lies in this direction. Another of its less sinister developments is perhaps a contemporary manifestation of that break, long considered necessary, between established morality and artistic freedom represented by the hetaira in Athens, the gifted actress in Paris, the geisha in Japan. Insofar as such women have been treated as independent human beings and prized for their mental and social charm, even although they are on a commercial basis, it makes for a humanization of this most sordid business. Such open manifestations of prostitution hasten social control, because publicity has ever been the first step toward community understanding and discipline.

Doubtless the attitude toward the victims of commercialized vice will be modified by many reactions upon the public consciousness, through a thousand manifestations of the great democratic movement which is developing all about us. Certainly we are safe in predicting that when the solidarity of human interest is actually realized, it will become unthinkable that one class of human beings should be sacrificed to the supposed needs of another; when the rights of human life have successfully asserted themselves in contrast to the rights of property, it will become impossible to sell the young and heedless into degradation. An age marked by its vigorous protests against slavery and class tyranny, will not continue to ignore the multitudes of women who are held in literal bondage; nor will an age characterized by a new tenderness for the losers in life's race, always persist in denying forgiveness to the woman who has lost all. A voice which has come across the centuries, filled with pity for her who has "sinned much," must at last be joined by the forgiving voices of others, to whom it has been revealed that it is hardness of heart which has ever thwarted the divine purposes of religion. A generation which has gone through so many successive revolts against commercial aggression and lawlessness, will at last lead one more revolt on behalf of the young girls who are the victims of the basest and vilest commercialism. As that consciousness of human suffering, which already hangs like a black cloud over thousands of our more sensitive contemporaries, increases in poignancy, it must finally include the women who for so many generations have received neither pity nor consideration; as the sense of justice fast widens to encircle all human relations, it must at length reach the women who have so long been judged without a hearing.

In that vast and checkered undertaking of its own moralization to which the human race is committed, it must constantly free itself from the survivals and savage infections of the primitive life from which it started. Now one and then another of the ancient wrongs and uncouth customs which have been so long familiar as to seem inevitable, rise to the moral consciousness of a passing generation; first for uneasy contemplation and then for gallant correction.

May America bear a valiant part in this international crusade of the compassionate, enlisting under its banner not only those sensitive to the wrongs of others, but those conscious of the destruction of the race itself, who form the standing army of humanity's self-pity, which is becoming slowly mobilized for a new conquest!

Twenty Years at Hull-House

Preface

Every preface is, I imagine, written after the book has been completed and now that I have finished this volume I will state several difficulties which may put the reader upon his guard unless he too postpones the preface to the very last.

Many times during the writing of these reminiscences, I have become convinced that the task was undertaken all too soon. One's fiftieth year is indeed an impressive milestone at which one may well pause to take an accounting, but the people with whom I have so long journeyed have become so intimate a part of my lot that they cannot be written of either in praise or blame; the public movements and causes with which I am still identified have become so endeared, some of them through their very struggles and failures, that it is difficult to discuss them.

It has also been hard to determine what incidents and experiences should be selected for recital, and I have found that I might give an accurate report of each isolated event and yet give a totally misleading impression of the whole, solely by the selection of the incidents. For these reasons and many others I have found it difficult to make a faithful record of the years since the autumn of 1889 when without any preconceived social theories or economic views, I came to live in an industrial district of Chicago.

If the reader should inquire why the book was ever undertaken in the face of so many difficulties, in reply I could instance two purposes, only one of which in the language of organized charity, is "worthy." Because Settlements have multiplied so easily in the United States I hoped that a simple statement of an earlier effort, including the stress and storm, might be of value in their interpretation and possibly clear them of a certain charge of superficiality. The unworthy motive was a desire to start a "backfire," as it were, to extinquish two biographies of myself, one of which had been submitted to me in outline, that made life in a Settlement all too smooth and charming.

The earlier chapters present influences and personal motives with a detail which will be quite unpardonable if they fail to make clear the personality upon whom various social and industrial movements in Chicago reacted during a period of twenty years. No effort is made in the recital to separate my own history from that of Hull-House during the years in which I was "launched deep into the stormy intercourse of human life" for, so far as a mind is pliant under the pressure of events and experiences, it becomes hard to detach it.

It has unfortunately been necessary to abandon the chronological order in favor of the topical, for during the early years at Hull-House, time seemed to afford a mere framework for certain lines of activity and I have found in writing this book, that after these activities have been recorded, I can scarcely recall the scaffolding.

More than a third of the material in the book has appeared in The American Magazine, one chapter of it in McClure's Magazine, and earlier statements of the Settlement motive, published years ago, have been utilized in chronological order because it seemed impossible to reproduce their enthusiasm.

It is a matter of gratification to me that the book is illustrated from drawings made by Miss Norah Hamilton of Hull-House, and the cover designed by another resident, Mr. Frank Hazenplug. I am indebted for the making of the index and for many other services to Miss Clara Landsberg, also of Hull-House.

If the conclusions of the whole matter are similar to those I have already published at intervals during the twenty years at Hull-House, I can only make the defense that each of the earlier books was an attempt to set forth a thesis supported by experience, whereas this volume endeavors to trace the experiences through which various conclusions were forced upon me.

Chapter I
Earliest Impressions

On the theory that our genuine impulses may be connected with our childish experiences, that one's bent may be tracked back to that "No-Man's Land" where character is formless but nevertheless settling into definite lines of future development, I begin this record with some impressions of my childhood.

All of these are directly connected with my father, although of course I recall many experiences apart from him. I was one of the younger members of a large family and an eager participant in the village life, but because my father was so distinctly the dominant influence and because it is quite impossible to set forth all of one's early impressions, it has seemed simpler to string these first memories on that single cord. Moreover, it was this cord which not only held fast my supreme affections, but also first drew me into the moral concerns of life, and later afforded a clew there to which I somewhat wistfully clung in the intricacy of its mazes.

It must have been from a very early period that I recall "horrid nights" when I tossed about in my bed because I had told a lie. I was held in the grip of a miserable dread of death, a double fear, first, that I myself should die in my sins and go straight to that fiery Hell which was never mentioned at home, but which I had heard all about from other children, and, second, that my father-representing the entire adult world which I had basely deceived-should himself die before I had time to tell him. My only method of obtaining relief was to go downstairs to my father's room and make full confession. The high resolve to do this would push me out of bed and carry me down the stairs without a touch of fear. But at the foot of the stairs I would be faced by the awful necessity of passing the front door-which my father, because of his Quaker tendencies, did not lock-and of crossing the wide and black expanse of the living room in order to reach his door. I would invariably cling to the newel post while I contemplated the perils of the situation, complicated by the fact that the literal first step meant putting my bare foot upon a piece of oilcloth in front of the door, only a few inches wide, but lying straight in my path. I would finally reach my father's bedside perfectly breathless and having panted out the history of my sin, invariable received the same assurance that if he "had a little girl who told lies," he was very glad that she "felt too bad to go to sleep afterward." No absolution was asked for or received, but apparently the sense that the knowledge of my wickedness was shared, or an obscure understanding of the affection which underlay the grave statement, was sufficient, for I always went back to bed as bold as a lion, and slept, if not the sleep of the just, at least that of the comforted.

I recall an incident which must have occurred before I was seven years old, for the mill in which my father transacted his business that day was closed in 1867. The mill stood in the neighboring town adjacent to its poorest quarter. Before then I had always seen the little city of ten thousand people with the admiring eyes of a country child, and it had never occurred to me that all its streets were not as bewilderingly attractive as the one which contained the glittering toyshop and the confectioner. On that day I had my first sight of the poverty which implies squalor, and felt the curious distinction between the ruddy poverty of the country and that which even a small city presents in its shabbiest streets. I remember launching at my father the pertinent inquiry why people lived in such horrid little houses so close together, and that after receiving his explanation I declared with much firmness when I grew up I should, of course, have a large house, but it would not be built among the other large houses, but right in the midst of horrid little houses like those.

That curious sense of responsibility for carrying on the world's affairs which little children often exhibit because "the old man clogs our earliest years," I remember in myself in a very absurd manifestation. I dreamed night after night that every one in the world was dead excepting myself, and that upon me rested the responsibility of making a wagon wheel. The village street remained as usual, the village blacksmith shop was "all there," even a glowing fire upon the forge and the anvil in its customary place near the door, but no human being was within sight. They had all gone around the edge of the hill to the village cemetery, and I alone remained alive in the deserted world. I always stood in the same spot in the blacksmith shop, darkly pondering as to how to begin, and never once did I know how, although I fully realized that the affairs of the world could not be resumed until at least one wheel should be made and something started. Every victim of nightmare is, I imagine, overwhelmed by an excessive sense of responsibility and the consciousness of a fearful handicap in the effort to perform what is required; but perhaps never were the odds more heavily against "a warder of the world" than in these reiterated dreams of mine, doubtless compounded in equal parts of a childish version of Robinson Crusoe and of the end-of-the-world predictions of the Second Adventists, a few of whom were found in the village. The next morning would often find me, a delicate little girl of six, with the further disability of a curved spine, standing in the doorway of the village blacksmith shop, anxiously watching the burly, red-shirted figure at work. I would store my mind with such details of the process of making wheels as I could observe, and sometimes I plucked up courage to ask for more. "Do you always have to sizzle the iron in water?" I would ask, thinking how horrid it would be to do. "Sure!" the good-natured blacksmith would reply, "that makes the iron hard." I would sigh heavily and walk away, bearing my responsibility as best I could, and this of course I confided to no one, for there is something too mysterious in the burden of "the winds that come from the fields of sleep" to be communicated, although it is at the same time too heavy a burden to be borne alone.

My great veneration and pride in my father manifested itself in curious ways. On several Sundays, doubtless occurring in two or three different years, the Union Sunday School of the village was visited by strangers, some of those "strange people" who live outside a child's realm, yet constantly thrill it by their close approach. My father taught the large Bible class in the lefthand corner of the church next to the pulpit, and to my eyes at least, was a most imposing figure in his Sunday frock coat, his fine head rising high above all the others. I imagined that the strangers were filled with admiration for this dignified person, and I prayed with all my heart that the ugly, pigeon-toed little girl, whose crooked back obliged her to walk with her head held very much upon one side, would never be pointed out to these visitors as the daughter of this fine man. In order to lessen the possibility of a connection being made, on these particular Sundays I did not walk beside my father, although this walk was the great event of the week, but attached myself firmly to the side of my Uncle James Addams, in the hope that I should be mistaken for his child, or at least that I should not remain so conspicuously unattached that troublesome questions might identify an Ugly Duckling with her imposing parent. My uncle, who had many children of his own, must have been mildly surprised at this unwonted attention, but he would look down kindly at me, and say, "So you are going to walk with me to-day?" "Yes, please, Uncle James," would be my meek reply. He fortunately never explored my motives, nor do I remember that my father ever did, so that in all probability my machinations have been safe from public knowledge until this hour.

It is hard to account for the manifestations of a child's adoring affection, so emotional, so irrational, so tangled with the affairs of the imagination. I simply could not endure the thought that "strange people" should know that my handsome father owned this homely little girl. But even in my chivalric desire to protect him from his fate, I was not quite easy in the sacrifice of my uncle, although I quieted my scruples with the reflection that the contrast was less marked and that, anyway, his own little girl "was not so very pretty." I do not know that I commonly dwelt much upon my personal appearance, save as it thrust itself as an incongruity into my father's life, and in spite of unending evidence to the contrary, there were even black moments when I allowed myself to speculate as to whether he might not share the feeling. Happily, however, this specter was laid before it had time to grow into a morbid familiar by a very trifling incident. One day I met my father coming out of his bank on the main street of the neighboring city which seemed to me a veritable whirlpool of society and commerce. With a playful touch of exaggeration, he lifted his high and shining silk hat and made me an imposing bow. This distinguished public recognition, this totally unnecessary identification among a mass of "strange people" who couldn't possibly know unless he himself made the sign, suddenly filled me with a sense of the absurdity of the entire feeling. It may not even then have seemed as absurd as it really was, but at least it seemed enough so to collapse or to pass into the limbo of forgotten specters.

I made still other almost equally grotesque attempts to express this doglike affection. The house at the end of the village in which I was born, and which was my home until I moved to Hull-House, in my earliest childhood had opposite to it-only across the road and then across a little stretch of greensward-two mills belonging to my father; one flour mill, to which the various grains were brought by the neighboring farmers, and one sawmill, in which the logs of the native timber were sawed into lumber. The latter offered the great excitement of sitting on a log while it slowly approached the buzzing saw which was cutting it into slabs, and of getting off just in time to escape a sudden and gory death. But the flouring mill was much more beloved. It was full of dusky, floury places which we adored, of empty bins in which we might play house; it had a basement, with piles of bran and shorts which were almost as good as sand to play in, whenever the miller let us wet the edges of the pile with water brought in his sprinkling pot from the mill-race.

In addition to these fascinations was the association of the mill with my father's activities, for doubtless at that time I centered upon him all that careful imitation which a little girl ordinarily gives to her mother's ways and habits. My mother had died when I was a baby and my father's second marriage did not occur until my eighth year.

I had a consuming ambition to posses a miller's thumb, and would sit contentedly for a long time rubbing between my thumb and fingers the ground wheat as it fell from between the millstones, before it was taken up on an endless chain of mysterious little buckets to be bolted into flour. I believe I have never since wanted anything more desperately than I wanted my right thumb to be flattened, as my father's had become, during his earlier years of a miller's life. Somewhat discouraged by the slow process of structural modification, I also took measures to secure on the backs of my hands the tiny purple and red spots which are always found on the hands of the miller who dresses millstones. The marks on my father's hands had grown faint, but were quite visible when looked for, and seemed to me so desirable that they must be procured at all costs. Even when playing in our house or yard, I could always tell when the millstones were being dressed, because the rumbling of the mill then stopped, and there were few pleasures I would not instantly forego, rushing at once to the mill, that I might spread out my hands near the mill-stones in the hope that the little hard flints flying form the miller's chisel would light upon their backs and make the longed-for marks. I used hotly to accuse the German miller, my dear friend Ferdinand, "of trying not to hit my hands," but he scornfully replied that he could not hit them if he did try, and that they were too little to be of use in a mill anyway. Although I hated his teasing, I never had the courage to confess my real purpose.

This sincere tribute of imitation, which affection offers to its adored object, had later, I hope, subtler manifestations, but certainly these first ones were altogether genuine. In this case, too, I doubtless contributed my share to that stream of admiration which our generation so generously poured forth for the self-made man. I was consumed by a wistful desire to apprehend the hardships of my father's earlier life in that faraway time when he had been a miller's apprentice. I knew that he still woke up punctually at three o'clock because for so many years he had taken his turn at the mill in the early morning, and if by chance I awoke at the same hour, as curiously enough I often did, I imagined him in the early dawn in my uncle's old mill reading through the entire village library, book after book, beginning with the lives of the signers of the Declaration of Independence. Copies of the same books, mostly bound in calfskin, were to be found in the library below, and I courageously resolved that I too would read them all and try to understand life as he did. I did in fact later begin a course of reading in the early morning hours, but I was caught by some fantastic notion of chronological order and early legendary form. Pope's translation of the "Iliad," even followed by Dryden's "Virgil," did not leave behind the residuum of wisdom for which I longed, and I finally gave them up for a thick book entitled "The History of the World" as affording a shorter and an easier path.

Although I constantly confided my sins and perplexities to my father, there are only a few occasions on which I remember having received direct advice or admonition; it may easily be true, however, that I have forgotten the latter, in the manner of many seekers after advice who enjoyably set forth their situation but do not really listen to the advice itself. I can remember an admonition on one occasion, however, when, as a little girl of eight years, arrayed in a new cloak, gorgeous beyond anything I had ever worn before, I stood before my father for his approval. I was much chagrined by his remark that it was a very pretty cloak-in fact so much prettier than any cloak the other little girls in the Sunday School had, that he would advise me to wear my old cloak, which would keep me quite as warm, with the added advantage of not making the other little girls feel badly. I complied with the request but I fear without inner consent, and I certainly was quite without the joy of self-sacrifice as I walked soberly through the village street by the side of my counselor. My mind was busy, however, with the old question eternally suggested by the inequalities of the human lot. Only as we neared the church door did I venture to ask what could be done about it, receiving the reply that it might never be righted so far as clothes went, but that people might be equal in things that mattered much more than clothes, the affairs of education and religion, for instance, which we attended to when we went to school and church, and that it was very stupid to wear the sort of clothes that made it harder to have equality even there.

It must have been a little later when I held a conversation with my father upon the doctrine of foreordination, which at one time very much perplexed my childish mind. After setting the difficulty before him and complaining that I could not make it out, although my best friend "understood it perfectly," I settled down to hear his argument, having no doubt that he could make it quite clear. To my delighted surprise, for any intimation that our minds were on an equality lifted me high indeed, he said that he feared that he and I did not have the kind of mind that would ever understand fore-ordination very well and advised me not to give too much time to it; but he then proceeded to say other things of which the final impression left upon my mind was, that it did not matter much whether one understood foreordination or not, but that it was very important not to pretend to understand what you didn't understand and that you must always be honest with yourself inside, whatever happened. Perhaps on the whole as valuable a lesson as the shorter catechism itself contains.

My memory merges this early conversation on religious doctrine into one which took place years later when I put before my father the situation in which I found myself at boarding school when under great evangelical pressure, and once again I heard his testimony in favor of "mental integrity above everything else."

At the time we were driving through a piece of timber in which the wood choppers had been at work during the winter, and so earnestly were we talking that he suddenly drew up the horses to find that he did not know where he was. We were both entertained by the incident, I that my father had been "lost in his own timber" so that various cords of wood must have escaped his practiced eye, and he on his side that he should have become so absorbed in this maze of youthful speculation. We were in high spirits as we emerged from the tender green of the spring woods into the clear light of day, and as we came back into the main road I categorically asked him:-

"What are you? What do you say when people ask you?"

His eyes twinkled a little as he soberly replied:

"I am a Quaker."

"But that isn't enough to say," I urged.

"Very well," he added, "to people who insist upon details, as some one is doing now, I add that I am a Hicksite Quaker"; and not another word on the weighty subject could I induce him to utter.

These early recollections are set in a scene of rural beauty, unusual at least for Illinois. The prairie around the village was broken into hills, one of them crowned by pine woods, grown up from a bag full of Norway pine seeds sown by my father in 1844, the very year he came to

Illinois, a testimony perhaps that the most vigorous pioneers gave at least an occasional thought to beauty. The banks of the mill stream rose into high bluffs too perpendicular to be climbed without skill, and containing caves of which one at least was so black that it could not be explored without the aid of a candle; and there was a deserted limekiln which became associated in my mind with the unpardonable sin of Hawthorne's "Lime-Burner." My stepbrother and I carried on games and crusades which lasted week after week, and even summer after summer, as only free-ranging country children can do. It may be in contrast to this that one of the most piteous aspects in the life of city children, as I have seen it in the neighborhood of Hull-House, is the constant interruption to their play which is inevitable on the streets, so that it can never have any continuity-the most elaborate "plan or chart" or "fragment from their dream of human life" is sure to be rudely destroyed by the passing traffic. Although they start over and over again, even the most vivacious become worn out at last and take to that passive "standing 'round" varied by rude horseplay, which in time becomes so characteristic of city children.

We had of course our favorite places and trees and birds and flowers. It is hard to reproduce the companionship which children establish with nature, but certainly it is much too unconscious and intimate to come under the head of aesthetic appreciation or anything of the sort. When we said that the purple wind-flowers —the anemone patens —"looked as if the winds had made them," we thought much more of the fact that they were wind-born than that they were beautiful: we clapped our hands in sudden joy over the soft radiance of the rainbow, but its enchantment lay in our half belief that a pot of gold was to be found at its farther end; we yielded to a soft melancholy when we heard the whippoorwill in the early twilight, but while he aroused in us vague longings of which we spoke solemnly, we felt no beauty in his call.

We erected an altar beside the stream, to which for several years we brought all the snakes we killed during our excursions, no matter how long the toil-some journey which we had to make with a limp snake dangling between two sticks. I remember rather vaguely the ceremonial performed upon this altar one autumn day, when we brought as further tribute one out of every hundred of the black walnuts which we had gathered, and then poured over the whole a pitcher full of cider, fresh from the cider mill on the barn floor. I think we had also burned a favorite book or two upon this pyre of stones. The entire affair carried on with such solemnity was probably the result of one of those imperative impulses under whose compulsion children seek a ceremonial which shall express their sense of identification with man's primitive life and their familiar kinship with the remotest past.

Long before we had begun the study of Latin at the village school, my brother and I had learned the Lord's Prayer in Latin out of an old copy of the Vulgate, and gravely repeated it every night in an execrable pronunciation because it seemed to us more religious than "plain English."

When, however, I really prayed, what I saw before my eyes was a most outrageous picture which adorned a song-book used in Sunday School, portraying the Lord upon his throne, surrounded by tiers and tiers of saints and angels all in a blur of yellow. I am ashamed to tell how old I was when that picture ceased to appear before my eyes, especially when moments of terror compelled me to ask protection from the heavenly powers.

I recall with great distinctness my first direct contact with death when I was fifteen years old: Polly was an old nurse who had taken care of my mother and had followed her to frontier Illinois to help rear a second generation of children. She had always lived in our house, but made annual visits to her cousins on a farm a few miles north of the village. During one of those visits, word came to us one Sunday evening that Polly was dying, and for a number of reasons I was the only person able to go to her. I left the lamp-lit, warm house to be driven four miles through a blinding storm which every minute added more snow to the already high drifts, with a sense of starting upon a fateful errand. An hour after my arrival all of the cousin's family went downstairs to supper, and I was left alone to watch with Polly. The square, old-fashioned chamber in the lonely farmhouse was very cold and still, with nothing to be heard but the storm outside. Suddenly the great change came. I heard a feeble call of "Sarah," my mother's name, as the dying eyes were turned upon me, followed by a curious breathing and in place of the face familiar from my earliest childhood and associated with homely household cares, there lay upon the pillow strange, august features, stern and withdrawn from all the small affairs of life. That sense of solitude, of being unsheltered in a wide world of relentless and elemental forces which is at the basis of childhood's timidity and which is far from outgrown at fifteen, seized me irresistibly before I could reach the narrow stairs and summon the family from below.

As I was driven home in the winter storm, the wind through the trees seemed laden with a passing soul and the riddle of life and death pressed hard; once to be young, to grow old and to die, everything came to that, and then a mysterious journey out into the Unknown. Did she mind faring forth alone? Would the journey perhaps end in something as familiar and natural to the aged and dying as life is to the young and living? Through all the drive and indeed throughout the night these thoughts were pierced by sharp worry, a sense of faithlessness because I had forgotten the text Polly had confided to me long before as the one from which she wished her funeral sermon to be preached. My comfort as usual finally came from my father, who pointed out what was essential and what was of little avail even in such a moment as this, and while he was much too wise to grow dogmatic upon the great theme of death, I felt a new fellowship with him because we had discussed it together.

Perhaps I may record here my protest against the efforts, so often made, to shield children and young people from all that has to do with death and sorrow, to give them a good time at all hazards on the assumption that the ills of life will come soon enough. Young people themselves often resent this attitude on the part of their elders; they feel set aside and belittled as if they were denied the common human experiences. They too wish to climb steep stairs and to eat their bread with tears, and they imagine that the problems of existence which so press upon them in pensive moments would be less insoluble in the light of these great happenings.

An incident which stands out clearly in my mind as an exciting suggestion of the great world of moral enterprise and serious undertakings must have occurred earlier than this, for in 1872, when I was not yet twelve years old, I came into my father's room one morning to find him sitting beside the fire with a newspaper in his hand, looking very solemn; and upon my eager inquiry what had happened, he told me that Joseph Mazzini was dead. I had never even heard Mazzini's name, and after being told about him I was inclined to grow argumentative, asserting that my father did not know him, that he was not an American, and that I could not understand why we should be expected to feel badly about him. It is impossible to recall the conversation with the complete breakdown of my cheap arguments, but in the end I obtained that which I have ever regarded as a valuable possession, a sense of the genuine relationship which may exist between men who share large hopes and like desires, even though they differ in nationality, language, and creed; that those things count for absolutely nothing between groups of men who are trying to abolish slavery in America or to throw off Hapsburg oppression in Italy. At any rate, I was heartily ashamed of my meager notion of patriotism, and I came out of the room exhilarated with the consciousness that impersonal and international relations are actual facts and not mere phrases. I was filled with pride that I knew a man who held converse with great minds and who really sorrowed and rejoiced over happenings across the sea. I never recall those early conversations with my father, nor a score of others like them, but there comes into my mind a line from Mrs. Browning in which a daughter describes her relations with her father: —

"He wrapt me in his large
Man's doublet, careless did it fit or no."

Chapter II
Influence of Lincoln

I suppose all the children who were born about the time of the Civil War have recollections quite unlike those of the children who are living now. Although I was but four and a half years old when Lincoln died, I distinctly remember the day when I found on our two white gateposts American flags companioned with black. I tumbled down on the harsh gravel walk in my eager rush into the house to inquire what they were "there for." To my amazement I found my father in tears, something that I had never seen before, having assumed, as all children do, that grown-up people never cried. The two flags, my father's tears, and his impressive statement that the greatest man in the world had died, constituted my initiation, my baptism, as it were, into the thrilling and solemn interests of a world lying quite outside the two white gateposts. The great war touched children in many ways: I remember an engraved roster of names, headed by the words "Addams' Guard," and the whole surmounted by the insignia of the American eagle clutching many flags, which always hung in the family living-room. As children we used to read this list of names again and again. We could reach it only by dint of putting the family Bible on a chair and piling the dictionary on top of it; using the Bible to stand on was always accompanied by a little thrill of superstitious awe, although we carefully put the dictionary above that our profane feet might touch it alone. Having brought the roster within reach of our eager fingers, —fortunately it was glazed, —we would pick out the names of those who "had fallen on the field" from those who "had come back from the war," and from among the latter those whose children were our schoolmates. When drives were planned, we would say, "Let us take this road," that we might pass the farm where a soldier had once lived; if flowers from the garden were to be given away, we would want them to go to the mother of one of those heroes whose names we knew from the "Addams' Guard." If a guest should become interested in the roster on the wall, he was at once led by the eager children to a small picture of Colonel Davis which hung next the opposite window, that he might see the brave Colonel of the Regiment. The introduction to the picture of the one-armed man seemed to us a very solemn ceremony, and long after the guest was tired of listening, we would tell each other all about the local hero, who at the head of his troops had suffered wounds unto death. We liked very much to talk to a gentle old lady who lived in a white farmhouse a mile north of the village. She was the mother of the village hero, Tommy, and used to tell us of her long anxiety during the spring of '62; how she waited day after day for the hospital to surrender up her son, each morning airing the white homespun sheets and holding the little bedroom in immaculate readiness. It was after the battle of Fort Donelson that Tommy was wounded and had been taken to the hospital at Springfield; his father went down to him and saw him getting worse each week, until it was clear that he was going to die; but there was so much red tape about the department, and affairs were so confused, that his discharge could not be procured. At last the hospital surgeon intimated to his father that he should quietly take him away; a man as sick as that, it would be all right; but when they told Tommy, weak as he was, his eyes flashed, and he said, "No, sir; I will go out of the front door or I'll die here." Of course after that every man in the hospital worked for it, and in two weeks he was honorably discharged. When he came home at last, his mother's heart was broken to see him so wan and changed. She would tell us of the long quiet days that followed his return, with the windows open so that the dying eyes might look over the orchard slope to the meadow beyond where the younger brothers were mowing the early hay. She told us of those days when his school friends from the Academy flocked in to see him, their old acknowledged leader, and of the burning words of earnest patriotism spoken in the crowded little room, so that in three months the Academy was almost deserted and the new Company who marched away in the autumn took as drummer boy Tommy's third brother, who was only seventeen and too young for a regular. She remembered the still darker days that followed, when the bright drummer boy was in Andersonville prison, and little by little she learned to be reconciled that Tommy was safe in the peaceful home graveyard.

However much we were given to talk of war heroes, we always fell silent as we approached an isolated farmhouse in which two old people lived alone. Five of their sons had enlisted in the Civil War, and only the youngest had returned alive in the spring of 1865. In the autumn of the same year, when he was hunting for wild ducks in a swamp on the rough little farm itself, he was accidently shot and killed, and the old people were left alone to struggle with the half-cleared land as best they might. When we were driven past this forlorn little farm our childish voices always dropped into speculative whisperings as to how the accident could have happened to this remaining son out of all the men in the world, to him who had escaped so many chances of death! Our young hearts swelled in first rebellion against that which Walter Pater calls "the inexplicable shortcoming or misadventure on the part of life itself"; we were overwhelmingly oppressed by that grief of things as they are, so much more mysterious and intolerable than those griefs which we think dimly to trace to man's own wrongdoing.

It was well perhaps that life thus early gave me a hint of one of her most obstinate and insoluble riddles, for I have sorely needed the sense of universality thus imparted to that mysterious injustice, the burden of which we are all forced to bear and with which I have become only too familiar.

My childish admiration for Lincoln is closely associated with a visit made to the war eagle, Old Abe, who, as we children well knew, lived in the state capital of Wisconsin, only sixty-five miles north of our house, really no farther than an eagle could easily fly! He had been carried by the Eighth Wisconsin Regiment through the entire war, and now dwelt an honored pensioner in the state building itself.

Many times, standing in the north end of our orchard, which was only twelve miles from that mysterious line which divided Illinois from Wisconsin, we anxiously scanned the deep sky, hoping to see Old Abe fly southward right over our apple trees, for it was clearly possible that he might at any moment escape from his keeper, who, although he had been a soldier and a sentinel, would have to sleep sometimes. We gazed with thrilled interest at one speck after another in the flawless sky, but although Old Abe never came to see us, a much more incredible thing happened, for we were at last taken to see him.

We started one golden summer's day, two happy children in the family carriage, with my father and mother and an older sister to whom, because she was just home from boarding school, we confidently appealed whenever we needed information. We were driven northward hour after hour, past harvest fields in which the stubble glinted from bronze to gold and the heavy-headed grain rested luxuriously in rounded shocks, until we reached that beautiful region of hills and lakes which surrounds the capital city of Wisconsin.

But although Old Abe, sitting sedately upon his high perch, was sufficiently like an uplifted ensign to remind us of a Roman eagle, and although his veteran keeper, clad in an old army coat, was ready to answer all our questions and to tell us of the thirty-six battles and skirmishes which Old Abe had passed unscathed, the crowning moment of the impressive journey came to me later, illustrating once more that children are as quick to catch the meaning of a symbol as they are unaccountably slow to understand the real world about them.

The entire journey to the veteran war eagle had itself symbolized that search for the heroic and perfect which so persistently haunts the young; and as I stood under the great white dome of Old Abe's stately home, for one brief moment the search was rewarded. I dimly caught a hint of what men have tried to say in their world-old effort to imprison a space in so divine a line that it shall hold only yearning devotion and high-hearted hopes. Certainly the utmost rim of my first dome was filled with the tumultuous impression of soldiers marching to death for freedom's sake, of pioneers streaming westward to establish self-government in yet another sovereign state. Only the great dome of St. Peter's itself has ever clutched my heart as did that modest curve which had sequestered from infinitude in a place small enough for my child's mind, the courage and endurance which I could not comprehend so long as it was lost in "the void of unresponsible space" under the vaulting sky itself. But through all my vivid sensations there persisted the image of the eagle in the corridor below and Lincoln himself as an epitome of all that was great and good. I dimly caught the notion of the martyred President as the standard bearer to the conscience of his countrymen, as the eagle had been the ensign of courage to the soldiers of the Wisconsin regiment.

Thirty-five years later, as I stood on the hill campus of the University of Wisconsin with a commanding view of the capitol building a mile directly across the city, I saw again the dome which had so uplifted my childish spirit. The University, which was celebrating it's fiftieth anniversary, had honored me with a doctor's degree, and in the midst of the academic pomp and the rejoicing, the dome again appeared to me as a fitting symbol of the state's aspiration even in its high mission of universal education.

Thousands of children in the sixties and seventies, in the simplicity which is given to the understanding of a child, caught a notion of imperishable heroism when they were told that brave men had lost their lives that the slaves might be free. At any moment the conversation of our elders might turn upon these heroic events; there were red-letter days, when a certain general came to see my father, and again when Governor Oglesby, whom all Illinois children called "Uncle Dick," spent a Sunday under the pine trees in our front yard. We felt on those days a connection with the great world so much more heroic than the village world which surrounded us through all the other days. My father was a member of the state senate for the sixteen years between 1854 and 1870, and even as a little child I was dimly conscious of the grave march of public affairs in his comings and goings at the state capital.

He was much too occupied to allow time for reminiscence, but I remember overhearing a conversation between a visitor and himself concerning the stirring days before the war, when it was by no means certain that the Union men in the legislature would always have enough votes to keep Illinois from seceding. I heard with breathless interest my father's account of the trip a majority of the legislators had made one dark day to St. Louis, that there might not be enough men for a quorum, and so no vote could be taken on the momentous question until the Union men could rally their forces.

My father always spoke of the martyred President as Mr. Lincoln, and I never heard the great name without a thrill. I remember the day-it must have been one of comparative leisure, perhaps a Sunday-when at my request my father took out of his desk a thin packet marked "Mr. Lincoln's Letters," the shortest one of which bore unmistakable traces of that remarkable personality. These letters began, "My dear Double-D'ed Addams," and to the inquiry as to how the person thus addressed was about to vote on a certain measure then before the legislature, was added the assurance that he knew that this Addams "would vote according to his conscience," but he begged to know in which direction the same conscience "was pointing." As my father folded up the bits of paper I fairly held my breath in my desire that he should go on with the reminiscence of this wonderful man, whom he had known in his comparative obscurity, or better still, that he should be moved to tell some of the exciting incidents of the Lincoln-Douglas debates. There were at least two pictures of Lincoln that always hung in my father's room, and one in our old-fashioned upstairs parlor, of Lincoln with little Tad. For one or all of these reasons I always tend to associate Lincoln with the tenderest thoughts of my father.

I recall a time of great perplexity in the summer of 1894, when Chicago was filled with federal troops sent there by the President of the United States, and their presence was resented by the governor of the state, that I walked the wearisome way from Hull-House to Lincoln Park-for no cars were running regularly at that moment of sympathetic strikes-in order to look at and gain magnanimous counsel, if I might, from the marvelous St. Gaudens statue which had been but recently been placed at the entrance of the park. Some of Lincoln's immortal words were cut into the stone at his feet, and never did a distracted town more sorely need the healing of "with charity towards all" than did Chicago at that moment, and the tolerance of the man who had won charity for those on both sides of "an irrepressible conflict."

Of the many things written of my father in that sad August in 1881, when he died, the one I cared for most was written by an old political friend of his who was then editor of a great Chicago daily. He wrote that while there were doubtless many members of the Illinois legislature who during the great contracts of the war time and the demoralizing reconstruction days that followed, had never accepted a bribe, he wished to bear testimony that he personally had known but this one man who had never been offered a bribe because bad men were instinctively afraid of him.

I feel now the hot chagrin with which I recalled this statement during those early efforts of Illinois in which Hull- House joined, to secure the passage of the first factory legislation. I was told by the representatives of an informal association of manufacturers that if the residents of Hull-House would drop this nonsense about a sweatshop bill, of which they knew nothing, certain business men would agree to give fifty thousand dollars within two years to be used for any of the philanthropic activities of the Settlement. As the fact broke upon me that I was being offered a bribe, the shame was enormously increased by the memory of this statement. What had befallen the daughter of my father that such a thing could happen to her? The salutary reflection that it could not have occurred unless a weakness in myself had permitted it, withheld me at least from an historic display of indignation before the two men making the offer, and I explained as gently as I could that we had no ambition to make Hull-House "the largest institution on the West Side," but that we were much concerned that our neighbors should be protected from untoward conditions of work, and-so much heroics, youth must permit itself-if to accomplish this the destruction of Hull-House was necessary, that we would cheerfully sing a Te Deum on its ruins. The good friend who had invited me to lunch at the Union League Club to meet two of his friends who wanted to talk over the sweat shop bill here kindly intervened, and we all hastened to cover the awkward situation by that scurrying away from ugly morality which seems to be an obligation of social intercourse.

Of the many old friends of my father who kindly came to look up his daughter in the first days of Hull-House, I recall none with more pleasure than Lyman Trumbull, whom we used to point out to members of the Young Citizen's Club as the man who had for days held in his keeping the Proclamation of Emancipation until his friend President Lincoln was ready to issue it. I remember the talk he gave at Hull-House on one of our early celebrations of Lincoln's birthday, his assertion that Lincoln was no cheap popular hero, that the "common people" would have to make an effort if they would understand his greatness, as Lincoln painstakingly made a long effort to understand the greatness of the people. There was something in the admiration of Lincoln's contemporaries, or at least of those men who had known him personally, which was quite unlike even the best of the devotion and reverent understanding which has developed since. In the first place, they had so large a fund of common experience; they too had pioneered in a western country, and had urged the development of canals and railroads in order that the raw prairie crops might be transported to market; they too had realized that if this last tremendous experiment in self-government failed here, it would be the disappointment of the centuries and that upon their ability to organize self-government in state, county, and town depended the verdict of history. These men also knew, as Lincoln himself did, that if this tremendous experiment was to come to fruition, it must be brought about by the people themselves; that there was no other capital fund upon which to draw. I remember an incident occurring when I was about fifteen years old, in which the conviction was driven into my mind that the people themselves were the great resource of the country. My father had made a little address of reminiscence at a meeting of "the old settlers of Stephenson County," which was held every summer in the grove beside the mill, relating his experiences in inducing the farmers of the county to subscribe for stock in the Northwestern Railroad, which was the first to penetrate the county and make a connection with the Great Lakes at Chicago. Many of the Pennsylvania German farmers doubted the value of "the whole new-fangled business," and had no use for any railroad, much less for one in which they were asked to risk their hard-earned savings. My father told of his despair in one farmers' community dominated by such prejudice which did not in the least give way under his argument, but finally melted under the enthusiasm of a high-spirited German matron who took a share to be paid for "out of butter and egg money." As he related his admiration of her, an old woman's piping voice in the audience called out:

"I'm here to-day, Mr. Addams, and I'd do it again if you asked me." The old woman, bent and broken by her seventy years of toilsome life, was brought to the platform and I was much impressed by my father's grave presentation of her as "one of the public-spirited pioneers to whose heroic fortitude we are indebted for the development of this country." I remember that I was at that time reading with great enthusiasm Carlyle's "Heroes and Hero Worship," but on the evening of "Old Settlers' Day," to my surprise, I found it difficult to go on. Its sonorous sentences and exaltation of the man who "can" suddenly ceased to be convincing. I had already written down in my commonplace book a resolution to give at least twenty-five copies of this book each year to noble young people of my acquaintance. It is perhaps fitting in this chapter that the very first Christmas we spent at Hull-House, in spite of exigent demands upon my slender purse for candy and shoes, I gave to a club of boys twenty-five copies of the then new Carl Schurz's "Appreciation of Abraham Lincoln."

In our early effort at Hull-House to hand on to our neighbors whatever of help we had found for ourselves, we made much of Lincoln. We were often distressed by the children of immigrant parents who were ashamed of the pit whence they were digged, who repudiated the language and customs of their elders, and counted themselves successful as they were able to ignore the past. Whenever I held up Lincoln for their admiration as the greatest American, I invariably pointed out his marvelous power to retain and utilize past experiences; that he never forgot how the plain people in Sangamon County thought and felt when he himself had moved to town; that this habit was the foundation for his marvelous capacity for growth; that during those distracting years in Washington it enabled him to make clear beyond denial to the American people themselves, the goal towards which they were moving. I was sometimes bold enough to add that proficiency in the art of recognition and comprehension did not come without effort, and that certainly its attainment was necessary for any successful career in our conglomerate America.

An instance of the invigorating and clarifying power of Lincoln's influence came to me many years ago in England. I had spent two days in Oxford under the guidance of Arnold Toynbee's old friend Sidney Ball of St. John's College, who was closely associated with the group of scholars we all identify with the beginnings of the Settlement movement. It was easy to claim the philosophy of Thomas Hill Green, the road-building episode of Ruskin, the experimental living in the east end by Frederick Maurice, the London Workingman's College of Edward Dennison, as foundations laid by university men for the establishment of Toynbee Hall. I was naturally much interested in the beginnings of the movement whose slogan was "Back to the People," and which could doubtless claim the Settlement as one of its manifestations. Nevertheless the processes by which so simple a conclusion as residence among the poor in East London was reached, seemed to me very involved and roundabout. However inevitable these processes might be for class-conscious Englishmen, they could not but seem artificial to a western American who had been born in a rural community where the early pioneer life had made social distinctions impossible. Always on the alert lest American Settlements should become mere echoes and imitations of the English movement, I found myself assenting to what was shown me only with that part of my consciousness which had been formed by reading of English social movements, while at the same time the rustic American looked on in detached comment.

Why should an American be lost in admiration of a group of Oxford students because they went out to mend a disused road, inspired thereto by Ruskin's teaching for the bettering of the common life, when all the country roads in America were mended each spring by self-respecting citizens, who were thus carrying out the simple method devised by a democratic government bent for providing highways. No humor penetrated my high mood even as I somewhat uneasily recalled certain spring thaws when I had been mired in roads provided by the American citizen. I continued to fumble for a synthesis which I was unable to make until I developed that uncomfortable sense of playing two roles at once. It was therefore almost with a dual consciousness that I was ushered, during the last afternoon of my Oxford stay, into the drawingroom of the Master of Balliol. Edward Caird's "Evolution of Religion," which I had read but a year or two before, had been of unspeakable comfort to me in the labyrinth of differing ethical teachings and religious creeds which the many immigrant colonies of our neighborhood presented. I remember that I wanted very much to ask the author himself how far it was reasonable to expect the same quality of virtue and a similar standard of conduct from these divers people. I was timidly trying to apply his method of study to those groups of homesick immigrants huddled together in strange tenement houses, among whom I seemed to detect the beginnings of a secular religion or at least of a wide humanitarianism evolved out of the various exigencies of the situation; somewhat as a household of children, whose mother is dead, out of their sudden necessity perform unaccustomed offices for each other and awkwardly exchange consolations, as children in happier households never dream of doing. Perhaps Mr. Caird could tell me whether there was any religious content in this

> Faith to each other; this fidelity
> Of fellow wanderers in a desert place.

But when tea was over and my opportunity came for a talk with my host, I suddenly remembered, to the exclusion of all other associations, only Mr. Caird's fine analysis of Abraham Lincoln, delivered in a lecture two years before.

The memory of Lincoln, the mention of his name, came like a refreshing breeze from off the prairie, blowing aside all the scholarly implications in which I had become so reluctantly involved, and as the philosopher spoke of the great American "who was content merely to dig the channels through which the moral life of his countrymen might flow," I was gradually able to make a natural connection between this intellectual penetration at Oxford and the moral perception which is always necessary for the discovery of new methods by which to minister to human needs. In the unceasing ebb and flow of justice and oppression we must all dig channels as best we may, that at the propitious moment somewhat of the swelling tide may be conducted to the barren places of life.

Gradually a healing sense of well-being enveloped me and a quick remorse for my blindness, as I realized that no one among his own countrymen had been able to interpret Lincoln's greatness more nobly than this Oxford scholar had done, and that vision and wisdom as well as high motives must lie behind every effective stroke in the continuous labor for human equality; I remembered that another Master of Balliol, Jowett himself, had said that it was fortunate for society that every age possessed at least a few minds, which, like Arnold Toynbee's, were "perpetually disturbed over the apparent inequalities of mankind." Certainly both the English and American settlements could unite in confessing to that disturbance of mind.

Traces of this Oxford visit are curiously reflected in a paper I wrote soon after my return at the request of the American Academy of Political and Social Science. It begins as follows: —

> The word "settlement," which we have borrowed from London, is apt to grate a little upon American ears. It is not, after all, so long ago that Americans who settled were those who had adventured into a new country, where they were pioneers in the midst of difficult surroundings. The word still implies migrating from one condition of life to another totally unlike it, and against this implication the resident of an American settlement takes alarm.
>
> We do not like to acknowledge that Americans are divided into two nations, as her prime minister once admitted of England. We are not willing, openly and professedly, to assume that American citizens are broken up into classes, even if we make that assumption the preface to a plea that the superior class has duties to the inferior. Our democracy is still our most precious possession, and we do well to resent any inroads upon it, even though they may be made in the name of philanthropy.

Is it not Abraham Lincoln who has cleared the title to our democracy? He made plain, once for all, that democratic government, associated as it is with all the mistakes and shortcomings of the common people, still remains the most valuable contribution America has made to the moral life of the world.

Chapter III
Boarding-School Ideals

As my three older sisters had already attended the seminary at Rockford, of which my father was trustee, without any question I entered there at seventeen, with such meager preparation in Latin and algebra as the village school had afforded. I was very ambitious to go to Smith College, although I well knew that my father's theory in regard to the education of his daughters implied a school as near at home as possible, to be followed by travel abroad in lieu of the wider advantages which the eastern college is supposed to afford. I was much impressed by the recent return of my sister from a year in Europe, yet I was greatly disappointed at the moment of starting to humdrum Rockford. After the first weeks of homesickness were over, however, I became very much absorbed in the little world which the boarding school in any form always offers to its students.

The school at Rockford in 1877 had not changed its name from seminary to college, although it numbered, on its faculty and among its alumnae, college women who were most eager that this should be done, and who really accomplished it during the next five years. The school was one of the earliest efforts for women's higher education in the Mississippi Valley, and from the beginning was called "The Mount Holyoke of the West."

It reflected much of the missionary spirit of that pioneer institution, and the proportion of missionaries among its early graduates was almost as large as Mount Holyoke's own. In addition there had been thrown about the founders of the early western school the glamour of frontier privations, and the first students, conscious of the heroic self-sacrifice made in their behalf, felt that each minute of the time thus dearly bought must be conscientiously used. This inevitably fostered an atmosphere of intensity, a fever of preparation which continued long after the direct making of it had ceased, and which the later girls accepted, as they did the campus and the buildings, without knowing that it could have been otherwise.

There was, moreover, always present in the school a larger or smaller group of girls who consciously accepted this heritage and persistently endeavored to fulfill its obligation. We worked in those early years as if we really believed the portentous statement from Aristotle which we found quoted in Boswell's Johnson and with which we illuminated the wall of the room occupied by our Chess Club; it remained there for months, solely out of reverence, let us hope, for the two ponderous names associated with it; at least I have enough confidence in human nature to assert that we never really believed that "There is the same difference between the learned and the unlearned as there is between the living and the dead." We were also too fond of quoting Carlyle to the effect, "'Tis not to taste sweet things, but to do noble and true things that the poorest son of Adam dimly longs."

As I attempt to reconstruct the spirit of my contemporary group by looking over many documents, I find nothing more amusing than a plaint registered against life's indistinctness, which I imagine more or less reflected the sentiments of all of us. At any rate here it is for the entertainment of the reader if not for his edification: "So much of our time is spent in preparation, so much in routine, and so much in sleep, we find it difficult to have any experience at all." We did not, however, tamely accept such a state of affairs, for we made various and restless attempts to break through this dull obtuseness.

At one time five of us tried to understand De Quincey's marvelous "Dreams" more sympathetically, by drugging ourselves with opium. We solemnly consumed small white powders at intervals during an entire long holiday, but no mental reorientation took place, and the suspense and excitement did not even permit us to grow sleepy. About four o'clock on the weird afternoon, the young teacher whom we had been obliged to take into our confidence, grew alarmed over the whole performance, took away our De Quincey and all the remaining powders, administrated an emetic to each of the five aspirants for sympathetic understanding of all human experience, and sent us to our separate rooms with a stern command to appear at family worship after supper "whether we were able to or not."

Whenever we had a chance to write, we took, of course, large themes, usually from the Greek because they were the most stirring to the imagination. The Greek oration I gave at our Junior Exhibition was written with infinite pains and taken to the Greek professor in Beloit College that there might be no mistakes, even after the Rockford College teacher and the most scholarly clergyman in town had both passed upon it. The oration upon Bellerophon and his successful fight with the Chimera contended that social evils could only be overcome by him who soared above them into idealism, as Bellerophon mounted upon the winged horse Pegasus, had slain the earthy dragon.

There were practically no Economics taught in women's colleges-at least in the fresh-water ones-thirty years ago, although we painstakingly studied "Mental" and "Moral" Philosophy, which, though far from dry in the classroom, became the subject of more spirited discussion outside, and gave us a clew for animated rummaging in the little college library. Of course we read a great deal of Ruskin and Browning, and liked the most abstruse parts the best; but like the famous gentleman who talked prose without knowing it, we never dreamed of connecting them with our philosophy. My genuine interest was history, partly because of a superior teacher, and partly because my father had always insisted upon a certain amount of historic reading ever since he had paid me, as a little girl, five cents a "Life" for each Plutarch hero I could intelligently report to him and twenty-five cents for every volume of Irving's "Life of Washington."

When we started for the long vacations, a little group of five would vow that during the summer we would read all of Motley's "Dutch Republic" or, more ambitious still, all of Gibbon's "Decline and Fall of the Roman Empire." When we returned at the opening of school and three of us announced we had finished the latter, each became skeptical of the other two. We fell upon each other in a sort of rough-and-tumble examination, in which no quarter was given or received; but the suspicion was finally removed that anyone had skipped. We took for a class motto the early Saxon word for lady, translated into breadgiver, and we took for our class color the poppy, because poppies grow among the wheat, as if Nature knew that wherever there was hunger that needed food there would be pain that needed relief. We must have found the sentiment in a book somewhere, but we used it so much it finally seemed like an idea of our own, although of course none of us had ever seen a European field, the only page upon which Nature has written this particular message.

That this group of ardent girls, who discussed everything under the sun with unabated interest, did not take it all out in talk may be demonstrated by the fact that one of the class who married a missionary founded a very successful school in Japan for the children of the English and Americans living there; another of the class became a medical missionary to Korea, and because of her successful treatment of the Queen, was made court physician at a time when the opening was considered of importance in the diplomatic as well as in the missionary world; still another became an unusually skilled teacher of the blind; and one of them a pioneer librarian in that early effort to bring "books to the people."

Perhaps this early companionship showed me how essentially similar are the various forms of social effort, and curiously enough, the actual activities of a missionary school are not unlike many that are carried on in a Settlement situated in a foreign quarter. Certainly the most sympathetic and comprehending visitors we have ever had at Hull-House have been returned missionaries; among them two elderly ladies, who had lived for years in India and who had been homesick and bewildered since their return, declared that the fortnight at Hull-House had been the happiest and most familiar they had had in America.

Of course in such an atmosphere a girl like myself, of serious not to say priggish tendency, did not escape a concerted pressure to push her into the "missionary field." During the four years it was inevitable that every sort of evangelical appeal should have been made to reach the comparatively few "unconverted" girls in the school. We were the subject of prayer at the daily chapel exercise and the weekly prayer meeting, attendance upon which was obligatory.

I was singularly unresponsive to all these forms of emotional appeal, although I became unspeakably embarrassed when they were presented to me at close range by a teacher during the "silent hour," which we were all required to observe every evening, and which was never broken into, even by a member of the faculty, unless the errand was one of grave import. I found these occasional interviews on the part of one of the more serious young teachers, of whom I was extremely fond, hard to endure, as was a long series of conversations in my senior year conducted by one of the most enthusiastic members of the faculty, in which the desirability of Turkey as a field for missionary labor was enticingly put before me. I suppose I held myself aloof from all these influences, partly owing to the fact that my father was not a communicant of any church, and I tremendously admired his scrupulous morality and sense of honor in all matters of personal and public conduct, and also because the little group to which I have referred was much given to a sort of rationalism, doubtless founded upon an early reading of Emerson. In this connection, when Bronson Alcott came to lecture at the school, we all vied with each other for a chance to do him a personal service because he had been a friend of Emerson, and we were inexpressibly scornful of our younger fellow-students who cared for him merely on the basis of his grandfatherly relation to "Little Women." I recall cleaning the clay of the unpaved streets off his heavy cloth overshoes in a state of ecstatic energy.

But I think in my case there were other factors as well that contributed to my unresponsiveness to the evangelical appeal. A curious course of reading I had marked out for myself in medieval history, seems to have left me fascinated by an ideal of mingled learning, piety and physical labor, more nearly exemplified by the Port Royalists than by any others.

The only moments in which I seem to have approximated in my own experience to a faint realization of the "beauty of holiness," as I conceived it, was each Sunday morning between the hours of nine and ten, when I went into the exquisitely neat room of the teacher of Greek and read with her from a Greek testament. We did this every Sunday morning for two years. It was not exactly a lesson, for I never prepared for it, and while I was held within reasonable bounds of syntax, I was allowed much more freedom in translation than was permitted the next morning when I read Homer; neither did we discuss doctrines, for although it was with this same teacher that in our junior year we studied Paul's Epistle to the Hebrews, committing all of it to memory and analyzing and reducing it to doctrines within an inch of our lives, we never allowed an echo of this exercise to appear at these blessed Sunday morning readings. It was as if the disputations of Paul had not yet been, for we always read from the Gospels. The regime of Rockford Seminary was still very simple in the 70's. Each student made her own fire and kept her own room in order. Sunday morning was a great clearing up day, and the sense of having made immaculate my own immediate surroundings, the consciousness of clean linen, said to be close to the consciousness of a clean conscience, always mingles in my mind with these early readings. I certainly bore away with me a lifelong enthusiasm for reading the Gospels in bulk, a whole one at a time, and an insurmountable distaste for having them cut up into chapter and verse, or for hearing the incidents in that wonderful Life thus referred to as if it were merely a record.

My copy of the Greek testament had been presented to me by the brother of our Greek teacher, Professor Blaisdell of Beloit College, a true scholar in "Christian Ethics," as his department was called. I recall that one day in the summer after I left college-one of the black days which followed the death of my father-this kindly scholar came to see me in order to bring such comfort as he might and to inquire how far I had found solace in the little book he had given me so long before. When I suddenly recall the village in which I was born, its steeples and roofs look as they did that day from the hilltop where we talked together, the familiar details smoothed out and merging, as it were, into that wide conception of the universe, which for the moment swallowed up my personal grief or at least assuaged it with a realization that it was but a drop in that "torrent of sorrow and aguish and terror which flows under all the footsteps of man." This realization of sorrow as the common lot, of death as the universal experience, was the first comfort which my bruised spirit had received. In reply to my impatience with the Christian doctrine of "resignation," that it implied that you thought of your sorrow only in its effect upon you and were disloyal to the affection itself, I remember how quietly the Christian scholar changed his phraseology, saying that sometimes consolation came to us better in the words of Plato, and, as nearly as I can remember, that was the first time I had ever heard Plato's sonorous argument for the permanence of the excellent.

When Professor Blaisdell returned to his college, he left in my hands a small copy of "The Crito." The Greek was too hard for me, and I was speedily driven to Jowett's translation. That old-fashioned habit of presenting favorite books to eager young people, although it degenerated into the absurdity of "friendship's offerings," had much to be said for it, when it indicated the wellsprings of literature from which the donor himself had drawn waters of healing and inspiration.

Throughout our school years, we were always keenly conscious of the growing development of Rockford Seminary into a college. The opportunity for our Alma Mater to take her place in the new movement of full college education for women filled us with enthusiasm, and it became a driving ambition with the undergraduates to share in this new and glorious undertaking. We gravely decided that it was important that some of the students should be ready to receive the bachelor's degree the very first moment that the charter of the school should secure the right to confer it. Two of us, therefore, took a course in mathematics, advanced beyond anything previously given in the school, from one of those early young women working for a Ph.D., who was temporarily teaching in Rockford that she might study more mathematics in Leipsic.

My companion in all these arduous labors has since accomplished more than any of us in the effort to procure the franchise for women, for even then we all took for granted the righteousness of that cause into which I at least had merely followed my father's conviction. In the old-fashioned spirit of that cause I might cite the career of this companion as an illustration of the efficacy of higher mathematics for women, for she possesses singular ability to convince even the densest legislators of their legal right to define their own electorate, even when they quote against her the dustiest of state constitutions or city charters.

In line with this policy of placing a woman's college on an equality with the other colleges of the state, we applied for an opportunity to compete in the intercollegiate oratorical contest of Illinois, and we succeeded in having Rockford admitted as the first woman's college. When I was finally selected as the orator, I was somewhat dismayed to find that, representing not only one school but college women in general, I could not resent the brutal frankness with which my oratorical possibilities were discussed by the enthusiastic group who would allow no personal feeling to stand in the way of progress, especially the progress of Woman's Cause. I was told among other things that I had an intolerable habit of dropping my voice at the end of a sentence in the most feminine, apologetic and even deprecatory manner which would probably lose Woman the first place.

Woman certainly did lose the first place and stood fifth, exactly in the dreary middle, but the ignominious position may not have been solely due to bad mannerisms, for a prior place was easily accorded to William Jennings Bryan, who not only thrilled his auditors with an almost prophetic anticipation of the cross of gold, but with a moral earnestness which we had mistakenly assumed would be the unique possession of the feminine orator.

I so heartily concurred with the decision of the judges of the contest that it was with a care-free mind that I induced my colleague and alternate to remain long enough in "The Athens of Illinois," in which the successful college was situated, to visit the state institutions, one for the Blind and one for the Deaf and Dumb. Dr Gillette was at that time head of the latter institution; his scholarly explanation of the method of teaching, his concern for his charges, this sudden demonstration of the care the state bestowed upon its most unfortunate children, filled me with grave speculations in which the first, the fifth, or the ninth place in the oratorical contest seemed of little moment.

However, this brief delay between our field of Waterloo and our arrival at our aspiring college turned out to be most unfortunate, for we found the ardent group not only exhausted by the premature preparations for the return of a successful orator, but naturally much irritated as they contemplated their garlands drooping disconsolately in tubs and bowls of water. They did not fail to make me realize that I had dealt the cause of woman's advancement a staggering blow, and all my explanations of the fifth place were haughtily considered insufficient before that golden Bar of Youth, so absurdly inflexible!

To return to my last year of school, it was inevitable that the pressure toward religious profession should increase as graduating day approached. So curious, however, are the paths of moral development that several times during subsequent experiences have I felt that this passive resistance of mine, this clinging to an individual conviction, was the best moral training I received at Rockford College. During the first decade of Hull-House, it was felt by propagandists of diverse social theories that the new Settlement would be a fine coign of vantage from which to propagate social faiths, and that a mere preliminary step would be the conversion of the founders; hence I have been reasoned with hours at a time, and I recall at least three occasions when this was followed by actual prayer. In the first instance, the honest exhorter who fell upon his knees before my astonished eyes, was an advocate of single tax upon land values. He begged, in that phraseology which is deemed appropriate for prayer, that "the sister might see the beneficent results it would bring to the poor who live in the awful congested districts around this very house."

The early socialists used every method of attack, —a favorite one being the statement, doubtless sometimes honestly made, that I really was a socialist, but "too much of a coward to say so." I remember one socialist who habitually opened a very telling address he was in the habit of giving upon the street corners, by holding me up as an awful example to his fellow socialists, as one of their number "who had been caught in the toils of capitalism." He always added as a final clinching of the statement that he knew what he was talking about because he was a member of the Hull-House Men's Club. When I ventured to say to him that not all of the thousands of people who belong to a class or club at Hull-House could possibly know my personal opinions, and to mildly inquire upon what he founded his assertions, he triumphantly replied that I had once admitted to him that I had read Sombart and Loria, and that anyone of sound mind must see the inevitable conclusions of such master reasonings.

I could multiply these two instances a hundredfold, and possibly nothing aided me to stand on my own feet and to select what seemed reasonable from this wilderness of dogma, so much as my early encounter with genuine zeal and affectionate solicitude, associated with what I could not accept as the whole truth.

I do not wish to take callow writing too seriously, but I reproduce from an oratorical contest the following bit of premature pragmatism, doubtless due much more to temperament than to perception, because I am still ready to subscribe to it, although the grandiloquent style is, I hope, a thing of the past: "Those who believe that Justice is but a poetical longing within us, the enthusiast who thinks it will come in the form of a millennium, those who see it established by the strong arm of a hero, are not those who have comprehended the vast truths of life. The actual Justice must come by trained intelligence, by broadened sympathies toward the individual man or woman who crosses our path; one item added to another is the only method by which to build up a conception lofty enough to be of use in the world."

This schoolgirl recipe has been tested in many later experiences, the most dramatic of which came when I was called upon by a manufacturing company to act as one of three arbitrators in a perplexing struggle between themselves, a group of trade-unionists and a non-union employee of their establishment. The non-union man who was the cause of the difficulty had ten years before sided with his employers in a prolonged strike and had bitterly fought the union. He had been so badly injured at that time, that in spite of long months of hospital care he had never afterward been able to do a full day's work, although his employers had retained him for a decade at full pay in recognition of his loyalty. At the end of ten years the once defeated union was strong enough to enforce its demands for a union shop and in spite of the distaste of the firm for the arrangement, no obstacle to harmonious relations with the union remained but for the refusal of the trade-unionists to receive as one of their members the old crippled employee, whose spirit was broken as last and who was now willing to join the union and to stand with his old enemies for the sake of retaining his place.

But the union men would not receive "a traitor," the firm flatly refused to dismiss so faithful an employee, the busy season was upon them, and everyone concerned had finally agreed to abide without appeal by the decision of the arbitrators. The chairman of our little arbitration committee, a venerable judge, quickly demonstrated that it was impossible to collect trustworthy evidence in regards to the events already ten years old which lay at the bottom of this bitterness, and we soon therefore ceased to interview the conflicting witnesses; the second member of the committee sternly bade the men remember that the most ancient Hebraic authority gave no sanction for holding even a just resentment for more than seven years, and at last we all settled down to that wearisome effort to secure the inner consent of all concerned, upon which alone the "mystery of justice" as Maeterlinck has told us, ultimately depends. I am not quite sure that in the end we administered justice, but certainly employers, trade-unionists, and arbitrators were all convinced that justice will have to be established in industrial affairs with the same care and patience which has been necessary for centuries in order to institute it in men's civic relationships, although as the judge remarked the search must be conducted without much help from precedent. The conviction remained with me, that however long a time might be required to establish justice in the new relationships of our raw industrialism, it would never be stable until it had received the sanction of those upon whom the present situation presses so harshly.

Towards the end of our four years' course we debated much as to what we were to be, and long before the end of my school days it was quite settled in my mind that I should study medicine and "live with the poor." This conclusion of course was the result of many things, perhaps epitomized in my graduating essay on "Cassandra" and her tragic fate "always to be in the right, and always to be disbelieved and rejected."

This state of affairs, it may readily be guessed, the essay held to be an example of the feminine trait of mind called intuition, "an accurate perception of Truth and Justice, which rests contented in itself and will make no effort to confirm itself or to organize through existing knowledge." The essay then proceeds —I am forced to admit, with overmuch conviction-with the statement that women can only "grow accurate and intelligible by the thorough study of at least one branch of physical science, for only with eyes thus accustomed to the search for truth can she detect all self-deceit and fancy in herself and learn to express herself without dogmatism." So much for the first part of the thesis. Having thus "gained accuracy, would woman bring this force to bear throughout morals and justice, then she must find in active labor the promptings and inspirations that come from growing insight." I was quite certain that by following these directions carefully, in the end the contemporary woman would find "her faculties clear and acute from the study of science, and her hand upon the magnetic chain of humanity."

This veneration for science portrayed in my final essay was doubtless the result of the statements the textbooks were then making of what was called the theory of evolution, the acceptance of which even thirty years after the publication of Darwin's "Origin of Species" had about it a touch of intellectual adventure. We knew, for instance, that our science teacher had accepted this theory, but we had a strong suspicion that the teacher of Butler's "Analogy" had not. We chafed at the meagerness of the college library in this direction, and I used to bring back in my handbag books belonging to an advanced brother-in-law who had studied medicine in Germany and who therefore was quite emancipated. The first gift I made when I came into possession of my small estate the year after I left school, was a thousand dollars to the library of Rockford College, with the stipulation that it be spent for scientific books. In the long vacations I pressed plants, stuffed birds and pounded rocks in some vague belief that I was approximating the new method, and yet when my stepbrother who was becoming a real scientist, tried to carry me along with him to the merest outskirts of the methods of research, it at once became evident that I had no aptitude and was unable to follow intelligently Darwin's careful observations on the earthworm. I made a heroic effort, although candor compels me to state that I never would have finished if I had not been pulled and pushed by my really ardent companion, who in addition to a multitude of earthworms and a fine microscope, possessed untiring tact with one of flagging zeal.

As our boarding-school days neared the end, in the consciousness of approaching separation we vowed eternal allegiance to our "early ideals," and promised each other we would "never abandon them without conscious justification," and we often warned each other of "the perils of self-tradition."

We believed, in our sublime self-conceit, that the difficulty of life would lie solely in the direction of losing these precious ideals of ours, of failing to follow the way of martyrdom and high purpose we had marked out for ourselves, and we had no notion of the obscure paths of tolerance, just allowance, and self-blame wherein, if we held our minds open, we might learn something of the mystery and complexity of life's purposes.

The year after I had left college I came back, with a classmate, to receive the degree we had so eagerly anticipated. Two of the graduating class were also ready and four of us were dubbed B.A. on the very day that Rockford Seminary was declared a college in the midst of tumultuous anticipations. Having had a year outside of college walls in that trying land between vague hope and definite attainment, I had become very much sobered in my desire for a degree, and was already beginning to emerge from that rose-colored mist with which the dream of youth so readily envelops the future.

Whatever may have been the perils of self-tradition, I certainly did not escape them, for it required eight years-from the time I left Rockford in the summer of 1881 until Hull-House was opened in the the autumn of 1889 —to formulate my convictions even in the least satis-factory manner, much less to reduce them to a plan for action. During most of that time I was absolutely at sea so far as any moral purpose was concerned, clinging only to the desire to live in a really living world and refusing to be content with a shadowy intellectual or aesthetic reflection of it.

Chapter IV
The Snare of Preparation

The winter after I left school was spent in the Woman's Medical College of Philadelphia, but the development of the spinal difficulty which had shadowed me from childhood forced me into Dr. Weir Mitchell's hospital for the late spring, and the next winter I was literally bound to a bed in my sister's house for six months. In spite of its tedium, the long winter had its mitigations, for after the first few weeks I was able to read with a luxurious consciousness of leisure, and I remember opening the first volume of Carlyle's "Frederick the Great" with a lively sense of gratitude that it was not Gray's "Anatomy," having found, like many another, that general culture is a much easier undertaking than professional study. The long illness inevitably put aside the immediate prosecution of a medical course, and although I had passed my examinations creditably enough in the required subjects for the first year, I was very glad to have a physician's sanction for giving up clinics and dissecting rooms and to follow his prescription of spending the next two years in Europe.

Before I returned to America I had discovered that there were other genuine reasons for living among the poor than that of practicing medicine upon them, and my brief foray into the profession was never resumed.

The long illness left me in a state of nervous exhaustion with which I struggled for years, traces of it remaining long after Hull-House was opened in 1889. At the best it allowed me but a limited amount of energy, so that doubtless there was much nervous depression at the foundation of the spiritual struggles which this chapter is forced to record. However, it could not have been all due to my health, for as my wise little notebook sententiously remarked, "In his own way each man must struggle, lest the moral law become a far-off abstraction utterly separated from his active life."

It would, of course, be impossible to remember that some of these struggles ever took place at all, were it not for these selfsame notebooks, in which, however, I no longer wrote in moments of high resolve, but judging from the internal evidence afforded by the books themselves, only in moments of deep depression when overwhelmed by a sense of failure.

One of the most poignant of these experiences, which occurred during the first few months after our landing upon the other side of the Atlantic, was on a Saturday night, when I received an ineradicable impression of the wretchedness of East London, and also saw for the first time the overcrowded quarters of a great city at midnight. A small party of tourists were taken to the East End by a city missionary to witness the Saturday night sale of decaying vegetables and fruit, which, owing to the Sunday laws in London, could not be sold until Monday, and, as they were beyond safe keeping, were disposed of at auction as late as possible on Saturday night. On Mile End Road, from the top of an omnibus which paused at the end of a dingy street lighted by only occasional flares of gas, we saw two huge masses of ill-clad people clamoring around two hucksters' carts. They were bidding their farthings and ha'pennies for a vegetable held up by the auctioneer, which he at last scornfully flung, with a gibe for its cheapness, to the successful bidder. In the momentary pause only one man detached himself from the groups. He had bidden in a cabbage, and when it struck his hand, he instantly sat down on the curb, tore it with his teeth, and hastily devoured it, unwashed and uncooked as it was. He and his fellows were types of the "submerged tenth," as our missionary guide told us, with some little satisfaction in the then new phrase, and he further added that so many of them could scarcely be seen in one spot save at this Saturday night auction, the desire for cheap food being apparently the one thing which could move them simultaneously. They were huddled into ill-fitting, cast-off clothing, the ragged finery which one sees only in East London. Their pale faces were dominated by that most unlovely of human expressions, the cunning and shrewdness of the bargain-hunter who starves if he cannot make a successful trade, and yet the final impression was not of ragged, tawdry clothing nor of pinched and sallow faces, but of myriads of hands, empty, pathetic, nerveless and workworn, showing white in the uncertain light of the street, and clutching forward for food which was already unfit to eat.

Perhaps nothing is so fraught with significance as the human hand, this oldest tool with which man has dug his way from savagery, and with which he is constantly groping forward. I have never since been able to see a number of hands held upward, even when they are moving rhythmically in a calisthenic exercise, or when they belong to a class of chubby children who wave them in eager response to a teacher's query, without a certain revival of this memory, a clutching at the heart reminiscent of the despair and resentment which seized me then.

For the following weeks I went about London almost furtively, afraid to look down narrow streets and alleys lest they disclose again this hideous human need and suffering. I carried with me for days at a time that curious surprise we experience when we first come back into the streets after days given over to sorrow and death; we are bewildered that the world should be going on as usual and unable to determine which is real, the inner pang or the outward seeming. In time all huge London came to seem unreal save the poverty in its East End. During the following two years on the continent, while I was irresistibly drawn to the poorer quarters of each city, nothing among the beggars of South Italy nor among the salt miners of Austria carried with it the same conviction of human wretchedness which was conveyed by this momentary glimpse of an East London street. It was, of course, a most fragmentary and lurid view of the poverty of East London, and quite unfair. I should have been shown either less or more, for I went away with no notion of the hundreds of men and women who had gallantly identified their fortunes with these empty-handed people, and who, in church and chapel, "relief works," and charities, were at least making an effort towards its mitigation.

Our visit was made in November, 1883, the very year when the Pall Mall Gazette exposure started "The Bitter Cry of Outcast London," and the conscience of England was stirred as never before over this joyless city in the East End of its capital. Even then, vigorous and drastic plans were being discussed, and a splendid program of municipal reforms was already dimly outlined. Of all these, however, I had heard nothing but the vaguest rumor.

No comfort came to me then from any source, and the painful impression was increased because at the very moment of looking down the East London street from the top of the omnibus, I had been sharply and painfully reminded of "The Vision of Sudden Death" which had confronted De Quincey one summer's night as he was being driven through rural England on a high mail coach. Two absorbed lovers suddenly appear between the narrow, blossoming hedgerows in the direct path of the huge vehicle which is sure to crush them to their death. De Quincey tries to send them a warning shout, but finds himself unable to make a sound because his mind is hopelessly entangled in an endeavor to recall the exact lines from the Iliad which describe the great cry with which Achilles alarmed all Asia militant. Only after his memory responds is his will released from its momentary paralysis, and he rides on through the fragrant night with the horror of the escaped calamity thick upon him, but he also bears with him the consciousness that he had given himself over so many years to classic learning-that when suddenly called upon for a quick decision in the world of life and death, he had been able to act only through a literary suggestion.

This is what we were all doing, lumbering our minds with literature that only served to cloud the really vital situation spread before our eyes. It seemed to me too preposterous that in my first view of the horror of East London I should have recalled De Quincey's literary description of the literary suggestion which had once paralyzed him. In my disgust it all appeared a hateful, vicious circle which even the apostles of culture themselves admitted, for had not one of the greatest among the moderns plainly said that "conduct, and not culture is three fourths of human life."

For two years in the midst of my distress over the poverty which, thus suddenly driven into my consciousness, had become to me the "Weltschmerz," there was mingled a sense of futility, of misdirected energy, the belief that the pursuit of cultivation would not in the end bring either solace or relief. I gradually reached a conviction that the first generation of college women had taken their learning too quickly, had departed too suddenly from the active, emotional life led by their grandmothers and great-grandmothers; that the contemporary education of young women had developed too exclusively the power of acquiring knowledge and of merely receiving impressions; that somewhere in the process of 'being educated' they had lost that simple and almost automatic response to the human appeal, that old healthful reaction resulting in activity from the mere presence of suffering or of helplessness; that they are so sheltered and pampered they have no chance even to make "the great refusal."

In the German and French pensions, which twenty-five years ago were crowded with American mothers and their daughters who had crossed the seas in search of culture, one often found the mother making real connection with the life about her, using her inadequate German with great fluency, gaily measuring the enormous sheets or exchanging recipes with the German Hausfrau, visiting impartially the nearest kindergarten and market, making an atmosphere of her own, hearty and genuine as far as it went, in the house and on the street. On the other hand, her daughter was critical and uncertain of her linguistic acquirements, and only at ease when in the familiar receptive attitude afforded by the art gallery and opera house. In the latter she was swayed and moved, appreciative of the power and charm of the music, intelligent as to the legend and poetry of the plot, finding use for her trained and developed powers as she sat "being cultivated" in the familiar atmosphere of the classroom which had, as it were, become sublimated and romanticized.

I remember a happy busy mother who, complacent with the knowledge that her daughter daily devoted four hours to her music, looked up from her knitting to say, "If I had had your opportunities when I was young, my dear, I should have been a very happy girl. I always had musical talent, but such training as I had, foolish little songs and waltzes and not time for half an hour's practice a day."

The mother did not dream of the sting her words left and that the sensitive girl appreciated only too well that her opportunities were fine and unusual, but she also knew that in spite of some facility and much good teaching she had no genuine talent and never would fulfill the expectations of her friends. She looked back upon her mother's girlhood with positive envy because it was so full of happy industry and extenuating obstacles, with undisturbed opportunity to believe that her talents were unusual. The girl looked wistfully at her mother, but had not the courage to cry out what was in her heart: "I might believe I had unusual talent if I did not know what good music was; I might enjoy half an hour's practice a day if I were busy and happy the rest of the time. You do not know what life means when all the difficulties are removed! I am simply smothered and sickened with advantages. It is like eating a sweet dessert the first thing in the morning."

This, then, was the difficulty, this sweet dessert in the morning and the assumption that the sheltered, educated girl has nothing to do with the bitter poverty and the social maladjustment which is all about her, and which, after all, cannot be concealed, for it breaks through poetry and literature in a burning tide which overwhelms her; it peers at her in the form of heavy-laden market women and underpaid street laborers, gibing her with a sense of her uselessness.

I recall one snowy morning in Saxe-Coburg, looking from the window of our little hotel upon the town square, that we saw crossing and recrossing it a single file of women with semi-circular, heavy, wooden tanks fastened upon their backs. They were carrying in this primitive fashion to a remote cooling room these tanks filled with a hot brew incident to one stage of beer making. The women were bent forward, not only under the weight which they were bearing, but because the tanks were so high that it would have been impossible for them to have lifted their heads. Their faces and hands, reddened in the cold morning air, showed clearly the white scars where they had previously been scalded by the hot stuff which splashed if they stumbled ever so little on their way. Stung into action by one of those sudden indignations against cruel conditions which at times fill the young with unexpected energy, I found myself across the square, in company with mine host, interviewing the phlegmatic owner of the brewery who received us with exasperating indifference, or rather received me, for the innkeeper mysteriously slunk away as soon as the great magnate of the town began to speak. I went back to a breakfast for which I had lost my appetite, as I had for Gray's "Life of Prince Albert" and his wonderful tutor, Baron Stockmar, which I had been reading late the night before. The book had lost its fascination; how could a good man, feeling so keenly his obligation "to make princely the mind of his prince," ignore such conditions of life for the multitude of humble, hard-working folk. We were spending two months in Dresden that winter, given over to much reading of "The History of Art" and after such an experience I would invariably suffer a moral revulsion against this feverish search after culture. It was doubtless in such moods that I founded my admiration for Albrecht Durer, taking his wonderful pictures, however, in the most unorthodox manner, merely as human documents. I was chiefly appealed to by his unwillingness to lend himself to a smooth and cultivated view of life, by his determination to record its frustrations and even the hideous forms which darken the day for our human imagination and to ignore no human complications. I believed that his canvases intimated the coming religious and social changes of the Reformation and the peasants' wars, that they were surcharged with pity for the down-trodden, that his sad knights, gravely standing guard, were longing to avert that shedding of blood which is sure to occur when men forget how complicated life is and insist upon reducing it to logical dogmas.

The largest sum of money that I ever ventured to spend in Europe was for an engraving of his "St. Hubert," the background of which was said to be from an original Durer plate. There is little doubt, I am afraid, that the background as well as the figures "were put in at a later date," but the purchase at least registered the high-water mark of my enthusiasm.

The wonder and beauty of Italy later brought healing and some relief to the paralyzing sense of the futility of all artistic and intellectual effort when disconnected from the ultimate test of the conduct it inspired. The serene and soothing touch of history also aroused old enthusiasms, although some of their manifestations were such as one smiles over more easily in retrospection than at the moment. I fancy that it was no smiling matter to several people in our party, whom I induced to walk for three miles in the hot sunshine beating down upon the Roman Campagna, that we might enter the Eternal City on foot through the Porta del Popolo, as pilgrims had done for centuries. To be sure, we had really entered Rome the night before, but the railroad station and the hotel might have been anywhere else, and we had been driven beyond the walls after breakfast and stranded at the very spot where the pilgrims always said "Ecco Roma," as they caught the first glimpse of St. Peter's dome. This melodramatic entrance into Rome, or rather pretended entrance, was the prelude to days of enchantment, and I returned to Europe two years later in order to spend a winter there and to carry out a great desire to systematically study the Catacombs. In spite of my distrust of "advantages" I was apparently not yet so cured but that I wanted more of them.

The two years which elapsed before I again found myself in Europe brought their inevitable changes. Family arrangements had so come about that I had spent three or four months of each of the intervening winters in Baltimore, where I seemed to have reached the nadir of my nervous depression and sense of maladjustment, in spite of my interest in the fascinating lectures given there by Lanciani of Rome, and a definite course of reading under the guidance of a Johns Hopkins lecturer upon the United Italy movement. In the latter I naturally encountered the influence of Mazzini, which was a source of great comfort to me, although perhaps I went too suddenly from a contemplation of his wonderful ethical and philosophical appeal to the work-ingmen of Italy, directly to the lecture rooms at Johns Hopkins University, for I was certainly much disillusioned at this time as to the effect of intellectual pursuits upon moral development.

The summers were spent in the old home in northern Illinois, and one Sunday morning I received the rite of baptism and became a member of the Presbyterian church in the village. At this time there was certainly no outside pressure pushing me towards such a decision, and at twenty-five one does not ordinarily take such a step from a mere desire to conform. While I was not conscious of any emotional "conversion," I took upon myself the outward expressions of the religious life with all humility and sincerity. It was doubtless true that I was

"Weary of myself and sick of asking
What I am and what I ought to be,"

and that various cherished safeguards and claims to self-dependence had been broken into by many piteous failures. But certainly I had been brought to the conclusion that "sincerely to give up one's conceit or hope of being good in one's own right is the only door to the Universe's deeper reaches." Perhaps the young clergyman recognized this as the test of the Christian temper, at any rate he required little assent to dogma or miracle, and assured me that while both the ministry and the officers of his church were obliged to subscribe to doctrines of well-known severity, the faith required to the laity was almost early Christian in its simplicity. I was conscious of no change from my childish acceptance of the teachings of the Gospels, but at this moment something persuasive within made me long for an outward symbol of fellowship, some bond of peace, some blessed spot where unity of spirit might claim right of way over all differences. There was also growing within me an almost passionate devotion to the ideals of democracy, and when in all history had these ideals been so thrillingly expressed as when the faith of the fisherman and the slave had been boldly opposed to the accepted moral belief that the well-being of a privileged few might justly be built upon the ignorance and sacrifice of the many? Who was I, with my dreams of universal fellowship, that I did not identify myself with the institutional statement of this belief, as it stood in the little village in which I was born, and without which testimony in each remote hamlet of Christendom it would be so easy for the world to slip back into the doctrines of selection and aristocracy?

In one of the intervening summers between these European journeys I visited a western state where I had formerly invested a sum of money in mortgages. I was much horrified by the wretched conditions among the farmers, which had resulted from a long period of drought, and one forlorn picture was fairly burned into my mind. A number of starved hogs-collateral for a promissory note-were huddled into an open pen. Their backs were humped in a curious, camel-like fashion, and they were devouring one of their own number, the latest victim of absolute starvation or possibly merely the one least able to defend himself against their voracious hunger. The farmer's wife looked on indifferently, a picture of despair as she stood in the door of the bare, crude house, and the two children behind her, whom she vainly tried to keep out of sight, continually thrust forward their faces almost covered by masses of coarse, sunburned hair, and their little bare feet so black, so hard, the great cracks so filled with dust that they looked like flattened hoofs. The children could not be compared to anything so joyous as satyrs, although they appeared but half-human. It seemed to me quite impossible to receive interest from mortgages placed upon farms which might at any season be reduced to such conditions, and with great inconvenience to my agent and doubtless with hardship to the farmers, as speedily as possible I withdrew all my investment. But something had to be done with the money, and in my reaction against unseen horrors I bought a farm near my native village and also a flock of innocent-looking sheep. My partner in the enterprise had not chosen the shepherd's lot as a permanent occupation, but hoped to speedily finish his college course upon half the proceeds of our venture. This pastoral enterprise still seems to me to have been essentially sound, both economically and morally, but perhaps one partner depended too much upon the impeccability of her motives and the other found himself too preoccupied with study to know that it is not a real kindness to bed a sheepfold with straw, for certainly the venture ended in a spectacle scarcely less harrowing than the memory it was designed to obliterate. At least the sight of two hundred sheep with four rotting hoofs each, was not reassuring to one whose conscience craved economic peace. A fortunate series of sales of mutton, wool, and farm enabled the partners to end the enterprise without loss, and they passed on, one to college and the other to Europe, if not wiser, certainly sadder for the experience.

It was during this second journey to Europe that I attended a meeting of the London match girls who were on strike and who met daily under the leadership of well-known labor men of London. The low wages that were reported at the meetings, the phossy jaw which was described and occasionally exhibited, the appearance of the girls themselves I did not, curiously enough, in any wise connect with what was called the labor movement, nor did I understand the efforts of the London trades-unionists, concerning whom I held the vaguest notions. But of course this impression of human misery was added to the others which were already making me so wretched. I think that up to this time I was still filled with the sense which Wells describes in one of his young characters, that somewhere in Church or State are a body of authoritative people who will put things to rights as soon as they really know what is wrong. Such a young person persistently believes that behind all suffering, behind sin and want, must lie redeeming magnanimity. He may imagine the world to be tragic and terrible, but it never for an instant occurs to him that it may be contemptible or squalid or self-seeking. Apparently I looked upon the efforts of the trades-unionists as I did upon those of Frederic Harrison and the Positivists whom I heard the next Sunday in Newton Hall, as a manifestation of "loyalty to humanity" and an attempt to aid in its progress. I was enormously interested in the Positivists during these European years; I imagined that their philosophical conception of man's religious development might include all expressions of that for which so many ages of men have struggled and aspired. I vaguely hoped for this universal comity when I stood in Stonehenge, on the Acropolis in Athens, or in the Sistine Chapel in the Vatican. But never did I so desire it as in the cathedrals of Winchester, Notre Dame, Amiens. One winter's day I traveled from Munich to Ulm because I imagined from what the art books said that the cathedral hoarded a medieval statement of the Positivists' final synthesis, prefiguring their conception of a "Supreme Humanity."

In this I was not altogether disappointed. The religious history carved on the choir stalls at Ulm contained Greek philosophers as well as Hebrew prophets, and among the disciples and saints stood the discoverer of music and a builder of pagan temples. Even then I was startled, forgetting for the moment the religious revolutions of south Germany, to catch sight of a window showing Luther as he affixed his thesis on the door at Wittenberg, the picture shining clear in the midst of the older glass of saint and symbol.

My smug notebook states that all this was an admission that "the saints but embodied fine action," and it proceeds at some length to set forth my hope for a "cathedral of humanity," which should be "capacious enough to house a fellowship of common purpose," and which should be "beautiful enough to persuade men to hold fast to the vision of human solidarity." It is quite impossible for me to reproduce this experience at Ulm unless I quote pages more from the notebook in which I seem to have written half the night, in a fever of composition cast in ill-digested phrases from Comte. It doubtless reflected also something of the faith of the Old Catholics, a charming group of whom I had recently met in Stuttgart, and the same mood is easily traced in my early hopes for the Settlement that it should unite in the fellowship of the deed those of widely differing religious beliefs.

The beginning of 1887 found our little party of three in very picturesque lodgings in Rome, and settled into a certain student's routine. But my study of the Catacombs was brought to an abrupt end in a fortnight by a severe attack of sciatic rheumatism, which kept me in Rome with a trained nurse during many weeks, and later sent me to the Riviera to lead an invalid's life once more. Although my Catacomb lore thus remained hopelessly superficial, it seemed to me a sufficient basis for a course of six lectures which I timidly offered to a Deaconess's Training School during my first winter in Chicago, upon the simple ground that this early interpretation of Christianity is the one which should be presented to the poor, urging that the primitive church was composed of the poor and that it was they who took the wonderful news to the more prosperous Romans. The open-minded head of the school gladly accepted the lectures, arranging that the course should be given each spring to her graduating class of Home and Foreign Missionaries, and at the end of the third year she invited me to become one of the trustees of the school. I accepted and attended one meeting of the board, but never another, because some of the older members objected to my membership on the ground that "no religious instruction was given at Hull-House." I remember my sympathy for the embarrassment in which the head of the school was placed, but if I needed comfort, a bit of it came to me on my way home from the trustees' meeting when an Italian laborer paid my street-car fare, according to the custom of our simpler neighbors. Upon my inquiry of the conductor as to whom I was indebted for the little courtesy, he replied roughly enough, "I cannot tell one dago from another when they are in a gang, but sure, any one of them would do it for you as quick as they would for the Sisters."

It is hard to tell just when the very simple plan which afterward developed into the Settlement began to form itself in my mind. It may have been even before I went to Europe for the second time, but I gradually became convinced that it would be a good thing to rent a house in a part of the city where many primitive and actual needs are found, in which young women who had been given over too exclusively to study might restore a balance of activity along traditional lines and learn of life from life itself; where they might try out some of the things they had been taught and put truth to "the ultimate test of the conduct it dictates or inspires." I do not remember to have mentioned this plan to anyone until we reached Madrid in April, 1888.

We had been to see a bull fight rendered in the most magnificent Spanish style, where greatly to my surprise and horror, I found that I had seen, with comparative indifference, five bulls and many more horses killed. The sense that this was the last survival of all the glories of the amphitheater, the illusion that the riders on the caparisoned horses might have been knights of a tournament, or the matadore a slightly armed gladiator facing his martyrdom, and all the rest of the obscure yet vivid associations of an historic survival, had carried me beyond the endurance of any of the rest of the party. I finally met them in the foyer, stern and pale with disapproval of my brutal endurance, and but partially recovered from the faintness and disgust which the spectacle itself had produced upon them. I had no defense to offer to their reproaches save that I had not thought much about the bloodshed; but in the evening the natural and inevitable reaction came, and in deep chagrin I felt myself tried and condemned, not only by this disgusting experience but by the entire moral situation which it revealed. It was suddenly made quite clear to me that I was lulling my conscience by a dreamer's scheme, that a mere paper reform had become a defense for continued idleness, and that I was making it a raison d'etre for going on indefinitely with study and travel. It is easy to become the dupe of a deferred purpose, of the promise the future can never keep, and I had fallen into the meanest type of self-deception in making myself believe that all this was in preparation for great things to come. Nothing less than the moral reaction following the experience at a bullfight had been able to reveal to me that so far from following in the wake of a chariot of philanthropic fire, I had been tied to the tail of the veriest ox-cart of self-seeking.

I had made up my mind that next day, whatever happened, I would begin to carry out the plan, if only by talking about it. I can well recall the stumbling and uncertainty with which I finally set it forth to Miss Starr, my old-time school friend, who was one of our party. I even dared to hope that she might join in carrying out the plan, but nevertheless I told it in the fear of that disheartening experience which is so apt to afflict our most cherished plans when they are at last divulged, when we suddenly feel that there is nothing there to talk about, and as the golden dream slips through our fingers we are left to wonder at our own fatuous belief. But gradually the comfort of Miss Starr's companionship, the vigor and enthusiasm which she brought to bear upon it, told both in the growth of the plan and upon the sense of its validity, so that by the time we had reached the enchantment of the Alhambra, the scheme had become convincing and tangible although still most hazy in detail.

A month later we parted in Paris, Miss Starr to go back to Italy, and I to journey on to London to secure as many suggestions as possible from those wonderful places of which we had heard, Toynbee Hall and the People's Palace. So that it finally came about that in June, 1888, five years after my first visit in East London, I found myself at Toynbee Hall equipped not only with a letter of introduction from Canon Fremantle, but with high expectations and a certain belief that whatever perplexities and discouragement concerning the life of the poor were in store for me, I should at least know something at first hand and have the solace of daily activity. I had confidence that although life itself might contain many difficulties, the period of mere passive receptivity had come to an end, and I had at last finished with the ever-lasting "preparation for life," however ill-prepared I might be.

It was not until years afterward that I came upon Tolstoy's phrase "the snare of preparation," which he insists we spread before the feet of young people, hopelessly entangling them in a curious inactivity at the very period of life when they are longing to construct the world anew and to conform it to their own ideals.

Chapter V
First Days at Hull-House

The next January found Miss Starr and myself in Chicago, searching for a neighborhood in which we might put our plans into execution. In our eagerness to win friends for the new undertaking, we utilized every opportunity to set forth the meaning of the Settlement as it had been embodied at Toynbee Hall, although in those days we made no appeal for money, meaning to start with our own slender resources. From the very first the plan received courteous attention, and the discussion, while often skeptical, was always friendly. Professor Swing wrote a commendatory column in the Evening Journal, and our early speeches were reported quite out of proportion to their worth. I recall a spirited evening at the home of Mrs. Wilmarth, which was attended by that renowned scholar, Thomas Davidson, and by a young Englishman who was a member of the then new Fabian society and to whom a peculiar glamour was attached because he had scoured knives all summer in a camp of high-minded philosophers in the Adirondacks. Our new little plan met with criticism, not to say disapproval, from Mr. Davidson, who, as nearly as I can remember, called it "one of those unnatural attempts to understand life through cooperative living."

It was in vain we asserted that the collective living was not an essential part of the plan, that we would always scrupulously pay our own expenses, and that at any moment we might decide to scatter through the neighborhood and to live in separate tenements; he still contended that the fascination for most of those volunteering residence would lie in the collective living aspect of the Settlement. His contention was, of course, essentially sound; there is a constant tendency for the residents to "lose themselves in the cave of their own companionship," as the Toynbee Hall phrase goes, but on the other hand, it is doubtless true that the very companionship, the give and take of colleagues, is what tends to keep the Settlement normal and in touch with "the world of things as they are." I am happy to say that we never resented this nor any other difference of opinion, and that fifteen years later Professor Davidson handsomely acknowledged that the advantages of a group far outweighed the weaknesses he had early pointed out. He was at that later moment sharing with a group of young men, on the East Side of New York, his ripest conclusions in philosophy and was much touched by their intelligent interest and absorbed devotion. I think that time has also justified our early contention that the mere foothold of a house, easily accessible, ample in space, hospitable and tolerant in spirit, situated in the midst of the large foreign colonies which so easily isolate themselves in American cities, would be in itself a serviceable thing for Chicago. I am not so sure that we succeeded in our endeavors "to make social intercourse express the growing sense of the economic unity of society and to add the social function to democracy". But Hull-House was soberly opened on the theory that the dependence of classes on each other is reciprocal; and that as the social relation is essentially a reciprocal relation, it gives a form of expression that has peculiar value.

In our search for a vicinity in which to settle we went about with the officers of the compulsory education department, with city missionaries, and with the newspaper reporters whom I recall as a much older set of men than one ordinarily associates with that profession, or perhaps I was only sent out with the older ones on what they must all have considered a quixotic mission. One Sunday afternoon in the late winter a reporter took me to visit a so-called anarchist sunday school, several of which were to be found on the northwest side of the city. The young man in charge was of the German student type, and his face flushed with enthusiasm as he led the children singing one of Koerner's poems. The newspaperman, who did not understand German, asked me what abominable stuff they were singing, but he seemed dissatisfied with my translation of the simple words and darkly intimated that they were "deep ones," and had probably "fooled" me. When I replied that Koerner was an ardent German poet whose songs inspired his countrymen to resist the aggressions of Napoleon, and that his bound poems were found in the most respectable libraries, he looked at me rather askance and I then and there had my first intimation that to treat a Chicago man, who is called an anarchist, as you would treat any other citizen, is to lay yourself open to deep suspicion.

Another Sunday afternoon in the early spring, on the way to a Bohemian mission in the carriage of one of its founders, we passed a fine old house standing well back from the street, surrounded on three sides by a broad piazza, which was supported by wooden pillars of exceptionally pure Corinthian design and proportion. I was so attracted by the house that I set forth to visit it the very next day, but though I searched for it then and for several days after, I could not find it, and at length I most reluctantly gave up the search.

Three weeks later, with the advice of several of the oldest residents of Chicago, including the ex-mayor of the city, Colonel Mason, who had from the first been a warm friend to our plans, we decided upon a location somewhere near the junction of Blue Island Avenue, Halsted Street, and Harrison Street. I was surprised and overjoyed on the very first day of our search for quarters to come upon the hospitable old house, the quest for which I had so recently abandoned. The house was of course rented, the lower part of it used for offices and storerooms in connection with a factory that stood back of it. However, after some difficulties were overcome, it proved to be possible to sublet the second floor and what had been a large drawing-room on the first floor.

The house had passed through many changes since it had been built in 1856 for the homestead of one of Chicago's pioneer citizens, Mr. Charles J. Hull, and although battered by its vicissitudes, was essentially sound. Before it had been occupied by the factory, it had sheltered a second-hand furniture store, and at one time the Little Sisters of the Poor had used it for a home for the aged. It had a half-skeptical reputation for a haunted attic, so far respected by the tenants living on the second floor that they always kept a large pitcher full of water on the attic stairs. Their explanation of this custom was so incoherent that I was sure it was a survival of the belief that a ghost could not cross running water, but perhaps that interpretation was only my eagerness for finding folklore.

The fine old house responded kindly to repairs, its wide hall and open fireplace always insuring it a gracious aspect. Its generous owner, Miss Helen Culver, in the following spring gave us a free leasehold of the entire house. Her kindness has continued through the years until the group of thirteen buildings, which at present comprises our equipment, is built largely upon land which Miss Culver has put at the service of the Settlement which bears Mr. Hull's name. In those days the house stood between an undertaking establishment and a saloon. "Knight, Death and the Devil," the three were called by a Chicago wit, and yet any mock heroics which might be implied by comparing the Settlement to a knight quickly dropped away under the genuine kindness and hearty welcome extended to us by the families living up and down the street.

We furnished the house as we would have furnished it were it in another part of the city, with the photographs and other impedimenta we had collected in Europe, and with a few bits of family mahogany. While all the new furniture which was bought was enduring in quality, we were careful to keep it in character with the fine old residence. Probably no young matron ever placed her own things in her own house with more pleasure than that with which we first furnished Hull-House. We believed that the Settlement may logically bring to its aid all those adjuncts which the cultivated man regards as good and suggestive of the best of the life of the past.

On the 18th of September, 1889, Miss Starr and I moved into it, with Miss Mary Keyser, who began performing the housework, but who quickly developed into a very important factor in the life of the vicinity as well as that of the household, and whose death five years later was most sincerely mourned by hundreds of our neighbors.

In our enthusiasm over "settling," the first night we forgot not only to lock but to close a side door opening on Polk Street, and we were much pleased in the morning to find that we possessed a fine illustration of the honesty and kindliness of our new neighbors.

Our first guest was an interesting young woman who lived in a neighboring tenement, whose widowed mother aided her in the support of the family by scrubbing a downtown theater every night. The mother, of English birth, was well bred and carefully educated, but was in the midst of that bitter struggle which awaits so many strangers in American cities who find that their social position tends to be measured solely by the standards of living they are able to maintain. Our guest has long since married the struggling young lawyer to whom she was then engaged, and he is now leading his profession in an eastern city. She recalls that month's experience always with a sense of amusement over the fact that the succession of visitors who came to see the new Settlement invariably questioned her most minutely concerning "these people" without once suspecting that they were talking to one who had been identified with the neighborhood from childhood. I at least was able to draw a lesson from the incident, and I never addressed a Chicago audience on the subject of the Settlement and its vicinity without inviting a neighbor to go with me, that I might curb any hasty generalization by the consciousness that I had an auditor who knew the conditions more intimately than I could hope to do.

Halsted Street has grown so familiar during twenty years of residence that it is difficult to recall its gradual changes, —the withdrawal of the more prosperous Irish and Germans, and the slow substitution of Russian Jews, Italians, and Greeks. A description of the street such as I gave in those early addresses still stands in my mind as sympathetic and correct.

Halsted Street is thirty-two miles long, and one of the great thoroughfares of Chicago; Polk Street crosses it midway between the stockyards to the south and the shipbuilding yards on the north branch of the Chicago River. For the six miles between these two industries the street is lined with shops of butchers and grocers, with dingy and gorgeous saloons, and pretentious establishments for the sale of ready-made clothing. Polk Street, running west from Halsted Street, grows rapidly more prosperous; running a mile east to State Street, it grows steadily worse, and crosses a network of vice on the corners of Clark Street and Fifth Avenue. Hull-House once stood in the suburbs, but the city has steadily grown up around it and its site now has corners on three or four foreign colonies. Between Halsted Street and the river live about ten thousand Italians-Neapolitans, Sicilians, and Calabrians, with an occasional Lombard or Venetian. To the south on Twelfth Street are many Germans, and side streets are given over almost entirely to Polish and Russian Jews. Still farther south, these Jewish colonies merge into a huge Bohemian colony, so vast that Chicago ranks as the third Bohemian city in the world. To the northwest are many Canadian-French, clannish in spite of their long residence in America, and to the north are Irish and first-generation Americans. On the streets directly west and farther north are well-to-do English speaking families, many of whom own their own houses and have lived in the neighborhood for years; one man is still living in his old farmhouse.

The policy of the public authorities of never taking an initiative, and always waiting to be urged to do their duty, is obviously fatal in a neighborhood where there is little initiative among the citizens. The idea underlying our self- government breaks down in such a ward. The streets are inexpressibly dirty, the number of schools inadequate, sanitary legislation unenforced, the street lighting bad, the paving miserable and altogether lacking in the alleys and smaller streets, and the stables foul beyond description. Hundreds of houses are unconnected with the street sewer. The older and richer inhabitants seem anxious to move away as rapidly as they can afford it. They make room for newly arrived immigrants who are densely ignorant of civic duties. This substitution of the older inhabitants is accomplished industrially also, in the south and east quarters of the ward. The Jews and Italians do the finishing for the great clothing manufacturers, formerly done by Americans, Irish, and Germans, who refused to submit to the extremely low prices to which the sweating system has reduced their successors. As the design of the sweating system is the elimination of rent from the manufacture of clothing, the "outside work" is begun after the clothing leaves the cutter. An unscrupulous contractor regards no basement as too dark, no stable loft too foul, no rear shanty too provisional, no tenement room too small for his workroom, as these conditions imply low rental. Hence these shops abound in the worst of the foreign districts where the sweater easily finds his cheap basement and his home finishers.

The houses of the ward, for the most part wooden, were originally built for one family and are now occupied by several. They are after the type of the inconvenient frame cottages found in the poorer suburbs twenty years ago. Many of them were built where they now stand; others were brought thither on rollers, because their previous sites had been taken by factories. The fewer brick tenement buildings which are three or four stories high are comparatively new, and there are few large tenements. The little wooden houses have a temporary aspect, and for this reason, perhaps, the tenement-house legislation in Chicago is totally inadequate. Rear tenements flourish; many houses have no water supply save the faucet in the back yard, there are no fire escapes, the garbage and ashes are placed in wooden boxes which are fastened to the street pavements. One of the most discouraging features about the present system of tenement houses is that many are owned by sordid and ignorant immigrants. The theory that wealth brings responsibility, that possession entails at length education and refinement, in these cases fails utterly. The children of an Italian immigrant owner may "shine" shoes in the street, and his wife may pick rags from the street gutter, laboriously sorting them in a dingy court. Wealth may do something for her self-complacency and feeling of consequence; it certainly does nothing for her comfort or her children's improvement nor for the cleanliness of anyone concerned. Another thing that prevents better houses in Chicago is the tentative attitude of the real estate men. Many unsavory conditions are allowed to continue which would be regarded with horror if they were considered permanent. Meanwhile, the wretched conditions persist until at least two generations of children have been born and reared in them.

In every neighborhood where poorer people live, because rents are supposed to be cheaper there, is an element which, although uncertain in the individual, in the aggregate can be counted upon. It is composed of people of former education and opportunity who have cherished ambitions and prospects, but who are caricatures of what they meant to be —"hollow ghosts which blame the living men." There are times in many lives when there is a cessation of energy and loss of power. Men and women of education and refinement come to live in a cheaper neighborhood because they lack the ability to make money, because of ill health, because of an unfortunate marriage, or for other reasons which do not imply criminality or stupidity. Among them are those who, in spite of untoward circumstances, keep up some sort of an intellectual life; those who are "great for books," as their neighbors say. To such the Settlement may be a genuine refuge.

In the very first weeks of our residence Miss Starr started a reading party in George Eliot's "Romola," which was attended by a group of young women who followed the wonderful tale with unflagging interest. The weekly reading was held in our little upstairs dining room, and two members of the club came to dinner each week, not only that they might be received as guests, but that they might help us wash the dishes afterwards and so make the table ready for the stacks of Florentine photographs.

Our "first resident," as she gaily designated herself, was a charming old lady who gave five consecutive readings from Hawthorne to a most appreciative audience, interspersing the magic tales most delightfully with recollections of the elusive and fascinating author. Years before she had lived at Brook Farm as a pupil of the Ripleys, and she came to us for ten days because she wished to live once more in an atmosphere where "idealism ran high." We thus early found the type of class which through all the years has remained most popular —a combination of a social atmosphere with serious study.

Volunteers to the new undertaking came quickly; a charming young girl conducted a kindergarten in the drawing room, coming regularly every morning from her home in a distant part of the North Side of the city. Although a tablet to her memory has stood upon a mantel shelf in Hull-House for five years, we still associate her most vividly with the play of little children, first in her kindergarten and then in her own nursery, which furnished a veritable illustration of Victor Hugo's definition of heaven —"a place where parents are always young and children always little." Her daily presence for the first two years made it quite impossible for us to become too solemn and self-conscious in our strenuous routine, for her mirth and buoyancy were irresistible and her eager desire to share the life of the neighborhood never failed, although it was often put to a severe test. One day at luncheon she gaily recited her futile attempt to impress temperance principles upon the mind of an Italian mother, to whom she had returned a small daughter of five sent to the kindergarten "in quite a horrid state of intoxication" from the wine-soaked bread upon which she had breakfasted. The mother, with the gentle courtesy of a South Italian, listened politely to her graphic portrayal of the untimely end awaiting so immature a wine bibber; but long before the lecture was finished, quite unconscious of the incongruity, she hospitably set forth her best wines, and when her baffled guest refused one after the other, she disappeared, only to quickly return with a small dark glass of whisky, saying reassuringly, "See, I have brought you the true American drink." The recital ended in seriocomic despair, with the rueful statement that "the impression I probably made on her darkened mind was, that it was the American custom to breakfast children on bread soaked in whisky instead of light Italian wine."

That first kindergarten was a constant source of education to us. We were much surprised to find social distinctions even among its lambs, although greatly amused with the neat formulation made by the superior little Italian boy who refused to sit beside uncouth little Angelina because "we eat our macaroni this way" —imitating the movement of a fork from a plate to his mouth — "and she eat her macaroni this way," holding his hand high in the air and throwing back his head, that his wide-open mouth might receive an imaginary cascade. Angelina gravely nodded her little head in approval of this distinction between gentry and peasant. "But isn't it astonishing that merely table manners are made such a test all the way along —" was the comment of their democratic teacher. Another memory which refuses to be associated with death, which came to her all too soon, is that of the young girl who organized our first really successful club of boys, holding their fascinated interest by the old chivalric tales, set forth so dramatically and vividly that checkers and jackstraws were abandoned by all the other clubs on Boys' Day, that their members might form a listening fringe to "The Young Heros."

I met a member of the latter club one day as he flung himself out of the House in the rage by which an emotional boy hopes to keep from shedding tears. "There is no use coming here any more, Prince Roland is dead," he gruffly explained as we passed. We encouraged the younger boys in tournaments and dramatics of all sorts, and we somewhat fatuously believed that boys who were early interested in adventurers or explorers might later want to know the lives of living statesmen and inventors. It is needless to add that the boys quickly responded to such a program, and that the only difficulty lay in finding leaders who were able to carry it out. This difficulty has been with us through all the years of growth and development in the Boys' Club until now, with its five-story building, its splendid equipment of shops, of recreation and study rooms, that group alone is successful which commands the services of a resourceful and devoted leader.

The dozens of younger children who from the first came to Hull- House were organized into groups which were not quite classes and not quite clubs. The value of these groups consisted almost entirely in arousing a higher imagination and in giving the children the opportunity which they could not have in the crowded schools, for initiative and for independent social relationships. The public schools then contained little hand work of any sort, so that naturally any instruction which we provided for the children took the direction of this supplementary work. But it required a constant effort that the pressure of poverty itself should not defeat the educational aim. The Italian girls in the sewing classes would count the day lost when they could not carry home a garment, and the insistence that it should be neatly made seemed a super-refinement to those in dire need of clothing.

As these clubs have been continued during the twenty years they have developed classes in the many forms of handicraft which the newer education is so rapidly adapting for the delight of children; but they still keep their essentially social character and still minister to that large number of children who leave school the very week they are fourteen years old, only too eager to close the schoolroom door forever on a tiresome task that is at last well over. It seems to us important that these children shall find themselves permanently attached to a House that offers them evening clubs and classes with their old companions, that merges as easily as possible the school life into the working life and does what it can to find places for the bewildered young things looking for work. A large proportion of the delinquent boys brought into the juvenile court in Chicago are the oldest sons in large families whose wages are needed at home. The grades from which many of them leave school, as the records show, are piteously far from the seventh and eighth where the very first introduction in manual training is given, nor have they been caught by any other abiding interest.

In spite of these flourishing clubs for children early established at Hull-House, and the fact that our first organized undertaking was a kindergarten, we were very insistent that the Settlement should not be primarily for the children, and that it was absurd to suppose that grown people would not respond to opportunities for education and social life. Our enthusiastic kindergartner herself demonstrated this with an old woman of ninety who, because she was left alone all day while her daughter cooked in a restaurant, had formed such a persistent habit of picking the plaster off the walls that one landlord after another refused to have her for a tenant. It required but a few week's time to teach her to make large paper chains, and gradually she was content to do it all day long, and in the end took quite as much pleasure in adorning the walls as she had formally taken in demolishing them. Fortunately the landlord had never heard the aesthetic principle that exposure of basic construction is more desirable than gaudy decoration. In course of time it was discovered that the old woman could speak Gaelic, and when one or two grave professors came to see her, the neighborhood was filled with pride that such a wonder lived in their midst. To mitigate life for a woman of ninety was an unfailing refutation of the statement that the Settlement was designed for the young.

On our first New Year's Day at Hull-House we invited the older people in the vicinity, sending a carriage for the most feeble and announcing to all of them that we were going to organize an Old Settlers' Party.

Every New Year's Day since, older people in varying numbers have come together at Hull-House to relate early hardships, and to take for the moment the place in the community to which their pioneer life entitles them. Many people who were formerly residents of the vicinity, but whom prosperity has carried into more desirable neighborhoods, come back to these meetings and often confess to each other that they have never since found such kindness as in early Chicago when all its citizens came together in mutual enterprises. Many of these pioneers, so like the men and women of my earliest childhood that I always felt comforted by their presence in the house, were very much opposed to "foreigners," whom they held responsible for a depreciation of property and a general lowering of the tone of the neighborhood. Sometimes we had a chance for championship; I recall one old man, fiercely American, who had reproached me because we had so many "foreign views" on our walls, to whom I endeavored to set forth our hope that the pictures might afford a familiar island to the immigrants in a sea of new and strange impressions. The old settler guest, taken off his guard, replied, "I see; they feel as we did when we saw a Yankee notion from Down East," —thereby formulating the dim kinship between the pioneer and the immigrant, both "buffeting the waves of a new development." The older settlers as well as their children throughout the years have given genuine help to our various enterprises for neighborhood improvement, and from their own memories of earlier hardships have made many shrewd suggestions for alleviating the difficulties of that first sharp struggle with untoward conditions.

In those early days we were often asked why we had come to live on Halsted Street when we could afford to live somewhere else. I remember one man who used to shake his head and say it was "the strangest thing he had met in his experience," but who was finally convinced that it was "not strange but natural." In time it came to seem natural to all of us that the Settlement should be there. If it is natural to feed the hungry and care for the sick, it is certainly natural to give pleasure to the young, comfort to the aged, and to minister to the deep-seated craving for social intercourse that all men feel. Whoever does it is rewarded by something which, if not gratitude, is at least spontaneous and vital and lacks that irksome sense of obligation with which a substantial benefit is too often acknowledged.

In addition to the neighbors who responded to the receptions and classes, we found those who were too battered and oppressed to care for them. To these, however, was left that susceptibility to the bare offices of humanity which raises such offices into a bond of fellowship.

From the first it seemed understood that we were ready to perform the humblest neighborhood services. We were asked to wash the new-born babies, and to prepare the dead for burial, to nurse the sick, and to "mind the children."

Occasionally these neighborly offices unexpectedly uncovered ugly human traits. For six weeks after an operation we kept in one of our three bedrooms a forlorn little baby who, because he was born with a cleft palate, was most unwelcome even to his mother, and we were horrified when he died of neglect a week after he was returned to his home; a little Italian bride of fifteen sought shelter with us one November evening to escape her husband who had beaten her every night for a week when he returned home from work, because she had lost her wedding ring; two of us officiated quite alone at the birth of an illegitimate child because the doctor was late in arriving, and none of the honest Irish matrons would "touch the likes of her"; we ministered at the deathbed of a young man, who during a long illness of tuberculosis had received so many bottles of whisky through the mistaken kindness of his friends, that the cumulative effect produced wild periods of exultation, in one of which he died.

We were also early impressed with the curious isolation of many of the immigrants; an Italian woman once expressed her pleasure in the red roses that she saw at one of our receptions in surprise that they had been "brought so fresh all the way from Italy." She would not believe for an instant that they had been grown in America. She said that she had lived in Chicago for six years and had never seen any roses, whereas in Italy she had seen them every summer in great profusion. During all that time, of course, the woman had lived within ten blocks of a florist's window; she had not been more than a five-cent car ride away from the public parks; but she had never dreamed of faring forth for herself, and no one had taken her. Her conception of America had been the untidy street in which she lived and had made her long struggle to adapt herself to American ways.

But in spite of some untoward experiences, we were constantly impressed with the uniform kindness and courtesy we received. Perhaps these first days laid the simple human foundations which are certainly essential for continuous living among the poor; first, genuine preference for residence in an industrial quarter to any other part of the city, because it is interesting and makes the human appeal; and second, the conviction, in the words of Canon Barnett, that the things that make men alike are finer and better than the things that keep them apart, and that these basic likenesses, if they are properly accentuated, easily transcend the less essential differences of race, language, creed, and tradition.

Perhaps even in those first days we made a beginning toward that object which was afterwards stated in our charter: "To provide a center for higher civic and social life; to institute and maintain educational and philanthropic enterprises, and to investigate and improve the conditions in the industrial districts of Chicago."

Chapter VI
Subjective Necessity for Social Settlements

The Ethical Culture Societies held a summer school at Plymouth, Massachusetts, in 1892, to which they invited several people representing the then new Settlement movement, that they might discuss with others the general theme of Philanthropy and Social Progress.

I venture to produce here parts of a lecture I delivered in Plymouth, both because I have found it impossible to formulate with the same freshness those early motives and strivings, and because, when published with other papers given that summer, it was received by the Settlement people themselves as a satisfactory statement.

I remember on golden summer afternoon during the sessions of the summer school that several of us met on the shores of a pond in a pine wood a few miles from Plymouth, to discuss our new movement. The natural leader of the group was Robert A. Woods. He had recently returned from a residence in Toynbee Hall, London, to open Andover House in Boston, and had just issued a book, "English Social Movements," in which he had gathered together and focused the many forms of social endeavor preceding and contemporaneous with the English Settlements. There were Miss Vida D. Scudder and Miss Helena Dudley from the College Settlement Association, Miss Julia C. Lathrop and myself from Hull-House. Some of us had numbered our years as far as thirty, and we all carefully avoided the extravagance of statement which characterizes youth, and yet I doubt if anywhere on the continent that summer could have been found a group of people more genuinely interested in social development or more sincerely convinced that they had found a clue by which the conditions in crowded cities might be understood and the agencies for social betterment developed.

We were all careful to avoid saying that we had found a "life work," perhaps with an instinctive dread of expending all our energy in vows of constancy, as so often happens; and yet it is interesting to note that of all the people whom I have recalled as the enthusiasts at that little conference have remained attached to Settlements in actual residence for longer or shorter periods each year during the eighteen years that have elapsed since then, although they have also been closely identified as publicists or governmental officials with movements outside. It is as if they had discovered that the Settlement was too valuable as a method as a way of approach to the social question to abandoned, although they had long since discovered it was not a "social movement" in itself. This, however, is anticipating the future, whereas the following paper on "The Subjective Necessity for Social Settlements" should have a chance to speak for itself. It is perhaps too late in the day to express regret for its stilted title.

This paper is an attempt to analyze the motives which underlie a movement based, not only upon conviction, but upon genuine emotion, wherever educated young people are seeking an outlet for that sentiment for universal brotherhood, which the best spirit of our times is forcing from an emotion into a motive. These young people accomplish little toward the solution of this social problem, and bear the brunt of being cultivated into unnourished, oversensitive lives. They have been shut off from the common labor by which they live which is a great source of moral and physical health. They feel a fatal want of harmony between their theory and their lives, a lack of coordination between thought and action. I think it is hard for us to realize how seriously many of them are taking to the notion of human brotherhood, how eagerly they long to give tangible expression to the democratic ideal. These young men and women, longing to socialize their democracy, are animated by certain hopes which may be thus loosely formulated; that if in a democratic country nothing can be permanently achieved save through the masses of the people, it will be impossible to establish a higher political life than the people themselves crave; that it is difficult to see how the notion of a higher civic life can be fostered save through common intercourse; that the blessings which we associate with a life of refinement and cultivation can be made universal and must be made universal if they are to be permanent; that the good we secure for ourselves is precarious and uncertain, is floating in mid-air, until it is secured for all of us and incorporated into our common life. It is easier to state these hopes than to formulate the line of motives, which I believe to constitute the trend of the subjective pressure toward the Settlement. There is something primordial about these motives, but I am perhaps overbold in designating them as a great desire to share the race life. We all bear traces of the starvation struggle which for so long made up the life of the race. Our very organism holds memories and glimpses of that long life of our ancestors, which still goes on among so many of our contemporaries. Nothing so deadens the sympathies and shrivels the power of enjoyment as the persistent keeping away from the great opportunities for helpfulness and a continual ignoring of the starvation struggle which makes up the life of at least half the race. To shut one's self away from that half of the race life is to shut one's self away from the most vital part of it; it is to live out but half the humanity to which we have been born heir and to use but half our faculties. We have all had longings for a fuller life which should include the use of these faculties. These longings are the physical complement of the "Intimations of Immortality," on which no ode has yet been written. To portray these would be the work of a poet, and it is hazardous for any but a poet to attempt it.

You may remember the forlorn feeling which occasionally seizes you when you arrive early in the morning a stranger in a great city: the stream of laboring people goes past you as you gaze through the plate-glass window of your hotel; you see hard working men lifting great burdens; you hear the driving and jostling of huge carts and your heart sinks with a sudden sense of futility. The door opens behind you and you turn to the man who brings you in your breakfast with a quick sense of human fellowship. You find yourself praying that you may never lose your hold on it all. A more poetic prayer would be that the great mother breasts of our common humanity, with its labor and suffering and its homely comforts, may never be withheld from you. You turn helplessly to the waiter and feel that it would be almost grotesque to claim from him the sympathy you crave because civilization has placed you apart, but you resent your position with a sudden sense of snobbery. Literature is full of portrayals of these glimpses: they come to shipwrecked men on rafts; they overcome the differences of an incongruous multitude when in the presence of a great danger or when moved by a common enthusiasm. They are not, however, confined to such moments, and if we were in the habit of telling them to each other, the recital would be as long as the tales of children are, when they sit down on the green grass and confide to each other how many times they have remembered that they lived once before. If these childish tales are the stirring of inherited impressions, just so surely is the other the striving of inherited powers.

"It is true that there is nothing after disease, indigence and a sense of guilt, so fatal to health and to life itself as the want of a proper outlet for active faculties." I have seen young girls suffer and grow sensibly lowered in vitality in the first years after they leave school. In our attempt then to give a girl pleasure and freedom from care we succeed, for the most part, in making her pitifully miserable. She finds "life" so different from what she expected it to be. She is besotted with innocent little ambitions, and does not understand this apparent waste of herself, this elaborate preparation, if no work is provided for her. There is a heritage of noble obligation which young people accept and long to perpetuate. The desire for action, the wish to right wrong and alleviate suffering haunts them daily. Society smiles at it indulgently instead of making it of value to itself. The wrong to them begins even farther back, when we restrain the first childish desires for "doing good", and tell them that they must wait until they are older and better fitted. We intimate that social obligation begins at a fixed date, forgetting that it begins at birth itself. We treat them as children who, with strong-growing limbs, are allowed to use their legs but not their arms, or whose legs are daily carefully exercised that after a while their arms may be put to high use. We do this in spite of the protest of the best educators, Locke and Pestalozzi. We are fortunate in the meantime if their unused members do not weaken and disappear. They do sometimes. There are a few girls who, by the time they are "educated", forget their old childish desires to help the world and to play with poor little girls "who haven't playthings". Parents are often inconsistent: they deliberately expose their daughters to knowledge of the distress in the world; they send them to hear missionary addresses on famines in India and China; they accompany them to lectures on the suffering in Siberia; they agitate together over the forgotten region of East London. In addition to this, from babyhood the altruistic tendencies of these daughters are persistently cultivated. They are taught to be self-forgetting and self-sacrificing, to consider the good of the whole before the good of the ego. But when all this information and culture show results, when the daughter comes back from college and begins to recognize her social claim to the "submerged tenth", and to evince a disposition to fulfill it, the family claim is strenuously asserted; she is told that she is unjustified, ill-advised in her efforts. If she persists, the family too often are injured and unhappy unless the efforts are called missionary and the religious zeal of the family carry them over their sense of abuse. When this zeal does not exist, the result is perplexing. It is a curious violation of what we would fain believe a fundamental law-that the final return of the deed is upon the head of the doer. The deed is that of exclusiveness and caution, but the return, instead of falling upon the head of the exclusive and cautious, falls upon a young head full of generous and unselfish plans. The girl loses something vital out of her life to which she is entitled. She is restricted and unhappy; her elders meanwhile, are unconscious of the situation and we have all the elements of a tragedy.

We have in America a fast-growing number of cultivated young people who have no recognized outlet for their active faculties. They hear constantly of the great social maladjustment, but no way is provided for them to change it, and their uselessness hangs about them heavily. Huxley declares that the sense of uselessness is the severest shock which the human system can sustain, and that if persistently sustained, it results in atrophy of function. These young people have had advantages of college, of European travel, and of economic study, but they are sustaining this shock of inaction. They have pet phrases, and they tell you that the things that make us all alike are stronger than the things that make us different. They say that all men are united by needs and sympathies far more permanent and radical than anything that temporarily divides them and sets them in opposition to each other. If they affect art, they say that the decay in artistic expression is due to the decay in ethics, that art when shut away from the human interests and from the great mass of humanity is self-destructive. They tell their elders with all the bitterness of youth that if they expect success from them in business or politics or in whatever lines their ambition for them has run, they must let them consult all of humanity; that they must let them find out what the people want and how they want it. It is only the stronger young people, however, who formulate this. Many of them dissipate their energies in so-called enjoyment. Others not content with that, go on studying and go back to college for their second degrees; not that they are especially fond of study, but because they want something definite to do, and their powers have been trained in the direction of mental accumulation. Many are buried beneath this mental accumulation with lowered vitality and discontent. Walter Besant says they have had the vision that Peter had when he saw the great sheet let down from heaven, wherein was neither clean nor unclean. He calls it the sense of humanity. It is not philanthropy nor benevolence, but a thing fuller and wider than either of these.

This young life, so sincere in its emotion and good phrases and yet so undirected, seems to me as pitiful as the other great mass of destitute lives. One is supplementary to the other, and some method of communication can surely be devised. Mr. Barnett, who urged the first Settlement, —Toynbee Hall, in East London, —recognized this need of outlet for the young men of Oxford and Cambridge, and hoped that the Settlement would supply the communication. It is easy to see why the Settlement movement originated in England, where the years of education are more constrained and definite than they are here, where class distinctions are more rigid. The necessity of it was greater there, but we are fast feeling the pressure of the need and meeting the necessity for Settlements in America. Our young people feel nervously the need of putting theory into action, and respond quickly to the Settlement form of activity.

Other motives which I believe make toward the Settlement are the result of a certain renaissance going forward in Christianity. The impulse to share the lives of the poor, the desire to make social service, irrespective of propaganda, express the spirit of Christ, is as old as Christianity itself. We have no proof from the records themselves that the early Roman Christians, who strained their simple art to the point of grotesqueness in their eagerness to record a "good news" on the walls of the catacombs, considered this good news a religion. Jesus had no set of truths labeled Religious. On the contrary, his doctrine was that all truth is one, that the appropriation of it is freedom. His teaching had no dogma to mark it off from truth and action in general. He himself called it a revelation—a life. These early Roman Christians received the Gospel message, a command to love all men, with a certain joyous simplicity. The image of the Good Shepherd is blithe and gay beyond the gentlest shepherd of Greek mythology; the hart no longer pants, but rushes to the water brooks. The Christians looked for the continuous revelation, but believed what Jesus said, that this revelation, to be retained and made manifest, must be put into terms of action; that action is the only medium man has for receiving and appropriating truth; that the doctrine must be known through the will.

That Christianity has to be revealed and embodied in the line of social progress is a corollary to the simple proposition, that man's action is found in his social relationships in the way in which he connects with his fellows; that his motives for action are the zeal and affection with which he regards his fellows. By this simple process was created a deep enthusiasm for humanity; which regarded man as at once the organ and the object of revelation; and by this process came about the wonderful fellowship, the true democracy of the early Church, that so captivates the imagination. The early Christians were preeminently nonresistant. They believed in love as a cosmic force. There was no iconoclasm during the minor peace of the Church. They did not yet denounce nor tear down temples, nor preach the end of the world. They grew to a mighty number, but it never occurred to them, either in their weakness or in their strength, to regard other men for an instant as their foes or as aliens. The spectacle of the Christians loving all men was the most astounding Rome had ever seen. They were eager to sacrifice themselves for the weak, for children, and for the aged; they identified themselves with slaves and did not avoid the plague; they longed to share the common lot that they might receive the constant revelation. It was a new treasure which the early Christians added to the sum of all treasures, a joy hitherto unknown in the world-the joy of finding the Christ which lieth in each man, but which no man can unfold save in fellowship. A happiness ranging from the heroic to the pastoral enveloped them. They were to possess a revelation as long as life had new meaning to unfold, new action to propose.

I believe that there is a distinct turning among many young men and women toward this simple acceptance of Christ's message. They resent the assumption that Christianity is a set of ideas which belong to the religious consciousness, whatever that may be. They insist that it cannot be proclaimed and instituted apart from the social life of the community and that it must seek a simple and natural expression in the social organism itself. The Settlement movement is only one manifestation of that wider humanitarian movement which throughout Christendom, but pre-eminently in England, is endeavoring to embody itself, not in a sect, but in society itself.

I believe that this turning, this renaissance of the early Christian humanitarianism, is going on in America, in Chicago, if you please, without leaders who write or philosophize, without much speaking, but with a bent to express in social service and in terms of action the spirit of Christ. Certain it is that spiritual force is found in the Settlement movement, and it is also true that this force must be evoked and must be called into play before the success of any Settlement is assured. There must be the overmastering belief that all that is noblest in life is common to men as men, in order to accentuate the likenesses and ignore the differences which are found among the people whom the Settlement constantly brings into juxtaposition. It may be true, as the Positivists insist, that the very religious fervor of man can be turned into love for his race, and his desire for a future life into content to live in the echo of his deeds; Paul's formula of seeking for the Christ which lieth in each man and founding our likenesses on him, seems a simpler formula to many of us.

In a thousand voices singing the Hallelujah Chorus in Handel's "Messiah," it is possible to distinguish the leading voices, but the differences of training and cultivation between them and the voices in the chorus, are lost in the unity of purpose and in the fact that they are all human voices lifted by a high motive. This is a weak illustration of what a Settlement attempts to do. It aims, in a measure, to develop whatever of social life its neighborhood may afford, to focus and give form to that life, to bring to bear upon it the results of cultivation and training; but it receives in exchange for the music of isolated voices the volume and strength of the chorus. It is quite impossible for me to say in what proportion or degree the subjective necessity which led to the opening of Hull-House combined the three trends: first, the desire to interpret democracy in social terms; secondly, the impulse beating at the very source of our lives, urging us to aid in the race progress; and, thirdly, the Christian movement toward humanitarianism. It is difficult to analyze a living thing; the analysis is at best imperfect. Many more motives may blend with the three trends; possibly the desire for a new form of social success due to the nicety of imagination, which refuses worldly pleasures unmixed with the joys of self-sacrifice; possibly a love of approbation, so vast that it is not content with the treble clapping of delicate hands, but wishes also to hear the bass notes from toughened palms, may mingle with these.

The Settlement then, is an experimental effort to aid in the solution of the social and industrial problems which are engendered by the modern conditions of life in a great city. It insists that these problems are not confined to any one portion of a city. It is an attempt to relieve, at the same time, the overaccumulation at one end of society and the destitution at the other; but it assumes that this overaccumulation and destitution is most sorely felt in the things that pertain to social and educational privileges. From its very nature it can stand for no political or social propaganda. It must, in a sense, give the warm welcome of an inn to all such propaganda, if perchance one of them be found an angel. The only thing to be dreaded in the Settlement is that it lose its flexibility, its power of quick adaptation, its readiness to change its methods as its environment may demand. It must be open to conviction and must have a deep and abiding sense of tolerance. It must be hospitable and ready for experiment. It should demand from its residents a scientific patience in the accumulation of facts and the steady holding of their sympathies as one of the best instruments for that accumulation. It must be grounded in a philosophy whose foundation is on the solidarity of the human race, a philosophy which will not waver when the race happens to be represented by a drunken woman or an idiot boy. Its residents must be emptied of all conceit of opinion and all self-assertion, and ready to arouse and interpret the public opinion of their neighborhood. They must be content to live quietly side by side with their neighbors, until they grow into a sense of relationship and mutual interests. Their neighbors are held apart by differences of race and language which the residents can more easily overcome. They are bound to see the needs of their neighborhood as a whole, to furnish data for legislation, and to use their influence to secure it. In short, residents are pledged to devote themselves to the duties of good citizenship and to the arousing of the social energies which too largely lie dormant in every neighborhood given over to industrialism. They are bound to regard the entire life of their city as organic, to make an effort to unify it, and to protest against its over-differentiation.

It is always easy to make all philosophy point one particular moral and all history adorn one particular tale; but I may be forgiven the reminder that the best speculative philosophy sets forth the solidarity of the human race; that the highest moralists have taught that without the advance and improvement of the whole, no man can hope for any lasting improvement in his own moral or material individual condition; and that the subjective necessity for Social Settlements is therefore identical with that necessity, which urges us on toward social and individual salvation.

Chapter VII
Some Early Undertakings at Hull-house

If the early American Settlements stood for a more exigent standard in philanthropic activities, insisting that each new undertaking should be preceded by carefully ascertained facts, then certainly Hull-House held to this standard in the opening of our new coffee-house first started as a public kitchen. An investigation of the sweatshops had disclosed the fact, that sewing women during the busy season paid little attention to the feeding of their families, for it was only by working steadily through the long day that the scanty pay of five, seven, or nine cents for finishing a dozen pairs of trousers could be made into a day's wage; and they bought from the nearest grocery the canned goods that could be most quickly heated, or gave a few pennies to the children with which they might secure a lunch from a neighboring candy shop.

One of the residents made an investigation, at the instance of the United States Department of Agriculture, into the food values of the dietaries of the various immigrants, and this was followed by an investigation made by another resident, for the United States Department of Labor, into the foods of the Italian colony, on the supposition that the constant use of imported products bore a distinct relation to the cost of living. I recall an Italian who, coming into Hull-House one day as we were sitting at the dinner table, expressed great surprise that Americans ate a variety of food, because he believed that they partook only of potatoes and beer. A little inquiry showed that this conclusion was drawn from the fact that he lived next to an Irish saloon and had never seen anything but potatoes going in and beer coming out.

At that time the New England kitchen was comparatively new in Boston, and Mrs. Richards, who was largely responsible for its foundation, hoped that cheaper cuts of meat and simpler vegetables, if they were subjected to slow and thorough processes of cooking, might be made attractive and their nutritive value secured for the people who so sadly needed more nutritious food. It was felt that this could be best accomplished in public kitchens, where the advantage of scientific training and careful supervision could be secured. One of the residents went to Boston for a training under Mrs. Richards, and when the Hull-House kitchen was fitted under her guidance and direction, our hopes ran high for some modification of the food of the neighborhood. We did not reckon, however, with the wide diversity in nationality and inherited tastes, and while we sold a certain amount of the carefully prepared soups and stews in the neigh- boring factories —a sale which has steadily increased throughout the years-and were also patronized by a few households, perhaps the neighborhood estimate was best summed up by the woman who frankly confessed, that the food was certainly nutritious, but that she didn't like to eat what was nutritious, that she liked to eat "what she'd ruther."

If the dietetics were appreciated but slowly, the social value of the coffee-house and the gymnasium, which were in the same building, were quickly demonstrated. At that time the saloon halls were the only places in the neighborhood where the immigrant could hold his social gatherings, and where he could celebrate such innocent and legitimate occasions as weddings and christenings.

These halls were rented very cheaply with the understanding that various sums of money should be "passed across the bar," and it was considered a mean host or guest who failed to live up to this implied bargain. The consequence was that many a reputable party ended with a certain amount of disorder, due solely to the fact that the social instinct was traded upon and used as a basis for money making by an adroit host. From the beginning the young people's clubs had asked for dancing, and nothing was more popular than the increased space for parties offered by the gymnasium, with the chance to serve refreshments in the room below. We tried experiments with every known "soft drink," from those extracted from an expensive soda water fountain to slender glasses of grape juice, but so far as drinks were concerned we never became a rival to the saloon, nor indeed did anyone imagine that we were trying to do so. I remember one man who looked about the cozy little room and said, "This would be a nice place to sit in all day if one could only have beer." But the coffee-house gradually performed a mission of its own and became something of a social center to the neighborhood as well as a real convenience. Business men from the adjacent factories and school teachers from the nearest public schools, used it increasingly. The Hull-House students and club members supped together in little groups or held their reunions and social banquets, as, to a certain extent, did organizations from all parts of the town. The experience of the coffee-house taught us not to hold to preconceived ideas of what the neighborhood ought to have, but to keep ourselves in readiness to modify and adapt our undertakings as we discovered those things which the neighborhood was ready to accept.

Better food was doubtless needed, but more attractive and safer places for social gatherings were also needed, and the neighborhood was ready for one and not for the other. We had no hint then in Chicago of the small parks which were to be established fifteen years later, containing the halls for dancing and their own restaurants in buildings where the natural desire of the young for gayety and social organization, could be safely indulged. Yet even in that early day a member of the Hull-House Men's Club who had been appointed superintendent of Douglas Park had secured there the first public swimming pool, and his fellow club members were proud of the achievement.

There was in the earliest undertakings at Hull-House a touch of the artist's enthusiasm when he translates his inner vision through his chosen material into outward form. Keenly conscious of the social confusion all about us and the hard economic struggle, we at times believed that the very struggle itself might become a source of strength. The devotion of the mothers to their children, the dread of the men lest they fail to provide for the family dependent upon their daily exertions, at moments seemed to us the secret stores of strength from which society is fed, the invisible array of passion and feeling which are the surest protectors of the world. We fatuously hoped that we might pluck from the human tragedy itself a consciousness of a common destiny which should bring its own healing, that we might extract from life's very misfortunes a power of cooperation which should be effective against them.

Of course there was always present the harrowing consciousness of the difference in economic condition between ourselves and our neighbors. Even if we had gone to live in the most wretched tenement, there would have always been an essential difference between them and ourselves, for we should have had a sense of security in regard to illness and old age and the lack of these two securities are the specters which most persistently haunt the poor. Could we, in spite of this, make their individual efforts more effective through organization and possibly complement them by small efforts of our own?

Some such vague hope was in our minds when we started the Hull-House Cooperative Coal Association, which led a vigorous life for three years, and developed a large membership under the skillful advice of its one paid officer, an English workingman who had had experience in cooperative societies at "'ome." Some of the meetings of the association, in which people met to consider together their basic dependence upon fire and warmth, had a curious challenge of life about them. Because the cooperators knew what it meant to bring forth children in the midst of privation and to see the tiny creatures struggle for life, their recitals cut a cross section, as it were, in that world-old effort-the "dying to live" which so inevitably triumphs over poverty and suffering. And yet their very familiarity with hardship may have been responsible for that sentiment which traditionally ruins business, for a vote of the cooperators that the basket buyers be given one basket free out of every six, that the presentation of five purchase tickets should entitle the holders to a profit in coal instead of stock "because it would be a shame to keep them waiting for the dividend," was always pointed to by the conservative quarter-of-a-ton buyers as the beginning of the end. At any rate, at the close of the third winter, although the Association occupied an imposing coal yard on the southeast corner of the Hull-House block and its gross receipts were between three and four hundred dollars a day, it became evident that the concern could not remain solvent if it continued its philanthropic policy, and the experiment was terminated by the cooperators taking up their stock in the remaining coal.

Our next cooperative experiment was much more successful, perhaps because it was much more spontaneous.

At a meeting of working girls held at Hull-House during a strike in a large shoe factory, the discussions made it clear that the strikers who had been most easily frightened, and therefore first to capitulate, were naturally those girls who were paying board and were afraid of being put out if they fell too far behind. After a recital of a case of peculiar hardship one of them exclaimed: "Wouldn't it be fine if we had a boarding club of our own, and then we could stand by each other in a time like this?" After that events moved quickly. We read aloud together Beatrice Potter's little book on "Cooperation," and discussed all the difficulties and fascinations of such an undertaking, and on the first of May, 1891, two comfortable apartments near Hull-House were rented and furnished. The Settlement was responsible for the furniture and paid the first month's rent, but beyond that the members managed the club themselves. The undertaking "marched," as the French say, from the very first, and always on its own feet. Although there were difficulties, none of them proved insurmountable, which was a matter for great satisfaction in the face of a statement made by the head of the United States Department of Labor, who, on a visit to the club when it was but two years old, said that his department had investigated many cooperative undertakings, and that none founded and managed by women had ever succeeded. At the end of the third year the club occupied all of the six apartments which the original building contained, and numbered fifty members.

It was in connection with our efforts to secure a building for the Jane Club, that we first found ourselves in the dilemma between the needs of our neighbors and the kind-hearted response upon which we had already come to rely for their relief. The adapted apartments in which the Jane Club was housed were inevitably more or less uncomfortable, and we felt that the success of the club justified the erection of a building for its sole use.

Up to that time, our history had been as the minor peace of the early Church. We had had the most generous interpretation of our efforts. Of course, many people were indifferent to the idea of the Settlement; others looked on with tolerant and sometimes cynical amusement which we would often encounter in a good story related at our expense; but all this was remote and unreal to us, and we were sure that if the critics could but touch "the life of the people," they would understand.

The situation changed markedly after the Pullman strike, and our efforts to secure factory legislation later brought upon us a certain amount of distrust and suspicion; until then we had been considered merely a kindly philanthropic undertaking whose new form gave us a certain idealistic glamour. But sterner tests were coming, and one of the first was in connection with the new building for the Jane Club. A trustee of Hull-House came to see us one day with the good news that a friend of his was ready to give twenty thousand dollars with which to build the desired new clubhouse. When, however, he divulged the name of his generous friend, it proved to be that of a man who was notorious for underpaying the girls in his establishment and concerning whom there were even darker stories. It seemed clearly impossible to erect a clubhouse for working girls with such money and we at once said that we must decline the offer. The trustee of Hull-House was put in the most embarrassing situation; he had, of course, induced the man to give the money and had had no thought but that it would be eagerly received; he would now be obliged to return with the astonishing, not to say insulting, news that the money was considered unfit.

In the long discussion which followed, it gradually became clear to all of us that such a refusal could be valuable only as it might reveal to the man himself and to others, public opinion in regard to certain methods of money-making, but that from the very nature of the case our refusal of this money could not be made public because a representative of Hull-House had asked for it. However, the basic fact remained that we could not accept the money, and of this the trustee himself was fully convinced. This incident occurred during a period of much discussion concerning "tainted money" and is perhaps typical of the difficulty of dealing with it. It is impossible to know how far we may blame the individual for doing that which all of his competitors and his associates consider legitimate; at the same time, social changes can only be inaugurated by those who feel the unrighteousness of contemporary conditions, and the expression of their scruples may be the one opportunity for pushing forward moral tests into that dubious area wherein wealth is accumulated.

In the course of time a new clubhouse was built by an old friend of Hull-House much interested in working girls, and this has been occupied for twelve years by the very successful cooperating Jane Club. The incident of the early refusal is associated in my mind with a long talk upon the subject of questionable money I held with the warden of Toynbee Hall, whom I visited at Bristol where he was then canon in the Cathedral. By way of illustration he showed me a beautiful little church which had been built by the last slave-trading merchant in Bristol, who had been much disapproved of by his fellow townsmen and had hoped by this transmutation of ill-gotten money into exquisite Gothic architecture to reconcile himself both to God and man. His impulse to build may have been born from his own scruples or from the quickened consciences of his neighbors who saw that the world-old iniquity of enslaving men must at length come to an end. The Abolitionists may have regarded this beautiful building as the fruit of a contrite heart, or they may have scorned it as an attempt to magnify the goodness of a slave trader and thus perplex the doubting citizens of Bristol in regard to the entire moral issue.

Canon Barnett did not pronounce judgment on the Bristol merchant. He was, however, quite clear upon the point that a higher moral standard for industrial life must be embodied in legislation as rapidly as possible, that it may bear equally upon all, and that an individual endeavoring to secure this legislation must forbear harsh judgment. This was doubtless a sound position, but during all the period of hot discussion concerning tainted money I never felt clear enough on the general principle involved, to accept the many invitations to write and speak upon the subject, although I received much instruction in the many letters of disapproval sent to me by radicals of various schools because I was a member of the university extension staff of the then new University of Chicago, the righteousness of whose foundation they challenged.

A little incident of this time illustrated to me the confusion in the minds of a least many older men between religious teaching and advancing morality. One morning I received a letter from the head of a Settlement in New York expressing his perplexity over the fact that his board of trustees had asked money from a man notorious for his unscrupulous business methods. My correspondent had placed his resignation in the hands of his board, that they might accept it at any time when they felt his utterances on the subject of tainted money were offensive, for he wished to be free to openly discuss a subject of such grave moral import. The very morning when my mind was full of the questions raised by this letter, I received a call from the daughter of the same business man whom my friend considered so unscrupulous. She was passing through Chicago and came to ask me to give her some arguments which she might later use with her father to confute the charge that Settlements were irreligious. She said, "You see, he has been asked to give money to our Settlement and would like to do it, if his conscience was only clear; he disapproves of Settlements because they give no religious instruction; he has always been a very devout man."

I remember later discussing the incident with Washington Gladden who was able to parallel it from his own experience. Now that this discussion upon tainted money has subsided, it is easy to view it with a certain detachment impossible at the moment, and it is even difficult to understand why the feeling should have been so intense, although it doubtless registered genuine moral concern.

There was room for discouragement in the many unsuccessful experiments in cooperation which were carried on in Chicago during the early nineties; a carpenter shop on Van Buren Street near Halsted, a labor exchange started by the unemployed, not so paradoxical an arrangement as it seems, and a very ambitious plan for a country colony which was finally carried out at Ruskin, Tennessee. In spite of failures, cooperative schemes went on, some of the same men appearing in one after another with irrepressible optimism. I remember during a cooperative congress, which met at Hull-House in the World's Fair summer that Mr. Henry D. Lloyd, who collected records of cooperative experiments with the enthusiasm with which other men collect coins or pictures, put before the congress some of the remarkable successes in Ireland

and North England, which he later embodied in his book on "Copartnership." One of the old-time cooperators denounced the modern method as "too much like cut-throat business" and declared himself in favor of "principles which may have failed over and over again, but are nevertheless as sound as the law of gravitation." Mr. Lloyd and I agreed that the fiery old man presented as fine a spectacle of devotion to a lost cause as either of us had ever seen, although we both possessed memories well stored with such romantic attachments.

And yet this dream that men shall cease to waste strength in competition and shall come to pool their powers of production is coming to pass all over the face of the earth. Five years later in the same Hull-House hall in which the cooperative congress was held, an Italian senator told a large audience of his fellow countrymen of the successful system of cooperative banks in north Italy and of their cooperative methods of selling produce to the value of millions of francs annually; still later Sir Horace Plunkett related the remarkable successes in cooperation in Ireland.

I have seldom been more infected by enthusiasm than I once was in Dulwich at a meeting of English cooperators where I was fairly overwhelmed by the fervor underlying the businesslike proceedings of the congress, and certainly when I served as a juror in the Paris Exposition of 1900, nothing in the entire display in the department of Social Economy was so imposing as the building housing the exhibit, which had been erected by cooperative trades-unions without the assistance of a single contractor.

And so one's faith is kept alive as one occasionally meets a realized ideal of better human relations. At least traces of successful cooperation are found even in individualistic America. I recall my enthusiasm on the day when I set forth to lecture at New Harmony, Indiana, for I had early been thrilled by the tale of Robert Owen, as every young person must be who is interested in social reform; I was delighted to find so much of his spirit still clinging to the little town which had long ago held one of his ardent experiments, although the poor old cooperators, who for many years claimed friendship at Hull-House because they heard that we "had once tried a cooperative coal association," might well have convinced me of the persistency of the cooperative ideal.

Many experiences in those early years, although vivid, seemed to contain no illumination; nevertheless they doubtless permanently affected our judgments concerning what is called crime and vice. I recall a series of striking episodes on the day when I took the wife and child, as well as the old godfather, of an Italian convict to visit him in the State Penitentiary. When we approached the prison, the sight of its heavy stone walls and armed sentries threw the godfather into a paroxysm of rage; he cast his hat upon the ground and stamped upon it, tore his hair, and loudly fulminated in weird Italian oaths, until one of the guards, seeing his strange actions, came to inquire if "the gentleman was having a fit." When we finally saw the convict, his wife, to my extreme distress, talked of nothing but his striped clothing, until the poor man wept with chagrin. Upon our return journey to Chicago, the little son aged eight presented me with two oranges, so affectionately and gayly that I was filled with reflections upon the advantage of each generation making a fresh start, when the train boy, finding the stolen fruit in my lap, violently threatened to arrest the child. But stranger than any episode was the fact itself that neither the convict, his wife, nor his godfather for a moment considered him a criminal. He had merely gotten excited over cards and had stabbed his adversary with a knife. "Why should a man who took his luck badly be kept forever from the sun?" was their reiterated inquiry.

I recall our perplexity over the first girls who had "gone astray" —the poor, little, forlorn objects, fifteen and sixteen years old, with their moral natures apparently untouched and un-awakened; one of them whom the police had found in a professional house and asked us to shelter for a few days until she could be used as a witness, was clutching a battered doll which she had kept with her during her six months of an "evil life." Two of these prematurely aged children came to us one day directly from the maternity ward of the Cook County hospital, each with a baby in her arms, asking for protection, because they did not want to go home for fear of "being licked." For them were no jewels nor idle living such as the storybooks portrayed.

The first of the older women whom I knew came to Hull-House to ask that her young sister, who was about to arrive from Germany, might live near us; she wished to find her respectable work and wanted her to have the "decent pleasures" that Hull-House afforded. After the arrangement had been completed and I had in a measure recovered from my astonishment at the businesslike way in which she spoke of her own life, I ventured to ask her history. In a very few words she told me that she had come from Germany as a music teacher to an American family. At the end of two years, in order to avoid a scandal involving the head of the house, she had come to Chicago where her child was born, but when the remittances ceased after its death, finding herself without home and resources, she had gradually become involved in her present mode of life. By dint of utilizing her family solicitude, we finally induced her to move into decent lodgings before her sister arrived, and for a difficult year she supported herself by her exquisite embroidery. At the end of that time, she gave up the struggle, the more easily as her young sister, well established in the dressmaking department of a large shop, had begun to suspect her past life.

But discouraging as these and other similar efforts often were, nevertheless the difficulties were infinitely less in those days when we dealt with "fallen girls" than in the years following when the "white slave traffic" became gradually established and when agonized parents, as well as the victims themselves, were totally unable to account for the situation. In the light of recent disclosures, it seems as if we were unaccountably dull not to have seen what was happening, especially to the Jewish girls among whom "the home trade of the white slave traffic" was first carried on and who were thus made to break through countless generations of chastity. We early encountered the difficulties of that old problem of restoring the woman, or even the child, into the society she has once outraged. I well remember our perplexity when we attempted to help two girls straight from a Virginia tobacco factory, who had been decoyed into a disreputable house when innocently seeking a lodging on the late evening of their arrival. Although they had been rescued promptly, the stigma remained, and we found it impossible to permit them to join any of the social clubs connected with Hull-House, not so much because there was danger of contamination, as because the parents of the club members would have resented their presence most hotly. One of our trustees succeeded in persuading a repentant girl, fourteen years old, whom we tried to give a fresh start in another part of the city, to attend a Sunday School class of a large Chicago church. The trustee hoped that the contact with nice girls, as well as the moral training, would help the poor child on her hard road. But unfortunately tales of her shortcomings reached the superintendent who felt obliged, in order to protect the other girls, to forbid her the school. She came back to tell us about it, defiant as well as discouraged, and had it not been for the experience with our own clubs, we could easily have joined her indignation over a church which "acted as if its Sunday School was a show window for candy kids."

In spite of poignant experiences or, perhaps, because of them, the memory of the first years at Hull-House is more or less blurred with fatigue, for we could of course become accustomed only gradually to the unending activity and to the confusion of a house constantly filling and refilling with groups of people. The little children who came to the kindergarten in the morning were followed by the afternoon clubs of older children, and those in turn made way for the educational and social organizations of adults, occupying every room in the house every evening. All one's habits of living had to be readjusted, and any student's tendency to sit with a book by the fire was of necessity definitely abandoned.

To thus renounce "the luxury of personal preference" was, however, a mere trifle compared to our perplexity over the problems of an industrial neighborhood situated in an unorganized city. Life pressed hard in many directions and yet it has always seemed to me rather interesting that when we were so distressed over its stern aspects and so impressed with the lack of municipal regulations, the first building erected for Hull-House should have been designed for an art gallery, for although it contained a reading-room on the first floor and a studio above, the largest space on the second floor was carefully designed and lighted for art exhibits, which had to do only with the cultivation of that which appealed to the powers of enjoyment as over against a wage-earning capacity. It was also significant that a Chicago business man, fond of pictures himself, responded to this first appeal of the new and certainly puzzling undertaking called a Settlement.

The situation was somewhat complicated by the fact that at the time the building was erected in 1891, our free lease of the land upon which Hull-House stood expired in 1895. The donor of the building, however, overcame the difficulty by simply calling his gift a donation of a thousand dollars a year. This restriction of course necessitated the simplest sort of a structure, although I remember on the exciting day when the new building was promised to us, that I looked up my European notebook which contained the record of my experience in Ulm, hoping that I might find a description of what I then thought "a Cathedral of Humanity" ought to be. The description was "low and widespreading as to include all men in fellowship and mutual responsibility even as the older pinnacles and spires indicated communion with God." The description did not prove of value as an architectural motive I am afraid, although the architects, who have remained our friends through all the years, performed marvels with a combination of complicated demands and little money. At the moment when I read this girlish outbreak it gave me much comfort, for in those days in addition to our other perplexities Hull-House was often called irreligious.

These first buildings were very precious to us and it afforded us the greatest pride and pleasure as one building after another was added to the Hull-House group. They clothed in brick and mortar and made visible to the world that which we were trying to do; they stated to Chicago that education and recreation ought to be extended to the immigrants. The boys came in great numbers to our provisional gymnasium fitted up in a former saloon, and it seemed to us quite as natural that a Chicago man, fond of athletics, should erect a building for them, as that the boys should clamor for more room.

I do not wish to give a false impression, for we were often bitterly pressed for money and worried by the prospect of unpaid bills, and we gave up one golden scheme after another because we could not afford it; we cooked the meals and kept the books and washed the windows without a thought of hardship if we thereby saved money for the consummation of some ardently desired undertaking.

But in spite of our financial stringency, I always believed that money would be given when we had once clearly reduced the Settlement idea to the actual deed. This chapter, therefore, would be incomplete if it did not record a certain theory of nonresistance or rather universal good will which I had worked out in connection with the Settlement idea and which was later so often and so rudely disturbed. At that time I had come to believe that if the activities of Hull-House were ever misunderstood, it would be either because there was not time to fully explain or because our motives had become mixed, for I was convinced that disinterested action was like truth or beauty in its lucidity and power of appeal.

But more gratifying than any understanding or response from without could possibly be, was the consciousness that a growing group of residents was gathering at Hull-House, held together in that soundest of all social bonds, the companionship of mutual interests. These residents came primarily because they were genuinely interested in the social situation and believed that the Settlement was valuable as a method of approach to it. A house in which the men residents lived was opened across the street, and at the end of the first five years the Hull-House residential force numbered fifteen, a majority of whom still remain identified with the Settlement.

Even in those early years we caught glimpses of the fact that certain social sentiments, which are "the difficult and cumulating product of human growth" and which like all higher aims live only by communion and fellowship, are cultivated most easily in the fostering soil of a community life.

Occasionally I obscurely felt as if a demand were being made upon us for a ritual which should express and carry forward the hope of the social movement. I was constantly bewildered by the number of requests I received to officiate at funeral services and by the curious confessions made to me by total strangers. For a time I accepted the former and on one awful occasion furnished "the poetic part" of a wedding ceremony really performed by a justice of the peace, but I soon learned to steadfastly refuse such offices, although I saw that for many people without church affiliations the vague humanitarianism the Settlement represented was the nearest approach they could find to an expression of their religious sentiments.

These hints of what the Settlement might mean to at least a few spirits among its contemporaries became clear to me for the first time one summer's day in rural England, when I discussed with John Trevor his attempts to found a labor church and his desire to turn the toil and danger attached to the life of the workingman into the means of a universal fellowship. That very year a papyrus leaf brought to the British Museum from Egypt, containing among other sayings of Jesus, "Raise the stone, and there thou shalt find me; cleave the wood and I am there," was a powerful reminder to all England of the basic relations between daily labor and Christian teaching.

In those early years at Hull-House we were, however, in no danger of losing ourselves in mazes of speculation or mysticism, and there was shrewd penetration in a compliment I received from one of our Scotch neighbors. He came down Polk Street as I was standing near the foundations of our new gymnasium, and in response to his friendly remark that "Hull-House was spreading out," I replied that "Perhaps we were spreading out too fast." "Oh, no," he rejoined, "you can afford to spread out wide, you are so well planted in the mud," giving the compliment, however, a practical turn, as he glanced at the deep mire on the then unpaved street. It was this same condition of Polk Street which had caused the crown prince of Belgium when he was brought upon a visit to Hull-House to shake his head and meditatively remark, "There is not such a street-no, not one-in all the territory of Belgium."

At the end of five years the residents of Hull-House published some first found facts and our reflections thereon in a book called "Hull-House Maps and Papers." The maps were taken from information collected by one of the residents for the United States Bureau of Labor in the investigation into "the slums of great cities" and the papers treated of various neighborhood matters with candor and genuine concern if not with skill. The first edition became exhausted in two years, and apparently the Boston publisher did not consider the book worthy of a second.

Chapter VII
Problems of Poverty

That neglected and forlorn old age is daily brought to the attention of a Settlement which undertakes to bear its share of the neighborhood burden imposed by poverty, was pathetically clear to us during our first months of residence at Hull-House. One day a boy of ten led a tottering old lady into the House, saying that she had slept for six weeks in their kitchen on a bed made up next to the stove; that she had come when her son died, although none of them had ever seen her before; but because her son had "once worked in the same shop with Pa she thought of him when she had nowhere to go." The little fellow concluded by saying that our house was so much bigger than theirs that he thought we would have more roomfor beds. The old woman herself said absolutely nothing, but looking on with that gripping fear of the poorhouse in her eyes, she was a living embodiment of that dread which is so heartbreaking that the occupants of the County Infirmary themselves seem scarcely less wretched than those who are making their last stand against it.

This look was almost more than I could bear for only a few days before some frightened women had bidden me come quickly to the house of an old German woman, whom two men from the country agent's office were attempting to remove to the County Infirmary. The poor old creature had thrown herself bodily upon a small and battered chest of drawers and clung there, clutching it so firmly that it would have been impossible to remove her without also taking the piece of furniture . She did not weep nor moan nor indeed make any human sound, but between her broken gasps for breath she squealed shrilly like a frightened animal caught in a trap. The little group of women and children gathered at her door stood aghast at this realization of the black dread which always clouds the lives of the very poor when work is slack, but which constantly grows more imminent and threatening as old age approaches. The neighborhood women and I hastened to make all sorts of promises as to the support of the old woman and the country officials, only too glad to be rid of their unhappy duty, left her to our ministrations. This dread of the poorhouse, the result of centuries of deterrent Poor Law administration, seemed to me not without some justification one summer when I found myself perpetually distressed by the unnecessary idleness and forlornness of the old women in the Cook County Infirmary, many of whom I had known in the years when activity was still a necessity, and when they yet felt bustlingly important. To take away from an old woman whose life has been spent in household cares all the foolish little belongings to which her affections cling and to which her very fingers have become accustomed, is to take away her last incentive to activity, almost to life itself. To give an old woman only a chair and a bed, to leave her no cupboard in which her treasures may be stowed, not only that she may take them out when she desires occupation, but that their mind may dwell upon them in moments of revery, is to reduce living almost beyond the limit of human endurance.

The poor creature who clung so desperately to her chest of drawers was really clinging to the last remnant of normal living —a symbol of all she was asked to renounce. For several years after this summer I invited five or six old women to take a two weeks' vacation from the poorhouse which was eagerly and even gayly accepted. Almost all the old men in the County Infirmary wander away each summer taking their chances for finding food or shelter and return much refreshed by the little "tramp," but the old women cannot do this unless they have some help from the outside, and yet the expenditure of a very little money secures for them the coveted vacation. I found that a few pennies paid their car fare into town, a dollar a week procured lodging with an old acquaintance; assured of two good meals a day in the Hull-House coffee-house they could count upon numerous cups of tea among old friends to whom they would airily state that they had "come out for a little change" and hadn't yet made up their minds about "going in again for the winter." They thus enjoyed a two weeks' vacation to the top of their bent and returned with wondrous tales of their adventures, with which they regaled the other paupers during the long winter.

The reminiscences of these old women, their shrewd comments upon life, their sense of having reached a point where they may at last speak freely with nothing to lose because of their frankness, makes them often the most delightful of companions. I recall one of my guests, the mother of many scattered children, whose one bright spot through all the dreary years had been the wedding feast of her son Mike, —a feast which had become transformed through long meditation into the nectar and ambrosia of the very gods. As a farewell fling before she went "in" again, we dined together upon chicken pie, but it did not taste like the "the chicken pie at Mike's wedding" and she was disappointed after all.

Even death itself sometimes fails to bring the dignity and serenity which one would fain associate with old age. I recall the dying hour of one old Scotchwoman whose long struggle to "keep respectable" had so embittered her that her last words were gibes and taunts for those who were trying to minister to her. "So you came in yourself this morning, did you? You only sent things yesterday. I guess you knew when the doctor was coming. Don't try to warm my feet with anything but that old jacket that I've got there; it belonged to my boy who was drowned at sea nigh thirty years ago, but it's warmer yet with human feelings than any of your damned charity hot-water bottles." Suddenly the harsh gasping voice was stilled in death and I awaited the doctor's coming shaken and horrified.

The lack of municipal regulation already referred to was, in the early days of Hull-House, parallelled by the inadequacy of the charitable efforts of the city and an unfounded optimism that there was no real poverty among us. Twenty years ago there was no Charity Organization Society in Chicago and the Visiting Nurse Association had not yet begun its beneficial work, while the relief societies, although conscientiously administered, were inadequate in extent and antiquated in method.

As social reformers gave themselves over to discussion of general principles, so the poor invariably accused poverty itself of their destruction. I recall a certain Mrs. Moran, who was returning one rainy day from the office of the county agent with her arms full of paper bags containing beans and flour which alone lay between her children and starvation. Although she had no money she boarded a street car in order to save her booty from complete destruction by the rain, and as the burst bags dropped "flour on the ladies' dresses" and ""beans all over the place," she was sharply reprimanded by the conductor, who was the further exasperated when he discovered she had no fare. He put her off, as she had hoped he would, almost in front of Hull-House. She related to us her state of mind as she stepped off the car and saw the last of her wares disappearing; she admitted she forgot the proprieties and "cursed a little," but, curiously enough, she pronounced her malediction, not against the rain nor the conductor, nor yet against the worthless husband who had been set up to the city prison, but, true to the Chicago spirit of the moment, went to the root of the matter and roundly "cursed poverty."

This spirit of generalization and lack of organization among the charitable forces of the city was painfully revealed in that terrible winter after the World's Fair, when the general financial depression throughout the country was much intensified in Chicago by the numbers of unemployed stranded at the close of the exposition. When the first cold weather came the police stations and the very corridors of the city hall were crowded by men who could afford no other lodging. They made huge demonstrations on the lake front, reminding one of the London gatherings in Trafalgar Square.

It was the winter in which Mr. Stead wrote his indictment of Chicago. I can vividly recall his visits to Hull-House, some of them between eleven and twelve o'clock at night, when he would come in wet and hungry from an investigation of the levee district, and while he was drinking hot chocolate before an open fire, would relate in one of his curious monologues, his experience as an out-of-door laborer standing in line without an overcoat for two hours in the sleet, that he might have a chance to sweep the streets; or his adventures with a crook, who mistook him for one of this own kind and offered him a place as an agent for a gambling house, which he promptly accepted. Mr. Stead was much impressed with the mixed goodness in Chicago, the lack of rectitude in many high places, the simple kindness of the most wretched to each other. Before he published "If Christ Came to Chicago" he made his attempt to rally the diverse moral forces of the city in a huge mass meeting, which resulted in a temporary organization, later developing into the Civic Federation. I was a member of the committee of five appointed to carry out the suggestions made in this remarkable meeting, and or first concern was to appoint a committee to deal with the unemployed. But when has a committee ever dealt satisfactorily with the unemployed? Relief stations were opened in various part of the city, temporary lodging houses were established, Hull-House undertaking to lodge the homeless women who could be received nowhere else; employment stations were opened giving sewing to the women, and street sweeping for the men was organized. It was in connection with the latter that the perplexing question of the danger of permanently lowering wages at such a crisis, in the praiseworthy effort to bring speedy relief, was brought home to me. I insisted that it was better to have the men work half a day for seventy-five cents than a whole day for a dollar, better that they should earn three dollars in two days than in three days. I resigned from the street-cleaning committee in despair of making the rest of the committee understand that, as our real object was not street cleaning but the help of the unemployed, we must treat the situation in such wise that the men would not be worse off when they returned to their normal occupations. The discussion opened up situations new to me and carried me far afield in perhaps the most serious economic reading I have ever done.

A beginning also was then made toward a Bureau of Organized Charities, the main office being put in charge of a young man recently come from Boston, who lived at Hull-House. But to employ scientific methods for the first time at such a moment involved difficulties, and the most painful episode of the winter came for me from an attempt on my part to conform to carefully received instructions. A shipping clerk whom I had known for a long time had lost his place, as so many people had that year, and came to the relief station established at Hull-House four or five times to secure help for his family. I told him one day of the opportunity for work on the drainage canal and intimated that if any employment were obtainable, he ought to exhaust that possibility before asking for help. The man replied that he had always worked indoors and that he could not endure outside work in winter. I am grateful to remember that I was too uncertain to be severe, although I held to my instructions. He did not come again for relief, but worked for two days digging on the canal, where he contracted pneumonia and died a week later. I have never lost trace of the two little children he left behind him, although I cannot see them without a bitter consciousness that it was at their expense I learned that life cannot be administered by definite rules and regulations; that wisdom to deal with a man's difficulties comes only through some knowledge of his life and habits as a whole; and that to treat an isolated episode is almost sure to invite blundering.

It was also during this winter that I became permanently impressed with the kindness of the poor to each other; the woman who lives upstairs will willingly share her breakfast with the family below because she knows they "are hard up"; the man who boarded with them last winter will give a month's rent because he knows the father of the family is out of work; the baker across the street who is fast being pushed to the wall by his downtown competitors, will send across three loaves of stale bread because he has seen the children looking longingly into his window and suspects they are hungry. There are also the families who, during times of business depression, are obliged to seek help from the county or some benevolent society, but who are themselves most anxious not to be confounded with the pauper class, with whom indeed they do not in the least belong. Charles Booth, in his brilliant chapter on the unemployed, expresses regret that the problems of the working class are so often confounded with the problems of the inefficient and the idle, that although working people live in the same street with those in need of charity, to thus confound two problems is to render the solution of both impossible.

I remember one family in which the father had been out of work for this same winter, most of the furniture had been pawned, and as the worn-out shoes could not be replaced the children could not go to school. The mother was ill and barely able to come for the supplies and medicines. Two years later she invited me to supper one Sunday evening in the little home which had been completely restored, and she gave as a reason for the invitation that she couldn't bear to have me remember them as they had been during that one winter, which she insisted had been unique in her twelve years of married life. She said that it was as if she had met me, not as I am ordinarily, but as I should appear misshapen with rheumatism or with a face distorted by neuralgic pain; that it was not fair to judge poor people that way. She perhaps unconsciously illustrated the difference between the relief-station relation to the poor and the Settlement relation to its neighbors, the latter wishing to know them through all the varying conditions of life, to stand by when they are in distress, but by no means to drop intercourse with them when normal prosperity has returned, enabling the relation to become more social and free from economic disturbance.

Possibly something of the same effort has to be made within the Settlement itself to keep its own sense of proportion in regard to the relation of the crowded city quarter to the rest of the country. It was in the spring following this terrible winter, during a journey to meet lecture engagements in California, that I found myself amazed at the large stretches of open country and prosperous towns through which we passed day by day, whose existence I had quite forgotten.

In the latter part of the summer of 1895, I served as a member on a commission appointed by the mayor of Chicago, to investigate conditions in the county poorhouse, public attention having become centered on it through one of those distressing stories, which exaggerates the wrong in a public institution while at the same time it reveals conditions which need to be rectified. However necessary publicity is for securing reformed administration, however useful such exposures may be for political purposes, the whole is attended by such a waste of the most precious human emotions, by such a tearing of living tissue, that it can scarcely be endured. Every time I entered Hull-House during the days of the investigation, I would find waiting for me from twenty to thirty people whose friends and relatives were in the suspected institution, all in such acute distress of mind that to see them was to look upon the victims of deliberate torture. In most cases my visitor would state that it seemed impossible to put their invalids in any other place, but if these stories were true, something must be done. Many of the patients were taken out only to be returned after a few days or weeks to meet the sullen hostility of their attendants and with their own attitude changed from confidence to timidity and alarm.

This piteous dependence of the poor upon the good will of public officials was made clear to us in an early experience with a peasant woman straight from the fields of Germany, whom we met during our first six months at Hull-House. Her four years in America had been spent in patiently carrying water up and down two flights of stairs, and in washing the heavy flannel suits of iron foundry workers. For this her pay had averaged thirty-five cents a day. Three of her daughters had fallen victims to the vice of the city. The mother was bewildered and distressed, but understood nothing. We were able to induce the betrayer of one daughter to marry her; the second, after a tedious lawsuit, supported his child; with the third we were able to do nothing. This woman is now living with her family in a little house seventeen miles from the city. She has made two payments on her land and is a lesson to all beholders as she pastures her cow up and down the railroad tracks and makes money from her ten acres. She did not need charity for she had an immense capacity for hard work, but she sadly needed the service of the State's attorney office, enforcing the laws designed for the protection of such girls as her daughters.

We early found ourselves spending many hours in efforts to secure support for deserted women, insurance for bewildered widows, damages for injured operators, furniture from the clutches of the installment store. The Settlement is valuable as an information and interpretation bureau. It constantly acts between the various institutions of the city and the people for whose benefit these institutions were erected. The hospitals, the county agencies, and State asylums are often but vague rumors to the people who need them most. Another function of the Settlement to its neighborhood resembles that of the big brother whose mere presence on the playground protects the little one from bullies.

We early learned to know the children of hard-driven mothers who went out to work all day, sometimes leaving the little things in the casual care of a neighbor, but often locking them into their tenement rooms. The first three crippled children we encountered in the neighborhood had all been injured while their mothers were at work: one had fallen out of a third-story window, another had been burned, and the third had a curved spine due to the fact that for three years he had been tied all day long to the leg of the kitchen table, only released at noon by his older brother who hastily ran in from a neighboring factory to share his lunch with him. When the hot weather came the restless children could not brook the confinement of the stuffy rooms, and, as it was not considered safe to leave the doors open because of sneak thieves, many of the children were locked out. During our first summer an increasing number of these poor little mites would wander into the cool hallway of Hull-House. We kept them there and fed them at noon, in return for which we were sometimes offered a hot penny which had been held in a tight little fist "ever since mother left this morning, to buy something to eat with." Out of kindergarten hours our little guests noisily enjoyed the hospitality of our bedrooms under the so-called care of any resident who volunteered to keep an eye on them, but later they were moved into a neighboring apartment under more systematic supervision.

Hull-House was thus committed to a day nursery which we sustained for sixteen years first in a little cottage on a side street and then in a building designed for its use called the Children's House. It is now carried on by the United Charities of Chicago in a finely equipped building on our block, where the immigrant mothers are cared for as well as the children, and where they are taught the things which will make life in America more possible. Our early day nursery brought us into natural relations with the poorest women of the neighborhood, many of whom were bearing the burden of dissolute and incompetent husbands in addition to the support of their children. Some of them presented an impressive manifestation of that miracle of affection which outlives abuse, neglect, and crime,—the affection which cannot be plucked from the heart where it has lived, although it may serve only to torture and torment. "Has your husband come back?" you inquire of Mrs. S., whom you have known for eight years as an overworked woman bringing her three delicate children every morning to the nursery; she is bent under the double burden of earning the money which supports them and giving them the tender care which alone keeps them alive. The oldest two children have at last gone to work, and Mrs. S. has allowed herself the luxury of staying at home two days a week. And now the worthless husband is back again-the "gentlemanly gambler" type who, through all vicissitudes, manages to present a white shirtfront and a gold watch to the world, but who is dissolute, idle and extravagant. You dread to think how much his presence will increase the drain upon the family exchequer, and you know that he stayed away until he was certain that the children were old enough to earn money for his luxuries. Mrs. S. does not pretend to take his return lightly, but she replies in all seriousness and simplicity, "You know my feeling for him has never changed. You may think me foolish, but I was always proud of his good looks and educated appearance. I was lonely and homesick during those eight years when the children were little and needed so much doctoring, but I could never bring myself to feel hard toward him, and I used to pray the good Lord to keep him from harm and bring him back to us; so, of course, I'm thankful now." She passes on with a dignity which gives one a new sense of the security of affection.

I recall a similar case of a woman who had supported her three children for five years, during which time her dissolute husband constantly demanded money for drink and kept her perpetually worried and intimidated. One Saturday, before the "blessed Easter," he came back from a long debauch, ragged and filthy, but in a state of lachrymose repentance. The poor wife received him as a returned prodigal, believed that his remorse would prove lasting, and felt sure that if she and the children went to church with him on Easter Sunday and he could be induced to take the pledge before the priest, all their troubles would be ended. After hours of vigorous effort and the expenditure of all her savings, he finally sat on the front doorstep the morning of Easter Sunday, bathed, shaved and arrayed in a fine new suit of clothes. She left him sitting there in the reluctant spring sunshine while she finished washing and dressing the children. When she finally opened the front door with the three shining children that they might all set forth together, the returned prodigal had disappeared, and was not seen again until midnight, when he came back in a glorious state of intoxication from the proceeds of his pawned clothes and clad once more in the dingiest attire. She took him in without comment, only to begin again the wretched cycle. There were of course instances of the criminal husband as well as of the merely vicious. I recall one woman who, during seven years, never missed a visiting day at the penitentiary when she might see her husband, and whose little children in the nursery proudly reported the messages from father with no notion that he was in disgrace, so absolutely did they reflect the gallant spirit of their mother.

While one was filled with admiration for these heroic women, something was also to be said for some of the husbands, for the sorry men who, for one reason or another, had failed in the struggle of life. Sometimes this failure was purely economic and the men were competent to give the children, whom they were not able to support, the care and guidance and even education which were of the highest value. Only a few months ago I met upon the street one of the early nursery mothers who for five years had been living in another part of the city, and in response to my query as to the welfare of her five children, she bitterly replied, "All of them except Mary have been arrested at one time or another, thank you." In reply to my remark that I thought her husband had always had such admirable control over them, she burst out, "That has been the whole trouble. I got tired taking care of him and didn't believe that his laziness was all due to his health, as he said, so I left him and said that I would support the children, but not him. From that minute the trouble with the four boys began. I never knew what they were doing, and after every sort of a scrape I finally put Jack and the twins into institutions where I pay for them. Joe has gone to work at last, but with a disgraceful record behind him. I tell you I ain't so sure that because a woman can make big money that she can be both father and mother to her children."

As I walked on, I could but wonder in which particular we are most stupid-to judge a man's worth so solely by his wage-earning capacity that a good wife feels justified in leaving him, or in holding fast to that wretched delusion that a woman can both support and nurture her children.

One of the most piteous revelations of the futility of the latter attempt came to me through the mother of "Goosie," as the children for years called a little boy who, because he was brought to the nursery wrapped up in his mother's shawl, always had his hair filled with the down and small feathers from the feather brush factory where she worked. One March morning, Goosie's mother was hanging out the washing on a shed roof before she left for the factory. Five-year-old Goosie was trotting at her heels handing her clothes pins, when he was suddenly blown off the roof by the high wind into the alley below. His neck was broken by the fall, and as he lay piteous and limp on a pile of frozen refuse, his mother cheerily called him to "climb up again," so confident do overworked mothers become that their children cannot get hurt. After the funeral, as the poor mother sat in the nursery postponing the moment when she must go back to her empty rooms, I asked her, in a futile effort to be of comfort, if there was anything more we could do for her. The overworked, sorrow-stricken woman looked up and replied, "If you could give me my wages for to-morrow, I would not go to work in the factory at all. I would like to stay at home all day and hold the baby. Goosie was always asking me to take him and I never had any time." This statement revealed the condition of many nursery mothers who are obliged to forego the joys and solaces which belong to even the most poverty-stricken. The long hours of factory labor necessary for earning the support of a child leave no time for the tender care and caressing which may enrich the life of the most piteous baby.

With all of the efforts made by modern society to nurture and educate the young, how stupid it is to permit the mothers of young children to spend themselves in the coarser work of the world! It is curiously inconsistent that with the emphasis which this generation has placed upon the mother and upon the prolongation of infancy, we constantly allow the waste of this most precious material. I cannot recall without indignation a recent experience. I was detained late one evening in an office building by a prolonged committee meeting of the Board of Education. As I came out at eleven o'clock, I met in the corridor of the fourteenth floor a woman whom I knew, on her knees scrubbing the marble tiling. As she straightened up to greet me, she seemed so wet from her feet up to her chin, that I hastily inquired the cause. Her reply was that she left home at five o'clock every night and had no opportunity for six hours to nurse her baby. Her mother's milk mingled with the very water with which she scrubbed the floors until she should return at midnight, heated and exhausted, to feed her screaming child with what remained within her breasts.

These are only a few of the problems connected with the lives of the poorest people with whom the residents in a Settlement are constantly brought in contact.

I cannot close this chapter without a reference to that gallant company of men and women among whom my acquaintance is so large, who are fairly indifferent to starvation itself because of their preoccupation with higher ends. Among them are visionaries and enthusiasts, unsuccessful artists, writers, and reformers. For many years at Hull-House, we knew a well-bred German woman who was completely absorbed in the experiment of expressing musical phrases and melodies by means of colors. Because she was small and deformed, she stowed herself into her trunk every night, where she slept on a canvas stretched hammock-wise from the four corners and her food was of the meagerest; nevertheless if a visitor left an offering upon her table, it was largely spent for apparatus or delicately colored silk floss, with which to pursue the fascinating experiment. Another sadly crippled old woman, the widow of a sea captain, although living almost exclusively upon malted milk tablets as affording a cheap form of prepared food, was always eager to talk of the beautiful illuminated manuscripts she had sought out in her travels and to show specimens of her own work as an illuminator. Still another of these impressive old women was an inveterate inventor. Although she had seen prosperous days in England, when we knew her, she subsisted largely upon the samples given away at the demonstration counters of the department stores, and on bits of food which she cooked on a coal shovel in the furnace of the apartment house whose basement back room she occupied. Although her inventions were not practicable, various experts to whom they were submitted always pronounced them suggestive and ingenious. I once saw her receive this complimentary verdict —"this ribbon to stick in her coat"—with such dignity and gravity that the words of condolence for her financial disappointment, died upon my lips.

These indomitable souls are but three out of many whom I might instance to prove that those who are handicapped in the race for life's goods, sometimes play a magnificent trick upon the jade, life herself, by ceasing to know whether or not they possess any of her tawdry goods and chattels.

Chapter IX
A Decade of Economic Discussion

The Hull-House residents were often bewildered by the desire for constant discussion which characterized Chicago twenty years ago, for although the residents in the early Settlements were in many cases young persons who had sought relief from the consciousness of social maladjustment in the "anodyne of work" afforded by philanthropic and civic activities, their former experiences had not thrown them into company with radicals. The decade between 1890-1900 was, in Chicago, a period of propaganda as over against constructive social effort; the moment for marching and carrying banners, for stating general principles and making a demonstration, rather than the time for uncovering the situation and for providing the legal measures and the civic organization through which new social hopes might make themselves felt.

When Hull-House was established in 1889, the events of the Haymarket riot were already two years old, but during that time Chicago had apparently gone through the first period of repressive measures, and in the winter of 1889-1890, by the advice and with the active participation of its leading citizens, the city had reached the conclusion that the only cure for the acts of anarchy was free speech and an open discussion of the ills of which the opponents of government complained. Great open meetings were held every Sunday evening in the recital hall of the then new auditorium, presided over by such representative citizens as Lyman Gage, and every possible shade of opinion was freely expressed. A man who spoke constantly at these meetings used to be pointed out to the visiting stranger as one who had been involved with the group of convicted anarchists, and who doubtless would have been arrested and tried, but for the accident of his having been in Milwaukee when the explosion occurred. One cannot imagine such meetings being held in Chicago to-day, nor that such a man should be encouraged to raise his voice in a public assemblage presided over by a leading banker. It is hard to tell just what change has come over our philosophy or over the minds of those citizens who were then convinced that if these conferences had been established earlier, the Haymarket riot and all its sensational results might have been avoided.

At any rate, there seemed a further need for smaller clubs, where men who differed widely in their social theories might meet for discussion, where representatives of the various economic schools might modify each other, and at least learn tolerance and the futility of endeavoring to convince all the world of the truth of one position. Fanaticism is engendered only when men, finding no contradiction to their theories, at last believe that the very universe lends itself as an exemplification of one point of view. "The Working People's Social Science Club" was organized at Hull-House in the spring of 1890 by an English workingman, and for seven years it held a weekly meeting. At eight o'clock every Wednesday night the secretary called to order from forty to one hundred people; a chairman for the evening was elected, a speaker was introduced who was allowed to talk until nine o'clock; his subject was then thrown open to discussion and a lively debate ensued until ten o'clock, at which hour the meeting was declared adjourned. The enthusiasm of this club seldom lagged. Its zest for discussion was unceasing, and any attempt to turn it into a study or reading club always met with the strong disapprobation of the members.

In these weekly discussions in the Hull-House drawing room everything was thrown back upon general principles and all discussion save that which "went to the root of things," was impatiently discarded as an unworthy, halfway measure. I recall one evening in this club when an exasperated member had thrown out the statement that "Mr. B. believes that socialism will cure the toothache." Mr. B. promptly rose to his feet and said that it certainly would, that when every child's teeth were systematically cared for from the beginning, toothaches would disappear from the face of the earth, belonging, as it did, to the extinct competitive order, as the black plague had disappeared from the earth with the ill-regulated feudal regime of the Middle Ages. "But," he added, "why do we spend time discussing trifles like the toothache when great social changes are to be considered which will of themselves reform these minor ills?" Even the man who had been humorous fell into the solemn tone of the gathering. It was, perhaps, here that the socialist surpassed everyone else in the fervor of economic discussion. He was usually a German or a Russian, with a turn for logical presentation, who saw in the concentration of capital and the growth of monopolies an inevitable transition to the socialist state. He pointed out that the concentration of capital in fewer hands but increased the mass of those whose interests were opposed to a maintenance of its power, and vastly simplified its final absorption by the community; that monopoly "when it is finished doth bring forth socialism." Opposite to him, springing up in every discussion was the individualist, or, as the socialist called him, the anarchist, who insisted that we shall never secure just human relations until we have equality of opportunity; that the sole function of the state is to maintain the freedom of each, guarded by the like freedom of all, in order that each man may be able to work out the problems of his own existence.

That first winter was within three years of the Henry George campaign in New York, when his adherents all over the country were carrying on a successful and effective propaganda. When Henry George himself came to Hull-House one Sunday afternoon, the gymnasium which was already crowded with men to hear Father Huntington's address on "Why should a free thinker believe in Christ," fairly rocked on its foundations under the enthusiastic and prolonged applause which greeted this great leader and constantly interrupted his stirring address, filled, as all of his speeches were, with high moral enthusiasm and humanitarian fervor. Of the remarkable congresses held in connection with the World's Fair, perhaps those inaugurated by the advocates of single tax exceeded all others in vital enthusiasm. It was possibly significant that all discussions in the department of social science had to be organized by partisans in separate groups. The very committee itself on social science composed of Chicago citizens, of whom I was one, changed from week to week, as partisan members had their feelings hurt because their cause did not receive "due recognition." And yet in the same building adherents of the most diverse religious creeds, eastern and western, met in amity and good fellowship. Did it perhaps indicate that their presentation of the eternal problems of life were cast in an older and less sensitive mold than this presentation in terms of social experience, or was it rather that the new social science was not yet a science at all but merely a name under cover of which we might discuss the perplexing problems of the industrial situation? Certainly the difficulties of our committee were not minimized by the fact that the then new science of sociology had not yet defined its own field. The University of Chicago, opened only the year before the World's Fair, was the first great institution of learning to institute a department of sociology.

In the meantime the Hull-House Social Science Club grew in numbers and fervor as various distinguished people who were visiting the World's Fair came to address it. I recall a brilliant Frenchwoman who was filled with amazement because one of the shabbiest men reflected a reading of Schopenhauer. She considered the statement of another member most remarkable—that when he saw a carriage driving through the streets occupied by a capitalist who was no longer even an entrepreneur, he felt quite as sure that his days were numbered and that his very lack of function to society would speedily bring him to extinction, as he did when he saw a drunkard reeling along the same street.

The club at any rate convinced the residents that no one so poignantly realizes the failures in the social structure as the man at the bottom, who has been most directly in contact with those failures and has suffered most. I recall the shrewd comments of a certain sailor who had known the disinherited in every country; of a Russian who had served his term in Siberia; of an old Irishman who called himself an atheist but who in moments of excitement always blamed the good Lord for "setting supinely" when the world was so horribly out of joint.

It was doubtless owing largely to this club that Hull-House contracted its early reputation for radicalism. Visitors refused to distinguish between the sentiments expressed by its members in the heat of discussion and the opinions held by the residents themselves. At that moment in Chicago the radical of every shade of opinion was vigorous and dogmatic; of the sort that could not resign himself to the slow march of human improvement; of the type who knew exactly "in what part of the world Utopia standeth."

During this decade Chicago seemed divided into two classes; those who held that "business is business" and who were therefore annoyed at the very notion of social control, and the radicals, who claimed that nothing could be done to really moralize the industrial situation until society should be reorganized.

A Settlement is above all a place for enthusiasms, a spot to which those who have a passion for the equalization of human joys and opportunities are early attracted. It is this type of mind which is in itself so often obnoxious to the man of conquering business faculty, to whom the practical world of affairs seems so supremely rational that he would never vote to change the type of it even if he could. The man of social enthusiasm is to him an annoyance and an affront. He does not like to hear him talk and considers him per se "unsafe." Such a business man would admit, as an abstract proposition, that society is susceptible of modification and would even agree that all human institutions imply progressive development, but at the same time he deeply distrusts those who seek to reform existing conditions. There is a certain common-sense foundation for this distrust, for too often the reformer is the rebel who defies things as they are, because of the restraints which they impose upon his individual desires rather than because of the general defects of the system. When such a rebel poses for a reformer, his shortcomings are heralded to the world, and his downfall is cherished as an awful warning to those who refuse to worship "the god of things as they are."

And yet as I recall the members of this early club, even those who talked the most and the least rationally, seem to me to have been particularly kindly and "safe." The most pronounced anarchist among them has long since become a convert to a religious sect, holding Buddhistic tenets which imply little food and a distrust of all action; he has become a wraith of his former self but he still retains his kindly smile.

In the discussion of these themes, Hull-House was of course quite as much under the suspicion of one side as the other. I remember one night when I addressed a club of secularists, which met at the corner of South Halsted and Madison streets, a rough-looking man called out: "You are all right now, but, mark my words, when you are subsidized by the millionaires, you will be afraid to talk like this." The defense of free speech was a sensitive point with me, and I quickly replied that while I did not intend to be subsidized by millionaires, neither did I propose to be bullied by workingmen, and that I should state my honest opinion without consulting either of them. To my surprise, the audience of radicals broke into applause, and the discussion turned upon the need of resisting tyranny wherever found, if democratic institutions were to endure. This desire to bear independent witness to social righteousness often resulted in a sense of compromise difficult to endure, and at many times it seemed to me that we were destined to alienate everybody. I should have been most grateful at that time to accept the tenets of socialism, and I conscientiously made my effort, both by reading and by many discussions with the comrades. I found that I could easily give an affirmative answer to the heated question "Don't you see that just as the hand mill created a society with a feudal lord, so the steam mill creates a society with an industrial capitalist?" But it was a little harder to give an affirmative reply to the proposition that the social relation thus established proceeds to create principles, ideas and categories as merely historical and transitory products.

Of course I use the term "socialism" technically and do not wish to confuse it with the growing sensitiveness which recognizes that no personal comfort, nor individual development can compensate a man for the misery of his neighbors, nor with the increasing conviction that social arrangements can be transformed through man's conscious and deliberate effort. Such a definition would not have been accepted for a moment by the Russians, who then dominated the socialist party in Chicago and among whom a crude interpretation of the class conflict was the test of faith.

During those first years on Halsted Street nothing was more painfully clear than the fact that pliable human nature is relentlessly pressed upon by its physical environment. I saw nowhere a more devoted effort to understand and relieve that heavy pressure than the socialists were making, and I should have been glad to have had the comradeship of that gallant company had they not firmly insisted that fellowship depends upon identity of creed. They repudiated similarity of aim and social sympathy as tests which were much too loose and wavering as they did that vague socialism which for thousands has come to be a philosophy or rather religion embodying the hope of the world and the protection of all who suffer.

I also longed for the comfort of a definite social creed, which should afford at one and the same time an explanation of the social chaos and the logical steps towards its better ordering. I came to have an exaggerated sense of responsibility for the poverty in the midst of which I was living and which the socialists constantly forced me to defend. My plight was not unlike that which might have resulted in my old days of skepticism regarding foreordination, had I then been compelled to defend the confusion arising from the clashing of free wills as an alternative to an acceptance of the doctrine. Another difficulty in the way of accepting this economic determinism, so baldly dependent upon the theory of class consciousness, constantly arose when I lectured in country towns and there had opportunities to read human documents of prosperous people as well as those of my neighbors who were crowded into the city. The former were stoutly unconscious of any classes in America, and the class consciousness of the immigrants was fast being broken into by the necessity for making new and unprecedented connections in the industrial life all about them.

In the meantime, although many men of many minds met constantly at our conferences, it was amazing to find the incorrigible good nature which prevailed. Radicals are accustomed to hot discussion and sharp differences of opinion and take it all in the day's work. I recall that the secretary of the Hull-House Social Science Club at the anniversary of the seventh year of its existence read a report in which he stated that, so far as he could remember, but twice during that time had a speaker lost his temper, and in each case it had been a college professor who "wasn't accustomed to being talked back to."

He also added that but once had all the club members united in applauding the same speaker; only Samuel Jones, who afterwards became the "golden rule" mayor of Toledo, had been able to overcome all their dogmatic differences, when he had set forth a plan of endowing a group of workingmen with a factory plant and a working capital for experimentation in hours and wages, quite as groups of scholars are endowed for research.

Chicago continued to devote much time to economic discussion and remained in a state of youthful glamour throughout the nineties. I recall a young Methodist minister who, in order to free his denomination from any entanglement in his discussion of the economic and social situation, moved from his church building into a neighboring hall. The congregation and many other people followed him there, and he later took to the street corners because he found that the shabbiest men liked that best. Professor Herron filled to overflowing a downtown hall every noon with a series of talks entitled "Between Caesar and Jesus"—an attempt to apply the teachings of the Gospel to the situations of modern commerce. A half dozen publications edited with some ability and much moral enthusiasm have passed away, perhaps because they represented pamphleteering rather than journalism and came to a natural end when the situation changed. Certainly their editors suffered criticism and poverty on behalf of the causes which they represented.

Trades-unionists, unless they were also socialists, were not prominent in those economic discussions, although they were steadily making an effort to bring order into the unnecessary industrial confusion. They belonged to the second of the two classes into which Mill divides all those who are dissatisfied with human life as it is, and whose feelings are wholly identified with its radical amendment. He states that the thoughts of one class are in the region of ultimate aims, of "the highest ideals of human life," while the thoughts of the other are in the region of the "immediately useful, and practically attainable."

The meetings of our Social Science Club were carried on by men of the former class, many of them with a strong religious bias who constantly challenged the Church to assuage the human spirit thus torn and bruised "in the tumult of a time disconsolate." These men were so serious in their demand for religious fellowship, and several young clergymen were so ready to respond to the appeal, that various meetings were arranged at Hull-House, in which a group of people met together to consider the social question, not in a spirit of discussion, but in prayer and meditation. These clergymen were making heroic efforts to induce their churches to formally consider the labor situation, and during the years which have elapsed since then, many denominations of the Christian Church have organized labor committees; but at that time there was nothing of the sort beyond the society in the established Church of England "to consider the conditions of labor."

During that decade even the most devoted of that pioneer church society failed to formulate the fervid desire for juster social conditions into anything more convincing than a literary statement, and the Christian Socialists, at least when the American branch held its annual meeting at Hull-House, afforded but a striking portrayal of that "between-age mood" in which so many of our religious contemporaries are forced to live. I remember that I received the same impression when I attended a meeting called by the canon of an English cathedral to discuss the relation of the Church to labor. The men quickly indicted the cathedral for its uselessness, and the canon asked them what in their minds should be its future. The men promptly replied that any new social order would wish, of course, to preserve beautiful historic buildings, that although they would dismiss the bishop and all the clergy, they would want to retain one or two scholars as custodians and interpreters. "And what next?" the imperturbable ecclesiastic asked. "We would democratize it," replied the men. But when it came to a more detailed description of such an undertaking, the discussion broke down into a dozen bits, although illuminated by much shrewd wisdom and affording a clue, perhaps as to the destruction of the bishop's palace by the citizens of this same town, who had attacked it as a symbol of swollen prosperity during the bread riots of the earlier part of the century.

On the other hand the workingmen who continue to demand help from the Church thereby acknowledge their kinship, as does the son who continues to ask bread from the father who gives him a stone. I recall an incident connected with a prolonged strike in Chicago on the part of the typographical unions for an eight-hour day. The strike had been conducted in a most orderly manner and the union men, convinced of the justice of their cause, had felt aggrieved because one of the religious publishing houses in Chicago had constantly opposed them. Some of the younger clergymen of the denominations who were friendly to the strikers' cause came to a luncheon at Hull-House, where the situation was discussed by the representatives of all sides. The clergymen, becoming much interested in the idealism with which an officer of the State Federation of Labor presented the cause, drew from him the story of his search for fraternal relation: he said that at fourteen years of age he had joined a church, hoping to find it there; he had later become a member of many fraternal organizations and mutual benefit societies, and, although much impressed by their rituals, he was disappointed in the actual fraternity. He had finally found, so it seemed to him, in the cause of organized labor, what these other organizations had failed to give him-an opportunity for sacrificial effort.

Chicago thus took a decade to discuss the problems inherent in the present industrial organization and to consider what might be done, not so much against deliberate aggression as against brutal confusion and neglect; quite as the youth of promise passed through a mist of rose-colored hope before he settles in the land of achievement where he becomes all too dull and literal minded. And yet as I hastily review the decade in Chicago which followed this one given over to discussion, the actual attainment of these early hopes, so far as they have been realized at all, seem to have come from men of affairs rather than from those given to speculation. Was the whole decade of discussion an illustration of that striking fact which has been likened to the changing of swords in Hamlet; that the abstract minds at length yield to the inevitable or at least grow less ardent in their propaganda, while the concrete minds, dealing constantly with daily affairs, in the end demonstrate the reality of abstract notions?

I remember when Frederick Harrison visited Hull-House that I was much disappointed to find that the Positivists had not made their ardor for humanity a more potent factor in the English social movement, as I was surprised during a visit from John Morley to find that he, representing perhaps the type of man whom political life seemed to have pulled away from the ideals of his youth, had yet been such a champion of democracy in the full tide of reaction. My observations were much too superficial to be of value and certainly both men were well grounded in philosophy and theory of social reform and had long before carefully formulated their principles, as the new English Labor Party, which is destined to break up the reactionary period, is now being created by another set of theorists. There were certainly moments during the heated discussions of this decade when nothing seemed so important as right theory: this was borne in upon me one brilliant evening at Hull-House when Benjamin Kidd, author of the much-read "Social Evolution," was pitted against Victor Berger of Milwaukee, even then considered a rising man in the Socialist Party.

At any rate the residents of Hull-House discovered that while their first impact with city poverty allied them to groups given over to discussion of social theories , their sober efforts to heal neighborhood ills allied them to general public movements which were without challenging creeds. But while we discovered that we most easily secured the smallest of much-needed improvements by attaching our efforts to those of organized bodies, nevertheless these very organizations would have been impossible, had not the public conscience been aroused and the community sensibility quickened by these same ardent theorists.

As I review these very first impressions of the workers in unskilled industries, living in a depressed quarter of the city, I realize how easy it was for us to see exceptional cases of hardship as typical of the average lot, and yet, in spite of alleviating philanthropy and labor legislation, the indictment of Tolstoy applied to Moscow thirty years ago still fits every American city: "Wherever we may live, if we draw a circle around us of a hundred thousand, or a thousand, or even of ten miles circumference, and look at the lives of those men and women who are inside our circle, we shall find half-starved children, old people, pregnant women, sick and weak persons, working beyond their strength, who have neither food nor rest enough to support them, and who, for this reason, die before their time; we shall see others, full grown, who are injured and needlessly killed by dangerous and hurtful tasks."

As the American city is awakening to self-consciousness, it slowly perceives the civic significance of these industrial conditions, and perhaps Chicago has been foremost in the effort to connect the unregulated overgrowth of the huge centers of population, with the astonishingly rapid development of industrial enterprises; quite as Chicago was foremost to carry on the preliminary discussion through which a basis was laid for likemindedness and the coordination of diverse wills. I remember an astute English visitor, who had been a guest in a score of American cities, observed that it was hard to understand the local pride he constantly encountered; for in spite of the boasting on the part of leading citizens in the western, eastern, and southern towns, all American cities seemed to him essentially alike and all equally the results of an industry totally unregulated by well-considered legislation.

I am inclined to think that perhaps all this general discussion was inevitable in connection with the early Settlements, as they in turn were the inevitable result of theories of social reform, which in their full enthusiasm reached America by way of England, only in the last decade of the century. There must have been tough fiber somewhere; for, although the residents of Hull-House were often baffled by the radicalism within the Social Science Club and harassed by the criticism from outside, we still continued to believe that such discussion should be carried on, for if the Settlement seeks its expression through social activity, it must learn the difference between mere social unrest and spiritual impulse.

The group of Hull-House residents, which by the end of the decade comprised twenty-five, differed widely in social beliefs, from the girl direct from the country who looked upon all social unrest as mere anarchy, to the resident, who had become a socialist when a student in Zurich, and who had long before translated from the German Engel's "Conditions of the Working Class in England," although at this time she had been read out of the Socialist Party because the Russian and German Impossibilists suspected her fluent English, as she always lightly explained. Although thus diversified in social beliefs, the residents became solidly united through our mutual experience in an industrial quarter, and we became not only convinced of the need for social control and protective legislation but also of the value of this preliminary argument.

This decade of discussion between 1890 and 1900 already seems remote from the spirit of Chicago of to-day. So far as I have been able to reproduce this earlier period, it must reflect the essential provisionality of everything; "the perpetual moving on to something future which shall supersede the present," that paramount impression of life itself, which affords us at one and the same time, ground for despair and for endless and varied anticipation.

Chapter X
Pioneer Labor Legislation in Illinois

Our very first Christmas at Hull-House, when we as yet knew nothing of child labor, a number of little girls refused the candy which was offered them as part of the Christmas good cheer, saying simply that they "worked in a candy factory and could not bear the sight of it." We discovered that for six weeks they had worked from seven in the morning until nine at night, and they were exhausted as well as satiated. The sharp consciousness of stern economic conditions was thus thrust upon us in the midst of the season of good will.

During the same winter three boys from a Hull-House club were injured at one machine in a neighboring factory for lack of a guard which would have cost but a few dollars. When the injury of one of these boys resulted in his death, we felt quite sure that the owners of the factory would share our horror and remorse, and that they would do everything possible to prevent the recurrence of such a tragedy. To our surprise they did nothing whatever, and I made my first acquaintance then with those pathetic documents signed by the parents of working children, that they will make no claim for damages resulting from "carelessness."

The visits we made in the neighborhood constantly discovered women sewing upon sweat-shop work, and often they were assisted by incredibly small children. I remember a little girl of four who pulled out basting threads hour after hour, sitting on a stool at the feet of her Bohemian mother, a little bunch of human misery. But even for that there was no legal redress, for the only child-labor law in Illinois, with any provision for enforcement, had been secured by the coal miners' unions, and was confined to children employed in mines.

We learned to know many families in which the working children contributed to the support of their parents, not only because they spoke English better than the older immigrants and were willing to take lower wages, but because their parents gradually found it easy to live upon their earnings. A South Italian peasant who has picked olives and packed oranges from his toddling babyhood cannot see at once the difference between the outdoor healthy work which he had performed in the varying seasons, and the long hours of monotonous factory life which his child encounters when he goes to work in Chicago. An Italian father came to us in great grief over the death of his eldest child, a little girl of twelve, who had brought the largest wages into the family fund. In the midst of his genuine sorrow he said: "She was the oldest kid I had. Now I shall have to go back to work again until the next one is able to take care of me." The man was only thirty-three and had hoped to retire from work at least during the winters. No foreman cared to have him in a factory, untrained and unintelligent as he was. It was much easier for his bright, English-speaking little girl to get a chance to paste labels on a box than for him to secure an opportunity to carry pig iron. The effect on the child was what no one concerned thought about, in the abnormal effort she made thus prematurely to bear the weight of life. Another little girl of thirteen, a Russian-Jewish child employed in a laundry at a heavy task beyond her strength, committed suicide, because she had borrowed three dollars from a companion which she could not repay unless she confided the story to her parents and gave up an entire week's wages-but what could the family live upon that week in case she did! Her child mind, of course, had no sense of proportion, and carbolic acid appeared inevitable.

While we found many pathetic cases of child labor and hard-driven victims of the sweating system who could not possibly earn enough in the short busy season to support themselves during the rest of the year, it became evident that we must add carefully collected information to our general impression of neighborhood conditions if we would make it of any genuine value.

There was at that time no statistical information on Chicago industrial conditions, and Mrs. Florence Kelley, an early resident of Hull-House, suggested to the Illinois State Bureau of Labor that they investigate the sweating system in Chicago with its attendant child labor. The head of the Bureau adopted this suggestion and engaged Mrs. Kelley to make the investigation. When the report was presented to the Illinois Legislature, a special committee was appointed to look into the Chicago conditions. I well recall that on the Sunday the members of this commission came to dine at Hull-House, our hopes ran high, and we believed that at last some of the worst ills under which our neighbors were suffering would be brought to an end.

As a result of its investigations, this committee recommended to the Legislature the provisions which afterward became those of the first factory law of Illinois, regulating the sanitary conditions of the sweatshop and fixing fourteen as the age at which a child might be employed. Before the passage of the law could be secured, it was necessary to appeal to all elements of the community, and a little group of us addressed the open meetings of trades-unions and of benefit societies, church organizations, and social clubs literally every evening for three months. Of course the most energetic help as well as intelligent understanding came from the trades-unions. The central labor body of Chicago, then called the Trades and Labor Assembly, had previously appointed a committee of investigation to inquire into the sweating system. This committee consisted of five delegates from the unions and five outside their membership. Two of the latter were residents of Hull-House, and continued with the unions in their well-conducted campaign until the passage of Illinois's first Factory Legislation was secured, a statute which has gradually been built upon by many public-spirited citizens until Illinois stands well among the States, at least in the matter of protecting her children. The Hull-House residents that winter had their first experience in lobbying. I remember that I very much disliked the word and still more the prospect of the lobbying itself, and we insisted that well-known Chicago women should accompany this first little group of Settlement folk who with trades-unionists moved upon the state capitol in behalf of factory legislation. The national or, to use its formal name, The General Federation of Woman's Clubs had been organized in Chicago only the year before this legislation was secured. The Federation was then timid in regard to all legislation because it was anxious not to frighten its new membership, although its second president, Mrs. Henrotin, was most untiring in her efforts to secure this law.

It was, perhaps, a premature effort, though certainly founded upon a genuine need, to urge that a clause limiting the hours of all women working in factories or workshops to eight a day, or forty-eight a week, should be inserted in the first factory legislation of the State. Although we had lived at Hull-House but three years when we urged this legislation, we had known a large number of young girls who were constantly exhausted by night work; for whatever may be said in defense of night work for men, few women are able to endure it. A man who works by night sleeps regularly by day, but a woman finds it impossible to put aside the household duties which crowd upon her, and a conscientious girl finds it hard to sleep with her mother washing and scrubbing within a few feet of her bed. One of the most painful impressions of those first years is that of pale, listless girls, who worked regularly in a factory of the vicinity which was then running full night time. These girls also encountered a special danger in the early morning hours as they returned from work, debilitated and exhausted, and only too easily convinced that a drink and a little dancing at the end of the balls in the saloon dance halls, was what they needed to brace them. One of the girls whom we then knew, whose name, Chloe, seemed to fit her delicate charm, craving a drink to dispel her lassitude before her tired feet should take the long walk home, had thus been decoyed into a saloon, where the soft drink was followed by an alcoholic one containing "knockout drops," and she awoke in a disreputable rooming house-too frightened and disgraced to return to her mother.

Thus confronted by that old conundrum of the interdependence of matter and spirit, the conviction was forced upon us that long and exhausting hours of work are almost sure to be followed by lurid and exciting pleasures; that the power to overcome temptation reaches its limit almost automatically with that of physical resistance. The eight-hour clause in this first factory law met with much less opposition in the Legislature than was anticipated, and was enforced for a year before it was pronounced unconstitutional by the Supreme Court of Illinois. During the halcyon months when it was a law, a large and enthusiastic Eight-Hour Club of working women met at Hull-House, to read the literature on the subject and in every way to prepare themselves to make public sentiment in favor of the measure which meant so much to them. The adverse decision in the test case, the progress of which they had most intelligently followed, was a matter of great disappointment. The entire experience left on my mind a mistrust of all legislation which was not preceded by full discussion and understanding. A premature measure may be carried through a legislature by perfectly legitimate means and still fail to possess vitality and a sense of maturity. On the other hand, the administration of an advanced law acts somewhat as a referendum. The people have an opportunity for two years to see the effects of its operation. If they choose to reopen the matter at the next General Assembly, it can be discussed with experience and conviction; the very operation of the law has performed the function of the "referendum" in a limited use of the term.

Founded upon some such compunction, the sense that the passage of the child labor law would in many cases work hardship, was never absent from my mind during the earliest years of its operation. I addressed as many mothers' meetings and clubs among working women as I could, in order to make clear the object of the law and the ultimate benefit to themselves as well as to their children. I am happy to remember that I never met with lack of understanding among the hard-working widows, in whose behalf many prosperous people were so eloquent. These widowed mothers would say, "Why, of course, that is what I am working for-to give the children a chance. I want them to have more education than I had"; or another, "That is why we came to America, and I don't want to spoil his start, even although his father is dead"; or "It's different in America. A boy gets left if he isn't educated." There was always a willingness, even among the poorest women, to keep on with the hard night scrubbing or the long days of washing for the children's sake.

The bitterest opposition to the law came from the large glass companies, who were so accustomed to use the labor of children that they were convinced the manufacturing of glass could not be carried on without it.

Fifteen years ago the State of Illinois, as well as Chicago, exhibited many characteristics of the pioneer country in which untrammeled energy and an "early start" were still the most highly prized generators of success. Although this first labor legislation was but bringing Illinois into line with the nations in the modern industrial world, which "have long been obliged for their own sakes to come to the aid of the workers by which they live-that the child, the young person and the woman may be protected from their own weakness and necessity?" nevertheless from the first it ran counter to the instinct and tradition, almost to the very religion of the manufacturers of the state, who were for the most part self-made men.

This first attempt in Illinois for adequate factory legislation also was associated in the minds of businessmen with radicalism, because the law was secured during the term of Governor Altgeld and was first enforced during his administration. While nothing in its genesis or spirit could be further from "anarchy" than factory legislation, and while the first law in Illinois was still far behind Massachusetts and New York, the fact that Governor Altgeld pardoned from the state's prison the anarchists who had been sentenced there after the Haymarket riot, gave the opponents of this most reasonable legislation a quickly utilized opportunity to couple it with that detested word; the State document which accompanied Governor Altgeld's pardon gave these ungenerous critics a further opportunity, because a magnanimous action was marred by personal rancor, betraying for the moment the infirmity of a noble mind. For all of these reasons this first modification of the undisturbed control of the aggressive captains of industry could not be enforced without resistance marked by dramatic episodes and revolts. The inception of the law had already become associated with Hull-House, and when its ministration was also centered there, we inevitably received all the odium which these first efforts entailed. Mrs. Kelley was appointed the first factory inspector with a deputy and a force of twelve inspectors to enforce the law. Both Mrs. Kelley and her assistant, Mrs. Stevens, lived at Hull-House; the office was on Polk Street directly opposite, and one of the most vigorous deputies was the president of the Jane Club. In addition, one of the early men residents, since dean of a state law school, acted as prosecutor in the cases brought against the violators of the law.

Chicago had for years been notoriously lax in the administration of law, and the enforcement of an unpopular measure was resented equally by the president of a large manufacturing concern and by the former victim of a sweatshop who had started a place of his own. Whatever the sentiments toward the new law on the part of the employers, there was no doubt of its enthusiastic reception by the trades-unions, as the securing of the law had already come from them, and through the years which have elapsed since, the experience of the Hull-House residents would coincide with that of an English statesman who said that "a common rule for the standard of life and the condition of labor may be secured by legislation, but it must be maintained by trades unionism."

This special value of the trades-unions first became clear to the residents of Hull-House in connection with the sweating system. We early found that the women in the sewing trades were sorely in need of help. The trade was thoroughly disorganized, Russian and Polish tailors competing against English-speaking tailors, unskilled Bohemian and Italian women competing against both. These women seem to have been best helped through the use of the label when unions of specialized workers in the trade are strong enough to insist that the manufacturers shall "give out work" only to those holding union cards. It was certainly impressive when the garment makers themselves in this way finally succeeded in organizing six hundred of the Italian women in our immediate vicinity, who had finished garments at home for the most wretched and precarious wages. To be sure, the most ignorant women only knew that "you couldn't get clothes to sew" from the places where they paid the best, unless "you had a card," but through the veins of most of them there pulsed the quickened blood of a new fellowship, a sense of comfort and aid which had been laid out to them by their fellow-workers.

During the fourth year of our residence at Hull-House we found ourselves in a large mass meeting ardently advocating the passage of a Federal measure called the Sulzer Bill. Even in our short struggle with the evils of the sweating system it did not seem strange that the center of the effort had shifted to Washington, for by that time we had realized that the sanitary regulation of sweatshops by city officials, and a careful enforcement of factory legislation by state factory inspectors will not avail, unless each city and State shall be able to pass and enforce a code of comparatively uniform legislation. Although the Sulzer Act failed to utilize the Interstate Commerce legislation for its purpose, many of the national representatives realized for the first time that only by federal legislation could their constituents in remote country places be protected from contagious diseases raging in New York or Chicago, for many country doctors testify as to the outbreak of scarlet fever in rural neighborhoods after the children have begun to wear the winter overcoats and cloaks which have been sent from infected city sweatshops.

Through our efforts to modify the sweating system, the Hull-House residents gradually became committed to the fortunes of the Consumers' League, an organization which for years has been approaching the question of the underpaid sewing woman from the point of view of the ultimate responsibility lodged in the consumer. It becomes more reasonable to make the presentation of the sweatshop situation through this League, as it is more effectual to work with them for the extension of legal provisions in the slow upbuilding of that code of legislation which is alone sufficient to protect the home from the dangers incident to the sweating system.

The Consumers' League seems to afford the best method of approach for the protection of girls in department stores; I recall a group of girls from a neighboring "emporium" who applied to Hull-House for dancing parties on alternate Sunday afternoons. In reply to our protest they told us they not only worked late every evening, in spite of the fact that each was supposed to have "two nights a week off," and every Sunday morning, but that on alternate Sunday afternoons they were required "to sort the stock." Over and over again, meetings called by the Clerks Union and others have been held at Hull-House protesting against these incredibly long hours. Little modification has come about, however, during our twenty years of residence, although one large store in the Bohemian quarter closes all day on Sunday and many of the others for three nights a week. In spite of the Sunday work, these girls prefer the outlying department stores to those downtown; there is more social intercourse with the customers, more kindliness and social equality between the saleswomen and the managers, and above all the girls have the protection naturally afforded by friends and neighbors and they are free from that suspicion which so often haunts the girls downtown, that their fellow workers may not be "nice girls."

In the first years of Hull-House we came across no trades-unions among the women workers, and I think, perhaps, that only one union, composed solely of women, was to be found in Chicago then-that of the bookbinders. I easily recall the evening when the president of this pioneer organization accepted an invitation to take dinner at Hull-House. She came in rather a recalcitrant mood, expecting to be patronized, and so suspicious of our motives that it was only after she had been persuaded to become a guest of the house for several weeks in order to find out about us for herself, that she was convinced of our sincerity and of the ability of "outsiders" to be of any service to working women. She afterward became closely identified with Hull-House, and her hearty cooperation was assured until she moved to Boston and became a general organizer for the American Federation of Labor.

The women shirt makers and the women cloak makers were both organized at Hull-House as was also the Dorcas Federal Labor Union, which had been founded through the efforts of a working woman, then one of the residents. The latter union met once a month in our drawing room. It was composed of representatives from all the unions in the city which included women in their membership and also received other women in sympathy with unionism. It was accorded representation in the central labor body of the city, and later it joined its efforts with those of others to found the Woman's Union Label League. In what we considered a praiseworthy effort to unite it with other organizations, the president of a leading Woman's Club applied for membership. We were so sure of her election that she stood just outside of the drawing-room door, or, in trades-union language, "the wicket gate," while her name was voted upon. To our chagrin, she did not receive enough votes to secure her admission, not because the working girls, as they were careful to state, did not admire her, but because she "seemed to belong to the other side." Fortunately, the big-minded woman so thoroughly understood the vote and her interest in working women was so genuine that it was less than a decade afterward when she was elected to the presidency of the National Woman's Trades Union League. The incident and the sequel registers, perhaps, the change in Chicago toward the labor movement, the recognition of the fact that it is a general social movement concerning all members of society and not merely a class struggle.

Some such public estimate of the labor movement was brought home to Chicago during several conspicuous strikes; at least labor legislation has twice been inaugurated because its need was thus made clear. After the Pullman strike various elements in the community were unexpectedly brought together that they might soberly consider and rectify the weakness in the legal structure which the strike had revealed. These citizens arranged for a large and representative convention to be held in Chicago on Industrial Conciliation and Arbitration. I served as secretary of the committee from the new Civic Federation having the matter in charge, and our hopes ran high when, as a result of the agitation, the Illinois legislature passed a law creating a State Board of Conciliation and Arbitration. But even a state board cannot accomplish more than public sentiment authorizes and sustains, and we might easily have been discouraged in those early days could we have foreseen some of the industrial disturbances which have since disgraced Chicago. This law embodied the best provisions of the then existing laws for the arbitration of industrial disputes. At the time the word arbitration was still a word to conjure with, and many Chicago citizens were convinced, not only of the danger and futility involved in the open warfare of opposing social forces, but further believed that the search for justice and righteousness in industrial relations was made infinitely more difficult thereby.

The Pullman strike afforded much illumination to many Chicago people. Before it, there had been nothing in my experience to reveal that distinct cleavage of society, which a general strike at least momentarily affords. Certainly, during all those dark days of the Pullman strike, the growth of class bitterness was most obvious. The fact that the Settlement maintained avenues of intercourse with both sides seemed to give it opportunity for nothing but a realization of the bitterness and division along class lines. I had known Mr. Pullman and had seen his genuine pride and pleasure in the model town he had built with so much care; and I had an opportunity to talk to many of the Pullman employees during the strike when I was sent from a so-called "Citizens' Arbitration Committee" to their first meetings held in a hall in the neighboring village of Kensington, and when I was invited to the modest supper tables laid in the model houses. The employees then expected a speedy settlement and no one doubted but that all the grievances connected with the "straw bosses" would be quickly remedied and that the benevolence which had built the model town would not fail them. They were sure that the "straw bosses" had misrepresented the state of affairs, for this very first awakening to class consciousness bore many traces of the servility on one side and the arrogance on the other which had so long prevailed in the model town. The entire strike demonstrated how often the outcome of far-reaching industrial disturbances is dependent upon the personal will of the employer or the temperament of a strike leader. Those familiar with strikes know only too well how much they are influenced by poignant domestic situations, by the troubled consciences of the minority directors, by the suffering women and children, by the keen excitement of the struggle, by the religious scruples sternly suppressed but occasionally asserting themselves, now on one side and now on the other, and by that undefined psychology of the crowd which we understand so little. All of these factors also influence the public and do much to determine popular sympathy and judgment. In the early days of the Pullman strike, as I was coming down in the elevator of the Auditorium hotel from one of the futile meetings of the Arbitration Committee, I met an acquaintance, who angrily said "that the strikers ought all to be shot." As I had heard nothing so bloodthirsty as this either from the most enraged capitalist or from the most desperate of the men, and was interested to find the cause of such a senseless outbreak, I finally discovered that the first ten thousand dollars which my acquaintance had ever saved, requiring, he said, years of effort from the time he was twelve years old until he was thirty, had been lost as the result of a strike; he clinched his argument that he knew what he was talking about, with the statement that "no one need expect him to have any sympathy with strikers or with their affairs."

A very intimate and personal experience revealed, at least to myself, my constant dread of the spreading ill will. At the height of the sympathetic strike my oldest sister, who was convalescing from a long illness in a hospital near Chicago, became suddenly very much worse. While I was able to reach her at once, every possible obstacle of a delayed and blocked transportation system interrupted the journey of her husband and children who were hurrying to her bedside from a distant state. As the end drew nearer and I was obliged to reply to my sister's constant inquiries that her family had not yet come, I was filled with a profound apprehension lest her last hours should be touched with resentment toward those responsible for the delay; lest her unutterable longing should at the very end be tinged with bitterness. She must have divined what was in my mind, for at last she said each time after the repetition of my sad news: "I don't blame any one, I am not judging them." My heart was comforted and heavy at the same time; but how many more such moments of sorrow and death were being made difficult and lonely throughout the land, and how much would these experiences add to the lasting bitterness, that touch of self-righteousness which makes the spirit of forgiveness well-nigh impossible.

When I returned to Chicago from the quiet country I saw the Federal troops encamped about the post office; almost everyone on Halsted Street wearing a white ribbon, the emblem of the strikers' side; the residents at Hull-House divided in opinion as to the righteousness of this or that measure; and no one able to secure any real information as to which side was burning the cars. After the Pullman strike I made an attempt to analyze in a paper which I called The Modern King Lear the inevitable revolt of human nature against the plans Mr. Pullman had made for his employees, the miscarriage of which appeared to him such black ingratitude. It seemed to me unendurable not to make some effort to gather together the social implications of the failure of this benevolent employer and its relation to the demand for a more democratic administration of industry. Doubtless the paper represented a certain "excess of participation," to use a gentle phrase of Charles Lamb's in preference to a more emphatic one used by Mr. Pullman himself. The last picture of the Pullman strike which I distinctly recall was three years later when one of the strike leaders came to see me. Although out of work for most of the time since the strike, he had been undisturbed for six months in the repair shops of a street-car company, under an assumed name, but he had at that moment been discovered and dismissed. He was a superior type of English workingman, but as he stood there, broken and discouraged, believing himself so black-listed that his skill could never be used again, filled with sorrow over the loss of his wife who had recently died after an illness with distressing mental symptoms, realizing keenly the lack of the respectable way of living he had always until now been able to maintain, he seemed to me an epitome of the wretched human waste such a strike implies. I fervently hoped that the new arbitration law would prohibit in Chicago forever more such brutal and ineffective methods of settling industrial disputes. And yet even as early as 1896, we found the greatest difficulty in applying the arbitration law to the garment workers' strike, although it was finally accomplished after various mass meetings had urged it. The cruelty and waste of the strike as an implement for securing the most reasonable demands came to me at another time, during the long strike of the clothing cutters. They had protested, not only against various wrongs of their own, but against the fact that the tailors employed by the custom merchants were obliged to furnish their own workshops and thus bore a burden of rent which belonged to the employer. One of the leaders in this strike, whom I had known for several years as a sober, industrious, and unusually intelligent man, I saw gradually break down during the many trying weeks and at last suffer a complete moral collapse.

He was a man of sensitive organization under the necessity, as is every leader during a strike, to address the same body of men day after day with an appeal sufficiently emotional to respond to their sense of injury; to receive callers at any hour of the day or night; to sympathize with all the distress of the strikers who see their families daily suffering; he must do it all with the sickening sense of the increasing privation in his own home, and in this case with the consciousness that failure was approaching nearer each day. This man, accustomed to the monotony of his workbench and suddenly thrown into a new situation, showed every sign of nervous fatigue before the final collapse came. He disappeared after the strike and I did not see him for ten years, but when he returned he immediately began talking about the old grievances which he had repeated so often that he could talk of nothing else. It was easy to recognize the same nervous symptoms which the broken-down lecturer exhibits who has depended upon the exploitation of his own experiences to keep himself going. One of his stories was indeed pathetic. His employer, during the busy season, had met him one Sunday afternoon in Lincoln Park whither he had taken his three youngest children, one of whom had been ill. The employer scolded him for thus wasting his time and roughly asked why he had not taken home enough work to keep himself busy through the day. The story was quite credible because the residents of Hull-House have had many opportunities to see the worker driven ruthlessly during the season and left in idleness for long weeks afterward. We have slowly come to realize that periodical idleness as well as the payment of wages insufficient for maintenance of the manual worker in full industrial and domestic efficiency, stand economically on the same footing with the "sweated" industries, the overwork of women, and employment of children.

But of all the aspects of social misery nothing is so heartbreaking as unemployment, and it was inevitable that we should see much of it in a neighborhood where low rents attracted the poorly paid worker and many newly arrived immigrants who were first employed in gangs upon railroad extensions and similar undertakings. The sturdy peasants eager for work were either the victims of the padrone who fleeced them unmercifully, both in securing a place to work and then in supplying them with food, or they became the mere sport of unscrupulous employment agencies. Hull-House made an investigation both of the padrone and of the agencies in our immediate vicinity, and the outcome confirming what we already suspected, we eagerly threw ourselves into a movement to procure free employment bureaus under State control until a law authorizing such bureaus and giving the officials intrusted with their management power to regulate private employment agencies, passed the Illinois Legislature in 1899. The history of these bureaus demonstrates the tendency we all have to consider a legal enactment in itself an achievement and to grow careless in regard to its administration and actual results; for an investigation into the situation ten years later discovered that immigrants were still shamefully imposed upon. A group of Bulgarians were found who had been sent to work in Arkansas where their services were not needed; they walked back to Chicago only to secure their next job in Oklahoma and to pay another railroad fare as well as another commission to the agency. Not only was there no method by which the men not needed in Arkansas could know that there was work in Oklahoma unless they came back to Chicago to find it out, but there was no certainty that they might not be obliged to walk back from Oklahoma because the Chicago agency had already sent out too many men.

This investigation of the employment bureau resources of Chicago was undertaken by the League for the Protection of Immigrants, with whom it is possible for Hull-House to cooperate whenever an investigation of the immigrant colonies in our immediate neighborhood seems necessary, as was recently done in regard to the Greek colonies of Chicago. The superintendent of this League, Miss Grace Abbott, is a resident of Hull-House and all of our later attempts to secure justice and opportunity for immigrants are much more effective through the League, and when we speak before a congressional committee in Washington concerning the needs of Chicago immigrants, we represent the League as well as our own neighbors.

It is in connection with the first factory employment of newly arrived immigrants and the innumerable difficulties attached to their first adjustment that some of the most profound industrial disturbances in Chicago have come about. Under any attempt at classification these strikes belong more to the general social movement than to the industrial conflict, for the strike is an implement used most rashly by unorganized labor who, after they are in difficulties, call upon the trades-unions for organization and direction. They are similar to those strikes which are inaugurated by the unions on behalf of unskilled labor. In neither case do the hastily organized unions usually hold after the excitement of the moment has subsided, and the most valuable result of such strikes is the expanding consciousness of the solidarity of the workers. This was certainly the result of the Chicago stockyard strike in 1905, inaugurated on behalf of the immigrant laborers and so conspicuously carried on without violence that, although twenty-two thousand workers were idle during the entire summer, there were fewer arrests in the stockyards district than the average summer months afford. However, the story of this strike should not be told from Hull-House, but from the University of Chicago Settlement, where Miss Mary McDowell performed such signal public service during that trying summer. It would be interesting to trace how much of the subsequent exposure of conditions and attempts at governmental control of this huge industry had their genesis in this first attempt of the unskilled workers to secure a higher standard of living. Certainly the industrial conflict when epitomized in a strike, centers public attention on conditions as nothing else can do. A strike is one of the most exciting episodes in modern life, and as it assumes the characteristics of a game, the entire population of a city becomes divided into two cheering sides. In such moments the fair-minded public, who ought to be depended upon as a referee, practically disappears. Anyone who tries to keep the attitude of nonpartisanship, which is perhaps an impossible one, is quickly under suspicion by both sides. At least that was the fate of a group of citizens appointed by the mayor of Chicago to arbitrate during the stormy teamsters' strike which occurred in 1905. We sat through a long Sunday afternoon in the mayor's office in the City Hall, talking first with the labor men and then with the group of capitalists. The undertaking was the more futile in that we were all practically the dupes of a new type of "industrial conspiracy" successfully inaugurated in Chicago by a close compact between the coal teamsters' union and the coal team owners' association, who had formed a kind of monopoly hitherto new to a monopoly-ridden public.

The stormy teamsters' strike, ostensibly undertaken in defense of the garment workers, but really arising from causes so obscure and dishonorable that they have never yet been made public, was the culmination of a type of trades-unions which had developed in Chicago during the preceding decade in which corruption had flourished almost as openly as it had previously done in the City Hall. This corruption sometimes took the form of grafting after the manner of Samuel Parks in New York; sometimes that of political deals in the "delivery of the labor vote"; and sometimes that of a combination between capital and labor hunting together. At various times during these years the better type of trades-unionists had made a firm stand against this corruption and a determined effort to eradicate it from the labor movement, not unlike the general reform effort of many American cities against political corruption. This reform movement in the Chicago Federation of Labor had its martyrs, and more than one man nearly lost his life through the "slugging" methods employed by the powerful corruptionists. And yet even in the midst of these things were found touching examples of fidelity to the earlier principles of brotherhood totally untouched by the corruption. At one time the scrubwomen in the downtown office buildings had a union of their own affiliated with the elevator men and the janitors. Although the union was used merely as a weapon in the fight of the coal teamsters against the use of natural gas in downtown buildings, it did not prevent the women from getting their first glimpse into the fellowship and the sense of protection which is the great gift of trades-unionism to the unskilled, unbefriended worker. I remember in a meeting held at Hull-House one Sunday afternoon, that the president of a "local" of scrubwomen stood up to relate her experience. She told first of the long years in which the fear of losing her job and the fluctuating pay were harder to bear than the hard work itself, when she had regarded all the other women who scrubbed in the same building merely as rivals and was most afraid of the most miserable, because they offered to work for less and less as they were pressed harder and harder by debt. Then she told of the change that had come when the elevator men and even the lordly janitors had talked to her about an organization and had said that they must all stand together. She told how gradually she came to feel sure of her job and of her regular pay, and she was even starting to buy a house now that she could "calculate" how much she "could have for sure." Neither she nor any of the other members knew that the same combination which had organized the scrubwomen into a union later destroyed it during a strike inaugurated for their own purposes.

That a Settlement is drawn into the labor issues of its city can seem remote to its purpose only to those who fail to realize that so far as the present industrial system thwarts our ethical demands, not only for social righteousness but for social order, a Settlement is committed to an effort to understand and, as far as possible, to alleviate it. That in this effort it should be drawn into fellowship with the local efforts of trades-unions is most obvious. This identity of aim apparently commits the Settlement in the public mind to all the faiths and works of actual trades-unions. Fellowship has so long implied similarity of creed that the fact that the Settlement often differs widely from the policy pursued by trades-unionists and clearly expresses that difference does not in the least change public opinion in regard to its identification. This is especially true in periods of industrial disturbance, although it is exactly at such moments that the trades-unionists themselves are suspicious of all but their "own kind." It is during the much longer periods between strikes that the Settlement's fellowship with trades-unions is most satisfactory in the agitation for labor legislation and similar undertakings. The first officers of the Chicago Woman's Trades Union League were residents of Settlements, although they can claim little share in the later record the League made in securing the passage of the Illinois Ten-Hour Law for Women and in its many other fine undertakings.

Nevertheless the reaction of strikes upon Chicago Settlements affords an interesting study in social psychology. For whether Hull-House is in any wise identified with the strike or not, makes no difference. When "Labor" is in disgrace we are always regarded as belonging to it and share the opprobrium. In the public excitement following the Pullman strike Hull-House lost many friends; later the teamsters' strike caused another such defection, although my office in both cases had been solely that of a duly appointed arbitrator.

There is, however, a certain comfort in the assumption I have often encountered that wherever one's judgment might place the justice of a given situation, it is understood that one's sympathy is not alienated by wrongdoing, and that through this sympathy one is still subject to vicarious suffering. I recall an incident during a turbulent Chicago strike which brought me much comfort. On the morning of the day of a luncheon to which I had accepted an invitation, the waitress, whom I did not know, said to my prospective hostess that she was sure I could not come. Upon being asked for her reason she replied that she had seen in the morning paper that the strikers had killed a "scab" and she was sure that I would feel quite too badly about such a thing to be able to keep a social engagement. In spite of the confused issues, she evidently realized my despair over the violence in a strike quite as definitely as if she had been told about it. Perhaps that sort of suffering and the attempt to interpret opposing forces to each other will long remain a function of the Settlement, unsatisfactory and difficult as the role often becomes.

There has gradually developed between the various Settlements of Chicago a warm fellowship founded upon a like-mindedness resulting from similar experiences, quite as identity of interest and endeavor develop an enduring relation between the residents of the same Settlement. This sense of comradeship is never stronger than during the hardships and perplexities of a strike of unskilled workers revolting against the conditions which drag them even below the level of their European life. At such time the residents in various Settlements are driven to a standard of life argument running somewhat in this wise-that as the very existence of the State depends upon the character of its citizens, therefore if certain industrial conditions are forcing the workers below the standard of decency, it becomes possible to deduce the right of State regulation. Even as late as the stockyard strike this line of argument was denounced as "socialism" although it has since been confirmed as wise statesmanship by a decision of the Supreme Court of the United States which was apparently secured through the masterly argument of the Brandeis brief in the Oregon ten-hour case.

In such wise the residents of an industrial neighborhood gradually comprehend the close connection of their own difficulties with national and even international movements. The residents in the Chicago Settlements became pioneer members in the American branch of the International League for Labor Legislation, because their neighborhood experiences had made them only too conscious of the dire need for protective legislation. In such a league, with its ardent members in every industrial nation of Europe, with its encouraging reports of the abolition of all night work for women in six European nations, with its careful observations on the results of employer's liability legislation and protection of machinery, one becomes identified with a movement of world-wide significance and manifold manifestation.

Chapter XI
Immigrants and Their Children

From our very first months at Hull-House we found it much easier to deal with the first generation of crowded city life than with the second or third, because it is more natural and cast in a simpler mold. The Italian and Bohemian peasants who live in Chicago still put on their bright holiday clothes on a Sunday and go to visit their cousins. They tramp along with at least a suggestion of having once walked over plowed fields and breathed country air. The second generation of city poor too often have no holiday clothes and consider their relations a "bad lot." I have heard a drunken man in a maudlin stage babble of his good country mother and imagine he was driving the cows home, and I knew that his little son who laughed loud at him would be drunk earlier in life and would have no pastoral interlude to his ravings. Hospitality still survives among foreigners, although it is buried under false pride among the poorest Americans. One thing seemed clear in regard to entertaining immigrants; to preserve and keep whatever of value their past life contained and to bring them in contact with a better type of Americans. For several years, every Saturday evening the entire families of our Italian neighbors were our guests. These evenings were very popular during our first winters at Hull-House. Many educated Italians helped us, and the house became known as a place where Italians were welcome and where national holidays were observed. They come to us with their petty lawsuits, sad relics of the vendetta, with their incorrigible boys, with their hospital cases, with their aspirations for American clothes, and with their needs for an interpreter.

An editor of an Italian paper made a genuine connection between us and the Italian colony, not only with the Neapolitans and the Sicilians of the immediate neighborhood, but with the educated connazionali throughout the city, until he went south to start an agricultural colony in Alabama, in the establishment of which Hull-House heartily cooperated.

Possibly the South Italians more than any other immigrants represent the pathetic stupidity of agricultural people crowded into city tenements, and we were much gratified when thirty peasant families were induced to move upon the land which they knew so well how to cultivate. The starting of this colony, however, was a very expensive affair in spite of the fact that the colonists purchased the land at two dollars an acre; they needed much more than raw land, and although it was possible to collect the small sums necessary to sustain them during the hard time of the first two years, we were fully convinced that undertakings of this sort could be conducted properly only by colonization societies such as England has established, or, better still, by enlarging the functions of the Federal Department of Immigration.

An evening similar in purpose to the one devoted to the Italians was organized for the Germans, in our first year. Owing to the superior education of our Teutonic guests and the clever leading of a cultivated German woman, these evenings reflected something of that cozy social intercourse which is found in its perfection in the fatherland. Our guests sang a great deal in the tender minor of the German folksong or in the rousing spirit of the Rhine, and they slowly but persistently pursued a course in German history and literature, recovering something of that poetry and romance which they had long since resigned with other good things. We found strong family affection between them and their English-speaking children, but their pleasures were not in common, and they seldom went out together. Perhaps the greatest value of the Settlement to them was in placing large and pleasant rooms with musical facilities at their disposal, and in reviving their almost forgotten enthusiams. I have seen sons and daughters stand in complete surprise as their mother's knitting needles softly beat time to the song she was singing, or her worn face turned rosy under the hand-clapping as she made an old-fashioned curtsy at the end of a German poem. It was easy to fancy a growing touch of respect in her children's manner to her, and a rising enthusiasm for German literature and reminiscence on the part of all the family, an effort to bring together the old life and the new, a respect for the older cultivation, and not quite so much assurance that the new was the best.

This tendency upon the part of the older immigrants to lose the amenities of European life without sharing those of America has often been deplored by keen observers from the home countries. When Professor Masurek of Prague gave a course of lectures in the University of Chicago, he was much distressed over the materialism into which the Bohemians of Chicago had fallen. The early immigrants had been so stirred by the opportunity to own real estate, an appeal perhaps to the Slavic land hunger, and their energies had become so completely absorbed in money-making that all other interests had apparently dropped away. And yet I recall a very touching incident in connection with a lecture Professor Masurek gave at Hull-House, in which he had appealed to his countrymen to arouse themselves from this tendency to fall below their home civilization and to forget the great enthusiasm which had united them into the Pan-Slavic Movement. A Bohemian widow who supported herself and her two children by scrubbing, hastily sent her youngest child to purchase, with the twenty-five cents which was to have supplied them with food the next day, a bunch of red roses which she presented to the lecturer in appreciation of his testimony to the reality of the things of the spirit.

An overmastering desire to reveal the humbler immigrant parents to their own children lay at the base of what has come to be called the Hull-House Labor Museum. This was first suggested to my mind one early spring day when I saw an old Italian woman, her distaff against her homesick face, patiently spinning a thread by the simple stick spindle so reminiscent of all southern Europe. I was walking down Polk Street, perturbed in spirit, because it seemed so difficult to come into genuine relations with the Italian women and because they themselves so often lost their hold upon their Americanized children. It seemed to me that Hull-House ought to be able to devise some educational enterprise which should build a bridge between European and American experiences in such wise as to give them both more meaning and a sense of relation. I meditated that perhaps the power to see life as a whole is more needed in the immigrant quarter of a large city than anywhere else, and that the lack of this power is the most fruitful source of misunderstanding between European immigrants and their children, as it is between them and their American neighbors; and why should that chasm between fathers and sons, yawning at the feet of each generation, be made so unnecessarily cruel and impassable to these bewildered immigrants? Suddenly I looked up and saw the old woman with her distaff, sitting in the sun on the steps of a tenement house. She might have served as a model for one of Michelangelo's Fates, but her face brightened as I passed and, holding up her spindle for me to see, she called out that when she had spun a little more yarn, she would knit a pair of stockings for her goddaughter. The occupation of the old woman gave me the clue that was needed. Could we not interest the young people working in the neighborhood factories in these older forms of industry, so that, through their own parents and grandparents, they would find a dramatic representation of the inherited resources of their daily occupation. If these young people could actually see that the complicated machinery of the factory had been evolved from simple tools, they might at least make a beginning toward that education which Dr. Dewey defines as "a continuing reconstruction of experience." They might also lay a foundation for reverence of the past which Goethe declares to be the basis of all sound progress.

My exciting walk on Polk Street was followed by many talks with Dr. Dewey and with one of the teachers in his school who was a resident at Hull-House. Within a month a room was fitted up to which we might invite those of our neighbors who were possessed of old crafts and who were eager to use them.

We found in the immediate neighborhood at least four varieties of these most primitive methods of spinning and three distinct variations of the same spindle in connection with wheels. It was possible to put these seven into historic sequence and order and to connect the whole with the present method of factory spinning. The same thing was done for weaving, and on every Saturday evening a little exhibit was made of these various forms of labor in the textile industry. Within one room a Syrian woman, a Greek, an Italian, a Russian, and an Irishwoman enabled even the most casual observer to see that there is no break in orderly evolution if we look at history from the industrial standpoint; that industry develops similarly and peacefully year by year among the workers of each nation, heedless of differences in language, religion, and political experiences.

And then we grew ambitious and arranged lectures upon industrial history. I remember that after an interesting lecture upon the industrial revolution in England and a portrayal of the appalling conditions throughout the weaving districts of the north, which resulted from the hasty gathering of the weavers into the new towns, a Russian tailor in the audience was moved to make a speech. He suggested that whereas time had done much to alleviate the first difficulties in the transition of weaving from hand work to steam power, that in the application of steam to sewing we are still in our first stages, illustrated by the isolated woman who tries to support herself by hand needlework at home until driven out by starvation, as many of the hand weavers had been.

The historical analogy seemed to bring a certain comfort to the tailor, as did a chart upon the wall showing the infinitesimal amount of time that steam had been applied to manufacturing processes compared to the centuries of hand labor. Human progress is slow and perhaps never more cruel than in the advance of industry, but is not the worker comforted by knowing that other historical periods have existed similar to the one in which he finds himself, and that the readjustment may be shortened and alleviated by judicious action; and is he not entitled to the solace which an artistic portrayal of the situation might give him? I remember the evening of the tailor's speech that I felt reproached because no poet or artist has endeared the sweaters' victim to us as George Eliot has made us love the belated weaver, Silas Marner. The textile museum is connected directly with the basket weaving, sewing, millinery, embroidery, and dressmaking constantly being taught at Hull-House, and so far as possible with the other educational departments; we have also been able to make a collection of products, of early implements, and of photographs which are full of suggestion. Yet far beyond its direct educational value, we prize it because it so often puts the immigrants into the position of teachers, and we imagine that it affords them a pleasant change from the tutelage in which all Americans, including their own children, are so apt to hold them. I recall a number of Russian women working in a sewing room near Hull-House, who heard one Christmas week that the House was going to give a party to which they might come. They arrived one afternoon, when, unfortunately, there was no party on hand and, although the residents did their best to entertain them with impromptu music and refreshments, it was quite evident that they were greatly disappointed. Finally it was suggested that they be shown the Labor Museum-where gradually the thirty sodden, tired women were transformed. They knew how to use the spindles and were delighted to find the Russian spinning frame. Many of them had never seen the spinning wheel, which has not penetrated to certain parts of Russia, and they regarded it as a new and wonderful invention. They turned up their dresses to show their homespun petticoats; they tried the looms; they explained the difficulty of the old patterns; in short, from having been stupidly entertained, they themselves did the entertaining. Because of a direct appeal to former experiences, the immigrant visitors were able for the moment to instruct their American hostesses in an old and honored craft, as was indeed becoming to their age and experience.

In some such ways as these have the Labor Museum and the shops pointed out the possibilities which Hull-House has scarcely begun to develop, of demonstrating that culture is an understanding of the long-established occupations and thoughts of men, of the arts with which they have solaced their toil. A yearning to recover for the household arts something of their early sanctity and meaning arose strongly within me one evening when I was attending a Passover Feast to which I had been invited by a Jewish family in the neighborhood, where the traditional and religious significance of the woman's daily activity was still retained. The kosher food the Jewish mother spread before her family had been prepared according to traditional knowledge and with constant care in the use of utensils; upon her had fallen the responsibility to make all ready according to Mosaic instructions that the great crisis in a religious history might be fittingly set forth by her husband and son. Aside from the grave religious significance in the ceremony, my mind was filled with shifting pictures of woman's labor with which travel makes one familiar; the Indian women grinding grain outside of their huts as they sing praises to the sun and rain; a file of white-clad Moorish women whom I had once seen waiting their turn at a well in Tangiers; south Italian women kneeling in a row along the stream and beating their wet clothes against the smooth white stones; the milking, the gardening, the marketing in thousands of hamlets, which are such direct expressions of the solicitude and affection at the basis of all family life.

There has been some testimony that the Labor Museum has revealed the charm of woman's primitive activities. I recall a certain Italian girl who came every Saturday evening to a cooking class in the same building in which her mother spun in the Labor Museum exhibit; and yet Angelina always left her mother at the front door while she herself went around to a side door because she did not wish to be too closely identified in the eyes of the rest of the cooking class with an Italian woman who wore a kerchief over her head, uncouth boots, and short petticoats. One evening, however, Angelina saw her mother surrounded by a group of visitors from the School of Education who much admired the spinning, and she concluded from their conversation that her mother was "the best stick-spindle spinner in America." When she inquired from me as to the truth of this deduction, I took occasion to describe the Italian village in which her mother had lived, something of her free life, and how, because of the opportunity she and the other women of the village had to drop their spindles over the edge of a precipice, they had developed a skill in spinning beyond that of the neighboring towns. I dilated somewhat on the freedom and beauty of that life-how hard it must be to exchange it all for a two-room tenement, and to give up a beautiful homespun kerchief for an ugly department store hat. I intimated it was most unfair to judge her by these things alone, and that while she must depend on her daughter to learn the new ways, she also had a right to expect her daughter to know something of the old ways.

That which I could not convey to the child, but upon which my own mind persistently dwelt, was that her mother's whole life had been spent in a secluded spot under the rule of traditional and narrowly localized observances, until her very religion clung to local sanctities-to the shrine before which she had always prayed, to the pavement and walls of the low vaulted church-and then suddenly she was torn from it all and literally put out to sea, straight away from the solid habits of her religious and domestic life, and she now walked timidly but with poignant sensibility upon a new and strange shore.

It was easy to see that the thought of her mother with any other background than that of the tenement was new to Angelina, and at least two things resulted; she allowed her mother to pull out of the big box under the bed the beautiful homespun garments which had been previously hidden away as uncouth; and she openly came into the Labor Museum by the same door as did her mother, proud at least of the mastery of the craft which had been so much admired.

A club of necktie workers formerly meeting at Hull-House persistently resented any attempt on the part of their director to improve their minds. The president once said that she "wouldn't be caught dead at a lecture," that she came to the club "to get some fun out of it," and indeed it was most natural that she should crave recreation after a hard day's work. One evening I saw the entire club listening to quite a stiff lecture in the Labor Museum and to my rather wicked remark to the president that I was surprised to see her enjoying a lecture, she replied that she did not call this a lecture, she called this "getting next to the stuff you work with all the time." It was perhaps the sincerest tribute we have ever received as to the success of the undertaking.

The Labor Museum continually demanded more space as it was enriched by a fine textile exhibit lent by the Field Museum, and later by carefully selected specimens of basketry from the Philippines. The shops have finally included a group of three or four women, Irish, Italian, Danish, who have become a permanent working force in the textile department which has developed into a self-supporting industry through the sale of its homespun products.

These women and a few men, who come to the museum to utilize their European skill in pottery, metal, and wood, demonstrate that immigrant colonies might yield to our American life something very valuable, if their resources were intelligently studied and developed. I recall an Italian, who had decorated the doorposts of his tenement with a beautiful pattern he had previously used in carving the reredos of a Neapolitan church, who was "fired" by his landlord on the ground of destroying property. His feelings were hurt, not so much that he had been put out of his house, as that his work had been so disregarded; and he said that when people traveled in Italy they liked to look at wood carvings but that in America "they only made money out of you."

Sometimes the suppression of the instinct of workmanship is followed by more disastrous results. A Bohemian whose little girl attended classes at Hull-House, in one of his periodic drunken spells had literally almost choked her to death, and later had committed suicide when in delirium tremens. His poor wife, who stayed a week at Hull-House after the disaster until a new tenement could be arranged for her, one day showed me a gold ring which her husband had made for their betrothal. It exhibited the most exquisite workmanship, and she said that although in the old country he had been a goldsmith, in America he had for twenty years shoveled coal in a furnace room of a large manufacturing plant; that whenever she saw one of his "restless fits," which preceded his drunken periods, "coming on," if she could provide him with a bit of metal and persuade him to stay at home and work at it, he was all right and the time passed without disaster, but that "nothing else would do it." This story threw a flood of light upon the dead man's struggle and on the stupid maladjustment which had broken him down. Why had we never been told? Why had our interest in the remarkable musical ability of his child blinded us to the hidden artistic ability of the father? We had forgotten that a long-established occupation may form the very foundations of the moral life, that the art with which a man has solaced his toil may be the salvation of his uncertain temperament.

There are many examples of touching fidelity to immigrant parents on the part of their grown children; a young man who day after day attends ceremonies which no longer express his religious convictions and who makes his vain effort to interest his Russian Jewish father in social problems; a daughter who might earn much more money as a stenographer could she work from Monday morning till Saturday night, but who quietly and docilely makes neckties for low wages because she can thus abstain from work Saturdays to please her father; these young people, like poor Maggie Tulliver, through many painful experiences have reached the conclusion that pity, memory, and faithfulness are natural ties with paramount claims.

This faithfulness, however, is sometimes ruthlessly imposed upon by immigrant parents who, eager for money and accustomed to the patriarchal authority of peasant households, hold their children in a stern bondage which requires a surrender of all their wages and concedes no time or money for pleasures.

There are many convincing illustrations that this parental harshness often results in juvenile delinquency. A Polish boy of seventeen came to Hull-House one day to ask a contribution of fifty cents "towards a flower piece for the funeral of an old Hull-House club boy." A few questions made it clear that the object was fictitious, whereupon the boy broke down and half-defiantly stated that he wanted to buy two twenty-five cent tickets, one for his girl and one for himself, to a dance of the Benevolent Social Twos; that he hadn't a penny of his own although he had worked in a brass foundry for three years and had been advanced twice, because he always had to give his pay envelope unopened to his father; "just look at the clothes he buys me" was his concluding remark.

Perhaps the girls are held even more rigidly. In a recent investigation of two hundred working girls it was found that only five per cent had the use of their own money and that sixty-two per cent turned in all they earned, literally every penny, to their mothers. It was through this little investigation that we first knew Marcella, a pretty young German girl who helped her widowed mother year after year to care for a large family of younger children. She was content for the most part although her mother's old-country notions of dress gave her but an infinitesimal amount of her own wages to spend on her clothes, and she was quite sophisticated as to proper dressing because she sold silk in a neighborhood department store. Her mother approved of the young man who was showing her various attentions and agreed that Marcella should accept his invitation to a ball, but would allow her not a penny toward a new gown to replace one impossibly plain and shabby. Marcella spent a sleepless night and wept bitterly, although she well knew that the doctor's bill for the children's scarlet fever was not yet paid. The next day as she was cutting off three yards of shining pink silk, the thought came to her that it would make her a fine new waist to wear to the ball. She wistfully saw it wrapped in paper and carelessly stuffed into the muff of the purchaser, when suddenly the parcel fell upon the floor. No one was looking and quick as a flash the girl picked it up and pushed it into her blouse. The theft was discovered by the relentless department store detective who, for "the sake of example," insisted upon taking the case into court. The poor mother wept bitter tears over this downfall of her "frommes Madchen" and no one had the heart to tell her of her own blindness.

I know a Polish boy whose earnings were all given to his father who gruffly refused all requests for pocket money. One Christmas his little sisters, having been told by their mother that they were too poor to have any Christmas presents, appealed to the big brother as to one who was earning money of his own. Flattered by the implication, but at the same time quite impecunious, the night before Christmas he nonchalantly walked through a neighboring department store and stole a manicure set for one little sister and a string of beads for the other. He was caught at the door by the house detective as one of those children whom each local department store arrests in the weeks before Christmas at the daily rate of eight to twenty. The youngest of these offenders are seldom taken into court but are either sent home with a warning or turned over to the officers of the Juvenile Protective Association. Most of these premature law breakers are in search of Americanized clothing and others are only looking for playthings. They are all distracted by the profusion and variety of the display, and their moral sense is confused by the general air of openhandedness.

These disastrous efforts are not unlike those of many younger children who are constantly arrested for petty thieving because they are too eager to take home food or fuel which will relieve the distress and need they so constantly hear discussed. The coal on the wagons, the vegetables displayed in front of the grocery shops, the very wooden blocks in the loosened street paving are a challenge to their powers to help out at home. A Bohemian boy who was out on parole from the old detention home of the Juvenile Court itself, brought back five stolen chickens to the matron for Sunday dinner, saying that he knew the Committee were "having a hard time to fill up so many kids and perhaps these fowl would help out." The honest immigrant parents, totally ignorant of American laws and municipal regulations, often send a child to pick up coal on the railroad tracks or to stand at three o'clock in the morning before the side door of a restaurant which gives away broken food, or to collect grain for the chickens at the base of elevators and standing cars. The latter custom accounts for the large number of boys arrested for breaking the seals on grain freight cars. It is easy for a child thus trained to accept the proposition of a junk dealer to bring him bars of iron stored in freight yards. Four boys quite recently had thus carried away and sold to one man two tons of iron.

Four fifths of the children brought into the Juvenile Court in Chicago are the children of foreigners. The Germans are the greatest offenders, Polish next. Do their children suffer from the excess of virtue in those parents so eager to own a house and lot? One often sees a grasping parent in the court, utterly broken down when the Americanized youth who has been brought to grief clings as piteously to his peasant father as if he were still a frightened little boy in the steerage.

Many of these children have come to grief through their premature fling into city life, having thrown off parental control as they have impatiently discarded foreign ways. Boys of ten and twelve will refuse to sleep at home, preferring the freedom of an old brewery vault or an empty warehouse to the obedience required by their parents, and for days these boys will live on the milk and bread which they steal from the back porches after the early morning delivery. Such children complain that there is "no fun" at home. One little chap who was given a vacant lot to cultivate by the City Garden Association insisted upon raising only popcorn and tried to present the entire crop to Hull-House "to be used for the parties," with the stipulation that he would have "to be invited every single time." Then there are little groups of dissipated young men who pride themselves upon their ability to live without working and who despise all the honest and sober ways of their immigrant parents. They are at once a menace and a center of demoralization. Certainly the bewildered parents, unable to speak English and ignorant of the city, whose children have disappeared for days or weeks, have often come to Hull-House, evincing that agony which fairly separates the marrow from the bone, as if they had discovered a new type of suffering, devoid of the healing in familiar sorrows. It is as if they did not know how to search for the children without the assistance of the children themselves. Perhaps the most pathetic aspect of such cases is their revelation of the premature dependence of the older and wiser upon the young and foolish, which is in itself often responsible for the situation because it has given the children an undue sense of their own importance and a false security that they can take care of themselves.

On the other hand, an Italian girl who has had lessons in cooking at the public school will help her mother to connect the entire family with American food and household habits. That the mother has never baked bread in Italy-only mixed it in her own house and then taken it out to the village oven-makes all the more valuable her daughter's understanding of the complicated cooking stove. The same thing is true of the girl who learns to sew in the public school, and more than anything else, perhaps, of the girl who receives the first simple instruction in the care of little children-that skillful care which every tenement-house baby requires if he is to be pulled through his second summer. As a result of this teaching I recall a young girl who carefully explained to her Italian mother that the reason the babies in Italy were so healthy and the babies in Chicago were so sickly, was not, as her mother had firmly insisted, because her babies in Italy had goat's milk and her babies in America had cow's milk, but because the milk in Italy was clean and the milk in Chicago was dirty. She said that when you milked your own goat before the door, you knew that the milk was clean, but when you bought milk from the grocery store after it had been carried for many miles in the country, you couldn't tell whether it was fit for the baby to drink until the men from the City Hall who had watched it all the way said that it was all right.

Thus through civic instruction in the public schools, the Italian woman slowly became urbanized in the sense in which the word was used by her own Latin ancestors, and thus the habits of her entire family were modified. The public schools in the immigrant colonies deserve all the praise as Americanizing agencies which can be bestowed upon them, and there is little doubt that the fast-changing curriculum in the direction of the vacation-school experiments will react more directly upon such households.

It is difficult to write of the relation of the older and most foreign-looking immigrants to the children of other people-the Italians whose fruit-carts are upset simply because they are "dagoes," or the Russian peddlers who are stoned and sometimes badly injured because it has become a code of honor in a gang of boys to thus express their derision. The members of a Protective Association of Jewish Peddlers organized at Hull-House related daily experiences in which old age had been treated with such irreverence, cherished dignity with such disrespect, that a listener caught the passion of Lear in the old texts, as a platitude enunciated by a man who discovers in it his own experience thrills us as no unfamiliar phrases can possibly do. The Greeks are filled with amazed rage when their very name is flung at them as an opprobrious epithet. Doubtless these difficulties would be much minimized in America, if we faced our own race problem with courage and intelligence, and these very Mediterranean immigrants might give us valuable help. Certainly they are less conscious than the Anglo-Saxon of color distinctions, perhaps because of their traditional familiarity with Carthage and Egypt. They listened with respect and enthusiasm to a scholarly address delivered by Professor Du Bois at Hull-House on a Lincoln's birthday, with apparently no consciousness of that race difference which color seems to accentuate so absurdly, and upon my return from various conferences held in the interest of "the advancement of colored people," I have had many illuminating conversations with my cosmopolitan neighbors.

The celebration of national events has always been a source of new understanding and companionship with the members of the contiguous foreign colonies not only between them and their American neighbors but between them and their own children. One of our earliest Italian events was a rousing commemoration of Garibaldi's birthday, and his imposing bust, presented to Hull-House that evening, was long the chief ornament of our front hall. It called forth great enthusiasm from the connazionali whom Ruskin calls, not the "common people" of Italy, but the "companion people" because of their power for swift sympathy.

A huge Hellenic meeting held at Hull-House, in which the achievements of the classic period were set forth both in Greek and English by scholars of well-known repute, brought us into a new sense of fellowship with all our Greek neighbors. As the mayor of Chicago was seated upon the right hand of the dignified senior priest of the Greek Church and they were greeted alternately in the national hymns of America and Greece, one felt a curious sense of the possibility of transplanting to new and crude Chicago some of the traditions of Athens itself, so deeply cherished in the hearts of this group of citizens.

The Greeks indeed gravely consider their traditions as their most precious possession and more than once in meetings of protest held by the Greek colony against the aggressions of the Bulgarians in Macedonia, I have heard it urged that the Bulgarians are trying to establish a protectorate, not only for their immediate advantage, but that they may claim a glorious history for the "barbarous country." It is said that on the basis of this protectorate, they are already teaching in their schools that Alexander the Great was a Bulgarian and that it will be but a short time before they claim Aristotle himself, an indignity the Greeks will never suffer!

To me personally the celebration of the hundredth anniversary of Mazzini's birth was a matter of great interest. Throughout the world that day Italians who believed in a United Italy came together. They recalled the hopes of this man who, with all his devotion to his country was still more devoted to humanity and who dedicated to the workingmen of Italy, an appeal so philosophical, so filled with a yearning for righteousness, that it transcended all national boundaries and became a bugle call for "The Duties of Man." A copy of this document was given to every school child in the public schools of Italy on this one hundredth anniversary, and as the Chicago branch of the Society of Young Italy marched into our largest hall and presented to Hull-House an heroic bust of Mazzini, I found myself devoutly hoping that the Italian youth, who have committed their future to America, might indeed become "the Apostles of the fraternity of nations" and that our American citizenship might be built without disturbing these foundations which were laid of old time.

Chapter XII
Tolstoyism

The administration of charity in Chicago during the winter following the World's Fair had been of necessity most difficult, for, although large sums had been given to the temporary relief organization which endeavored to care for the thousands of destitute strangers stranded in the city, we all worked under a sense of desperate need and a paralyzing consciousness that our best efforts were most inadequate to the situation.

During the many relief visits I paid that winter in tenement houses and miserable lodgings, I was constantly shadowed by a certain sense of shame that I should be comfortable in the midst of such distress. This resulted at times in a curious reaction against all the educational and philanthropic activities in which I had been engaged. In the face of the desperate hunger and need, these could not but seem futile and superficial. The hard winter in Chicago had turned the thoughts of many of us to these stern matters. A young friend of mine who came daily to Hull-House consulted me in regard to going into the paper warehouse belonging to her father that she might there sort rags with the Polish girls; another young girl took a place in a sweatshop for a month, doing her work so simply and thoroughly that the proprietor had no notion that she had not been driven there by need; still two others worked in a shoe factory; —and all this happened before such adventures were undertaken in order to procure literary material. It was in the following winter that the pioneer effort in this direction, Walter Wyckoff's account of his vain attempt to find work in Chicago, compelled even the sternest businessman to drop his assertion that "any man can find work if he wants it."

The dealing directly with the simplest human wants may have been responsible for an impression which I carried about with me almost constantly for a period of two years and which culminated finally in a visit to Tolstoy-that the Settlement, or Hull-House at least, was a mere pretense and travesty of the simple impulse "to live with the poor," so long as the residents did not share the common lot of hard labor and scant fare.

Actual experience had left me in much the same state of mind I had been in after reading Tolstoy's "What to Do," which is a description of his futile efforts to relieve the unspeakable distress and want in the Moscow winter of 1881, and his inevitable conviction that only he who literally shares his own shelter and food with the needy can claim to have served them.

Doubtless it is much easier to see "what to do" in rural Russia, where all the conditions tend to make the contrast as broad as possible between peasant labor and noble idleness, than it is to see "what to do" in the interdependencies of the modern industrial city. But for that very reason perhaps, Tolstoy's clear statement is valuable for that type of conscientious person in every land who finds it hard, not only to walk in the path of righteousness, but to discover where the path lies.

I had read the books of Tolstoy steadily all the years since "My Religion" had come into my hands immediately after I left college. The reading of that book had made clear that men's poor little efforts to do right are put forth for the most part in the chill of self-distrust; I became convinced that if the new social order ever came, it would come by gathering to itself all the pathetic human endeavor which had indicated the forward direction. But I was most eager to know whether Tolstoy's undertaking to do his daily share of the physical labor of the world, that labor which is "so disproportionate to the unnourished strength" of those by whom it is ordinarily performed, had brought him peace!

I had time to review carefully many things in my mind during the long days of convalescence following an illness of typhoid fever which I suffered in the autumn of 1895. The illness was so prolonged that my health was most unsatisfactory during the following winter, and the next May I went abroad with my friend, Miss Smith, to effect if possible a more complete recovery.

The prospect of seeing Tolstoy filled me with the hope of finding a clue to the tangled affairs of city poverty. I was but one of thousands of our contemporaries who were turning toward this Russian, not as to a seer-his message is much too confused and contradictory for that-but as to a man who has had the ability to lift his life to the level of his conscience, to translate his theories into action.

Our first few weeks in England were most stimulating. A dozen years ago London still showed traces of "that exciting moment in the life of the nation when its youth is casting about for new enthusiasms," but it evinced still more of that British capacity to perform the hard work of careful research and self-examination which must precede any successful experiments in social reform. Of the varied groups and individuals whose suggestions remained with me for years, I recall perhaps as foremost those members of the new London County Council whose far-reaching plans for the betterment of London could not but enkindle enthusiasm. It was a most striking expression of that effort which would place beside the refinement and pleasure of the rich, a new refinement and a new pleasure born of the commonwealth and the common joy of all the citizens, that at this moment they prized the municipal pleasure boats upon the Thames no less than the extensive schemes for the municipal housing of the poorest people. Ben Tillet, who was then an alderman, "the docker sitting beside the duke," took me in a rowboat down the Thames on a journey made exciting by the hundreds of dockers who cheered him as we passed one wharf after another on our way to his home at Greenwich; John Burns showed us his wonderful civic accomplishments at Battersea, the plant turning street sweepings into cement pavements, the technical school teaching boys brick laying and plumbing, and the public bath in which the children of the Board School were receiving a swimming lesson-these measures anticipating our achievements in Chicago by at least a decade and a half. The new Education Bill which was destined to drag on for twelve years before it developed into the children's charter, was then a storm center in the House of Commons. Miss Smith and I were much pleased to be taken to tea on the Parliament terrace by its author, Sir John Gorst, although we were quite bewildered by the arguments we heard there for church schools versus secular.

We heard Keir Hardie before a large audience of workingmen standing in the open square of Canning Town outline the great things to be accomplished by the then new Labor Party, and we joined the vast body of men in the booming hymn

When wilt Thou save the people,
O God of Mercy, when!

finding it hard to realize that we were attending a political meeting. It seemed that moment as if the hopes of democracy were more likely to come to pass on English soil than upon our own. Robert Blatchford's stirring pamphlets were in everyone's hands, and a reception given by Karl Marx's daughter, Mrs. Aveling, to Liebknecht before he returned to Germany to serve a prison term for his lese majeste speech in the Reichstag, gave us a glimpse of the old-fash-ioned orthodox Socialist who had not yet begun to yield to the biting ridicule of Bernard Shaw although he flamed in their midst that evening.

Octavia Hill kindly demonstrated to us the principles upon which her well-founded business of rent collecting was established, and with pardonable pride showed us the Red Cross Square with its cottages marvelously picturesque and comfortable, on two sides, and on the third a public hall and common drawing room for the use of all the tenants; the interior of the latter had been decorated by pupils of Walter Crane with mural frescoes portraying the heroism in the life of the modern workingman.

While all this was warmly human, we also had opportunities to see something of a group of men and women who were approaching the social problem from the study of economics; among others Mr. and Mrs. Sidney Webb who were at work on their Industrial Democracy; Mr. John Hobson who was lecturing on the evolution of modern capitalism.

We followed factory inspectors on a round of duties performed with a thoroughness and a trained intelligence which were a revelation of the possibilities of public service. When it came to visiting Settlements, we were at least reassured that they were not falling into identical lines of effort. Canon Ingram, who has since become Bishop of London, was then warden of Oxford House and in the midst of an experiment which pleased me greatly, the more because it was carried on by a churchman. Oxford House had hired all the concert halls-vaudeville shows we later called them in Chicago-which were found in Bethnal Green, for every Saturday night. The residents had censored the programs, which they were careful to keep popular, and any workingman who attended a show in Bethnal Green on a Saturday night, and thousands of them did, heard a program the better for this effort.

One evening in University Hall Mrs. Humphry Ward, who had just returned from Italy, described the effect of the Italian salt tax in a talk which was evidently one in a series of lectures upon the economic wrongs which pressed heaviest upon the poor; at Browning House, at the moment, they were giving prizes to those of their costermonger neighbors who could present the best cared-for donkeys, and the warden, Herbert Stead, exhibited almost the enthusiasm of his well-known brother, for that crop of kindliness which can be garnered most easily from the acreage where human beings grow the thickest; at the Bermondsey Settlement they were rejoicing that their University Extension students had successfully passed the examinations for the University of London. The entire impression received in England of research, of scholarship, of organized public spirit, was in marked contrast to the impressions of my next visit in 1900, when the South African War had absorbed the enthusiasm of the nation and the wrongs at "the heart of the empire" were disregarded and neglected.

London, of course, presented sharp differences to Russia where social conditions were written in black and white with little shading, like a demonstration of the Chinese proverb, "Where one man lives in luxury, another is dying of hunger."

The fair of Nijni-Novgorod seemed to take us to the very edge of civilization so remote and eastern that the merchants brought their curious goods upon the backs of camels or on strange craft riding at anchor on the broad Volga. But even here our letter of introduction to Korolenko, the novelist, brought us to a realization of that strange mingling of a remote past and a self-conscious present which Russia presents on every hand. This same contrast was also shown by the pilgrims trudging on pious errands to monasteries, to tombs, and to the Holy Land itself, with their bleeding feet bound in rags and thrust into bast sandals, and, on the other hand, by the revolutionists even then advocating a Republic which should obtain not only in political but also in industrial affairs.

We had letters of introduction to Mr. and Mrs. Aylmer Maude of Moscow, since well known as the translators of "Resurrection" and other of Tolstoy's later works, who at that moment were on the eve of leaving Russia in order to form an agricultural colony in South England where they might support themselves by the labor of their hands. We gladly accepted Mr. Maude's offer to take us to Yasnaya Polyana and to introduce us to Count Tolstoy, and never did a disciple journey toward his master with more enthusiasm than did our guide. When, however, Mr. Maude actually presented Miss Smith and myself to Count Tolstoy, knowing well his master's attitude toward philanthropy, he endeavored to make Hull-House appear much more noble and unique than I should have ventured to do.

Tolstoy, standing by clad in his peasant garb, listened gravely but, glancing distrustfully at the sleeves of my traveling gown which unfortunately at that season were monstrous in size, he took hold of an edge and pulling out one sleeve to an interminable breadth, said quite simply that "there was enough stuff on one arm to make a frock for a little girl," and asked me directly if I did not find "such a dress" a "barrier to the people." I was too disconcerted to make a very clear explanation, although I tried to say that monstrous as my sleeves were they did not compare in size with those of the working girls in Chicago and that nothing would more effectively separate me from "the people" than a cotton blouse following the simple lines of the human form; even if I had wished to imitate him and "dress as a peasant," it would have been hard to choose which peasant among the thirty-six nationalities we had recently counted in our ward. Fortunately the countess came to my rescue with a recital of her former attempts to clothe hypothetical little girls in yards of material cut from a train and other superfluous parts of her best gown until she had been driven to a firm stand which she advised me to take at once. But neither Countess Tolstoy nor any other friend was on hand to help me out of my predicament later, when I was asked who "fed" me, and how did I obtain "shelter"? Upon my reply that a farm a hundred miles from Chicago supplied me with the necessities of life, I fairly anticipated the next scathing question: "So you are an absentee landlord? Do you think you will help the people more by adding yourself to the crowded city than you would by tilling your own soil?" This new sense of discomfort over a failure to till my own soil was increased when Tolstoy's second daughter appeared at the five-o'clock tea table set under the trees, coming straight from the harvest field where she had been working with a group of peasants since five o'clock in the morning, not pretending to work but really taking the place of a peasant woman who had hurt her foot. She was plainly much exhausted, but neither expected nor received sympathy from the members of a family who were quite accustomed to see each other carry out their convictions in spite of discomfort and fatigue. The martyrdom of discomfort, however, was obviously much easier to bear than that to which, even to the eyes of the casual visitor, Count Tolstoy daily subjected himself, for his study in the basement of the conventional dwelling, with its short shelf of battered books and its scythe and spade leaning against the wall, had many times lent itself to that ridicule which is the most difficult form of martyrdom.

That summer evening as we sat in the garden with a group of visitors from Germany, from England and America, who had traveled to the remote Russian village that they might learn of this man, one could not forbear the constant inquiry to one's self, as to why he was so regarded as sage and saint that this party of people should be repeated each day of the year. It seemed to me then that we were all attracted by this sermon of the deed, because Tolstoy had made the one supreme personal effort, one might almost say the one frantic personal effort, to put himself into right relations with the humblest people, with the men who tilled his soil, blacked his boots, and cleaned his stables. Doubtless the heaviest burden of our contemporaries is a consciousness of a divergence between our democratic theory on the one hand, that working people have a right to the intellectual resources of society, and the actual fact on the other hand, that thousands of them are so overburdened with toil that there is no leisure nor energy left for the cultivation of the mind. We constantly suffer from the strain and indecision of believing this theory and acting as if we did not believe it, and this man who years before had tried "to get off the backs of the peasants," who had at least simplified his life and worked with his hands, had come to be a prototype to many of his generation.

Doubtless all of the visitors sitting in the Tolstoy garden that evening had excused themselves from laboring with their hands upon the theory that they were doing something more valuable for society in other ways. No one among our contemporaries has dissented from this point of view so violently as Tolstoy himself, and yet no man might so easily have excused himself from hard and rough work on the basis of his genius and of his intellectual contributions to the world. So far, however, from considering his time too valuable to be spent in labor in the field or in making shoes, our great host was too eager to know life to be willing to give up this companionship of mutual labor. One instinctively found reasons why it was easier for a Russian than for the rest of us to reach this conclusion; the Russian peasants have a proverb which says: "Labor is the house that love lives in," by which they mean that no two people nor group of people can come into affectionate relations with each other unless they carry on together a mutual task, and when the Russian peasant talks of labor he means labor on the soil, or, to use the phrase of the great peasant, Bondereff, "bread labor." Those monastic orders founded upon agricultural labor, those philosophical experiments like Brook Farm and many another have attempted to reduce to action this same truth. Tolstoy himself has written many times his own convictions and attempts in this direction, perhaps never more tellingly than in the description of Lavin's morning spent in the harvest field, when he lost his sense of grievance and isolation and felt a strange new brotherhood for the peasants, in proportion as the rhythmic motion of his scythe became one with theirs.

At the long dinner table laid in the garden were the various traveling guests, the grown-up daughters, and the younger children with their governess. The countess presided over the usual European dinner served by men, but the count and the daughter, who had worked all day in the fields, ate only porridge and black bread and drank only kvas, the fare of the hay-making peasants. Of course we are all accustomed to the fact that those who perform the heaviest labor eat the coarsest and simplest fare at the end of the day, but it is not often that we sit at the same table with them while we ourselves eat the more elaborate food prepared by someone else's labor. Tolstoy ate his simple supper without remark or comment upon the food his family and guests preferred to eat, assuming that they, as well as he, had settled the matter with their own consciences.

The Tolstoy household that evening was much interested in the fate of a young Russian spy who had recently come to Tolstoy in the guise of a country schoolmaster, in order to obtain a copy of "Life," which had been interdicted by the censor of the press. After spending the night in talk with Tolstoy, the spy had gone away with a copy of the forbidden manuscript but, unfortunately for himself, having become converted to Tolstoy's views he had later made a full confession to the authorities and had been exiled to Siberia. Tolstoy, holding that it was most unjust to exile the disciple while he, the author of the book, remained at large, had pointed out this inconsistency in an open letter to one of the Moscow newspapers. The discussion of this incident, of course, opened up the entire subject of nonresidence, and curiously enough I was disappointed in Tolstoy's position in the matter. It seemed to me that he made too great a distinction between the use of physical force and that moral energy which can override another's differences and scruples with equal ruthlessness.

With that inner sense of mortification with which one finds one's self at difference with the great authority, I recalled the conviction of the early Hull-House residents; that whatever of good the Settlement had to offer should be put into positive terms, that we might live with opposition to no man, with recognition of the good in every man, even the most wretched. We had often departed from this principle, but had it not in every case been a confession of weakness, and had we not always found antagonism a foolish and unwarrantable expenditure of energy?

The conversation at dinner and afterward, although conducted with animation and sincerity, for the moment stirred vague misgivings within me. Was Tolstoy more logical than life warrants? Could the wrongs of life be reduced to the terms of unrequited labor and all be made right if each person performed the amount necessary to satisfy his own wants? Was it not always easy to put up a strong case if one took the naturalistic view of life? But what about the historic view, the inevitable shadings and modifications which life itself brings to its own interpretation? Miss Smith and I took a night train back to Moscow in that tumult of feeling which is always produced by contact with a conscience making one more of those determined efforts to probe to the very foundations of the mysterious world in which we find ourselves. A horde of perplexing questions, concerning those problems of existence of which in happier moments we catch but fleeting glimpses and at which we even then stand aghast, pursued us relentlessly on the long journey through the great wheat plains of South Russia, through the crowded Ghetto of Warsaw, and finally into the smiling fields of Germany where the peasant men and women were harvesting the grain. I remember that through the sight of those toiling peasants, I made a curious connection between the bread labor advocated by Tolstoy and the comfort the harvest fields are said to have once brought to Luther when, much perturbed by many theological difficulties, he suddenly forgot them all in a gush of gratitude for mere bread, exclaiming, "How it stands, that golden yellow corn, on its fine tapered stem; the meek earth, at God's kind bidding, has produced it once again!" At least the toiling poor had this comfort of bread labor, and perhaps it did not matter that they gained it unknowingly and painfully, if only they walked in the path of labor. In the exercise of that curious power possessed by the theorist to inhibit all experiences which do not enhance his doctrine, I did not permit myself to recall that which I knew so well-that exigent and unremitting labor grants the poor no leisure even in the supreme moments of human suffering and that "all griefs are lighter with bread."

I may have wished to secure this solace for myself at the cost of the least possible expenditure of time and energy, for during the next month in Germany, when I read everything of

Tolstoy's that had been translated into English, German, or French, there grew up in my mind a conviction that what I ought to do upon my return to Hull-House was to spend at least two hours every morning in the little bakery which we had recently added to the equipment of our coffeehouse. Two hours' work would be but a wretched compromise, but it was hard to see how I could take more time out of each day. I had been taught to bake bread in my childhood not only as a household accomplishment, but because my father, true to his miller's tradition, had insisted that each one of his daughters on her twelfth birthday must present him with a satisfactory wheat loaf of her own baking, and he was most exigent as to the quality of this test loaf. What could be more in keeping with my training and tradition than baking bread? I did not quite see how my activity would fit in with that of the German union baker who presided over the Hull-House bakery, but all such matters were secondary and certainly could be arranged. It may be that I had thus to pacify my aroused conscience before I could settle down to hear Wagner's "Ring" at Beyreuth; it may be that I had fallen a victim to the phrase, "bread labor"; but at any rate I held fast to the belief that I should do this, through the entire journey homeward, on land and sea, until I actually arrived in Chicago when suddenly the whole scheme seemed to me as utterly preposterous as it doubtless was. The half dozen people invariably waiting to see me after breakfast, the piles of letters to be opened and answered, the demand of actual and pressing wants-were these all to be pushed aside and asked to wait while I saved my soul by two hours' work at baking bread?

Although my resolution was abandoned, this may be the best place to record the efforts of more doughty souls to carry out Tolstoy's conclusions. It was perhaps inevitable that Tolstoy colonies should be founded, although Tolstoy himself has always insisted that each man should live his life as nearly as possible in the place in which he was born. The visit Miss Smith and I made a year or two later to a colony in one of the southern States portrayed for us most vividly both the weakness and the strange august dignity of the Tolstoy position. The colonists at Commonwealth held but a short creed. They claimed in fact that the difficulty is not to state truth but to make moral conviction operative upon actual life, and they announced it their intention "to obey the teachings of Jesus in all matters of labor and the use of property." They would thus transfer the vindication of creed from the church to the open field, from dogma to experience.

The day Miss Smith and I visited the Commonwealth colony of threescore souls, they were erecting a house for the family of a one-legged man, consisting of a wife and nine children who had come the week before in a forlorn prairie schooner from Arkansas. As this was the largest family the little colony contained, the new house was to be the largest yet erected. Upon our surprise at this literal giving "to him that asketh," we inquired if the policy of extending food and shelter to all who applied, without test of creed or ability, might not result in the migration of all the neighboring poorhouse population into the colony. We were told that this actually had happened during the winter until the colony fare of corn meal and cow peas had proved so unattractive that the paupers had gone back, for even the poorest of the southern poorhouses occasionally supplied bacon with the pone if only to prevent scurvy from which the colonists themselves had suffered. The difficulty of the poorhouse people had thus settled itself by the sheer poverty of the situation, a poverty so biting that the only ones willing to face it were those sustained by a conviction of its righteousness. The fields and gardens were being worked by an editor, a professor, a clergyman, as well as by artisans and laborers, the fruit thereof to be eaten by themselves and their families or by any other families who might arrive from Arkansas. The colonists were very conventional in matters of family relationship and had broken with society only in regard to the conventions pertaining to labor and property. We had a curious experience at the end of the day, when we were driven into the nearest town. We had taken with us as a guest the wife of the president of the colony, wishing to give her a dinner at the hotel, because she had girlishly exclaimed during a conversation that at times during the winter she had become so eager to hear good music that it had seemed to her as if she were actually hungry for it, almost as hungry as she was for a beefsteak. Yet as we drove away we had the curious sensation that while the experiment was obviously coming to an end, in the midst of its privations it yet embodied the peace of mind which comes to him who insists upon the logic of life whether it is reasonable or not-the fanatic's joy in seeing his own formula translated into action. At any rate, as we reached the common-place southern town of workaday men and women, for one moment its substantial buildings, its solid brick churches, its ordered streets, divided into those of the rich and those of the poor, seemed much more unreal to us than the little struggling colony we had left behind. We repeated to each other that in all the practical judgments and decisions of life, we must part company with logical demonstration; that if we stop for it in each case, we can never go on at all; and yet, in spite of this, when conscience does become the dictator of the daily life of a group of men, it forces our admiration as no other modern spectacle has power to do. It seemed but a mere incident that this group should have lost sight of the facts of life in their earnest endeavor to put to the test the things of the spirit.

I knew little about the colony started by Mr. Maude at Purleigh containing several of Tolstoy's followers who were not permitted to live in Russia, and we did not see Mr. Maude again until he came to Chicago on his way from Manitoba, whither he had transported the second group of Dukhobors, a religious sect who had interested all of Tolstoy's followers because of their literal acceptance of non-resistance and other Christian doctrines which are so strenuously advocated by Tolstoy. It was for their benefit that Tolstoy had finished and published "Resurrection," breaking through his long-kept resolution against novel writing. After the Dukhobors were settled in Canada, of the five hundred dollars left from the "Resurrection" funds, one half was given to Hull-House. It seemed possible to spend this fund only for the relief of the most primitive wants of food and shelter on the part of the most needy families.

Chapter XIII
Public Activities and Investigations

One of the striking features of our neighborhood twenty years ago, and one to which we never became reconciled, was the presence of huge wooden garbage boxes fastened to the street pavement in which the undisturbed refuse accumulated day by day. The system of garbage collecting was inadequate throughout the city but it became the greatest menace in a ward such as ours, where the normal amount of waste was much increased by the decayed fruit and vegetables discarded by the Italian and Greek fruit peddlers, and by the residuum left over from the piles of filthy rags which were fished out of the city dumps and brought to the homes of the rag pickers for further sorting and washing.

The children of our neighborhood twenty years ago played their games in and around these huge garbage boxes. They were the first objects that the toddling child learned to climb; their bulk afforded a barricade and their contents provided missiles in all the battles of the older boys; and finally they became the seats upon which absorbed lovers held enchanted converse. We are obliged to remember that all children eat everything which they find and that odors have a curious and intimate power of entwining themselves into our tenderest memories, before even the residents of Hull-House can understand their own early enthusiasm for the removal of these boxes and the establishment of a better system of refuse collection.

It is easy for even the most conscientious citizen of Chicago to forget the foul smells of the stockyards and the garbage dumps, when he is living so far from them that he is only occasionally made conscious of their existence but the residents of a Settlement are perforce constantly surrounded by them. During our first three years on Halsted Street, we had established a small incinerator at Hull-House and we had many times reported the untoward conditions of the ward to the city hall. We had also arranged many talks for the immigrants, pointing out that although a woman may sweep her own doorway in her native village and allow the reuse to innocently decay in the open air and sunshine, in a crowded city quarter, if the garbage is not properly collected and destroyed, a tenement-house mother may see her children sicken and die, and that the immigrants must therefore not only keep their own houses clean, but must also help the authorities to keep the city clean.

Possibly our efforts slightly modified the worst conditions, but they still remained intolerable, and the fourth summer the situation became for me absolutely desperate when I realized in a moment of panic that my delicate little nephew for whom I was guardian, could not be with me at Hull-House at all unless the sickening odors were reduced. I may well be ashamed that other delicate children who were torn from their families, not into boarding school but into eternity, had not long before driven me to effective action. Under the direction of the first man who came as a resident to Hull-House we began a systematic investigation of the city system of garbage collection, both as to its efficiency in other wards and its possible connection with the death rate in the various wards of the city.

The Hull-House Woman's Club had been organized the year before by the resident kindergartner who had first inaugurated a mother's meeting. The new members came together, however, in quite a new way that summer when we discussed with them the high death rate so persistent in our ward. After several club meetings devoted to the subject, despite the fact that the death rate rose highest in the congested foreign colonies and not in the streets in which most of the Irish American club women lived, twelve of their number undertook in connection with the residents, to carefully investigate the conditions of the alleys. During August and September the substantiated reports of violations of the law sent in from Hull-House to the health department were one thousand and thirty-seven. For the club woman who had finished a long day's work of washing or ironing followed by the cooking of a hot supper, it would have been much easier to sit on her doorstep during a summer evening than to go up and down ill-kept alleys and get into trouble with her neighbors over the condition of their garbage boxes. It required both civic enterprise and moral conviction to be willing to do this three evenings a week during the hottest and most uncomfortable months of the year. Nevertheless, a certain number of women persisted, as did the residents, and three city inspectors in succession were transferred from the ward because of unsatisfactory services. Still the death rate remained high and the condition seemed little improved throughout the next winter. In sheer desperation, the following spring when the city contracts were awarded for the removal of garbage, with the backing of two well-known business men, I put in a bid for the garbage removal of the nineteenth ward. My paper was thrown out on a technicality but the incident induced the mayor to appoint me the garbage inspector of the ward.

The salary was a thousand dollars a year, and the loss of that political "plum" made a great stir among the politicians. The position was no sinecure whether regarded from the point of view of getting up at six in the morning to see that the men were early at work; or of following the loaded wagons, uneasily dropping their contents at intervals, to their dreary destination at the dump; or of insisting that the contractor must increase the number of his wagons from nine to thirteen and from thirteen to seventeen, although he assured me that he lost money on every one and that the former inspector had let him off with seven; or of taking careless landlords into court because they would not provide the proper garbage receptacles; or of arresting the tenant who tried to make the garbage wagons carry away the contents of his stable.

With the two or three residents who nobly stood by, we set up six of those doleful incinerators which are supposed to burn garbage with the fuel collected in the alley itself. The one factory in town which could utilize old tin cans was a window weight factory, and we deluged that with ten times as many tin cans as it could use-much less would pay for. We made desperate attempts to have the dead animals removed by the contractor who was paid most liberally by the city for that purpose but who, we slowly discovered, always made the police ambulances do the work, delivering the carcasses upon freight cars for shipment to a soap factory in Indiana where they were sold for a good price although the contractor himself was the largest stockholder in the concern. Perhaps our greatest achievement was the discovery of a pavement eighteen inches under the surface in a narrow street, although after it was found we triumphantly discovered a record of its existence in the city archives. The Italians living on the street were much interested but displayed little astonishment, perhaps because they were accustomed to see buried cities exhumed. This pavement became the casus belli between myself and the street commissioner when I insisted that its restoration belonged to him, after I had removed the first eight inches of garbage. The matter was finally settled by the mayor himself, who permitted me to drive him to the entrance of the street in what the children called my "garbage phaeton" and who took my side of the controversy.

A graduate of the University of Wisconsin, who had done some excellent volunteer inspection in both Chicago and Pittsburg, became my deputy and performed the work in a most thoroughgoing manner for three years. During the last two she was under the regime of civil service for in 1895, to the great joy of many citizens, the Illinois legislature made that possible.

Many of the foreign-born women of the ward were much shocked by this abrupt departure into the ways of men, and it took a great deal of explanation to convey the idea even remotely that if it were a womanly task to go about in tenement houses in order to nurse the sick, it might be quite as womanly to go through the same district in order to prevent the breeding of so-called "filth diseases." While some of the women enthusiastically approved the slowly changing conditions and saw that their housewifely duties logically extended to the adjacent alleys and streets, they yet were quite certain that "it was not a lady's job." A revelation of this attitude was made one day in a conversation which the inspector heard vigorously carried on in a laundry. One of the employees was leaving and was expressing her mind concerning the place in no measured terms, summing up her contempt for it as follows: "I would rather be the girl who goes about in the alleys than to stay here any longer!"

And yet the spectacle of eight hours' work for eight hours' pay, the even-handed justice to all citizens irrespective of "pull," the dividing of responsibility between landlord and tenant, and the readiness to enforce obedience to law from both, was, perhaps, one of the most valuable demonstrations which could have been made. Such daily living on the part of the office holder is of infinitely more value than many talks on civics for, after all, we credit most easily that which we see. The careful inspection combined with other causes, brought about a great improvement in the cleanliness and comfort of the neighborhood and one happy day, when the death rate of our ward was found to have dropped from third to seventh in the list of city wards and was so reported to our Woman's Club, the applause which followed recorded the genuine sense of participation in the result, and a public spirit which had "made good." But the cleanliness of the ward was becoming much too popular to suit our all-powerful alderman and, although we felt fatuously secure under the regime of civil service, he found a way to circumvent us by eliminating the position altogether. He introduced an ordinance into the city council which combined the collection of refuse with the cleaning and repairing of the streets, the whole to be placed under a ward superintendent. The office of course was to be filled under civil service regulations but only men were eligible to the examination. Although this latter regulation was afterwards modified in favor of one woman, it was retained long enough to put the nineteenth ward inspector out of office.

Of course our experience in inspecting only made us more conscious of the wretched housing conditions over which we had been distressed from the first. It was during the World's Fair summer that one of the Hull-House residents in a public address upon housing reform used as an example of indifferent landlordism a large block in the neighborhood occupied by small tenements and stables unconnected with a street sewer, as was much similar property in the vicinity. In the lecture the resident spared neither a description of the property nor the name of the owner. The young man who owned the property was justly indignant at this public method of attack and promptly came to investigate the condition of the property. Together we made a careful tour of the houses and stables and in the face of the conditions that we found there, I could not but agree with him that supplying South Italian peasants with sanitary appliances seemed a difficult undertaking. Nevertheless he was unwilling that the block should remain in its deplorable state, and he finally cut through the dilemma with the rash proposition that he would give a free lease of the entire tract to Hull-House, accompanying the offer, however, with the warning remark, that if we should choose to use the income from the rents in sanitary improvements we should be throwing our money away.

Even when we decided that the houses were so bad that we could not undertake the task of improving them, he was game and stuck to his proposition that we should have a free lease. We finally submitted a plan that the houses should be torn down and the entire tract turned into a playground, although cautious advisers intimated that it would be very inconsistent to ask for subscriptions for the support of Hull-House when we were known to have thrown away an income of two thousand dollars a year. We, however, felt that a spectacle of inconsistency was better than one of bad landlordism and so the worst of the houses were demolished, the best three were sold and moved across the street under careful provision that they might never be used for junk- shops or saloons, and a public playground was finally established. Hull-House became responsible for its management for ten years, at the end of which time it was turned over to the City Playground Commission although from the first the city detailed a policeman who was responsible for its general order and who became a valued adjunct of the House.

During fifteen years this public-spirited owner of the property paid all the taxes, and when the block was finally sold he made possible the playground equipment of a near-by schoolyard. On the other hand, the dispossessed tenants, a group of whom had to be evicted by legal process before their houses could be torn down, have never ceased to mourn their former estates. Only the other day I met upon the street an old Italian harness maker, who said that he had never succeeded so well anywhere else nor found a place that "seemed so much like Italy."

Festivities of various sorts were held on this early playground, always a May day celebration with its Maypole dance and its May queen. I remember that one year that honor of being queen was offered to the little girl who should pick up the largest number of scraps of paper which littered all the streets and alleys. The children that spring had been organized into a league, and each member had been provided with a stiff piece of wire upon the sharpened point of which stray bits of paper were impaled and later soberly counted off into a large box in the Hull-House alley. The little Italian girl who thus won the scepter took it very gravely as the just reward of hard labor, and we were all so absorbed in the desire for clean and tidy streets that we were wholly oblivious to the incongruity of thus selecting "the queen of love and beauty."

It was at the end of the second year that we received a visit from the warden of Toynbee Hall and his wife, as they were returning to England from a journey around the world. They had lived in East London for many years, and had been identified with the public movements for its betterment. They were much shocked that, in a new country with conditions still plastic and hopeful, so little attention had been paid to experiments and methods of amelioration which had already been tried; and they looked in vain through our library for blue books and governmental reports which recorded painstaking study into the conditions of English cities.

They were the first of a long line of English visitors to express the conviction that many things in Chicago were untoward not through paucity of public spirit but through a lack of political machinery adapted to modern city life. This was not all of the situation but perhaps no casual visitor could be expected to see that these matters of detail seemed unimportant to a city in the first flush of youth, impatient of correction and convinced that all would be well with its future. The most obvious faults were those connected with the congested housing of the immigrant population, nine tenths of them from the country, who carried on all sorts of traditional activities in the crowded tenements. That a group of Greeks should be permitted to slaughter sheep in a basement, that Italian women should be allowed to sort over rags collected from the city dumps, not only within the city limits but in a court swarming with little children, that immigrant bakers should continue unmolested to bake bread for their neighbors in unspeakably filthy spaces under the pavement, appeared incredible to visitors accustomed to careful city regulations. I recall two visits made to the Italian quarter by John Burns-the second, thirteen years after the first. During the latter visit it seemed to him unbelievable that a certain house owned by a rich Italian should have been permitted to survive. He remembered with the greatest minuteness the positions of the houses on the court, with the exact space between the front and rear tenements, and he asked at once whether we had been able to cut a window into a dark hall as he had recommended thirteen years before. Although we were obliged to confess that the landlord would not permit the window to be cut, we were able to report that a City Homes Association had existed for ten years; that following a careful study of tenement conditions in Chicago, the text of which had been written by a Hull-House resident, the association had obtained the enactment of a model tenement-house code, and that their secretary had carefully watched the administration of the law for years so that its operation might not be minimized by the granting of too many exceptions in the city council. Our progress still seemed slow to Mr. Burns because in Chicago, the actual houses were quite unchanged, embodying features long since declared illegal in London. Only this year could we have reported to him, had he again come to challenge us, that the provisions of the law had at last been extended to existing houses and that a conscientious corps of inspectors under an efficient chief, were fast remedying the most glaring evils, while a band of nurses and doctors were following hard upon the "trail of the white hearse."

The mere consistent enforcement of existing laws and efforts for their advance often placed Hull-House, at least temporarily, into strained relations with its neighbors. I recall a continuous warfare against local landlords who would move wrecks of old houses as a nucleus for new ones in order to evade the provisions of the building code, and a certain Italian neighbor who was filled with bitterness because his new rear tenement was discovered to be illegal. It seemed impossible to make him understand that the health of the tenants was in any wise as important as his undisturbed rents.

Nevertheless many evils constantly arise in Chicago from congested housing which wiser cities forestall and prevent; the inevitable boarders crowded into a dark tenement already too small for the use of the immigrant family occupying it; the surprisingly large number of delinquent girls who have become criminally involved with their own fathers and uncles; the school children who cannot find a quiet spot in which to read or study and who perforce go into the streets each evening; the tuberculosis superinduced and fostered by the inadequate rooms and breathing spaces. One of the Hull-House residents, under the direction of a Chicago physician who stands high as an authority on tuberculosis and who devotes a large proportion of his time to our vicinity, made an investigation into housing conditions as related to tuberculosis with a result as startling as that of the "lung block" in New York.

It is these subtle evils of wretched and inadequate housing which are often the most disastrous. In the summer of 1902 during an epidemic of typhoid fever in which our ward, although containing but one thirty-sixth of the population of the city, registered one sixth of the total number of deaths, two of the Hull-House residents made an investigation of the methods of plumbing in the houses adjacent to conspicuous groups of fever cases. They discovered among the people who had been exposed to the infection, a widow who had lived in the ward for a number of years, in a comfortable little house of her own. Although the Italian immigrants were closing in all around her, she was not willing to sell her property and to move away until she had finished the education of her children. In the meantime she held herself quite aloof from her Italian neighbors and could never be drawn into any of the public efforts to secure a better code of tenement-house sanitation. Her two daughters were sent to an eastern college. One June when one of them had graduated and the other still had two years before she took her degree, they came to the spotless little house and their self-sacrificing mother for the summer holiday. They both fell ill with typhoid fever and one daughter died because the mother's utmost efforts could not keep the infection out of her own house. The entire disaster affords, perhaps, a fair illustration of the futility of the individual conscience which would isolate a family from the rest of the community and its interests.

The careful information collected concerning the juxtaposition of the typhoid cases to the various systems of plumbing and nonplumbing was made the basis of a bacteriological study by another resident, Dr. Alice Hamilton, as to the possibility of the infection having been carried by flies. Her researches were so convincing that they have been incorporated into the body of scientific data supporting that theory, but there were also practical results from the investigation. It was discovered that the wretched sanitary appliances through which alone the infection could have become so widely spread, would not have been permitted to remain, unless the city inspector had either been criminally careless or open to the arguments of favored landlords.

The agitation finally resulted in a long and stirring trial before the civil service board of half of the employees in the Sanitary Bureau, with the final discharge of eleven out of the entire force of twenty-four. The inspector in our neighborhood was a kindly old man, greatly distressed over the affair, and quite unable to understand why he should have not used his discretion as to the time when a landlord should be forced to put in modern appliances. If he was "very poor," or "just about to sell his place," or "sure that the house would be torn down to make room for a factory," why should one "inconvenience" him? The old man died soon after the trial, feeling persecuted to the very last and not in the least understanding what it was all about. We were amazed at the commercial ramifications which graft in the city hall involved and at the indignation which interference with it produced. Hull-House lost some large subscriptions as the result of this investigation, a loss which, if not easy to bear, was at least comprehensible. We also uncovered unexpected graft in connection with the plumbers' unions, and but for the fearless testimony of one of their members, could never have brought the trial to a successful issue.

Inevitable misunderstanding also developed in connection with the attempt on the part of Hull-House residents to prohibit the sale of cocaine to minors, which brought us into sharp conflict with many druggists. I recall an Italian druggist living on the edge of the neighborhood, who finally came with a committee of his countryman to see what Hull-House wanted of him, thoroughly convinced that no such effort could be disinterested. One dreary trial after another had been lost through the inadequacy of the existing legislation and after many attempts to secure better legal regulation of its sale, a new law with the cooperation of many agencies was finally secured in 1907. Through all this the Italian druggist, who had greatly profited by the sale of cocaine to boys, only felt outraged and abused. And yet the thought of this campaign brings before my mind with irresistible force, a young Italian boy who died, —a victim of the drug at the age of seventeen. He had been in our kindergarten as a handsome merry child, in our clubs as a vivacious boy, and then gradually there was an eclipse of all that was animated and joyous and promising, and when I at last saw him in his coffin, it was impossible to connect that haggard shriveled body with what I had known before.

A midwife investigation, undertaken in connection with the Chicago Medical Society, while showing the great need of further state regulation in the interest of the most ignorant mothers and helpless children, brought us into conflict with one of the most venerable of all customs. Was all this a part of the unending struggle between the old and new, or were these oppositions so unexpected and so unlooked for merely a reminder of that old bit of wisdom that "there is no guarding against interpretations"? Perhaps more subtle still, they were due to that very super-refinement of disinterestedness which will not justify itself, that it may feel superior to public opinion. Some of our investigations of course had no such untoward results, such as "An Intensive Study of Truancy" undertaken by a resident of Hull-House in connection with the compulsory education department of the Board of Education and the Visiting Nurses Association. The resident, Mrs. Britton, who, having had charge of our children's clubs for many years, knew thousands of children in the neighborhood, made a detailed study of three hundred families tracing back the habitual truancy of the child to economic and social causes. This investigation preceded a most interesting conference on truancy held under a committee of which I was a member from the Chicago Board of Education. It left lasting results upon the administration of the truancy law as well as the cooperation of volunteer bodies.

We continually conduct small but careful investigations at Hull-House, which may guide us in our immediate doings such as two recently undertaken by Mrs. Britton, one upon the reading of school children before new books were bought for the children's club libraries, and another on the proportion of tuberculosis among school children, before we opened a little experimental outdoor school on one of our balconies. Some of the Hull-House investigations are purely negative in result; we once made an attempt to test the fatigue of factory girls in order to determine how far overwork superinduced the tuberculosis to which such a surprising number of them were victims. The one scientific instrument it seemed possible to use was an ergograph, a complicated and expensive instrument kindly lent to us from the physiological laboratory of the University of Chicago. I remember the imposing procession we made from Hull-House to the factory full of working women, in which the proprietor allowed us to make the tests; first there was the precious instrument on a hand truck guarded by an anxious student and the young physician who was going to take the tests every afternoon; then there was Dr. Hamilton the resident in charge of the investigation, walking with a scientist who was interested to see that the instrument was properly installed; I followed in the rear to talk once more to the proprietor of the factory to be quite sure that he would permit the experiment to go on. The result of all this preparation, however, was to have the instrument record less fatigue at the end of the day than at the beginning, not because the girls had not worked hard and were not "dog tired" as they confessed, but because the instrument was not fitted to find it out.

For many years we have administered a branch station of the federal post office at Hull-House, which we applied for in the first instance because our neighbors lost such a large percentage of the money they sent to Europe, through the commissions to middle men. The experience in the post office constantly gave us data for urging the establishment of postal savings as we saw one perplexed immigrant after another turning away in bewilderment when he was told that the United States post office did not receive savings.

We find increasingly, however, that the best results are to be obtained in investigations as in other undertakings, by combining our researches with those of other public bodies or with the State itself. When all the Chicago Settlements found themselves distressed over the condition of the newsboys who, because they are merchants and not employees, do not come under the provisions of the Illinois child labor law, they united in the investigation of a thousand young newsboys, who were all interviewed on the streets during the same twenty-four hours. Their school and domestic status was easily determined later, for many of the boys lived in the immediate neighborhoods of the ten Settlements which had undertaken the investigation. The report embodying the results of the investigation recommended a city ordinance containing features from the Boston and Buffalo regulations, and although an ordinance was drawn up and a strenuous effort was made to bring it to the attention of the aldermen, none of them would introduce it into the city council without newspaper backing. We were able to agitate for it again at the annual meeting of the National Child Labor Committee which was held in Chicago in 1908, and which was of course reported in papers throughout the entire country. This meeting also demonstrated that local measures can sometimes be urged most effectively when joined to the efforts of a national body. Undoubtedly the best discussions ever held upon the operation and status of the Illinois law were those which took place then. The needs of the Illinois children were regarded in connection with the children of the nation and advanced health measures for Illinois were compared with those of other states.

The investigations of Hull-House thus tend to be merged with those of larger organizations, from the investigation of the social value of saloons made for the Committee of Fifty in 1896, to the one on infant mortality in relation to nationality, made for the American Academy of Science in 1909. This is also true of Hull-House activities in regard to public movements, some of which are inaugurated by the residents of other Settlements, as the Chicago School of Civics and Philanthropy, founded by the splendid efforts of Dr. Graham Taylor for many years head of Chicago Commons. All of our recent investigations into housing have been under the department of investigation of this school with which several of the Hull-House residents are identified, quite as our active measures to secure better housing conditions have been carried on with the City Homes Association and through the cooperation of one of our residents who several years ago was appointed a sanitary inspector on the city staff.

Perhaps Dr. Taylor himself offers the best possible example of the value of Settlement experience to public undertakings, in his manifold public activities of which one might instance his work at the moment upon a commission recently appointed by the governor of Illinois to report upon the best method of Industrial Insurance or Employer's Liability Acts, and his influence in securing another to study into the subject of Industrial Diseases. The actual factory investigation under the latter is in charge of Dr. Hamilton, of Hull-House, whose long residence in an industrial neighborhood as well as her scientific attainment, give her peculiar qualifications for the undertaking.

And so a Settlement is led along from the concrete to the abstract, as may easily be illustrated. Many years ago a tailors' union meeting at Hull-House asked our cooperation in tagging the various parts of a man's coat in such wise as to show the money paid to the people who had made it; one tag for the cutting and another for the buttonholes, another for the finishing and so on, the resulting total to be compared with the selling price of the coat itself. It quickly became evident that we had no way of computing how much of this larger balance was spent for salesmen, commercial travelers, rent and management, and the poor tagged coat was finally left hanging limply in a closet as if discouraged with the attempt. But the desire of the manual worker to know the relation of his own labor to the whole is not only legitimate but must form the basis of any intelligent action for his improvement. It was therefore with the hope of reform in the sewing trades that the Hull-House residents testified before the Federal Industrial Commission in 1900, and much later with genuine enthusiasm joined with trades-unionists and other public-spirited citizens in an industrial exhibit which made a graphic presentation of the conditions and rewards of labor. The large casino building in which it was held was filled every day and evening for two weeks, showing how popular such information is, if it can be presented graphically. As an illustration of this same moving from the smaller to the larger, I might instance the efforts of Miss McDowell of the University of Chicago Settlement and others in urging upon Congress the necessity for a special investigation into the conditions of women and children in industry because we had discovered the insuperable difficulties of smaller investigations, notably one undertaken for the Illinois Bureau of Labor by Mrs. Van der Vaart of Neighborhood House and by Miss Breckinridge of the University of Chicago. This investigation made clear that it was as impossible to detach the girls working in the stockyards from their sisters in industry as it was to urge special legislation on their behalf.

In the earlier years of the American Settlements, the residents were sometimes impatient with the accepted methods of charitable administration and hoped, through residence in an industrial neighborhood, to discover more cooperative and advanced methods of dealing with the problems of poverty which are so dependent upon industrial maladjustment. But during twenty years, the Settlements have seen the charitable people, through their very knowledge of the poor, constantly approach nearer to those methods formerly designated as radical. The residents, so far from holding aloof from organized charity, find testimony, certainly in the National Conferences, that out of the most persistent and intelligent efforts to alleviate poverty will in all probability arise the most significant suggestions for eradicating poverty. In the hearing before a congressional committee for the establishment of a Children's Bureau, residents in American Settlements joined their fellow philanthropists in urging the need of this indispensable instrument for collecting and disseminating information which would make possible concerted intelligent action on behalf of children.

Mr. Howells has said that we are all so besotted with our novel reading that we have lost the power of seeing certain aspects of life with any sense of reality because we are continually looking for the possible romance. The description might apply to the earlier years of the American settlement, but certainly the later years are filled with discoveries in actual life as romantic as they are unexpected. If I may illustrate one of these romantic discoveries from my own experience, I would cite the indications of an internationalism as sturdy and virile as it is unprecedented which I have seen in our cosmopolitan neighborhood: when a South Italian Catholic is forced by the very exigencies of the situation to make friends with an Austrian Jew representing another nationality and another religion, both of which cut into all his most cherished prejudices, he finds it harder to utilize them a second time and gradually loses them. He thus modifies his provincialism, for if an old enemy working by his side has turned into a friend, almost anything may happen. When, therefore, I became identified with the peace movement both in its International and National Conventions, I hoped that this internationalism engendered in the immigrant quarters of American cities might be recognized as an effective instrument in the cause of peace. I first set it forth with some misgiving before the Convention held in Boston in 1904 and it is always a pleasure to recall the hearty assent given to it by Professor William James.

I have always objected to the phrase "sociological laboratory" applied to us, because Settlements should be something much more human and spontaneous than such a phrase connotes, and yet it is inevitable that the residents should know their own neighborhoods more thoroughly than any other, and that their experiences there should affect their convictions.

Years ago I was much entertained by a story told at the Chicago Woman's Club by one of its ablest members in the discussion following a paper of mine on "The Outgrowths of Toynbee Hall." She said that when she was a little girl playing in her mother's garden, she one day discovered a small toad who seemed to her very forlorn and lonely, although she did not in the least know how to comfort him, she reluctantly left him to his fate; later in the day, quite at the other end of the garden, she found a large toad, also apparently without family and friends. With a heart full of tender sympathy, she took a stick and by exercising infinite patience and some skill, she finally pushed the little toad through the entire length of the garden into the company of the big toad, when, to her inexpressible horror and surprise, the big toad opened his mouth and swallowed the little one. The moral of the tale was clear applied to people who lived "where they did not naturally belong," although I protested that was exactly what we wanted-to be swallowed and digested, to disappear into the bulk of the people.

Twenty years later I am willing to testify that something of the sort does take place after years of identification with an industrial community.

Chapter XIV
Civic Cooperation

One of the first lessons we learned at Hull-House was that private beneficence is totally inadequate to deal with the vast numbers of the city's disinherited. We also quickly came to realize that there are certain types of wretchedness from which every private philanthropy shrinks and which are cared for only in those wards of the county hospital provided for the wrecks of vicious living or in the city's isolation hospital for smallpox patients.

I have heard a broken-hearted mother exclaim when her erring daughter came home at last too broken and diseased to be taken into the family she had disgraced, "There is no place for her but the top floor of the County Hospital; they will have to take her there," and this only after every possible expedient had been tried or suggested. This aspect of governmental responsibility was unforgettably borne in upon me during the smallpox epidemic following the World's Fair, when one of the residents, Mrs. Kelley, as State Factory Inspector, was much concerned in discovering and destroying clothing which was being finished in houses containing unreported cases of smallpox. The deputy most successful in locating such cases lived at Hull-House during the epidemic because he did not wish to expose his own family. Another resident, Miss Lathrop, as a member of the State Board of Charities, went back and forth to the crowded pest house which had been hastily constructed on a stretch of prairie west of the city. As Hull-House was already so exposed, it seemed best for the special smallpox inspectors from the Board of Health to take their meals and change their clothing there before they went to their respective homes. All of these officials had accepted without question and as implicit in public office the obligation to carry on the dangerous and difficult undertakings for which private philanthropy is unfitted, as if the commonalty of compassion represented by the State was more comprehending than that of any individual group.

It was as early as our second winter on Halsted Street that one of the Hull-House residents received an appointment from the Cook County agent as a county visitor. She reported at the agency each morning, and all the cases within a radius of ten blocks from Hull-House were given to her for investigation. This gave her a legitimate opportunity for knowing the poorest people in the neighborhood and also for understanding the county method of outdoor relief. The commissioners were at first dubious of the value of such a visitor and predicted that a woman would be a perfect "coal chute" for giving away county supplies, but they gradually came to depend upon her suggestion and advice.

In 1893 this same resident, Miss Julia C. Lathrop, was appointed by the governor a member of the Illinois State Board of Charities. She served in this capacity for two consecutive terms and was later reappointed to a third term. Perhaps her most valuable contribution toward the enlargement and reorganization of the charitable institutions of the State came through her intimate knowledge of the beneficiaries, and her experience demonstrated that it is only through long residence among the poor that an official could have learned to view public institutions as she did, from the standpoint of the inmates rather than from that of the managers. Since that early day, residents of Hull-House have spent much time in working for the civil service methods of appointment for employees in the county and State institutions; for the establishment of State colonies for the care of epileptics; and for a dozen other enterprises which occupy that borderland between charitable effort and legislation. In this borderland we cooperate in many civic enterprises for I think we may claim that Hull-House has always held its activities lightly, ready to hand them over to whosoever would carry them on properly.

Miss Starr had early made a collection of framed photographs, largely of the paintings studied in her art class, which became the basis of a loan collection first used by the Hull-House students and later extended to the public schools. It may be fair to suggest that this effort was the nucleus of the Public School Art Society which was later formed in the city and of which Miss Starr was the first president.

In our first two summers we had maintained three baths in the basement of our own house for the use of the neighborhood, and they afforded some experience and argument for the erection of the first public bathhouse in Chicago, which was built on a neighboring street and opened under the city Board of Health. The lot upon which it was erected belonged to a friend of Hull-House who offered it to the city without rent, and this enabled the city to erect the first public bath from the small appropriation of ten thousand dollars. Great fear was expressed by the public authorities that the baths would not be used, and the old story of the bathtubs in model tenements which had been turned into coal bins was often quoted to us. We were supplied, however, with the incontrovertible argument that in our adjacent third square mile there were in 1892 but three bathtubs and that this fact was much complained of by many of the tenement-house dwellers. Our contention was justified by the immediate and overflowing use of the public baths, as we had before been sustained in the contention that an immigrant population would respond to opportunities for reading when the Public Library Board had established a branch reading room at Hull-House.

We also quickly discovered that nothing brought us so absolutely into comradeship with our neighbors as mutual and sustained effort such as the paving of a street, the closing of a gambling house, or the restoration of a veteran police sergeant.

Several of these earlier attempts at civic cooperation were undertaken in connection with the Hull-House Men's Club, which had been organized in the spring of 1893, had been incorporated under a State charter of its own, and had occupied a club room in the gymnasium building. This club obtained an early success in one of the political struggles in the ward and thus fastened upon itself a specious reputation for political power. It was at last so torn by the dissensions of two political factions which attempted to capture it that, although it is still an existing organization, it has never regained the prestige of its first five years. Its early political success came in a campaign Hull-House had instigated against a powerful alderman who has held office for more than twenty years in the nineteenth ward, and who, although notoriously corrupt, is still firmly intrenched among his constituents.

Hull-House has had to do with three campaigns organized against him. In the first one he was apparently only amused at our "Sunday School" effort and did little to oppose the election to the aldermanic office of a member of the Hull-House Men's Club who thus became his colleague in the city council. When Hull-House, however, made an effort in the following spring against the re-election of the alderman himself, we encountered the most determined and skillful opposition. In these campaigns we doubtless depended too much upon the idealistic appeal for we did not yet comprehend the element of reality always brought into the political struggle in such a neighborhood where politics deal so directly with getting a job and earning a living.

We soon discovered that approximately one out of every five voters in the nineteenth ward at that time held a job dependent upon the good will of the alderman. There were no civil service rules to interfere, and the unskilled voter swept the street and dug the sewer, as secure in his position as the more sophisticated voter who tended a bridge or occupied an office chair in the city hall. The alderman was even more fortunate in finding places with the franchise-seeking corporations; it took us some time to understand why so large a proportion of our neighbors were street-car employees and why we had such a large club composed solely of telephone girls. Our powerful alderman had various methods of entrenching himself. Many people were indebted to him for his kindly services in the police station and the justice courts, for in those days Irish constituents easily broke the peace, and before the establishment of the Juvenile Court, boys were arrested for very trivial offenses; added to these were hundreds of constituents indebted to him for personal kindness, from the peddler who received a free license to the businessman who had a railroad pass to New York. Our third campaign against him, when we succeeded in making a serious impression upon his majority, evoked from his henchmen the same sort of hostility which a striker so inevitably feels against the man who would take his job, even sharpened by the sense that the movement for reform came from an alien source.

Another result of the campaign was an expectation on the part of our new political friends that Hull-House would perform like offices for them, and there resulted endless confusion and misunderstanding because in many cases we could not even attempt to do what the alderman constantly did with a right good will. When he protected a law breaker from the legal consequences of his act, his kindness appeared, not only to himself but to all beholders, like the deed of a powerful and kindly statesman. When Hull-House on the other hand insisted that a law must be enforced, it could but appear like the persecution of the offender. We were certainly not anxious for consistency nor for individual achievement, but in a desire to foster a higher political morality and not to lower our standards, we constantly clashed with the existing political code. We also unwittingly stumbled upon a powerful combination of which our alderman was the political head, with its banking, its ecclesiastical, and its journalistic representatives, and as we followed up the clue and naively told all we discovered, we of course laid the foundations for opposition which has manifested itself in many forms; the most striking expression of it was an attack upon Hull-House lasting through weeks and months by a Chicago daily newspaper which has since ceased publication.

During the third campaign I received many anonymous letters-those from the men often obscene, those from the women revealing that curious connection between prostitution and the lowest type of politics which every city tries in vain to hide. I had offers from the men in the city prison to vote properly if released; various communications from lodging-house keepers as to the prices of the vote they were ready to deliver; everywhere appeared that animosity which is evoked only when a man feels that his means of livelihood is threatened.

As I look back, I am reminded of the state of mind of Kipling's newspapermen who witnessed a volcanic eruption at sea, in which unbelievable deep-sea creatures were expelled to the surface, among them an enormous white serpent, blind and smelling of musk, whose death throes thrashed the sea into a fury. With professional instinct unimpaired, the journalists carefully observed the uncanny creature never designed for the eyes of men; but a few days later, when they found themselves in a comfortable second-class carriage, traveling from Southampton to London between trim hedgerows and smug English villages, they concluded that the experience was too sensational to be put before the British public, and it became improbable even to themselves.

Many subsequent years of living in kindly neighborhood fashion with the people of the nineteenth ward has produced upon my memory the soothing effect of the second-class railroad carriage and many of these political experiences have not only become remote but already seem improbable. On the other hand, these campaigns were not without their rewards; one of them was a quickened friendship both with the more substantial citizens in the ward and with a group of fine young voters whose devotion to Hull-House has never since failed; another was a sense of identification with public-spirited men throughout the city who contributed money and time to what they considered a gallant effort against political corruption. I remember a young professor from the University of Chicago who with his wife came to live at Hull-House, traveling the long distance every day throughout the autumn and winter that he might qualify as a nineteenth-ward voter in the spring campaign. He served as a watcher at the polls and it was but a poor reward for his devotion that he was literally set upon and beaten up, for in those good old days such things frequently occurred. Many another case of devotion to our standard so recklessly raised might be cited, but perhaps more valuable than any of these was the sense of identification we obtained with the rest of Chicago.

So far as a Settlement can discern and bring to local consciousness neighborhood needs which are common needs, and can give vigorous help to the municipal measures through which such needs shall be met, it fulfills its most valuable function. To illustrate from our first effort to improve the street paving in the vicinity, we found that when we had secured the consent of the majority of the property owners on a given street for a new paving, the alderman checked the entire plan through his kindly service to one man who had appealed to him to keep the assessments down. The street long remained a shocking mass of wet, dilapidated cedar blocks, where children were sometimes mired as they floated a surviving block in the water which speedily filled the holes whence other blocks had been extracted for fuel. And yet when we were able to demonstrate that the street paving had thus been reduced into cedar pulp by the heavily loaded wagons of an adjacent factory, that the expense of its repaving should be borne from a general fund and not by the poor property owners, we found that we could all unite in advocating reform in the method of repaving assessments, and the alderman himself was obliged to come into such a popular movement. The Nineteenth Ward Improvement Association which met at Hull-House during two winters, was the first body of citizens able to make a real impression upon the local paving situation. They secured an expert to watch the paving as it went down to be sure that their half of the paving money was well expended. In the belief that property values would be thus enhanced, the common aim brought together the more prosperous people of the vicinity, somewhat as the Hull-House Cooperative Coal Association brought together the poorer ones.

I remember that during the second campaign against our alderman, Governor Pingree of Michigan came to visit at Hull-House. He said that the stronghold of such a man was not the place in which to start municipal regeneration; that good aldermen should be elected from the promising wards first, until a majority of honest men in the city council should make politics unprofitable for corrupt men. We replied that it was difficult to divide Chicago into good and bad wards, but that a new organization called the Municipal Voters' League was attempting to give to the well-meaning voter in each ward throughout the city accurate information concerning the candidates and their relation, past and present, to vital issues. One of our trustees who was most active in inaugurating this League always said that his nineteenth-ward experience had convinced him of the unity of city politics, and that he constantly used our campaign as a challenge to the unaroused citizens living in wards less conspicuously corrupt.

Certainly the need for civic cooperation was obvious in many directions, and in none more strikingly than in that organized effort which must be carried on unceasingly if young people are to be protected from the darker and coarser dangers of the city. The cooperation between Hull-House and the Juvenile Protective Association came about gradually, and it seems now almost inevitably. From our earliest days we saw many boys constantly arrested, and I had a number of most enlightening experiences in the police station with an Irish lad whose mother upon her deathbed had begged me "to look after him." We were distressed by the gangs of very little boys who would sally forth with an enterprising leader in search of old brass and iron, sometimes breaking into empty houses for the sake of the faucets or lead pipe which they would sell for a good price to a junk dealer. With the money thus obtained they would buy cigarettes and beer or even candy, which could be conspicuously consumed in the alleys where they might enjoy the excitement of being seen and suspected by the "coppers." From the third year of Hull-House, one of the residents held a semiofficial position in the nearest police station; at least, the sergeant agreed to give her provisional charge of every boy and girl under arrest for a trivial offense.

Mrs. Stevens, who performed this work for several years, became the first probation officer of the Juvenile Court when it was established in Cook County in 1899. She was the sole probation officer at first, but at the time of her death, which occurred at Hull-House in 1900, she was the senior officer of a corps of six. Her entire experience had fitted her to deal wisely with wayward children. She had gone into a New England cotton mill at the age of thirteen, where she had promptly lost the index finger of her right hand, through "carelessness" she was told, and no one then seemed to understand that freedom from care was the prerogative of childhood. Later she became a typesetter and was one of the first women in America to become a member of the typographical union, retaining her "card" through all the later years of editorial work. As the Juvenile Court developed, the committee of public-spirited citizens who first supplied only Mrs. Stevens' salary later maintained a corps of twenty-two such officers; several of these were Hull-House residents who brought to the house for many years a sad little procession of children struggling against all sorts of handicaps. When legislation was secured which placed the probation officers upon the payroll of the county, it was a challenge to the efficiency of the civil service method of appointment to obtain by examination men and women fitted for this delicate human task. As one of five people asked by the civil service commission to conduct this first examination for probation officers, I became convinced that we were but at the beginning of the nonpolitical method of selecting public servants, but even stiff and unbending as the examination may be, it is still our hope of political salvation.

In 1907, the Juvenile Court was housed in a model court building of its own, containing a detention home and equipped with a competent staff. The committee of citizens largely responsible for this result thereupon turned their attention to the conditions which the records of the court indicated had led to the alarming amount of juvenile delinquency and crime. They organized the Juvenile Protective Association, whose twenty-two officers meet weekly at Hull-House with their executive committee to report what they have found and to discuss city conditions affecting the lives of children and young people.

The association discovers that there are certain temptations into which children so habitually fall that it is evident that the average child cannot withstand them. An overwhelming mass of data is accumulated showing the need of enforcing existing legislation and of securing new legislation, but it also indicates a hundred other directions in which the young people who so gaily walk our streets, often to their own destruction, need safeguarding and protection.

The effort of the association to treat the youth of the city with consideration and understanding has rallied the most unexpected forces to its standard. Quite as the basic needs of life are supplied solely by those who make money out of the business, so the modern city has assumed that the craving for pleasure must be ministered to only by the sordid. This assumption, however, in a large measure broke down as soon as the Juvenile Protective Association courageously put it to the test. After persistent prosecutions, but also after many friendly interviews, the Druggists' Association itself prosecutes those of its members who sell indecent postal cards; the Saloon Keepers' Protective Association not only declines to protect members who sell liquor to minors, but now takes drastic action to prevent such sales; the Retail Grocers' Association forbids the selling of tobacco to minors; the Association of Department Store Managers not only increased the vigilance in their waiting rooms by supplying more matrons, but as a body they have become regular contributors to the association; the special watchmen in all the railroad yards agree not to arrest trespassing boys but to report them to the association; the firms manufacturing moving picture films not only submit their films to a volunteer inspection committee, but ask for suggestions in regard to new matter; and the Five-Cent Theaters arrange for "stunts" which shall deal with the subject of public health and morals, when the lecturers provided are entertaining as well as instructive.

It is not difficult to arouse the impulse of protection for the young, which would doubtless dictate the daily acts of many a bartender and poolroom keeper if they could only indulge it without giving their rivals an advantage. When this difficulty is removed by an even-handed enforcement of the law, that simple kindliness which the innocent always evoke goes from one to another like a slowly spreading flame of good will. Doubtless the most rewarding experience in any such undertaking as that of the Juvenile Protective Association is the warm and intelligent cooperation coming from unexpected sources-official and commercial as well as philanthropic. Upon the suggestion of the association, social centers have been opened in various parts of the city, disused buildings turned into recreation rooms, vacant lots made into gardens, hiking parties organized for country excursions, bathing beaches established on the lake front, and public schools opened for social purposes. Through the efforts of public-spirited citizens a medical clinic and a Psychopathic Institute have become associated with the Juvenile Court of Chicago, in addition to which an exhaustive study of court-records has been completed. To this carefully collected data concerning the abnormal child, the Juvenile Protective Association hopes in time to add knowledge of the normal child who lives under the most adverse city conditions.

It was not without hope that I might be able to forward in the public school system the solution of some of these problems of delinquency so dependent upon truancy and ill-adapted education that I became a member of the Chicago Board of Education in July, 1905. It is impossible to write of the situation as it became dramatized in half a dozen strong personalities, but the entire experience was so illuminating as to the difficulties and limitations of democratic government that it would be unfair in a chapter on Civic Cooperation not to attempt an outline.

Even the briefest statement, however, necessitates a review of the preceding few years. For a decade the Chicago school teachers, or rather a majority of them who were organized into the Teachers' Federation, had been engaged in a conflict with the Board of Education both for more adequate salaries and for more self-direction in the conduct of the schools. In pursuance of the first object, they had attacked the tax dodger along the entire line of his defense, from the curbstone to the Supreme Court. They began with an intricate investigation which uncovered the fact that in 1899, $235,000,000 of value of public utility corporations paid nothing in taxes. The Teachers' Federation brought a suit which was prosecuted through the Supreme Court of Illinois and resulted in an order entered against the State Board of Equalization, demanding that it tax the corporations mentioned in the bill. In spite of the fact that the defendant companies sought federal aid and obtained an order which restrained the payment of a portion of the tax, each year since 1900, the Chicago Board of Education has benefited to the extent of more than a quarter of a million dollars. Although this result had been attained through the unaided efforts of the teachers, to their surprise and indignation their salaries were not increased. The Teachers' Federation, therefore, brought a suit against the Board of Education for the advance which had been promised them three years earlier but never paid. The decision of the lower court was in their favor, but the Board of Education appealed the case, and this was the situation when the seven new members appointed by Mayor Dunne in 1905 took their seats. The conservative public suspected that these new members were merely representatives of the Teachers' Federation. This opinion was founded upon the fact that Judge Dunne had rendered a favorable decision in the teachers' suit and that the teachers had been very active in the campaign which had resulted in his election as mayor of the city. It seemed obvious that the teachers had entered into politics for the sake of securing their own representatives on the Board of Education. These suspicions were, of course, only confirmed when the new board voted to withdraw the suit of their predecessors from the Appellate Court and to act upon the decision of the lower court. The teachers, on the other hand, defended their long effort in the courts, the State Board of Equalization, and the Legislature against the charge of "dragging the schools into politics," and declared that the exposure of the indifference and cupidity of the politicians was a well-deserved rebuke, and that it was the politicians who had brought the schools to the verge of financial ruin; they further insisted that the levy and collection of taxes, tenure of office, and pensions to civil servants in Chicago were all entangled with the traction situation, which in their minds at least had come to be an example of the struggle between the democratic and plutocratic administration of city affairs. The new appointees to the School Board represented no concerted policy of any kind, but were for the most part adherents to the new education. The teachers, confident that their cause was identical with the principles advocated by such educators as Colonel Parker, were therefore sure that the plans of the "new education" members would of necessity coincide with the plans of the Teachers' Federation. In one sense the situation was an epitome of Mayor Dunne's entire administration, which was founded upon the belief that if those citizens representing social ideals and reform principles were but appointed to office, public welfare must be established.

During my tenure of office I many times talked to the officers of the Teachers' Federation, but I was seldom able to follow their suggestions and, although I gladly cooperated in their plans for a better pension system and other matters, only once did I try to influence the policy of the Federation. When the withheld salaries were finally paid to the representatives of the Federation who had brought suit and were divided among the members who had suffered both financially and professionally during this long legal struggle, I was most anxious that the division should voluntarily be extended to all of the teachers who had experienced a loss of salary although they were not members of the Federation. It seemed to me a striking opportunity to refute the charge that the Federation was self-seeking and to put the whole long effort in the minds of the public, exactly where it belonged, as one of devoted public service. But it was doubtless much easier for me to urge this altruistic policy than it was for those who had borne the heat and burden of the day to act upon it.

The second object of the Teachers' Federation also entailed much stress and storm. At the time of the financial stringency, and largely as a result of it, the Board had made the first substantial advance in a teacher's salary dependent upon a so-called promotional examination, half of which was upon academic subjects entailing a long and severe preparation. The teachers resented this upon two lines of argument: first, that the scheme was unprofessional in that the teacher was advanced on her capacity as a student rather than on her professional ability; and, second, that it added an intolerable and unnecessary burden to her already overfull day. The administration, on the other hand, contended with much justice that there was a constant danger in a great public school system that teachers lose pliancy and the open mind, and that many of them had obviously grown mechanical and indifferent. The conservative public approved the promotional examinations as the symbol of an advancing educational standard, and their sympathy with the superintendent was increased because they continually resented the affiliation of the Teachers' Federation with the Chicago Federation of Labor, which had taken place several years before the election of Mayor Dunne on his traction platform.

This much talked of affiliation between the teachers and the trades-unionists had been, at least in the first instance, but one more tactic in the long struggle against the tax-dodging corporations. The Teachers' Federation had won in their first skirmish against that public indifference which is generated in the accumulation of wealth and which has for its nucleus successful commercial men. When they found themselves in need of further legislation to keep the offending corporations under control, they naturally turned for political influence and votes to the organization representing workingmen. The affiliation had none of the sinister meaning so often attached to it. The Teachers' Federation never obtained a charter from the American Federation of Labor, and its main interest always centered in the legislative committee.

And yet this statement of the difference between the majority of the grade-school teachers and the Chicago School Board is totally inadequate, for the difficulties were stubborn and lay far back in the long effort of public school administration in America to free itself from the rule and exploitation of politics. In every city for many years the politician had secured positions for his friends as teachers and janitors; he had received a rake-off in the contract for every new building or coal supply or adoption of school-books. In the long struggle against this political corruption, the one remedy continually advocated was the transfer of authority in all educational matters from the Board to the superintendent. The one cure for "pull" and corruption was the authority of the "expert." The rules and records of the Chicago Board of Education are full of relics of this long struggle honestly waged by honest men, who unfortunately became content with the ideals of an "efficient business administration." These businessmen established an able superintendent with a large salary, with his tenure of office secured by State law so that he would not be disturbed by the wrath of the balked politician. They instituted impersonal examinations for the teachers both as to entrance into the system and promotion, and they proceeded "to hold the superintendent responsible" for smooth-running schools. All this, however, dangerously approximated the commercialistic ideal of high salaries only for the management with the final test of a small expense account and a large output.

In this long struggle for a quarter of a century to free the public schools from political interference, in Chicago at least, the high wall of defense erected around the school system in order "to keep the rascals out" unfortunately so restricted the teachers inside the system that they had no space in which to move about freely and the more adventurous of them fairly panted for light and air. Any attempt to lower the wall for the sake of the teachers within was regarded as giving an opportunity to the politicians without, and they were often openly accused, with a show of truth, of being in league with each other. Whenever the Dunne members of the Board attempted to secure more liberty for the teachers, we were warned by tales of former difficulties with the politicians, and it seemed impossible that the struggle so long the focus of attention should recede into the dullness of the achieved and allow the energy of the Board to be free for new effort.

The whole situation between the superintendent supported by a majority of the Board and the Teachers' Federation had become an epitome of the struggle between efficiency and democracy; on one side a well-intentioned expression of the bureaucracy necessary in a large system but which under pressure had become unnecessarily self-assertive, and on the other side a fairly militant demand for self-government made in the name of freedom. Both sides inevitably exaggerated the difficulties of the situation, and both felt that they were standing by important principles.

I certainly played a most inglorious part in this unnecessary conflict; I was chairman of the School Management Committee during one year when a majority of the members seemed to me exasperatingly conservative, and during another year when they were frustratingly radical, and I was of course highly unsatisfactory to both. Certainly a plan to retain the undoubted benefit of required study for teachers in such wise as to lessen its burden, and various schemes devised to shift the emphasis from scholarship to professional work, were mostly impatiently repudiated by the Teachers' Federation, and when one badly mutilated plan finally passed the Board, it was most reluctantly administered by the superintendent.

I at least became convinced that partisans would never tolerate the use of stepping-stones. They are much too impatient to look on while their beloved scheme is unstably balanced, and they would rather see it tumble into the stream at once than to have it brought to dry land in any such half-hearted fashion. Before my School Board experience, I thought that life had taught me at least one hard-earned lesson, that existing arrangements and the hoped for improvements must be mediated and reconciled to each other, that the new must be dovetailed into the old as it were, if it were to endure; but on the School Board I discerned that all such efforts were looked upon as compromising and unworthy, by both partisans. In the general disorder and public excitement resulting from the illegal dismissal of a majority of the "Dunne" board and their reinstatement by a court decision, I found myself belonging to neither party. During the months following the upheaval and the loss of my most vigorous colleagues, under the regime of men representing the leading Commercial Club of the city who honestly believed that they were rescuing the schools from a condition of chaos, I saw one beloved measure after another withdrawn. Although the new president scrupulously gave me the floor in the defense of each, it was impossible to consider them upon their merits in the lurid light which at the moment enveloped all the plans of the "uplifters." Thus the building of smaller schoolrooms, such as in New York mechanically avoid overcrowding, the extension of the truant rooms so successfully inaugurated, the multiplication of school playgrounds, and many another cherished plan was thrown out or at least indefinitely postponed.

The final discrediting of Mayor Dunne's appointees to the School Board affords a very interesting study in social psychology; the newspapers had so constantly reflected and intensified the ideals of a business Board, and had so persistently ridiculed various administration plans for the municipal ownership of street railways, that from the beginning any attempt the new Board made to discuss educational matters only excited their derision and contempt. Some of these discussions were lengthy and disorderly and deserved the discipline of ridicule, but others which were well conducted and in which educational problems were seriously set forth by men of authority were ridiculed quite as sharply. I recall the surprise and indignation of a University professor who had consented to speak at a meeting arranged in the Board rooms, when next morning his nonpartisan and careful disquisition had been twisted into the most arrant uplift nonsense and so connected with a fake newspaper report of a trial marriage address delivered, not by himself, but by a colleague, that a leading clergyman of the city, having read the newspaper account, felt impelled to preach a sermon, calling upon all decent people to rally against the doctrines which were being taught to the children by an immoral School Board. As the bewildered professor had lectured in response to my invitation, I endeavored to find the animus of the complication, but neither from editor in chief nor from the reporter could I discover anything more sinister than that the public expected a good story out of these School Board "talk fests," and that any man who even momentarily allied himself with a radical administration must expect to be ridiculed by those papers which considered the traction policy of the administration both foolish and dangerous.

As I myself was treated with uniform courtesy by the leading papers, I may perhaps here record my discouragement over this complicated difficulty of open discussion, for democratic government is founded upon the assumption that differing policies shall be freely discussed and that each party shall have an opportunity for at least a partisan presentation of its contentions. This attitude of the newspapers was doubtless intensified because the Dunne School Board had instituted a lawsuit challenging the validity of the lease for the school ground occupied by a newspaper building. This suit has since been decided in favor of the newspaper, and it may be that in their resentment they felt justified in doing everything possible to minimize the prosecuting School Board. I am, however, inclined to think that the newspapers but reflected an opinion honestly held by many people, and that their constant and partisan presentation of this opinion clearly demonstrates one of the greatest difficulties of governmental administration in a city grown too large for verbal discussions of public affairs.

It is difficult to close this chapter without a reference to the efforts made in Chicago to secure the municipal franchise for women. During two long periods of agitation for a new city charter, a representative body of women appealed to the public, to the charter convention, and to the Illinois legislature for this very reasonable provision. During the campaign when I acted as chairman of the federation of a hundred women's organizations, nothing impressed me so forcibly as the fact that the response came from bodies of women representing the most varied traditions. We were joined by a church society of hundreds of Lutheran women, because Scandinavian women had exercised the municipal franchise since the seventeenth century and had found American cities strangely conservative; by organizations of working women who had keenly felt the need of the municipal franchise in order to secure for their workshops the most rudimentary sanitation and the consideration which the vote alone obtains for workingmen; by federations of mothers' meetings, who were interested in clean milk and the extension of kindergartens; by property-owning women, who had been powerless to protest against unjust taxation; by organizations of professional women, of university students, and of collegiate alumnae; and by women's clubs interested in municipal reforms. There was a complete absence of the traditional women's rights clamor, but much impressive testimony from busy and useful women that they had reached the place where they needed the franchise in order to carry on their own affairs. A striking witness as to the need of the ballot, even for the women who are restricted to the most primitive and traditional activities, occurred when some Russian women waited upon me to ask whether under the new charter they could vote for covered markets and so get rid of the shocking Chicago grime upon all their food; and when some neighboring Italian women sent me word that they would certainly vote for public washhouses if they ever had the chance to vote at all. It was all so human, so spontaneous, and so direct that it really seemed as if the time must be ripe for political expression of that public concern on the part of women which had so long been forced to seek indirection. None of these busy women wished to take the place of men nor to influence them in the direction of men's affairs, but they did seek an opportunity to cooperate directly in civic life through the use of the ballot in regard to their own affairs.

A Municipal Museum which was established in the Chicago public library building several years ago, largely through the activity of a group of women who had served as jurors in the departments of social economy, of education, and of sanitation in the World's Fair at St. Louis, showed nothing more clearly than that it is impossible to divide any of these departments from the political life of the modern city which is constantly forced to enlarge the boundary of its activity.

Chapter XV
The Value of Social Clubs

From the early days at Hull-House, social clubs composed of English speaking American born young people grew apace. So eager were they for social life that no mistakes in management could drive them away. I remember one enthusiastic leader who read aloud to a club a translation of "Antigone," which she had selected because she believed that the great themes of the Greek poets were best suited to young people. She came into the club room one evening in time to hear the president call the restive members to order with the statement, "You might just as well keep quiet for she is bound to finish it, and the quicker she gets to reading, the longer time we'll have for dancing." And yet the same club leader had the pleasure of lending four copies of the drama to four of the members, and one young man almost literally committed the entire play to memory.

On the whole we were much impressed by the great desire for self-improvement, for study and debate, exhibited by many of the young men. This very tendency, in fact, brought one of the most promising of our earlier clubs to an untimely end. The young men in the club, twenty in number, had grown much irritated by the frivolity of the girls during their long debates, and had finally proposed that three of the most "frivolous" be expelled. Pending a final vote, the three culprits appealed to certain of their friends who were members of the Hull-House Men's Club, between whom and the debating young men the incident became the cause of a quarrel so bitter that at length it led to a shooting. Fortunately the shot missed fire, or it may have been true that it was "only intended for a scare," but at any rate, we were all thoroughly frightened by this manifestation of the hot blood which the defense of woman has so often evoked. After many efforts to bring about a reconciliation, the debating club of twenty young men and the seventeen young women, who either were or pretended to be sober minded, rented a hall a mile west of Hull-House severing their connection with us because their ambitious and right-minded efforts had been unappreciated, basing this on the ground that we had not urged the expulsion of the so-called "tough" members of the Men's Club, who had been involved in the difficulty. The seceding club invited me to the first meeting in their new quarters that I might present to them my version of the situation and set forth the incident from the standpoint of Hull-House. The discussion I had with the young people that evening has always remained with me as one of the moments of illumination which life in a Settlement so often affords. In response to my position that a desire to avoid all that was "tough" meant to walk only in the paths of smug self-seeking and personal improvement leading straight into the pit of self-righteousness and petty achievement and was exactly what the Settlement did not stand for, they contended with much justice that ambitious young people were obliged for their own reputation, if not for their own morals, to avoid all connection with that which bordered on the tough, and that it was quite another matter for the Hull-House residents who could afford a more generous judgment. It was in vain I urged that life teaches us nothing more inevitably than that right and wrong are most confusingly confounded; that the blackest wrong may be within our own motives, and that at the best, right will not dazzle us by its radiant shining and can only be found by exerting patience and discrimination. They still maintained their wholesome bourgeois position, which I am now quite ready to admit was most reasonable.

Of course there were many disappointments connected with these clubs when the rewards of political and commercial life easily drew the members away from the principles advocated in club meetings. One of the young men who had been a shining light in the advocacy of municipal reform deserted in the middle of a reform campaign because he had been offered a lucrative office in the city hall; another even after a course of lectures on business morality, "worked" the club itself to secure orders for custom-made clothing from samples of cloth he displayed, although the orders were filled by ready-made suits slightly refitted and delivered at double their original price. But nevertheless, there was much to cheer us as we gradually became acquainted with the daily living of the vigorous young men and women who filled to overflowing all the social clubs.

We have been much impressed during our twenty years, by the ready adaptation of city young people to the prosperity arising from their own increased wages or from the commercial success of their families. This quick adaptability is the great gift of the city child, his one reward for the hurried changing life which he has always led. The working girl has a distinct advantage in the task of transforming her whole family into the ways and connections of the prosperous when she works down town and becomes conversant with the manners and conditions of a cosmopolitan community. Therefore having lived in a Settlement twenty years, I see scores of young people who have successfully established themselves in life, and in my travels in the city and outside, I am constantly cheered by greetings from the rising young lawyer, the scholarly rabbi, the successful teacher, the prosperous young matron buying clothes for blooming children. "Don't you remember me? I used to belong to a Hull-House club." I once asked one of these young people, a man who held a good position on a Chicago daily, what special thing Hull-House had meant to him, and he promptly replied, "It was the first house I had ever been in where books and magazines just lay around as if there were plenty of them in the world. Don't you remember how much I used to read at that little round table at the back of the library? To have people regard reading as a reasonable occupation changed the whole aspect of life to me and I began to have confidence in what I could do."

Among the young men of the social clubs a large proportion of the Jewish ones at least obtain the advantages of a higher education. The parents make every sacrifice to help them through the high school after which the young men attend universities and professional schools, largely through their own efforts. From time to time they come back to us with their honors thick upon them; I remember one who returned with the prize in oratory from a contest between several western State universities, proudly testifying that he had obtained his confidence in our Henry Clay Club; another came back with a degree from Harvard University saying that he had made up his mind to go there the summer I read Royce's "Aspects of Modern Philosophy" with a group of young men who had challenged my scathing remark that Herbert Spencer was not the only man who had ventured a solution of the riddles of the universe. Occasionally one of these learned young folk does not like to be reminded he once lived in our vicinity, but that happens rarely, and for the most part they are loyal to us in much the same spirit as they are to their own families and traditions. Sometimes they go further and tell us that the standards of tastes and code of manners which Hull-House has enabled them to form, have made a very great difference in their perceptions and estimates of the larger world as well as in their own reception there. Five out of one club of twenty-five young men who had held together for eleven years, entered the University of Chicago but although the rest of the Club called them the "intellectuals," the old friendships still held.

In addition to these rising young people given to debate and dramatics, and to the members of the public school alumni associations which meet in our rooms, there are hundreds of others who for years have come to Hull-House frankly in search of that pleasure and recreation which all young things crave and which those who have spent long hours in a factory or shop demand as a right. For these young people all sorts of pleasure clubs have been cherished, and large dancing classes have been organized. One supreme gayety has come to be an annual event of such importance that it is talked of from year to year. For six weeks before St. Patrick's day, a small group of residents put their best powers of invention and construction into preparation for a cotillion which is like a pageant in its gayety and vigor. The parents sit in the gallery, and the mothers appreciate more than anyone else perhaps, the value of this ball to which an invitation is so highly prized; although their standards of manners may differ widely from the conventional, they know full well when the companionship of the young people is safe and unsullied.

As an illustration of this difference in standard, I may instance an early Hull-House picnic arranged by a club of young people, who found at the last moment that the club director could not go and accepted the offer of the mother of one of the club members to take charge of them.

When they trooped back in the evening, tired and happy, they displayed a photograph of the group wherein each man's arm was carefully placed about a girl; no feminine waist lacked an arm save that of the proud chaperon, who sat in the middle smiling upon all. Seeing that the photograph somewhat surprised us, the chaperon stoutly explained, "This may look queer to you, but there wasn't one thing about that picnic that wasn't nice," and her statement was a perfectly truthful one.

Although more conventional customs are carefully enforced at our many parties and festivities, and while the dancing classes are as highly prized for the opportunity they afford for enforcing standards as for their ostensible aim, the residents at Hull-House, in their efforts to provide opportunities for clean recreation, receive the most valued help from the experienced wisdom of the older women of the neighborhood. Bowen Hall is constantly used for dancing parties with soft drinks established in its foyer. The parties given by the Hull-House clubs are by invitation and the young people themselves carefully maintain their standard of entrance so that the most cautious mother may feel safe when her daughter goes to one of our parties. No club festivity is permitted without the presence of a director; no young man under the influence of liquor is allowed; certain types of dancing often innocently started are strictly prohibited; and above all, early closing is insisted upon. This standardizing of pleasure has always seemed an obligation to the residents of Hull-House, but we are, I hope, saved from that priggishness which young people so heartily resent, by the Mardi Gras dance and other festivities which the residents themselves arrange and successfully carry out.

In spite of our belief that the standards of a ball may be almost as valuable to those without as to those within, the residents are constantly concerned for those many young people in the neighborhood who are too hedonistic to submit to the discipline of a dancing class or even to the claim of a pleasure club, but who go about in freebooter fashion to find pleasure wherever it may be cheaply on sale.

Such young people, well meaning but impatient of control, become the easy victims of the worst type of public dance halls, and of even darker places, whose purposes are hidden under music and dancing. We were thoroughly frightened when we learned that during the year which ended last December, more than twenty-five thousand young people under the age of twenty-five passed through the Juvenile and Municipal Courts of Chicago-approximately one out of every eighty of the entire population, or one out of every fifty-two of those under twenty-five years of age. One's heart aches for these young people caught by the outside glitter of city gayety, who make such a feverish attempt to snatch it for themselves. The young people in our clubs are comparatively safe, but many instances come to the knowledge of Hull-House residents which make us long for the time when the city, through more small parks, municipal gymnasiums, and schoolrooms open for recreation, can guard from disaster these young people who walk so carelessly on the edge of the pit.

The heedless girls believe that if they lived in big houses and possessed pianos and jewelry, the coveted social life would come to them. I know a Bohemian girl who surreptitiously saved her overtime wages until she had enough money to hire for a week a room with a piano in it where young men might come to call, as they could not do in her crowded untidy home. Of course she had no way of knowing the sort of young men who quickly discover an unprotected girl.

Another girl of American parentage who had come to Chicago to seek her fortune, found at the end of a year that sorting shipping receipts in a dark corner of a warehouse not only failed to accumulate riches but did not even bring the "attentions" which her quiet country home afforded. By dint of long sacrifice she had saved fifteen dollars; with five she bought an imitation sapphire necklace, and the balance she changed into a ten dollar bill. The evening her pathetic little snare was set, she walked home with one of the clerks in the establishment, told him that she had come into a fortune, and was obliged to wear the heirloom necklace to insure its safety, permitted him to see that she carried ten dollars in her glove for carfare, and conducted him to a handsome Prairie Avenue residence. There she gayly bade him good-by and ran up the steps shutting herself in the vestibule from which she did not emerge until the dazzled and bewildered young man had vanished down the street.

Then there is the ever-recurring difficulty about dress; the insistence of the young to be gayly bedecked to the utter consternation of the hardworking parents who are paying for a house and lot. The Polish girl who stole five dollars from her employer's till with which to buy a white dress for a church picnic was turned away from home by her indignant father who replaced the money to save the family honor, but would harbor no "thief" in a household of growing children who, in spite of the sister's revolt, continued to be dressed in dark heavy clothes through all the hot summer. There are a multitude of working girls who for hours carry hair ribbons and jewelry in their pockets or stockings, for they can wear them only during the journey to and from work. Sometimes this desire to taste pleasure, to escape into a world of congenial companionship takes more elaborate forms and often ends disastrously. I recall a charming young girl, the oldest daughter of a respectable German family, whom I first saw one spring afternoon issuing from a tall factory. She wore a blue print gown which so deepened the blue of her eyes that Wordsworth's line fairly sung itself:

The pliant harebell swinging in the breeze
On some gray rock.

I was grimly reminded of that moment a year later when I heard the tale of this seventeen-year-old girl, who had worked steadily in the same factory for four years before she resolved "to see life." In order not to arouse her parents' suspicions, she borrowed thirty dollars from one of those loan sharks who require no security from a pretty girl, so that she might start from home every morning as if to go to work. For three weeks she spent the first part of each dearly bought day in a department store where she lunched and unfortunately made some dubious acquaintances; in the afternoon she established herself in a theater and sat contentedly hour after hour watching the endless vaudeville until the usual time for returning home. At the end of each week she gave her parents her usual wage, but when her thirty dollars was exhausted it seemed unendurable that she should return to the monotony of the factory. In the light of her newly acquired experience she had learned that possibility which the city ever holds open to the restless girl.

That more such girls do not come to grief is due to those mothers who understand the insatiable demand for a good time, and if all of the mothers did understand, those pathetic statistics which show that four fifths of all prostitutes are under twenty years of age would be marvelously changed. We are told that "the will to live" is aroused in each baby by his mother's irresistible desire to play with him, the physiological value of joy that a child is born, and that the high death rate in institutions is increased by "the discontented babies" whom no one persuades into living. Something of the same sort is necessary in that second birth at adolescence. The young people need affection and understanding each one for himself, if they are to be induced to live in an inheritance of decorum and safety and to understand the foundations upon which this orderly world rests. No one comprehends their needs so sympathetically as those mothers who iron the flimsy starched finery of their grown-up daughters late into the night, and who pay for a red velvet parlor set on the installment plan, although the younger children may sadly need new shoes. These mothers apparently understand the sharp demand for social pleasure and do their best to respond to it, although at the same time they constantly minister to all the physical needs of an exigent family of little children. We often come to a realization of the truth of Walt Whitman's statement, that one of the surest sources of wisdom is the mother of a large family.

It is but natural, perhaps, that the members of the Hull-House Woman's Club whose prosperity has given them some leisure and a chance to remove their own families to neighborhoods less full of temptations, should have offered their assistance in our attempt to provide recreation for these restless young people. In many instances their experience in the club itself has enabled them to perceive these needs. One day a Juvenile Court officer told me that a woman's club member, who has a large family of her own and one boy sufficiently difficult, had undertaken to care for a ward of the Juvenile Court who lived only a block from her house, and that she had kept him in the path of rectitude for six months. In reply to my congratulations upon this successful bit of reform to the club woman herself, she said that she was quite ashamed that she had not undertaken the task earlier for she had for years known the boy's mother who scrubbed a downtown office building, leaving home every evening at five and returning at eleven during the very time the boy could most easily find opportunities for wrongdoing. She said that her obligation toward this boy had not occurred to her until one day when the club members were making pillowcases for the Detention Home of the Juvenile Court, it suddenly seemed perfectly obvious that her share in the salvation of wayward children was to care for this particular boy and she had asked the Juvenile Court officer to commit him to her. She invited the boy to her house to supper every day that she might know just where he was at the crucial moment of twilight, and she adroitly managed to keep him under her own roof for the evening if she did not approve of the plans he had made. She concluded with the remark that it was queer that the sight of the boy himself hadn't appealed to her, but that the suggestion had come to her in such a roundabout way.

She was, of course, reflecting upon a common trait in human nature, —that we much more easily see the duty at hand when we see it in relation to the social duty of which it is a part. When she knew that an effort was being made throughout all the large cities in the United States to reclaim the wayward boy, to provide him with reasonable amusement, to give him his chance for growth and development, and when she became ready to take her share in that movement, she suddenly saw the concrete case which she had not recognized before.

We are slowly learning that social advance depends quite as much upon an increase in moral sensibility as it does upon a sense of duty, and of this one could cite many illustrations. I was at one time chairman of the Child Labor Committee in the General Federation of Woman's Clubs, which sent out a schedule asking each club in the United States to report as nearly as possible all the working children under fourteen living in its vicinity. A Florida club filled out the schedule with an astonishing number of Cuban children who were at work in sugar mills, and the club members registered a complaint that our committee had sent the schedule too late, for if they had realized the conditions earlier, they might have presented a bill to the legislature which had now adjourned. Of course the children had been working in the sugar mills for years, and had probably gone back and forth under the very eyes of the club women, but the women had never seen them, much less felt any obligation to protect them, until they joined a club, and the club joined a Federation, and the Federation appointed a Child Labor Committee who sent them a schedule. With their quickened perceptions they then saw the rescue of these familiar children in the light of a social obligation. Through some such experiences the members of the Hull-House Woman's Club have obtained the power of seeing the concrete through the general and have entered into various undertakings.

Very early in its history the club formed what was called "A Social Extension Committee." Once a month this committee gives parties to people in the neighborhood who for any reason seem forlorn and without much social pleasure. One evening they invited only Italian women, thereby crossing a distinct social "gulf," for there certainly exists as great a sense of social differ- ence between the prosperous Irish-American women and the South-Italian peasants as between any two sets of people in the city of Chicago. The Italian women, who were almost eastern in their habits, all stayed at home and sent their husbands, and the social extension committee entered the drawing room to find it occupied by rows of Italian workingmen, who seemed to prefer to sit in chairs along the wall. They were quite ready to be "socially extended," but plainly puzzled as to what it was all about. The evening finally developed into a very successful party, not so much because the committee were equal to it, as because the Italian men rose to the occasion.

Untiring pairs of them danced the tarantella; they sang Neapolitan songs; one of them per- formed some of those wonderful sleight-of-hand tricks so often seen on the streets of Naples; they explained the coral finger of St. Januarius which they wore; they politely ate the strange American refreshments; and when the evening was over, one of the committee said to me, "Do you know I am ashamed of the way I have always talked about 'dagos,' they are quite like other people, only one must take a little more pains with them. I have been nagging my husband to move off M Street because they are moving in, but I am going to try staying awhile and see if I can make a real acquaintance with some of them." To my mind at that moment the speaker had passed from the region of the uncultivated person into the possibilities of the cultivated person. The former is bounded by a narrow outlook on life, unable to overcome differences of dress and habit, and his interests are slowly contracting within a circumscribed area; while the latter constantly tends to be more a citizen of the world because of his growing understanding of all kinds of people with their varying experiences. We send our young people to Europe that they may lose their provincialism and be able to judge their fellows by a more universal test, as we send them to college that they may attain the cultural background and a larger outlook; all of these it is possible to acquire in other ways, as this member of the woman's club had discovered for herself.

This social extension committee under the leadership of an ex-president of the Club, a Hull-House resident with a wide acquaintance, also discover many of those lonely people of which every city contains so large a number. We are only slowly apprehending the very real danger to the individual who fails to establish some sort of genuine relation with the people who surround him. We are all more or less familiar with the results of isolation in rural districts; the Bronte sisters have portrayed the hideous immorality and savagery of the remote dwellers on the bleak moorlands of northern England; Miss Wilkins has written of the overdeveloped will of the solitary New Englander; but tales still wait to be told of the isolated city dweller. In addition to the lonely young man recently come to town, and the country family who have not yet made their connections, are many other people who, because of temperament or from an estimate of themselves which will not permit them to make friends with the "people around here," or who, because they are victims to a combination of circumstances, lead a life as lonely and untouched by the city about them as if they were in remote country districts. The very fact that it requires an effort to preserve isolation from the tenement-house life which flows all about them, makes the character stiffer and harsher than mere country solitude could do.

Many instances of this come into my mind; the faded, ladylike hairdresser, who came and went to her work for twenty years, carefully concealing her dwelling place from the "other people in the shop," moving whenever they seemed too curious about it, and priding herself that no neighbor had ever "stepped inside her door," and yet when discovered through an asthma which forced her to crave friendly offices, she was most responsive and even gay in a social atmosphere. Another woman made a long effort to conceal the poverty resulting from her husband's inveterate gambling and to secure for her children the educational advantages to which her family had always been accustomed. Her five children, who are now university graduates, do not realize how hard and solitary was her early married life when we first knew her, and she was beginning to regret the isolation in which her children were being reared, for she saw that their lack of early companionship would always cripple their power to make friends. She was glad to avail herself of the social resources of Hull-House for them, and at last even for herself.

The leader of the social extension committee has also been able, through her connection with the vacant lot garden movement in Chicago, to maintain a most flourishing "friendly club" largely composed of people who cultivate these garden plots. During the club evening at least, they regain something of the ease of the man who is being estimated by the bushels per acre of potatoes he has raised, and not by that flimsy city judgment so often based upon store clothes. Their jollity and enthusiasm are unbounded, expressing itself in clog dances and rousing old songs often in sharp contrast to the overworked, worn aspects of the members.

Of course there are surprising possibilities discovered through other clubs, in one of Greek women or in the "circolo Italiano," for a social club often affords a sheltered space in which the gentler social usages may be exercised, as the more vigorous clubs afford a point of departure into larger social concerns.

The experiences of the Hull-House Woman's Club constantly react upon the family life of the members. Their husbands come with them to the annual midwinter reception, to club concerts and entertainments; the little children come to the May party, with its dancing and games; the older children, to the day in June when prizes are given to those sons and daughters of the members who present a good school record as graduates either from the eighth grade or from a high school.

It seemed, therefore, but a fit recognition of their efforts when the president of the club erected a building planned especially for their needs, with their own library and a hall large enough for their various social undertakings, although of course Bowen Hall is constantly put to many other uses.

It was under the leadership of this same able president that the club achieved its wider purposes and took its place with the other forces for city betterment. The club had begun, as nearly all women's clubs do, upon the basis of self-improvement, although the foundations for this later development had been laid by one of their earliest presidents, who was the first probation officer of the Juvenile Court, and who had so shared her experiences with the club that each member felt the truth as well as the pathos of the lines inscribed on her memorial tablet erected in their club library:-

"As more exposed to suffering and distress
Thence also more alive to tenderness."

Each woman had discovered opportunities in her own experience for this same tender understanding, and under its succeeding president, Mrs. Pelham, in its determination to be of use to the needy and distressed, the club developed many philanthropic undertakings from the humble beginnings of a linen chest kept constantly filled with clothing for the sick and poor. It required, however, an adequate knowledge of adverse city conditions so productive of juvenile delinquency and a sympathy which could enkindle itself in many others of divers faiths and training, to arouse the club to its finest public spirit. This was done by a later president, Mrs. Bowen, who, as head of the Juvenile Protective Association, had learned that the moralized energy of a group is best fitted to cope with the complicated problems of a city; but it required ability of an unusual order to evoke a sense of social obligation from the very knowledge of adverse city conditions which the club members possessed, and to connect it with the many civic and philanthropic organizations of the city in such wise as to make it socially useful. This financial and representative connection with outside organizations, is valuable to the club only as it expresses its sympathy and kindliness at the same time in concrete form. A group of members who lunch with Mrs. Bowen each week at Hull-House discuss, not only topics of public interest, sometimes with experts whom they have long known through their mutual undertakings, but also their own club affairs in the light of this larger knowledge.

Thus the value of social clubs broadens out in one's mind to an instrument of companionship through which many may be led from a sense of isolation to one of civic responsibility, even as another type of club provides recreational facilities for those who have had only meaningless excitements, or, as a third type, opens new and interesting vistas of life to those who are ambitious.

The entire organization of the social life at Hull-House, while it has been fostered and directed by residents and others, has been largely pushed and vitalized from within by the club members themselves. Sir Walter Besant once told me that Hull-House stood in his mind more nearly for the ideal of the "Palace of Delight" than did the "London People's Palace" because we had depended upon the social resources of the people using it. He begged me not to allow Hull-House to become too educational. He believed it much easier to develop a polytechnic institute than a large recreational center, but he doubted whether the former was as useful.

The social clubs form a basis of acquaintanceship for many people living in other parts of the city. Through friendly relations with individuals, which is perhaps the sanest method of approach, they are thus brought into contact, many of them for the first time, with the industrial and social problems challenging the moral resources of our contemporary life. During our twenty years hundreds of these non-residents have directed clubs and classes, and have increased the number of Chicago citizens who are conversant with adverse social conditions and conscious that only by the unceasing devotion of each, according to his strength, shall the compulsions and hardships, the stupidities and cruelties of life be overcome. The number of people thus informed is constantly increasing in all our American cities, and they may in time remove the reproach of social neglect and indifference which has so long rested upon the citizens of the new world. I recall the experience of an Englishman who, not only because he was a member of the Queen's Cabinet and bore a title, but also because he was an able statesman, was entertained with great enthusiasm by the leading citizens of Chicago. At a large dinner party he asked the lady sitting next to him what our tenement-house legislation was in regard to the cubic feet of air required for each occupant of a tenement bedroom; upon her disclaiming any knowledge of the subject, the inquiry was put to all the diners at the long table, all of whom showed surprise that they should be expected to possess this information. In telling me the incident afterward, the English guest said that such indifference could not have been found among the leading citizens of London, whose public spirit had been aroused to provide such housing conditions as should protect tenement dwellers at least from wanton loss of vitality and lowered industrial efficiency. When I met the same Englishman in London five years afterward, he immediately asked me whether Chicago citizens were still so indifferent to the conditions of the poor that they took no interest in their proper housing. I was quick with that defense which an American is obliged to use so often in Europe, that our very democracy so long presupposed that each citizen could care for himself that we are slow to develop a sense of social obligation. He smiled at the familiar phrases and was still inclined to attribute our indifference to sheer ignorance of social conditions.

The entire social development of Hull-House is so unlike what I predicted twenty years ago, that I venture to quote from that ancient writing as an end to this chapter.

The social organism has broken down through large districts of our great cities. Many of the people living there are very poor, the majority of them without leisure or energy for anything but the gain of subsistence.

They live for the moment side by side, many of them without knowledge of each other, without fellowship, without local tradition or public spirit, without social organization of any kind. Practically nothing is done to remedy this. The people who might do it, who have the social tact and training, the large houses, and the traditions and customs of hospitality, live in other parts of the city. The club houses, libraries, galleries, and semi-public conveniences for social life are also blocks away. We find workingmen organized into armies of producers because men of executive ability and business sagacity have found it to their interests thus to organize them. But these workingmen are not organized socially; although lodging in crowded tenement houses, they are living without a corresponding social contact. The chaos is as great as it would be were they working in huge factories without foremen or superintendent. Their ideas and resources are cramped, and the desire for higher social pleasure becomes extinct. They have no share in the traditions and social energy which make for progress. Too often their only place of meeting is a saloon, their only host a bartender; a local demagogue forms their public opinion. Men of ability and refinement, of social power and university cultivation, stay away from them. Personally, I believe the men who lose most are those who thus stay away. But the paradox is here; when cultivated people do stay away from a certain portion of the population, when all social advantages are persistently withheld, it may be for years, the result itself is pointed to as a reason and is used as an argument, for the continued withholding.

It is constantly said that because the masses have never had social advantages, they do want them, that they are heavy and dull, and that it will take political or philanthropic machinery to change them. This divides a city into rich and poor; into the favored, who express their sense of the social obligation by gifts of money, and into the unfavored, who express it by clamoring for a "share"—both of them actuated by a vague sense of justice. This division of the city would be more justifiable, however, if the people who thus isolate themselves on certain streets and use their social ability for each other, gained enough thereby and added sufficient to the sum total of social progress to justify the withholding of the pleasures and results of that progress from so many people who ought to have them. But they cannot accomplish this for the social spirit discharges itself in many forms, and no one form is adequate to its total expression.

Chapter XVI

Arts at Hull-House

The first building erected for Hull-House contained an art gallery well lighted for day and evening use, and our first exhibit of loaned pictures was opened in June, 1891, by Mr. And Mrs. Barnett of London. It is always pleasant to associate their hearty sympathy with that first exhibit, and thus to connect it with their pioneer efforts at Toynbee Hall to secure for working people the opportunity to know the best art, and with their establishment of the first permanent art gallery in an industrial quarter.

We took pride in the fact that our first exhibit contained some of the best pictures Chicago afforded, and we conscientiously insured them against fire and carefully guarded them by night and day.

We had five of these exhibits during two years, after the gallery was completed: two of oil paintings, one of old engravings and etchings, one of water colors, and one of pictures especially selected for use in the public schools. These exhibits were surprisingly well attended and thousands of votes were cast for the most popular pictures. Their value to the neighborhood of course had to be determined by each one of us according to the value he attached to beauty and the escape it offers from dreary reality into the realm of the imagination. Miss Starr always insisted that the arts should receive adequate recognition at Hull-House and urged that one must always remember "the hungry individual soul which without art will have passed unsolaced and unfed, followed by other souls who lack the impulse his should have given."

The exhibits afforded pathetic evidence that the older immigrants do not expect the solace of art in this country; an Italian expressed great surprise when he found that we, although Americans, still liked pictures, and said quite naively that he didn't know that Americans cared for anything but dollars-that looking at pictures was something people only did in Italy.

The extreme isolation of the Italian colony was demonstrated by the fact that he did not know that there was a public art gallery in the city nor any houses in which pictures were regarded as treasures.

A Greek was much surprised to see a photograph of the Acropolis at Hull-House because he had lived in Chicago for thirteen years and had never before met any Americans who knew about this foremost glory of the world. Before he left Greece he had imagined that Americans would be most eager to see pictures of Athens, and as he was a graduate of a school of technology, he had prepared a book of colored drawings and had made a collection of photographs which he was sure Americans would enjoy. But although from his fruit stand near one of the large railroad stations he had conversed with many Americans and had often tried to lead the conversation back to ancient Greece, no one had responded, and he had at last concluded that "the people of Chicago knew nothing of ancient times."

The loan exhibits were continued until the Chicago Art Institute was opened free to the public on Sunday afternoons and parties were arranged at Hull-House and conducted there by a guide. In time even these parties were discontinued as the galleries became better known in all parts of the city and the Art Institute management did much to make pictures popular.

From the first a studio was maintained at Hull-House which has developed through the changing years under the direction of Miss Benedict, one of the residents who is a member of the faculty in the Art Institute. Buildings on the Hull-House quadrangle furnish studios for artists who find something of the same spirit in the contiguous Italian colony that the French artist is traditionally supposed to discover in his beloved Latin Quarter. These artists uncover something of the picturesque in the foreign colonies, which they have reproduced in painting, etching, and lithography. They find their classes filled not only by young people possessing facility and sometimes talent, but also by older people to whom the studio affords the one opportunity of escape from dreariness; a widow with four children who supplemented a very inadequate income by teaching the piano, for six years never missed her weekly painting lesson because it was "her one pleasure"; another woman, whose youth and strength had gone into the care of an invalid father, poured into her afternoon in the studio once a week, all of the longing for self-expression which she habitually suppressed.

Perhaps the most satisfactory results of the studio have been obtained through the classes of young men who are engaged in the commercial arts, and who are glad to have an opportunity to work out their own ideas. This is true of young engravers and lithographers; of the men who have to do with posters and illustrations in various ways. The little pile of stones and the lithographer's handpress in a corner of the studio have been used in many an experiment, as has a set of beautiful type loaned to Hull-House by a bibliophile.

The work of the studio almost imperceptibly merged into the crafts and well within the first decade a shop was opened at Hull-House under the direction of several residents who were also members of the Chicago Arts and Crafts Society. This shop is not merely a school where people are taught and then sent forth to use their teaching in art according to their individual initiative and opportunity, but where those who have already been carefully trained, may express the best they can in wood or metal. The Settlement soon discovers how difficult it is to put a fringe of art on the end of a day spent in a factory. We constantly see young people doing overhurried work. Wrapping bars of soap in pieces of paper might at least give the pleasure of accuracy and repetition if it could be done at a normal pace, but when paid for by the piece, speed becomes the sole requirement and the last suggestion of human interest is taken away. In contrast to this the Hull-House shop affords many examples of the restorative power in the exercise of a genuine craft; a young Russian who, like too many of his countrymen, had made a desperate effort to fit himself for a learned profession, and who had almost finished his course in a night law school, used to watch constantly the work being done in the metal shop at Hull-House. One evening in a moment of sudden resolve, he took off his coat, sat down at one of the benches, and began to work, obviously as a very clever silversmith. He had long concealed his craft because he thought it would hurt his efforts as a lawyer and because he imagined an office more honorable and "more American" than a shop. As he worked on during his two leisure evenings each week, his entire bearing and conversation registered the relief of one who abandons the effort he is not fitted for and becomes a man on his own feet, expressing himself through a familiar and delicate technique.

Miss Starr at length found herself quite impatient with her role of lecturer on the arts, while all the handicraft about her was untouched by beauty and did not even reflect the interest of the workman. She took a training in bookbinding in London under Mr. Cobden-Sanderson and established her bindery at Hull-House in which design and workmanship, beauty and thoroughness are taught to a small number of apprentices.

From the very first winter, concerts which are still continued were given every Sunday afternoon in the Hull-House drawing-room and later, as the audiences increased, in the larger halls. For these we are indebted to musicians from every part of the city. Mr. William Tomlins early trained large choruses of adults as his assistants did of children, and the response to all of these showed that while the number of people in our vicinity caring for the best music was not large, they constituted a steady and appreciative group. It was in connection with these first choruses that a public-spirited citizen of Chicago offered a prize for the best labor song, competition to be open to the entire country. The responses to the offer literally filled three large barrels and speaking at least for myself as one of the bewildered judges, we were more disheartened by their quality than even by their overwhelming bulk. Apparently the workers of America are not yet ready to sing, although I recall a creditable chorus trained at Hull-House for a large meeting in sympathy with the anthracite coal strike in which the swinging lines

> "Who was it made the coal?
> Our God as well as theirs."

seemed to relieve the tension of the moment. Miss Eleanor Smith, the head of the Hull-House Music School, who had put the words to music, performed the same office for the "Sweatshop" of the Yiddish poet, the translation of which presents so graphically the bewilderment and tedium of the New York shop that it might be applied to almost any other machinery industry as the first verse indicates: —

> "The roaring of the wheels has filled my ears,
>   The clashing and the clamor shut me in,
> Myself, my soul, in chaos disappears,
>   I cannot think or feel amid the din."

It may be that this plaint explains the lack of labor songs in this period of industrial maladjustment when the worker is overmastered by his very tools. In addition to sharing with our neighborhood the best music we could procure, we have conscientiously provided careful musical instruction that at least a few young people might understand those old usages of art; that they might master its trade secrets, for after all it is only through a careful technique that artistic ability can express itself and be preserved.

From the beginning we had classes in music, and the Hull-House Music School, which is housed in quarters of its own in our quieter court, was opened in 1893. The school is designed to give a thorough musical instruction to a limited number of children. From the first lessons they are taught to compose and to reduce to order the musical suggestions which may come to them, and in this wise the school has sometimes been able to recover the songs of the immigrants through their children. Some of these folk songs have never been committed to paper, but have survived through the centuries because of a touch of undying poetry which the world has always cherished; as in the song of a Russian who is digging a post hole and finds his task dull and difficult until he strikes a stratum of red sand, which in addition to making digging easy, reminds him of the red hair of his sweetheart, and all goes merrily as the song lifts into a joyous melody. I recall again the almost hilarious enjoyment of the adult audience to whom it was sung by the children who had revived it, as well as the more sober appreciation of the hymns taken from the lips of the cantor, whose father before him had officiated in the synagogue.

The recitals and concerts given by the school are attended by large and appreciative audiences. On the Sunday before Christmas the program of Christmas songs draws together people of the most diverging faiths. In the deep tones of the memorial organ erected at Hull-House, we realize that music is perhaps the most potent agent for making the universal appeal and inducing men to forget their differences.

Some of the pupils in the music school have developed during the years into trained musicians and are supporting themselves in their chosen profession. On the other hand, we constantly see the most promising musical ability extinguished when the young people enter industries which so sap their vitality that they cannot carry on serious study in the scanty hours outside of factory work. Many cases indisputably illustrate this: a Bohemian girl, who, in order to earn money for pressing family needs, first ruined her voice in a six months' constant vaudeville engagement, returned to her trade working overtime in a vain effort to continue the vaudeville income; another young girl whom Hull-House had sent to the high school so long as her parents consented, because we realized that a beautiful voice is often unavailable through lack of the informing mind, later extinguished her promise in a tobacco factory; a third girl who had supported her little sisters since she was fourteen, eagerly used her fine voice for earning money at entertainments held late after her day's work, until exposure and fatigue ruined her health as well as a musician's future; a young man whose music-loving family gave him every possible opportunity, and who produced some charming and even joyous songs during the long struggle with tuberculosis which preceded his death, had made a brave beginning, not only as a teacher of music but as a composer. In the little service held at Hull-House in his memory, when the children sang his composition, "How Sweet is the Shepherd's Sweet Lot," it was hard to realize that such an interpretive pastoral could have been produced by one whose childhood had been passed in a crowded city quarter.

Even that bitter experience did not prepare us for the sorrowful year when six promising pupils out of a class of fifteen, developed tuberculosis. It required but little penetration to see that during the eight years the class of fifteen school children had come together to the music school, they had approximately an even chance, but as soon as they reached the legal working age only a scanty moiety of those who became self-supporting could endure the strain of long hours and bad air. Thus the average human youth, "With all the sweetness of the common dawn," is flung into the vortex of industrial life wherein the everyday tragedy escapes us save when one of them becomes conspicuously unfortunate. Twice in one year we were compelled

> "To find the inheritance of this poor child
> His little kingdom of a forced grave."

It has been pointed out many times that Art lives by devouring her own offspring and the world has come to justify even that sacrifice, but we are unfortified and unsolaced when we see the children of Art devoured, not by her, but by the uncouth stranger, Modern Industry, who, needlessly ruthless and brutal to her own children, is quickly fatal to the offspring of the gentler mother. And so schools in art for those who go to work at the age when more fortunate young people are still sheltered and educated, constantly epitomize one of the haunting problems of life; why do we permit the waste of this most precious human faculty, this consummate possession of civilization? When we fail to provide the vessel in which it may be treasured, it runs out upon the ground and is irretrievably lost.

The universal desire for the portrayal of life lying quite outside of personal experience evinces itself in many forms. One of the conspicuous features of our neighborhood, as of all industrial quarters, is the persistency with which the entire population attends the theater. The very first day I saw Halsted Street a long line of young men and boys stood outside the gallery entrance of the Bijou Theater, waiting for the Sunday matinee to begin at two o'clock, although it was only high noon. This waiting crowd might have been seen every Sunday afternoon during the twenty years which have elapsed since then. Our first Sunday evening in Hull-House, when a group of small boys sat on our piazza and told us "about things around here," their talk was all of the theater and of the astonishing things they had seen that afternoon.

But quite as it was difficult to discover the habits and purposes of this group of boys because they much preferred talking about the theater to contemplating their own lives, so it was all along the line; the young men told us their ambitions in the phrases of stage heroes, and the girls, so far as their romantic dreams could be shyly put into words, possessed no others but those soiled by long use in the melodrama. All of these young people looked upon an afternoon a week in the gallery of a Halsted Street theater as their one opportunity to see life. The sort of melodrama they see there has recently been described as "the ten commandments written in red fire." Certainly the villain always comes to a violent end, and the young and handsome hero is rewarded by marriage with a beautiful girl, usually the daughter of a millionaire, but after all that is not a portrayal of the morality of the ten commandments any more than of life itself.

Nevertheless the theater, such as it was, appeared to be the one agency which freed the boys and girls from that destructive isolation of those who drag themselves up to maturity by themselves, and it gave them a glimpse of that order and beauty into which even the poorest drama endeavors to restore the bewildering facts of life. The most prosaic young people bear testimony to this overmastering desire. A striking illustration of this came to us during our second year's residence on Halsted Street through an incident in the Italian colony, where the men have always boasted that they were able to guard their daughters from the dangers of city life, and until evil Italians entered the business of the "white slave traffic," their boast was well founded. The first Italian girl to go astray known to the residents of Hull-House, was so fascinated by the stage that on her way home from work she always loitered outside a theater before the enticing posters. Three months after her elopement with an actor, her distracted mother received a picture of her dressed in the men's clothes in which she appeared in vaudeville.

Her family mourned her as dead and her name was never mentioned among them nor in the entire colony. In further illustration of an overmastering desire to see life as portrayed on the stage are two young girls whose sober parents did not approve of the theater and would allow no money for such foolish purposes. In sheer desperation the sisters evolved a plot that one of them would feign a toothache, and while she was having her tooth pulled by a neighboring dentist the other would steal the gold crowns from his table, and with the money thus procured they could attend the vaudeville theater every night on their way home from work. Apparently the pain and wrongdoing did not weigh for a moment against the anticipated pleasure. The plan was carried out to the point of selling the gold crowns to a pawnbroker when the disappointed girls were arrested.

All this effort to see the play took place in the years before the five-cent theaters had become a feature of every crowded city thoroughfare and before their popularity had induced the attendance of two and a quarter million people in the United States every twenty-four hours. The eagerness of the penniless children to get into these magic spaces is responsible for an entire crop of petty crimes made more easy because two children are admitted for one nickel at the last performance when the hour is late and the theater nearly deserted. The Hull-House residents were aghast at the early popularity of these mimic shows, and in the days before the inspection of films and the present regulations for the five-cent theaters we established at Hull-House a moving picture show. Although its success justified its existence, it was so obviously but one in the midst of hundreds that it seemed much more advisable to turn our attention to the improvement of all of them or rather to assist as best we could, the successful efforts in this direction by the Juvenile Protective Association.

However, long before the five-cent theater was even heard of, we had accumulated much testimony as to the power of the drama, and we would have been dull indeed if we had not availed ourselves of the use of the play at Hull-House, not only as an agent of recreation and education, but as a vehicle of self-expression for the teeming young life all about us.

Long before the Hull-House theater was built we had many plays, first in the drawing-room and later in the gymnasium. The young people's clubs never tired of rehearsing and preparing for these dramatic occasions, and we also discovered that older people were almost equally ready and talented. We quickly learned that no celebration at Thanksgiving was so popular as a graphic portrayal on the stage of the Pilgrim Fathers, and we were often put to it to reduce to dramatic effects the great days of patriotism and religion.

At one of our early Christmas celebrations Longfellow's "Golden Legend" was given, the actors portraying it with the touch of the miracle play spirit which it reflects. I remember an old blind man, who took the part of a shepherd, said, at the end of the last performance, "Kind Heart," a name by which he always addressed me, "it seems to me that I have been waiting all my life to hear some of these things said. I am glad we had so many performances, for I think I can remember them to the end. It is getting hard for me to listen to reading, but the different voices and all made this very plain." Had he not perhaps made a legitimate demand upon the drama, that it shall express for us that which we have not been able to formulate for ourselves, that it shall warm us with a sense of companionship with the experiences of others; does not every genuine drama present our relations to each other and to the world in which we find ourselves in such wise as may fortify us to the end of the journey?

The immigrants in the neighborhood of Hull-House have utilized our little stage in an endeavor to reproduce the past of their own nations through those immortal dramas which have escaped from the restraining bond of one country into the land of the universal.

A large colony of Greeks near Hull-House, who often feel that their history and classic background are completely ignored by Americans, and that they are easily confused with the more ignorant immigrants from other parts of southeastern Europe, welcome an occasion to present Greek plays in the ancient text. With expert help in the difficulties of staging and rehearsing a classic play, they reproduced the Ajax of Sophocles upon the Hull-House stage. It was a genuine triumph to the actors who felt that they were "showing forth the glory of

Greece" to "ignorant Americans." The scholar who came with a copy of Sophocles in hand and followed the play with real enjoyment, did not in the least realize that the revelation of the love of Greek poets was mutual between the audience and the actors. The Greeks have quite recently assisted an enthusiast in producing "Electra," while the Lithuanians, the Poles, and other Russian subjects often use the Hull-House stage to present plays in their own tongue, which shall at one and the same time keep alive their sense of participation in the great Russian revolution and relieve their feelings in regard to it. There is something still more appealing in the yearning efforts the immigrants sometimes make to formulate their situation in America. I recall a play written by an Italian playwright of our neighborhood, which depicted the insolent break between Americanized sons and old country parents, so touchingly that it moved to tears all the older Italians in the audience. Did the tears of each express relief in finding that others had had the same experience as himself, and did the knowledge free each one from a sense of isolation and an injured belief that his children were the worst of all?

This effort to understand life through its dramatic portrayal, to see one's own participation intelligibly set forth, becomes difficult when one enters the field of social development, but even here it is not impossible if a Settlement group is constantly searching for new material.

A labor story appearing in the Atlantic Monthly was kindly dramatized for us by the author who also superintended its presentation upon the Hull-House stage. The little drama presented the untutored effort of a trades-union man to secure for his side the beauty of self-sacrifice, the glamour of martyrdom, which so often seems to belong solely to the nonunion forces. The presentation of the play was attended by an audience of trades-unionists and employers and those other people who are supposed to make public opinion. Together they felt the moral beauty of the man's conclusion that "it's the side that suffers most that will win out in this war-the saints is the only ones that has got the world under their feet-we've got to do the way they done if the unions is to stand," so completely that it seemed quite natural that he should forfeit his life upon the truth of this statement.

The dramatic arts have gradually been developed at Hull-House through amateur companies, one of which has held together for more than fifteen years. The members were originally selected from the young people who had evinced talent in the plays the social clubs were always giving, but the association now adds to itself only as a vacancy occurs. Some of them have developed almost a professional ability, although contrary to all predictions and in spite of several offers, none of them have taken to a stage career. They present all sorts of plays from melodrama and comedy to those of Shaw, Ibsen, and Galsworthy. The latter are surprisingly popular, perhaps because of their sincere attempt to expose the shams and pretenses of contemporary life and to penetrate into some of its perplexing social and domestic situations. Through such plays the stage may become a pioneer teacher of social righteousness.

I have come to believe, however, that the stage may do more than teach, that much of our current moral instruction will not endure the test of being cast into a lifelike mold, and when presented in dramatic form will reveal itself as platitudinous and effete. That which may have sounded like righteous teaching when it was remote and wordy, will be challenged afresh when it is obliged to simulate life itself.

This function of the stage, as a reconstructing and reorganizing agent of accepted moral truths, came to me with overwhelming force as I listened to the Passion Play at Oberammergau one beautiful summer's day in 1900. The peasants who portrayed exactly the successive scenes of the wonderful Life, who used only the very words found in the accepted version of the Gospels, yet curiously modernized and reorientated the message. They made clear that the opposition to the young Teacher sprang from the merchants whose traffic in the temple He had disturbed and from the Pharisees who were dependent upon them for support. Their query was curiously familiar, as they demanded the antecedents of the Radical who dared to touch vested interests, who presumed to dictate the morality of trade, and who insulted the marts of honest merchants by calling them "a den of thieves." As the play developed, it became clear that this powerful opposition had friends in Church and State, that they controlled influences which ramified in all directions. They obviously believed in their statement of the case and their very wealth and position in the community gave their words such weight that finally all of their hearers were convinced that the young Agitator must be done away with in order that the highest interests of society might be conserved. These simple peasants made it clear that it was the money power which induced one of the Agitator's closest friends to betray him, and the villain of the piece, Judas himself, was only a man who was so dazzled by money, so under the domination of all it represented, that he was perpetually blind to the spiritual vision unrolling before him. As I sat through the long summer day, seeing the shadows on the beautiful mountain back of the open stage shift from one side to the other and finally grow long and pointed in the soft evening light, my mind was filled with perplexing questions. Did the dramatization of the life of Jesus set forth its meaning more clearly and conclusively than talking and preaching could possibly do as a shadowy following of the command "to do the will"?

The peasant actors whom I had seen returning from mass that morning had prayed only to portray the life as He had lived it and, behold, out of their simplicity and piety arose this modern version which even Harnack was only then venturing to suggest to his advanced colleagues in Berlin. Yet the Oberammergau fold were very like thousands of immigrant men and women of Chicago, both in their experiences and in their familiarity with the hard facts of life, and throughout that day as my mind dwelt on my far-away neighbors, I was reproached with the sense of an ungarnered harvest.

Of course such a generally uplifted state comes only at rare moments, while the development of the little theater at Hull-House has not depended upon the moods of any one, but upon the genuine enthusiasm and sustained effort of a group of residents, several of them artists who have ungrudgingly given their time to it year after year. This group has long fostered junior dramatic associations, through which it seems possible to give a training in manners and morals more directly than through any other medium. They have learned to determine very cleverly the ages at which various types of the drama are most congruous and expressive of the sentiments of the little troupes, from the fairy plays such as "Snow-White" and "Puss-in-Boots" which appeal to the youngest children, to the heroic plays of "William Tell," "King John," and "Wat Tyler" for the older lads, and to the romances and comedies which set forth in stately fashion the elaborated life which so many young people admire. A group of Jewish boys gave a dramatic version of the story of Joseph and his brethren and again of Queen Esther. They had almost a sense of proprietorship in the fine old lines and were pleased to bring from home bits of Talmudic lore for the stage setting. The same club of boys at one time will buoyantly give a roaring comedy and five years later will solemnly demand a drama dealing with modern industrial conditions. The Hull-House theater is also rented from time to time to members of the Young People's Socialist League who give plays both in Yiddish and English which reduce their propaganda to conversation. Through such humble experiments as the Hull-House stage, as well as through the more ambitious reforms which are attempted in various parts of the country, the theatre may at last be restored to its rightful place in the community.

There have been times when our little stage was able to serve the theatre libre. A Chicago troupe, finding it difficult to break into a trust theater, used it one winter twice a week for the presentation of Ibsen and old French comedy. A visit from the Irish poet Yeats inspired us to do our share towards freeing the stage from its slavery to expensive scene setting, and a forest of stiff conventional trees against a gilt sky still remains with us as a reminder of an attempt not wholly unsuccessful, in this direction.

This group of Hull-House artists have filled our little foyer with a series of charming playbills and by dint of painting their own scenery and making their own costumes have obtained beguiling results in stage setting. Sometimes all the artistic resources of the House unite in a Wagnerian combination; thus, the text of the "Troll's Holiday" was written by one resident, set to music by another; sung by the Music School, and placed upon the stage under the careful direction and training of the dramatic committee; and the little brown trolls could never have tumbled about so gracefully in their gleaming caves unless they had been taught in the gymnasium.

Some such synthesis takes place every year at the Hull-House annual exhibition, when an effort is made to bring together in a spirit of holiday the nine thousand people who come to the House every week during duller times. Curiously enough the central feature at the annual exhibition seems to be the brass band of the boys' club which apparently dominates the situation by sheer size and noise, but perhaps their fresh boyish enthusiasm expresses that which the older people take more soberly.

As the stage of our little theater had attempted to portray the heroes of many lands, so we planned one early spring seven years ago, to carry out a scheme of mural decoration upon the walls of the theater itself, which should portray those cosmopolitan heroes who have become great through identification with the common lot, in preference to the heroes of mere achievement. In addition to the group of artists living at Hull-House several others were in temporary residence, and they all threw themselves enthusiastically into the plan. The series began with Tolstoy plowing his field which was painted by an artist of the Glasgow school, and the next was of the young Lincoln pushing his flatboat down the Mississippi River at the moment he received his first impression of the "great iniquity." This was done by a promising young artist of Chicago, and the wall spaces nearest to the two selected heroes were quickly filled with their immortal sayings.

A spirited discussion thereupon ensued in regard to the heroes for the two remaining large wall spaces, when to the surprise of all of us the group of twenty-five residents who had lived in unbroken harmony for more than ten years, suddenly broke up into cults and even camps of hero worship. Each cult exhibited drawings of its own hero in his most heroic moment, and of course each drawing received enthusiastic backing from the neighborhood, each according to the nationality of the hero. Thus Phidias standing high on his scaffold as he finished the heroic head of Athene; the young David dreamily playing his harp as he tended his father's sheep at Bethlehem; St. Francis washing the feet of the leper; the young slave Patrick guiding his master through the bogs of Ireland, which he later rid of their dangers; the poet Hans Sachs cobbling shoes; Jeanne d'Arc dropping her spindle in startled wonder before the heavenly visitants, naturally all obtained such enthusiastic following from our cosmopolitan neighborhood that it was certain to give offense if any two were selected. Then there was the cult of residents who wished to keep the series contemporaneous with the two heroes already painted, and they advocated William Morris at his loom, Walt Whitman tramping the open road, Pasteur in his laboratory, or Florence Nightingale seeking the wounded on the field of battle. But beyond the socialists, few of the neighbors had heard of William Morris, and the fame of Walt Whitman was still more apocryphal; Pasteur was considered merely a clever scientist without the romance which evokes popular affection and in the provisional drawing submitted for votes, gentle Florence Nightingale was said "to look more as if she were robbing the dead than succoring the wounded." The remark shows how high the feeling ran, and then, as something must be done quickly, we tried to unite upon strictly local heroes such as the famous fire marshal who had lived for many years in our neighborhood — but why prolong this description which demonstrates once more that art, if not always the handmaid of religion, yet insists upon serving those deeper sentiments for which we unexpectedly find ourselves ready to fight. When we were all fatigued and hopeless of compromise, we took refuge in a series of landscapes connected with our two heroes by a quotation from Wordsworth slightly distorted to meet our dire need, but still stating his impassioned belief in the efficacious spirit capable of companionship with man which resides in "particular spots." Certainly peace emanates from the particular folding of the hills in one of our treasured mural landscapes, yet occasionally when a guest with a bewildered air looks from one side of the theater to the other, we are forced to conclude that the connection is not convincing.

In spite of its stormy career this attempt at mural decoration connects itself quite naturally with the spirit of our earlier efforts to make Hull-House as beautiful as we could, which had in it a desire to embody in the outward aspect of the House something of the reminiscence and aspiration of the neighborhood life.

As the House enlarged for new needs and mellowed through slow-growing associations, we endeavored to fashion it from without, as it were, as well as from within. A tiny wall fountain modeled in classic pattern, for us penetrates into the world of the past, but for the Italian immigrant it may defy distance and barriers as he dimly responds to that typical beauty in which Italy has ever written its message, even as classic art knew no region of the gods which was not also sensuous, and as the art of Dante mysteriously blended the material and the spiritual.

Perhaps the early devotion of the Hull-House residents to the pre-Raphaelites recognized that they above all English speaking poets and painters reveal "the sense of the expressiveness of outward things" which is at once the glory and the limitation of the arts.

Chapter XVII
Echoes of the Russian Revolution

The residents of Hull-House have always seen many evidences of the Russian Revolution; a forlorn family of little children whose parents have been massacred at Kishinev are received and supported by their relatives in our Chicago neighborhood; or a Russian woman, her face streaming with tears of indignation and pity, asks you to look at the scarred back of her sister, a young girl, who has escaped with her life from the whips of the Cossack soldiers; or a studious young woman suddenly disappears from the Hull-House classes because she has returned to Kiev to be near her brother while he is in prison, that she may earn money for the nourishing food which alone will keep him from contracting tuberculosis; or we attend a protest meeting against the newest outrages of the Russian government in which the speeches are interrupted by the groans of those whose sons have been sacrificed and by the hisses of others who cannot repress their indignation. At such moments an American is acutely conscious of our ignorance of this greatest tragedy of modern times, and at our indifference to the waste of perhaps the noblest human material among our contemporaries. Certain it is, as the distinguished Russian revolutionists have come to Chicago, they have impressed me, as no one else ever has done, as belonging to that noble company of martyrs who have ever and again poured forth blood that human progress might be advanced. Sometimes these men and women have addressed audiences gathered quite outside the Russian colony and have filled to overflowing Chicago's largest halls with American citizens deeply touched by this message of martyrdom. One significant meeting was addressed by a member of the Russian Duma and by one of Russia's oldest and sanest revolutionists; another by Madame Breshkovsky, who later languished a prisoner in the fortress of St. Peter and St. Paul.

In this wonderful procession of revolutionists, Prince Kropotkin, or, as he prefers to be called, Peter Kropotkin, was doubtless the most distinguished. When he came to America to lecture, he was heard throughout the country with great interest and respect; that he was a guest of Hull-House during his stay in Chicago attracted little attention at the time, but two years later, when the assassination of President McKinley occurred, the visit of this kindly scholar, who had always called himself an "anarchist" and had certainly written fiery tracts in his younger manhood, was made the basis of an attack upon Hull-House by a daily newspaper, which ignored the fact that while Prince Kropotkin had addressed the Chicago Arts and Crafts Society at Hull-House, giving a digest of his remarkable book on "Fields, Factories, and Workshops," he had also spoken at the State Universities of Illinois and Wisconsin and before the leading literary and scientific societies of Chicago. These institutions and societies were not, therefore, called anarchistic. Hull-House had doubtless laid itself open to this attack through an incident connected with the imprisonment of the editor on an anarchistic paper, who was arrested in Chicago immediately after the assassination of President McKinley. In the excitement following the national calamity and the avowal by the assassin of the influence of the anarchistic lecture to which he had listened, arrests were made in Chicago of every one suspected of anarchy, in the belief that a widespread plot would be uncovered. The editor's house was searched for incriminating literature, his wife and daughter taken to a police station, and his son and himself, with several other suspected anarchists, were placed in the disused cells in the basement of the city hall.

It is impossible to overstate the public excitement of the moment and the unfathomable sense of horror with which the community regarded an attack upon the chief executive of the nation, as a crime against government itself which compels an instinctive recoil from all law-abiding citizens. Doubtless both the horror and recoil have their roots deep down in human experience; the earliest forms of government implied a group which offered competent resistance to outsiders, but assuming no protection was necessary between any two of its own members, promptly punished with death the traitor who had assaulted anyone within. An anarchistic attack against an official thus furnishes an accredited basis both for unreasoning hatred and for prompt punishment. Both the hatred and the determination to punish reached the highest pitch in Chicago after the assassination of President McKinley, and the group of wretched men detained in the old-fashioned, scarcely habitable cells, had not the least idea of their ultimate fate. They were not allowed to see an attorney and were kept "in communicado" as their excited friends called it. I had seen the editor and his family only during Prince Kropotkin's stay at Hull-House, when they had come to visit him several times. The editor had impressed me as a quiet, scholarly man, challenging the social order by the philosophic touchstone of Bakunin and of Herbert Spencer, somewhat startled by the radicalism of his fiery young son and much comforted by the German domesticity of his wife and daughter. Perhaps it was but my hysterical symptom of the universal excitement, but it certainly seemed to me more than I could bear when a group of his individualistic friends, who had come to ask for help, said: "You see what becomes of your boasted law; the authorities won't even allow an attorney, nor will they accept bail for these men, against whom nothing can be proved, although the veriest criminals are not denied such a right." Challenged by an anarchist, one is always sensitive for the honor of legally constituted society, and I replied that of course the men could have an attorney, that the assassin himself would eventually be furnished with one, that the fact that a man was an anarchist had nothing to do with his rights before the law! I was met with the retort that that might do for a theory, but that the fact still remained that these men had been absolutely isolated, seeing no one but policemen, who constantly frightened them with tales of public clamor and threatened lynching.

The conversation took place on Saturday night and, as the final police authority rests in the mayor, with a friend who was equally disturbed over the situation, I repaired to his house on Sunday morning to appeal to him in the interest of a law and order that should not yield to panic. We contended that to the anarchist above all men it must be demonstrated that law is impartial and stands the test of every strain. The mayor heard us through with the ready sympathy of the successful politician. He insisted, however, that the men thus far had merely been properly protected against lynching, but that it might now be safe to allow them to see some one; he would not yet, however, take the responsibility of permitting an attorney, but if I myself chose to see them on the humanitarian errand of an assurance of fair play, he would write me a permit at once. I promptly fell into the trap, if trap it was, and within half an hour was in a corridor in the city hall basement, talking to the distracted editor and surrounded by a cordon of police, who assured me that it was not safe to permit him out of his cell. The editor, who had grown thin and haggard under his suspense, asked immediately as to the whereabouts of his wife and daughter, concerning whom he had heard not a word since he had seen them arrested. Gradually he became composed as he learned, not that his testimony had been believed to the effect that he had never seen the assassin but once and had then considered him a foolish half-witted creature, but that the most thoroughgoing "dragnet" investigations on the part of the united police of the country had failed to discover a plot and that the public was gradually becoming convinced that the dastardly act was that of a solitary man with no political or social affiliations.

The entire conversation was simple and did not seem to me unlike, in motive or character, interviews I had had with many another forlorn man who had fallen into prison. I had scarce returned to Hull-House, however, before it was filled with reporters, and I at once discovered that whether or not I had helped a brother out of a pit, I had fallen into a deep one myself. A period of sharp public opprobrium followed, traces of which, I suppose, will always remain. And yet in the midst of the letters of protest and accusation which made my mail a horror every morning came a few letters of another sort, one from a federal judge whom I had never seen and another from a distinguished professor in the constitutional law, who congratulated me on what they termed a sane attempt to uphold the law in time of panic.

Although one or two ardent young people rushed into print to defend me from the charge of "abetting anarchy," it seemed to me at the time that mere words would not avail. I had felt that the protection of the law itself extended to the most unpopular citizen was the only reply to the anarchistic argument, to the effect that this moment of panic revealed the truth of their theory of government; that the custodians of law and order have become the government itself quite as the armed men hired by the medieval guilds to protect them in the peaceful pursuit of their avocations, through sheer possession of arms finally made themselves rulers of the city. At that moment I was firmly convinced that the public could only be convicted of the blindness of its course, when a body of people with a hundred-fold of the moral energy possessed by a Settlement group, should make clear that there is no method by which any community can be guarded against sporadic efforts on the part of half- crazed, discouraged men, save by a sense of mutual rights and securities which will include the veriest outcast.

It seemed to me then that in the millions of words uttered and written at that time, no one adequately urged that public-spirited citizens set themselves the task of patiently discovering how these sporadic acts of violence against government may be understood and averted. We do not know whether they occur among the discouraged and unassimilated immigrants who might be cared for in such a way as enormously to lessen the probability of these acts, or whether they are the result of anarchistic teaching. By hastily concluding that the latter is the sole explanation for them, we make no attempt to heal and cure the situation. Failure to make a proper diagnosis may mean treatment of a disease which does not exist, or it may furthermore mean that the dire malady from which the patient is suffering be permitted to develop unchecked. And yet as the details of the meager life of the President's assassin were disclosed, they were a challenge to the forces for social betterment in American cities. Was it not an indictment to all those whose business it is to interpret and solace the wretched, that a boy should have grown up in an American city so uncared for, so untouched by higher issues, his wounds of life so unhealed by religion that the first talk he ever heard dealing with life's wrongs, although anarchistic and violent, should yet appear to point a way of relief?

The conviction that a sense of fellowship is the only implement which will break into the locked purpose of a half-crazed creature bent upon destruction in the name of justice, came to me through an experience recited to me at this time by an old anarchist.

He was a German cobbler who, through all the changes in the manufacturing of shoes, had steadily clung to his little shop on a Chicago thoroughfare, partly as an expression of his individualism and partly because he preferred bitter poverty in a place of his own to good wages under a disciplinary foreman. The assassin of President McKinley on his way through Chicago only a few days before he committed his dastardly deed had visited all the anarchists whom he could find in the city, asking them for "the password" as he called it. They, of course, possessed no such thing, and had turned him away, some with disgust and all with a certain degree of impatience, as a type of the ill-balanced man who, as they put it, was always "hanging around the movement, without the slightest conception of its meaning." Among other people, he visited the German cobbler, who treated him much as the others had done, but who, after the event had made clear the identity of his visitor, was filled with the most bitter remorse that he had failed to utilize his chance meeting with the assassin to deter him from his purpose. He knew as well as any psychologist who has read the history of such solitary men that the only possible way to break down such a persistent and secretive purpose, was by the kindliness which might have induced confession, which might have restored the future assassin into fellowship with normal men.

In the midst of his remorse, the cobbler told me a tale of his own youth; that years before, when an ardent young fellow in Germany, newly converted to the philosophy of anarchism, as he called it, he had made up his mind that the Church, as much as the State, was responsible for human oppression, and that this fact could best be set forth "in the deed" by the public destruction of a clergyman or priest; that he had carried firearms for a year with this purpose in mind, but that one pleasant summer evening, in a moment of weakness, he had confided his intention to a friend, and that from that moment he not only lost all desire to carry it out, but it seemed to him the most preposterous thing imaginable. In concluding the story he said; "That poor fellow sat just beside me on my bench; if I had only put my hand on his shoulder and said, 'Now, look here, brother, what is on your mind? What makes you talk such nonsense? Tell me. I have seen much of life, and understand all kinds of men. I have been young and hot-headed and foolish myself,' if he had told me of his purpose then and there, he would never have carried it out. The whole nation would have been spared this horror." As he concluded he shook his gray head and sighed as if the whole incident were more than he could bear-one of those terrible sins of omission; one of the things he "ought to have done," the memory of which is so hard to endure.

The attempt a Settlement makes to interpret American institutions to those who are bewildered concerning them either because of their personal experiences, or because of preconceived theories, would seem to lie in the direct path of its public obligation, and yet it is apparently impossible for the overwrought community to distinguish between the excitement the Settlements are endeavoring to understand and to allay and the attitude of the Settlement itself. At times of public panic, fervid denunciation is held to be the duty of every good citizen, and if a Settlement is convinced that the incident should be used to vindicate the law and does not at the moment give its strength to denunciation, its attitude is at once taken to imply a championship of anarchy itself.

The public mind at such a moment falls into the old medieval confusion-he who feeds or shelters a heretic is upon prima facie evidence a heretic himself-he who knows intimately people among whom anarchists arise is therefore an anarchist. I personally am convinced that anarchy as a philosophy is dying down, not only in Chicago, but everywhere; that their leading organs have discontinued publication, and that their most eminent men in America have deserted them. Even those groups which have continued to meet are dividing, and the major half in almost every instance calls itself socialist-anarchists, an apparent contradiction of terms, whose members insist that the socialistic organization of society must be the next stage of social development and must be gone through with, so to speak, before the ideal state of society can be reached, so nearly begging the question that some orthodox socialists are willing to recognize them. It is certainly true that just because anarchy questions the very foundations of society, the most elemental sense of protection demands that the method of meeting the challenge should be intelligently considered.

Whether or not Hull-House has accomplished anything by its method of meeting such a situation, or at least attempting to treat it in a way which will not destroy confidence in the American institutions so adored by refugees from foreign governmental oppression, it is of course impossible for me to say.

And yet it was in connection with an effort to pursue an intelligent policy in regard to a so-called "foreign anarchist" that Hull-House again became associated with that creed six years later. This again was an echo of the Russian revolution, but in connection with one of its humblest representatives. A young Russian Jew named Averbuch appeared in the early morning at the house of the Chicago chief of police upon an obscure errand. It was a moment of panic everwhere in regard to anarchists because of a recent murder in Denver which had been charged to an Italian anarchist, and the chief of police, assuming that the dark young man standing in his hallway was an anarchist bent upon his assassination, hastily called for help. In a panic born of fear and self-defense, young Averbuch was shot to death. The members of the Russian-Jewish colony on the west side of Chicago were thrown into a state of intense excitement as soon as the nationality of the young man became known. They were filled with dark forebodings from a swift prescience of what it would mean to them were the oduim of anarchy rightly or wrongly attached to one of their members. It seemed to the residents of Hull-House most important that every effort should be made to ascertain just what did happen, that every means of securing information should be exhausted before a final opinion should be formed, and this odium fastened upon a colony of law-abiding citizens. The police might be right or wrong in their assertion that the man was an anarchist. It was, to our minds, also most unfortunate that the Chicago police in the determination to uncover an anarchistic plot should have utilized the most drastic methods of search within the Russian-Jewish colony composed of families only too familiar with the methods of Russian police. Therefore, when the Chicago police ransacked all the printing offices they could locate in the colony, when they raided a restaurant which they regarded as suspicious because it had been supplying food at cost to the unemployed, when they searched through private houses for papers and photographs of revolutionaries, when they seized the library of the Edelstadt group and carried the books, including Shakespeare and Herbert Spencer, to the city hall, when they arrested two friends of young Averbuch and kept them in the police station forty-eight hours, when they mercilessly "sweated" the sister, Olga, that she might be startled into a confession-all these things so poignantly reminded them of Russian methods that indignation fed both by old memory and bitter disappointment in America, swept over the entire colony. The older men asked whether constitutional rights gave no guarantee against such violent aggression of police power, and the hot-headed younger ones cried out at once that the only way to deal with the police was to defy them, which was true of police the world over. It was said many times that those who are without influence and protection in a strange country fare exactly as hard as do the poor in Europe; that all the talk of guaranteed protection through political institutions is nonsense.

Every Settlement has classes in citizenship in which the principles of American institutions are expounded, and of these the community, as a whole, approves. But the Settlements know better than anyone else that while these classes and lectures are useful, nothing can possibly give lessons in citizenship so effectively and make so clear the constitutional basis of a self-governing community as the current event itself. The treatment at a given moment of that foreign colony which feels itself outraged and misunderstood, either makes its constitutional rights clear to it, or forever confuses it on the subject.

The only method by which a reasonable and loyal conception of government may be substituted for the one formed upon Russian experiences is that the actual experience of refugees with government in America shall gradually demonstrate what a very different thing government means here. Such an event as the Averbuch affair affords an unprecedented opportunity to make clear this difference and to demonstrate beyond the possibility of misunderstanding that the guarantee of constitutional rights implies that officialism shall be restrained and guarded at every point, that the official represents, not the will of a small administrative body, but the will of the entire people, and that methods therefore have been constituted by which official aggression may be restrained. The Averbuch incident gave an opportunity to demonstrate this to that very body of people who need it most; to those who have lived in Russia where autocratic officers represent autocratic power and where government is officialism. It seemed to the residents in the Settlements nearest the Russian-Jewish colony that it was an obvious piece of public spirit to try out all the legal value involved, to insist that American institutions were stout enough to break down in times of stress and public panic.

The belief of many Russians that the Averbuch incident would be made a prelude to the constant use of the extradition treaty for the sake of terrorizing revolutionists both at home and abroad received a certain corroboration when an attempt was made in 1908 to extradite a Russian revolutionist named Rudovitz who was living in Chicago. The first hearing before a United States Commissioner gave a verdict favorable to the Russian Government although this was afterward reversed by the Department of State in Washington. Partly to educate American sentiment, partly to express sympathy with the Russian refugees in their dire need, a series of public meetings was arranged in which the operations of the extradition treaty were discussed by many of us who had spoken at a meeting held in protest against its ratification fifteen years before. It is impossible for anyone unacquainted with the Russian colony to realize the consternation produced by this attempted extradition. I acted as treasurer of the fund collected to defray the expenses of halls and printing in the campaign against the policy of extradition and had many opportunities to talk with members of the colony. One old man, tearing his hair and beard as he spoke, declared that all his sons and grandsons might thus be sent back to Russia; in fact, all of the younger men in the colony might be extradited, for every high-spirited young Russian was, in a sense, a revolutionist.

Would it not provoke to ironic laughter that very nemesis which presides over the destinies of nations, if the most autocratic government yet remaining in civilization should succeed in utilizing for its own autocratic methods the youngest and most daring experiment in democratic government which the world has ever seen? Stranger results have followed a course of stupidity and injustice resulting from blindness and panic!

It is certainly true that if the decision of the federal office in Chicago had not been reversed by the department of state in Washington, the United States government would have been committed to return thousands of spirited young refugees to the punishments of the Russian autocracy.

It was perhaps significant of our need of what Napoleon called a "revival of civic morals" that the public appeal against such a reversal of our traditions had to be based largely upon the contributions to American progress made from other revolutions; the Puritans from the English, Lafayette from the French, Carl Schurz and many another able man from the German upheavals in the middle of the century.

A distinguished German scholar writing at the end of his long life a description of his friends of 1848 who made a gallant although premature effort to unite the German states and to secure a constitutional government, thus concludes: "But not a few saw the whole of their lives wrecked, either in prison or poverty, though they had done no wrong, and in many cases were the finest characters it has been my good fortune to know. They were before their time; the fruit was not ripe, as it was in 1871, and Germany but lost her best sons in those miserable years." When the time is ripe in Russia, when she finally yields to those great forces which are molding and renovating contemporary life, when her Cavour and her Bismark finally throw into the first governmental forms all that yearning for juster human relations which the idealistic Russian revolutionists embody, we may look back upon these "miserable years" with a sense of chagrin at our lack of sympathy and understanding.

Again it is far from easy to comprehend the great Russian struggle. I recall a visit from the famous revolutionist Gershuni, who had escaped from Siberia in a barrel of cabbage rolled under the very fortress of the commandant himself, had made his way through Manchuria and China to San Francisco, and on his way back to Russia had stopped in Chicago for a few days. Three months later we heard of his death, and whenever I recall the conversation held with him, I find it invested with that dignity which last words imply. Upon the request of a comrade, Gershuni had repeated the substance of the famous speech he had made to the court which sentenced him to Siberia. As representing the government against which he had rebelled, he told the court that he might in time be able to forgive all of their outrages and injustices save one; the unforgivable outrage would remain that hundreds of men like himself, who were vegetarians because they were not willing to participate in the destruction of living creatures, who had never struck a child even in punishment, who were so consumed with tenderness for the outcast and oppressed that they had lived for weeks among starving peasants only that they might cheer and solace them,—that these men should have been driven into terrorism, until impelled to "execute," as they call it,—"assassinate" the Anglo-Saxon would term it,—public officials, was something for which he would never forgive the Russian government. It was, perhaps, the heat of the argument, as much as conviction, which led me to reply that it would be equally difficult for society to forgive these very revolutionists for one thing they had done, their institution of the use of force in such wise that it would inevitably be imitated by men of less scruple and restraint; that to have revived such a method in civilization, to have justified it by their disinterestedness of purpose and nobility of character, was perhaps the gravest responsibility that any group of men could assume. With a smile of indulgent pity such as one might grant to a mistaken child, he replied that such Tolstoyan principles were as fitted to Russia as "these toilettes," pointing to the thin summer gowns of his listeners, "were fitted to a Siberian winter." And yet I held the belief then, as I certainly do now, that when the sense of justice seeks to express itself quite outside the regular channels of established government, it has set forth on a dangerous journey inevitably ending in disaster, and that this is true in spite of the fact that the adventure may have been inspired by noble motives.

Still more perplexing than the use of force by the revolutionists is the employment of the agent-provocateur on the part of the Russian government. The visit of Vladimir Bourtzeff to Chicago just after his exposure of the famous secret agent, Azeff, filled one with perplexity in regard to a government which would connive at the violent death of a faithful official and that of a member of the royal household for the sake of bringing opprobrium and punishment to the revolutionists and credit to the secret police.

The Settlement has also suffered through its effort to secure open discussion of the methods of the Russian government. During the excitement connected with the visit of Gorki to this country, three different committees of Russians came to Hull-House begging that I would secure a statement in at least one of the Chicago dailies of their own view, that the agents of the Czar had cleverly centered public attention upon Gorki's private life and had fomented a scandal so successfully that the object of Gorki's visit to America had been foiled; he who had known intimately the most wretched of the Czar's subjects, who was best able to sympathetically portray their wretchedness, not only failed to get a hearing before an American audience, but could scarcely find the shelter of a roof. I told two of the Russian committees that it was hopeless to undertake any explanation of the bitter attack until public excitement had somewhat subsided; but one Sunday afternoon when a third committee arrived, I said that I would endeavor to have reprinted in a Chicago daily the few scattered articles written for the magazines which tried to explain the situation, one by the head professor in political economy of a leading university, and others by publicists well informed as to Russian affairs.

I hoped that a cosmopolitan newspaper might feel an obligation to recognize the desire for fair play on the part of thousands of its readers among the Russians, Poles, and Finns, at least to the extent of reproducing these magazine articles under a noncommittal caption. That same Sunday evening, in company with one of the residents, I visited a newspaper office only to hear its representative say that my plan was quite out of the question, as the whole subject was what newspaper men called "a sacred cow." He said, however, that he would willingly print an article which I myself should write and sign. I declined this offer with the statement that one who had my opportunities to see the struggles of poor women in securing support for their children, found it impossible to write anything which would however remotely justify the loosening of marriage bonds, even if the defense of Gorki made by the Russian committees was sound. We left the newspaper office somewhat discouraged with what we thought one more unsuccessful effort to procure a hearing for the immigrants.

I had considered the incident closed, when to my horror and surprise several months afterward it was made the basis of a story with every possible vicious interpretation. One of the Chicago newspapers had been indicted by Mayor Dunne for what he considered an actionable attack upon his appointees to the Chicago School Board of whom I was one, and the incident enlarged and coarsened was submitted as evidence to the Grand Jury in regard to my views and influence. Although the evidence was thrown out, an attempt was again made to revive this story by the managers of Mayor Dunne's second campaign, this time to show how "the protector of the oppressed" was traduced. The incident is related here as an example of the clever use of that old device which throws upon the radical in religion, in education, and in social reform, the oduim of encouraging "harlots and sinners" and of defending their doctrines.

If the under dog were always right, one might quite easily try to defend him. The trouble is that very often he is but obscurely right, sometimes only partially right, and often quite wrong; but perhaps he is never so altogether wrong and pig-headed and utterly reprehensible as he is represented to be by those who add the possession of prejudices to the other almost insuperable difficulties of understanding him. It was, perhaps, not surprising that with these excellent opportunities for misjudging Hull-House, we should have suffered attack from time to time whenever any untoward event gave an opening as when an Italian immigrant murdered a priest in Denver, Colorado. Although the wretched man had never been in Chicago, much less at Hull-House, a Chicago ecclesiastic asserted that he had learned hatred of the Church as a member of the Giordano Bruno Club, an Italian Club, one of whose members lived at Hull-House, and which had occasionally met there, although it had long maintained clubrooms of its own. This club had its origin in the old struggles of united Italy against the temporal power of the Pope, one of the European echoes with which Chicago resounds. The Italian resident, as the editor of a paper representing new Italy, had come in sharp conflict with the Chicago ecclesiastic, first in regard to naming a public school of the vicinity after Garibaldi, which was of course not tolerated by the Church, and then in regard to many another issue arising in anticlericalism, which, although a political party, is constantly involved, from the very nature of the case, in theological difficulties. The contest had been carried on with a bitterness impossible for an American to understand, but its origin and implications were so obvious that it did not occur to any of us that it could be associated with Hull-House either in its motive or direction.

The ecclesiastic himself had lived for years in Rome, and as I had often discussed the problems of Italian politics with him, I was quite sure he understood the raison d'etre for the Giordano Bruno Club. Fortunately in the midst of the rhetorical attack, our friendly relations remained unbroken with the neighboring priests from whom we continued to receive uniform courtesy as we cooperated in cases of sorrow and need. Hundreds of devout communicants identified with the various Hull-House clubs and classes were deeply distressed by the incident, but assured us it was all a misunderstanding. Easter came soon afterwards, and it was not difficult to make a connection between the attack and the myriad of Easter cards which filled my mail.

Thus a Settlement becomes involved in the many difficulties of its neighbors as its experiences make vivid the consciousness of modern internationalism. And yet the very fact that the sense of reality is so keen and the obligation of the Settlement so obvious may perhaps in itself explain the opposition Hull-House has encountered when it expressed its sympathy with the Russian revolution. We were much entertained, although somewhat ruefully, when a Chicago woman withdrew from us a large annual subscription because Hull-House had defended a Russian refugee while she, who had seen much of the Russian aristocracy in Europe, knew from them that all the revolutionary agitation was both unreasonable and unnecessary!

It is, of course impossible to say whether these oppositions were inevitable or whether they were indications that Hull-House had somehow bungled at its task. Many times I have been driven to the confession of the blundering Amiel: "It requires ability to make what we seem agree with what we are."

Chapter XVIII
Socialized Education

In a paper written years ago I deplored at some length the fact that educational matters are more democratic in their political than in their social aspect, and I quote the following extract from it as throwing some light upon the earlier educational undertakings at Hull-House:-

Teaching in a Settlement requires distinct methods, for it is true of people who have been allowed to remain undeveloped and whose facilities are inert and sterile, that they cannot take their learning heavily. It has to be diffused in a social atmosphere, information must be held in solution, in a medium of fellowship and good will.

Intellectual life requires for its expansion and manifestation the influences and assimilation of the interests and affections of others. Mazzini, that greatest of all democrats, who broke his heart over the condition of the South European peasantry, said: "Education is not merely a necessity of true life by which the individual renews his vital force in the vital force of humanity; it is a Holy Communion with generations dead and living, by which he fecundates all his faculties. When he is withheld from this Communion for generations, as the Italian peasant has been, we say, 'He is like a beast of the field; he must be controlled by force.'" Even to this it is sometimes added that it is absurd to educate him, immoral to disturb his content. We stupidly use the effect as an argument for a continuance of the cause. It is needless to say that a Settlement is a protest against a restricted view of education.

In line with this declaration, Hull-House in the very beginning opened what we called College Extension Classes with a faculty finally numbering thirty-five college men and women, many of whom held their pupils for consecutive years. As these classes antedated in Chicago the University Extension and Normal Extension classes and supplied a demand for stimulating instruction, the attendance strained to their utmost capacity the spacious rooms in the old house. The relation of students and faculty to each other and to the residents was that of guest and hostess, and at the close of each term the residents gave a reception to students and faculty which was one of the chief social events of the season. Upon this comfortable social basis some very good work was done.

In connection with these classes a Hull-House summer school was instituted at Rockford College, which was most generously placed at our disposal by the trustees. For ten years one hundred women gathered there for six weeks, in addition there were always men on the faculty, and a small group of young men among the students who were lodged in the gymnasium building. The outdoor classes in bird study and botany, the serious reading of literary masterpieces, the boat excursions on the Rock River, the cooperative spirit of doing the housework together, the satirical commencements in parti-colored caps and gowns, lent themselves toward a reproduction of the comradeship which college life fosters.

As each member of the faculty, as well as the students, paid three dollars a week, and as we had little outlay beyond the actual cost of food, we easily defrayed our expenses. The undertaking was so simple and gratifying in results that it might well be reproduced in many college buildings which are set in the midst of beautiful surroundings, unused during the two months of the year when hundreds of people, able to pay only a moderate price for lodgings in the country, can find nothing comfortable and no mental food more satisfying than piazza gossip.

Every Thursday evening during the first years, a public lecture came to be an expected event in the neighborhood, and Hull-House became one of the early University Extension centers, first in connection with an independent society and later with the University of Chicago. One of the Hull-House trustees was so impressed with the value of this orderly and continuous presentation of economic subjects that he endowed three courses in a downtown center, in which the lectures were free to anyone who chose to come. He was much pleased that these lectures were largely attended by workingmen who ordinarily prefer that an economic subject shall be presented by a partisan, and who are supremely indifferent to examinations and credits.

They also dislike the balancing of pro and con which scholarly instruction implies, and prefer to be "inebriated on raw truth" rather than to sip a carefully prepared draught of knowledge.

Nevertheless Bowen Hall, which seats seven hundred and fifty people, is often none too large to hold the audiences of men who come to Hull-House every Sunday evening during the winter to attend the illustrated lectures provided by the faculty of the University of Chicago and others who kindly give their services. These courses differ enormously in their popularity: one on European capitals and their social significance was followed with the most vivid attention and sense of participation indicated by groans and hisses when the audience was reminded of an unforgettable feud between Austria and her Slavic subjects, or when they wildly applauded a Polish hero endeared through his tragic failure.

In spite of the success of these Sunday evening courses, it has never been an easy undertaking to find acceptable lectures. A course of lectures on astronomy illustrated by stereopticon slides will attract a large audience the first week, who hope to hear of the wonders of the heavens and the relation of our earth thereto, but instead are treated to spectrum analyses of star dust, or the latest theory concerning the milky way. The habit of research and the desire to say the latest word upon any subject often overcomes the sympathetic understanding of his audience which the lecturer might otherwise develop, and he insensibly drops into the dull terminology of the classroom. There are, of course, notable exceptions; we had twelve gloriously popular talks on organic evolution, but the lecturer was not yet a professor-merely a university instructor-and his mind was still eager over the marvel of it all. Fortunately there is an increasing number of lecturers whose matter is so real, so definite, and so valuable, that in an attempt to give it an exact equivalence in words, they utilize the most direct forms of expression.

It sometimes seems as if the men of substantial scholarship were content to leave to the charletan the teaching of those things which deeply concern the welfare of mankind, and that the mass of men get their intellectual food from the outcasts of scholarship, who provide millions of books, pictures, and shows, not to instruct and guide, but for the sake of their own financial profit. A Settlement soon discovers that simple people are interested in large and vital subjects, and the Hull-House residents themselves at one time, with only partial success, undertook to give a series of lectures on the history of the world, beginning with the nebular hypothesis and reaching Chicago itself in the twenty-fifth lecture! Absurd as the hasty review appears, there is no doubt that the beginner in knowledge is always eager for the general statement, as those wise old teachers of the people well knew, when they put the history of creation on the stage and the monks themselves became the actors. I recall that in planning my first European journey I had soberly hoped in two years to trace the entire pattern of human excellence as we passed from one country to another, in the shrines popular affection had consecrated to the saints, in the frequented statues erected to heroes, and in the "worn blasonry of funeral brasses" —an illustration that when we are young we all long for those mountaintops upon which we may soberly stand and dream of our own ephemeral and uncertain attempts at righteousness. I have had many other illustrations of this; a statement was recently made to me by a member of the Hull-House Boys' club, who had been unjustly arrested as an accomplice to a young thief and held in the police station for three days, that during his detention he "had remembered the way Jean Valjean behaved when he was everlastingly pursued by that policeman who was only trying to do right"; "I kept seeing the pictures in that illustrated lecture you gave about him, and I thought it would be queer if I couldn't behave well for three days when he had kept it up for years."

The power of dramatic action may unfortunately be illustrated in other ways. During the weeks when all the daily papers were full of the details of a notorious murder trial in New York and all the hideous events which preceded the crime, one evening I saw in the street a knot of working girls leaning over a newspaper, admiring the clothes, the beauty, and "sorrowful expression" of the unhappy heroine. In the midst of the trial a woman whom I had known for years came to talk to me about her daughter, shamefacedly confessing that the girl was trying to dress and look like the notorious girl in New York, and that she had even said to her mother in a moment of defiance, "Some day I shall be taken into court and then I shall dress just as Evelyn did and face my accusers as she did in innocence and beauty."

If one makes calls on a Sunday afternoon in the homes of the immigrant colonies near Hull-House, one finds the family absorbed in the Sunday edition of a sensational daily newspaper, even those who cannot read, quite easily following the comic adventures portrayed in the colored pictures of the supplement or tracing the clew of a murderer carefully depicted by a black line drawn through a plan of the houses and streets.

Sometimes lessons in the great loyalties and group affections come through life itself and yet in such a manner that one cannot but deplore it. During the teamsters' strike in Chicago several years ago when class bitterness rose to a dramatic climax, I remember going to visit a neighborhood boy who had been severely injured when he had taken the place of a union driver upon a coal wagon. As I approached the house in which he lived, a large group of boys and girls, some of them very little children, surrounded me to convey the exciting information that "Jack T. was a 'scab'," and that I couldn't go in there. I explained to the excited children that his mother, who was a friend of mine, was in trouble, quite irrespective of the way her boy had been hurt. The crowd around me outside of the house of the "scab" constantly grew larger and I, finally abandoning my attempt at explanation, walked in only to have the mother say: "Please don't come here. You will only get hurt, too." Of course I did not get hurt, but the episode left upon my mind one of the most painful impressions I have ever received in connection with the children of the neighborhood. In addition to all else are the lessons of loyalty and comradeship to come to them as the mere reversals of class antagonism? And yet it was but a trifling incident out of the general spirit of bitterness and strife which filled the city.

Therefore the residents of Hull-House place increasing emphasis upon the great inspirations and solaces of literature and are unwilling that it should ever languish as a subject for class instruction or for reading parties. The Shakespeare club has lived a continuous existence at Hull-House for sixteen years during which time its members have heard the leading interpreters of Shakespeare, both among scholars and players. I recall that one of its earliest members said that her mind was peopled with Shakespeare characters during her long hours of sewing in a shop, that she couldn't remember what she thought about before she joined the club, and concluded that she hadn't thought about anything at all. To feed the mind of the worker, to lift it above the monotony of his task, and to connect it with the larger world, outside of his immediate surroundings, has always been the object of art, perhaps never more nobly fulfilled than by the great English bard. Miss Starr has held classes in Dante and Browning for many years, and the great lines are conned with never failing enthusiasm. I recall Miss Lathrop's Plato club and an audience who listened to a series of lectures by Dr. John Dewey on "Social Psychology" as geniune intellectual groups consisting largely of people from the immediate neighborhood, who were willing to make "that effort from which we all shrink, the effort of thought." But while we prize these classes as we do the help we are able to give to the exceptional young man or woman who reaches the college and university and leaves the neighborhood of his childhood behind him, the residents of Hull-House feel increasingly that the educational efforts of a Settlement should not be directed primarily to reproduce the college type of culture, but to work out a method and an ideal adapted to the immediate situation. They feel that they should promote a culture which will not set its possessor aside in a class with others like himself, but which will, on the contrary, connect him with all sorts of people by his ability to understand them as well as by his power to supplement their present surroundings with the historic background. Among the hundreds of immigrants who have for years attended classes at Hull-House designed primarily to teach the English language, dozens of them have struggled to express in the newly acquired tongue some of these hopes and longings which had so much to do with their emigration.

A series of plays was thus written by a young Bohemian; essays by a Russian youth, outpouring sorrows rivaling Werther himself and yet containing the precious stuff of youth's perennial revolt against accepted wrong; stories of Russian oppression and petty injustices throughout which the desire for free America became a crystallized hope; an attempt to portray the Jewish day of Atonement, in such wise that even individualistic Americans may catch a glimpse of that deeper national life which has survived all transplanting and expresses itself in forms so ancient that they appear grotesque to the ignorant spectator. I remember a pathetic effort on the part of a young Russian Jewess to describe the vivid inner life of an old Talmud scholar, probably her uncle or father, as of one persistently occupied with the grave and important things of the spirit, although when brought into sharp contact with busy and overworked people, he inevitably appeared self-absorbed and slothful. Certainly no one who had read her paper could again see such an old man in his praying shawl bent over his crabbed book, without a sense of understanding.

On the other hand, one of the most pitiful periods in the drama of the much-praised young American who attempts to rise in life, is the time when his educational requirements seem to have locked him up and made him rigid. He fancies himself shut off from his uneducated family and misunderstood by his friends. He is bowed down by his mental accumulations and often gets no farther than to carry them through life as a great burden, and not once does he obtain a glimpse of the delights of knowledge.

The teacher in a Settlement is constantly put upon his mettle to discover methods of instruction which shall make knowledge quickly available to his pupils, and I should like here to pay my tribute of admiration to the dean of our educational department, Miss Landsberg, and to the many men and women who every winter come regularly to Hull-House, putting untiring energy into the endless task of teaching the newly arrived immigrant the first use of a language of which he has such desperate need. Even a meager knowledge of English may mean an opportunity to work in a factory versus nonemployment, or it may mean a question of life or death when a sharp command must be understood in order to avoid the danger of a descending crane.

In response to a demand for an education which should be immediately available, classes have been established and grown apace in cooking, dressmaking, and millinery. A girl who attends them will often say that she "expects to marry a workingman next spring," and because she has worked in a factory so long she knows "little about a house." Sometimes classes are composed of young matrons of like factory experiences. I recall one of them whose husband had become so desperate after two years of her unskilled cooking that he had threatened to desert her and go where he could get "decent food," as she confided to me in a tearful interview, when she followed my advice to take the Hull-House courses in cooking, and at the end of six months reported a united and happy home.

Two distinct trends are found in response to these classes; the first is for domestic training, and the other is for trade teaching which shall enable the poor little milliner and dressmaker apprentices to shorten the years of errand running which is supposed to teach them their trade.

The beginning of trade instruction has been already evolved in connection with the Hull-House Boys' club. The ample Boys' club building presented to Hull-House three years ago by one of our trustees has afforded well-equipped shops for work in wood, iron, and brass; for smithing in copper and tin; for commercial photography, for printing, for telegraphy, and electrical construction. These shops have been filled with boys who are eager for that which seems to give them a clew to the industrial life all about them. These classes meet twice a week and are taught by intelligent workingmen who apparently give the boys what they want better than do the strictly professional teachers. While these classes in no sense provide a trade training, they often enable a boy to discover his aptitude and help him in the selection of what he "wants to be" by reducing the trades to embryonic forms. The factories are so complicated that the boy brought in contact with them, unless he has some preliminary preparation, is apt to become confused. In pedagogical terms, he loses his "power of orderly reaction" and is often so discouraged or so overstimulated in his very first years of factory life that his future usefulness is seriously impaired.

One of Chicago's most significant experiments in the direction of correlating the schools with actual industry was for several years carried on in a public school building situated near

Hull-House, in which the bricklayers' apprentices were taught eight hours a day in special classes during the non-bricklaying season. This early public school venture anticipated the very successful arrangement later carried on in Cincinnati, in Pittsburgh and in Chicago itself, whereby a group of boys at work in a factory alternate month by month with another group who are in school and are thus intelligently conducted into the complicated processes of modern industry. But for a certain type of boy who has been demoralized by the constant change and excitement of street life, even these apprenticeship classes are too strenuous, and he has to be lured into the path of knowledge by all sorts of appeals.

It sometimes happens that boys are held in the Hull-House classes for weeks by their desire for the excitement of placing burglar alarms under the door mats. But to enable the possessor of even a little knowledge to thus play with it, is to decoy his feet at least through the first steps of the long, hard road of learning, although even in this, the teacher must proceed warily. A typical street boy who was utterly absorbed in a wood-carving class, abruptly left never to return when he was told to use some simple calculations in the laying out of the points. He evidently scented the approach of his old enemy, arithmetic, and fled the field. On the other hand, we have come across many cases in which boys have vainly tried to secure such opportunities for themselves. During the trial of a boy of ten recently arrested for truancy, it developed that he had spent many hours watching the electrical construction in a downtown building, and many others in the public library "reading about electricity." Another boy who was taken from school early, when his father lost both of his legs in a factory accident, tried in vain to find a place for himself "with machinery." He was declared too small for any such position, and for four years worked as an errand boy, during which time he steadily turned in his unopened pay envelope for the use of the household. At the end of the fourth year the boy disappeared, to the great distress of his invalid father and his poor mother whose day washings became the sole support of the family. He had beaten his way to Kansas City, hoping "they wouldn't be so particular there about a fellow's size." He came back at the end of six weeks because he felt sorry for his mother who, aroused at last to a realization of his unbending purpose, applied for help to the Juvenile Protective Association. They found a position for the boy in a machine shop and an opportunity for evening classes.

Out of the fifteen hundred members of the Hull-House Boy's club, hundreds seem to respond only to the opportunities for recreation, and many of the older ones apparently care only for the bowling and the billiards. And yet tournaments and match games under supervision and regulated hours are a great advance over the sensual and exhausting pleasures to be found so easily outside the club. These organized sports readily connect themselves with the Hull-House gymnasium and with all those enthusiasms which are so mysteriously aroused by athletics.

Our gymnasium has been filled with large and enthusiastic classes for eighteen years in spite of the popularity of dancing and other possible substitutes, while the Saturday evening athletic contests have become a feature of the neighborhood. The Settlement strives for that type of gymnastics which is at least partly a matter of character, for that training which presupposes abstinence and the curbing of impulse, as well as for those athletic contests in which the mind of the contestant must be vigilant to keep the body closely to the rules of the game. As one sees in rhythmic motion the slim bodies of a class of lads, "that scrupulous and uncontaminate purity of form which recommended itself even to the Greeks as befitting messengers from the gods, if such messengers should come," one offers up in awkward prosaic form the very essence of that old prayer, "Grant them with feet so light to pass through life." But while the glory stored up for Olympian winners was at the most a handful of parsley, an ode, fame for family and city, on the other hand, when the men and boys from the Hull-House gymnasium bring back their cups and medals, one's mind is filled with something like foreboding in the reflection that too much success may lead the winners into the professionalism which is so associated with betting and so close to pugilism. Candor, however, compels me to state that a long acquaintance with the acrobatic folk who have to do with the circus, a large number of whom practice in our gymnasium every winter, has raised our estimate of that profession.

Young people who work long hours at sedentary occupations, factories and offices, need perhaps more than anything else the freedom and ease to be acquired from a symmetrical muscular development and are quick to respond to that fellowship which athletics apparently affords more easily than anything else. The Greek immigrants form large classes and are eager to reproduce the remnants of old methods of wrestling, and other bits of classic lore which they still possess, and when one of the Greeks won a medal in a wrestling match which represented the championship of the entire city, it was quite impossible that he should present it to the Hull-House trophy chest without a classic phrase which he recited most gravely and charmingly.

It was in connection with a large association of Greek lads that Hull-House finally lifted its long restriction against military drill. If athletic contests are the residuum of warfare first waged against the conqueror without and then against the tyrants within the State, the modern Greek youth is still in the first stage so far as his inherited attitude against the Turk is concerned. Each lad believes that at any moment he may be called home to fight this long-time enemy of Greece. With such a genuine motive at hand, it seemed mere affectation to deny the use of our boys' club building and gymnasium for organized drill, although happily it forms but a small part of the activities of the Greek Educational Association.

Having thus confessed to military drill countenanced if not encouraged at Hull-House, it is perhaps only fair to relate an early experience of mine with the "Columbian Guards," and organization of the World's Fair summer. Although the Hull-House squad was organized as the others were with the motto of a clean city, it was very anxious for military drill. This request not only shocked my nonresistant principles, but seemed to afford an opportunity to find a substitute for the military tactics which were used in the boys' brigades everywhere, even in those connected with churches. As the cleaning of the filthy streets and alleys was the ostensible purpose of the Columbian guards, I suggested to the boys that we work out a drill with sewer spades, which with their long narrow blades and shortened handles were not so unlike bayoneted guns in size, weight, and general appearance, but that much of the usual military drill could be readapted. While I myself was present at the gymnasium to explain that it was nobler to drill in imitation of removing disease-breeding filth than to drill in simulation of warfare; while I distractedly readapted tales of chivalry to this modern rescuing of the endangered and distressed, the new drill went forward in some sort of fashion, but so surely as I withdrew, the drillmaster would complain that our troops would first grow self-conscious, then demoralized, and finally flatly refuse to go on. Throughout the years since the failure of this Quixotic experiment, I occasionally find one of these sewer spades in a Hull-House storeroom, too truncated to be used for its original purpose and too prosaic to serve the purpose for which it was bought. I can only look at it in the forlorn hope that it may foreshadow that piping time when the weapons of warfare shall be turned into the implements of civic salvation.

Before closing this chapter on Socialized Education, it is only fair to speak of the education accruing to the Hull-House residents themselves during their years of living in what at least purports to be a center for social and educational activity.

While a certain number of the residents are primarily interested in charitable administration and the amelioration which can be suggested only by those who know actual conditions, there are other residents identified with the House from its earlier years to whom the groups of immigrants make the historic appeal, and who use, not only their linguistic ability, but all the resource they can command of travel and reading to qualify themselves for intelligent living in the immigrant quarter of the city. I remember one resident lately returned from a visit in Sicily, who was able to interpret to a bewildered judge the ancient privilege of a jilted lover to scratch the cheek of his faithless sweetheart with the edge of a coin. Although the custom in America had degenerated into a knife slashing after the manner of foreign customs here, and although the Sicilian deserved punishment, the incident was yet lifted out of the slough of mere brutal assault, and the interpretation won the gratitude of many Sicilians.

There is no doubt that residents in a Settlement too often move toward their ends "with hurried and ignoble gait," putting forth thorns in their eagerness to bear grapes. It is always easy for those in pursuit of ends which they consider of overwhelming importance to become themselves thin and impoverished in spirit and temper, to gradually develop a dark mistaken eagerness alternating with fatigue, which supersedes "the great and gracious ways" so much more congruous with worthy aims.

Partly because of this universal tendency, partly because a Settlement shares the perplexities of its times and is never too dogmatic concerning the final truth, the residents would be glad to make the daily life at the Settlement "conform to every shape and mode of excellence."

It may not be true

  "That the good are always the merry
Save by an evil chance,"

but a Settlement would make clear that one need not be heartless and flippant in order to be merry, nor solemn in order to be wise. Therefore quite as Hull-House tries to redeem billiard tables from the association of gambling, and dancing from the temptations of the public dance halls, so it would associate with a life of upright purpose those more engaging qualities which in the experience of the neighborhood are too often connected with dubious aims.

Throughout the history of Hull-House many inquiries have been made concerning the religion of the residents, and the reply that they are as diversified in belief and in the ardor of the inner life as any like number of people in a college or similar group, apparently does not carry conviction. I recall that after a house for men residents had been opened on Polk Street and the residential force at Hull-House numbered twenty, we made an effort to come together on Sunday evenings in a household service, hoping thus to express our moral unity in spite of the fact that we represented many creeds. But although all of us reverently knelt when the High Church resident read the evening service and bowed our heads when the evangelical resident led in prayer after his chapter, and although we sat respectfully through the twilight when a resident read her favorite passages from Plato and another from Abt Vogler, we concluded at the end of the winter that this was not religious fellowship and that we did not care for another reading club. So it was reluctantly given up, and we found that it was quite as necessary to come together on the basis of the deed and our common aim inside the household as it was in the neighborhood itself. I once had a conversation on the subject with the warden of Oxford House, who kindly invited me to the evening service held for the residents in a little chapel on the top floor of the Settlement. All the residents were High Churchmen to whom the service was an important and reverent part of the day. Upon my reply to a query of the warden that the residents of Hull-House could not come together for religious worship because there were among us Jews, Roman Catholics, English Churchmen, Dissenters, and a few agnostics, and that we had found unsatisfactory the diluted form of worship which we could carry on together, he replied that it must be most difficult to work with a group so diversified, for he depended upon the evening service to clear away any difficulties which the day had involved and to bring the residents to a religious consciousness of their common aim. I replied that this diversity of creed was part of the situation in American Settlements, as it was our task to live in a neighborhood of many nationalities and faiths, and that it might be possible that among such diversified people it was better that the Settlement corps should also represent varying religious beliefs.

A wise man has told us that "men are once for all so made that they prefer a rational world to believe in and to live in," but that it is no easy matter to find a world rational as to its intellectual, aesthetic, moral, and practical aspects. Certainly it is no easy matter if the place selected is of the very sort where the four aspects are apparently furthest from perfection, but an undertaking resembling this is what the Settlement gradually becomes committed to, as its function is revealed through the reaction on its consciousness of its own experiences. Because of this fourfold undertaking, the Settlement has gathered into residence people of widely diversified tastes and interests, and in Hull-House, at least, the group has been surprisingly permanent. The majority of the present corp of forty residents support themselves by their business and professional occupations in the city, giving only their leisure time to Settlement undertakings.

This in itself tends to continuity of residence and has certain advantages. Among the present staff, of whom the larger number have been in residence for more than twelve years, there are the secretary of the City club, two practicing physicians, several attorneys, newspapermen, businessmen, teachers, scientists, artists, musicians, lecturers in the School of Civics and Philanthropy, officers in The Juvenile Protective Association and in The League for the Protection of Immigrants, a visiting nurse, a sanitary inspector, and others.

We have also worked out during our years of residence a plan of living which may be called cooperative, for the families and individuals who rent the Hull-House apartments have the use of the central kitchen and dining room so far as they care for them; many of them work for hours every week in the studios and shops; the theater and drawing-rooms are available for such social organization as they care to form; the entire group of thirteen buildings is heated and lighted from a central plant. During the years, the common human experiences have gathered about the House; funeral services have been held there, marriages and christenings, and many memories hold us to each other as well as to our neighbors. Each resident, of course, carefully defrays his own expenses, and his relations to his fellow residents are not unlike those of a college professor to his colleagues. The depth and strength of his relation to the neighborhood must depend very largely upon himself and upon the genuine friendships he has been able to make. His relation to the city as a whole comes largely through his identification with those groups who are carrying forward the reforms which a Settlement neighborhood so sadly needs and with which residence has made him familiar.

Life in the Settlement discovers above all what has been called "the extraordinary pliability of human nature," and it seems impossible to set any bounds to the moral capabilities which might unfold under ideal civic and educational conditions. But in order to obtain these conditions, the Settlement recognizes the need of cooperation, both with the radical and the conservative, and from the very nature of the case the Settlement cannot limit its friends to any one political party or economic school.

The Settlement casts side none of those things which cultivated men have come to consider reasonable and goodly, but it insists that those belong as well to that great body of people who, because of toilsome and underpaid labor, are unable to procure them for themselves. Added to this is a profound conviction that the common stock of intellectual enjoyment should not be difficult of access because of the economic position of him who would approach it, that those "best results of civilization" upon which depend the finer and freer aspects of living must be incorporated into our common life and have free mobility through all elements of society if we would have our democracy endure.

The educational activities of a Settlement, as well its philanthropic, civic, and social undertakings, are but differing manifestations of the attempt to socialize democracy, as is the very existence of the Settlement itself.

Why Women Should Vote

For many generations it has been believed that woman's place is within the walls of her home, and it is indeed impossible to imagine the time when her duty there shall be ended or to forecast any social change which shall release her from that paramount obligation.

This paper is an attempt to show that many women today are failing to discharge their duties to their own households properly simply because they do not perceive that as society grows more complicated it is necessary that woman shall extend her sense of responsibility to many things outside of her own home if she would continue to preserve the home in its entirety. One could illustrate in many ways. A woman's simplest duty, one would say, is to keep her house clean and wholesome and to feed her children properly. Yet if she lives in a tenement house, as so many of my neighbors do, she cannot fulfill these simple obligations by her own efforts because she is utterly dependent upon the city administration for the conditions which render decent living possible. Her basement will not be dry, her stairways will not be fireproof, her house will not be provided with sufficient windows to give light and air, nor will it be equipped with sanitary plumbing, unless the Public Works Department sends inspectors who constantly insist that these elementary decencies be provided. Women who live in the country sweep their own dooryards and may either feed the refuse of the table to a flock of chickens or allow it innocently to decay in the open air and sunshine. In a crowded city quarter, however, if the street is not cleaned by the city authorities no amount of private sweeping will keep the tenement free from grime; if the garbage is not properly collected and destroyed a tenement-house mother may see her children sicken and die of diseases from which she alone is powerless to shield them, although her tenderness and devotion are unbounded. She cannot even secure untainted meat for her household, she cannot provide fresh fruit, unless the meat has been inspected by city officials, and the decayed fruit, which is so often placed upon sale in the tenement districts, has been destroyed in the interests of public health. In short, if woman would keep on with her old business of caring for her house and rearing her children she will have to have some conscience in regard to public affairs lying quite outside of her immediate household. The individual conscience and devotion are no longer effective.

Chicago one spring had a spreading contagion of scarlet fever just at the time the school nurses had been discontinued because business men had pronounced them too expensive. If the women who sent their children to the schools had been sufficiently public-spirited and had been provided with an implement through which to express that public spirit they would have insisted that the schools be supplied with nurses in order that their own children might be protected from contagion. In other words, if women would effectively continue their old avocations they must take part in the slow upbuilding of that code of legislation which is alone sufficient to protect the home from the dangers incident to modern life. One might instance the many deaths of children from contagious diseases; the germs of which had been carried in tailored clothing. Country doctors testify as to the outbreak of scarlet fever in remote neighborhoods each autumn, after the children have begun to wear the winter overcoats and cloaks which have been sent from infected city sweatshops. That their mothers mend their stockings and guard them from "taking cold" is not a sufficient protection when the tailoring of the family is done in a distant city under conditions which the mother cannot possibly control. The sanitary regulation of sweatshops by city officials is all that can be depended upon to prevent such needless destruction. Who shall say that women are not concerned in the enactment and enforcement of such legislation if they would preserve their homes?

Even women who take no part in public affairs in order that they may give themselves entirely to their own families, sometimes going so far as to despise those other women who are endeavoring to secure protective legislation, may illustrate this point. The Hull-House neighborhood was at one time suffering from a typhoid epidemic. A careful investigation was made by which we were able to establish a very close connection between the typhoid and a mode of plumbing which made it most probable that the infection had been carried by flies. Among the people who been exposed to the infection was a widow who had lived in the ward for a number of years, in a comfortable little house which she owned. Although the Italian immigrants were closing in all around her she was not willing to sell her property and to move away until she had finished the education of her children. In the mean time she held herself quite aloof from her Italian neighbors and could never be drawn into any of the public efforts to protect them by securing a better code of tenement-house sanitation. Her two daughters were sent to an Eastern college; one June, when one of them had graduated and the other still had two years before she took her degree, they came to the spotless little house and to their self-sacrificing mother for the summer's holiday. They both fell ill, not because their own home was not clean, not because their mother was not devoted, but because next door to them and also in the rear were wretched tenements, and because the mother's utmost efforts could not keep the infection out of her own house. One daughter died and one recovered but was an invalid for two years following. This is, perhaps, a fair illustration of the futility of the individual conscience when woman insists upon isolating her family from the rest of the community and its interests. The result is sure to be a pitiful failure.

One of the interesting experiences in the Chicago campaign for inducing the members of the Charter Convention to recommend municipal franchise for women in the provisions of the new charter was the unexpected enthusiasm and help which came from large groups of foreign-born women. The Scandinavian women represented in many Lutheran Church societies said quite simply that in the old country they had had the municipal franchise upon the same basis as men since the seventeenth century; all the women formerly living under the British Government, in England, Australia or Canada, pointed out that Chicago women were asking now for what the British women had long had. But the most unexpected response came from the foreign colonies in which women had never heard such problems discussed and took the prospect of the municipal ballot as a simple device-which it is-to aid them in their daily struggle with adverse city conditions. The Italian women said that the men engaged in railroad construction were away all summer and did not know anything about their household difficulties. Some of them came to Hull-House one day to talk over the possibility of a public wash-house. They do not like to wash in their own tenements, they have never seen a washing-tub until they came to America, and find it very difficult to use it in the restricted space of their little kitchens and to hang the clothes within the house to dry. They say that in the Italian villages the women all go to the streams together; in the town they go to the public washhouse; and washing, instead of being lonely and disagreeable, is made pleasant by cheerful conversation. It is asking a great deal of these women to change suddenly all their habits of living, and their contention that the tenement-house kitchen is too small for laundry-work is well taken. If women in Chicago knew the needs of the Italian colony they would realize that any change bringing cleanliness and fresh clothing into the Italian household would be a very sensible and hygienic measure. It is, perhaps, asking a great deal that the members of the City Council should understand this, but surely a comprehension of the needs of these women and efforts toward ameliorating their lot might be regarded as matters of municipal obligation on the part of voting women.

The same thing is true of the Jewish women in their desire for covered markets which have always been a municipal provision in Russia and Poland. The vegetables piled high upon the wagons standing in the open markets of Chicago become covered with dust and soot. It seems to these women a violation of the most rudimentary decencies and they sometimes say quite simply: " If women had anything to say about it they would change all that."

...The duty of a woman toward the schools which her children attend is so obvious that it is not necessary to dwell upon it. But even this simple obligation cannot be effectively carried out without some form of social organization as the mothers' school clubs and mothers' congresses testify, and to which the most conservative women belong because they feel the need of wider reading and discussion concerning the many problems of childhood. It is, therefore, perhaps natural that the public should have been more willing to accord a vote to women in school matters than in any other, and yet women have never been members of a Board of Education in sufficient numbers to influence largely actual school curriculi. If they had been kindergartens, domestic science courses and school playgrounds would be far more numerous than they are. More than one woman has been convinced of the need of the ballot by the futility of her efforts in persuading a businessman that young children need nurture in something besides the three r's. Perhaps, too, only women realize the influence which the school might exert upon the home if a proper adaptation to actual needs were considered. An Italian girl who has had lessons in cooking at the public school will help her mother to connect the entire family with American food and household habits. That the mother has never baked bread in Italy-only mixed it in her own house and then taken it out to the village oven-makes it all the more necessary that her daughter should understand the complication of a cooking-stove. The same thing is true of the girl who learns to sew in the public school, and more than anything else, perhaps, of the girl who receives the first simple instruction in the care of little children, that skillful care which every tenement-house baby requires if he is to be pulled through his second summer. The only time, to my knowledge, that lessons in the care of children were given in the public schools of Chicago was one summer when the vacation schools were being managed by a volunteer body of women. The instruction was eagerly received by the Italian girls, who had been "little mothers" to younger children every since they could remember.

As a result of this teaching I recall a young girl who carefully explained to her Italian mother that the reason the babies in Italy were so healthy and the babies in Chicago were so sickly was not, as her mother had always firmly insisted, because her babies in Italy had goat's milk and her babies in America had cow's milk, but because the milk in Italy was clean and the milk in Chicago was dirty.... She also informed her mother that the "City Hall wanted to fix up the milk so that it couldn't make the baby sick, but that they hadn't quite enough votes for it yet." The Italian mother believed what her child had been taught in the big school; it seemed to her quite as natural that the city should be concerned in providing pure milk for her younger children as it should provide big schools and teachers for her older children. She reached this naive conclusion because she had never heard those arguments which make it seem reasonable that a woman should be given the school franchise but no other.

But women are also beginning to realize that children need attention outside of school hours; that much of the petty vice in cities is merely the love of pleasure gone wrong, the overrestrained boy or girl seeking improper recreation and excitement. It is obvious that a little study of the needs of children, a sympathetic understanding of the conditions under which they go astray, might save hundreds of them. Women traditionally have had an opportunity to observe the plays of children and the needs of youth, and yet in Chicago, at least, they had done singularly little in this vexed problem of juvenile delinquency until they helped to inaugurate the juvenile Court movement a dozen years ago. The juvenile Court Committee, made up largely of women, paid the salaries of the probation officers connected with the court for the first six years of its existence, and after the salaries were cared for by the county the same organization turned itself into a juvenile Protective League, and through a score of paid officers are doing valiant service in minimizing some of the dangers of city life which boys and girls encounter....

The more extensively the modern city endeavors on the one hand to control and on the other hand to provide recreational facilities for its young people the more necessary it is that women should assist in their direction and extension. After all, a care for wholesome and innocent amusement is what women have for many years assumed. When the reaction comes on the part of taxpayers women's votes may be necessary to keep the city to its beneficent obligations toward its own young people.

...Ever since steam power has been applied to the processes of weaving and spinning woman's traditional work has been carried on largely outside of the home. The clothing and household linen are not only spun and woven, but also usually sewed, by machinery; the preparation of many foods has also passed into the factory and necessarily a certain number of women have been obliged to follow their work there, although it is doubtful, in spite of the large numbers of factory girls, whether women now are doing as large a proportion of the world's work as they used to do. Because many thousands of those working in factories and shops are girls between the ages of fourteen and twenty-two there is a necessity that older women should be interested in the conditions of industry. The very fact that these girls are not going to remain in industry permanently makes it more important that some one should see to it that they shall not be incapacitated for their future family life because they work for exhausting hours and under insanitary [sic] conditions.

If woman's sense of obligation had enlarged as the industrial conditions changed she might naturally and almost imperceptibly have inaugurated the movements for social amelioration in the line of factory legislation and shop sanitation. That she has not done so is doubtless due to the fact that her conscience is slow to recognize any obligation outside of her own family circle, and because she was so absorbed in her own household that she failed to see what the conditions outside actually were. It would be interesting to know how far the consciousness that she had no vote and could not change matters operated in this direction. After all, we see only those things to which our attention has been drawn, we feel responsibility for those things which are brought to us as matters of responsibility. If conscientious women were convinced that it was a civic duty to be informed in regard to these grave industrial affairs, and then to express the conclusions which they had reached by depositing a piece of paper in a ballot box, one cannot imagine that they would shirk simply because the action ran counter to old traditions.

To those of my readers who would admit that although woman has no right to shirk her old obligations, that all of these measures could be secured more easily through her influence upon the men of her family than through the direct use of the ballot; I should like to tell a little story. I have a friend in Chicago who is the mother of four sons and the grandmother of twelve grandsons who are voters. She is a woman of wealth, of secured social position, of sterling character and clear intelligence, and may, therefore, quite fairly be cited as a "woman of influence"....I happened to call at her house on the day that Mr. McKinley was elected President against Mr. Bryan for the first time. I found my friend much disturbed. She said somewhat bitterly that she had at last discovered what the much-vaunted influence of woman was worth; that she had implored each one of her sons and grandsons, had entered into endless arguments and moral appeals to induce one of them to represent her convictions by voting for Bryan! That, although sincerely devoted to her, each one had assured her that his convictions forced him to vote the Republican ticket....I contended that a woman had no right to persuade a man to vote against his own convictions; that I respected the men of her family for following their own judgement regardless of the appeal which the honored head of the house had made to their chivalric devotion. To this she replied that she would agree with that point of view when a woman had the same opportunity as a man to register her convictions by vote. I believed then as I do now, that nothing is gained when independence of judgement is assailed by "influence," sentimental or otherwise, and that we test advancing civilization somewhat by our power to respect differences and by our tolerance of another's honest conviction.

This is, perhaps, the attitude of many busy women who would be glad to use the ballot to further public measures in which they are interested and for which they have been working for years. It offends the taste of such a woman to be obliged to use "indirect influence" when she is accustomed to well-bred, open action in other affairs, and she very much resents the time spent in persuading a voter to take her point of view, and possibly to give up his own, quite as honest and valuable as hers, although different because resulting from a totally different experience. Public-spirited women who wish to use the ballot, as I know them, do not wish to do the work of men nor to take over men's affairs. They simply want an opportunity to do their own work and to take care of those affairs which naturally and historically belong to women, but which are constantly being overlooked and slighted in our political institutions....To turn the administration of our civic affairs wholly over to men may mean that the American city will continue to push forward in its commercial and industrial development, and continue to lag behind in those things which make a city healthful and beautiful. After all, woman's traditional function has been to make her dwelling-place both clean and fair. Is that dreariness in city life, that lack of domesticity which the humblest farm dwelling presents, due to a withdrawal of one of the naturally cooperating forces? If women have in any sense been responsible for the gentler side of life which softens and blurs some of its harsher conditions, may they not have a duty to perform in our American cities?

In closing, may I recapitulate that if woman would fulfill her traditional responsibility to her own children; if she would educate and protect from danger factory children who must find their recreation on the street; if she would bring the cultural forces to bear upon our materialistic civilization; and if she would do it all with the dignity and directness fitting one who carries on her immemorial duties, then she must bring herself to the use of the ballot-that latest implement for self government. May we not fairly say that American women need this implement in order to preserve the home? Notes

Belated Industry

The industry which the title of this paper designates as belated is that of domestic labor, which is belated, both ethically and industrially; the status of its ethics operating very largely as the determining factor in its industrial situation.

It may be well to make clear at once that this paper does not treat of this occupation as a domestic art, in which the members of the household engage and spend time which would otherwise have no economic value. As an art it is charming and destined to endure so long as women cherish their homes and express affection by personal service. This paper treats of the occupation solely as an industry, by means of which large numbers of women are earning a livelihood. An attempt is made to present this industry from the point of view of those women who are working in households for wages.[1]

This industry was little affected by the industrial revolution of the eighteenth century, and is a surviving remnant of the household system which preceded the factory system. Both employers and employés, for the most part, hold moral conceptions and notions of duty which are tinged with feudalism. There is a tendency for each worker to become isolated from her fellow workers; to be dependent upon the protection and goodwill of her employer, and to have little share in the corporate life of the community. The employés in this industry practically lead the lives of those who have not discovered the power to combine; of those who "cannot create a sufficiently coherent organization to sustain themselves under changing conditions."

We are all more or less familiar with the conditions of the trades affected most quickly by the industrial revolution. If we have not read the reports of the investigations undertaken by the distracted English Parliament, we have at least read the German poems and English stories concerning the misery of the displaced weavers who, upon the application of steam power to weaving, were obliged to leave their hand looms in the country and adjust themselves to the conditions of hastily-built towns. We know that there were painstaking, industrious and virtuous men among the weavers, who were too dull to seize upon the changed conditions of their trades, and who continued to work many hours a day at their hand looms until they and their families perished miserably. The possession of certain individual virtues did not make them of industrial value.

This breaking-up of long established industrial habits and occupations and the necessity for a difficult readjustment comes about constantly with changing conditions, and it is easy to believe that we are in the midst of one of these sweeping industrial changes now; in fact, that it has already come about in regard to many commodities formerly produced in the household which are now produced in factories; that it would naturally come about in regard to most of them, if women did not oppose it and fatuously believe that within these old methods is bound up the sanctity of family life. Most of us can remember the conscientious struggle with which our grandmothers slowly gave up homemade candles, and some of us may dimly recall homespun sheets. All of us know something of the conservative reserve with which our mothers, later, gave up the pleasures and economies of homemade soap in spite of the lively competition and seductive advertisements offered by the factory product

As industrial conditions have changed, the household has become simplified, from the mediæval affair of journeymen, apprentices and maidens who spun and brewed, to the family proper; to those who love each other and live together in ties of affection and consanguinity. Were this process complete, we should have no problem of household employment. But, even in households comparatively humble, there is still one alien, one who is neither loved nor loving. The modern family has dropped the man who made its shoes, the woman who spun its clothes, and to a large extent the woman who washes them, but it stoutly refuses to drop the woman who cooks its food; it strangely insists that to do that would be to destroy family life. The cook is uncomfortable, the family is uncomfortable; but it will not drop her as all her fellow-workers have been dropped, although the cook herself insists upon it. So far has this insistance gone that every possible concession is made to retain her. I know an employer in one of the suburbs who built a bay at the back of her house so that her cook might have a pleasant room in which to sleep, and one in which to receive her friends. This employer naturally felt aggrieved when the cook refused to stay in her bay. Viewed in an historic light, this employer might just as well have added a bay to her house for her shoemaker, and then deemed him ungrateful because he declined to live in it. The employer misunderstood the situation. She did not realize that the desire to live with one's kinsfolk is stronger in most of us than the desire for the comforts to be found in a bay.

The household employe has no regular opportunity for meeting other workers of her trade, and of attaining with them the dignity of a corporate body. The industrial isolation of the household employé results, as isolation in a trade must always result, in a lack of progress in the methods and products of that trade and a lack of aspiration and education in the workman. Whether we recognize this isolation as a cause or not, I think we are all ready to acknowledge that household labor has been in some way belated; that the improvements there have not kept up with the improvement in other occupations. It is said that the last revolution in the processes of cooking was brought about by Count Rumford, who died a hundred years ago. This is largely due to lack of *esprit de corps* among the employés, which keeps them collectively from fresh achievements, as the absence of education in the individual keeps her from improving her implements.

Under this isolation, not only must one set of utensils serve divers purposes, and as a consequence tend to a lessened volume, and lower quality of work, but inasmuch as the appliances are not made to perform the fullest work, there is an amount of capital invested disproportionate to the result when measured by the achievement in other branches of industry. More important than this is the result of the isolation upon the worker herself. There is nothing more devastating to the inventive faculty, nor fatal to a flow of mind and spirit, than the constant feeling of loneliness and the absence of that fellowship which makes our public opinion.

If an angry foreman reprimands a girl for breaking a machine, twenty other girls hear him, and the culprit knows perfectly well their opinion as to the justice or injustice of her situation. In either case she bears it better for knowing that, and for not thinking it over in solitude. If a household employé breaks a utensil or a piece of porcelain and is reprimanded by her employer, too often the invisible jury is the family of the latter, who naturally uphold her censorious position and intensify the feeling of loneliness in the employé.

The isolation of the household employe is perhaps inevitable so long as the employer holds her belated ethics; but the situation is made even more difficult by the character and capacity of the girls who enter this industry. In any great industrial change the workmen who are permanently displaced are those who are too dull to seize upon changed conditions. The workmen who have knowledge and insight, and who are in touch with their time, quickly reorganize. There are many noble exceptions, but it follows that on the whole the enterprising girls of the community go into factories, and the less enterprising go into households. It is not a question of skill, of energy, of conscientious work, which will enable a girl to rise industrially while she is in the household; she is not in the rising movement. She is belated in a class composed of the unprogressive elements of the community, and which is recruited constantly from the victims of misfortune and incompetence, by girls who are learning the language, girls who are timid and slow, or girls who look at life solely from the savings bank point of view. The distracted housekeeper struggles with these unprogressive girls, holding to them not even the well-defined and independent relation of employer and employed, but the hazy and constantly changing one of mistress to servant. A listener attentive to a conversation between two employers of household labor, and we certainly all have opportunity to hear such conversations, would often discover a tone implying that the employer was abused and put upon; that she was struggling with it solely because she was thus serving her family and performing her social duties; that otherwise it would be a great relief to her to throw up the whole thing and "never have a servant in her house again." Did she follow this impulse she would simply yield to the trend of her times, and accept the system of factory production. She would be in line with the industrial organization of her age. Were she in line ethically, she would have to believe that the sacredness and beauty of family life do not consist in the processes of the separate preparation of food, but in sharing the corporate life of the community, and in making the family the unit of that life.

The selfishness of a modern mistress, who, in her narrow social ethics, insists that those who minister to the comforts of her family, shall minister to it alone, that they shall not only be celibate, but shall be cut off more or less from their natural social ties, excludes the best working people from her service. A man of dignity and ability is quite willing to come into a house to tune a piano. Another man of mechanical skill will come to put up window shades. Another of less skill, but perfect independence, will come to clean and lay a carpet. These men would all resent the situation and consider it quite impossible if it implied the giving up of their family and social ties, and living under the roof of the household requiring their services. Most of the cooking and serving and cleaning of a household could be done by women living outside and coming into a house as a skilled workmen does, having no "personal service" relation to the employer. There is no reason why the woman who cleans windows in a house, should not live as full a domestic and social life as the man who cleans windows in an office. If the "servant" attitude were once eliminated from household industry, and the well-established one of employer and employé substituted, the first step would be taken toward overcoming many difficulties.

Although this household industry survives in the midst of the factory system, it must, of course, constantly compete with it. To all untrained women seeking employment-save those with little children or invalids depending upon them, to whom both factory and household labor are impossible, and who are practically confined to the sewing trades —a choice is open between these two forms of labor.

There are few women so dull that they cannot paste labels on a box, or do some form of factory work, few so dull that some perplexed housekeeper will not receive them at least for a trial into her household. Household labor then has to compete constantly with factory labor, and women seeking employment, more or less consciously compare these two forms of labor in point of hours, in point of permanency of employment, in point of wages and in point of the advantage afforded for family and social life. Three points are easily disposed of: (1) In regard to hours there is no doubt that the factory has the advantage. The average factory hours are from seven in the morning to six in the evening, with the chance of working over time in busy seasons. This leaves most of the evenings and Sundays entirely free. The average hours of household labor are from six in the morning until eight at night, with little difference in seasons. There is one afternoon a week, with an occasional evening, but Sunday is almost never wholly free. (2) In regard to permanency of position the advantage is found clearly on the side of the household employe, if she proves in any measure satisfactory to her employer, for she encounters much less competition. (3) In point of wages the household is again fairly ahead, if we consider not the money received but the opportunity offered for saving money. This is greater among household employes because they do not pay board, the clothing required is simpler, and the temptation to spend money in recreation is less frequent. The minimum wages paid an adult in household labor may be fairly put at two dollars and a half a week; the maximum at six dollars, this excluding the comparatively rare opportunities for women to cook at forty dollars a month, and the housekeeper's position at fifty dollars a month. The factory wages, viewed from the savings bank standpoint, may be smaller in the average, but this I believe to be counterbalanced in the minds of the employes by the greater chance which the factory offers for increased wages. A girl over sixteen seldom works in a factory for less than four dollars a week, and she always cherishes the hope of at last being a forewoman with a permanent salary of fifteen or twenty-five dollars a week. Whether she attains this or not, she runs a fair chance of earning ten dollars a week as a skilled worker. A girl finds it easier to be content with four dollars a week, when she pays for board, in a scale of wages rising towards ten dollars, than to be content with four dollars a week and pay no board in a scale of wages rising towards six dollars, and the girl well knows that there are scores of forewomen at sixty dollars a month for one forty-dollar cook or fifty-dollar housekeeper. In many cases this position is well taken economically for, although the opportunity for saving may be better for the employes in the household than in the factory, her family saves more when she works in a factory and lives with them. The rent is no more when she is at home. The two dollars and fifty cents a week which she pays into the family fund more than covers the cost of her actual food, and at night she can often contribute towards the family labor by helping her mother wash and sew.

This brings us easily to the fourth point of comparison, that of the possibilities afforded for family life. It is well to remember that women, as a rule, are devoted to their families; that they want to live with their parents, their brothers and sisters and kinsfolk, and will sacrifice a good deal to accomplish this. This devotion is so universal that it is impossible to ignore it when we consider women as employés. Young unmarried women are not detached from family claims and requirement as young men are, and, so far as my observation goes, are more ready and steady in their response to the needs of the aged parents and helpless members of the family. But women performing labor in households find peculiar difficulties in the way of enjoying family life, and are more or less dependent upon their employers for possibilities to see their relatives and friends. Curiously enough the same devotion to family life and quick response to its claims on the part of the employer, operates against the girl in household labor and places her in a unique position of isolation. The employer of household labor, in her zeal to preserve her family life intact and free from intrusion, acts inconsistently and grants to her cook, for instance, but once or twice a week such opportunity for untrammelled association with her relatives as the employer's family claims constantly. This devotion to the narrow conception of family life the men of the family also share. The New York gentleman who lunches at Delmonico's eats food cooked by a *chef* with a salary of five thousand dollars a year, and prepared with all modern appliances. He comes home hungry and with a tantalizing memory of his lunch to a dinner cooked by a woman with a salary of forty dollars a month, with only those appliances possible in a small kitchen. The contrast between the lunch and dinner is great, but the aforesaid gentleman quiets his discontent by his reflection, that, in eating a dinner cooked under his own roof, he is in some occult manner contributing to the sanctity of family life; though his business mind knows full well that, in actual money, he is paying more for his badly cooked dinner than for his well-cooked lunch; that in submitting to such conditions he is failing to use the powers of organization and combination which have made his business so successful.

The household employé, in addition to her industrial isolation, is also isolated socially. It is well to remember that the household employés, for the better quarters of the city and suburbs, are largely drawn from the poorer quarters, which are nothing if not gregarious. The girl is born and reared in a tenement house full of children. She goes to school with them, and there she learns to march, to read and write in companionship with forty others. When she is old enough to go to parties, those she attends are usually held in a public hall and are crowded with dancers. If she works in a factory, she walks home with many other girls, in much the same spirit as she formerly walked in school with them. She mingles with the young men she knows, in frank economic and social equality. Until she marries she remains at home with no special break or change in her family and social life.

If she is employed in a household, this is not true. Suddenly all the conditions of her life are changed. This change may be wholesome for her, but it is not easy, and the thought of the savings bank does not cheer one much, when one is twenty. She is isolated from the people with whom she has been reared, with whom she has gone to school, and among whom she expects to live when she marries. She is naturally lonely and constrained away from them, and the "new girl" often seems "queer" to her employer's family. She does not care to mingle socially with the people in whose house she is employed, as the girl in the country when she "works for" a country neighbor often does, and she suffers horribly from loneliness. This wholesome instinctive dread of social isolation is so strong that, as every city intelligence office can testify, the filling of situations is easier or more difficult just in proportion as the place offers more or less companionship. Thus, the easy situation to fill is always the city house with five or six employés, shading off into the more difficult suburban home with two, and the utterly impossible lonely country house.

There are suburban employers of household labor who make heroic efforts to supply domestic and social life to their employés, who take the domestic employé to drive, arrange to have her invited out occasionally, who supply her with books and papers and companionship. Nothing could be more praiseworthy in motive, but it is seldom successful in actual operation. In the first place it is a forced relationship, and nothing in the world can be worse than a simulacrum of companionship. The employé may have a genuine friendship for her employer and a pleasure in her companionship, or she may not, and the unnaturalness of the situation comes from the insistence that she has, merely because of the propinquity. I should consider myself an unpardonable snob if, because a woman did my cooking, I should not hold myself ready to have her for my best friend, to drive, to read, to attend receptions with her, but that friendship might or might not come about, according to her nature and mine, just as it might or might not come about between me and my college colleague. On the other hand, I should consider myself very stupid if merely because a woman cooked my food and lived in my house I should insist upon having a friendship with her, whether her nature and mine responded to it or not. It would be folly to force the companionship of myself or my family upon her when doubtless she would vastly prefer the companionship of her own friends and her own family. The unnaturalness of the situation is brought about by the fact that she is practically debarred by distance and lack of leisure from her own natural ties, and then her employer feeling sorry, insists upon filling the vacancy in interests and affections by her own tastes and friendship. She may or may not succeed, but the employé should not be thus dependent upon the good will of her employer. That in itself is feudal.

Added to all this is a social distinction which the household employé feels keenly against her, and in favor of the factory girls, in the minds of the young men of her acquaintance. A woman who has worked in households for twenty years told me that when she was a young and pretty nurse girl, the only young men who "paid her attention" were coachmen and unskilled laborers. The skill in the trades of her suitors increased as her position in the household in- creased in dignity. When she was a housekeeper, forty years old, skilled mechanics appeared, one of whom she married. Women seeking employment understand perfectly well this feeling, quite unjustifiable I am willing to admit, among mechanics, and it acts as a strong inducement towards factory labor.

I have long ceased to apologize for the views and opinions of working people. I am quite sure that on the whole they are just about as wise and just about as foolish as the views and opinions of other people, but that this particularly foolish opinion of young mechanics is widely shared by the employing class can be easily demonstrated. The contrast is further accentuated by the better social position of the factory girl, and the advantages provided for her in the way of lunch clubs, social clubs, and vacation homes, from which girls performing household labor are practically excluded by their hours of work, their geographical situation, and a curious feeling that they are not as interesting as factory girls.

It is not the object of this paper to suggest remedies; but if the premise in regard to the isolation of the household employé is well taken, and if the position can be sustained that this isolation proves the determining factor in the situation, then certainly an effort should be made to remedy this, at least in its domestic and social aspects. To allow household employés to live with their own families and among their own friends, as factory employes now do, would be to relegate more production to industrial centers administered on the factory system, and to secure shorter hours for that which remains to be done in the household.

It might be possible that the employer of household labor would have to go back, at least during the period of transition, to the original office of "lady," that of "bread giving" to her household. It might be necessary for her to receive the prepared food and drink and serve it herself to her family and guests, but truly that is no hardship, which may be made a grace and a token, and there is no reason why in time the necessary serving at a table should not be done by a trained corps of women as fine as the Swiss men who make the table d'hôte of the European hotel such a marvel of celerity. In the fewer cases in which the household employés have no family ties, doubtless a remedy against social isolation would be the formation of residence clubs, at least in the suburbs, where the isolation is most keenly felt. Indeed the beginnings of these clubs are already seen in the servants' quarters at the summer hotels. In these residence clubs the household employé could have the independent life which only one's abiding place can afford. This, of course, presupposes a higher grade of ability than household employés at present possess; on the other hand it is only by offering such possibilities that the higher grades of intelligence can be secured for household employment. As the plan of separate clubs for household employés will probably come first in the suburbs, where the difficulty of securing and holding "servants" under the present system is most keenly felt, so the plan of buying cooked food from an outside kitchen and of having more and more of the household product relegated to the factory will probably come from the comparatively poor people in the city, who feel most keenly the pressure of the present system. They already consume a much larger proportion of canned goods and baker's wares and "prepared meats" than the more prosperous people do,[2] because they cannot command the skill nor the time for the more tedious preparation of the raw material. It is comparatively easy for an employer to manage her household industry with a cook, a laundress, a waitress, etc. The difficulties really begin when the family income is so small that but one person can be employed in the household for all these varied functions, and the difficulties increase and grow almost insurmountable as they fall altogether upon the mother of the family, who is living in a flat, or worse still, in a tenement house, where one stove and one set of utensils must be put to all sorts of uses, fit or unfit, making the living room of the family a horror in summer, and perfectly insupportable in rainy washing days in winter. Such a woman is living in a complicated age, totally without the differentiation of functions and utensils which that age demands.

A fuller social and domestic life among household employés would be the first step toward securing their entrance into the larger industrial organizations by which the needs of a community are most successfully administered. Many a girl who complains of loneliness, and who relinquishes her situation with that as her sole excuse, feebly tries to formulate her sense of restraint and social mal-adjustment. She sometimes says that she "feels so unnatural all the time."[3] And when she leaves her employer her reasons are often incoherent and totally incomprehensible to that good lady, who naturally concludes that she wishes to get away from the work and back to her dances and giddy life, content to stand many hours in an unsanitary factory, if she has these. The charge of the employer is only a half truth. These dances may be the only organized form of social life which the disheartened employé is able to mention; but she has felt the social trend of her times, and is trying to say what an old English poet said five centuries ago: "Forsooth, brothers, fellowship is heaven, and lack of fellowship is hell; fellowship is life and lack of fellowship is death; and the deeds that ye do upon earth, it is for fellowship's sake that ye do them."

Two other contemporary industries are similar in condition and situation to that of domestic labor. The workers in these two industries are also isolated. The worker in the first is the woman who endeavors to support herself "by taking in sewing." She is the last unit of the sweating system-the home finisher. The majority of her sisters in all the other trades have gone into the factories, she alone remains at home and turns her already uncomfortable tenement into a workshop. Isolated as the sewing woman is, industrially she still has advantages over the household employé, in that she may remain in the same part of town with her kinsfolk and her natural social associations. In that respect she is nearer the conditions of factory life. Indeed, there is a detectable tendency to absorb her into the factory, a tendency hastened by the sweating investigations, workshop acts, the trades unions slowly being formed among sewing women, and one might add by the conscience more slowly still being evolved amongst the consumers in regard to clothing manufactured in tenement houses. These causes all operate toward the establishment of factories.[4]

Farming is another unorganized industry depending upon isolated workers, which is not in the least holding its own in our industrial development. There are doubtless many causes to explain the increase of cities, and the steady depopulation of the country. In a careful estimate, however, it should not be ignored that the farmer relies more and more upon the labor of the few people living upon his farm. The gathering together of all the neighbors for hay-making and house-raising, the apple-paring parties, and the corn-husking bees are all experiences of the past. These mixed the pleasures of social intercourse with the labor of production, and implied the vicinage in their very conception.

Much discussion has of late been expended on the discontent of the farmer. It has been discovered that while one-half of the entire population of the United States is agricultural, in the last two decades this one-half of the population have amassed but one-tenth of the wealth of the country. This failure to amass their share of wealth, in spite of their almost incessant exertions, doubtless arises chiefly from the lack of association and cooperation among farmers, from the diffusion rather than the concentration of their energies. To quote from a recent writer, in the *Forum,* "Not only does a lack of organized effort among farmers result in much misdirected energy and consequent economic loss, but it works an even more serious injury by placing the farmer population at a disadvantage in the great industrial contest in which other and coordinated industries-by virtue of their ability for thorough concentration and organization-have a superior advantage. The American farmer has not yet mastered the problem of combined action, consequently he has not fully "realized" upon his energies. The economic loss, however, great as it is, is but a trifle, compared with the woeful waste of social energy. From this comes that abiding soul weariness suffered by so many farmers, and still more by their wives and their children. This, again, reacts against their economic value."

If the farmer is doomed to have a poorer social life than men in other vocations, then the bright farmer's boys, naturally craving those things which sweeten and brighten human life, will not stay upon the farm, and the force which drives them into their share of associated life is just as natural and just as much to be counted upon as the force which drives the wind through the tree tops. If the girl who engages in domestic labor is doomed to a narrow social life, if she is isolated from her family and natural industrial associations, then it follows that the brightest girl will not engage in domestic labor, but will follow the natural trend of their times, towards factory work and associated effort.

The cry of the whip-poor-will never struck so lonely upon the heart of the young man sitting in the dusk upon the farmhouse porch as it did last summer, because the farm work itself and the farmhouse production has never been so far away from the spirit and tendency of its times. All over the country various experiments are being made to reorganize the conditions of farm life, that the farmers may live in villages, where may be sustained some of the higher forms of education and social civilization. Will women again fail in this time of reorganization, as they utterly failed to reorganize their half of the world's work, upon the introduction of the factory system? Will they utterly disregard the lonely girl within their household, and when she demands a fuller life, and leaves that household, will they weakly continue to complain, rather than make a vigorous effort for bringing household industry into the trend of the times? To fail to apprehend the tendency of one's age, and to fail to adapt the conditions of an industry to it is to leave that industry ill adjusted and belated.

Jane Addams

Hull-House.

Footnotes

1. The opinions in it have been largely gained through experiences in a Woman's Labor Bureau, and through conversations held there with women returning from the "situations," which they had voluntarily relinquished in Chicago households of all grades. These same women seldom gave up a place in a factory, although many of the factory situations involved long hours and hard work.

2. The writer has seen a tenement house mother pass by a basket of green peas at the door of a local grocery store, to purchase a tin of canned peas, because they could be easily prepared for supper and "the children liked the tinny taste."

3. The writer has known the voice of a girl to change so much during three weeks of "service" that she could not recognize it when the girl returned to the bureau. It alternated between the high falsetto in which a shy child "speaks a piece," and the husky gulp with which the *globus hystericus* is swallowed. The alertness and *bonhomie* of the voice of the tenement-house child had totally disappeared.

4. The industrial and ethical situation of the sewing woman has been so fully discussed in "Hull-House Maps and Papers" that it is needless to repeat it here. (See pp. 27-45, 184-187.)

www.ingramcontent.com/pod-product-compliance
Lightning Source LLC
Chambersburg PA
CBHW051733250726
48659CB00001B/34